RACE
INDIVIDUAL AND COLLECTIVE BEHAVIOR

ADVISORS

H. C. BREARLEY

WILLIAM O. BROWN

WERNER CAHNMAN

HILDA HERTZ GOLDEN

RUDOLF HEBERLE

BERNARD HORMANN

FORREST LAVIOLETTE

I. D. MACCRONE

J. MASUOKA

DONALD PIERSON

RACE

INDIVIDUAL AND COLLECTIVE BEHAVIOR

EDITED BY

EDGAR T. THOMPSON, DUKE UNIVERSITY

AND

EVERETT C. HUGHES, UNIVERSITY OF CHICAGO

THE FREE PRESS

THE FREE PRESS, *New York*
COLLIER-MACMILLAN LIMITED, *London*

Copyright © 1958 by The Free Press, A Corporation

Printed in the United States of America

For information, address:

THE FREE PRESS
A DIVISION OF THE MACMILLAN COMPANY
60 Fifth Avenue, New York, N.Y. 10011

Collier-Macmillan Canada, Ltd., Toronto, Ontario

DESIGNED BY SIDNEY SOLOMON

Library of Congress Catalog Card Number: 58–6490
FIRST FREE PRESS PAPERBACK EDITION 1965

CONTENTS

INTRODUCTION

I. The Need to Know Who We Are

A. OF WHAT RACE AM I?

B. RACE AS BEHAVIOR

C. POPULAR CLASSIFICATION AND THE PROBLEM OF NAMING

D. SOME MORE FORMAL CONCEPTIONS RELATING TO RACE

[v]

II. Race and Region

III. The Ecology of Race Relations

IV. The Idea of Race

V. Race Conflict

VI. Status and Change

VII. Race and Human Nature

VIII. The Study and Control of Race Relations

IX.

X.

INTRODUCTION

THIS *Reader* BELONGS to that class of books which seeks to gain perspective. "In the absence of perspective," Whitehead said, "there is only triviality." Here we seek perspective on the problem of race from a large number of authors and from a wide range of documentary material dealing with lore, myths, rationalizations, doctrines, poetry, and social fiction as well as from serious scientific studies and reports.

The race problem is a problem so immediately in the minds of so many people, a problem so insistently demanding action, even drastic action, right now, that a sense of balance and proportion is not easily come by and held to. When men are caught in the meshes of racial feeling it is next to impossible to view the matter with the degree of objective consideration necessary to understanding and rational action. On the other hand, those who have not experienced the emotions of race probably are not in the best position to understand and to act upon the race problem either. For all of us some method for gaining greater depth and distance is needed.

The readings in this book are organized around the race problem. What is this problem? There have been many answers. Here it may be suggested that, fundamentally, it is the problem of understanding and dealing with an idea, the idea of race. In particular areas the race problem is identified with relations of tension between two or more specific peoples, but this is only a local expression of the problem. In every region where race relations are problematic they are implicated in concrete social, political, demographic, and biological problems, but these same problems can and do exist where there is no racial involvement. The race problem is everywhere accompanied by charges of discrimination, segregation, and injustice, but these same charges are made where the idea of race is absent. The idea is not limited to men of ill-will; in the same community it is entertained by men regarded by their fellows as well as by themselves as men of good-will and responsibility. Neither is it limited, where it exists, to members of only one race; men of the "inferior" race will not agree to many things done in its name, especially when done to them, but they may be almost as completely possessed by the idea as the men of the "superior" race. The people of the community can divide themselves into different races only because they all hold the idea of race in common. And not only do they hold it but they believe in it, and, believing in it, are moved to action by it. Thus the problem becomes a race problem, and ceases to be some other kind of social and political or demographic problem, when it becomes implicated in "a way of life" or "a civilization" which, of course, must be defended at all costs. When this happens the ordinary problems of a society have been pushed down into its deeper structure where they have become a part of its constitutional organization.

The idea of race is only one of many schismatic myths which have divided mankind into warring groups throughout history. But in perhaps no other form of ethnocentrism have the divisions been regarded as so wide and so deep as the divisions that are believed to be based upon race. Here the separation is not to be bridged by learning a new language, or by conversion to a different religion, or by changing to another costume, or by professing loyalty to another ruler or set of laws. Race does not result in a mere estrangement of peoples; it is presumed to effect nothing short of an abysmal separation. The idea of race is present, says Yves R. Simon, "the moment one admits that there exists, apart from individual and sociological causes of infamy, a mark of degradation which is properly biological, permanent, transmissible by physical generation, inherent in the chromosomes, independent of all good will and all good conduct, ineffaceable, fatal in the way death is fatal."[1] Race is ultimate and final.

It is a terrible idea. Europe, which has given the world so many energizing ideas, gave this one too, but Europeans seem not to have fully realized the drastic quality of their contribution. It might almost be said of Europe as a whole, as Vidal de la Blache said of Germany, that it came to represent "above everything else an ethnic idea."[2] Yet no matter how full of error, the idea has been a source of tremendous energy within Europe itself as well as along the frontiers of European colonization and trade. It still is powerful, but almost everywhere it is at least beginning to decline and to assume a defensive position. The facts of biology and genetics are beginning to be apparent even among ordinary people, race is becoming more and more identified with the general problem of democracy and subject to all the pressures of the democratic ideal, and more and more of us are experiencing the discovery that in the people of other races there are other lives to learn about and to learn from. The idea of race is beginning to decline before the facts of biology, of politics, and of human nature.

It is at the point of their decline, it seems, that the dominating ideas and forces of history come to be recognized and studied, when already, perhaps, some new ideas are beginning to take the place of the old. At any rate, so far as the subject of race is concerned, the volume of popular literature and serious study grows greater and greater.

In this book a good deal of information and a good many insights about race are passed along to the reader through the generosity of the authors and publishers who have given permission to reprint parts of their works. It is hoped that the excerpts and adaptations offered here will stimulate readers to consult the original papers in the periodicals and books in which they are published and where they are documented and annotated in footnotes.

This book also shows how two people, the editors, have organized for themselves the materials which are at hand. Some readers will doubtless complain of our selections, and some will decry the mood of detachment in which they have been made. They may suspect our motives. We hasten to say that we are of the race called white. (There are said to be other terms applied to our kind in various parts of the world.) One of us was born and reared in the plantation society of the South; both his grandfathers fought hard in the War Between the States to take the South out of the Union and one of them died in the attempt. The two grandfathers of the other fought for the Union in the Civil War, and

---

[1] "Secret Sources of the Success of the Racist Ideology," *Review of Politics*, VII (January, 1945), 75.

[2] *Histoire de France*, Paris, 1903. I, 50.

his father's uncompromising sermons on racial equality led to the burning of a fiery cross in his honor in southern Ohio in the 1920's. The two of us might not agree on all points of short-run policy and action concerning the race problem in our country. But we do fully agree on the value of the detached look at this and all other great human problems. For only to the extent that one is passionately attached to the human race—all of it—can one really be detached about the particular errors and oddities of its member groups. Nothing is so devastatingly equalitarian as detachment.

The readings in this book are neither inclusive nor comprehensive. The reader may wish to substitute a better selection of documents under the same series of concepts and chapter headings utilized here or he may organize the same materials according to some better plan. What is important, if the book is to be useful, is that the book's users and readers make themselves participators in the work from which it has come in order to think critically and creatively beyond it. We have tried to present the materials in a form which will arouse curiosity and lead the student to question conventional knowledge on the subject of race. The reader is not asked to accept anything on the authority of the editors, the contributors, or of anyone else. This is why our introductions to the chapters take the form of questions rather than of conclusions. It is not only possible but highly desirable that the user of this book ask himself other and better questions than those we have put to him. As far as possible his own experience and the facts of the community in which he lives should first be taxed to supply the answers. Then let him go to the literature and read widely, but not worshipfully.

By agreement between us, the greater initiative in preparing this book was taken by Thompson.

In addition to the scholars and writers and publishers who have permitted the use of their work in this book we are under obligations to Florence Blakely, Mary Canada, Mary Francis Morris, Margaret Thompson, and Emerson Ford of the Duke University Libraries for generous assistance in its preparation. Alma Lee Thompson helped with the typing and proofreading. We are particularly indebted to Alma Macy Thompson for a considerable amount of tedious work in typing, library checking, and proofreading. Her help has been indispensable. We wish, too, to acknowledge the assistance of colleagues who have suggested readings and offered constructive criticism. These include Robert Redfield, Leo Kuper, and Herbert Collins.

Edgar T. Thompson
Everett C. Hughes

PART I

The Need to Know Who We Are

INTRODUCTION

THE QUESTION "Of What Race Am I?" is part of the larger question "Who Am I?" which in turn is the usual way of asking the more abstract question "What Is the Self?" It is part of the problem of self-definition or identification. Why do we need to know who we are? How do we in our society ordinarily go about identifying ourselves, and to what extent do people proceed differently toward this end in other societies?

Does not everyone know the race to which he belongs? Under what circumstances is one likely to be uncertain of his race, and under what circumstances would this uncertainty make some practical difference? If race is a matter of living, and not primarily a matter of intellect, might we not expect to learn most from those people or peoples who suffer from interraciality in situations where racial belongingness is emphasized? Is such "marginality" to be found in cases other than those of racial and cultural hybrids? If so, what is the essential nature of this phenomenon? Do we not, all of us, suffer some uncertainty when people of the other race or races fail to accord us traditional treatment? Is not to lose racial identity also to lose some sense of self, to cease by so much to know who we are? Is it surprising that we do not willingly surrender ourselves, in the literal sense of this expression, and that in these times of rapid social change white men especially face with some fear the loss of the racial aspect of their selves?

Whatever else it is, a race is a group analyzable into a number of people not all of whom are contemporaries of one another. Not all human beings belong to it. It therefore is constituted by a selection on the part of someone or another group of individuals. To ask what the race is to ask how we identify the individuals belonging to it. When do two individuals belong to the same race? As we identify friends so do we identify races without knowing exactly how we go about it. How can we make explicit the process whereby in a given situation the people themselves work out a scheme of identification and classification? What are the requirements for a scheme adequate for a popular or conventional racial classification? What accounts for historical shifts in the criteria of popular or discriminatory classification? How do biologists and anthropologists go about making racial identification and classification explicit?

Why do we need to classify people at all? Is it possible to deal with a large number of people without positing categories and sub-categories? Is classification by race possible in the absence of some distinctive physical trait? Under what circumstances does religion, language, costume, or surname serve to classify a group of people as a racial or a near racial group?

An old Russian proverb says, "We do not hate the wolf because his fur is gray, but because he eats our sheep." What appears to be the nature of the real connection between physical marking, behavior and race? What is the connection between the identifying and classifying process and the naming process? How far is it true that race is merely a tag or a name attached to a readily identifiable group and having much the same function as an epithet? To the extent that this is true does it mean that race is merely a matter of semantics, and that if words like "Negro" and "Jew" could be banished from our vocabulary race problems would disappear?

A French scientist complains that "the popular conception of race is entirely lacking in precision." If it were precise would it any longer be a popular conception? What is the importance of the fact that in the minds of people generally race remains a vague and imprecise thing? What changes in perspective appear to emerge when professors and scientists attempt conscious and formal definitions of race, and undertake to distinguish between such concepts as *people, nationality, ethnic,* and *race?*

THE MULATTO'S CONCEPTION OF

HIMSELF

By E. C. L. Adams

Tad: Who is you an' wuh is you? I ain' 'member to axe you 'fore dis. Who is you an' wuh is you an' wey you come from?

Yellow Jack: You axe me who I is an' wuh I is an' wey I come from? You axe a heap er question all in one, an' I guh axe you a question:

Who business is it who I is an' wuh I is an' wey I come from? Is you care

---

Reprinted from "A Yellow Bastard" in *Nigger to Nigger* by E. C. L. Adams, pp. 33–35, by permission of the owners of the copyright: George C. S. Adams and Stephen B. Adams.

'bout me? Is you my friend? I ain' think so. Is you my enemy? I ain' think dat neither. Is you axe me jes for talk an' compersation? Maybe you axe me who I is for laugh an' game makin'. Well, it do not matter. It ain't make no diff'ence wuh you' reason. I guh tell you who I is an' wuh I is. It ain't matter ef you laugh or cry.

It ain't make no diff'ence, wuh I is I is. An' when dey puts me in de ground, I is wuh everybody is, or guh be is. You axe me wuh I is. Laugh, ef you has a mind to. I ain' care. Grin, ef you wants to. I ain't to fault, an' I ain' care.

I have thought an' dream, an' I dream beautiful dream, but it seem like I ain' kin tell my dream. I ain' seems rough enough. I ain' seems man enough to make my feelin's known. My dream ain' nothin' but for laughter for other folks, an' my dream is tear for me an' torment. But I dreams—dat's all dere is for me.

You axe who I is an' wuh I is an' wey I come from.

I come from wey de door is shet, an' I come to wey it still is closed. All I got is dreams, an' dey is drownded. I ain' kin make my feelin's known. Laughin' ain' make no diff'ence now. God has overlooked me. I is not strong enough. I ain' kin make my feelin's known.

You axe me wuh I is an' I guh tell you. I is wuh I is. I isn't wuh I mought er been. To my lonesome self I ain' nothin' but a yellow bastard—laugh, I ain' care—a yellow bastard wid no place—wid no place amongst de white folks an' a poorly place amongst de niggers.

De door is shet to me. Hemmed in on every side, I has nothin' but dreams. An' my thoughts is floatin' out, floatin' far above de tall tree tops, here an' dere, listenin' to de wind's soft tune above de tree tops an' de clouds. Across de stars dey wander for a lonely moment, an' den back again an' down, down, down into de mire. For de door is shet to me. Hemmed in, hemmed in on every side.

I ain' kin make my feelin's known, for I ain' nothin'—nothin' but a yellow bastard to white an' black alike. I is wuh I is—nothin' but a yellow bastard— an' I ain' kin make my feelin's known. Laugh, I ain't care.

Tad: I hear wuh you say. I ain' guh laugh an' I ain' guh cry. I ain' know wuh you is.

Scip: Le's we finish move dis fertilizer.

THE GROUP'S CONCEPTION OF THE

MULATTO

By E. C. L. Adams

Scip: Gentlemen's!
Voices: How do, Scip?
Scip: Sorter slow.

Voice: Is you well?

Scip: Middlin', is you hear de news?

Voice: We ain't hear no news, tell us, brother?

Scip: Well, de law got Simon.

Voice: Who got Simon?

Scip: De law got him.

Voice: How come, what he do?

Scip: Kilt a white 'ooman.

Voice: How come he kilt a white 'ooman?

Scip: I ain't know, and if I know I ain't say. All I say Simon kilt a white 'ooman an' de law got him. I see him an' he face twis' an' swell up, an' he eye red, an' he ain't say nothin' an' de law got him. He ain't say nothin' kaze he heart black an' he mind white an' de law got Simon.

Voice: Have mercy!

Second Voice: Dey ain't no mercy.

Third Voice: Jesus!

Fourth Voice: God have mercy!

Scip: Ain't I tell you de law got Simon?

Old Daniel: Simon ain't nothin'. He ain't bird-dog an' he ain't houn'. He ain't nothin'.

Voice: How come Simon ain't nothin'?

Old Daniel: Simon Daddy white, Simon' mammy black, Simon ain't nothin'. He got a nigger heart an' a white man head, an' dat's a mighty po' mixtry. What Simon head say Simon heart ain't know, an' what Simon heart say Simon head tangle up. He ain't white an' he ain't black, an' he ain't nothin'. White man spiles the nigger in him an' nigger spiles the white man. He born tangle up an' he guh die tangle up, an' all I can say is God forgive he Daddy and God love he Mammy an' God have mercy on Simon. He ain't nigger, en he ain't white, an' he ain't nothin'. He born tangle up.

Scip: Well, all I say is, de law got Simon.

DIFFERENTLY BORN

By Kathleen Tamagawa Eldridge

THE TROUBLE WITH ME is my ancestry. I really should not have been born. No, I am not illegitimate, but just an outlawed product of a legal marriage. Illegitimacy is often inconspicuous and easily concealed and sometimes it is even paraded for purposes of publicity. My problem goes deeper than that, for no law can change, no later ceremony right it—the problem of ancestry will remain.

My parents came from two small islands on opposite sides of the Earth. My mother was "North of Ireland," my father is Japanese and I have faced the traditions of two worlds, so to speak; an occidental and an oriental. Ireland and Japan! Even an instant's consideration of that combination will convey the thought that such a field of battle for life must needs be a "scene of tragedy and intense gaiety."

My father came to America when he was a little boy of eleven. In those days when Japan was first opened, it was progressive for young Japan to accept gracefully and completely the new world. So father was sent here as a child to enter our Chicago public schools and study our strange barbaric customs.

He must have been a likeable chap for in my long and intimate dealings with him as a parent, he has always won my total admiration. It was in high school that he met my Uncle Frank, who became his best friend. Uncle Frank was not an ordinary person; in fact, none of the Adamses were ordinary.

Some one sent me a newspaper clipping just the other day headed, "The Adams Still Survive." Most of it spoke of the American branch but toward the end it said, "As a family they have been inclined to advocate unpopular causes, to speak out in meeting and sometimes to make themselves obnoxious. But no one has ever questioned their ability, their patriotism, their honesty of purpose, or their integrity of character." I can't resist the temptation to quote this, because it so typically describes my mother. I don't know whether she included my father among her early advocacy of unpopular causes, but when Uncle Frank brought him home she promptly fell in love with him.

Grandmother disapproved. She disapproved all over the map, so much so, in fact, that when her husband's sisters sent for one of the children to "finish" in Europe, at the time of my Grandfather's death, it was mother who was chosen. I'm sure my Grandmother must have recognised all the danger my father was to her daughter, who was a real Adams—"inclined to advocate unpopular causes, to speak out in meeting and to make themselves obnoxious." I can see her now, in that old Chicago house, settling that "outlandish affair of Kate's"—packing mother off to Europe to "get her senses."

My mother stayed six years in Europe, yet all the while was answering father's missives. Perhaps words are nothing, nothing but pleasant little tinkling symbols blown upon white fields of blank paper, unless they might be judged by their effectiveness upon the reader. Father's words brought mother home from Europe, brought her home against the wishes of the Adams' aunts, of my inflexible Grandmother and her own better judgment, and were, in a way, responsible for my very being.

Her marriage to father was the result of so many causes that one might almost believe it to have been fate. Besides my father's love for her there was this lack of sympathy at home and her own desire for the extraordinary. Someone called her a woman with a "flair." She revelled in adventure and daring; after all she was the daughter of "Dare-Devil-Dick-Adams," who had been arrested time and again for driving six horses tandem through the streets of Londonderry. Then, too, my father was very much in the position of an "unpopular cause."

They eloped.

For mother an elopement seems quite in season, but for my father it seems too fantastic to be true. Young men in Japan still marry according to the dictates of their family . . . and these two eloped in eighteen eighty something. For him to marry anyone of a different race was astonishing enough, for he came of good family, but for him to marry without his family's consent and against the wishes of hers is, indeed, inconceivable from a Japanese standpoint.

Grandmother was essentially cold, but when she heard the news, she simply froze. This blue white glacier in her soul remained intact, until I unconsciously began thawing it at the age of three. During the interim Kate's name was non-existent in that household and woe to any reference to Japan. It was Uncle Frank who, making a trip east, went a little out of his way to see the banished Kate. He begged mother to forget, forgive and take father and me home to Chicago, to Grandmother. . . .

I don't know the exact details of the war which he must have fought with Grandmother on his return to Chicago, but the result was that my earliest memories are all of that rather grim household with its ultra polished floors and its slippery Turkish rugs.

It's well that tonsils and appendixes had not become the rage then, or I should undoubtedly have lost mine. Everything was "done," everything that could possibly improve me, but the thing they could not change and which I did not escape, was my heritage—the "Japanese." This thought-stimulating, imagination-firing label which inevitably leads to complications.

To the friends who visited us in those days, I felt myself to be a comicality, a toy. I was often spoken of as a "Japanese doll," or worse still as the "cute" little Japanese. My mother's guests found in me what Pierre Loti found in all Japan, "qui n'a pas l'air serieux, qui fait l'effet d'une chose pour rire." I felt this more keenly than I understood it. I had never been to Japan; I was as innocent of any real knowledge of the Japanese as those who visited us, but whatever I did, of good or of bad, was sure to be because I was Japanese.

These mental pit-falls surprised me, and alienated me from all the rest of the world, even from old, fat Nan, the colored wash woman.

One lovely summer's afternoon when I was about six, I was down in the basement, where I spent much of my time. Our cat had had kittens and while Nan was busy with the family washing, I watched the antics of the sprawling kittens over their languid mother. Suddenly it occurred to me that the large collie dog across the street might also be interested in the new kittens. Mother was in the attic when she heard my voice in the side yard, "Come along Friskey, I want to show you our nice, new kittens. . . ."

She rushed down three long flights of stairs only to find a revolving mass of cat and dog among the furnace pipes. Nan's wig had been snatched from her head in the mix-up and every movable article in the laundry room displaced.

"Oh Mother," I cried, choking on my tears, "I didn't know they would do that!"

I shall never forget how funny Nan looked without her wig or how thought-inspiring were her words. "Maybe cats and dogs don't have no fights in Japan, but they sure do in the U-u-United States."

Strange, distant and delightful Japan, land of childhood dreams, where anything might be! But all of my encounters with this mythical Japan were not so fascinating. There was the dirty-faced boy who sat on the back fence calling,

"Chink! Chink!" whenever I ventured into his presence in search of a playmate.

Hurrying back to my mother and weeping real tears brought small comfort for she only said, "Why didn't you tell him you were not a Chink?" She did not seem to understand my problem, for she never, even to her dying day, admitted that there was, or could be, a problem.

"But Mother," I parried, on that first occasion, "you told me never to contradict."

This sent the family into peals of mirth.

But I see it as an early tragedy, however funny, for what could I have told the young warrior on the back fence? That I was not a "Chink"—only a "Jap?" My childish instinct had but introduced me to the polite withdrawal, as one of the few possible responses to other people's little phantasms concerning me. True, I have long since reached the saturation point, and now frequently view with intense gaiety the mental gyrations of my critics.

At that time I was attending John Dewey's school of Education, but there I was the ever conspicuous Japanese. This was exactly what they strove to avoid, but their constant reassurance made one doubt. There was Barr, a Mexican girl who came each day with her swarthy Mexican nurse, there was a Dutch boy with a peculiarly blurred accent, there was a french Miss whose dresses were always copied by sewing mothers, there was Aie Fujita, a real Japanese child, the consul's little girl and there were still a good majority of thorough Anglo-Saxons for contrast. Our teachers constantly reiterated that, "All nations are the same. Though the little Dutch boys wear wooden shoes and the little Chinese ladies pinch their feet and the little Eskimos wear fur boots, we are all the same, we are just alike. One human family." Dear teachers, kind, well meaning souls who so earnestly fought to blanket the word "human." But this little polyglot community of my early school days was "human" enough to make us feel our differences. We were a collection of freaks, of children with race contrasts or faddist mothers and we never doubted it for an instant! How many internationalists make this same mistake! Do they ever convince?

Every summer Mother and I made a pilgrimage to Forest Hall. The long summer months spent there brought me a fulfillment of love for America, which can never be broken. Slowly and secretly this country became my native land. Secretly, because at the time my mother had taught me to say, "Grandmother, Mother and Uncle Frank are British, but Father and I are Japanese," and to look forward to a time when I should find my real home in that remote, unknown Japan.

But the peace and security of these early days were all shattered and broken by the death of my Uncle Frank. My Grandmother for the only time in my remembrance of her, seemed crushed. But strangest of all my mother and father seemed to have lost something vital from their relationship. All the pleasant chatter and intimacy were gone. As for myself, I buried all of my happiest childhood in his grave. And then, one day, I was thirteen at the time, my mother announced that we were going to Japan as father was being sent out by the Corticelli Silk Company as a silk buyer.

I dreaded leaving my Grandmother, for I could not readjust myself so suddenly to the new order, and my cousins became doubly dear. Now that I was actually going, I lost my curiosity about Japan, I was not at all sure that I wanted to see Japan after all. I began to understand that what was for my mother a flaring adventure, and for my father a turning homeward, was for me only the tragedy of tearing away all my early roots of home and homeland.

My only consoling thought was that at last I would cease to be "une chose pour rire"—"the little Japanese"—a toy for the passing whim of the public mind. In other words I was at last to become ordinary, inconspicuous. I was to feel a oneness with a people. I should no longer be "different." It is only when one can understand my utter faith in my Orientalism, that one can glimpse the extent of my disappointment and disillusionment!

Disillusionment can be a comedy and a tragedy all rolled into one! I had believed that I was Japanese and that Japan was my home. Why should I have doubted this when no one had ever suggested otherwise, when everyone, in fact, had assured me that it was so?

Fear is said to be man's greatest emotion and with fear I greeted Japan. And with every step I took after alighting from our ship at Yokohama, my original fear increased. Nothing I had been taught, told or imagined was in the least like Japan and this much being true, what was I to expect? Such disillusionment gave me an uncertainty as to everything in the world. No kitten was ever put in a cage with wild cats with more instincts for self-preservation than I and to me Japan was even worse than wild cats—it was gargoyles and disenchantment.

In Chicago I had been merely conspicuous in what now appeared to have been a limited social group. In Yokohama I was something far worse than conspicuous, I was a regular show for the entire city! I was not even going to be able to walk down the street without a crowd forming. This was demolition of illusion with vengeance. My only alternative was not to care and this I could not quite do, for I was half Japanese.

"What does the word *Ijin san* mean?" I asked at last of my father.

His look was full of sympathy as he answered quietly, " It means foreigner."

The facts were these—in America I was Japanese. In Japan I was an American. I had an Oriental father who wished to live like an Occidental and an Irish mother who wished to live like a Japanese. I had a series of eccentric traditions on my Western side and a thousand unknown, silent Tamagawas, buried in their own family cemetery on the other.

My mother's friends had thought of me as a decoration, or a gimcrack; and my father's friends now thought of me as a barbarism and a blemish. I had had an uncle in America who had played doll's store on the ironing board for my amusement, and I now had an uncle in Japan who sat on a cushion, in the mysterious dimness of an inner temple and "thought he was God"—Was this to be for my amusement also?

Somewhere in between all this, I existed. I was neither American, nor Irish, nor Japanese. I had no race, nationality or home. Everybody, who seriously considered me at all, immediately focused upon me an eye glued to a microscope or monocle. I was a curiosity, of that I was certain and I could see little concealment or delicacy in it all. What I wanted to know was whether I was a pleasing or an unpleasing curiosity, for I could not spend my life chasing other people's trains of thought and missing one train after another. That was annoying even to an Irish-Japanese of thirteen years.

There was something vitally wrong with the logic of the whole situation. I was as far from being what I now recognized as the "Japanese doll," as a monkey is from being a jelly fish. But on the other hand, could I be as completely crude and boorish as my father's friends evidently thought me? My thinking resulted in chaos. There were no answers to these questions. They were all perplexing whirlpools of thought to me, aged thirteen, and instead of becoming quiet lakes of reflections, some of them have become regular maelstroms, now that I am thirty-six. I began to see that people thought in groups, in societies, in nations and in whole races, and they all thought differently. The unaccepted, the unexpected, like myself, must remain forever outside of it all, but nature fortunately left such exceptions with a sense of humor.

I lived on in Japan and yet never as a Japanese would live, and I was Japanese and I was not Japanese. For no one who had even the most superficial knowledge of Japan considered that I was Japanese, and the Japanese themselves considered me as a foreigner, and yet was I a real American? Would I ever be completely anything? Or must I always be the exception? Unanswerable questions.

Meanwhile I grew up in the foreign community of Yokohama, and reached at last the leisurely years of 1910–12. I made my debut and was "popular" as all we girls bred in the foreign community were. It was an October evening in 1911 that I first met Frank Eldridge, "one of the boys from the American Consulate," at one of the most festive of consular parties. I fell in love with him immediately because I thought him divinely ordinary.

If there was one thing I longed for above all others at that point of my existence, it was the ordinary. To be simple—insignificant—and to melt inconspicuously into some environment—seemed to me worth the ambition of a lifetime. This was quite understandable for I had found my seat on the bucking bronco of internationalism, anything but restful. . . . Try as I would I could never find the charm in being raceless, countryless, and now to all intents and purposes practically relativeless as well—though mother said it was charming and many agreed with her. Like the old song from the opera Pinafore, I "might have been a Roosian or a French or Turk or Proosian, or perhaps Itali-an." For by the time I was introduced to my prince of the proletariats, I had had the opportunity of dismissing a number of worldly and attractive men of different nationalities. But I had had my practical lessons in trying to be native in two countries and I lacked any curiosity for a third splicing of my nationality.

We were married a year later. I was nineteen at the time and Frank was twenty three. Of course, I was to find that the most actually extraordinary man of the lot was my husband. But I did not discover this until I was so firmly rooted in the character of the conservative Mrs. Eldridge, that I had forgotten I had ever been considered, or had considered myself a freak, and from that safe viewpoint could even admire his unexpectedness.

In the spring of 1914 Frank sailed for America to enter private business. The plan was for me to stay on in Japan and await the success of his business affairs before following him and so it was not till the next spring that he sent for me.

There were many, many things that entered into my feeling about my homegoing. I wanted to go. I had never really loved Japan, though I had been deeply interested. Nevertheless the language, the habits, the Bushido had made a stranger of me; to Japan I was always a foreigner.

I sailed on the *S. S. China*. My destination in the United States was the

South. That meant only a place "where Frank was" to me then, but it turned out to be a place where a lot of other people were as well.

To live in a small southern town, to do my own work and be Mrs. Eldridge, —a nice insignificant, every-day sort of person was just what I had most wished to do. I had never discussed the matter with my husband. Needless to say I had not stressed the fact that I especially admired what I considered his "divine ordinariness" and it never occurred to me that he might have admired me for any of my unusualness. This I had always believed to be but an illusion in other people's minds. But Frank had been a whole year in that southern town and he had been enthusiastically expecting me for months. He met me filled with desire to present me to his new-found friends, and attentions were heaped upon me by everyone.

It is of these attentions which I wish to speak. They are the "prayers in the horse's ear." They came to me in that southern town and they come to me still from the majority of the people I meet. They surprise me. They seem to me to be vague utterances of a mystic Western philosophy, which my horse's ear refuses to understand. They are definite schools of thought with which people here in the United States make their friendly onslaughts upon me.

As a little girl when I went to Japan I had thought I was to be Japanese, but the Japanese themselves had gaped at me and decided differently. Now that I had returned to America, the problem was something complex and at first confusing to me in that quiet southern town.

People did a great deal more than gape at me. They had "ideas" about me, theories, preconceptions—*beliefs!*

One type thought of me as "cute." I remember once being taken to an Arts Club by one of these persons, and being introduced as the "little Japanese lady."

Then there are the people who insist that I am an Oriental and when I even meekly suggest that I have certain doubts on the subject, they assume the attitude that I am posing as an Occidental but that they are too clever and have discovered me. They usually end by getting very sentimental over Oriental art and religion and find in my reticence all sorts of mysterious and beautiful philosophies which I, being an Oriental, do not reveal.

There are the moderns who analyze my sentences as I talk, "Ah, now—that's your Irish," "Ah, now—that's your Japanese." These are usually the most annoying, for they consistently refuse to be human. They generally close their ears to what I am saying in their efforts to have me properly assorted and psychologically tabulated.

There are the anthropological hounds. They are not half bad, because in their intellectual peregrinations they have discovered that mixed races have existed since the world began. Their examinations are limited to the shape of my nose and the quality of my hair.

There are the dramatists who are interested in what they call my "racial pulls." What am I feeling? In America, do I long for Japan? In Japan do I long for America? Or do my feelings explode when they clash somewhere in the middle of the Pacific as they rush violently in both directions?

The educationalists (and not all of them are confined to the schools and colleges) have a keen desire to make something out of me. Meanwhile they consider me a sort of Oriental information bureau. "Are the Japanese becoming a

Christian Nation?" "Is it true that the Chinese are more honest than the Japanese?"—and so on.

There are the people who are actually afraid of me. I am a menace! I find them in all classes of society from the most charming of Californians to my colored scrub-woman, whom I found one night sitting on the front door-step.

"Lucy, what are you doing out here?"

"Oh Miss Eldridge, I'se afeared. I never did like to work with them idols in the house nohow, and money ain't gwine to hire me to stay in thar after it gits dark."

Fortunately for the welfare of my soul, however, there is a great middle class who after they have discovered my heredity, do accept the "is" where they find it. They start by asking me, "Just when did you learn to eat with a knife and fork?" "How long did it take your feet to grow?" Then they urge me to "say something in Japanese so I can hear what it's like," and by that time they are feeling almost as foolish as they care to feel and begin to be human by "say, which do you think it is better to lead from, a sneak or just follow the fourth-highest-of-your-longest-suit rule?"

Frank introduced me to all these varieties of thought in that southern town. After several months of their attention and consideration, I began to wonder seriously if I was actually as phenomenal as without doubt I was supposed to be.

My eldest son, Francis, was expected in July 1916. It was decided that I was to go to the hospital to receive him. At the time I was miserable and depressed. I was very happy with my husband but I had not found myself living the nice sequestered life I had pictured. Though I had been supplied with all the materials, a good husband, a small salary; a quiet town, life's most conventional domestic situation; a coming baby . . . and so far as I could see, it should have been the most ordinary of all American situations and I the most average and usual of all American girls—I was not!

As soon as I reached the hospital I was greeted by a young nurse who ushered me into the stifling hot little room where my son was to be born, and when I gave my name, she grinned a knowing assurance, "Oh, we all know *all* about you. We are all so interested."

I think most women feel when they enter the hospital on these occasions that they are victims of one of Nature's dreadful traps, but I suddenly felt as I looked at my neat uniformed attendant, that I was trapped by Humanity as well. I had not crawled into some impersonal hole wherein I could have my baby in peace. Instead, I had been heralded by Heaven alone knew what mysterious beliefs about me. Was I a Japanese doll, or a menace? Her sickly sweet smile informed me that in her case at least it was the Japanese doll.

After a while another nurse whisked into the room. She was cold and formal, but I soon felt that she too "knew all about me." She dismissed the first with a quiet stare and jammed a thermometer into my mouth with a do-or-die attitude that was provoking. To this one I was a menace, but at least I could hope to count on her impersonal service.

Then, a long animal-like cry shattered my thoughts.

"What's that?"

"That?" She dismissed it with a sniff. "One of those half-nigger girls in the ward. It is her first baby. She has been going on like that for hours. You can hear her all over the place every time the door is opened."

"Poor, poor thing. Can't something be done for her?"

"Oh, she's alright. These niggers make an awful 'to-do' about nothing."

"Oh—" the pain had wrenched my back. But I must not let this woman say that about me. I must be silent. This place wasn't a hospital. No. It was a sort of moral testing ground. Whatever happened I would be "decent." No one would ever say, "It's that Jap girl in room 31, making an awful 'to-do' about nothing."

Hours after hour the pains grew more terrible. But I was silent. With each new racking attack of horror I drew on every atom of my will power not to cry out, not to betray my mother, my father and husband who believed me to be *decent*.

The room, the doctor and the nurses all faded away from my sight into a blazing world of pain. Then suddenly as if suffering were only an asbestos curtain at the theatre, it lifted and I was conscious of the room and the people and my coral-colored son who was being held up by his heels and shaken by the doctor.

I must admit that just for a second or so I felt heroic. Everyone in the room seemed to be feeling that emotional relief that can but be called happiness. But all this feeling of ecstasy lasted for only five or ten minutes. It was the youngest nurse who smashed it all with, "Isn't the baby too cute! It's not often that the Stork brings us a little Japanese baby!"

Next morning the old nurse was as ungracious as ever. My heroism of the night before had not melted her.

I dared to question her, "Was there anything unusual about the birth?"

"No, absolutely normal."

That was something to be glad about. I could at least have an average birth to my credit. I was not unusual or extraordinary in that.

But half an hour later the younger nurse had destroyed my illusions.

"The doctor says it's a perfectly *marvelous* case. Of course these things have been known to be true in the Orient. But to have it happen right here in our own hospital!"

"What happened?"—"What is it?"

"A PAINLESS birth!"

Nineteen seventeen—the war, and we were off to Washington, Frank accepting the post of assistant Chief of the Far Eastern Division, Department of Commerce. In Washington I found that I was no longer an Adams or a Tamagawa,—I was Mrs. Eldridge. I baked and scrubbed and attended functions and played bridge with the other wives of the Department officials. Most of the other Department officials' wives were doing the same thing. I was not sequestered, nor even rooted, but, at least, I was ordinary.

I belonged completely and absolutely to this international group of roving diplomats and cruising Trade Commissioners and Attaches and their families. I felt and knew their esprit de corps and was one with them as I never have been one with any other group. These people were filled with too many other interests to bother about whether I was Japanese or not. Who-is-who and why was a far more interesting question than whether or not I was a little Japanese lady, or a menace.

The years went on in Washington, happy, satisfying years. Although our

Washington friends still arrived and departed we ourselves had now begun to feel like old residents. In fact, never before had I felt such delusions of a rooted security. Day followed day without the tremor of a change,—nothing seemed to indicate the slightest disturbance of my happily dull and calm existence. . . .

And then, a shattering event took place on the other side of the world which was to vitally effect our lives—September first 1923, the great earthquake of Japan! This tremendous cataclysm changed the destinies of almost all those who had even the remotest connections over there, however far they were scattered over the world. It shook us out of our smugness of mind, scattered our peace, demolished our illusions of security. It brought Mother back to America, shaken in spirit, in faith and in her ability to "flair."

My mother's presence in our household made us face facts that might otherwise have been buried in our busy lives. When she came to us she brought Japan with her and renewed my own mental confusion regarding my ancestry without meaning to do so. In fact, her intention was just the opposite, to make me forget my Japanese. Her expressed position was that there was no problem in an Eurasian marriage and she retained her viewpoint until the day she died.

However, I do not approve of Eurasian marriages. I do not approve of international marriages. Because this world is full of uncertainties, confusions and insecurities for all of us. Occidental and Oriental alike are afraid to climb down from the psychological horses they are riding however many prayers our priests of philosophy, science, economy and travel may be muttering. We must stick to our horses or fall, because we have not yet learned to unhorse gracefully. I disapprove of Eurasian marriages because there are so few among the many in Europe, in Asia or in America who have the wit and ability or the moral and spiritual stamina and determination, or the keen, blind, deaf and dumb intellect that will allow them to drive their psychological horse in triumph to its goal.

And now with my mother gone and my father in Japan the problem of their marriage should have ended. But I now find that it has only just seriously begun, for the Japanese Government now tells me that I do not exist, that I never have existed, as far as they are concerned, because I was never registered as a Japanese. Here, then, is an official refusal to accept the "is" of the thing. Legally I am not and never was; therefore, I cannot be the lineal descendant of my parents or an inheritor of my mother's estate.

My lawyers say that I am "an ultimate, international, legal absurdity." As a citizen of Nowhere, I don't know whether it's better to be a born Oriental, or a born Occidental. I don't know whether Japan is the delightful fairyland of Lafcadio Hearn, or the dangerous yellow peril of the Californians. I don't know whether I have had the ideal home and the perfectly mated parents that my mother said I had, or whether I was the victim of one of the most horrible marital combinations ever perpetrated. I'm not even sure that I'm not the world's prize freak, though I believe myself to be addicted to the conventional life. Who can say whether it's better to dance on your heels with your toes turned in, or on your toes with your heels turned in?

Perhaps it's wise to be foolish and foolish to be wise. But it's safer, much safer, to ride a nice, still, conventional wooden horse secured to a merry-go-round than a wild, untrained and untamed international steed.

For, only the non-existent can stand on their feet in mid-Pacific!

A NATIVE ALIEN

By W. E. B. DuBois

BETWEEN ME AND THE OTHER WORLD there is ever an unasked question: unasked by some through feelings of delicacy; by others through the difficulty of rightly framing it. All, nevertheless, flutter round it. They approach me in a half-hesitant sort of way, eye me curiously or compassionately, and then, instead of saying directly, How does it feel to be a problem? they say, I know an excellent colored man in my town; or, I fought at Mechanicsville; or, Do not these Southern outrages make your blood boil? At these I smile, or am interested, or reduce the boiling to a simmer, as the occasion may require. To the real question, How does it feel to be a problem? I answer seldom a word.

And yet, being a problem is a strange experience,—peculiar even for one who has never been anything else, save perhaps in babyhood and in Europe. It is in the early days of rollicking boyhood that the revelation first bursts upon one, all in a day, as it were. I remember well when the shadow swept across me. I was a little thing, away up in the hills of New England, where the dark Housatonic winds between Hoosac and Taghkanic to the sea. In a wee wooden schoolhouse, something put it into the boys' and girls' heads to buy gorgeous visiting-cards—ten cents a package—and exchange. The exchange was merry, till one girl, a tall newcomer, refused my card,—refused it peremptorily, without a glance. Then it dawned upon me with a certain suddenness that I was different from the others; or like, mayhap, in heart and life and longing, but shut out from their world by a vast veil. I had thereafter no desire to tear down that veil, to creep through; I held all beyond it in common contempt, and lived above it in a region of blue sky and great wandering shadows. That sky was bluest when I could beat my mates at examination-time, or beat them at a foot-race, or even beat their stringy heads. Alas, with the years all this fine contempt began to fade; for the worlds I longed for, and all their dazzling opportunities, were theirs, not mine. But they should not keep these prizes, I said; some, all, I would wrest from them. Just how I would do it I could never decide: by reading law, by healing the sick, by telling the wonderful tales that swam in my head,—some way. With other black boys the strife was not so fiercely sunny: their youth shrunk into tasteless sycophancy, or into silent hatred of the pale world about them and mocking distrust of everything white; or wasted itself in a bitter cry, Why did God make me an outcast and a stranger in mine own house? The shades of the prison-house closed round about us all: walls strait and stubborn to the whitest, but relentlessly narrow, tall, and unscalable to sons of night who must plod darkly on in resignation, or beat unavailing palms against the stone, or steadily, half hopelessly, watch the streak of blue above.

After the Egyptian and Indian, the Greek and Roman, the Teuton and Mongolian, the Negro is a sort of seventh son, born with a veil, and gifted with second-sight in this American world,—a world which yields him no true self-consciousness, but only lets him see himself through the revelation of the other world. It is a peculiar sensation, this double-consciousness, this sense of always looking at one's self through the eyes of others, of measuring one's soul by the tape of a world that looks on in amused contempt and pity. One ever feels his two-ness,—an American, a Negro; two souls, two thoughts, two unreconciled strivings; two warring ideals in one dark body, whose dogged strength alone keeps it from being torn asunder.

ENGLISHMAN OR JEW?

By Maurice Samuel

"WHATEVER STANDS BETWEEN MAN AND MAN, as God made us, is error," I said. "Take me as I am. What if my father does tell me I am a Jew? What he tells me does not alter me, except as I permit it, sentimentally, unreasonably. Suppose, to your confusion, I were a changeling, an English child left in Roumania, brought up by Jews here in your midst. I would still, for all my blood relationship, feel myself a stranger to your pride of heritage—and only because of a thing said to me. This barrier which rises between us is something unreal, then. It has no foundation in the nature of things; that which only words create, words can uncreate.

"This past," I said, "this tyrannous past—you and I make it. The past *is not,* except as you and I will it to be. I have willed the English past to exist in me, as you have willed it to exist in you. Why, then, is it yours more than mine? Are the experiences of your fathers stamped into your blood, making you more fit than another to carry on the civilization which they founded?"

"Assuredly it is so," I was answered. "Only Englishmen have, in the first place, that attitude toward things which has produced England's institutions and her civilization. The Frenchman has his own way of reacting toward life. The Russian, the Italian—each is fashioned in a general mold. There may be overlappings—but Englishmen could not have produced the civilization of France, nor Frenchmen the civilization of England. Each race produces after its own fashion. You, a Jew, can produce, feel, think, only in the fashion of your race. And further, if there is such a thing as a racial type (and can you deny it? Look at the world around you, the tone and temper of lands), whence can it arise but from inherited memory, worked into our fiber: we say the blood, but we mean the entirety of the man. It is not you who make the past; it is the past which makes you. It made you a Jew, as it made us Englishmen."

This statement, plausible, convincing, was a sufficient and final argument—if only it were true. If a race, from generation to generation, is an organism with its record written into the structure of its children, if the past is in our blood, in this special and immediate sense, then my extrusion was real, and my distress corresponded not to sentimentalities, but to ultimate human realities. I was then a stranger, in the midst of others than my own kind—to be received, welcomed, befriended, made an equal in all things, except in what matters most—a misfortune to be faced, but not be argued away.

But *was* it true? I sought the answer among scientists, and they said, "It is not true." There was nothing in the world of science which bore out this quiet assumption of racial aptitudes, with its corollary of racial memory. It was impossible to define races even on a purely physical basis—let alone in the tenuous terminology of the romantic psychologists.

"The Englishman is slow, steady; the Frenchman volatile, but logical; the Russian dreamy, mystical." It was the easiest thing in the world to say this and to illustrate it with all manner of quotations and incidents. One could as easily say the reverse, and argue it with equal plausibility. But in actual fact they could not demonstrate any acceptable difference between the Englishman and the Frenchman. To whatever test and measurement you submitted a number of Frenchmen, you obtained practically the same results from the same number of Englishmen. Cephalic indices either on the plan of the skull or on the end elevation, nasal indices, whatever ingenuities anthropometry has devised, yielded the same result. The body of man was the same everywhere; the same nerves reacted in the same fashion to the same stimuli. The babies of all races were identical in all respects that mattered. One was not born an Englishman, with an English inheritance. One was born merely a human being, and the "pride," the "inheritance," the "share in the past" were the result of education, or "conditioning." Any human being could be brought up to be moved by pride of English heritage.

There were differences, of course. The Chinaman is yellow, even as a baby; the negro is black. There is some rough correspondence of skull shapes among Eskimos, or among Australian aborigines. There may even be a classification of this kind holding between Nordics, Alpines, and Mediterraneans. Certain groups of human beings may be successfully classified according to the cross index of their hair. But who has yet proved that any of these physical characteristics are related to any psychological predispositions? You may say with safety that southern Europeans are darker-skinned than northern Europeans. But on what basis do you go on from this classification to assert that darker skins go with "more violent passions?" If you find a number of blonds among darker southern races, will you single them out as being less emotional than their neighbors? If you find a number of brunets among lighter northern races, will you single them out as being more temperamental? Suppose we grant that the Alpine type is more frequently brachycephalous than the Nordic. And suppose we grant that Nordics are by nature mystics, Alpines logicians (an almost meaningless classification), will you then go on to say that brachycephalous Nordics are more logical than their neighbors, dolichocephalous Alpines more mystical?

My Englishmen said one thing; dispassionate study said something else; namely, that race in the sense my Englishmen spoke of did not exist. Nature does not know of races, psychically. It knows only of man. Nobody is an Englishman or a Jew or a Frenchman "by birth." In the matter of mental predisposition or faculties, nobody is even a negro or a Chinaman.

Such is the verdict of science, and it was the verdict I needed. I could thenceforth look upon the tacit exclusiveness of the Englishman as something quite irrelevant to the true situation. His pride was an error. As such it need not disturb me. True, he clung to his error, acting, as human beings do, not on what is the truth, but on what they conceive to be the truth. Theoretically, at least, I did not let this disturb me. I was rehabilitated in equality. Science had demonstrated that in all respects he and I were the same.

But what had begun as a revolt against the tyranny of the recorded past developed into something which carried me far beyond the limits of my original problem. I had set out to prove myself an Englishman, by proving that I was the same as my neighbor. And science proved for me that I was the same as my neighbor, but neither of us was an Englishman or anything else. As the barrier fell between Jew and Englishman, it fell also between Englishman and Frenchman, and German and Russian. This delight of race (not to speak of its pride) was the illusion of a savage; the historic past transmitted nothing to any man. The Englishman's assertion that his race was by inward nature the guardian of certain human values, individual and social, was devoid of meaning. Equally invalid were the similar claims of all other peoples.

There was lifted for me, at that time, the veil which concealed the treacherous and tremendous conspiracy of environment against the pure intelligence of man. It was a conspiracy which subtly corrupted the intelligence at its source, and extended into almost every subject connected with human progress. I was interested at first only in the problem of individual identity, the basis of all true advance, in the mind, as it should be, *could* be—an instrument of clear perception—were it not for the fine, all-persuasive net of rationalized prejudices which the world offers us as "education." A child was subjected, during the years of its extremest sensitiveness, to unrelenting mental pressure resulting in a deformity which was practically incurable. At home, in the school, in its first social contacts, it was taught that it was an "Englishman." The huge machinery of its environment was directed to one end—the warping of its natural intelligence. So effectively was the task performed that assumptions utterly repugnant to logic became "self-evident truths"; efforts to dislodge them were received with bitter resentment as an assault on man's dearest possessions, and the disinterested idealism of the free-thinker was interpreted as a sort of original evil, the pure *Schadenfreude* of Satan; men became infatuated with stupidity, not only taking pride in it, but defending it with an involved and passionate ingenuity, one half of which, soberly applied to human problems, might prepare the millennium for the next generation. Part of this huge machine (*part,* because after all there had been the counter-conspiracy of a Jewish home) had sufficed to convince me that I was "an Englishman." The accident of birth (I might never have rebelled if I had not been born "a Jew") later compelled me to revise this conviction. Between the two conspiracies I arrived at the truth, as, when thieves fall out, honest men come by their own.

And I saw the objective, as well as the subjective, evil in which this culminated. I had been excluded from the ultimate spiritual benefit of being an Englishman because, born of Jewish parents, I was assumed to have inherited a mysterious biological quantity which marked me off from the rest of mankind.

My first sufferings had been intense. I had been made to feel a stranger, with no ultimate share in the life around me. But the case of the individual was of little importance, and mine particularly so because, realizing that I was not being excluded from anything real (unless it were from the prejudices of my friends) I could learn to accept the gesture of expulsion with tolerance, perhaps amusement. The case as between nation and nation involved the most fearful consequences. Here were great, civilized, and intelligent groups of human beings who regarded each other as belonging to different species. Their mentality warped by patriotic histories, by shallow and unjustified differentiations, they grew up in the belief that an unbridgeable gulf separated them. Out of this sense of fundamental separation grew suspicion and dislike, a fertile breeding-ground for sudden outbursts of hatred, for wars, for the most monstrous sort of perversions.

RACE IS AS RACE DOES

TRIED BEFORE Mr. Justice Evans, at Barnwell—Spring Term, 1835.

Indictment for larceny. On the trial, two of the principal witnesses for the prosecution were objected to as incompetent, on the ground that they were persons of color. An issue was made up and this question submitted to the jury. It appeared that the father of the witnesses was a white man, and their mother a descendant in the third degree of a half breed who had a white wife; their mother's father was the issue of this marriage, and he also married a white woman; so that the witnesses had one-sixteenth part of African blood. The maternal grandfather of the witnesses, although of dark complexion, had been recognized as a white man, received into society, and exercised political privileges as such; their mother was uniformly treated as a white woman; their relations of the same admixture have married into respectable families, and one of them had been a candidate for the legislature. The witnesses were ordinarily fair, and exhibited none of the distinctive marks of the African race; they are respectable, have always been received into society, and recognized as white men—one of them is a militia officer, and their caste has never been questioned until now. His honor charged the jury, that if there be a clear visible admixture evidenced by the color of the skin, the hair or features, the person is to be regarded as of the degraded class; but if these distinctive characteristics be wanting, and the person has been received and treated as white, although there may be proof of some admixture derived from a remote ancestor, yet such person is to be accounted white, and entitled to privileges as such. The jury found that the witnesses were not persons of color; they were then sworn, and the defendant found guilty.

Reprinted from State v. Cantey, 2 Hill, *South Carolina Reports* (1835), 613–618.

On a motion for a new trial the only questions were as to the correctness of this charge, and the competence of these witnesses.

(The opinion, rendered in this case by Justice Harper, shows that it was necessary to take a very broad interpretation of the term mulatto.)

HARPER, J. We feel no disposition to depart from the rule laid down in the State v. Davis and Hannah, 2 Bail. 558. The ground of that decision is, that neither of the several statutes which speak of "negroes, mulattoes and persons of color," nor the constitution of the State, which restricts political privileges to "free white men," give any definition of those terms, nor is there any known technical meaning affixed to them. We must of necessity then suppose them to have been used in their ordinary and popular signification; and to the ordinary and popular signification we must resort for the interpretation of the laws. From what possible source could a definition be drawn which would make a person who has no visible mixture of negro blood, as evidenced by complexion, features or favor, and who is received in society and generally reputed to be a free white person, mulatto or person of color? Indeed it would be an absurdity in terms to say that such an one is, in the popular sense of the word, a person of color. If we should say that such an one is to be regarded as a person of color, on account of any mixture of negro blood, however slight or remote, we should be making, instead of declaring the law, and making a very cruel and mischievous law. It is this which makes the question peculiarly proper for a jury. It belongs to them to settle questions of common usage and the meaning of popular terms, though their decisions may be matured into rules of law.

The principal argument urged against the rule we have adopted, is its want of precision. We cannot say what admixture of negro blood will make a colored person, and, by a jury, one may be found a colored person, while another of the same degree of blood may be declared a white man. In general it is very desirable that rules of law should be certain and precise. But it is not always practicable, nor is it practicable in this instance. Nor do I know that it is desirable. The condition of the individual is not to be determined solely by the distinct and visible mixture of negro blood, but by reputation, by his reception into society, and his having commonly exercised the privileges of a white man. But his admission to these privileges, regulated by the public opinion of the community in which he lives, will very much depend on his own character and conduct; and it may be well and proper, that a man of worth, honesty, industry and respectability, should have the rank of a white man, while a vagabond of the same degree of blood should be confined to the inferior caste. It will be a stimulus to the good conduct of these persons, and security for their fidelity as citizens. It is hardly necessary to say that a slave cannot be a white man. In the case before us, the grandfather of the witnesses in question exercised all the privileges of a free white person; his descendants have continued to do so till the present day. Shall time and prescription, which secure and consecrate all other rights, have no effect in fixing the civil condition of an individual?

It is perhaps not necessary to advert particularly to some of the arguments which were urged. It seemed to be argued as if there were no necessary connexion between the degree of negro blood and its appearance in the person; that an individual of unmixed European descent, may approach to the negro features and complexion, and one having a large proportion of negro blood may be free from these distinctive marks. But in general this is not so. I doubt whether a person of unmixed European blood, though he might be darker than many a colored person, would ever be mistaken for one. And it can hardly happen that a person having more than an eighth of negro blood will not betray it in his person. It is true that some individuals retain the distinctive marks of their descent much longer than others, and it may be that one who has lost these marks in his own person, may see them re-appear in some degree in his children. But if such cases should occur, a jury will be aided by the circumstances of reputation, &c., to which I have referred, and if there should be extraordinary departures from the general course of mixture, the questions arising out of them may, I have no doubt, be satisfactorily determined by the jury. It is indeed rather a question of fact for them, than referable to any definitive rule of law.

We wish it to be understood that this matter is regarded as settled, that it is not every admixture of negro blood, however slight and remote that will make a person of color, within the meaning of the law; and that this Court will very rarely feel itself authorized to interfere with the verdict of a jury. I think it to be regretted that the question was made in the present case, and hope that the same question will not be again made under the same circumstances. It is doing unnecessary violence to the feelings of persons, who in this instance are admitted to be of much worth and respectability.

WHICH BROTHER IS THE JEW?

By Budd Schulberg

AFTER THE WAR, prices went higher, but there was no change in the pushcart business. The talk at meals was always money now. The Glicksteins were behind in their rent. A newsboys' take was no longer enough to complement the old man's income. The boys had to find regular jobs.

Sammy and [his brother] Israel both answered a call for messenger boys. There were hundreds of others. For hours they cussed and fought each other for places near the door because their parents had sent them all out with the same fight talk, spoken in English, Yiddish, Italian, and with a brogue—Sammy, Israel, Joe, Pete, Tony, Mike, if you don't get that job today we don't know what we'll do.

Israel was just ahead of Sammy. They had been waiting since six in the morning for the doors to open at eight. They were chilled outside, nervous inside.

When the doors opened at last and Israel was finally standing before the checker, he was told:

"Sorry, kid—Ain't hirin' no Hebes."

Reprinted from Budd Schulberg, *What Makes Sammy Run?* (Garden City: The Sun Dial Press, 1943), pp. 240–1; copyright 1941 by Budd Schulberg and used with the kind permission of Random House, Inc.

As Israel hesitated there, crying inside, Sammy suddenly threw himself at him and knocked him down.

"What the hell did you do that for?" said the checker.

"That dirty kike cut in ahead of me," Sammy screamed.

The checker looked at Sammy curiously. Sammy stood there, small, spider-like, intense, snarling at Israel.

"Fer Chris'sake, you look like a Jew-boy yerself."

"Oh, Jesus, everybody's always takin' me for one of them goddam sheenies," Sammy yelled. Then he broke into gibberish Italian.

ACTIONS, NOT APPEARANCE,
DECIDE RACE

United Press

BERLIN, MARCH 28, 1936.—(UP)—A German may be tall, blonde, and have a long skull and not be a Nordic; and again, he may be short, with brown eyes and curls, and yet be a Nordic, for in this country not looks, but actions, decide the race.

This is the latest criterion propagated by Nazi racial experts. It at once reveals the ramifications of the racial problem for the Nazi party among whose most eminent leaders even a wellmeaning person will find it hard to detect one who, according to outward appearance, conforms to the Nordic ideal.

Fuehrer Adolf Hitler is dark. Paul Goebbels, minister of propaganda, is even more so. Hermann Goering, air force commander, although blonde and blue-eyed is rather the "Falian" type, Dr. Hjalmer Schacht, director of the Reichsbank, is perhaps the only Nordic in the whole cabinet.

So far, the new criterion has been set forth most pointedly by Dr. Eugen Staehle, ministerial councillor in the Wuerttemberg Ministry of the Interior. His axioms, moreover, have been distributed as guidance to all Nazi district headquarters.

Writing in "Volksgesundheitswacht," the organ of the party's special committee for public health, Staehle explained: "He who always struggles and makes sacrifices, he who without regard to himself devotes his entire strength in the party for the furtherance of a heroic aim, he who never shirks if a new honorary burden is added to his previous burdens, is a Nordic, no matter how he looks."

Without this spiritual attitude, blondness, blue eyes and the rest of outward attributes generally considered to make a Nordic, count for little. If they be the

United Press Dispatch from Berlin, Germany, March 28, 1936. Reprinted with the kind permission of the United Press Association.

attributes of a man not belonging to the Nazi party, so much the worse; for according to Staehle, "all the true Nordic people are already party members, while those still outside are of inferior race even if they be tall, blonde, and have long skulls."

Staehle also explains the "true" racial distinctions of the other European races. Here they are: "He who always carries a chip on his shoulder, who loves incense, the crosier, and the pompousness of overladen churches, who advocates authority and totality only in the realm of church dogma, who like Tannhäuser, first sings the praise of sin and afterwards begs for remission and clemency, is Western, even if he has a mop of blonde hair on his head.

"He who anxiously clings to denomination and in his thoughts is circling only around his own church spire, who when asked to buy a buttonhole for the Winter Relief wails: 'What! Again 20 pfennings? Doesn't that sort of thing ever stop?'—who miserly keeps his pennies and democratically grouses about everything without himself doing better, is Eastern, even though his eyes be blue as cornflowers.

"He who always criticizes the government because his father used to do it for tradition's sake, who carouses in hot beer halls, sings popular hits, drinks enormous quantities of the brew, and out of sheer goodwill breaks his neighbor's head by hitting him with a beer mug, is Dinarian, even though he has no peaked skull or aquiline nose.

"He who out of hatred inflicts wounds on an enemy and subsequently flows over with hypocritical repentence and piousness, who takes unemployment as something sent by fate and who at the most whines about it to higher powers, who yesterday yelled 'Hail Moscow,' and today as loudly cries, 'Hail Hitler,' is East Baltic and permanently needs a strong fist to keep him down lest treason spring from his deceptive racial soul.

"But he who destroys everything that is holy to others, who considers the flag a piece of red cloth with a white circle and something black in the center, who when he says 'work' means 'business' and always wants to live in luxury by the sweat of others, is a Jewish Bolshevist."

MOTIVES AND BASES OF POPULAR CLASSIFICATION

By N. S. Shaler

IT IS COMMONLY SUPPOSED that the process of classification is of a recondite nature to be used only in learned inquiries. It is, in fact, a necessary part of all thinking, and is more trusted to by untrained simple minds than by

Adapted from N. S. Shaler, *The Neighbor* (Boston: Houghton Mifflin Co., 1904), pp. 192–197, 207–208; copyright 1904 by N. S. Shaler and used with the kind permission of the estate of Gabriella Shaler Webb.

those whose thoughts are of a higher order. This desire for classification which I shall, for brevity, term the categoric motive, is recognizable in the lower animals, as well as in man. When a brute, as for instance a horse, sees a large moving object which is unfamiliar, he is at once frightened, and this for the reason that he has by ages of ancestral experience learned to form a group or category of such objects which it is profitable to be afraid of, for the reason that enemies lie in that group. If the thing is a sheet of paper blown by the wind, or an automobile, and the creature is forced to encounter it often, he will form a new category, or rather a subdivision of the old, of moving things with the particular features belonging to the paper or the horseless carriage, of which the individuals are not harmful. Of course, all this process of categorizing objects performed by the lower animals, and by lower man as well, is done without a trace of consciousness of what they are about. They do it after the manner of untrained men, for the reason that it is the only way in which intelligence can deal with the practically infinite number and variety of things that come to its attention. They have to divide these presentations of the universe into groups, those that may include enemies, those in which their species belong, those good to eat, etc., etc., and neglect all the rest as in no wise concerning them. The groups which are important to them are evidently subdivided, so that they hold quite a variety of genera and species in their limited minds.

When we observe the instinctive categoric motive in man, we find that it works exactly as in the vertebrates of lowlier estate, with the difference that it is much more important, leading to the construction of far more divisions and to a better definition of them. Thus while a horse has probably not more than a score of categories, the lowliest savage cannot do his work with his fellows or with the world without, it may be, a thousand of them. Each of these categories is represented in his mind by a type, usually a composite image made from his various seeings of objects included in it. Naturally, but not necessarily, there is a word or phrase by which the group may be called to mind. It is easy to see that success in life, in savage as in beast, depends upon the sufficiency of these categories. They must contain what needs be known for success and no more; they must be sharp, clear, and to the point; else some enemy, man or beast, not properly included, may slay him, or some improperly classified plant, unhappily categorized as good for eating, may poison him. In fact, I fear that some of my excessively Darwinian friends will, if they happen to note these statements, proceed at once to show that the survival of man has depended altogether on the fitness of his categories. I am myself inclined to think that the ability to classify effectively has had a considerable share in the myriad influences which have given our genus its marvelous success.

Assuming then the point that man does his thinking largely by the aid of his categories, let us note certain features which necessarily characterize these groups. First let us remark that in no case do these mental pictures approach accuracy. Even the naturalist, who with all his skill and patience sets down his description of a species, knows that he has done no more than describe certain salient points of the group; he is well aware that a life-time of observation on a single group would leave the task incomplete. In our ordinary categories we evidently include no more than experience teaches us to do, which is to regard only what immediately concerns us. Here and there a wise man, and his is the supreme task of wisdom, sets to work to widen the scope of his categories, particularly those which relate to mankind. With the common folk, the categories into which they fit the kinds of men are as gross as the others, such as may be denoted by good or bad; my sort or other sort, savage or civilized, Jew, "nigger," gentleman, and by scores of other words by which for our rude purposes we divide up our fellow-men.

When a category has been made it is thereafter recalled by some striking feature or features which can be easily seized on by eye or other senses, and becomes, so to say, the label of the thing, one that can be seen at a distance and one not likely to be mistaken. Thus the color of the skin is sufficient to categorize the Negro, or the shape of the nose the Jew. It does not seriously matter that an Arab may be blacker than a true African; for the reason that all these groups have to be made in a rough-and-ready way there is no time or skill for finished work. The main point being not so much to exclude all that should be put out, but to include all that by any chance should go in. Thus, for instance, it is better for a horse in the wilds to shy at many an innocuous object than to have the category of dangerous things insufficient in its extent. So with men it is safer in the various groups of enemies to include objects that are not inimical, rather than to leave any dangers out. So it comes to pass that with the primitive man all others than his own tribe are counted as enemies, or, with ourselves, all who are black are reckoned as of one kind. The result is that nearly all these groups which are the bases of our thinking are taken as indicating universal likeness among the included objects, while in fact they may denote only some relatively unimportant feature which conveniently serves as a sign of the category.

As soon as a category is established in the observational way there begin to accumulate about it certain emotional qualities; the states of mind aroused by contact with the things included in the group come to be associated with the name of it. This is true of inanimate objects, but it is vastly more true of the categories we form of men. There the traditional and literary impulses serve to gather about the name of a human group a body of emotions which awake when the word is spoken and which prevent any change in its connotation. Thus it is that such terms as Jew, "nigger," and the like become barriers to sympathetic advance. They are to common people insuperable obstacles to further understanding of the facts, and even to persons of well-trained minds they are hard to clear away, for they are founded not alone on human nature, but on that of all intelligence of man and brute. It is not too much to say that all social advance intimately depends on the extent to which we may be able to break down these ancient barriers and reconstruct our primitive classifications in the light of inquiry.

Let us consider what takes place when two men, mere strangers to one another, come together. The motive of classification leads each of them at once to recognize the approaching object first as living, then as human. The shape and dress carry the categorizing process yet further, so that they are placed in groups, as of this or that tribe or social class, and as these determinations are made they arouse the appropriate sympathies or hatreds such as by experience have become associated with the several categories. Be it observed that these judgments are spontaneous, instinctive, and unnoticed. They are made so by immemorial education in the art of contact which man has inherited from the life of the ancestral beasts and men; they have most likely been in some measure affirmed by selection, for these determinations as to the nature of the neighbor were in the lower stages of existence in brute and man of critical importance, the creatures lived or died according as they determined well or ill, swiftly or slowly. If we observe what takes place in our own minds at such meetings we will see that the action in its immediateness is like that of the eye-lids when the eye is threatened. As we say, it is done before we know it.

LANGUAGE AS A BASIS OF RACIAL CLASSIFICATION

By Edward Augustus Freeman

IT IS NO VERY GREAT TIME since the readers of English newspapers were, perhaps a little amused, perhaps a little startled, at the story of a deputation of Hungarian students going to Constantinople to present a sword of honor to an Ottoman general. The address and the answer enlarged on the ancient kindred of Turks and Magyars, on the long alienation of the dissevered kinsfolk, on the return of both in these later times to a remembrance of the ancient kindred and to the friendly feelings to which such kindred gave birth. The discourse has a strange sound when we remember the reigns of Sigismund and Wladislaus, when we think of the dark days of Nikopolis and Varna, when we think of Huniades encamped at the foot of Haemus, and of Belgrade beating back Mahomet the Conqueror from her gates. The Magyar and the Ottoman embracing with the joy of reunited kinsfolk is a sight which certainly no man would have looked forward to in the fourteenth or fifteenth century. Yet the Magyar students seem to have meant their address quite seriously. And the Turkish general, if he did not take it seriously, at least thought it wise to shape his answer as if he did. The thing sounds like comedy, almost like conscious comedy. But it is a kind of comedy which may become tragedy, if the idea from which it springs gets so deeply rooted in men's minds as to lead to any practical consequences.

To allege the real or supposed primeval kindred between Magyars and Ottomans as a ground for political action, or at least for political sympathy, in the affairs of the present moment, is an extreme case of the whole range of doctrines and sentiments which have in modern days gained a great power over men's minds. To make any practical inference from the primeval kindred of Magyar and Turk is indeed pushing the doctrine of race, and of sympathies arising from race, as far as it well can be pushed. As far as the great facts of history go, the kindred is of the vaguest and most shadowy kind. It comes to

Adapted from Edward Augustus Freeman, "Race and Language," *Historical Essays* (Third Series, 1879).

little more than the fact that Magyars and Ottomans are alike non-Aryan invaders who have made their way into Europe within recorded times, and that both have, rightly or wrongly, been called by the name of Turks. These do seem rather slender grounds on which to build up a fabric of national sympathy between two nations, when several centuries of living practical history all pull the other way. But it is the very wildness of the thing which gives it its importance. The doctrine of race, and of sympathies springing from race, must have taken very firm hold indeed of men's minds before it could be carried out in a shape which we are tempted to call so grotesque as this.

The plain fact is that the new lines of scientific and historical inquiry which have been opened in modern times have had a distinct and deep effect upon the politics of the age. Not in a merely scientific or literary point of view, but in one strictly practical, the world is not the same world as it was when men had not yet dreamed of the kindred between Sanscrit, Greek, and English, when it was looked on as something of a paradox that there was a distinction between Celtic and Teutonic tongues and nations. Ethnological and philological researches have opened the way for new national sympathies, new national antipathies, such as would have been unintelligible a hundred years ago. A hundred years ago the political community of which a man was a member had its traditional alliances and traditional enmities but these were seldom determined by theories about language or race. Not a soul then would have understood the feelings which have allowed Panslavism to be a great practical agent in the affairs of Europe, and which have made talk about "the Latin race," if not practical, at least possible. Least of all, would it have been possible to give any touch of political importance to what would have then seemed so wild a dream as a primeval kindred between Magyar and Ottoman.

That feelings such as these, and the practical consequences which have flowed from them, are distinctly due to scientific and historical teaching there can, I think, be no doubt. Religious sympathy and purely national sympathy are both feelings of much simpler growth, which need no deep knowledge nor any special teaching. The cry which resounded through Christendom when the Holy City was taken by the Mussulmans, the cry which resounded through Islam when the same city was taken by the Christians, the spirit which armed England to support French Huguenots and which armed Spain to support French Leaguers, all spring from motives which lie on the surface. Nor need we seek for any explanation but such as lies on the surface for the natural wish for closer union which arose among Germans or Italians who found themselves parted off by purely dynastic arrangements from men who were their countrymen in everything else. Such a feeling has to strive with the counter-feeling which springs from local jealousies and local dislikes; but it is a perfectly simple feeling, which needs no subtle research either to arouse or to understand it. The feeling here is that of nationality in the strictest sense, nationality in a purely local or geographical sense. It would exist all the same if Panslavism had never been heard of; it might exist though those who feel it had never heard of the Slavonic race at all. It is altogether another thing when we come to the doctrine of race, and of sympathies founded on race, in the wider sense. Here we have a feeling which professes to bind together, and which as a matter of fact has had a real effect in binding together, men whose kindred to one another is not so obvious at first sight as the kindred of Germans,

Italians, or Serbs who are kept asunder by nothing but a purely artificial political boundary. It is a feeling at whose bidding the call to union goes forth
to men whose dwellings are geographically far apart, to men who may have
had no direct dealings with one another for years or for ages, to men whose
languages, though the scholar may at once see that they are closely akin, may
not be so closely akin as to be mutually intelligible for common purposes. A
hundred years back the Servian might have cried for help to the Russian on
the ground of common Orthodox faith; he would hardly have called for help
on the ground of common Slavonic speech and origin. If he had done so, it
would have been rather by way of grasping at any chance, however desperate or
far-fetched, than as putting forward a serious and well understood claim which
he might expect to find accepted and acted on by large masses of men. He
might have received help, either out of genuine sympathy springing from
community of faith or from the baser thought that he could be made use of as
a convenient political tool. He would have got but little help purely on the
ground of a community of blood and speech which had had no practical result
for ages.

There is then a distinct doctrine of race, and of sympathies founded on
race, distinct from the feeling of community of religion, and distinct from the
feeling of nationality in the narrower sense. It is not so simple or easy a feeling
as either of those two. It does not in the same way lie on the surface; it is not
in the same way grounded on obvious facts which are plain to every man's
understanding. The doctrine of race is essentially an artificial doctrine, a
learned doctrine. It is an inference from facts which the mass of mankind could
never have found out for themselves; facts which, without a distinctly learned
teaching, could never be brought home to them in any intelligible shape. Now
what is the value of such a doctrine? Does it follow that, because it is con-
fessedly artificial, because it springs, not from a spontaneous impulse, but from
a learned teaching, it is therefore necessarily foolish, mischievous, perhaps
unnatural? It may perhaps be safer to hold that like many other doctrines, many
other sentiments, it is neither universally good nor universally bad, neither
inherently wise nor inherently foolish. A belief or a feeling which has a practical effect on the conduct of great masses of men, sometimes on the conduct of
whole nations, may be very false and very mischievous; but it is in every case
a great and serious fact, to be looked gravely in the face. Men who sit at their
ease and think that all wisdom is confined to themselves and their own clique
may think themselves vastly superior to the great emotions which stir our
times, as they would doubtless have thought themselves vastly superior to the
emotions which stirred the first Saracens or the first Crusaders. But the emotions are there all the same, and they do their work all the same. The most
highly educated man in the most highly educated society cannot sneer them out
of being.

The doctrine of race, in its popular form, is the direct offspring of the study
of scientific philology; and yet it is just now, in its popular form at least, somewhat under the ban of scientific philologers. It may often happen that, while
the scientific statement is the only true one for scientific purposes, the popular
version may also have a kind of practical truth for the somewhat rough and
ready purposes of a popular version. In our present case scientific philologers
are beginning to complain, with perfect truth and perfect justice from their own

point of view, that the popular doctrine of race confounds race and language. They tell us, and they do right to tell us, that language is no certain test of race, that men who speak the same tongue are not therefore necessarily men of the same blood. And they tell us further, that from whatever quarter the alleged popular confusion came, it certainly did not come from any teaching of scientific philologers.

The truth of all this cannot be called in question. We have too many instances in recorded history of nations laying aside the use of one language and taking to the use of another, for anyone who cares for accuracy to set down language as any sure test of race. There are men who by speech belong to one nation, by actual descent to another. If they lose the physical characteristics of the race to which the original settler belonged, it will be due to inter-marriage, to climate, to some cause altogether independent of language. Every nation will have some adopted children of this kind, more or fewer; men who belong to it by speech, but who do not belong to it by race. And what happens in the case of individuals happens in the case of whole nations. The pages of history are crowded with cases in which nations have cast aside the tongue of their forefathers, and have taken instead the tongue of some other people. Greek in the East, Latin in the West, became the familiar speech of millions who had not a drop of Greek or Italian blood in their veins. The same has been the case in later times with Arabic, Persian, Spanish, German, English. Each of those tongues has become the familiar speech of vast regions where the mass of the people are not Arabian, Spanish, or English, otherwise than by adoption. The Briton of Cornwall has, slowly but in the end thoroughly, adopted the speech of England.

But on the other hand, it is quite possible that the truth to which our attention is just now most fittingly called may, if put forth too broadly and without certain qualifications, lead to error quite as great as the error at which it is aimed. I do not suppose that anyone ever thought that language was, necessarily and in all cases, an absolute and certain test. If anybody does think so, he has put himself altogether out of court by shutting his eyes to the most manifest facts of the case. But there can be no doubt that many people have given too much importance to language as a test of race. Though they have not wholly forgotten the facts which tell the other way, they have not brought them out with enough prominence. But I can also believe that many people have written and spoken on the subject in a way which cannot be justified from a strictly scientific point of view, but which may have been fully justified from the point of view of the writers and speakers themselves. It may often happen that a way of speaking may not be scientifically accurate, but may yet be quite near enough to the truth for the purposes of the matter in hand. It may, for some practical or even historical purpose, be really more true than the statement which is scientifically more exact. Language is no certain test of race; but if a man, struck by this wholesome warning, should run off into the belief that language and race have absolutely nothing to do with one another, he had better have gone without the warning. For in such a case the last error would be worse than the first. The natural instinct of mankind connects race and language. It does not assume that language is an infallible test of race; but it does assume that language and race have something to do with one another. It assumes, that though language is not an accurately scientific test of race, yet it is a rough and ready test which does for many practical purposes. To make something more of an exact definition, one might say, that though language is not a test of race, it is, in the absence of evidence to the contrary, a presumption of race; that though it is not a test of race, yet it is a test of something which, for many practical purposes, is the same as race. Professor Max Müller warned us long ago that we must not speak of a Celtic skull. Mr. Sayce has more lately warned us that we must not infer from community of Aryan speech that there is any kindred in blood between this or that Englishman and this or that Hindoo. And both warnings are scientifically true. Yet anyone who begins his studies on these matters with Professor Müller's famous Oxford Essay will practically come to another way of looking at things. He will fill his mind with a vivid picture of the great Aryan family, as yet one, dwelling in one place, speaking one tongue, having already taken the first steps towards settled society, recognizing the domestic relations, possessing the first rudiments of government and religion, and calling all these first elements of culture by names of which traces still abide here and there among the many nations of the common stock. He will go on to draw pictures equally vivid of the several branches of the family parting off from the primeval home. He traces out how each branch starts with its own share of the common stock—how the language, the creed, the institutions, once common to all, grow up into different, yet kindred, shapes, among the many parted branches which grew up, each with an independent life and strength of its own. And, in drawing out the picture, we cannot avoid, our teachers themselves do not avoid, the use of words which imply that the strictly family relation, the relation of community of blood, is at the root of the whole matter. We cannot help talking about the family and its branches, about parents, children, brothers, sisters, cousins. The nomenclature of natural kindred exactly fits the case; it fits it so exactly that no other nomenclature could enable us to set forth the case with any clearness.

If races and nations, though largely formed by the workings of an artificial law, are still real and living things, groups in which the idea of kindred is the idea around which everything has grown, how are we to define our races and our nations? How are we to mark them off one from the other? Bearing in mind cautions and qualifications and certain large classes of exceptions, I say unhesitatingly that for practical purposes there is one test, and one only, and that that test is language. It is hardly needful to show that races and nations cannot be defined by the merely political arrangements which group men under various governments. So far as a nation and a government coincide, we accept it as the natural state of things, and ask no question as to the cause. So far as they do not coincide, we mark the case as exceptional, by asking what is the cause. And by saying that a government and a nation should coincide we mean that, as far as possible, the boundaries of governments should be so laid out as to agree with the boundaries of nations. That is, we assume the nation as something already existing, something primary, to which the secondary arrangements of government should, as far as possible, conform. How then do we define the nation, which is, if there is no especial reason to the contrary, to fix the limits of a government? Primarily, I say, as a rule, but a rule subject to exception—as a *prima facie* standard, subject to special reasons to the contrary—we define the nation by language. We may at least apply the test negatively. It would be unsafe to rule that all speakers of the same language must have a common nationality; but we may safely say that where there is not community of language, there is no common nationality in the highest sense. It is true that without community of language there may be an artificial nationality, a nationality which may be good for all political purposes, and which may engender a common national feeling. Still this is not quite the same thing as that fuller national unity which is felt where there is community of language. In fact, mankind instinctly takes language as the badge of nationality. We so far take it as the badge, that we instinctly assume community of language in a nation as the rule, and we set down anything that departs from that rule as an exception. The first idea suggested by the word Frenchman or German or any other national name, is that he is a man who speaks French or German as his mother-tongue. We take for granted, in the absence of anything to make us think otherwise, that a Frenchman is a speaker of French, and that a speaker of French is a Frenchman. Where in any case it is otherwise, we mark that case as an exception, and we ask the special cause. Again, the rule is none the less the rule, nor the exceptions the exceptions, because the exceptions may easily outnumber the instances which conform to the rule. The rule is still the rule, because we take the instances which conform to it as a matter of course, while in every case which does not conform to it we ask for the explanation. All the larger countries of Europe provide us with exceptions; but we treat them all as exceptions. We do not ask why a native of France speaks French. But when a native of France speaks as his mother-tongue some other tongue than French, when French, or something which popularly passes for French, is spoken as his mother-tongue by someone who is not a native of France, we at once ask the reason. And the reason will be found in each case in some special historical cause which withdraws that case from the operation of the general law. A very good reason can be given why French, or something which popularly passes for French, is spoken in parts of Belgium and Switzerland, whose inhabitants are certainly not Frenchmen. But the reason has to be given, and it may fairly be asked.

Thus, wherever we go, we find language to be the rough practical test of nationality. Community of language does not imply community of blood; it might be added that diversity of language does not imply diversity of blood. But community of language is, in the absence of any evidence to the contrary, a presumption of the community of blood, and it is proof of something which for practical purposes is the same as community of blood. To talk of "the Latin race" is in strictness absurd. We know that the so-called race is simply made up of those nations which adopted the Latin language. The Celtic, Teutonic, and Slavonic races may conceivably have been formed by a like artificial process. But the presumption is the other way; and if such a process ever took place, it took place long before history began. The Celtic, Teutonic, and Slavonic races come before us as groups of mankind marked out by the test of language. Within those races separate nations are again marked out by a stricter application of the test of language. Within the race we may have languages which are clearly akin to each other, but which need not be mutually intelligible. Within the nation we have only dialects which are mutually intelligible, or which, at all events, gather round some one central dialect which is intelligible to all. We take this standard of races and nations, fully aware that it will not stand a physiological test, but holding that for all practical purposes adoption must pass as equivalent to natural descent. And, among the practical purposes which are affected by the facts of race and nationality, we must, as long as a man is what he is, as long as he has not been created afresh according to some new scientific pattern, not shrink from reckoning those generous emotions which, in the present state of European feeling, are beginning to bind together the greater as well as the lesser groups of mankind. The sympathies of men are beginning to reach wider than could have been dreamed of a century ago. The feeling which was once confined to the mere household extended itself to the tribe or city. From the tribe or city it extended itself to the nation; from the nation it is beginning to extend itself to the whole race. In some cases it can extend itself to the whole race far more easily than in others. In some cases historical causes have made nations of the same race bitter enemies, while they have made nations of different races friendly allies. The same thing happened in earlier days between tribes and cities of the same nation. But, when hindrances of this kind do not exist, the feeling of race, as something beyond the narrower feeling of nationality, is beginning to be a powerful agent in the feelings and actions of men and of nations. A long series of mutual wrongs, conquest, and oppression on one side, avenged by conquest and oppression on the other side, have made the Slave of Poland and the Slave of Russia the bitterest of enemies. No such hindrance exists to stop the flow of natural and generous feeling between the Slave of Russia and the Slave of the southeastern lands. Those whose statesmanship consists in some hand-to-mouth shift for the moment, whose wisdom consists in refusing to look either back to the past or onward to the future, cannot understand this great fact of our times; and what they cannot understand they mock at. But the fact exists, and does its work in spite of them. And it does its work none the less because in some cases the feeling of sympathy is awakened by a claim of kindred, where, in the sense of the physiologist or the genealogist, there is no kindred at all. The practical view, historical or political, will accept as members of this or that race or nation many members whom the physiologist would shut out, whom the English lawyer would shut out, but whom the Roman lawyer would gladly welcome to every privilege of the stock on which they were grafted. The line of the Scipios, of the Caesars, and of the Antonines was continued by adoption; and for all practical purposes the nations of the earth have agreed to follow the examples set them by their masters.

RELIGION AS A BASIS OF RACIAL CLASSIFICATION

By W. M. Flinders Petrie

THE DEFINITION of the nature of race is the most requisite element for any clear ideas about man. Our present conception of the word has been modified recently more than may be supposed by our realising the antiquity of the species. When only a few thousand years had to be dealt with nothing seemed easier or more satisfactory than to map out races on the assumption that so many million people were descended from one ancestor and so many from another. Mixed races were glibly separated from pure races, and all humanity was partitioned off into well-defined divisions. But when the long ages of man's history and the incessant mixtures that have taken place during the brief end of it that is recorded come to be realised, the meaning of "race" must be wholly revised. And this revision has not yet taken effect on the modes of thought, though it may have demanded the assent of the judgment. The only meaning that a "race" can have is a group of persons whose type has become unified by their rate of assimilation and affection, by their conditions exceeding the rate of change produced by foreign elements. If the rate of mixture exceeds that of assimilation, then the people are a mixed race, or a mere agglomeration, like the population of the United States. The greatest problems awaiting solution are the conditions and rate of assimilation of races, namely, what period and kind of life is needed for climatic and other causes to have effect on the constitution and structure, what are the causes of permanence of type, and what relative powers of absorption one race has over the other. Until these problems are reduced to something that can be reasonably estimated we shall only grope in the dark as to all racial questions.

How, then, can these essential problems be attacked? Not by any study of the lower races, but rather by means of those whose history is best recorded. The great mode of isolation on which we can work is religious difference, and oppressed religious minorities are the finest anthropological material. The first question is (given a mixture of various races in approximately known proportions, isolated, and kept under uniform conditions), how soon does uniformity of type prevail, or what proportions of diversity will be found after a given number of generations? A perfect case of this awaits study in the Copts, who have, by monogamy and the fanaticism of a hostile majority been rigorously isolated during 1,200 years from any appreciable admixture, and who before this settling time were compounded of eight or ten different races, whose nature and extent of combination can be tolerably appraised. A thorough study of the present people and their forefathers, whose tombs of every age provide abundant material for examination, promises to clear up one of the greatest

From W. M. Flinders Petrie, "Race and Civilization," *Annual Report of the Board of Regents of the Smithsonian Institution to July* (1895), pp. 589–600. Originally printed in the report of the British Association for Advancement of Science, 1895, pp. 816–824. By permission of the British Association for the Advancement of Science.

questions—the effect of climate and conditions on assimilating mixed peoples. The other great problem is, How far can a type resist changes of conditions, provided it be not mixed in blood so as to disturb its equilibrium of constitution? This is to be answered by the Jews and the Parsis. As with the Copts, an oppressed religious minority has no chance of mixture, as all mixed marriages are abhorrent to its exclusiveness, and are at once swept into the hostile majority. The study is, however, far more difficult, owing to the absence of such good conditions of the preservation of material. But nothing could throw so much light on this as an excavation of some Jewish cemeteries of a thousand years or so ago in various European countries, and the comparison of the skeletons with the proportions of the Jews now living. The countries least affected by the various proscriptions and emigrations of the race would be the proper ground for inquiry. When these studies have been made we shall begin to understand what the constants of a race really are.

POPULAR CLASSIFICATION BY
COSTUME AND SURNAME
IN YUCATAN

By Robert Redfield

THE LANGUAGE of every society has terms for denoting the races and classes that matter to its members, and in the development of these terms may be read something of the history of that society. Where two ethnic groups occupy the same or adjacent territories, or where a society is made up of classes or castes, there are local words to distinguish them, and in the connotations of the words are to be found the attitudes by which convention has defined the position of the groups with reference to one another. "Barbarian," "helot," "villein," "lord," "Yankee," "greaser," "goy," and "Jew" might serve as gateways to an immense amount of history of social relations. And what significant changes in the societal position of people of African origin are briefly recorded in three forms of the same word: negro, nigger, Negro! From this approach one may consider the history and the outcome of Spanish-Indian contacts in the peninsula of Yucatan.

If the few Negroes, Chinese, Koreans, and Europeans are disregarded, there are in Merida just two contrasting kinds of people which the local community clearly defines: *mestizos* and *gente de vestido*. The terms "rich" and "poor," "upper class" and "lower class" are not precisely denotative; there are

Adapted from Robert Redfield, "Race and Class in Yucatan," in *Cooperation in Research*, Carnegie Institution of Washington, Publication No. 501 (1938). Pp. 511–532. By permission of the Carnegie Institution of Washington.

many people who are neither rich nor poor, and many whose class position is uncertain. The terms "Indian" and "White" do not denote significant groups in Merida. But with *mestizo* and its opposite, *gente de vestido,* there is practically no doubt because the words have reference to contrasting kinds of costume, and every individual either is wearing one of the two costumes or is wearing the other. If a man wears cotton trousers, cotton shirt, and especially sandals, he is a *mestizo;* if a woman wears the *huipil* and *rebozo,* she is a *mestiza;* and it does not matter what be the color of their skin. Correspondingly any wearer of modern European clothes is *de vestido.*

This distinction is recognized almost everywhere in Yucatan. The basic terms by which Yucatecan society classifies its members refer not to race, nor to genealogy, nor to wealth, but to costume. The costume is, however, connotative of class position. *Mestizos* are members of the lower class; costume is the paramount symbol of lower class position. If you see a *mestizo* costume you see someone who may be a laborer, or a house servant; he could not be a lawyer, or a business man, or even a street car conductor. The basic terms *mestizo* and *de vestido* recognize an essential division of society into two classes: the élite and the non-élite, the classes and the masses. These terms imply a stable social order so constituted. The children of *mestizos* should be *mestizos;* the children of *gente de vestido* are expected to have children who wear European dress.

But the society is not stable. The *mestizo-de vestido* distinction is not as important as it is remembered to have been. The society is undergoing great change. In Merida especially the *mestizos* are giving up the folk attire and putting on European dress. They are doing it so rapidly that the folk costume is likely to become extinct, at least in the city, in a few decades. The degree to which the folk costume has been given up is evidenced by the fact that today while there are only four social clubs for *mestizos,* there are at least twenty-eight for the recently *de vestido.* Had we no other knowledge of the change we should nevertheless be informed of it from the fact that there are derogatory terms (*cuch-vestido, dzul del pueblo, dzul falso*) for such costume changers. To conservative *mestizos,* proud of their class and the garb which is its badge, such persons are to be condemned. "To the conservative," writes Dr. Hansen of Merida *mestizos,* "the *vestido* garb has a semi-sacred quality. It is entirely inappropriate in the type of life the lower class must lead. To carry a basket in the market or to wash clothes while wearing the *vestido,* almost defiles the costume."

Nevertheless the change goes on. European garb is the symbol nowadays not so much of the status of a priviledged class as of opportunity in a freer and more individuated society. It is identified with education and a better job. If a *mestizo* lacks the courage to make the change in costume himself, he can make it through his children by putting them in European dress. If the question be asked directly, people will often reply that there are *three* classes in Merida; they will describe these three classes in terms of occupation and wealth, and they will recognize a middle class composed of people fallen from the old upper class and of new arrivals from the old lower, *mestizo* class.

Today, there are many *de vestido* people in humble occupations. To say "we *mestizos*" means less than it did; the tendency nowadays is to say "we poor people." The old-established upper class person, on his part, is less likely to use *gente de vestido* to denote his class; so many pushing people claim the term

now and with it identify themselves with the old aristocracy. So the terms with
which Merida in fact describes itself today are many and vague: the upper
class, the middle class, the lower class; the poor and the rich; the professional and business and other occupational groups; the *mestizos,* the *gente de
vestido,* and the people-who-used-to-be-*mestizo*-but-are-now-*de-vestido-or-are*-
on-their-way.

The terminology now in use makes known to us a society that is in process
of change, in which social position is in considerable degree a matter of individual accident, choice, and initiative. But the basic pair of terms, impaired
though they are in definition, record a condition of society in which two status
groups, almost like castes in their fixity, composed the society of Yucatan.

This two-class society existed in its full vigor, apparently, just before the
memory of the oldest natives now living. Dr. Asael T. Hansen and Sr. J. Ignacio
Rubio Mañé have investigated some of the documentary sources on Yucatan
in the early decades of the nineteenth century. With Dr. Hansen's permission
I quote from his unpublished manuscript on the subject. Intra-class movements,
he says, "rarely led to crossing the boundary between the two main classes. No
matter what reverses a person in the upper grouping suffered, he remained in
that category. Not a single example to the contrary was ever encountered. The
line was not absolutely inviolable from the other direction." In six decades of
the nineteenth century not more than a few dozen *mestizos,* having amassed
wealth, abandoned the folk costume. "All of these cases were isolated achievements. They probably did not blur the line in the least." *Mestizos* "accepted
their general place in the social scale without question. They tended to rank
themselves with reference to other members of the category rather than with
reference to the total range of status. The goal that the ambitious sought was
to attain an enviable position in the lower class; to be able to do lower class
things that were out of the reach of most of their fellows. Such an accomplishment brought complete satisfaction. Upper class people could strive for other
ends; ends that members of the lower class recognized as higher than their own."
In such a society, where the status of every individual was sure and was obviously announced in his costume, "superiors and inferiors could rub shoulders
without danger of offending either, and they did so in patron fiestas and on
many other occasions." Norman, writing in 1841, was struck with the easy
intimacy of the social classes. It is apparent that the connotation of *mestizo* as
used by a conservative older person of Yucatan reaches back to a state of society which the historical investigations of Sr. Rubio Mañé and Dr. Hansen
recall for us.

We are not yet done with the word *mestizo.* There is a puzzle written on
its face. Why should a word which ordinarily refers to a person of mixed racial
ancestry, in present-day Yucatan mean in nineteen uses out of twenty a person
wearing a certain sort of costume? This question reminds us of others: What
has become of the Indians? Who, in Merida today, is "an Indian"?

An answer to the last question leads toward an answer of the first. To the
Meridano the Indians are, generally speaking, not to be found in Merida, but
in the villages and settlements out in the bush. The word *indio* is, however,
sometimes applied to those relatively few city dwellers who wear the folk
costume and who bear Maya surnames. Such persons are included among the
mestizos in the common general meaning of the word. But in a less common

and special sense a *mestizo* is a person who wears the folk costume and who bears a Spanish surname. Although the difference between a person with a Maya surname and one with a Spanish patronymic is of little importance in Merida today, yet one who wishes to speak depreciatively of another may call him an Indian, and if the latter bears an Indian surname he cannot cast off the epithet. The distinction, on the basis of surname, between two stratified divisions of the lower class is a mere vestige in Merida.

Once the distinction must have been clear. The early lists of population recognize three groups: Indians, *mestizos,* and Whites (Spaniards). The very existence of the word *mestizo* testifies to the previous recognition of a threefold division of the population along ethnic lines. When Indians mixed with Whites it became necessary to call the marginal individual by some term. *Mestizo,* in the primary sense of racial hybrid, was applied. The problem arose, inevitably, in any situation of racial intermixture, of the social position of the mixed person. Should he be identified with the Indian group? Should he be identified with the Spanish group? Should he be recognized as constituting an intermediate social category? Without the benefit of particular knowledge of historical fact it is nevertheless safe to say that all three of these results took place. The offspring of casual unions between Spanish man and Indian woman, unrecognized by the father and hence bearing an Indian surname, were brought up with Indians and must have been identified with the Indian group. If certain such individuals were marked out as having Spanish blood, the tendency to do so must have declined with the spread of white admixture throughout the socially Indian group. On the other hand the offspring of legitimate marriage between Spaniard and Indian (of which there were a few) must, at least in some cases where the mother was an Indian of prestige and where the Spanish father gave the children education, have been identified with the Spanish group. At the same time many offspring of nonlegal but enduring unions of Spaniard and Indian involving the setting up of a domestic establishment must have occupied an intermediate position. The father, associated with his offspring in familial intimacy, could not repudiate them entirely; frequently, we know, he allowed them to take his surname. Yet as illegitimate halfbreeds, raised by Indian mothers, they could not, in most cases, be identified with the Conquerors. Thus there came about a socially intermediate group of racial hybrids. Some children of formal intermarriages and some resulting from casual union also probably came to be associated with the intermediate group.

At this period—during, let us say, early Colonial times—a *mestizo* was, we may suppose, a person of mixed Indian-Spanish ancestry who wore folk costume but who bore a Spanish surname. In the former character they were like the Indians; in the latter like the Whites. Together Indians and *mestizos* constituted the lower classes, but they were discriminated, Dr. Hansen tells me, in both the civil and the ecclesiastical law: there were certain differences as to religious privilege; *mestizos* were under the direct municipal government of Merida, while Indians had their own municipal government subordinated to Spanish authority; *mestizos* but not Indians were obliged to perform military service, while *mestizos* were free from obligatory labor of all kinds; the Church discouraged intermarriage between the two groups. There were also certain distinctions recognized by custom alone, as in details of the folk costume and in the division of labor between the two groups. But in important essentials

Indians and *mestizos* were alike: they were the common people, doing the common labor and accepting lower status; and they wore essentially the same costume.

The word *mestizo* must have come to mean primarily a member of the lower class wearing the folk costume as the line between Indian and *mestizo* became blurred. Dr. Hansen puts it thus: "The development may be viewed as a linguistic response to the fading of the Indian-*mestizo* demarcation and as further evidence that the basic status groups were White and non-White or what we have called the upper class and the lower class." The number of *mestizos* increased relative to the number of Indians. In spite of restrictions against marriage between Indians and mixed-bloods with Spanish names, many such marriages occurred. Sr. Rubio Mañé tells us that in the eighteenth and nineteenth centuries a practice flourished whereby upper class fathers had their illegitimate children by Indian mothers baptized as foundlings. "In some years," says Dr. Hansen reporting on Sr. Rubio Mañé's investigations, "foundlings made up more than one-fourth of the total baptisms in the cathedral of Mérida —the church of the whites." In certain cases white godparents gave their surnames to Indian godchildren. In these ways the *mestizo* population multiplied. At the same time differences in costume between Indian and *mestizo*—they had never been great—gradually disappeared. Dr. Hansen's references to conditions in the early part of the nineteenth century indicate that by that time the two groups had the same occupations and the same dress. The legal restrictions on the Indians were revoked or fell into disuse after independence from Spain. By the middle of the nineteenth century the mixed-bloods with Spanish names and the Indians—now also largely mixed in blood—with Indian surnames looked alike, dressed alike, and were treated substantially alike. There were many more of the former than there were of the latter, and it was easy to apply the term earlier reserved for this subgroup to the entire, uniform-wearing lower class. A word for a biological hybrid had come to designate the lower of two social classes. This coalescence of mixed-blood and Indian groups suggests the manner in which mulatto and Negro came in the United States to form a single caste-like class, but with the important differences that Yucatan, like the rest of Latin America, drew no color line, and that the badge of the Yucatecan class was a costume, not a skin color. And now it comes about that with the breakdown of other features of the old social organization of the penninsula, and with the freedom of the individual to give up the folk costume and no matter what his birth to compete with others for status, the class lines tend to disappear.

We have seen that in Merida there is now a shifting three-class system with much individual mobility. At the same time the terms *mestizo* and *de vestido* represent a two-class system that no longer completely exists. Some reasonable speculations, developed from consideration of the word *mestizo,* supported by a little historical data, led us back to a condition of Yucatecan society in which there were three ethnically defined classes, or, perhaps it would be better to say, in which the lower class was divided into two stratified parts: the people with Indian surnames and the people with Spanish surnames. Of this class division there is in Merida today hardly a trace. In Yucatan, however, if one wants to find an older condition of society represented currently, all he needs to do in many cases is to go farther away from the one city into the rural communities. One can go back either in time or in space and, speaking broadly, arrive at the same condition of society.

The people of the little town of Dzitas, like those of Merida, exhibit every shade and combination of Indian and Spanish racial intermixture. There is relatively more Indian blood in the population, and much more Maya is spoken. There is the same difference between *mestizos* and *gente de vestido* that is recognized in Merida, but there are proportionately more *mestizos* than there are in the city. In general the people who dwell on the outskirts of the town are Maya-speaking, *mestizo* people who carry on a simple agriculture. In news from Dzitas sent to the Merida newspaper by the local correspondent these people are referred to as "members of our working class." The writer of such notices, like others of the prestige-enjoying people who have their homes near the central plaza, is a Spanish-speaking *de vestido* person with a specialized occupation. Included in his group are such specialists as carpenters, masons, storekeepers, and barbers. These occupations are open to anyone, and many persons apparently of all-Indian ancestry are to be found in them. Dzitas, it soon appears, recognizes two social classes, the lower and middle class of present-day Merida; the outlines of the classes are ill defined and ethnic origin or pedigree does not determine class membership, a combination of factors determining the social position of the individual.

This is, however, only the apparent, the public, class structure. Behind it exists another, remembered rather than actual. People in Dzitas, especially older people, divide their neighbors into two groups: *vecinos* and *indios*. A *vecino* is anyone with a Spanish surname. An *indio* is anyone with a Maya surname. The older distinction to which the conservative people still cling is that between the Peches, Poots, and Nahs on the one hand and the Leals, Arceos, and Aguilars on the other. The former are, or should be, the lower class; the latter, the upper class. Any *indio* is theoretically inferior to any *vecino*. No matter how poor or how dark-skinned a man or a woman may be, or how humble his occupation, if he has a Spanish surname it is proof that he is not an Indian, that he is a descendant of Spaniards, and that *indios* should recognize that he is better than they. One case, well known to the writer, illustrates the force and tenacity of this old genealogical class division. The case is that of an old man, dark-skinned as any Indian, a wearer of the folk costume. He speaks no Spanish; he carries on primitive agriculture like any of his neighbors, and participates in the pagan agricultural ceremonies. But he has a Spanish surname; therefore he looks down upon his neighbors with Maya names. On one occasion he came to the plaza and watched the activities of the municipal government—since the Revolution in the hands chiefly of Indians—"to see," he said, "what a bad job those Indians are making of the town government."

As may be supposed, the *vecino-indio* distinction is emphasized especially by *vecinos,* and still more specially by *vecinos* who have lost the other indicia of status: those who are poor, who have no longer specialized occupations, and who cannot afford *vestido* attire. A person with three *indio* grandparents and one, the father's father, a *vecino* grandparent clings to the prestige attached to the Spanish surname. A woman, impoverished to beggary, with four *vecino* grandparents does her best to look down upon her well-to-do *indio* neighbors, is scornful of *indios* who get into trade or take houses near the plaza, and complains of the fact that *indios* do not show her respect. Although marriages between *indios* and *vecinos* are fairly common, and informal unions are even commoner, nevertheless when an *india* becomes the wife of a member of a *vecino* family that maintains some cohesiveness and class pride, she is not readily accepted, and the bride's *indio* pedigree may be a matter of embarrassment.

It is clear that the *vecino-indio* distinction is that between the two levels of the fundamental Yucatecan lower class. It is the distinction which we have seen was once more clearly recognized in Merida, but which is there practically extinct. In the thinking of the older generation in Dzitas it is *the* important social distinction. Either the upper white class was never clearly represented in Dzitas, or it early disappeared. The *vecinos* are the upper division of the old lower class; but in old Dzitas they were the highest class that local society recognized. A division was formed between the Indians, on the one hand, and the mixed-bloods on the other. With intermixture, surname came to be the essential symbol of class membership.

Apparently the old class structure still flourished in the youth of the oldest natives of Dzitas now living. They give many details of the conditions which then prevailed. Only *vecinos* lived near the plaza, and all the *indios* lived on the outskirts of the town. The posts in the local government were filled, with only the rarest exceptions, by *vecinos*. The *indios* had their own separate municipal government, subordinated to that of the *vecinos*. The *indios* met in a separate place of public meeting, called *audiencia*. The decisions and orders of the *vecino* government were transmitted to them through their own chieftain (*batab* or *alcalde*) whom they themselves selected. Only a *vecino* might be a soldier; in military activities the *indios* were permitted to be watchmen and messengers. In short, the *vecinos* were politically dominant; they were the real citizens of Dzitas; the *indios* maintained a separate government for matters concerning exclusively *indios;* and the *vecinos* ruled the *indios,* making use of the *indio* officers.

The *indios* occupied positions of less dignity and acknowledged their inferior position in name, costume, occupation, and place of residence. An older *indio* was addressed with a term of respect, recognizing his years, but the term (*yum*) was not the same by which a *vecino* was addressed; only *vecinos* were called *don*. By the manner of salutation the *indio* expressed deference, while the *vecino* received it. In domestic life both classes wore the folk costume, but there were many small differences in costume associated with the difference in status. The *huipils* of the *indias* had little or very simple embroidery, while the *huipils* of the *vecinas* (*ternos*) had cross-stitch embroidery. "If an *india* had worn a *terno* it would have been taken from her and burned at the door of the church." The *vecinas* wore petticoats, coral hairpins, fine combs, and head scarves of fine cloth; the *indias* had to content themselves with hairpins of native tortoise shell, wooden combs, and head scarves of crude cotton cloth. It was the *vecinas* who responded to the fashions. They went to mass in the costume of the city (*de vestido*), and as each novelty in dress or display reached Dzitas—gold chains, good shoes, new embroidery designs—it was the *vecinas* who took it up, and public opinion allowed the *indias* to assume these modes only when they had been abandoned by the class above theirs. It is said that in those times the Church discouraged intermarriage between the classes by charging a higher fee for such marriages, and indeed the books of the Dzitas civil registry, which go back to 1867, tend to confirm this assertion.

An examination of the distribution of cultural, linguistic, and occupational characters among the *vecinos* and *indios* of present-day Dzitas reveals the discrepancy that has developed between the old ethnic classes and the present more flexible status groups. Out of 225 households of Dzitas, thirty-nine are of Spanish-speaking, *de vestido* people carrying on specialized occupations. These people are with very few exceptions *vecinos*. At the other extreme are 136 households of Maya-speaking, *mestizo milperos* and woodcutters. All these people, in the thinking of the conservative native, ought to be *indios;* in fact, most of them are; the minority that are *vecinos* tend to regard their position as an anomaly. Furthermore (besides 12 households for which data are lacking), there are 38 households in which the social factors are inconsistently distributed; included are Maya-speaking *mestizos* who have specialized occupations, Maya-speaking *de vestido* people, and Spanish-speaking people, with the woman only *de vestido,* some of whom are simple agriculturalists and others of whom carry on specialized occupations. Of these intermediate families some have Spanish names and some Indian names. In the thinking of the old conservative these "mixed people" should not be there at all. The Indians have "got out of their place." They control the municipal government; they are becoming barbers and brakemen; they put on city clothes; they join the social club; they do not, in gesture or speech, show respect for *vecinos*. Meanwhile some *vecinos* have lost power, grown poor, and given up their Sunday *de vestido* attire. Left behind in the changing world, bereft of the symbols of the status which traditionally they should have, save the Spanish name, they emphasize the worth of this and cling to the memory of a definite class society in which membership was decided at birth.

As in the case of the word *mestizo,* there is a question as to how *vecino* ("neighbor," "citizen") came to denote a member of a social class. In Merida today the word means "neighbor"; it is not used there to mean a non-Indian, although people in Merida know that in such places as Dzitas it does have this meaning. Formerly, however, according to Dr. Hansen, "at least from 1847 to 1881, the population of Yucatan was legally divided into two categories, Indians and *vecinos*." It may be that the term *vecino,* though recognized in law, was never popularly employed in Merida for the higher division of the lower class because in Merida there was an important upper class of white aristocracy who of course also enjoyed all civil rights. *Vecino* meant non-Indian and so included two groups socially distinguished: Whites and mixed-bloods. But in such a place as Dzitas, where this supreme class was unrepresented, the mixed-bloods with Spanish names were the only ones who enjoyed full civil, military, and ecclesiastical rights; they were complete citizens, in a sense in which the Indians were not. So the word *vecino* came, especially in such communities, to denote the upper of the two classes.

The situation in Dzitas may be summarized. The society maintains in a moribund condition a two-class structure. These classes correspond to the division within the lower (*mestizo*) class in Merida, where the division is practically lost. The Dzitas classes are defined as Indians and non-Indians, but as assimilation and amalgamation had distributed racial features of physiognomy throughout the population and developed a single culture for all, the surname, a certificate of ancestry, had become the symbol of class position. Nevertheless these ethnic or genealogical classes, no longer supported by legal provisions and undermined as a result of freedom of economic and educational opportunity for all, exist more in retrospect than in current fact. Their place is taken by a vague distinction between "the working people" and "the best people" (there are no accepted terms for these groups). The status of the individual is not determined by his birth; he may seek it and make it for himself.

THE PHYSICAL TRAIT AS A PRINCIPLE
OF CLASSIFICATION

By Arnold J. Toynbee

IT IS AN ESTABLISHED FACT of Physiology that, in all human beings, the pigment secreted in the skin is qualitatively the same; and that the different shades of colour which strike the eye and affect the feelings and give rise to theories and classifications correspond to mere differences in the quantity in which this qualitatively uniform human pigment happens to be present beneath the skin of any given specimen of the Human Race. We can verify this on the body of an African Negro; for the palms of his hands and the soles of his feet are of a different shade from the rest of his skin and of practically the same shade as the whole skin of a White man—the explanation being that, on his palms and soles, a Negro has about the same quantity of pigment that a White man has all over, while on the rest of his body the Negro has rather more. This fact indicates that our colour-prejudice has not a shadow of physiological justification and shows it up for what it is: a particular instance of the irrational but universal aversion from whatever is abnormal. 'Nordic Man,' who rejoices in the rather low quantity of pigment in his skin, eyes, and hair which happens to be normal in human beings of his kind, is repelled by the abnormal case in which this quantity is reduced to zero and 'the Blond Beast' transformed into an albino, though logically, if colourlessness is the pink of perfection, the rare albino ought to be hailed by his commonplace Nordic relatives as a king of men. Again, even the relative lack of colour which is normal and therefore comely in the sight of a White man is abnormal and therefore unbecoming in the sight of a Red Indian, who expresses his aversion by calling the White man a 'pale-face.' It even happens that a human being comes to regard his own colour with aversion if he lives for some time in a minority of one among people of a different colour—the colour of the majority setting the norm. For

Reprinted from Arnold J. Toynbee, *A Study of History* (London: Oxford University Press, 1936), I, 227–230; by permission of Oxford University Press and The Royal Institute of International Affairs.

example, it is said that David Livingstone, on one of his expeditions, after passing many months in Central Africa with no White companions and none but Negroes round him, began to find that the sight of his own naked skin turned him sick, as though he were looking at some deformity of nature.

This craving for the normal in physical appearance (whatever the normal may be in the particular circumstances) is not of course confined to the single feature of colour. For example, in the United States, where the physical appearance of the White people is the norm for the Coloured people, the Coloured women try to lessen their unlikeness from the White women by straightening their hair. On the other hand, the White women, who have no fear of looking like Negroes, take pleasure, as White women do in other countries, in having their hair waved or curled. Thus, in the same American town at the same moment, some barbers may be busy straightening women's hair in the Negro quarter while others are busy curling women's hair in the White quarter—in both cases alike, for the satisfaction of the universal human craving to be 'in the fashion.'

Hair, indeed, is just as good—or just as bad—a criterion of Race as pigment. The North American Whites and Negroes are sensitive to the straightness or curliness of the hair on the head. The Japanese are sensitive to the general hairiness of the human body, because, in Japan, this happens to be a more significant feature than the colour of the skin. The Japanese people (like almost every other people that has ever distinguished itself) is of mixed race; and its original racial components must have differed widely in colour; for there is a considerable diversity of colour among the Japanese people to this day. In the same district and in the same social class and in the same family you may find skins varying from copper-colour to what White people call white. Hence, the differences of colour within this range do not excite race-feeling among the Japanese any more than this is excited among Europeans by differences in the quantity of hair on their bodies. On the other hand, Japanese of all shades of skin are alike in being more or less hairless except on their heads, in contrast to the aboriginal inhabitants of the Japanese Islands who, like Nordic Man in the unshaven state of nature, have bushy beards and hairy chests. For this reason, the Japanese call these aborigines (the remnant of whom are now philanthropically preserved, on the northern island of Hokkaido, in 'reservations') 'the Hairy Ainu'. In the local circumstances of Japan, it is just as natural to emphasize the hairiness of the inferior race as it is in the United States or in the Union of South Africa to emphasize their colour; and as the people of European origin apply the colour-classification, which suggests itself in their own local circumstances, to the whole of Mankind, so we might expect the Japanese to divide the human family, not into a 'White Race' and a 'Coloured Race' but into a 'Hairless Race' and a 'Hairy'.

Logically there is nothing to choose between one classification and the other; but it may be edifying for us to glance at the classification with which we are less familiar. It yields what, to our minds, are disconcerting results. It brackets 'Nordic Man' with the Hairy Ainu of Hokkaido and the Blackfellows of Australia and the Veddahs of Ceylon and the Todas of the Nilgiri Hills in Southern India, as one of the representatives of a race whose abnormal hairiness makes them not as other men are.

'What nonsense', the indignant Nordic ethnologist exclaims. 'Is it likely that there is any racial relation between these tribes, considering that their homes are separated by the whole breadth of Europe and Asia?' But the Japanese ethnologist has his answer up his sleeve. Courteously he points out to his Nordic colleague that 'the Hairy Race' is the nearest of all living races to the Apes in that feature which is fundamental for Japanese purposes of racial classification. It follows that 'the Hairy Race' is the nearest of all living breeds of Man to the common ancestor of Apes and Men. In other words, 'the Hairy Race' is the most primitive, rudimentary experiment in *Homo Sapiens* that survives; and it is natural enough that it should only survive in holes and corners. If we assume that the original breeding-ground of Mankind lay somewhere in the heart of the Old World, and that 'the Hairy Race' was one of the earliest human swarms to hive off, then we should expect to find *Homo Hirsutus* pushed outwards in all directions, to the ends of the Earth, to Australia and to Hokkaido and to Ultima Thule, by younger and superior races—*Homo Mediterraneus* and *Homo Dravidicus, Homo Alpinus* and *Homo Mongolicus*—which have issued from the common breeding-ground at later dates to multiply and replenish the Earth in their turns. Thus the vast distances which separate the several surviving tribes of *Homo Hirsutus* to-day are presumptive evidence for and not against the racial kinship of these tribes which their common shagginess betrays. Their present homes are not their respective cradles but their respective retreats from a common birthplace. They are fragments of the circumference of the circle in which *Homo Hirsutus* has spread—or has been chevied—over the face of the Earth from his original centre of dispersion. We may compare his now widely dispersed representatives with the disturbances which remain here and there on the surface of a pond when the last of the ripples produced by the fall of a stone into the water is dying away. If the Japanese ethnologist presents his case on these lines, it will be difficult for the Nordic ethnologist to rebut it.

A PEOPLE IN SEARCH OF A NAME

By Cedric Dover

THE EURASIANS are the answer to Kipling's ignorant but persistent couplet. Among them the new style 'Anglo-Indians' or Eurindians form the largest, most misrepresented, and oldest group, its origin dating from the Portuguese occupation in the early sixteenth century, but more especially from intermarriages in the days of the East India Company between Britishers and native women or the indigenous descendants of previous European invasions. Portu-

By Cedric Dover. Extracted with minor modifications by the author and reprinted with his permission as holder of the copyright from his *Half-Caste* (London: Secker and Warburg, 1937), Ch. VI.

guese, Dutch and French ancestry, however, is more prevalent than is generally supposed, since British domination has induced a natural tendency to give foreign names a patriotic flavour—Leal to Lea, Correa to Currie, D'Silva to Silver, Rozario to Rose, Ingels to Inglis, and so on.

It is difficult to draw sharp lines of demarcation between these Eurasians and other groups resulting from the march of European civilisation. The Domiciled Europeans, who would be more accurately described as Domiciled Indians, are socially identified with them, and so are the West Indians in India; Anglophilic Indian Christians seep in at the lower income groups; and the Portuguese-Indians leak in continuously at all levels. The latter are the remnants of early Luso-Indian mixture, and have lost their Lusitanian physical characteristics so considerably that, as far back as 1826, Bishop Heber was able to observe that 'the Portuguese have become as black as Caffres'. But they retain some connexion with the land of their fathers through the Portuguese colony of Goa on the west coast, speak a patois of the Lusitanian tongue (as well as English and a vernacular), dress in Westernised mode, and perpetuate the lofty names of their paternal ancestors, whose customs and Catholic religion they proudly maintain.

Their associations with a defeated Power, and their occupations as musicians, cooks, stewards, small hotel-keepers and workers outside the privileged circle of Anglo-Indian employment, have created a vulgar contempt for the Goans which they certainly do not deserve. But the power of ridicule has stimulated attempts to distinguish between Goans and the more obvious and successful Lusitanian hybrids by introducing the isolating term 'Luso-Indians'—without much success, for the academic charm of the new name could not compete with the greater attractions of being known as 'Anglo-Indians'.

The interactions of prejudice are further illustrated by the evolution of Eurasian attitudes towards communal nomenclature. In the early days of the British insinuation into India, they were referred to as 'half-castes', 'mixed bloods', 'countryborns' and 'members of the mixed races', and appear to have accepted these terms without significant protest. By the beginning of the nineteenth century, these names were widely understood as derogatory epithets rather than descriptive terms; and the growth of communal pride expressed itself at a public meeting held at Calcutta in 1825 which decided that 'East Indian' should be adopted as 'the most appropriate and applicable designation'. But the East Indians' Petition, which was carried to the British Parliament in 1830, variously describes the petitioners as 'Indo-Britons' or 'persons of mixed blood'. Thereafter, the term 'Indo-Briton' found much popular usage, but its suggestion of blood relationship with the ruling class was not strong enough to survive the consciousness of Empire which followed Queen Victoria's Proclamation of 1848.

Meanwhile, the Marquess of Hastings had used the name 'Eurasian' in his despatches (1813–1823); and by the mid-nineteenth century it was so commonly accepted that 'The Eurasian and Anglo-Indian Association', founded in 1876, adopted it as the preferred communal designation. The 'Anglo-Indians' in this Association were the locally born and less privileged whites who later came to be known as Domiciled Europeans; and it seemed to many, both Eurasians and Anglo-Indians, that status and unity would be better served by a simple deletion from the name of this body. By the end of the century this feeling had grown so strong that Dr. J. R. Wallace could lead a fully supported delegation to the Secretary of State for India with the principle purpose of acquiring for the term 'Anglo-Indian' a wider, and officially recognised, meaning; but that dignitary remained unimpressed. Undeterred, the energetic doctor founded on his return 'The Imperial Anglo-Indian Association', for he was convinced that 'Britishers we are and Britishers we ever must and shall be. Once we relinquish this name (Anglo-Indian) and permit ourselves to be styled "Eurasians" or "Statutory Natives of India" we become estranged from our proud heritage as Britishers.'

The reward of these patriotic exercises was the publicly expressed sarcasm of Lord Curzon, then Viceroy of India, and the neglect of the stolen cognomen outside the community itself. But Lord Hardinge, acting upon representations by 'The Anglo-Indian Empire League', authorised the use of 'Anglo-Indian' in the desired manner in the Indian Census of 1911; and this encouragement, together with the impact of the Montagu-Chelmsford Reforms of 1918, promoted the emergence of 'The Anglo-Indian and Domiciled European Association of India' in 1919. Its president became the representative of the community in the Central Legislative Assembly.

In these ways the Eurindians appropriated the elegant label which the resident Britishers had invented for themselves. It is now officially employed as a useful concession to communal pride without being universally recognised, though the changed meaning of 'Anglo-Indian' is beginning to find occasional expression in print, often with the satirical qualification 'new style'. Moreover, the nomenclatorial concession has not released the new Anglo-Indians from their old statutory definition as 'Natives of India', nor their occupational definition as 'European British Subjects'. This anomalous position exposes the Eurindians to utilisation according to official convenience. As natives they are excluded from certain British privileges; as European British Subjects they enlarge the British electoral and military strength, and are prevented from orienting themselves to complete acceptance of their statutory position.

The transparent diplomacy of this situation has recently been further emphasised by giving Eurasians of direct European paternity the definite status of European voters, leaving those whose European paternal connexions are more remote to vote as 'Anglo-Indian Natives of India'; those who derive their white ancestry from the maternal side are merely regarded as unqualified natives. The members of many Eurindian families therefore share with some 'Anglo-Indians' of West Indies origin the curious privilege of being able to exercise their votes in different constituencies.

The disruptive effects of Anglo-Indianism became dramatically clear during the last days of British rule in India and they continue to be operative seven years after the establishment of the Indian Republic. Large numbers of Eurindians tried, often without success, to escape the consequences of their own folly by emigration; but the majority had to accommodate themselves, without adequate training or full understanding of the necessary adjustments, to the ferment and expansion which accompanied the release of the national spirit. Cultural Anglo-Indianism not only continues but is now enlarged by English-speaking Indians who have moved into 'the Anglo-Indian quarter', send their children to Anglo-Indian schools, and generally expand a way of life that is recognisably and literally Anglo-Indian—with the differences brought about by

British power being substituted by the continuation of the British connexion. The whole situation is rich in materials for students of cultural contacts and survivals.

So serious are the consequences of the psychological and other disadvantages implicit in the use of the term 'Anglo-Indian' that it is comforting to recall that Eurasian critics of Anglophily have never been lacking. As far back as 1881, an anonymous critic of 'The Eurasian and Anglo-Indian Association' pointed out that over a hundred pounds had been wasted in assuring the Queen of the Association's loyalty. He was sure that Her Majesty knew, as well as Eurasians knew themselves, that 'we dare not be disloyal'.

This spirit of clear-minded independence has responded creatively to changing conditions in the East; and part of this response has been the attempts made by the younger generation of Eurasians to renew the employment of the more logical designation as a first contribution to fuller participation in national struggle. They had before them the example of Burma, where the Eurasians protested to the Simon Commission against being regarded as 'Anglo-Indians'; and also defined as a member of their community 'any person of mixed European and Indian or Burmese descent, whether of legitimate parentage or not, or whether the European strain be derived from the paternal or the maternal side.'

This definition must be regarded as a forward step, though it is not as comprehensive as it should be, and the alternative designation 'Anglo-Burman' is as inept as any attempt to inject the 'Anglo' into the names of mixed communities in the East. While they remain comparatively free from recent African elements, usage, logic and a sense of cohesion dictate the general use of the word 'Eurasion' as the only appropriate designation for communities of very diverse Eur-Asiatic origins, with such geographical variations as 'Eurindian' when convenience demands. Therefore, I continue to hope that the folly and degenerating temper of its petty Anglicism will be increasingly rejected by contemporary Eurasian thought. For when Eurasians see themselves in the contexts of their own societies, when they view the neem and tamarind rather than the ash and oak, when they share the burdens and aspirations of their national kinsfolk, they will have earned the right to live constructively, with the privilege of having no privileges, as free men in a free Asia.

Let them know what they are and they will know what they can be.

RACE IN OUR PAPER CULTURE

By C. A. Weslager

THE CHESWOLD MOORS have no false pretenses in the question of their racial positions. When the interrogator asked if they were white, he was given a negative reply. Are they Negroes? Again the reply was a decisive negative. Well, if they were not whites or blacks, what is their race. The answer was, "We are Moors."

The question of color must be answered on birth certificates, income tax reports, drivers' licenses, insurance policies, employment applications, draft questionnaires, and similar documents where racial identity is demanded of the applicant. Once again the classifications are arbitrary, inconsistent, and often unjust. Nothing illustrates this better than life insurance records. Life insurance rates are generally higher for Negroes than for whites, inasmuch as the black man is known to be a greater insurance risk. The environment to which he has been relegated is generally not a healthy one. He is seemingly more susceptible than whites to certain diseases. The insurance companies know that the average Negro does not live as long as the average white person, and must set their rates accordingly.

When an insurance agent suspects that an applicant may have a trace of Negro blood, it is to his company's financial interest to insure that person's life under the higher Negro rates, even though he is not a pure Negro. Naturally the insurance companies must accept their commitments with care. Nevertheless observations indicate that many Moors and Indians have been wrongly classified for insurance purposes as Negroes. Some who are so categorized do not admit of a drop of black blood in their veins. It would be impossible to prove that they have it. Still their position in society as mixed-bloods, with the questionable status and instability of that position, renders them ineligible for the insurance rates applying to white persons. It should be said in fairness that not all mixed-bloods are insured under the Negro rates. Some light-complexioned persons have white insurance and pay less for their protection than their swarthy neighbors. This is an example of the paradox that can accompany the segregation of a people on the color scale of their skins. If one carries such arbitrary reasoning to its logical conclusion, every Caucasian brunette would be assessed higher insurance rates than those with lighter complexions.

Intolerance, both political and social, has prevented many of these folk from sharing privileges accorded white people. A few examples will serve as illustrations:

One Cheswold mother found it necessary to go to Dover to obtain a birth certificate for her eighteen-year old daughter. The girl was asked to produce the certificate to obtain employment. Like her parents she was no different in appearance from a white person. Nothing about her appearance would suggest

Adapted from C. A. Weslager, *Delaware's Forgotten Folk: The Story of the Moors and Nanticokes* (Philadelphia: University of Pennsylvania Press, 1943), pp. 18–20, 143; copyright 1943 by University of Pennsylvania Press and used with the permission of the publisher.

the slightest thought of African mixture. In fact, she later married a white man. Imagine the mother's embarrassment to find her daughter's birth recorded as a Negro. The presentation of such a certificate would have made the girl ineligible for consideration in a position where a white person was wanted. The mother objected strenuously and asked that the clerk show the birth record of a younger daughter for comparison. The second certificate was produced, and thereon the second daughter's birth was recorded simply as a Moor. Fortunately for those concerned, the clerk was intelligent and liberal-minded enough to recognize the unanswerable objection that was raised, and a satisfactory adjustment was made in the records.

Here we see what can happen to a leaderless Indian blood group after ruinous contact with other races. Just as the Indian blood was diluted, so the folklore and native customs and practices have been falling away. Among the younger generation, a feeling of racial insecurity and skepticism as to their identities has begun to appear. They are so far removed from their Indian ancestors that their consciousness of native ancestry has become latent. Their perplexity may be due to a disinterested or a disillusioned parent who refuses to discuss the racial question with them, or who is himself ignorant of his background. Several Moors in their teens have come to me and asked: "Who do you think we are? How did we get the name of Moors?" Moreover, unkind whites have been heard to comment facetiously that Moor (pronounced More) means "more-or-less nigger." One of the lads overheard the remark and took it quite seriously. He said to me afterwards "What's the use of trying to be different? If everyone thinks a Moor is a mulatto, I guess that's what we must be, even though we think we are not."

SOME WORDS AND TERMS DESIGNATING,
OR RELATING TO, RACIALLY MIXED
PERSONS OR GROUPS

Compiled by Salme Pekkala, Marian B. Hamilton
and Wiley Alford.

AFRO-ASIAN. South Africa. A newer element in the population of South Africa; the progeny or unions between Indians and Africans, often due to the insufficient numbers of Indian women compared with men; such unions occurring chiefly in Natal and a few in other parts of South Africa. (Fantham, H. B., "Some Race Problems in South Africa," *Scientific Monthly,* 42 (Feb., 1936), 162–165.)

ANGLO-INDIAN. India. Used in India to denote mixed European and Indian stock; since 1911 has been officially designated by the government of India as the Anglo-Indian community, the term "community" referring to a cultural group in regard to the ecological aspects of its distribution. (Cressey, P., "The Anglo-Indians: A Disorganized Marginal Group," *Social Forces,* 14 (Dec., 1935), 263.)

ASIATIC-HAWAIIANS. Hawaii. The one statistical group employed in the censuses taken under the authority of the United States Congress under which is included the Chinese-Hawaiians, Japanese-Hawaiians, Korean-Hawaiians, and the Filipino-Hawaiians. (Adams, R., *Interracial Marriage in Hawaii,* 1937, p. 87.)

BASTAARDS. South Africa. A hybrid African people who arose from matings between Boers and Hottentot women. (Boas, F., "Fallacies of Racial Inferiority," *Current History,* 25 (Feb., 1927), 676–682). One group of the Bastaards, so-called by the white population, came to call themselves Griquas. (Campbell, J., *Travels in South Africa,* 1816, pp. 235–237.)

BOVIANDERS. British Guiana. A mixture of native Indians and Negroes. It is reported that the Indian women much prefer Negro men to men of their own race as husbands, and out of this intermixture a new native stock is emerging. (Schomburgk, R., *Travels in New Guiana,* 1922, Vol. 1, p. 45.)

CABOSLOS. Brazil. Indian-white mixture. (Ramos, A., "Contact of Races in Brazil," *Social Forces,* 19 (May, 1941), 535.)

CAFUSOS. Brazil. Negro-Indian mixture. (Ramos, A., "Contact of Races in Brazil," *Social Forces,* 19 (May, 1941), 535.)

CAJUNS. Louisiana and Alabama. A corruption of Acadian; people reputed to be of Acadian French descent. (Bond, H. M., "Two Racial Islands in Alabama: Creoles and Cajuns," *American Journal of Sociology,* 36 (Jan., 1931), 552–567.)

CAPE COLOURED. South Africa. An Eurafrican group found chiefly in the Cape Province. In origin they go back to early inter-mixture between the Portuguese, the Hottentots, the Dutch, slaves brought in from West Africa, Mozambique and Madagascar, Malays imported from the East, and the Bantu peoples advancing from the northeast. (Stonequist, E. V., *Marginal Man,* 1937, pp. 18–24.)

CARIBOCO. North American. Term given to the offspring of an inter-racial union when the father is Negro and the mother North American Indian (probably an adaptation from "caribobo," the Spanish word meaning stupid or dumb-looking.) (Appleton's *New Spanish Dictionary,* 1941, p. 91, "Spanish-English" section.)

CASCOS. Southern United States. Name given by the French in the southern part of the United States to the offspring of two mulattoes. This is one among other terms given to colored people by the French to classify them according to the greater or lesser preponderance of Negro blood. (Reuter, E. B., *The Mulatto in the United States,* 1918, p. 12.)

CAUCASIAN-HAWAIIAN. Hawaii. Intermixture of Caucasian and Hawaiian groups. Primarily a statistical term, Adams states that the "racial classification and definitions used for census and other statistical purposes are of such a character as to isolate those part-Hawaiians who claim their non-Hawaiian blood and subdivide them into two classes, the Caucasian-Hawaiian and the Asiatic-Hawaiian, at least a third of the latter class having both Caucasian and Asiatic as well as Hawaiian blood." (Adams, R., *Interracial Marriage in Hawaii,* 1937, p. 12.)

CHINO. Spanish America. A zambo, specifically, a person of one quarter Indian and three quarters negro blood. (Funk and Wagnalls, *New Standard Dictionary of the English Language,* 1942, p. 1585.) In Brazil, an offspring of a

Negro father and Indian mother. (Wyndham, H. A., *The Atlantic and Slavery*, 1935, pp. 246–247.)

CHOLO. Spanish America. Used in Peru, Costa Rica, Chile, Argentina, Ecuador and Bolivia of Negro-Indian-White hybrids or in Bolivia of Indian-Spanish hybrids. The cholos form about one-fourth of the population of Peru and Chile. The name has a connotation of "civilized Indian" and is usually applied to persons with Indian features predominating. (Woodbridge, H.C., "Glossary of Names Used in Colonial Latin America for Crosses Among Indians, Negroes and Whites," *Journal of the Washington Academy of Sciences*, 38 (Nov., 1948), 357.)

CROATAN. North Carolina. A mixed white, Indian and Negro group centered in Robeson County, North Carolina. (Johnson, G. B., "Personality in a White-Indian-Negro Community," *American Sociological Review*, 4 (Aug., 1939), 516–523.)

CUATERON. Spanish America. The offspring of an inter-racial union when the father is white and the mother Mulatto. (Funk and Wagnalls, *New Standard Dictionary of the English Language*, 1942, p. 1585.)

EMABASITELA. Africa. The illegitimate offspring of European men and Native women in Swaziland. (Kuper, H., *The Uniform of Colour*, 1947, p. 46.)

ESKIMO HALF-BREEDS. Greenland. Dating their origin from the establishment of the Danish missionary settlements on the West Coast in 1721, the resulting intermixture has, for the most part, been extra-matrimonial. "In comparison with the native Eskimo the mixed-bloods are considered to be superior men." (Reuter, E. B., *The Mulatto in the United States*, 1918, pp. 31–33.)

EURASIAN. India. Used to denote the offspring of Indian mothers and European, especially Portuguese, fathers. Ostracized by both English and Indians, the term "Eurasian" carries the stigma of contemptibility. (Hedin, P., "Anglo-Indian Community," *American Journal of Sociology*, 39 (Sept., 1934), 165–179.)

FERINGHI. India. The word *Feringhi* (Frank), originally merely a geographical reference to the origin of the white man, is now used with offensive intent as a name for Europeans. (Burns, A. C., *Colour Prejudice*, 1948, p. 64.)

GRIFFE (also GRIFF, GRIFFO, GRIFFIN). Louisiana. A type of mulatto. Was used constantly in Louisiana, both in conversation and print for a mulatto, particularly the woman. It meant the product of a Negro and a mulatto, containing one-fourth white blood, and three-fourths Negro; also, used to refer to any offspring of a Negro and a mulatto. (Murray, J. A. H., *A New English Dictionary*, 1888, Vol. 5, p. 419.)

GRIQUAS. South Africa. A hybrid people in South Africa, who arose from matings between early Dutch colonists and Hottentot and Bush women. Originally the Bastaards, so-called by the white population, the group migrated north of the Orange River, successfully established a settlement, and abandoned the name Bastaards and adopted that of Griquas. (Fantham, H. B., "Some Race Problems in South Africa," *Scientific Monthly*, 42 (Feb., 1936), 158.)

GUINEAS. West Virginia. Used of a Negro-Indian-White hybrid group in West Virginia and Maryland. (Gilbert, Jr., W. H., "Mixed Bloods of the Upper Monangahela Valley, West Virginia," *Journal of the Washington Academy of Sciences*, 36 (Jan., 1946), 1–13.)

JACKSON WHITE. New York. Used of Negro-Indian-White hybrids in the State of New York. The name is a very derogatory one. (Speck, F. G., "The Jackson Whites," *The Southern Workman*, 40 (Feb., 1911), 104–107.)

JIBARO. Mexico and Puerto Rica. Used to denote a mixture of white, Negro, and

Indian strains. In Peurto Rica this group constitutes three-fourths of the population. (Lovett, R. M., *All Our Years,* 1948, p. 312.)

KAZ DZUL. Yucatan. A term used for marginal individuals which has the connotation of lessened respect mingled with a tinge of contempt. A man living in Chan Kom who has a Spanish surname is *half-dzul* (kaz dzul). The Chan Kom people say that such persons are not "genuine Indians," but they are treated no differently from other members of the community. (Redfield, R., *The Folk Culture of Yucatan,* 1941, pp. 62–63.)

LEPEROS. Mexico. The lowest class of Mexicans. They are pariah mestizos who are so numerous as to be given the distinct name, leperos. Mostly town dwellers, subject "to all manner of diseases" with a language that is " an unintelligible argot." "Many of the leperos are astonishingly white, apparently showing a large admixture of Spanish blood." (Kelly, J., *Physical Anthropology of a Mexican Population in Texas,* 1947, p. 14.)

LOBO. Mexico. Term used for a Mexican half-breed who is half-Chinese and half-Negro. (Appleton's *New Spanish Dictionary,* 1941, p. 311, "Spanish-English" section.)

LUSO-INDIAN. India. The offspring resulting from the intermarriage of Portuguese males and Indian women. Relatively few in numbers today, they had the high status of their fathers so long as the Portuguese remained in power, but when the Dutch and English took over, the children were absorbed into the maternal stock or intermarried with British soldiers, partly loosing themselves in the British-Indian community. (Dover, C., *Cimmerii,* 1929, pp. 2–4.)

MANGO. United States. A particular type of hybrid—the product of the cross between the Sambo and Negro. (Reuter, E. B., *The Mulatto in the United States,* 1918, p. 13.)

MARABON. United States. The name given by the French in the Southern United States to the offspring of a mulatto and a griffe. (Reuter, E. B., *The Mulatto in the United States,* 1918, p. 12.)

MELUNGEONS. Eastern Tennessee. Believed to be a mixture of white, Indian and Negro strains, but the Melungeons themselves say they are of Portuguese descent. (Burnett, S. M., "A Note on the Melungeons," *American Anthropologist,* 2 (Oct., 1889), 342–349.)

METIS. Brazil. The mixed bloods of Brazil. In a general sense this term applies to all those who have mixed blood of two or more races, the specific groups in Brazil being the Portuguese, Indian, and Negro. (Stonequist, E., *The Marginal Man,* 1937, pp. 44–48.)

MOORS. Delaware and Southern New Jersey. The term is applied to a Negro-Indian-White hybrid group thinly scattered throughout this general area. (Weslanger, C. A., *Delaware's Forgotten Folk: The Story of the Moors and Nanticokes,* 1943, p. 215.)

MOPLAH. India. One of a class of Mohammedan inhabitants of southwestern India, especially Malabar, descended from Arab settlers and native women. (*The New Century Dictionary,* 1931, p. 1091.)

MORISCO. Mexico. The term used to distinguish one who is three-fourths Negro and one-fourth white (quadroon); the caste name for the children of Spanish and mulatto. (Appleton's *New Spanish Dictionary,* 1941, p. 339, "Spanish-English" section.)

MOTHRAKES. Sparta. In ancient Sparta, the half-caste offspring of Spartan fathers and helot mothers, treated as and brought up with pure Spartans but denied full citizenship rights. (Maunier, R., *The Sociology of Colonies,* 1949, Vol. 1, p. 127.)

MULATTO. General. Widely used term for the Negro-white hybrid. Specifically, it may refer to the first generation offspring of a pure Negro and a white. In a general and more popular way, a mulatto is any person of mixed Caucasian and Negro blood. (Stonequist, E. V., *The Marginal Man*, 1937, pp. 24–27.)

MUSTIFEE. United States. A particular type of hybrid—the product of the cross between the octoroon and white. (Reuter, E. B., *The Mulatto in the United States*, 1918, p. 13.)

MUSTIFINO. United States. A particular type of hybrid—the product of the cross between the mustifee and white. (Reuter, E. B., *The Mulatto in the United States*, 1918, p. 13.)

MULADIS. Mediterranean Area. Formerly to be found in this general area, a cross between the Muslim Arab and Spanish Christian. (Maunier, R., *The Sociology of Colonies*, 1949, Vol. 1, p. 125.)

NIGGER. General. A Negro (colloquial or vulgar, and commonly contemptuous); loosely, a member of any dark skinned race. (Murray, J. A. H., *New English Dictionary*, 1888, Vol. 6, p. 137.) "Nigger is really only an English form of the Portuguese *niger*—black. It was long in use before the more acceptable 'negro' was commonly accepted." (Wright, A., *The Romance of Colonization*, 1923, pp. 108–109.)

OCTOROON. United States and Mexico. In the United States a person having one-eighth Negro blood; the offspring of a quadroon and a white. In Mexico it applies to those who are one-fourth Negro and three-fourths white. (Murray, J. A. H., *New English Dictionary*, 1888, Vol. 7, p. 56.)

PAROS. Brazil. "To the offspring of races where it was impossible to distinguish the originators, we give the general name *pardos* (brown and light brown)." (Ramos, A., "Contact of Races in Brazil," *Social Forces*, 19 (May, 1941), 535.)

PERANAKAN. Dutch Indonesia. The Indo-Chinese, the Indo-Europeans, and the Indo-Arabs of Dutch Indonesia. Under Dutch rule these enjoyed a preferred position above that of the full-blooded Indonesians. Listed in the official census as Europeans. (Earle, F. M., "Eurasians—Dutch or Indonesian?" *Far Eastern Survey*, 17 (Dec. 22, 1948), 288–290.)

POULAIN. Eastern Mediterranean Area. "In the French kingdoms of the Latin Orient, the offspring of Crusaders and Syrian women were known as *poulains*." (Maunier, R., *The Sociology of Colonies*, 1949, Vol. 1, p. 70.)

QUADROON. General. One who is the offspring of a white person and a mulatto; one who is fourth in descent from a Negro, one of the parents in each genera-tion being white. In early Spanish usage, the term was applied to the offspring of a white and a mestizo, a half-breed Indian. (Murray, J. A. H., *A New English Dictionary*, 1888, Vol. 8, p. 8.)

SABINES. Louisiana. A community of mixed Indian, white and Negro ancestry bordering the Gulf of Mexico. (Parenton, V. J., and Pellegrin, R. J., "The 'Sabines': A Study of Racial Hybrids in a Louisiana Coastal Parish," *Social Forces*, 29 (Dec., 1950), 148–154.)

SACATRA. Louisiana. The name given to the offspring of a griffe and a negress. (Murray, J. A. H., *A New English Dictionary*, 1888, Vol. 8, p. 7.)

SALTOS ATRAS (jump back). Mexico. The name given to those reversions to primitive type which were most likely to occur in the crossing of Zambos and Mulattoes. (Kelly, A. R., *Physical Anthropology of a Mexican Population in Texas*, 1947, p. 12.)

SARAKOLLE. Africa. The Sarakolle, who lay claim to white ancestry, are an endogamous, long-haired, dark-skinned people in Senegal, Mauritania, and the French Sudan. The term means 'white man.' (Maunier, R., *The Sociology of Colonies*, 1949, Vol. 1, p. 119.)

TURKS. South Carolina. Used of a Negro-Indian-White hybrid group found mainly in the coastal area of South Carolina. A term of derision applied by the whites, the group is also known as "Redbones," "Red Legs," "Brass Ankles," "Buckheads," "Marlboro Blues," and "Yellow Hammers." (Berry, B., "The Mestizos of South Carolina," *America Journal of Sociology*, 51 (July, 1945). 31–41.)

VECINOS. Central America. In Dzitas, Yucatan, the great degree of racial intermixture makes any social stratification based upon determined degrees of biological intermixture or upon skin color impossible. It is probable that there is no one without Indian ancestry, and there is more Indian than European blood in the population as a whole. The mixed bloods with Spanish surnames are denoted vacinos (meaning neighboring, next, near, like, resembling) and accorded superior status. (Redfield, R., *Folk Culture of Yucatan*, 1941, p. 66.)

WESORTS. Southern Maryland. Said to be mainly white and Indian with some Negro infusion. (Gilbert, Jr., W. H., "The Wesorts of Southern Maryland," *Journal of the Washington Academy of Sciences*, 35 (April 15, 1945), 237–246.)

ZAMBOS (or SAMBOS). United States and Mexico. Name given to the children of a mulatto and a Negro in America; also the offspring of the imported Negro and native Indian stock. In Mexico, the cross of the Negro with the ancient inhabitants of the country; also the half-caste offspring of a Mulatto father and a Zamba mother; also half cambujo and half Indian. (Funk and Wagnalls, *New Standard Dictionary of the English Language*, 1942, p. 1585; Murray, J. A. H., *A New English Dictionary*, 1888, Vol. 10, p. 85.)

THE ANTHROPOLOGICAL AND

STATISTICAL CONCEPTION

OF RACE

*

By Alexander Goldenweiser

MAN IS PART OF NATURE. In more respects than one he is like other things on earth. Man is a physical thing. He has size and weight and shape, like a stone. Also, he has color and smell and is subject to the influence of heat and cold. When he drops he falls like a stone, and the law of falling bodies applies to him as it does to the rest of nature. Man is a chemical thing. Many processes in his body are like those of a chemical laboratory: for example, digestion, respiration, vision and glandular secretions. Man is like a plant: He comes from a cell, he absorbs foreign substances into his body, transforms them into parts of his own tissues, grows, and reproduces his kind. Also, the substance he is

From Alexander Goldenweiser, *Race and Race Relations* (American Council, Institute of Pacific Relations, 1931), p. 5.

made of is sensitive to external and internal stimuli. Man is like an animal, for in addition to having the properties of a plant, he also can move about freely at his own volition, as most animals do. In particular, man is like all vertebrate animals; his skeleton is built around a spinal column, symmetrically and bilaterally. While supporting the muscular tissues, the skeletal framework also articulates with the nervous system and especially with the spinal cord which extends along the vertebral column to the brain incased in the skull. So it is also with other vertebrates. Again, man is a mammal, bringing live offspring into the world and feeding them with the mother's milk. Among mammals the monkeys are even closer to man than the rest, in so far as they have arms and hands like man and are closer to him in mental capacity than most other animals. Over and above the monkeys, man is most like the great apes, the gorilla, orang-outang, chimpanzee and gibbon, who on account of their great resemblance to man, are called anthropoids. We no longer believe, as people once did, that the great apes are man's direct ancestors, but there can be no doubt that both belong to a common ancestral stem.

Man then is part of nature, and for purposes of science must be regarded as such.

* *

By Frank H. Hankins

THE BASIS OF ALL ACCURATE THINKING regarding racial matters is the fact of human variability. This is merely a special case of that variability which is universal in animate nature. There is no measurable trait, either physical or mental, with respect to which the members of any human group, however limited in numbers, are equal. Even a small body of adults of the same sex will show considerable variations in stature, weight, hair-color, eye-color, head-form, brain-size, body-build, length of span, size of foot, etc., through the whole list of physical measurements. The same may be said of the much more important physiological characteristics, such as vitality, energy, endurance, resistance to disease, and longevity, which are so basic to individual success whether in the struggle for existence on the savage plane or the struggle for a certain standard of living in a civilized community. This fact of human variability scarcely needs further elaboration since it is a matter of common observation, though too frequently ignored in the democratic philosophizings of a humanitarian age. So universal is this tendency to vary that children of the same family differ one from another. They may frequently exhibit a general family resemblance, but sometimes they differ as much as children of different families. Even identical twins, evolved from the same zygote, will, according to the find-

Reprinted from *The Racial Basis of Civilization: A Critique of the Nordic Doctrine*, pp. 258–274, by Frank H. Hankins, by permission of Alfred A. Knopf, Inc. Copyright 1926 by Alfred A. Knopf, Inc.

ings of Professors H. H. Newman and H. H. Wilder, show some, though slight, variation one from another.

If one turn his attention to mental differences he meets with the same general fact. In any considerable group there is a range from idiocy to genius. If the group is made small and relatively homogeneous the range of variation is narrowed but the variability still exists. Children of the same age, pupils of the same school grades, adult males of the same occupation, differ one from another in their sensory powers, speed of reaction to stimulus, memory, judgment and reasoning ability. These differences are at any time and place due to the combined effects of both hereditary potentialities and environmental conditions. But it is worth while to note that, even if the environmental conditions are made as nearly equal as possible the variations persist. The variations in mental traits rest, on their biological side, on variations in brain and nerve size and structure, and there is no ground for supposing that these do not vary through wide limits in consequence of purely hereditary factors.

We see then, in the first place, that any conception of race must include this fact of universal variability. How then can this variability be graphically represented? For nearly a century now, or since the work of the Belgian astronomer and anthropometrist, Adolphe Quetelet, it has been clear that the physical traits of a homogeneous group of men are distributed after the manner of the probability integral pictured in the curve of distribution of errors in measurement. The work of three generations of anthropologists and biometricians makes it clear that the same general form of distribution is found for all traits. In the light of the voluminous researches of recent years under the leadership of Galton and Pearson, Thorndike, Terman and the army psychologists it now appears clear that mental traits also follow this same general form of distribution. In the theoretically ideal case a perfectly symmetrical curve of distribution would result because the variations would be due to the chance combinations of an infinitude of infinitesimal factors each of which had an equal probability of being present or absent. This would be like the frequency distribution of all the possible combinations of say a thousand coins thrown an exceedingly great number of times, a statistical distribution being made of the numbers of heads and tails in each throw.

If, for example, one were graphically representing the distribution of stature in a given racial group he would indicate units of stature on the base line and units of frequency on the vertical ordinate. His curve would then tell him what were the limits of stature in the group, how many individuals will be found having each degree of stature, and what the central tendency of the group is as to stature. If one call this central tendency the mode or average, it is clear that more persons have statures near the average than elsewhere and that the frequency diminishes with departure therefrom. In the same, or much the same, manner other traits will be found distributed. We need not concern ourselves here with departures from symmetry as they do not affect the general nature of the concepts we are elucidating.

We have in the foregoing statistical theory the only valid method of conceiving a race. When we speak of the characteristics of a race it is necessary to think in terms of average values for given traits about which are grouped the members of the race in a more or less symmetrical manner through a greater or less range of variability. To think of a race as having certain well-defined traits without at the same time taking account of its variability is to leave out an essential datum for accurate thinking. Our Nordic propagandists, for example, customarily attribute high intelligence to the Nordic, thus leaving out of account the fact that Nordic intellects range downward through imbecility to idiocy.

We may then ask: what is a race? In the first place, race designates a group of human beings set apart from others by one or more marks of physical difference. It is a taxonomic, zoological term and it is thus similar to such terms as variety, subspecies, species, genus. These terms designate groups of quite different inclusiveness, but the term race is commonly used, in the case of the human species, to designate all such groupings and hence all degrees of inclusiveness. Thus we have the human race, the Caucasian race, the Caledonian race. But in all cases the word means a group of men set apart by certain physical traits implied in the qualifying adjective. Thus when one speaks of the human race he means to set off all mankind as distinct in certain physical respects from the rest of the animal world. In this case the range of variability is very great and the elements found in common among all members of the group are general rather than specific. The terms Caucasian or Mongolian applied to races are likewise recognized as broad and general in nature. They call attention to certain obvious differences between some of the major ethnic stocks of mankind which include within themselves a variety of minor divisions.

But this last statement holds true of all groups included in every known classification of races including those of Bernier in 1684 and Linnaeus in 1735. The term Caucasian, originated by Blumenbach (1775), included Arabs and Swedes. Cuvier (1769–1832) found in Noah's three sons, Shem, Ham and Japheth, the progenitors of three primary varieties of man, a classification still extant in certain religious circles. With the growth of knowledge and development of scientific methods there was a tendency among anthropologists to multiply the races and varieties of man. Haeckel found twelve races in 1873 but thirty-four in 1879; Topinard found sixteen in 1878 but increased the number to nineteen seven years later; and Deniker's classification in 1889 included thirteen races and thirty sub-divisions but in 1900 had seventeen races with twenty-nine divisions.

Meanwhile it had become evident to a few that, as Pritchard said: "The different races of man are not distinguished from each other by strongly-marked and permanent distinctions. . . . All the diversities which exist are variable, and pass into each other by insensible gradations." Indeed, this same fact had been perceived by Blumenbach a generation earlier when he said: "The innumerable varieties of mankind run into one another by insensible degrees." Topinard said: "Race in the present state of things is an abstract conception, a notion of continuity in discontinuity, of unity in diversity. It is the rehabilitation of a real, but directly unattainable thing." Keane classified mankind into many varieties all of which were derived from three or four original or primary, that is, "ideal" or "generalized" types.

A little reflection on these efforts will show that there is no simple and exhaustive conception of race. If we begin with the concept "Primates" we include with man the anthropoids and in so doing will call attention to their numerous fundamental similarities, and will set off the race of primates from the rest of the animal world. If we begin with the human race as the most inclusive group we can steadily narrow the number of individuals included and hence the range of variation by a more and more precise definition of requisite traits. If, for example, we add to the trait human, the trait white, or near-white, skin we set apart the Caucasian division. Let us add blond hair, and our group diminishes and the range narrows; if we add blue eyes, it contracts still further. It should be evident that we can go on adding traits of more and more specificity until we distinguish one stirp or kinship group from another; and in this we could set families off one from another; until, in last analysis, we come to the individual, who is the only creature in the world like himself in all respects. We can thus arrange a series ranging down from Primates through humanity to such narrower groups as Caucasian, Nordic, Nordic varieties and sub-varieties, or stirps or clans and families to individuals. Such a series would be comparable to the zoologist's series: kingdom, phylum, class, order, genus, species, variety, individual.

The term race in the sense of a group with distinctive hereditary traits would apply to every category in such a series, except the last. Each category is included in the one which precedes it and to that extent bears a fundamental resemblance to it; but each is also distinctive in possessing traits peculiar to itself. One may thus say that all men are human, and since he would mean by this that they are set apart from the anthropoids he would be warranted in saying that their similarities one with another are obvious in their universal contrasts with the apes. This would not be a denial of man's fundamental unity with the anthropoids but would emphasize his differences in certain respects. Similarly with each narrowing category. Hence one must beware of unconsciously assuming that because all men are human that, therefore, their differences are negligible. There is probably no point of demarcation where the differences are negligible, even down to the individuals who represent the smallest possible sub-division. We may not, however, as yet be able to measure the significance for human affairs of some of these differences. It is thus apparent why the concept of race is so elusive. We can say only that, in its general meaning, the concept of race, first of all, includes the idea of distinctive hereditary traits.

In the second place, since the concept must allow for a certain variability among the members of the designated group, the two ideas of type and variation about the type become essential elements in the definition of race. If we think of a race as a group set apart by some *single* trait, as stature, these ideas may be represented in their simplest form by graphs for Japanese and American soldiers. The one group has a typical or average stature of 63.24 inches but varies in height from just under 56 inches to 69 inches; the other has an average stature of 67.51 inches and varies in height from under 62 inches to nearly 75 inches.

This simple illustration also serves to bring out the overlapping of races though the overlapping is here much less than will be found in most cases. If we had only stature to go by we should not be able to determine whether many of the individuals measured belonged to the taller or to the shorter race. This fact of overlapping constitutes, then, a third primary feature in our concept of race. As the above quotations from Blumenbach and Topinard indicate, the races or types of man shade into one another—there is a "continuity in discontinuity." This is true of all the customary indices of racial difference, viz., stature, cephalic-index, hair-color, eye-color, skin-color, nasal-index, hair-form, alveolar-index, etc. As regards any one index, therefore, it is possible to arrange the types of man into a series with large overlapping areas so that it would be impossible to tell where one race ends or the next begins. This over-lapping is primarily a consequence of the fact that all men may be traced back through hundreds of thousands of years to a common ancestral stem; in spite of their differentiation into varieties all men retain some combination of those traits which distinguish men from the other primates. The overlapping is due in part also to the universal tendency of all living things to vary about their own hereditary center. Thus Professor Jennings and his laboratory associates have shown that even in pure-line paramecia, bred from single individuals, there is a considerable variability, and a great deal of overlapping of strains nearest each other.

It follows from this extensive overlapping of racial categories when only a single trait is measured, that we must combine a number of traits in order to distinguish one race from another. Even white and negro cannot be distin-guished by stature or by cephalic index; even as regards skin-color and hair-form the border areas of distribution overlap. It is this overlapping that makes it necessary to think of a race as a complex of traits inherited together within a limited range of variability. Since tall shades into short, long into round, and dark into light, it must be shown that with tall stature are found also a certain head-form, eye-color, shape of hair, etc. But even with a combination of traits there is considerable difficulty in distinguishing one race from another in areas where the two have long been in contact with each other and produced inter-mediate types of varying degrees of composition.

And it is here that we come upon the central difficulty of race discrimination, namely, the fact that through geologic periods one human stem has crossed with another so that traits tend to spread widely from the center of their first specialization. In other words, as regards man, there is no such thing as a pure line in either modern or extinct races. There has always been a certain amount of cross-breeding, though among peoples living in great isolation, such as the extinct Tasmanians, this must have been slight. All peoples living in accessible, and especially all those living in fertile areas, have been so subject to immigra-tion, war and conquest as well as wife stealing and other variations of matri-monial institutions as to make impossible the maintenance of racial purity in an unalloyed state.

The human groups now existent will range, therefore, all the way from a high degree of racial purity in small isolated groups found here and there which for many generations have remained in complete freedom from outside influ-ence, such as certain Eskimo tribes mentioned by Boas, to the extreme hybridity characteristic of such great cosmopolitan centers as Constantinople.

But the problem of racial definition is not beyond a certain degree of possible clarification. The primary difficulty is the difficulty of thinking in terms of relatives rather than absolutes, of probabilities rather than certainties. The average mind wants its science like its religion and its ethics dished up to it in terms of absolutes and eternal verities, whereas the actual world is a world of variability, constant alteration, and relativity. We shall find that racial types are themselves in a state of flux and that the differences between types are rela-tive rather than absolute. This does not mean that the differences are without significance, but that they must be conceived as what they are, variations of certain fundamental attributes which belong to all mankind. Just as all men of a certain group have stature or intelligence, but some are taller or brighter than others, so all the different varieties of men have stature and intelligence but some are taller than others and some are brighter.

If Sir Arthur Keith be correct in assuming that the human stem differentiated from the anthropoid stem about 2,000,000 years ago and that the fundamental types of modern men were differentiated from each other at least 400,000 years ago, there has been plenty of time for both race specialization and race crossing. White, Yellow and Black—each during all this time has undergone mutation, variation and selection and varying degrees of geographic isolation for varying lengths of time. Groups have repeatedly split off from parent stems, undergone greater or less differentiation, and then crossed with other variates of the same general stock. Crosses have now been between closely related types and now between those widely separated. They have taken the form sometimes of small infusions of alien elements, sometimes of large ones, and sometimes large, fairly heterogeneous groups have been absorbed into others. These crossings have sometimes been the result of temporary contacts between settled and migratory groups, sometimes long continued interchange between contiguous settled communities. All sorts of human interests have played their part in such intermixture of blood, from war and slavery, through drought and enforced migration, adventure, exploration and trade, to wife capture and purchase, and even religious wars and crusades.

The result is that the populations found within any considerable geographical area will present a certain broad similarity which sets them off from the populations of other distant areas, as Africans from Europeans, Chinese or Hindus. But within each such area viewed by itself there is great diversity; these large areas may be broken up into smaller ones each showing a certain distinction from others, as is seen in the case of Europe where the south, northwest and east form more or less distinctive anthropological provinces. Then these provinces may be further sub-divided until one reaches those small and very special differences which distinguish the people of one mountain valley from their neighbors. Here again we see that the concept of race must vary constantly with the number of traits which are brought into consideration and the extent of their variation. We may move from such broad terms as Caucasian, through Ripley's well-known designations of European races, to the sub-varieties under each of the latter.

And as we thus give definiteness and concreteness to the concept we meet with an increasing difficulty of finding perfect exemplars of it. Thus Ripley found that the European peoples were so mixed that any given combination of hair-color and eye-color would exclude two-thirds of the population in nearly every area. If to these two traits be added head-form, then only a small portion of the population in any European area would be found to combine all three traits. "Imagine a fourth trait, stature, or a fifth, nasal-index, to be added, and our proportion of pure types becomes almost infinitesimal." So that, when Ripley asked Ammon for a photograph of a pure Alpine type, the latter, although he had measured thousands of Rhenish recruits, replied that he had never found a specimen of the Alpine type perfect in all details. "All his round-headed men were either blond, or tall, or narrow-nosed, or something else they ought not to be."

This means that when we define a race in terms of a series of physical traits we necessarily describe an idealized type. Thus the Baltic, Teutonic or Nordic race is said to have tall stature, long heads, narrow noses, clear blue, green or gray eyes, and blond hair.

All these traits are variable, even the blue eyes, though the range of variation is narrowly restricted in each case. If now, one studies the population of a presumably "Nordic" community he might begin by singling out all the tall people; among these he might select out those with long heads; and from among these in turn those with narrow noses, etc. He would end by having all those of his assumed race, and they would be only a small fraction of those with whom he began. If now, these were judged by an exacting standard, such as is used in judging animals at the cattle show, an even smaller fraction of them, a truly infinitesimal portion of them, would exemplify the true or perfect type. It is much like the "average man" of common parlance. All of us represent him in some respect; many of us in more than one; but almost none, if any, of us represent him in all respects. He is purely ideal because so many variants of him are embodied in all sorts of persons.

In other words, when one speaks of a race he must bear in mind the following considerations. There is, first, the general fact of human variability. There is, secondly, the idea of type about which individual copies more or less inexact are grouped in a more or less regular manner. There is, thirdly, the overlapping with reference to any specific traits of the exemplars of one type and of related or contiguous types. This in itself would tend to prevent the easy separation of types but such is made immensely more difficult by the fact of race crossing. This brings it about, fourthly, that the determination of race types in any given area (except long isolated ones) becomes a process of the abstraction of traits from existing individuals and their recombination into a generalized or ideal type represented by few or no living individuals.

We thus see that the concept "race" is plastic and relative. In what sense, if any, can there be said to be pure races? This question already has been largely answered. So frequent have been human migrations and so constant the contacts of tribes that a perfect purity could not be maintained. Purity of a very high degree could only be preserved in areas of geographic isolation, such as islands, mountain valleys, or desert oases. But, if one is interested in the role of race in cultural evolution, it must be evident that completely isolated groups have counted for naught. On the other hand, all those conditions which enable a race to play such a role have favored its commingling with other stocks. When, therefore, one thinks of those groups which have swept across the pages of European history in either prehistoric or historic times he must conceive them as being already more or less heterogeneous. The acquisition of the very cultural equipment which enabled them to migrate and conquer was doubtless due in large part to those contacts which, while facilitating a diffusion of culture, would also involve a crossing of strains. It is for such reasons taken in conjunction with the discussion of earlier pages that we are warranted in holding on strong *a priori* grounds as well as on both recent and Palaeo-anthropological evidence that there has been no considerable area at any time inhabited by a simon-pure Nordic race.

It is this universal hybridity which has made necessary the idealization of the type as illustrated by the terms Nordic, Alpine and Mediterranean. Professor Ripley's discussion makes it clear as we have seen that the traits ascribed to these races are arrived at only in consequence of processes of elimination and idealization. It is wholly improbable that there is anywhere in Europe any sizable area inhabited by a people whose blood has remained since Neolithic times unmixed with that of some more or less different stock. The proof is in the fact that "at the present time rarely, if indeed ever, do we discover a single individual corresponding to our racial type in every detail." Similar considerations apply to other areas and peoples. It appears on a superficial survey that there are vast groups of Europeans unmixed with negro blood, as also considerable areas of negroid and mongoloid stocks unaffected by European admixture. But within each grand division of mankind and even down to particular tribal bodies within them there has everywhere been an absence of that complete segregation of groups which would have given perfect homogeneity. Indeed, the facts presented by Dixon's survey of extant anthropological data show that everywhere on the globe, and at all times for which data are available, head-forms have been quite variable. This conclusion holds whether his theory of the original ingredients be correct or not. In almost exactly the same manner Fleure has shown that extreme dolichocephaly and certain associated characters are found in such widely separated places as Wales, Ireland, France, the Iberian Peninsula, North and East Africa, Australia (Aborigines), Fiji Islands and East Brazil.

All this has an intimate bearing on one's conception of such populations as the assumed original Aryans, the Nordics, the Wiros. Thus Peake, Nordic Aryanist, while giving them rather typical traditional characteristics, admits their heterogeneity. In fact, he argues that there probably has never been a human group living in complete isolation long enough to have produced a close homogeneity. Thus the evidence of Palaeolithic skulls of the steppe-folk of several thousand years ago, studied by Sergi and Bogdanov, show a range in cephalic index from 65 to 79 even with the exclusion of certain broad skulls found in the same burial mounds. This is more than a third of the whole human range and fully one-half the range of all but extreme forms; it is wide enough to include many sub-types. His conclusion is: "We can then imagine our Wiros as a somewhat variable race, with heads that conform to the narrow rather than the broad type, tall and robust, though probably neither so tall nor so robust as many of the modern Nordics. There is reason for believing them to have been fair, though it is likely enough that in coloration, too, there was considerable variation." This is a circumspect statement, but one may add to its circumspection. The only evidences for blondness are scrappy bits of mythology. We do not know what proportion may have approached pure blonds. Peake is himself inclined to think the extreme blondness found among the Swedes is a later specialization. We do not know for certain whether in ancient times blondness was associated with the long heads or the round heads and in what proportions; nor do we know in what proportions tallness, blondness and long-headedness were found in the same persons. All the evidence presented by Peake indicates that his mythical Wiros, the possible ancestors of the Achaean heroes, of the Celts and the Teutons, were highly hybridized 5000 to 8000 years ago. It is doubtful whether they have ever been less so at any time since, except in small isolated areas, where they would be of no historical significance.

We think then of a race as an ensemble of physical traits, each more or less variable, all inherited as an ensemble within their limits of variation, and sufficiently distinctive when taken together to mark off their possessors from other members of the human species. Such a conception is plastic and adaptable. It applies to all anthropological types, but in view of the excessive tendency toward crossing of lines such a concept of race makes it clear that such historical groups as the Aryan, Greek, Latin, German, or English cannot be looked upon as pure races, or even approximately pure. Such terms as Slav, Celtic and Teutonic, when applied to those tribes and peoples who have moved across the arena of European history must be reserved for political and ethnological groupings rather than anthropological types. It should be clear also that if the term Nordic is to be used to designate one of the racial types entering into the composition of European peoples, then it should not be applied to historical groups. There have been and still are some groups containing more Nordic blood than others but no investigation has yet been made which shows how much such nations owe to their Nordic ingredients and how much to other elements.

RACE AS A SOCIAL PHENOMENON

By Robert Redfield

THE PHYSICAL CHARACTERISTICS used by anthropologists to classify people racially have, so far as we know, practically no significance for cultural achievement. We can not validly say that skin color, hair form and other racial differences, of themselves and without reference to the attention paid to them, are of any consequence in human behavior. If we were to take no notice of the shape of the nose, we could not say that people with noses of one shape would not be just as well prepared to run governments or to write books as people with noses of another shape. We have no reason to conclude that the lips of Negroes are not as good instruments as other kinds of lips for speaking beautiful French or perfect English, as well as excellent Bantu. The brains of Chinese, African and North European are boxed in bony containers that differ somewhat in their characteristic shapes, but we have no real evidence that, on the average, the brains contained in the skulls of representatives of one of these racial groups are better organs for thinking than those occupying the skulls of representatives of the other groups.

Reprinted from Robert Redfield, "What Do We Know About Race," *The Scientific Monthly*, LVII (September, 1943), pp. 193–195; copyright 1943 by American Association for the Advancement of Science and used with the kind permission of the publisher.

What we do know to be important about race is known about the races that people see and recognize, or believe to exist. Physical anthropologists are concerned with race as a biological phenomenon. In this paper we are concerned with race as a social phenomenon. We might speak of the "socially supposed races." Such races have a reality, too, but it is different from the reality of biological races. If people took special notice of red automobiles, were attracted to or repelled by the color of red automobiles, and believed that the redness of automobiles was connected inseparably with their mechanical effectiveness, then red automobiles would constitute a real and important category. It is something like that with the socially supposed races. The real differences among biologically different groups may have little consequences for the affairs of men. The believed-in differences, and the visible differences of which notice is taken, do have consequence for the affairs of men. This is what we know about race. It is on the level of habit, custom, sentiment and attitude that race, as a matter of practical significance, is to be understood. Race is, so to speak, a human invention.

The biological differences which enable us to classify the human species into races are superficial differences. There are few racial differences deep inside our bodies. Racial differences are mostly in the outermost layer. This fact is important for the social significance of race, because, being in the outermost layer, racial differences are easily visible. It is skin color, hair form, the shape of the nose, the lips and the eyelids that enter into our awareness and become connected with attitudes and judgments. The relative flatness of the shin bone has been used as a criterion in the biological classification of races. But there is no prejudice against flat-shinned races as such, because nobody, except perhaps a few anthropologists, know they exist. The visible racial characteristics constitute a marker, a label, for all to read. When the label has not been put there by nature, and if the identification of the group has become important in the thinking of people, there is a disposition to exaggerate it or even to manufacture it. When one drop of African blood makes a Negro, it may be believed advisable to look at the fingernails or the whites of the eyes of an individual to discover to which racial category he belongs. The anthropologists tell us that the Jews are not a race. They are not a biological race because the people known as Jews are not enough like each other and are too much like other people to be distinguishable from them. But as people act with reference to Jews, and to some extent connect the attitudes they have about them with real or imagined biological characteristics, they are a socially supposed race. As such, they lack a clear and consistent natural label. The Nazis require them to wear yellow arm bands or the Star of David. A cartoon stereotype of the Jew has comparable effect.

It is the association of some such label with cultural differences and in combination with real or imagined biological differences that brings about a socially supposed race. The observable physical difference is alone not enough. Red-haired people are not collectively noticed and judged any more than are red automobiles. They do not constitute a cultural group. But Negroes are, or have been, a cultural group, and the same is true of Chinese and Japanese, Italians, Jews and Swedes and, indeed, of lawyers, gangsters and professors. These are in varying degrees cultural groups, but in the cases of those named toward the end of this list there is little or no physical label, and much less disposition to identify the cultural difference with real or supposed biological difference. So lawyers, gangsters and professors, whatever else they may be, are not socially supposed races.

√   In the Negro, the Chinese, the Jew and the White Gentile, the apparent marks of difference become identified with the sentiments and collective judgments that are held about these groups. In the first place these visible markers serve to assign a marked individual to the class to which others feel he belongs or to which he feels he belongs. If members of my group look down upon Negroes, then any person with a black skin is recognized as one to be looked down upon. In the second place the racial labels and the biological differences which are believed to lie in, or be connected with, these labels become the reasons and the supposed proofs of the sentiments and judgments borne toward the marked group. When the rise of the cotton industry induced Southern leaders before the Civil War to stop apologizing for slavery and to begin defending it, it was asserted that the Negro lacked the native intelligence to be more than a slave. It was said that the low skull of the Negro pressed upon his brain and prevented him from becoming intelligent.

It was not, of course, the Negro's skull that pressed upon him. It was slavery and ignorance that pressed upon him. But the skull got the blame. The skulls always do. When people have prejudices it is convenient to support them by referring to the will of God or the wisdom of science. The latter is as innocent as the former. The beliefs of people about the physical features of race become a sort of false science. Or we might call them a modern mythology. We believe many things about people who are different from ourselves, many of which are not true. It is not now widely believed in this country that Jews perform ritual murder; the belief that they control the present Federal Government or American business is more commonly encountered. In so far as the Jews are thought of racially, these are beliefs as to race, and so relevant to our discussion.

We now review some of the things that we do know to be important about race. We do know that the cultural differences between groups come to be associated with noticed and imagined physical differences and that sometimes the latter are regarded as the explanation of the former. We learn that this happens and something about how it happens from the history of race relations. The racial explanation of cultural differences has great antiquity and has followed a varying career. In a great many societies where groups looking and acting differently have dwelt together, the differences between them and the kinds of relationships established between them have been explained racially. They are also often commonly justified racially. Greek writers offered a justification in racial terms for the subordination of helots to Athenian citizens. Negro slavery and discrimination against Negroes have been regularly supported by similar argument. The doctrine of a master race, capable of ruling and of creation, as contrasted with lesser breeds, such as Poles and Jews, capable only of being ruled and of imitating and obeying, was developed by a number of nineteenth-century writers. By the Nazis it has been elevated to a cardinal dogma and a principle of statecraft. At present, in this country, the Japanese, who used to be regarded as a wonderful little people are being radically reinterpreted. Our enemies, they tend also to be set away so far from us racially that it seems as if now they had connection with us hardly humanly at all but only as co-members of the Animal Kingdom.

We are saying that the social significance of race, which is its only practical significance, is a product of history. It results from the interaction of human nature with situations of group difference and group relationship. It is not always the same. It does not even always exist.

For the small child there is, characteristically, no significance in race. There is surely no instinct of racial prejudice or of racial recognition. Children brought up in societies where there are racial prejudices ordinarily begin to share them —or perhaps to rebel against them—at the age when self-consciousness begins. In the first years they exhibit no special sort of behavior toward representatives of other races. They may not even pay much attention to the physical differences. A small White child drawing a picture of the Negro cook in the kitchen, may run into the kitchen to see whether her black friend's eyes are blue or brown. It is clear that attitudes about racial groups have to be learned.

When racial groups come into contact with each other for the first time, it does not always follow that they at once dislike each other. Certainly, under such circumstances, they do not at once pronounce judgment as to the worth or character of each other. The white skin of the European was interesting to the Indian and to the African when first seen. It drew the native to look further into these odd-looking invaders. In some cases the appearance of the newcomer was found to be fearful, and the native fled. Physical difference, within limits, attracts, else the exotic would not be appreciated. The first Negroes brought to Europe by White explorers of Africa were welcomed into intimate household association with aristocratic Englishmen; they were interesting oddities. It took time for the attitude of the North European toward the black man to develop its characteristic form.

The dependence of racial attitudes upon historical events is likewise shown by the varying course of these changing attitudes with regard to any one racial group. The American Indian has passed through an almost complete cycle of collective judgment; he has been the Noble Red Man, that "varmint," good only when dead, and that appreciated and interesting fellow-American whose blood in one's veins is considered desirable rather than otherwise. I have mentioned the case of the Japanese. It is humbling to a lesser student of race relations to read what one of our greatest sociologists and students of race relations wrote about the Japanese in 1905: "It is indeed probable that in the event of a successful struggle with Russia, little will remain of prejudice against (the Japanese) this smallish, yellow people, or of impediment to social and matrimonial, as well as political and commercial, association with it."

Let it be said again that what we do know about race is that it is significant as account is taken of it at any time and place, and that the significance changes as the time and the place change. In some interracial situations peoples come together freshly; neither has a traditional view of the other; then the character of race relations will be determined largely by immediate circumstances. So it was that some Indian tribes welcomed the White man and regarded him favorably; others sought to destroy him. In such a situation the whole difference could be determined by one gift or one bullet. On the other hand, some interracial situations are the product of long histories, and new events can only modify, one way or the other, the character of those relations. The situation of the Jew is of this sort. He has been so long an international scapegoat that he is likely to be the unfortunate candidate in any new situation that requires a scapegoat.

It follows that the factor of race—the visible marker with its assumed implications as to inherent differences—gets itself attached to groups that are separated or segregated or stigmatized. As people think and feel themselves different from, or better than, other people, and there is a racial marker, so there arises a race-relations problem. In the case of the Chinese on the Pacific Coast, in the early days of anti-Asiatic sentiment, there was an association of a racial marker with an economically conflicting cultural group. The Japanese today is at once the enemy with whom we have come to closest grips and also the wearer of a face notably different from our own. The influence of the racial marker may be so strong as to overcome even the knowledge gained by personal acquaintance with members of the racial group. To cite one example I mention the situation of many young American citizens of Japanese descent who are today confined in relocation centers. In one of these centers an American of, I think, Swedish descent was employed as a garage foreman in charge of six or seven mechanics. Finally he gave up the job after trying for weeks to be happy in it. "It's no use," he said, "I look at them and I can't help thinking of them as Japs." He meant, of course, as our Japanese enemies on the other side of the lines on Guadalcanal. Yet his mechanics were boys born and brought up in Oakland and Los Angeles and educated in our schools. Had they looked like his own sons, the foreman would have got along with them, and would, probably, have forgotten the fact that they had enemy-alien parents.

The effectiveness of race as an indicator of the relations between groups is probably greatest where it indicates higher and lower social status. When there are castes within a society, and the one caste is racially different from the others, then race is of greatest social consequence. The whole system depends on it. Our Old South is the most familiar example of this situation. In that society the fundamental castes are social castes. The significance of race is to identify the members of the two castes and to keep the one below the other. Negro and White may have close personal relations. White and Negro may be linked in intimate sympathetic association. A White child caresses his Negro mammy. But the black skin, the conception of one drop of Negro blood, and a great many secondary indicators of the subordinated racial group serve to keep the castes sharply separated in terms of "aboveness" and "belowness." It is all right for Negro and White to be close together provided that the one is, without doubt, below the other. Hence come such Southern usages as the separation of Whites and Blacks at a lunch counter by a single symbolic vertical brass pole, or the practice of certain Southern banks to send out monthly statements of account to all White customers with the name at the head of the sheet prefixed with "Mr." or "Mrs.," while the bank statements of Negro customers are made up without this designation.

In the North, on the other hand, and to a growing extent in the South, racial markers are not so clearly arrangements for the maintenance of caste lines. Negroes have education and enter the professions, and the intimate families and small communities of both Negroes and Whites give way to looser and more impersonal communities. So the Negro and the White drift apart from each other as the Negro to some degree gets out from under the White. The Negro and the White do not look directly up and directly down at each other; they come, almost, to look across at each other. Race is still important, but it serves to mark separation more and subordination less. So it is sometimes said that there is more race prejudice in the North than in the South. By this is meant that in the North the Negro is kept away from the White by the factor of race. Human relations between the two groups are restricted by the difference of color. A man is prejudged as unworthy, or as merely inappropriate, to associate with because he is a Negro. In the Old South the individual Negro was treated humanly just because he did not compete with the White for status. But when and if, in the South, he did or does challenge the status position of the White man, the response of the White man was or is correspondingly vigorous.

ETHNICS

By E. K. Francis

FRIEDRICH MEINECKE, in his book *Weltbürgertum und Nationalstaat,* has put his finger on a difference in concepts which distinguished Western and central European thought on the phenomenon of the nation. Meinecke was mostly concerned with the political and historical implications of this difference when he set the idea of *Staatsnation* against that of *Kulturnation.* But his dichotomy indicates more than that; namely, two scientific approaches to a distinctive category of social facts; two sociologies, as it were; two philosophies of society, based on different sets of attitudes and scales of values.

This was almost forty years ago. But even today we find that the prevailing trend of thought differs among students of society who have grown up under German influence and those who are working in the Anglo-Saxon scientific climate. The latter put their main emphasis either on the political implications of nations or on the psychological and historical genesis of nationalism. Now, nationalism, taken either as a psychological or as a historical phenomenon, is not identical with the social fact called "a nation." It is, however, significant that probably the most thoroughgoing essay on the nation which has been published in the English language not only bears the title *Nationalism* (London, 1939) but gives as one of the characteristics of nation the following: "The idea of a common government whether as a reality in the present or past, or as an aspiration of the future."

The other class of Continental sociologists have tended to separate the concept of nation from that of the state; they also have emphasized the onto-logical and phenomeno-logical analysis of nation rather than a genetical inter-

E. K. Francis, "The Nature of the Ethnic Group," *The American Journal of Sociology,* LII (March, 1947), 393–400. By permission.

pretation. Thus we find among them a great number of book titles, such as *Nation und Staat, Nation und Nationalität, Volk und Nation,* and *Das eigenständige Volk.* It is significant that the French sociologist J.-T. Delos of Lille divides his recent publication on *La Nation* into two volumes: the first, *Sociologie de la nation,* and the second, *Le Nationalisme et l'ordre de droit.*

There is, however, general agreement that the modern nation signifies a definite stage of social organization which is limited not only in time but also in space. As E. H. Carr has pointed out, nation is not a definable and clearly recognizable entity but "is confined to certain periods of history and to certain parts of the world." "Today," he continues, "—in the most nation-conscious of all epochs—it would still probably be fair to say that a large numerical majority of the population of the world feel no allegiance to any nation." It is of secondary importance whether we hold that nations sprang into existence with the waning of the Middle Ages, with the absolute monarchies of the sixteenth and the seventeenth centuries, or with the French Revolution. As the Chatham House report suggests, "a good case can be made for each of these views, which are indeed only incompatible so long as the term 'nation' is assumed to be used in each case in an identical sense." For the present purpose we may adopt Carr's procedure, which distinguishes three stages of nationalism, apart from a fourth—the present one.

In the first period the national unit was identified with the person of the sovereign, the absolute monarch. As Carr recalls: "Louis XIV thought that the French nation 'resided wholly in the person of the King.'" The second period is characterized by the democratization of the nation, which eventually was considered as a corporate personality centered around the *bourgeoisie.* Eventually the nineteenth century brought the socialization of the nation by including the masses of the people. This resulted in the social service state, which claims the absolute loyalty of the whole people to a nation as the instrument of collective interests and ambitions. This description, however, seems to be correct only if we consider Western society in general. The fact is that in many countries, particularly in Germany and in the Slavic regions east of it, the first-named stage seems to be missing. Neither the German princes nor the emperor ever succeeded in creating nation-states in the same sense in which France or England became a nation-state. They did not appeal to national sentiments but to patriotic sentiments. The *Vaterland,* not the *Nation,* was here the central idea of absolutism. Thus, students of the history of nationalism in these parts of Europe have emphasized the transition, which started in the latter part of the eighteenth century, from dynastic and territorial patriotism to nationalism in the modern sense. The Bohemian revivalists of that time, who were backed by the Bohemian aristocracy, originally propagated Bohemian patriotism against Hapsburg patriotism. Only with the spread of the ideas of romanticism and the French Revolution was Bohemian patriotism transformed into a Czech (ethnic) nationalism.

The different ways in which national ideology has become foremost in the minds of Europeans east and west of the Rhine has apparently determined their sociological theories. Since there were no clearly defined nations in the Western sense, German and Slavic authors were moved to seek symbols for the entity of nation in a common language or in the biological concept of the race. Although in the nineteenth century nationalism in central Europe traversed approximately the same stages which Carr describes as the second and third periods, the idea remained alive that *Kultur* and *Rasse* indicate some more basic social fact than *Staat and Staatsnation* or, in other words, that *Staat* and *Staatsnation* are nothing but the ephemeral manifestations of human groups which are always present in society; the *Volk,* these scholars maintain, is a basic form of social organization, even *the* basic form, while nation and nation-states are the result of a historical process and may disappear without affecting the existence of *Völker.*

This concept of *Volk* or *narod* cannot be symbolized adequately by any commonly used English word, such as "race," "people," or "nation." Now, in the field of the social sciences it is often a helpful methodological device to adopt the most colorless term to indicate an elusive or difficult social fact. Pareto aptly used algebraic symbols. In order to find out whether the Continental concept of *Volk* is a legitimate one, we propose to use the term "ethnic group" to describe it. This phrase coincides philologically with the French *groupe ethnique* and with the German *Volksgruppe.* Moreover, the Greek described with *ethnos* about the same social unit, which is called in other languages *people, popolo, peuple, Volk, narod.* Finally, the term "group" is being used by many sociologists as the *genus proximum* in defining the various types of plurality patterns.

(The term "ethnic" has been adopted by some American authors in a much narrower sense. L. Warner and L. Srole have proposed the following definition: "The term ethnic refers to any individual who considers himself, or is considered, to be a member of a group with a foreign culture and who participates in the activities of the group. Ethnics may be either of foreign or native birth." *The Social Systems of American Ethnic Groups,* 1945, p. 28. Here the main emphasis is given to the individual, while the sociological aspect is almost lost. Moreover, undue distinction is made between minority and majority groups, although both seem to belong basically to the same type of plurality patterns. Cf. also the article "Ethnic Community" in the *Encyclopedia of the Social Sciences.* We need not emphasize that in this context "ethnic group" is not limited to ethnic fragments and minorities within a larger culture. In our terminology not only the French-Canadians or the Pennsylvania Dutch would be ethnic groups but also the French of France or the Irish in Ireland. In his study on *Group Settlement* in western Canada, C. A. Dawson subsumed—and to our opinion correctly—under the heading "Ethnic Communities" not only the French Canadians but also the Doukhobors, Mormons, or Mennonites.)

In trying to clarify our hypothetical category, "ethnic group," we find it easier to say what it is not than what it is. An ethnic group is not a race, if we take race in the anthropological sense as a group of people with common physical characteristics. Moreover, an ethnic group is not a nation, if we understand nation to mean a society united under a common government or an aggregation of individuals united by political ties as well as by common language or common territory or common race or common tradition or any combination thereof. Our problem becomes more difficult if we wish to distinguish ethnic group from such phenomena as a definite local or regional community, a patriarchical family, a clan, and similar face-to-face groups. However, this is a problem that occurs with every attempt at a classification, be it of social or of physical facts.

If we adopt for the moment Ferdinand Tönnies' typological dichotomy, *Gemeinschaft* and *Gesellschaft,* we would have to classify an ethnic group as a rather pure type of *Gemeinschaft.* We will recall that, according to Tönnies, a group of the association type is based on a definite purpose, although not necessarily on *ad hoc* contractural agreements. It is a means by which the individual attains his own ends. In a community the parties are treated and act as a unit of solidarity. Institutional sanctions, if present, are concerned rather with attitudes than with specific acts. While groups of the community type always live in relatively local as well as social and mental segregation from other groups, such local, social, and mental barriers to social contact, exchange, and circulation are absent in associations. Based on emotional bonds and endowed with a homogeneous cultural heritage, the community aims at the preservation of the group. Based on rational, contractual bonds and endowed with a heterogeneous social heritage, the association aims at the preservation of the individual. In the language of Freud, a community can be said to be derived mainly from subconscious experiences, while an association is derived from direct knowledge.

Culture is usually regarded as a fundamental factor of an ethnic group. However, the concept of culture is as elusive and contradictory as that of the ethnic group itself. The words *Kultur, culture,* appear to mean almost the opposite of what English speakers understand by "culture." While to them civilization usually refers to the late phases or to a superior stage of cultural development, to Continental students *Kultur* is essentially different from civilization. According to them, civilization is a means to an end. Culture is an end in itself; it includes folkways and mores and their manifestations in art and artifact which, persisting through tradition, characterize a human group. While civilization spreads and accumulates through cross-fertilization and diffusion, culture tends to produce itself indefinitely. We may say that every ethnic group has a distinctive culture, but a common culture pattern does not necessarily constitute an ethnic group. The peasants of all times and regions, for instance, show more or less identical culture traits. Yet they do not form a social group at all, still less an ethnic group. They belong to the same culture *type,* not to the same culture *group.* An ethnic group may also modify and change its culture without losing its identity.

Every group is defined by social interrelationship. All social relations presuppose contacts and communication. Language is one of the most important means of communication between human persons. Thus, we may say that face-to-face relationship is essential in preliterate societies only, but in literate societies the language spoken by the members of an ethnic group must at least be intelligible without much difficulty to all of them. Nevertheless, there seems to be a limit in size beyond which intimate relationship cannot be maintained when the ties become too spurious and weak to uphold the existence of the group.

Racial affinity, too, has been associated with the ethnic group. Now, ethnic groups usually are endogamous; marriages with members of the outgroup are frequently tabooed. However, the laws of genetics do not suggest that inbreeding alone, without selection, results in homogeneous racial strains. How far selection operates in ethnic groups remains largely a controversial matter. Nevertheless, it cannot be denied that the composition of hereditary traits varies from one ethnic group to another. More significant than the real racial composition is an assumed common descent. Awareness of blood relationship and kinship seems to strengthen the ties between the members of a group. And yet the actual genetic composition is apparently irrelevant; for instance, family names follow either the patrilineal or, more rarely, the matrilineal sequence, and only occasionally both. The device of myths to establish a common ancestry for an ethnic group is a very ancient one. At all times man seems to have tampered with the mystery of biological heredity.

Physical and mental traits, which are really or only supposedly based on heredity and common descent, influence social behavior in yet another sense. Community or difference of objective characteristics affects human behavior in various ways. Physical traits, being obvious and usually indelible, lend themselves—even if they have gone unnoticed for a long time—readily to rationalizations of attitudes of sympathy and antipathy. Conflict situations, whether between ethnic groups or individuals, often—and not only since Hitler—hinge, as it were, on racial characteristics. The same is probably true of sympathetic sentiments and we-feeling.

Since humans are spatial entities, the attribution of a territory to ethnic groups is actually only a corollary to local affinity and size which we have discussed before. The only distinction of an ethnic group seems to lie in the exclusiveness with which it usually occupies a definite space. Finally, there is the time factor. Since an ethnic group is based on an elementary feeling of solidarity, we must suppose that mutual adjustment has been achieved over a considerable length of time and that the memory of having possibly belonged to another system of social relationships must have been obliterated.

The we-feeling present in the members of any group of the community type is, of course, also a characteristic of the ethnic group. We would not have introduced it expressedly if it did not offer a key to the distinction which we proposed to make between ethnic group and nation. Delos suggests that the transition from ethnic group to nation is characterized by *la passage de la communauté de conscience à la conscience de former une communauté*. The phrase cannot be translated literally without conjuring up great confusion. Since Delos himself uses *conscience de "nous"* to describe the same phenomenon, we may translate *communauté de conscience* with "we-feeling." The ethnic group, he continues, is *une réalité objective*, although there is no *conscience réflexe*. Two elements transform the ethnic group into a nation: (1) the knowledge of forming an original entity and (2) the value attached to this fact. *Elle se manifeste par la volonté de perpétuer la vie commune*. Consequently, *une nation est un peuple [sic!] qui prend conscience de lui-même selon ce que l'histoire l'a fait; il se replie donc sur soi et sur son passé; ce qu'il aime, c'est lui-même tel qu'il se connaît ou se figure être*. We thus seem to have arrived at a certain solution. Nationalism, the sentiment of forming a community and the will to perpetuate it by—as we would add—political devices, is indeed the prerequisite. But it apparently presupposes another social fact. To describe it Delos uses the term *groupe ethnique*, although, in one place at least, he inadvertently substitutes the word *peuple*.

If sentiment and will are the factors which transform the ethnic group into a nation, the question arises: Which are the constitutional factors of the ethnic group itself?

There are a number of characteristics widely ascribed to the ethnic group: common language, folkways and mores, attitudes and standards, territory, descent, history, and, we may now add, common government. In fact, we know that the subjection of a group of people to a common political organization may directly or, more often, indirectly by imposition of common laws, religion, language, feeling of loyalty, etc., not only forge together different ethnic elements into a new ethnic group but also divide an ethnic group or deliberately alter its structure, culture, and character. This, however, does not answer our question, for upon closer inspection it appears that two or more distinct ethnic groups may share in common certain characteristics, such as language, descent, religion. On the other hand, many ethnic groups are obviously not at all homogeneous as to their descent or religion, for instance. Still worse, the differences in the general culture pattern of different social strata within all the more developed and complex ethnic groups are very marked. It may even be doubtful whether the peasant culture in one ethnic group is not more closely related to the peasant culture in another than to urban culture in the same ethnic group. Thus, we cannot define the ethnic group as a plurality pattern which is characterized by a distinct language, culture, territory, religion, and so on.

It was exactly the attempt to reach a conclusion as to the nature of the ethnic group, inductively, by analyzing objective characteristics of concrete social facts of this kind, which so far has defied the ingenuity of a long series of writers of treatises dealing with our problem. The main reason for this failure must be sought in the fact that the essentially dynamic character of ethnic groups has been largely neglected, for these may represent different stages of development. It may well be the case that factors which have contributed to the formation of an ethnic group will lose their significance—once a certain degree of group coherence has been reached—or will be, later on, replaced by other factors not present in the beginning but contributing to the preservation of the group. In order to decide the issue it would be necessary to analyze the genesis of a great number of existing ethnic groups. Unfortunately, the origins of most ethnic groups lie in the distant and uncertain past. Dubious guesswork alone is our guide in their analysis. The emergence of new ethnic groups in the New World, however, offers more reliable material for the study of our problem. It should be possible from available historical sources to reconstruct their genesis in such a way as to reach definite conclusions. What seems clear even on the basis of our limited knowledge is that it is too early yet to reach any definite conclusions.

Here we find, for example, sectarian groups which show all the traits and typical behavior of ethnic groups, although, originally, they were joined together from various ethnic elements under the impact of a distinct religious persuasion and church organization and not on the basis of a distinct language, territory, and so on. Moreover, some of them have in the meantime undergone numerous schisms and religious splits which nevertheless have left untouched their identity and coherence. On the other hand, the major ethnic groups which have sprung up in the Americas seem to have been formed not so much by religion as by politics and geography. It should be possible to reconstruct from the available historical sources their genesis in such a way that definite generalizations could be reached. Yet even on the ground of our limited knowledge it becomes clear that, generally speaking, the stages of development traversed by ethnic groups are: expansion—fission—new combination. The factors which condition fission and new combination, however, appear to vary from case to case.

The thought suggests itself to us that allegiance to some external object is the most essential single factor in the formation or revival of ethnic groups. But the object of allegiance shifts from period to period, from country to country. It may be a monarch, a religion, language and literature, other forms of a higher culture, a political ideology centered around some type of government, a class, a "race." The type of catalyst apparently changes, as culture and the interests and ideas of man change—but, it seems, there always is a catalyst necessary to join the elements together into an ethnic group.

Delos suggests that a social fact is a relationship that unites a person to other persons not directly but by the mediation of another term, which he calls *l'objet,* because it is exterior to the *sujets individuels,* the persons whom it puts into a relationship. According to him, all institutions and all groups present this triad: person—object—person. If Delos' position is correct, the element which we have called figuratively a catalyst seems to coincide with his *objet extraindividuel et extérieur.* Yet this object, he maintains, is an element common to all social facts. Should we, therefore, rather choose the type of objects as a principle of classification? Religious groups would be those which have religion as an "object"; culture groups, those which have culture as their "object"—and so on. Which specific object, however, shall we attribute to an ethnic group? And why does a religious group, under certain conditions, behave exactly as any ethnic group? We even may ask ourselves whether the ideologies and we-feelings which constitute the formative forces in a nation are typologically different from those which constitute the formative forces in a religious group. Hans Kohn said that "today . . . . . nationalism is the most universal religion of all times." This statement, though exaggerated in a measure, tends to defy any attempt to classify the phenomena under discussion according to "objects." An ethnic group, if we understand Delos rightly, would almost be identical with a nation which has not yet become fully conscious of itself. Would this not be, so to say, a definition *ex post facto?* Or is ethnic group a more universal, perhaps the most universal, fact of human society, while all other social facts are arrived at by way of elimination?

We hestitate to draw any definite conclusions from the few reflections presented in this paper. But we may state tentatively the following propositions as a working hypothesis for further investigation:

1. In their usual connotation the words "nation," "race," "nationality," "people," "religious group," etc., do not indicate any valid and definite categories of sociological classification. Neither do they describe *entia realia* in the philosophical sense, if such exist at all, or even definite types of social facts which would be useful for sociological generalizations.

2. The term "ethnic group," however, seems to be valuable to describe a variation of the community type. This subtype deserves a special name and formulation because it includes a considerable number of phenomena which are of practical interest to various social sciences. The basic type of the community includes many other phenomena such as the family, caste, or residential community. Nevertheless, we believe it is possible to distinguish them from the ethnic group. While the family or residential community is unable to satisfy

all the basic societal needs of human nature, the ethnic group not only permits a high degree of self-sufficiency and segregation but tends to enforce and preserve it.

On the other hand, the ethnic group is not so much dependent on fact-to-face relationship as other types of communities. We find that the pattern of social interaction which is characteristic of the primary group permits its extension under certain conditions to a larger, locally less well-defined, and culturally less homogeneous group. We may, for instance, think of a peasant village as an ideal primary group. Now, under certain conditions, the we-feeling of this community *can be made* to include the natives of a valley or of a wider region, even a whole country. Thus, a larger, but secondary, group is being formed which presents most of the characteristics originally attached to the primary group. In this way, we may say, the ethnic group is the most inclusive, cumulative, and realistic type of *secondary* community.

3. The catalyst, or principal factor, which brings about such an extension of we-feeling is a mental process based on abstraction and hypostatical transposition of characteristics from the primary to the secondary group. We may say that every ethnic group presupposes an ideology, however vague and unreflective it may be. The followers of a new religion, for instance, are moved by the overriding value they attach to their faith to withdraw their we-feeling from the non-believing members of their original community and to extend it to all fellow-believers. Since human nature seems to crave a pattern of social interaction which is of the community type, the wish and will become effective to substitute a community of all fellow-believers for the original community. In the same way, a national ideology tends to substitute or to widen a pre-existing community.

4. All ethnic groups behave in the same typical manner, regardless of whether the underlying ideologies hinge on religious, political, cultural, racial, or other characteristics and regardless of whether these characteristics are real or fictitious. Once an ethnic group is well integrated it makes little difference whether the underlying ideology is rationally disproved; for, by then, the community has become real, that is, a social fact, and it will find new rationalizations for its coherence, if ever its ideological basis should be challenged.

5. It is quite likely that the quest for "objective" characteristics by which one concrete ethnic group could be distinguished from any other is futile. But there are certain elements that must be present or which must be deliberately created in the early stages of its genesis, such as a distinctive territory, some sort of distinctive political organization, a common language, a common scale of values. Yet, once the ethnic group has reached a certain maturity, the elements which have conditioned it in the beginning may disappear, change, or be supplanted by others,without affecting its coherence and the *communauté de conscience* among its members. The dissolution of a community is brought about not so much by the loss of external characteristics as by the collision of conflicting values, solidarities, and loyalties.

6. Finally, no individual group, which is always a singular and unrepeatable phenomenon, will ever coincide with that type of plurality pattern which we have described as an ethnic group. As in the case with every other *type,* it will be quite legitimate to state that some concrete social group is an ethnic group to a lesser or greater degree. It appears that the modern nation belongs

in the category of ethnic groups just as much as the religious communities of other stages of history. It is the result of deliberate political action by which all the ethnic groups that pre-exist within the actual or visualized territory of a state are molded into a new unit of we-feeling, into a new more or less homogeneous ethnic group.

In the preceding discussion we have been experimenting with a hypothetical sociological category which we thought could cover a number of phenomena popularly classed together. We have ventured to construe the ethnic type of cumulative groups as a device of sociological research, and we have proposed to term it "ethnic group." Whether this is a useful device can be ascertained only by operating with it for some time and by applying it experimentally to a considerable number of concrete cases.

PEOPLES

By Oswald Spengler

NOW AT LAST it is possible to approach—if with extreme precaution —the conception "people," and to bring order into that chaos of people-forms that the historical research of the present day has only succeeded in making worse confounded than before. There is no word that has been used more freely and more utterly uncritically, yet none that calls for a stricter critique, than this. Very careful historians, even, after going to much trouble to clear their theoretical basis (up to a point) slide back thereafter into treating peoples, race-parts, and speech-communities as completely equivalent. If they find the name of a people, it counts without more ado as the designation of a language as well. If they discover an inscription of three words, they believe they have established a racial connexion. If a few "roots" correspond, the curtain rises at once on a primitive people with a primitive habitat in the background. And the modern nationalist spirit has only enhanced this "thinking in terms of peoples."

But is it the Hellenes, the Dorians, or the Spartans that are a people? If the Romans were a people, what are we to say about the Latins? And what kind of a unit within the population of Italy at *c.* 400 do we mean by the name "Etruscan?" Has not their "Nationality," like that of Basques and Thracians, been made actually to depend upon the build of their language? What ethnic idea underlies the words "American," "Swiss," "Jew," "Boer"? Blood, speech, faith, State, landscape—what in all these is determinative in the formation of a people? In general, relationships of blood and language are determined only by way of scholarship, and the ordinary individual is perfectly unconscious of them. "Indo-

Reprinted from *The Decline of the West*, Vol. II, pp. 159–162, 165, by Oswald Spengler, by permission of Alfred A. Knopf, Inc. Copyright 1932 by Alfred A. Knopf, Inc.

germanic" is purely and simply a scientific, more particularly a philological, concept. The attempt of Alexander the Great to fuse Greeks and Persians together was a complete failure, and we have recently had experience of the real strength of Anglo-German community of feeling. But "people" is a linkage of which one is *conscious*. In ordinary usage, one designates as one's "people"— and with feeling—that community, out of the many to which one belongs, which inwardly stands nearest to one. And then he extends the use of this concept, which is really quite particular and derived from personal experience, to collectivities of the most varied kinds. For Caesar the Arverni were a *"civitas";* for us the Chinese are a "nation." On this basis, it was the Athenians and not the Greeks who constituted a nation, and in fact there were only a few individuals who, like Isocrates, felt themselves *primarily* as Hellenes. On this basis, one of two brothers may call himself a Swiss and the other, with equal right, a German. These are not philosophical concepts, but historical facts. A people is an aggregate of men which feels itself a unit. The Spartiates felt themselves a people in *this* sense; the "Dorians" of 1100, too, probably, but those of 400 certainly not. The Crusaders became genuinely a people in taking the oath of Clermont; the Mormons in their expulsion from Missouri, in 1839; the Mamertines by their need of winning for themselves a stronghold of refuge. Was the formative principle very different with the Jacobins and Hyksos? How many peoples may have originated in a chief's following or a band of fugitives? Such a group can change race, like the Osmanli, who appeared in Asia Minor as Mongols; or language, like the Sicilian Normans; or name, like Achæans and Danaoi. So long as the common feeling is there, the people as such is there.

We have to distinguish the destiny of a people from its name. The latter is often the only thing about which information remains to us; but can we fairly conclude from a name anything about the history, the descent, the language, or even merely the identify of those who bore it? Here again the historical researcher is to blame, in that, whatever his theory may have been, he has in practice treated the relation between name and bearer as simply as he would treat, say, the personal names of today. Have we any conception of the number of unexplored possibilities in this field? To begin with, the very act of name-giving is of enormous importance in early associations. For with a name the human group consciously sets itself up with a sort of sacral dignity. But, here, cult-and war-names may exist side by side; others the land or the heritage may provide; the tribal name may be exchanged for that of an eponymous hero, as with the Osmanli; lastly, an unlimited number of alien names can be applied along the frontiers of a group without more than a part of the community ever hearing them at all. If only such names as these be handed down, it becomes practically inevitable that conclusions about the bearers of them will be wrong. The indubitably sacral names of Franks, Alemanni, and Saxons have superseded a host of names of the period of the Varus battle—but if we did not happen to know this, we should long ago have been convinced that an expulsion or annihilation of old tribes by new intruders had taken place here. The names "Romans" and "Quirites," "Spartans" and "Lacedæmonians," "Carthaginian" and "Punic" have endured side by side—here again there was a risk of supposing two peoples instead of one. In what relation the names "Pelasgi," "Achæans," "Danai," stand to one another we shall never learn, and had we nothing more than these names, the scholar would long ago have assigned to each a separate people, complete with language and racial affinities. Has it not been attempted to draw from the regional designation "Doric" conclusions as to the course of the Dorian migration? How often may a people have adopted a land-name and taken it along with them? This is the case with the modern Prussians, but also with the modern Parsees, Jews, and Turks, while the opposite is the case in Burgundy and Normandy. The name "Hellenes" arose about 650, and, therefore, cannot be connected with any movement of population. Lorraine (Lothringen) received the name of a perfectly unimportant prince, and that, in connexion with the decision of a heritage and not a folk-migration. Paris called the Germans Allemands in 1814, Prussians in 1770, Boches in 1914—in other circumstances three distinct peoples might have been supposed to be covered by these names. The West-European is called in the East a Frank, the Jew a Spaniole—the fact is readily explained by historical circumstances, but what would a philologist have produced from the *words alone?*

It is not to be imagined at what results the scholars of A.D. 3000 might arrive if they worked by present-day methods on names, linguistic remains, and the notion of original homes and migration. For example, the Teutonic Knights about 1300 drove out the heathen "Prussians," and in 1870 these people suddenly appear on their wanderings at the gates of Paris! The Romans, pressed by the Goths, emigrate from the Tiber to the lower Danube! Or a part of them perhaps settled in Poland, where Latin was spoken? Charlemagne on the Weser defeated the Saxons, who thereupon emigrated to the neighborhood of Dresden, their places being taken by the Hanoverians, whose original settlement, according to the dynasty-name, was on the Thames! The historian who writes down the history of names instead of that of peoples, forgets that names, too, have their destinies. So also languages, which, with their migrations, modifications, victories, and defeats, are inconclusive even as to the existence of peoples associated with them. This is the basic error of Indo-Germanic research in particular. If in historic times the names "Pfalz" and "Calagria" have moved about, if Hebrew has been driven from Palestine to Warsaw, and Persian from the Tigris to India, what conclusions can be drawn from the history of the Etruscan name and the alleged "Tyrsenian" inscription at Lemnos? Or did the French and the Haytian Negroes, as shown by their common language, once form a single primitive people? In the region between Budapest and Constantinople today two Mongolian, one Semitic, two Classical, and three Slavonic languages are spoken, and these speech-communities all feel themselves essentially as peoples. If we were to build up a migration-story here, the error of the method would be manifested in some singular results. "Doric" is a dialect designation—that we know, and that is all we know. No doubt some few dialects of this group spread rapidly, but that is no proof of the spread or even of the existence of a human stock belonging with it.

For me, the "people" is a *unit of the soul.* The great events of history were not really achieved by peoples; *they themselves created the peoples.* Every act alters the soul of the doer. Even when the event is preceded by some grouping around or under a famous name, the fact that there is a people and not merely a band behind the prestige of that name is not a condition, but a result of the event. It was the fortunes of their migrations that made the Ostrogoths and the Osmanli what they afterwards were. The "Americans" did not immigrate from Europe; the name of the Florentine geographer Amerigo Vespucci designates today not only a continent, but also a people in the true sense of the word, whose specific character was born in the spiritual upheavals of 1775 and, above all, 1861–5.

This is the one and only connotation of the word "people." Neither unity of speech nor physical descent is decisive. That which distinguishes the people from the population, raises it up out of the population, and will one day let it find its level again in the population is always the inwardly lived experience of the "we." The deeper this feeling is, the stronger is the *vis viva* of the people. There are energetic and tame, ephemeral and indestructible, forms of peoples. They can change speech, name, race, and land, but so long as their soul lasts, they can gather to themselves and transform human material of any and every provenance. The Roman name in Hannibal's day meant a people, in Trajan's time nothing more than a population.

PART II

Race and Region

INTRODUCTION

ONE OF THE FIRST THINGS to be noticed about race and the relationships of race is that invariably they are associated in our minds with geography and place. They seem never to be wholly independent of territory. "From the beginning of the era of voyages and explorations," said Vidal de la Blache, "it is the spectacle of social diversities associated with diversities of places that has aroused man's attention." Indeed, territorialism was and continues to be such a universal phenomenon among men that the original and most natural principle of ethnic classification appears to have been that of geographic origin.

How and by what agencies are the physical races formed and distributed over the earth? How does Europe compare with the other continents with reference to the number and distribution of isolated areas? What appears to be the nature and influence of the cradle land in the formation of a race? Do races have histories? What do you understand by the term "historical races"? How do physical anthropologists go about the mapping of race regions?

If the relations between the different races and peoples of the world were first geographical then how, when, and under what conditions have they become commercial, industrial and social? What type of facts would you consider necessary to make a cartographic representation of existing political relations between races and peoples and which tends increasingly to make the world a political unit? In the world so conceived there are a large number of areas in each of which there is a rich mixture of peoples or economies or languages or religions, or all of these, and which we seek to analyze and classify into a societal system of some sort.

Among them are the areas we call race relations regions. Do race relations inevitably and invariably result from the contact of peoples of diverse culture and physical marking? At what point are we justified in speaking of the region as a "race relations region"? How would you distinguish between a race region and a race relations region? Do the two "regions" ever coincide? How would you go about delimiting race relations regions?

If one reads widely in the literature he will sense the fact that conceptions of race and of race relations vary widely and vary regionally. Where the idea of race exists at all it is locally involved in biological, linguistic, national, and cultural phenomena in such varied ways and to such varying degrees as seemingly to justify reference to "varieties" of race relations situations or regions. This chapter presents materials descriptive of only a few such regions and intended to illustrate their range. Do you think it possible usefully to classify these regions? On the basis of what criteria might they be classified? What are the characteristics of regions where there are only two racially defined groups? Three? Four? Many? Does there seem to be a tendency in each region for race relations to polarize around two groups? What do you know about areas where color differences are present but where the people appear to be insensitive to them? What do you know about areas where color differences are almost imperceptible to outsiders but where the local people are highly sensitive to them? What do you know about areas where certain segments of society are sensitive to such color differences as there are but other segments are not sensitive to them? In these areas how do these differences in sensitivity to physical traits register themselves in ordinary conduct? In institutions? What difference does the presence or absence of a plantation system, ex-territoriality, bilingualism, a creole or pidgin language, mixed-bloods, white women, poor whites, colonialism, or nationalism make in the character of a race relations region? At what point in the evolution of a race relations region does a "race problem" appear? What seems to be the role of the city in the development of a race relations region?

A race relations region is a region in which the matter of history is concerned, or largely concerned, with racial and ethnic conflict. In what regions is the idea of race apparently becoming stronger? Where is it becoming weaker? What regions have entirely ceased to be race relations regions? What regions are now in the process of being defined as race relations regions?

RACE AND HABITAT

By Oswald Spengler

A RACE has roots. Race and landscape belong together. Where a plant takes root, there it dies also. There is certainly a sense in which we can, without absurdity, work backwards from a race to its "home," but it is much more important to realize that the race adheres permanently to this home with some of its most essential characters of body and soul. If in that home the race cannot

Reprinted from *The Decline of the West*, Vol. II, pp. 119–120, by Oswald Spengler, by permission of Alfred A. Knopf, Inc. Copyright 1932 by Alfred A. Knopf, Inc.

now be found, this means that the race has ceased to exist. A race does not migrate. Men migrate, and their successive generations are born in ever-changing landscapes; but the landscape exercises a secret force upon the plant-nature in them, and eventually the race-expression is completely transformed by the extinction of the old and the appearance of a new one. Englishmen and Germans did not migrate to America, but human beings migrated thither *as* Englishmen and Germans, and their descendants are there *as* Americans. It has long been obvious that the soil of the Indians has made its mark upon them —generation by generation they become more and more like the people they eradicated. Gould and Baxter have shown that Whites of all races, Indians, and Negroes have come to the same average in size of body and time of maturity— and that so rapidly that Irish immigrants, arriving young and developing very slowly, come under this power of the landscape within the same generation. Boas has shown that the American-born children of long-headed Sicilian and short-headed German Jews at once conform to the same head-type. This is not a special case, but a general phenomenon, and it should serve to make us very cautious in dealing with those migrations of history about which we know nothing more than some names of vagrant tribes and relics of languages (e.g., Danai, Etruscans, Pelasgi, Achæans, and Dorians). As to the race of these "peoples" we can conclude nothing whatever. That which flowed into the lands of southern Europe under the diverse names of Goths, Lombards, and Vandals was without doubt a race in itself. But already by Renaissance times it had completely grown itself into the root characters of the Provençal, Castilian, and Tuscan soil.

Not so with language. The home of a language means merely the accidental place of its formation, and this has no relation to its inner form. Languages migrate in that they spread by carriage from tribe to tribe. Above all, they are capable of being, and are, exchanged—indeed, in studying the early history of races we need not, and should not, feel the slightest hesitation about postulating such speech-changes. It is, I repeat, the form-content and not the speaking of a language that is taken over, and it is taken over (as primitives are for ever taking over ornament-motives) in order to be used with perfect sureness as elements of their own form-language. In early times the fact that a people has shown itself the stronger, or the feeling that its language possesses superior efficacy, is enough to induce others to give up their own language and—with genuinely religious awe—to take its language to themselves. Follow out the speech-changes of the Normans, whom we find in Normandy, England, Sicily, and Constantinople with different languages in each place, and ever ready to exchange one for another. Piety towards the mother tongue—the very term testifies to deep ethical forces, and accounts for the bitterness of our ever-recurring language-battles—is a trait of the *Late* Western soul, almost un-knowable for the men of other Cultures and entirely so for the primitive. Un-fortunately, our historians not only are sensible of this, but tacitly extend it as a postulate over their entire field, which leads to a multitude of fallacious con-clusions as to the bearing of linguistic discoveries upon the fortunes of "peoples" —think of the reconstruction of the "Dorian migration," argued from the distribution of later Greek dialects. It is impossible, therefore, to draw con-clusions as to the fortunes of the race side of peoples from mere place-names,

personal names, inscriptions, and dialects. Never do we know *a priori,* whether
a folkname stands for a language-body, or a race-part, or both, or neither—
besides which, folknames themselves, and even land-names, have, as such,
Destinies of their own.

THE CRADLE LANDS OF THE RACES

By N. S. Shaler

THE CONTINENT of Europe differs from the other great land-masses in
the fact that it is a singular aggregation of peninsulas and islands, originating
in separate centers of mountain growth, and of enclosed valleys walled about
from the outer world by elevated summits. Other continents are somewhat
peninsulated; Asia approaches Europe in that respect; North America has a
few great dependencies in its larger islands and considerable promontories; but
Africa, South America, and Australia are singularly united lands.

The highly divided state of Europe has greatly favored the development
within its area of isolated fields, each fitted for the growth of a separate state,
adapted even in this day of local life although commerce in our time binds
lands together in a way which it did not of old. These separated areas were
marvelously suited to be the cradles of peoples; and if we look over the map
of Europe we readily note the geographic insulations which that remarkably
varied land affords.

Beginning with the eastern Mediterranean, we have the peninsula on which
Constantinople stands—a region only partly protected from assault by its
geographic peculiarities; and yet it owes to its partial separation from the main-
lands on either side a large measure of local historic development. Next, we
have Greece and its associated islands, which—a safe stronghold for centuries
—permitted the nurture of the most marvelous life the world has ever known.
Farther to the west the Italian peninsula, where during three thousand years
the protecting envelope of the sea and the walls of Alps and Apennines have
enabled a score of states to attain a development; where the Roman nation,
absorbing, with its singular power of taking in other life, a number of primitive
centers of civilization, grew to power which made it dominant in the ancient
world. Sicily, Sardinia, Corsica, have each profited by their isolation, and have
bred diverse qualities in man and contributed motives which have interacted
in the earth's history. Again, in Spain we have a region well fitted to be the
cradle of a great people; to its geographic position it owed the fact that it became the seat of the most cultivated Mahometanism the world has ever known.
To the Pyrenees, the mountain wall of the north, we owe in good part the limi-

Adapted from N. S. Shaler, *Nature and Man in America* (New York: Charles Scribner's Sons,
1900), pp. 151–166.

tation of that Mussulman invasion and the protection of central Europe from its forward movement, until luxury and half-faith had sapped its energies. Going northward, we find in the region of Normandy the place of growth of that fierce but strong folk, the ancient Scandinavians, who, transplanted there, held their ground, and grew until they were strong enough to conquer Britain and give it a large share of the quality which belongs to our own state.

To a trifling geographic accident we owe the isolation of Great Britain from the European continent; and all the marvelous history of the English folk, as we all know, hangs upon the existence of that narrow strip of sea between the Devon coast and the kindred lowlands of northern France.

East of Britain lie two peninsulas which have been the cradle of very important peoples. That of Sweden and Norway is the result of mountain development; that of Denmark appears to be in the main the product of glacial and marine erosion, differing in its non-mountainous origin from all the other peninsulas and islands of the European border. Thus on the periphery of Europe we have at least a dozen geographical isolated areas, sufficiently large and well separated from the rest of the world to make them the seats of independent social life. The interior of the country has several similarly, though less perfectly, detached areas. Of these the most important lie fenced within the highlands of the Alps. In that extensive system of mountain disturbances we have the geographical conditions which most favor the development of peculiar divisions of men, and which guard such cradled peoples from the destruction which so often awaits them on the plains. Thus, while the folk of the European lowlands have been overrun by the successive tides of invasion, their qualities confused, and their succession of social life interrupted, Switzerland has to a great extent, by its mountain walls, protected its people from the troubles to which their lowland neighbors have been subjected. The result is that within an area not twice as large as Massachusetts we find a marvelous diversity of folk, as is shown by the variety in physical aspect, moral quality, language, and creed in the several important valleys and other divisions of that complicated topography.

After a race has been formed and bred to certain qualities within a limited field, after it has come to possess a certain body of characteristics which gives it its particular stamp, the importance of the original cradle passes away. There is something very curious in the permanence of race conditions after they have been fixed for a thousand years or so in a people. When the assemblage of physical and mental motives are combined in a body of country folk, they may endure under circumstances in which they could not have originated; thus, even in our domesticated animals and plants, we find that varieties created under favorable conditions, obtaining their inheritances in suitable conditions, may then flourish in many conditions of environment in which they could not by any chance have originated. The barnyard creatures of Europe, with their established qualities, may be taken to Australia, and there retain their nature for many generations; even where the form falls away from the parent stock, the decline is generally slow and may not for a great time become apparent.

This fixity of race characteristics has enabled the several national varieties of men to go forth from their nurseries, carrying the qualities bred in their earlier conditions through centuries of life in other climes. The Gothic blood of Italy and of Spain still keeps much of its parent strength; the Aryan's of India, though a world apart in its conditions from those which gave it character in its cradle, is still, in many of its qualities, distinctly akin to that of the home people. Moor, Hun and Turk—all the numerous folk we find in the present condition of the world so far from their cradle-lands—are still to a great extent what their primitive nurture made them. On this rigidity which comes to mature races in the lower life as well as in man, depends the vigor with which they do their appointed work.

THE RACE REGION AND THE RACE RELATIONS REGION

By Edgar T. Thompson

THE RACIAL GROUP which emerges from the measurements of anthropologists and the dissections of biologists is quite a different thing from the racial group which exists in the minds of its members. In different racially conscious groups the criterion of membership varies. It may be language, religion, temperament, or pigmentation, but whatever it is the race group is composed of those who regard themselves as belonging to it and who are so regarded by others. The uncopyrighted word "race" means what the generality of people think it means as well as what anthropologists, biologists and sociologists think it should mean. The social scientists are much concerned to formulate a precise and accurate definition; the generality of people are not. Yet the absence among the people of a clearly formulated definition of race, far from weakening it, actually adds to the potency of the race idea. We can each assume that our individual view of the matter is also the view of every other right-thinking member of our group since we are not aware of any fixed and objective rule the conscious interpretation of which would put us at odds. Whatever our individual assumptions about race are, we can feel that we have our group behind us, and we are united.

The different ethnic stocks studied by anthropologists seem to have developed originally under conditions of regional segregation in close adaptation to food, climate, water, enemies, and the general habitat. Under circumstances of geographical isolation, relatively close in-breeding over long periods of time, and the cumulative effect of mutations it was inevitable that groups of men physically distinct from each other in varying degree should result. Such a race,

Adapted from Edgar T. Thompson, "Race in the Modern World," *The Journal of Negro Education*, XIII (Summer, 1944), 272–273, with the kind permission of the publisher, Howard University, Washington D.C. and Robert E. Park, "The Nature of Race Relations," in Edgar T. Thompson (ed.), *Race Relations and the Race Problem* (Durham: Duke University Press, 1939), pp. 3–5; copyright 1939 by The Duke University Press and used with the kind permission of the publisher.

as Demolins said, "n'est pas une cause, c'est une consequence." But the physical characteristics produced through the long ages of relative isolation "when providence set apart the nations" were not realized by the people possessing them and bore no special significance in their minds. Negroes in the middle of Africa did not know themselves to be Negroes and white men in the middle of Europe did not know themselves as Caucasians. Such groupings were known best to the physical anthropologists who, in the privacy of their studies and laboratories, plotted the distributions of various physical trait criteria on the map and sought to determine some system of racial isolates kept apart by geographical and social forces. We call race regions the different geographical areas occupied by whatever races are identified and located by the methods of the physical anthropologists.

It was not until the nations of Europe began to expand overseas, to invade and to conquer the populations of new continents, not until, with new developments in navigation in the sixteenth and seventeenth centuries, the world began to shrink enough for men of strikingly diverse cultures and noticeably different physical appearances to come suddenly and shockingly into close and continuous contact that the stage was set for the emergence of race consciousness and race ideas.

What is popularly called "race" must be understood, therefore, not in isolation, but in contact situations, and the focus for such an understanding must be upon race relations and not upon race differences. The alleged differences, it would seem, are an incident of the relations and can be understood only by understanding the circumstances under which the relations originally were defined and established and the circumstances under which they subsequently developed.

In the following paragraphs, written in 1939, Robert E. Park formulated his conception of the "nature" of race relations:

"Race relations, as that term is defined in use and wont in the United States, are the relations existing between peoples distinguished by marks of racial descent, particularly when these racial differences enter into the consciousness of the individuals and groups so distinguished, and by so doing determine in each case the individual's conception of himself as well as his status in the community. Thus anything that intensifies race consciousness; anything, particularly if it is a permanent physical trait, that increases an individual's visibility and by so doing makes more obvious his identity with a particular ethnic unit or genetic group, tends to create and maintain the conditions under which race relations, as here defined, may be said to exist. Race consciousness, therefore, is to be regarded as a phenomenon, like class or caste consciousness, that enforces social distances. Race relations, in this sense, are not so much the relations that exist between individuals of different races as between individuals conscious of these differences.

"Thus one may say, without doing injustice to the sense in which the term is ordinarily used, that there are, to be sure, races in Brazil—there are, for example, Europeans and Africans—but not race relations because there is in that country no race consciousness, or almost none. One speaks of race relations when there is a race problem, and there is no race problem in Brazil, or if there is, it is very little if at all concerned with the peoples of African and European origin.

"On the other hand, when one speaks of race relations and the race problem in South Africa one does not think of the African and the European. The African does, to be sure, constitute a problem, but in South Africa, it is described as 'the native problem.' South Africa has, also, the problem of the Cape Coloured, a hybrid people of mixed Hottentot and European origin. The native, as the term is there used, is a Bantu, and of a quite different racial origin than the 'native.' South Africa has, likewise, the problem of the East Indian. Hindus were first imported into Natal about 1860 in the interest of the sugar industry in that province. However, when one speaks or writes in common parlance of the race problem in South Africa, it is to the relations existing between the English and the native Dutch or Africanders that this expression refers.

"In this context and in this sense the expression race relations seems to describe merely the sentiments and attitudes which racial contacts invariably provoke and for which there is, apparently, no more substantial basis than an existing state of the public mind. For the purpose of this chapter, however, the term has been employed in a somewhat wider universe of discourse, in which it includes all the relations that ordinarily exist between members of different ethnic and genetic groups which are capable of provoking race conflict and race consciousness or of determining the relative status of the racial groups of which a community is composed.

"Race relations, in this more inclusive sense, might comprise, therefore, all those situations in which some relatively stable equilibrium between competing races has been achieved and in which the resulting social order has become fixed in custom and tradition.

"Under such circumstances the intensity of the race consciousness which a struggle for status inevitably arouses, where it did not altogether disappear, would be greatly diminished. The biracial organizations of certain social institutions that have come into existence in Southern states since emancipation exhibit the form which such racial accommodations sometimes take. Some of these, as in the case of the churches and the labor organizations, seem to have grown up quite spontaneously and have been accepted by both races as offering a satisfactory *modus vivendi.* In other instances, as in the case of the public school, the segregation which such dual or biracial organizations necessitate, in spite of certain advantages they offer, has been bitterly opposed even when they have later been reluctantly accepted by the colored people. They were opposed (1) because of the discrimination they inevitably involve and (2) because the separation of the races in the schools as elsewhere has seemed to imply the acceptance of an inferior civic and social status.

"All this suggests that the term *race relations,* as here conceived, include relations which are not now conscious or personal, though they have been; relations which are fixed in and enforced by the custom, convention, and the routine of the expected social order of which there may be at the moment no very lively consciousness. . . .

"What then, finally, is the precise nature of race relations that distinguish them, in all the variety of conditions in which they arise, from other fundamental forms of human relations? It is the essence of race relations that they are the relations of strangers; of peoples who are associated primarily for secular and practical purposes; for the exchange of goods and services. They are otherwise the relations of people of diverse races and cultures who have been thrown together by the fortunes of war, and who, for any reason, have not been sufficiently knit together by intermarriage and interbreeding to constitute a single ethnic community, with all that it implies."

The areas around the world where race relations are, according to Park's conception, more or less problematic and more or less involved in the existing political and social arrangements bear no necessary relation to the original race homelands. However, the different systems of racial relationships, with their accompanying codes, attitudes and patterns, are also geographical expressions. Race relations are bound up with the general culture of a society, and culture is generally a local and regional phenomenon. Each system of racial relationships must be understood, therefore, in the setting of its own habitat.

We have a large and growing literature dealing with problems in a number of race relations regions, but the systematic use of this literature for the comparative study of race relations has scarcely begun.

WHERE RACE RELATIONS BECOME

PROBLEMATIC

By E. B. Reuter

DURING THE LONG PERIOD of American slavery there was no race problem. There were, of course, various problems having to do with the control and discipline of the slaves, the profitable use of their vital force, the provisions for their feeding and shelter, the maintenance of their health and morale, and numerous similar items. But these were problems of labor and management, not race problems; they were essentially the same problems that face the employer of free labor and entertain the professors of personnel management.

The plantation system—an adjustment to the more fundamental facts of climatic conditions, sparseness of population, and the state of world economy and markets—set the pattern of social organization and defined the conditions in which a social and moral order could develop. It determined the class structure, the social values, the division of labor, the incidence of rewards, and other items that give individuality and character to a culture area. The race relations were those of white superiority and Negro subordination and dependence. The period was of sufficient duration and stability for the patterns of racial adjustment to find lodgement, not only in the institutional structures and their dependent philosophies, but also in the social sentiments and moral attitudes of the masters and the slaves.

Reprinted from E. B. Reuter, "Why the Presence of the Negro Constitutes a Problem in the American Social Order," *The Journal of Negro Education*, VIII (July, 1939), 291–298, with the kind permission of the publisher, Howard University, Washington, D.C.

The accommodation of the races, even in the period of national slavery, was seldom or never perfect. It hardly reached that stage of dependence and protection that normally prevails in the relations of the parents and the children in the household, or even the stage of social and psychological superiority and inferiority that for so long characterized the adjustment of the sexes in the Western world. There was no complete consensus among the whites as to the wisdom and necessity of the slave institution and their treatment of the Negroes was far from uniform. The slave order was not entirely static, and slavery presented many rather than a single set of patterns. The racial accommodation was most nearly complete where the institution was most stable. Each change in relations resulting from the development of the institution disturbed in a measure the racial adjustments and modified the habits of mind and behavior that define perfect accommodation. The character of slavery varied somewhat according to the type of agriculture and the nature of the labor to be performed. The treatment of slaves and the degree of racial accommodation varied somewhat from one area to another and from one plantation or household to another.

But there was very general acceptance of the slave institution and the racial status that it implied and enforced. Both the slaves and the masters were habituated to the arrangements and generally unable to visualize any other tolerable system. The definitions growing out of and supporting the economic structure were generally accepted. The dogma of the racial superiority of the whites and the racial inferiority of the Negroes was accepted by the one race as by the other. The right of the whites to rule and the duty of the Negro to serve were as seldom questioned by the slave as by the master.

In the situation, there could be no real race problem. The fundamental institutions and the consequent personal relations were accepted. Each race knew its place in the social order and accepted it. Both adjusted to the system and each adjusted to the other. There was perhaps everywhere some degree of friction which, under hard and unusual treatment and physical deprivation sometimes rose to the level of rebellion and conflict. But these indications of imperfect accommodation were few in number and never widespread. The general pattern was an acceptance of the status as something reasonably in accord with nature and the Divine plan.

The American race problem is a consequence of emancipation and racial freedom. It dates from the breakdown of the slave status. That event disorganized the economic structure as well as the system of political control; it initiated a period of racial competition and social instability. It was the beginning of a period of transition from an old and familiar status, deeply entrenched in the habits and sentiments, to some new and as yet not clearly defined status and system of human relations.

The breakdown of the old status was not exclusively, perhaps not primarily, a change in economic and political relations; it disorganized the whole complex of ideas and attitudes basic to the old structure. The old definitions no longer worked.

The Negroes developed a new body of behavior and new traits of mind and character. Their efforts to live and their desire to prosper brought them into new relations with the whites. Their invasion of new fields of labor brought a new type of direct competition. Their struggle for education, for a decent scale of living, for human dignity and self-respect undermined the basis of the traditional order.

The negative attitudes of the whites made impossible immediately any workable system of adjustments looking toward the progressive establishment of a democracy in race relations. They were scandalized by the self-respecting or aggressive behavior on the part of the freedmen. They opposed all efforts to change the old order; they suppressed, so far as it was in their power, behavior not in harmony with the old definitions. They struggled to retain control and to perpetuate a social order long after its foundations had crumbled.

The period since the Emancipation is one of blind fumbling for a new basis of racial accommodation. The basis of the old order is gone; the basis for a democratic equality has not developed. The race problem is that of maintaining some sort of tolerable working relations between the races during the transition to a new social status. From the point of view of one group, it is that of achieving equal status in the common social order; from the point of view of the other, it is that of preventing the achievement of a democratic equality. *The Negro is a problem in the American social order because his aspirations and his behavior are oriented toward a goal that a dominant majority does not want realized.*

THE CITY AND THE RACE
PROBLEM

By Jitsuichi Masuoka

IT IS IN THE EMPORIUM that divergent races agglomerate and carry on symbiotic relations; that is to say, they live side by side without each dreaming the dreams of others. But sooner or later there emerge more or less abiding economic, political, and cultural relationships among peoples occupying a common territory. Each individual, in his effort to find a proper niche in the highly competitive urban life, becomes mobile, acquires self-respect, and creates a common culture—civilization. It is in this sense that the denizen of the city is a creature and creator of civilization; that of the isolated community a creature and preserver of culture.

It is precisely because life in the city is based upon the nexus of money that the city lures the people. Here, in the confines of a relatively small area, a large number of people of the most extraordinary racial and cultural origins live in close physical proximity and yet maintain their individuality. Furthermore, a far-reaching effect of money upon human relations is to liberate persons from the bondage of intimate personal obligations and expectations. Human relations become impersonal, abstract, and fragmentary; and customs and mores of the traditional social order lose their constraining forces. In the anomalous situation

From Jitsuichi Masuoka, "Race and Culture Contacts in the Emporium," *The American Journal of Sociology*, L (November, 1944), 200–201.

of urban life, therefore, oppressed groups and the "socially undesirables" find a kind of natural habitat.

In the freedom of city life the oppressed racial groups become organized through news and public opinion and learn to act collectively and, therefore, effectively. Through organization they make their wishes known; they define their problems in terms of race and give them political and moral significance. Finally, they channelize their concerted efforts toward the betterment of their life in the city, in the nation, and in the world as a whole. In short, what we call the "race problem," as distinguished from the "native problem," has been cradled in the city.

Every great city has its own written history. But in the emporium are found newspapers—the great papers—for the news, as so aptly characterized by Desmond, is the "stuff of civilization." It is no small wonder, therefore, that the city is a journalist's paradise. Likewise, to a littérateur the emporium is a happy hunting ground for the materials on human nature, for nowhere is the conflict between human nature and civilization so dramatically revealed as in the city. Other kinds of documents are also found in the city, for here people of divergent origins leave their ink-prints as well as their footprints. Hard-boiled business-men write about the cities, and what they write portrays the symbiotic aspects of the city life. Missionaries, too, write about the cities; they write movingly of "the heathen," who, catching glimpses of heaven, dream the same dreams. Dr. R. E. Park used to characterize missionary letters as "the living documents of the Great Society in evolution." One of the significant implications of his statement is, I take it, that the missionaries, freed from things earthly—economics and politics—enter into the lives of the people with whom they come in contact and establish an intimate personal relationship. Perhaps the most interesting documents, although not the most useful, are the letters written by tourists. They lament the fact that the big commercial city is much the same everywhere, and thus indicate the extent to which civilization has superimposed itself upon the divergent subcultures of wider environment. All these documents, whatever their value, demonstrate the telling effects of the city and civilization upon the human mind.

* *

The tension or conflict approach to the study of race and ethnic groups is indeed in accord with the spirit and thought of many present-day sociologists. Tensions and conflicts are inherent in the very nature of the urban community as well as in "race" and culture contacts. High mobility of the city people makes the situation of multiple contacts part and parcel of the daily life of city people —so much so that they have virtually lost their sustained curiosity toward the people whom they meet. It is out of this "city atmosphere" of freedom of movement and thought, and, of impersonal relationship, that cultural and ethnic diversities find their active roots. As the city expands, it loses its consensus based upon neighborhood prides and loyalties; the consensus in the city is dependent chiefly on the functional coordination of its various formal and

Reprinted from Jitsuichi Masuoka, "The City and Racial Adjustment," *Social Forces*, XXVII (October, 1948), 38–40; copyright 1948 by the Williams and Wilkins Company, Baltimore, Md., for the University of North Carolina Press and used with the kind permission of the publishers.

informal organizations, systems of transportation, and media for mass communication.

In this world of more or less orderly human associations and functions, tensions and conflicts assume two distinct forms—personal and intergroup. They are fundamentally the same but are given different treatments in the process of mass communication. The personal conflict is treated as an aspect of "human interest stories," whereas the intergroup conflict is treated as a dramatic event needing an organized attack to stem such a tide. In short, group conflict is an event to be reported in the press; to be discussed by individuals; to be formulated in public opinion; and eventually to be taken up and put into use by politicians and other so-called "public spirited" citizens.

It is inevitable that as the people become concerned with the way of life of their society, some forms of communication will ensue. Whether the process operates within the private circle of friends or out in the open is immaterial in so far as the end product is concerned. The more people talk about the present state of the Negro-white relationship, the more difficult it will be for them to remain indifferent to the issue. Not too infrequently do they find themselves forced to entertain all or some of the claims advanced by others. But as the people talk about "how Negroes should live and behave" and entertain new ideas on this subject, it may, and generally does, assume the character of an issue—a social issue. An issue having been formulated and brought out in the open invites a dialectic process. It is out of such an unintentional and unplanned discourse that the traditional definition of the Negro-white relationship becomes progressively up-rooted from the mores of the southern society. In and through such a dialectic process, so-called, "the southern liberals" are born in the society. As this group gains in numerical strength, increases in *esprit de corps,* and morale, it gives an active support to "pro-Negro" sentiments and opinions. The liberal is essentially a city man—in actuality or in potentiality. In the future, it seems that "the balance of power" pertaining to race relations in the South will rest more and more in the hands of the enlightened liberals. This is the area of sociological investigations that needs to be carried out. Who are these liberals? What is the life cycle of a typical southern liberal? What role in race relations do these liberals play? How do they play these roles? How does the playing of this role affect their social status in the southern society?

Moreover, in the city human relationships lose much of the earmarks of etiquette. In a moving cultural environment of the urban community, personal relations based on ceremonial observance, give way to the form of relations based on functional usefulness. Broadly speaking, it is to the moving hands of time and not to ceremonial observance that human beings in the city adjust their daily activities. Thus in the urban milieu the traditional Negro-white relationship is inevitably modified. If to a white person the conduct of a Negro appears less polite or less "child-like" it is because the long existing racial etiquette is breaking down in southern cities. On the whole, the urban Negro is increasingly making it evident that the archaic racial etiquette is altogether unnecessary. Moreover, in the freedom of the city an infringement upon racial etiquette does not call out in white persons the same degree of emotional disgust and anger as it does in the isolated rural area. What keeps the groups apart in the city are the Jim Crow laws together with "the natural segregation" resulting from competitive struggle. But, like most of the man-made barriers, the categorical segregation is not inviolable. In fact, it can be, and frequently is, circumvented; it is done, however, in a none too spectacular manner. Then, too, as relations become more formal, as they inevitably do in the city, adjustment is achieved more through formal channels and less through the media of personal sentiment, attitude, and loyalty.

When the traditional relationship breaks down, there may be and generally is a period of social disorganization, with characteristic symptoms of increase in crimes, juvenile delinquency, suicide, family and other institutional disorganization. In view of the fact that Negroes in the city live in a moving environment, personal demoralization and social disorganization must be subjected to more critical investigation in relation to adjustment processes. Is the type of disorganization "a real but frustrated tendency to organize on a higher plane," or one more correspondent with the moving environment and that type of disorganization which is simply the abandonment of patterns of behavior? If the rate of disorganization due to the abandonment of standards is disproportionately larger among Negroes than among whites, it is perhaps because the Negro regards the laws as discriminatory imposition of the dominant group upon him. At least he has no share in making and enforcing these laws.

Even in the heyday of slavery, cities were havens of refuge for elements of the Negro population who were not disposed to fit themselves into the niche carved out for them in the traditional southern social organization. Thus, the free Negroes and mulattoes alike tended to aggregate in the cities of the South: they constituted the southern colored city-folk and enjoyed greater educational and economic opportunities. In the relative greater freedom of the city they acquired a more or less secure foothold in the urban economic order. But, as they succeeded in carving out for themselves their economic niche outside the rim of the plantation order, they became the real source of threats to white urban populations. One might say, therefore, that in the South it was this group of nondescript elements that ushered in a "race problem," as that term is now used by sociologists.

SOVIET RUSSIA

By Walter Kolarz

NEITHER OFFICIAL NOR UNOFFICIAL RUSSIA knew any racial prejudice. It would, therefore, be an unjustified over-simplification of Russian history to describe the Russians as 'oppressors' and the non-Russians as the 'oppressed' in the conquered and colonized territories of the Russian Empire. There was,

Reprinted from Walter Kolarz, *Russia and Her Colonies* (London: George Philip and Son, Ltd., 1952), pp. 5–7; (American edition, New York: Frederick A. Praeger, Inc.); with the kind permission of both publishers.

of course, a Russian upper class in the new Eastern territories, i.e. the Volga region, the Urals and Siberia, but there was no Russian master race since the serfs of the Russian squires were not only 'natives' but Russians as well. Some nationalities such as the Tartars also had an upper class whose prestige did not rank below that of the Russian squires. Russian and native oppressed classes joined hands in common action against economic oppression. Russian and Tartar nobility on the other hand established close social relations with each other which were not marred by any racial antipathies.

At no time in Russia's development was there any need for a book like *Uncle Tom's Cabin* since racial intermixture and assimilation were the basic principles on which Russian colonization was built. The classic work of Russian literature depicting the relationship of the Russians towards Tartars, Bashkirs, Kalmucks, etc. in the multi-national Volga region is the *Chronicles of a Russian Family* by S. T. Aksakov, a striking illustration of the Russian-oriental synthesis which came into existence during the centuries following the conquest of Kazan.

The author of this remarkable work was no revolutionary but a conservative country gentleman belonging to a family tracing its origin back to the ninth century. This family after transferring its seat to Bashkiria had no objection to establishing the closest possible ties with Tartars and Bashkirs, which Aksakov illustrates by numerous examples. He mentions one of his uncles, a wealthy nobleman who was so attracted by the Bashkirs that he used to spend the greater part of the summer with them. 'He spoke their language like one of themselves, and would remain whole days in the saddle never alighting even for a moment, so that his legs were as bowed as any Bashkir horseman's.' Another of Aksakov's relatives married a beautiful Tartar girl whose family had then (at the end of the eighteenth century) already adopted 'an external European culture and spoke good Russian but retained the strictest Mohammedan faith.' The young Russian-Tartar couple soon enjoyed a 'firm and honourable position' in Russian provincial society and the Tartar lady turned out to be 'a most graceful and interesting woman of the highest fashion causing no little sensation and envy.' The most remarkable evidence of the gradual growing together of Russians and non-Russians in the Volga valley and the Transvolga region was the personality of Aksakov's own tutor at Kazan University, Nikolay Mikhailovich Ibragimov. His family name and his external appearance were completely Tartar or Bashkir; he had an enormous head, wide cheek bones and small piercing eyes. Culturally, however, he was so totally Russian and Slav that he wrote an *Introduction to the Slavonic Grammar* for the perusal of Russian secondary schools. It was he who encouraged Aksakov to take up a literary career.

In Siberia, where the local nationalities were more primitive than in the Volga region, the lack of racial prejudice expressed itself in a far more robust way than in Aksakov's refined family circle. Rape and barbarian acts of violence towards native women marked the first stage of the 'physical *rapprochement*' between Russian Cossacks and the Siberian peoples. This intermixture between Russians and natives was later carried on on a voluntary basis with the blessing of the Orthodox Church. As a result of intermarriage with the natives the Russians in many parts of Siberia lost all similarity to the Russians of Kiev and Novgorod. Thus in the Lower Ob region, in the Northern part of the Tobolsk province, the 'Russians' assumed the characteristic features of the Ostyaks: round face and slanting eyes; in the Tomsk area, Russians mixed with Tartars,

Kalmucks and Kirghiz and assumed their physical characteristics; in the area of Lake Baikal black-haired and black-eyed 'Russians' bear witness to Russian-Buryat mixed marriages.

Absence of racial pride and prejudice is thus for Russia not a revolutionary principle, but is both the natural prerequisite of the growth of the Russian Empire and the natural outcome of centuries of racial intermixture. A conservative Russian nobleman would have been as proud of being a descendant of Genghis Khan as of the most highly-born Slavonic ancestry. The Soviet régime may have transformed antiracialism into a dogmatic principle, it may have formulated this principle legally and politically, but Russian anti-racialism is no Bolshevik creation, it is a component part of Russian history.

At the time of the establishment of the Soviet régime Russian colonization was still unfinished. The Russians had colonized the Eastern part of European Russia, the Volga region and the Urals from the sixteenth century onwards, they had colonized the Black Sea coast and the North Caucasus region in the eighteenth and nineteenth centuries. A great effort was made to colonize Siberia in the period between 1886 and 1916 when 4,500,000 persons went to that vast area, of whom, it is true, 1,000,000 returned to Europe. But all these and many other colonizing activities amounted to little when related to the gigantic potentialities of the Russian Empire. The North, not only the Far North, was a huge empty space. Siberia had hardly any major towns. The Russian Far East was badly underpopulated.

NORTHERN ALASKA

By Robert Marshall

AL WEST HAS TOLD ME that when he was living alone as the only white man in Alatna, Little Mary would frequently come around to invite him to her house for meals. "You no cook for yourself, open cans all time, no good," she would say. After a while, when he commenced to feel embarrassed at the number of times she was inviting him without any reciprocation on his part, she adopted a more tactful approach. She would send one of her little sons just before lunch time to ask Al to help her with some trivial matter, and then he would have to stay for lunch. She would always have some special reason. "You never eat white-fish eggs, you got to try them," she might say, and of course Al could not refuse such an invitation.

This story could just as well be reversed to illustrate the innumerable acts of white kindness to Eskimos. Either way it illustrates the fact that two such divergent races as the whites and the Eskimos are actually living together in

From Robert Marshall, *Arctic Village* (New York: H. Smith and R. Haas, 1933), pp. 230–236. Copyright 1933 by Robert Marshall. By permission of Random House.

almost perfect amity. They are continually exchanging visits in each other's homes, mingling together in conversation, eating together at meals, sharing the same cabins on the trail. At all social events they have standing of equal importance, except that the Eskimo girls are in greater demand than the white women at the dances because they are younger. There are absolutely no legal inequalities set up, no restrictive regulations which do not apply to both races. From every standpoint the Eskimos and whites treat each other as equals.

This gives rise to the natural question whether the Eskimos and whites also think of each other as equals. I have attempted to obtain some measure of belief, not by questionnaire, not by the superficial method of direct oral inquiry, but by close observation and intimate personal acquaintance.

I have conceived of four different attitudes which the white people could entertain toward the Eskimos. Each of these viewpoints could be subdivided almost indefinitely, but I prefer to use rather broad categories. I have tried to augment my definitions with quotations expressing the viewpoints held in each of these groups.

I. In this class I include anybody who takes the attitude that the Eskimos are too low to associate with. It is the typical attitude of the Southerner toward the negro. I cannot give any quotations for this category because no white person in the entire Koyukuk held such views.

II. In this class I include those who believe the Eskimos are distinctly inferior to the whites in every way, who tend to treat them coldly, and who constantly make uncomplimentary remarks behind their backs. In spite of this attitude some of them have been exceptionally generous to the Eskimos when they have needed help. Here are a few of the expressions which typify the attitude of this class of people:

"Fancy treating the natives as equals! It's simply out of the question. They have nothing but children's minds. All I have to do is smile at them and be friendly and give them a little food now and then and they think I'm a goddess. Just like children. No, they're simply below the white man's level, that's all there's to it." (The Eskimos, who have secret nicknames in their language for every white person, call this "goddess" by two titles. One means "she paints her lips red," with reference to her desperate efforts to maintain a youthful appearance. The other means "The camp robber.")

"I always considered an Eskimo a good shot, but of course he ain't good at nothing compared with a white man."

"When you try to compare the natives to the whites it's like comparing night to day. You just can't talk about the two together. Tell me, did a native ever invent a typewriter or make anything like a can of milk or a rifle cartridge? No, you're God damn right they didn't. There are thousands of things like that which whites have invented and not one did a native ever make. But they're so God damn conceited they think they're better than the whites. 'White man fool,' they always say. Why, they never have a thought which is more than skin deep."

III. In this class I include those who regard the Eskimos as inferior to the whites in intelligence and culture, though they treat them as equals. Their attitude may be summarized by the remark: "They're not quite our equals, but it isn't their fault." Here are a few sample viewpoints from this group of people.

"I get along with the natives fine, just as well as with the whites. But they're peculiar people in many ways. They seem to think it's wrong to save up any money. As long as they've got two bits they're never happy until they've spent it. It doesn't matter if their kids may be starving next month, they'll spend what they've got now on clothes, on useless contraptions, on drinking or gambling. Then when they've got it all spent they'll go back to work."

"She's a pretty good woman for a squaw."

"I figure the native is to white man almost just like a dog. You can train a native to be good or you can train a native to be bad. Bad native, it ain't his fault, it's because he's gotten mixed up with bad white men. A native could be the finest man in the world or the worst man in the world. It all depends on how he's brought up."

IV. In this class I include those who consider the Eskimos to be fully as admirable a people as the whites, though undeniably a very different people. This group may criticize various traits of the Eskimos, but they feel that other good points fully balance these defects. The following quotations are representative of the attitude of this class:

"The Lithuanians (from whom this man came) aren't my people any more. The natives here are my people. The land here really all belongs to them. They just let us live here through kindness. They have always been very kind to me. I want to do what I can for them. At first I wanted to destroy their superstitions, but then I thought of the superstitions of all the white men around me and decided I'd better leave them alone. I think it's time we stopped patronizing the native. He's just as good as the white man and we ought to treat him so."

"They're fine people to get along with. Poor devils, they haven't got a thing in the world, but what they have got they'll share with you. I've lived with the natives here for thirty-four years and I've found them better people to live with than the whites. In all the years I've lived with them I've only found one who ever stole anything from me and that was only a ball of twine. No, I've bunked with them from Dawson to the Siberian coast for better than thirty years and I'd never ask to find a finer people."

"There's lots of things you can say against the Eskimos. They're forever squabbling and they're terribly superstitious and they don't think anything of a debt. But on the other side, look at all you can say. For all their little fights they don't ever carry resentments like the white people. They're not all the time scheming to get the better of you. They're the most honest people you can find if you treat them squarely. They know how to enjoy themselves to-day without worrying over what's going to happen to-morrow. And you know, I believe they have on the average greater mental capacity and more intelligence than the whites. Anyway, they're the most good-hearted people in the world, and that's a lot more important than whether they pay their bills at the store."

I think these quotations define the viewpoints of the groups I have mentioned. It is now pertinent to present my census of how these different attitudes were distributed among the seventy-seven white people of the upper Koyukuk.

Included among the nine people who regarded the Eskimos as distinctly inferior were the whites with the first, second, fourth, and fifth most enemies among their own race. Not a single one of the nine people was ranked by his fellow whites among the top half in popularity. This hints at an interesting psychological relationship. A person is disliked by his own people, so in order to assuage the feeling of inferiority which this must at least subconsciously create, he bolsters his pride by stressing how much superior his entire race is to another race.

Attitude of Whites Toward Eskimos

	Number Holding This View
I. Eskimos are too low to associate with	0
II. Eskimos are distinctly inferior to the whites in every way	9
III. Eskimos are somewhat inferior to the whites but should be treated as equals	38
IV. Eskimos are fully as admirable a people as the whites	30

If a white person treats the Eskimos as equals, is interested in and sympathetic to what interests them, is honest, jolly, and fairly generous, is neither stupid nor conceited, and does not try to get their women drunk in order to have sexual intercourse with them, it is almost certain that he will be regarded enthusiastically by the Eskimos. Just about one quarter of all the whites qualify in this class, and the amount of affection which the Eskimos heap upon them is enormous.

The majority of the white people fail to meet all these requirements. The Eskimos feel friendly toward most of these people, but they lack the great enthusiasm with which they regard the first group. It is also true that they are not averse to ridiculing many of these white people. I recollect an exceptionally gay evening in Ekok's cabin when one elderly man who was ardently courting a fifteen-year-old Eskimo girl, another fellow who was a terrible liar, a third who erroneously thought he was immensely popular with the Eskimos, and a fourth who was merely dull-minded, were successively derided.

As to positive dislikes, the Eskimos have surprisingly few. There is one white man, who when he used to be commissioner, heckled them pretty badly. Many of them hate him. But the whites who are most genuinely scorned are the ones who treat the Eskimos as inferiors. One of these people imagines that the natives are too childish to understand serious talk, so he only speaks nonsense to them. They laugh perfunctorily at his silliness, but behind his back, they ridicule him and call him "the crazy old man." The woman, whom I have previously mentioned as being called "the camp robber," is a constant butt for their jokes. It is important to note, however, that all these instances of unpopularity are individual cases. Unlike most of the whites, the Eskimos almost never generalize about an entire race.

Of course one of the most interesting aspects of interracial relations is the sexual. Here I merely want to mention that there is almost no prejudice in the Koyukuk against intermarriage and a sufficient amount of it actually occurring that a third of all the children in the Koyukuk have mixed blood.

HAWAII

By Romanzo Adams

WHEN PEOPLES WHO DIFFER markedly in language, manners, customs, and technical skill, as well as in color and other physical race traits, come to live together in the same community, their differences tend to become matters of interest. Such coming together is never a mere matter of spatial approach; it is always associated with the development of an economic system in which the two or more racial groups play dissimilar parts. The members of the one race may be merchants while the others produce raw materials for the market. The one may be organized as a military class of superior power and privilege while the others are expected to obey. The teachers may be of one race, the pupils of the other. One may possess the capital and the superior technology while the other furnishes the brawn. To one may belong the masters; to the other the slaves. There is always the dissimilarity of function and this is associated with a difference in power and privilege.

As the initial system of relationships gets established as custom, they represent a sort of vested interest for the people of the race of superior privilege. Before the customs have hardened into tradition the people of inferior privilege —or some of them, at least—may be dissatisfied and there may be a struggle on their part to readjust the system in their own interest; and it may be that they will be aided by some of the members of the other race. Such a struggle may, in one of its aspects, involve the use of clubs and swords, but always there is the intellectual aspect. If the race of superior privilege is to maintain its own integrity of purpose and hence its vigor and unity of action, it must have a system of theories or doctrines from the standpoint of which their practice appears to be reasonable and just. Unless the race of inferior privilege also has a suitable equipment of theories and doctrines, its struggle tends to be meaningless and is abandoned. To the extent that beliefs are associated with sentiment they are not mere theories but doctrines, and they call for a sort of loyalty. The man who fails to maintain the doctrine of his group is regarded as a heretic and, perhaps, as a traitor.

Where there is a strong and long-continued interest, the doctrines come to be associated with a code. The code may be concerned with practical matters to some extent, but it is most important when it takes the form of a ritual. The prescriptions of a code are ritualistic when they are chiefly important for what they symbolize. For example, in many places a white man may not, in addressing a Negro, use the title of respect "Mister." The street-car rules in southern cities are, in fact, ritualistic, but not so obviously so. Negroes and whites travel on the same street car, enter by the same door and sit, not side by side, but not far apart. The seat occupied by Negroes in the early morning may be used by whites in the mid-forenoon. But the little movable sign attached to the back of

By Romanzo Adams, "The Unorthodox Race Doctrine of Hawaii." By permission from *Race and Culture Contacts*, by E. B. Reuter (ed.), copyright 1934, McGraw-Hill Book Company, Inc. Ch. IX.

some seat serves as a boundary line between the white and the "colored" sections and so meets the requirements of the situation. Racial inequality is symbolized without the expense that an extra car would entail.

Under the provisions of even a very strict code based on the caste principle, there may be personal relationships between representatives of the two or more races of a very intimate and friendly sort, provided each "keeps his place," that is, observes the provisions of the code designed to symbolize the difference of status.

In the long run the ritual is the most important thing in race relations. Unless supported by ritual the doctrines tend to be subverted by the facts of experience. If doctrines are to be stabilized in a world of change they must have the support of a ritual which tends to fix habit and to control opinion by a method that lies below the level of reflective thought.

When a traveler familiar with race doctrines and practices in other places visits Hawaii, he is impressed with the apparent absence of what is commonly called race prejudice. One man said, "Humanly speaking, you have no race prejudice in Hawaii." The things observed relate largely to ritual. A man of any race is addressed as "Mister" in Hawaii. A man from Texas saw and heard a Negro in the legislature—a Negro treated with respect and as an equal—and he went away in disgust. If our visitor has traveled in China he knows that the Chinese are not admitted as guests to Shanghai hotels intended for whites. But in Honolulu a Chinese man or a man of any other race may be entertained in any hotel and white men may sit at the table with him. In cities of the United States, Negroes occupy a separate section in theatres, away in the rear. In Hawaii a man of any race may be seated in the best section. If our traveler were to visit the public schools he might find a Negro woman as principal of a school in which she is the only Negro, or he might find one whose principal is an American Indian. He might be shocked to discover that men of dark complexion can and do arrest white criminals and act as their jailers. If he goes to the governor's reception he will see men of all colors shaking hands and holding friendly conversation with each other. If he is entertained at the home of a leading citizen, and if he is believed not to have sentiments antagonistic thereto, he may sit at the table with guests some of whom are not of his own race. If he is taken to a university social affair he will see young men and young women of several races and mixed races dancing on the same floor and to the same music. Should our traveler visit the industrial or the commercial sections of the city, he might find a white man who takes orders from a man of some other race or a white man who deposits his money in a bank with a Chinese or a Japanese manager. If he consults the report of the Bureau of Vital Statistics he will find that men and women of all races are intermarrying and that, in the general process of interracial amalgamation through marriage, the white race is taking an important part. Possibly our traveler may attend a church wedding to witness a white young woman marry a man of some other race, while the friends of both or several races give their sanction by sitting in the pews.

If our visitor talks freely with white men who have lived in the Territory long enough to have accepted the doctrinal implications of Hawaii's ritual of race relations he will hear expressions of opinion and sentiment consonant with the practices. When a white man familiar with a different ritual comes to Hawaii —if he comes into social contact with the local people at all—he is soon made to feel the pertinence of the old saying "when in Rome do as the Romans do," and he does, in a measure, conform. One must do what "everybody" does—what is expected of him. It would not be in good form to do otherwise. There is a code for gentlemen. A man may observe the rules of the local code with his fingers crossed but he does observe them. In the Hawaiian language there is a name for such. A *malahini* is a newcomer not yet in sympathy with the local race mores.

If, however, the *malahini* remains long enough, and if he is normal in his social attitudes, desiring to be really a part of the society in which he lives and not a permanent outsider, he will, early or late, begin to readjust his theories or doctrines. One begins to feel humiliated at the thought of yielding to a code contrary to his doctrines—"principles." But he cannot change the code or yet violate it without some sort of penalty, the penalty involved in placing himself "outside." His doctrines are, therefore, reconstructed; and in this way he achieves a comfortable social status without violating his conscience or standing condemned by it as a coward. When he has made this adjustment he is no longer a *malahini,* but a *kamaaina,* an old-timer, a member of the "we-group."

Perhaps our *kamaaina,* if a white man and if not to be quoted, will qualify the doctrines somewhat. He may not accept all the implications of the ritual and he may have misgivings as to the future. In minor crises he may even manifest attitudes quite antagonistic to the code he commonly observes and, within the intimate circle, he may profess doctrines of a contrary character. But the existence of these contrary sentiments and beliefs is a matter of second-rate importance. The really important thing is the general body of tradition that inhibits the open and constant avowal of such attitudes. In the conflict between antagonistic mores, the sentiment that cannot be openly avowed, that cannot be expressed in slogans, and that cannot influence the civil law or the social code is ineffective or, at most, effective only in a rear-guard action to cover a retreat.

In short, the race mores of Hawaii are, or tend to be, the mores of race equality, and the doctrines are, therefore, unorthodox from the standpoint of white people, especially of most English-speaking white people.

At this point no question is raised as to equality of stature, beauty, strength, inborn mental ability, temperamental traits, education, or technical skill. It is just a question of what the social ritual symbolizes. The use of the title Mister, the front-door welcome, the sitting together at dinner, and many other things symbolize equality of social status in Hawaii, just as the denial of the title Mister, the back-door entrance, and other rules of similar import symbolize social inequality in other places.

In the long run, the ritual affects the relations of a more directly practical sort in a very important way. Under the code of racial equality, it is possible for men of superior character and ability to attain to positions of power and dignity and to exercise authority without limitation as to race. Personal status comes to depend more on personal merit and less on racial antecedents.

Before undertaking to account for the special race mores that tend to prevail in Hawaii it is necessary to make certain admissions. In the first place, the opposing race doctrines and rituals of the white people, even of the English-speaking white people or of those who live in the United States, are not strictly uniform in character. In some places there are so few colored people that they have not attracted much attention, and so there are no obviously well-established ideas and practices relating to race contacts. In other cases the experience of race contact has been too recent to permit of the development of a definite set of mores. What is said relative to these mores must be taken to refer either to the somewhat undeveloped tendencies or to the doctrines and practices of those communities in which the contacts have been important for a long time. On the other hand, the experience of most of the actual residents of Hawaii with its system of race relations has been too recent to permit of the general and full acceptance of the code; and the number and influence of the people of more recent arrival, many of whom are but temporary residents, is not without influence on the general situation. For many, the local race mores are accepted only in a superficial sense; they are not supported by strong sentiment—they lack the sacredness suggested by the word mores. The term, then, must be understood as referring to the trend of attitude or to the attitude of the people of more stable residence. The race mores of Hawaii are still in the making.

If one wishes to discover the things that were most important in creating Hawaii's pattern of race relations he must turn to experience—to the experience of particular men and women as revealed in case studies. In the stories of the early white residents one sees the mores at the very beginning of their development.

Any explanation of the special sort of race relations that has come into existence in Hawaii must deal with the factors that have conditioned the development of ritual. It is not that the white people of Hawaii differed from the white people of Virginia in color, in character, in the religion professed, in temperamental traits, or in their initial theories or doctrines about race. Nor were they different essentially in their attitudes relating to economic affairs. Business always seeks a profit, and a high profit is preferred to a low. Nor has there been in Hawaii an absence of the sorts of personal attitude which in American colonial times contributed toward the development of slavery and its social code. The problem is to discover the things that, in Hawaii, favored the development of one sort of code and tended to inhibit behavior consonant with the other—the series of historic situations.

In the beginning the things that tended to favor a sort of behavior that was based on the assumption of race equality may be considered as accidents of history—a series of situations in which it seemed to the white people and to the Hawaiians to be advantageous to treat each other with respect and, sometimes, with deference, the respect and deference not being a one-way affair. Behavior of this sort became habitual. Custom was established. There came to be a normal expectation—an incipient tradition.

The native Hawaiians, while representatives of a stone-age culture, were so far developed in this culture that they were able to produce in considerable quantity certain commodities—fruits, vegetables, meat, salt, and timber—which were desired by the masters of European and American trading ships. They were also of such cultural advancement that they wanted articles made of iron, cotton goods, and other commodities available for exchange. That is, they were of such cultural advancement that trade was possible and the trade was important to vessels operating in the Pacific in the early nineteenth century. The Hawaiians were under the rule of a strong and shrewd king or chief who was able to maintain order among his people and to control trade relations. It was advantageous to white traders to recognize his authority. Since the king symbolized the dignity of his people as a whole, the recognition of his authority, in a subtle way, involved for the people as a whole a status superior to what would have existed had there been no such chiefly authority.

The king secured the services of a number of white men, men who understood how to build and operate ships, to use firearms, to negotiate in relation to trade, etc. From such accounts as we have, it appears that they served him loyally and, while they did not symbolize their respect according to the native ritual, they did show it in a way that was understood and accepted. These men, because of the value of their services, were given positions of honor and were given native women of chiefly rank to be their wives. They were recognized as chiefs in the Hawaiian system and their half-blood children were, by the Hawaiians, accorded high rank. These early white residents were, by the nature of their services and on account of the rank and position they held and also by virtue of their family relationships, absorbed into the Hawaiian society. Through their services they added to the power and dignity of the king and to the ability of their society to command the respect of transient foreigners.

It is not necessary to inquire into the early upbringing of these men, whether they were taught to believe in the inferiority of the dark-colored peoples or were wholly ignorant of the existence of such peoples. Doubtless, if they had gone to Virginia to live they would have accepted the system of race relations that prevailed in Virginia. Coming to Hawaii, they found no pattern of race relations and so they had to establish one.

When men live among relatives and friends as members of a we-group they must observe the prevailing code. But when they are spatially and spiritually isolated from their old home people they may be free. These men had not come from their old homes directly to Hawaii with a fresh memory of the paternal benediction. They had knocked about over the world and had met peoples of many varying customs and standards, so that those of their old home did not seem to be so important. They were emancipated men.

The case of a high-born Scottish lad who ran away from home may serve as an example. He left home because he did not get along well with his stepmother. He changed his name, taking that of his own mother's father, thus symbolizing his ill will toward his father. According to the story, he fought under Lord Nelson at Trafalgar. Eventually he reached Hawaii, where he remained and probably never after had any communication with anyone in Scotland. Because of his qualifications, King Kamehameha desired his services and so he appointed him to positions of dignity and gave him a Hawaiian woman of chiefly rank to be his wife. As a man of special qualifications and as one closely associated with the king he could not fail to have prestige among the Hawaiians. As a man in the service of the king and as one taken into Hawaiian society he could not assume the airs of racial superiority. His superiority, on the one side, was a matter of personal qualification and, on the other, a matter of accepting honor under the Hawaiian system and at the hands of Hawaiians. Through his children (there are over four hundred living descendants) he was permanently identified with the Hawaiians. He inevitably had to support the doctrine of racial equality if he responded in a normal way to the requirements of his situation.

Man is so fundamentally a social being that when he comes into contact with strange peoples he tends to make such adjustments as are necessary to the enjoyment of normal human relationships. It seems to be more important to a man to enjoy such relationships than to maintain the standards of his former people, and this is especially true if he is not only spatially but also spiritually isolated from them. These men were free from the control of the old home mores and they were in a practical situation that called for a special sort of behavior. Under the circumstances they had to act as if the king was their superior and the other high chiefs equals. They had to show respect and to accept the status given them by the natives—a status which was, in fact, higher than they had ever enjoyed before.

Not only were the white men who thus early helped to set the pattern of race relations men of the emancipated type, but in all periods, down even to our own time, there have been in Hawaii considerable numbers of white men of this sort —men away from home and, therefore, more or less free from home standards. Sometimes these men contribute to the strengthening of the race mores of Hawaii, not directly, by accepting them at first, but as a result of an unintended commitment. Being nearly free from all mores, they follow the course of least difficulty in their social relations and cross the Rubicon by marrying Hawaiian women. Of course, there are many such out-marriages by old residents who are under the mores, but the percentage of out-marriages is much higher among the newcomers, many of whom are merely emancipated, than among the white men of more extended residence who are more or less fully under the local mores. In such cases it is not at all certain that it makes any difference whether a man comes from a place where race standards are strictly maintained or from a place in which little attention is given to matters of race. For example, a young man from a southern state is said to have sung with the rest,

> "You may call 'em Hawaiians, but they look
> like niggers to me,"

when he first came to Hawaii, but within a year or two he was married to a Hawaiian woman and for years he has been working to support his wife and half-white children. When he was married he was merely emancipated from the mores of his old home, but gradually he tended to come under those of Hawaii.

Gradually, through the mixed marriages, there comes into existence a population of mixed racial ancestry and, since the mixed bloods typically have their origin in a socially sanctioned marriage relationship, they enjoy a status impossible where marriage is forbidden and where, consequently, the mixed bloods are supposed to have had their origin in temporary and unsanctioned unions. The influence of this group of increasing size and prestige is bound to be for a continuation of the mores of racial equality and they contribute not a little to the developing sentiment that makes custom sacred.

Within permissible limits it is not possible to refer to all of the significant situations in which the incipient mores were exposed to the danger of overturn. Suffice it to say that there has been a succession of challenging situations and that, in one case at least, the outcome seemed doubtful for a time. It was finally settled, thanks to favoring circumstances as well as to the strength of a partially established tradition, in harmony with the earlier practice.

The coming of the American missionaries, in just one aspect, represented a possible influence for reversal. The missionaries tended to destroy the freedom of the emancipated white men in Hawaii. To a considerable extent they estab-

lished communication with the outside English-speaking world and in that way
tended to establish in Hawaii the standards of England and America. This was
bitterly resented by some of the emancipated, but it could not be avoided.
Moreover, the missionaries brought their wives and established white family
life with New England standards. After a while the white wives of business men
came. Here was a chance, at least, that there would grow up a strictly white
social group with standards adverse to interracial marriage and hence to the
type of social relations that normally leads to marriage. This would supply a
theoretical basis for a whole code of the typical American sort.

But when the missionaries applied for permission to reside in the Islands
and to teach, the request was referred by the chiefs to an old white man of thirty
years' residence who had served the king with honor and who had a Hawaiian
wife and a family of mixed-blood children. The missionary cause rested on this
man's advice. Since the advice was favorable, they were permitted to remain in
the land. Being under such obligations to this old man, they were under the
necessity of accepting his family arrangements formally, even if there was some
feeling adverse thereto.

But in any case the strategy of the missionary position was such that they
had to make concessions on matters of race. They saw many things in the
behavior of the Hawaiians which they disapproved. Even after many natives
were baptized as Christians, they did not commonly live up to the standards set
by the missionaries. Now if the missionaries had said that these deficiencies of
conduct were in consequence of certain racial traits—of traits conditioned by
biological heredity—they would have found it hard to answer the question,
"Why are you here?" But if the defects of character were regarded as due to
the lack of the Christian religion, that is, to a cultural rather than to a racial
trait, they could feel that there was a reason for their presence.

The missionaries having accepted the incipient race traditions, at least as
far as the ritual symbolizing respect and good will was concerned, they were
destined to furnish a strong support for the Hawaiian social order at a critical
juncture. When, due to the multiplication of white residents and transient
sailors, there was danger of a complete overturn of all Hawaiian authority, it
was the missionaries who turned the scale. The old strong-willed king Kamehameha was dead and the young king lacked resoluteness and shrewdness. The
transient sailors and some men of more permanent residence manifested the
common tendency of white exploiters and irresponsible transients to break
down the native order. After such a breakdown the next step commonly is for
the foreigners to plead native incompetence and thus to secure the assistance
of their national governments to set up a control of their own. At times the king
of Hawaii was forced to submit to unjust demands backed up by foreign war-
ships. Sometimes these demands were of such a character as to suggest that they
were not expected ever to come to the attention of the civilized world.

The missionaries, because they had access to some of the agencies of civilized public opinion and were able even to influence the foreign policy of some
of the great nations, played at this time a most important rôle. Some of them
resigned from their missionary connection and, as advisers to the king, helped
to reorganize the government so that it could maintain order at home and so
that it could meet its international obligations. As administrators they helped
to maintain the king in a position of dignity and to protect the people against

disorderly white residents and transients and also against cheating by shrewd traders.

All this automatically tended to favor the mores of race equality. It was necessary to treat the king, the members of his family, and other high chiefs in such a way as to symbolize respect. If one who thus treated the king and other Hawaiian dignitaries with respect did, at some other time, refuse social recognition to Hawaiians of lower rank, such discrimination had to be regarded as based on rank or class, not race. If white people commonly had their more intimate associations, according to preference, with each other, such association could not be made to symbolize what must be symbolized in a caste system of race mores. Their social relations with the king inhibited that.

If the whole story were to be told it would be necessary to refer to the new situations of each generation. At one time the Chinese were involved and, in a different way, the Portuguese immigrants. There is a Japanese and a Filipino chapter to the story and even the small groups such as the Korean and the Porto Rican have had a place in the developing situation.

If a superpatriotic orator in Minneapolis wishes to propagandize against the kind of people who live in Cicero, Ill., he must not refer to them merely as foreigners, lest the Swedes take offense. So in the height of the anti-Chinese agitation in Hawaii nearly fifty years ago, the whites could not use the terms necessary to make it a race issue without offense to their Hawaiian friends. They had to forego a most effective method of propaganda and, hence, the inferior status of the Chinese was of a less permanent character—so transient that no regular doctrines and codes were developed. With such modifications of behavior as came naturally with time and changing circumstance, the Chinese escaped from the early odium and were welcomed into the general community life and this, of course, committed them to the formal support of the race doctrines that worked in their favor.

So far, the tradition based on early practice has been maintained—maybe waveringly at times but, on the whole, maintained. The sentiment is coming to be more widely shared and the doctrines are being more definitely formulated. At each critical juncture there have been at least some factors in the situation that have favored a continuation of the early customs, and the developing traditions have been strong enough to cast the deciding vote.

The coming of comparatively large numbers of white citizens from the mainland, especially the men and officers in army and navy service, constitutes the most recent challenge to Hawaii's race mores. These men and officers belong to organizations with their own traditions; in their traditions, distinctions of rank are highly important. Such traditions make it easy for them to accept the traditions of a racial caste system, and most of those who have the greatest influence were brought up in, or have lived in, sections of the country in which the doctrines of race inequality are definitely professed and practiced. Naturally, they are irritated by the practices and attitudes of the local people, and in minor crises their opposing attitudes become manifest. Because of the very definite character of their traditions and because of the temporary character of their residence, there is no tendency to accept the local mores. Because of their access to the agencies of public opinion on the mainland their attitude constitutes a challenge of more than common importance. Hawaii's race mores are still in the making.

In the beginning the social contacts between the Hawaiians and the early white residents were between a people who had no memory of race relations, and hence no traditions relative thereto, and some white newcomers who were emancipated from the mores of their native lands. The situation came uncommonly near to one of absolute freedom from all predisposing tradition and, in effect, the early system of race relations was almost an unbiased response to the practical demands of the situation. These demands were such that behavior, dominated at first merely by a consideration of practical interests, was free from any implied assumption of racial superiority or inferiority. Out of the early practices came habit, custom, normal expectation. There were people of influence whose interests were best subserved by a continuation of the sorts of relationship that were becoming customary. In challenging situations there were, therefore, people who would struggle for the maintenance of custom, and in such struggle sentiment would be strengthened. The logical implications of the situation would come to the surface, receiving some more or less formal statement. That is, there came to be beliefs and theories and, when sentiment was sufficiently strong, these were doctrines.

The doctrines were, of course, in harmony with the habitual behavior, and as the doctrines came to be more clearly formulated the behavior acquired significance for what it symbolized; it tended to become a ritual. That is, the practices were becoming traditional. In later times these traditions, even the traditions of a not very well-established character, were able to cast the deciding vote in challenging situations and the early tradition tended to be self-perpetuating. In its struggle for self-maintenance it has, on the whole, been successful because there is a ritualistic code which supports the beliefs and theories and serves for the expression of sentiment. But also there has been, to some extent, a continuation of favoring circumstance.

BRAZIL

*

By Henriqueta Chamberlain

UNTIL MY FIRST DAY AT SCHOOL I always thought I was like all other Brazilian girls. But that day for the first time I saw myself in a mirror.

Mother did not send me to the usual parochial Catholic school for girls because she was a Protestant missionary and a Southern Baptist. She sent us to a private school, which must have been all right or she never would have allowed us to go.

Reprinted from Henriqueta Chamberlain, *Where the Sabia Sings* (New York: The Macmillan Co., 1947), pp. 1–3, 129–134; copyright 1947 by the Macmillan Co., and used with the kind permission of the publisher.

It was the first time I ever wore the standard schoolgirl's uniform of navy-blue skirt and white blouse, and I felt very proud as I trotted down the street holding my mother by the hand. Everything in school was just as I had expected. There I met other Brazilian girls like me, excited, shy, a little uncertain of what to expect.

In the great reception room of this school, which was a former private residence, a teacher came in and asked us politely to line up along the wall. And that was when I first saw this large mirror.

I had been watching my teacher intently. She was an attractive mulatta who wore her hair parted in the middle, combed tightly down the side, and rolled into a large bun on the back of her neck. Her face was calm, even though she was pushing us around trying to get us to form a straight line. Then I looked into the mirror.

I could see us standing stiffly in line, and we all looked exactly alike. All had on black stockings, navy-blue pleated skirts, white blouses. Everybody had black hair, swarthy skin, black eyes, except me. I was mortified. My hair was red. My eyes were blue. And my skin was white, sprinkled with lots of brown freckles. I could have died. I was different. It had never occurred to me before that I did not look exactly like my friends.

When I followed the line marching into my classroom, my eyes were brimful of tears. The letters of my primer, "B-a, Ba, Be, Be," all blurred before me. I prayed to God and begged him to change me and make me a brunette and beautiful like the other girls.

I was born in a small town in North Brazil between Natal and Recife. My story is the story of an American girl living in Brazil as a Brazilian. Never once did my parents take us to live in an American or English colony. We did not join country clubs, nor did we attend English-speaking schools. We were brought up as Brazilians, with Brazilians, and our loyalty and passionate love of country were for Brazil.

Portuguese was my native language. At home my parents spoke English, but I would always answer in Portuguese. In fact, I was convinced that English was a sacred language. I heard it spoken only by my missionary parents and their friends. And the only literature I had ever heard of in English was the Bible. It was a great shock to me when I first heard an American businessman casually speaking English.

It wasn't only the Brazilians and the Baptist Mission that sent people to our house, but other organizations such as the Y.M.C.A. They got into the habit of offering our home to any young person who seemed to be getting out of hand, or who was lonely and in need of contact with wholesome family life. That was how a young American named Andy came into our life.

Andy had been jilted by a girl in the States, and in a great dramatic gesture had packed his belongings and come to Brazil to forget it all and start life over again. When the Y.M.C.A. found him he was in a miserable, blue frame of mind, and they decided we should be good for him. So he moved in with all his trunks and suitcases, and, because he was American, mother gave him our best guest room.

I hadn't met an unmarried young American before, and I was fluttering around with excitement when he walked in. Nor was I disappointed. He was everything I had hoped for: tall, with blond wavy hair and sky-blue eyes. His skin was tanned and smooth-shaven and shone like a child's newly scrubbed face. Our hearts went out to him, and we wondered what American women were like if one was stupid enough to give him up, unless, of course, all American men were that beautiful.

In the first five minutes he told us he planned to go far into the interior to prospect for diamonds; but he didn't know Portuguese, and he had been told not to start the trip until he could speak the language like a native. Would we teach it to him?

Would we? We all promptly fell in love with him and got very busy teaching him all the Portuguese we knew. All our neighbors got busy, too, especially the German girls who lived back of us, and the Brazilian girls. We were all fired with zeal to teach this young man, and a great rivalry arose among us.

Because he was American, and therefore trustworthy to mother, she didn't think a chaperon would be necessary. So she let us walk around the garden and talk to him. But, being a lonely American in a tropical paradise, surrounded by all the adoring females of the neighborhood, he soon forgot his old love in the States, and also his inhibitions. He began to take a walk in the garden every night after supper with one of the Brazilian girls, and one night I saw him try to kiss her. It was a casual gesture on his part, but she thought he was going to propose marriage the next day.

At the breakfast table mother tried to explain these things to him. She said he mustn't walk around the garden alone with that girl any more, or her father would be calling on him. They were respectable Brazilians and were not to be played with.

"Gosh!" he said. "Can't I even flirt a little bit?"

Mother told him he had better play safe and flirt only with American girls who would not attach too much significance to his actions.

"Well, I guess you're right," he said contemptuously. "They're most of them negroid anyhow, aren't they?"

We looked up, surprised. We had never heard Negro blood spoken of with a sneer.

Mother said hastily that there was a great racial mixture in Brazil and probably many Brazilians had a touch of color; but there were also many, many pure white, of the brunette variety, descendants of the Portuguese.

"God damn it!" he burst out. "How can you tell the difference?"

I smiled to myself as I remembered a passage with some Brazilian girls from the interior on that very subject. After dinner they gathered in my room. I don't remember how the conversation started, but someone said that everybody in the world had a dark shadow, a sort of brown line, on the skin over the spinal column, and that all women had brownish nipples.

"Oh, no!" I blurted out. "You're wrong. Because I know I haven't any such shadow on my spinal column, nor are my breasts brown."

"We'll bet on it," one girl said. "You just haven't noticed. Let's look at you. We'll show you."

I blushed furiously, as usual, and said they would have to take my word for it. But they were insistent. They ganged up on me.

"Come on, take your dress off, and let's see you. We'll find the brown spots. That's the way people are made, you know. God made us all alike. You don't think you're a wonderful exception of His, do you?"

Reluctantly I slipped off my dress and my slip. And in the interest of science and truth I turned my back to them and let them examine freely my spinal column.

"God above! She's right," they said. "Her skin is white—white as milk; not a shadow anywhere."

"Now turn around," they commanded.

"She's right," they finally agreed. "There's nothing brown on her." Then one of the girls burst out laughing. "Whoever heard of pink-tipped breasts. You must be an albino. What light coloring!"

I said I was perfectly normal, and I also said I thought most of the white people they knew in the interior had brownish shadows and undertones because there was Negro blood somewhere in the family.

"But of course!" the girl said. "That's what we were talking about. Everybody has some Negro blood in them. We all have."

Looking at me critically again, she had to admit, regretfully so as not to hurt my feelings, that I probably didn't have any.

"Your parents are foreigners anyhow," she said. "But take us Brazilians, if we go back far enough in our family tree we'll all probably find a *negra* somewhere—and a *padre*."

This is an old joke in Brazil, and you're supposed to snicker when you hear it.

Now our American friend Andy was quite excited about this mixture of blood. "Can you always tell when someone has Negro blood?" he asked.

"Well, yes," we said. "By the fingernails, by the eyes—"

"Do you have to know?" someone interrupted.

"Well," he said, "I'd hate to think I'd fallen in love with someone who had nigger blood in her."

"Why?" I asked, surprised.

"Why?" he repeated, exasperated and horrified. "Why?" he said again, at a loss to explain himself to us.

We were frankly staring at him, the first person we had ever met who was so seriously upset about the color of a person's skin.

Father came into the conversation then. Pushing aside his golden papaya, he explained: "These children have grown up here in this land where there is no color distinction. They know nothing at all about race prejudice. All their lives they've chosen their friends because they liked them as people, and these friends range in every shade from white to black. Isn't that so, children?"

"Of course," we answered.

Another friend staying with us at the time, a Brazilian-Lithuanian said: "Brazil is the one country in the world where the white man doesn't consider himself better than the red or the black. You see, here the original Indians were not exterminated or isolated. They were incorporated into the body of the new Brazilian. And when the Negro slaves were freed they became an important element of the Brazilian race. When they got their liberty they became 'free and equal' in every sense of the word."

As he talked I remembered a story every schoolgirl in Brazil knows, the story of how Princess Isabella established a great precedent. At a fashionable court ball where all the leading government dignitaries were mingling socially, a question of etiquette came up as between a white man inviting a negroid woman to the dance floor and a Negro man inviting a white woman to dance with him. One of the high officials invited to the ball was a coal-black Negro. He was at a loss when the dancing began; nobody knew just how to deal with the situation. And the Negro in his natural gentility hesitated to ask a white lady to dance, for fear she would feel humilated.

But Princess Isabella, a sparkling and glowing white Portuguese Brazilian, gave the cue to the court beauties. She walked over to the embarrassed Negro and asked him to share the first dance with her.

The precedent there established has been recited for generations in the schools of our country, just as the story of Washington suffering with his soldiers at Valley Forge to free his country and Lincoln dying to perpetuate the Union is told to every schoolboy in America.

* *

By Charles Wagley

BRAZIL IS WELL KNOWN throughout the world for its racial democracy. Throughout the country racial prejudice and discrimination are relatively subdued, in comparison to the situation in the United States of America, South Africa, and most of Europe. This does not mean that race prejudice is entirely lacking or that physical characteristics are not symbols of social status and thus barriers or aids to social mobility. It does mean, however, that race relations are essentially peaceful and harmonious. The Amazon Valley shares the traditional Brazilian patterns of race relations. Yet the attitudes in regard to different racial groups and the relations between racial groups in Amazon society reflect the distinctive aspects of Amazon history and regional society.

Throughout most of Brazil, Indians rapidly gave way to imported African slaves as the major source of labor. Thus, the descendants of Negro slaves came to form the majority of the lower classes in contemporary society. The Indian, as the memory of his early slave position in colonial society faded, became a romantic figure, and it is today a point of pride for many aristocratic families in South Brazil to number Indians among their forebears. In the Amazon, on the other hand, colonists were not wealthy enough to purchase many African slaves. The few Negroes who did reach such communities as Itá during the colonial period must have been valuable property, men to be instructed and treated with great care—or they were already freemen. In the Amazon the majority of slaves were always Indians.

In Itá all three racial stocks which make up the Brazilian population; namely, the European, the African, and the Indian, are represented. All possible crossings of the three races have taken place to such an extent that classifica-

Reprinted with minor deletions from Charles Wagley, *Amazon Town: A Study of Man in the Tropics* (New York: The Macmillan Co., 1953), pp. 128–140; copyright 1953 by the Macmillan Co., and used with the kind permission of the publisher and the author.

tion of the population of Itá as to physical race is difficult, if not scientifically impossible. Roughly, however, the population of Itá appears to be about 15 per cent European, about 50 per cent mixtures of Europeans with Negroes and Indians in various degrees, about 25 per cent American Indian, and about 10 per cent Negro. It is doubtful whether any of those classed as European, Negro, or Indian are genetically pure; they are classified according to apparent physical characteristics. Our general observations in Itá, as well as the historical evidence, indicates that the American Indian genetic strain predominates in this mixed population.

The people of Itá have their own categories by which they classify their fellow citizens as to physical type. The most frequent ones used are *branco* (white) for those of apparent European or Caucasoid physical type; *moreno* (brunette) for mixtures of various types; *caboclo* for those of apparent Indian physical characteristics; and *preto* (black) for those of apparent Negro physical type. The term *mulato,* so often used elsewhere in Brazil, is only used in Itá in the feminine gender to refer to an attractive woman (for example, *uma mulatinha bonita* [pretty little mulatta] or *uma mulata boa* [good mulatta], but having the meaning of "a well formed wench"). As in most of Brazil, the term "Negro" is seldom heard, and then only in anger. Against anyone who has physical traits suggesting Negroid ancestry, the label *Negro ruim* (bad Negro) is a powerful insult. The term *pardo,* which is so often used in Brazilian newspapers and in official census data to include people of various racial mixtures who are not clearly Negroid, Indian, or European, is not used in Itá except by a few government officials.

The most important criterion for arriving at such classifications in Itá is the quality of the hair and the amount of body hair. The branco has thin straight hair and a heavy beard. The caboclo has black coarse hair. He has "three hairs on his chin for a beard and his hair stands on end despite all efforts to comb it." The kinky hair of the preto is described as *quebra pente* (break-a-comb); people laugh when they tell how such hair strips the teeth from a comb when the preto tries to comb it. Other criteria which are sometimes used as indicators of racial types are a flat nose and thick lips, which are signs of Negroid ancestry; and slant eyes, indicative of Indian parental stock. Skin color is frequently mentioned, but the common diagnostic trait is hair. Itá people say that skin color and facial features are not trustworthy: "They fool one."

The general rule of thumb for Brazil—"The lighter the skin, the higher the class; the darker the skin, the lower the class"—may be said to apply in Itá. The majority of the Itá First Class are in physical appearance either Europeans or mestizos (mixtures) with predominantly European ancestry. The majority of the lower-class groups (the urban Second Class, the farmers, and the collectors) are in physical appearance mestizos with predominantly Indian or Negro ancestry, or they are of apparently pure Indian or Negro physical type.

In Itá the descendants of the Indian and the Negro continue to occupy the lower positions in the social hierarchy. Despite the relatively large population of freemen in the Amazon Valley of Indian and Negro ancestry in the nineteenth century, those inhabitants of Itá with Indian, Negroid, and mestizo physical characteristics are derived ultimately from slave ancestry. As a group, they have not, during the last half-century, been able to rise in the social hierarchy. In Itá, where the effects of mass education and industrialism have not as yet been felt, Indian and Negro physical characteristics are still a symbol of low social status and of slave ancestry. European physical appearance is a symbol of aristocratic slaveowning descent.

Yet there are individuals of all racial types in all social strata. The mayor of Itá, who is, of course, classified as a "white" or First Class, has the copper skin color and the high cheekbones of an Indian. The widow Dona Dora Cesar Andrade, the individual who has perhaps the highest social position in Itá, is a dark mulatta. Her husband was a Negro. The local porter and the town drunk, Oswaldo Costa, at the other extreme of the social scale, is clearly of European descent, having light pigmentation and a heavy beard. His father, some old people remember, was a Portuguese immigrant. There are other cases of dark mestizos and even a few caboclos in the upper class and of European physical types in the lower-class groups. The people of non-European physical types who figure in the upper class are numerous enough to indicate that racial character-istics are not immutable barriers to social advancement. Social position and class membership are economically and socially determined. Physical race is an important but uncertain diagnostic of social position.

Perhaps because of the enormous variety of different racial types in their society, the people of Itá seem acutely conscious of physical characteristics When one wants to describe a specific person, it is usual to do so by saying *aquele branco* (that white) or *aquele preto* (that black), and so on, in about the same way that we might say "that short fat fellow." The relative lack of racial prejudice or discrimination does not mean that people are unaware of physical appearance. On the contrary, they seem more conscious of minute details of racial characteristics than people in the United States.

People do not always agree on the racial classification of people whose physical traits are not clear-cut, who are obviously of mixed racial descent, or whose physical characteristics conflict, so to speak, with their expected social position. Thus, Dona Branquinha was found to be a branca by five people and a morena by six. The vice mayor was classed as a branco by three, a caboclo by three, and a moreno by five people. In classifying Oswaldo Costa, five people out of eleven classified him as a caboclo, despite his marked European features, which the other six took into consideration in calling him a branco. "How can Oswaldo be a branco?" one informant exclaimed, referring to his low social position. Conversely, Dona Dora Cesar Andrade was classed as a morena by nine people, while two others placed her as a branca. Dona Dora had a "white father and a negro mother," one man reasoned, "but her money whitens her skin," He implied that if Dona Dora were of low social rank she might even be classed as a preta. The conflict between race appearance and expected social position reminds one of the Brazilian expression, "A rich Negro is a white and a poor white is a Negro," and of the story told by Henry Koster, the nineteenth century English traveler to Brazil. When Koster asked if a certain high official (*capitão-mór*) was not a "mulatto man," his informant replied, "He was but he is no longer." When Koster asked for an explanation, his informant replied, "Can a *capitão-mór* be a mulatto man?" Social position tends in many cases to override observable physical characteristics in the classification of individuals in terms of "race."

A series of stereotyped concepts and cultural values persists in Itá, re-flecting the social position of people of different racial stocks in the colonial society. Light complexion and the fine facial features of the European, for example, are considered beautiful. In the slave society of the past, it was an advantage for children to inherit the features of their European fathers rather than the Indian or Negroid features of their slave mothers. In Itá, mothers frequently boast of the "fine nose, the light skin, and the fine hair" of their children. Itá men consider the morena, varying from dark brunette to mulatta, to be the most attractive feminine type. They like the "long straight hair of the Tapuia" [Indian], the regular features of the European, and a dark skin. On the other hand, women prefer lighter men. In colonial times it was to the advantage of the Indian or Negro woman to be the concubine or the wife of a European. Emilia, a young girl of Indian-Portuguese descent, made it quite clear that she would not marry a Negro "even if he were perfumed." She would like to marry a "light moreno." Yet Marcos Dias, the twenty-year-old son of the Negro Alfredo Dias, who is a dark mulatto, was considered handsome by many women "in spite of his color and his 'bad' [kinky] hair." Despite their stated preferences, however, people actually seek mates of approximately the same physical type.

Marriages between people of the same physical type or between people of approximately the same skin color are not determined by any restrictions against interracial marriages. They result from the fact that in Itá people tend to marry roughly within the same social stratum. Since people of a social stratum tend to be generally of similar physical type, marriage in one's own social stratum results in marriage between people roughly similar in physical type. That marriages between people of different physical type are not prohibited or even discouraged, was attested by our Itá informants, who remembered numerous cases of branco men marrying women of American Indian or Negro physical type and of pretos and caboclos marrying branco wives. In Itá, whatever segregation exists is based on social class rather than on physical or socially defined race.

The fixed ideas which the people of Itá maintain regarding the innate abilities of people of each "racial" category also reflect the position of each of these groups in colonial society. In Itá, people say that the branco is always "good at business," and a man who is physically a branco arriving in the community would be considered per se "intelligent and well educated," obviously a persistence from the time when most Europeans were landed aristocrats, owners of great rubber-producing forests, or important officials from the capital. Our informants in Itá told us with some amusement of strangers who were brancos but who came dressed in poor clothes and who were found to be illiterate. In asking for a favor, people in Itá are apt to address others as "*Meu branco!*" (My white!), a term which indicates high respect.

As in other parts of Brazil and, for that matter, other parts of the New World, people of mixed Negro and Caucasoid parentage (the moreno of Itá and the mulatto of other regions) are considered treacherous, irascible, and difficult to deal with. Especially those with light skin, "who seem almost branco," are thought to have *mau génio* (bad character), a term used to indicate an irritable person whose mood shifts easily to anger, and not to describe a person's moral character.

The number and variety of the stereotypes held in Itá in regard to the preto seem strangely out of keeping with the small number of Negroes in the present population. There is a veritable aura of prestige tied to the "old Negroes" (*os velhos pretos,* as they are called). The preto is known as a fluent conversationalist and a good storyteller. People say that the "old Negroes" who lived in Itá over a generation ago knew more stories than anyone else and told them better, and a local saying has it that "whoever talks a lot is a Negro." In Itá the Negro is known, in addition, as particularly witty and crafty. And the Negro male is thought of as especially potent sexually. Men tell of the sexual exploits of pretos of their acquaintance and of their greater sexual abilities. The Negro woman and the dark morena are also considered to have greater sexual appetites than the cabocla or the white woman. But the craftiness of the Negro is not limited to situations involving his sexual exploits. There are stories of how the preto outsmarted his master who would punish him for not working, and how the Negro equalized matters with a trader-patron who overcharged him for the goods he purchased.

The stereotypes of the Negro as a good storyteller, and of the Negro as especially potent sexually, are similar indeed to stereotypes regarding the Negro encountered in North America. Furthermore, a series of jokes, many of which are pornographic, are told in the North American South about the Negro. Undoubtedly, these similar stereotypes result from the background of Negro slavery which is common both to southern North America and to northern Brazil. But here the similarity ends. The picture of the "old Negro" as a good storyteller in Itá is not that of Uncle Remus who mildly recounts folk tales to a younger audience. In Itá the picture evoked is that of the colorful raconteur of stories of all kinds, both for the family and for the ears of men in the bar.

The stereotype of the sexual ability of the Negro male may well arise from sexual envy on the part of non-Negro males in Itá, as it seems to in the South of the United States. But it does not serve, as Gunnar Myrdal indicates, for the North American South, "as part of the social control devices to aid in preventing intercourse between Negro males and white females." This very situation is part of the plot of many "off-color" stories, and both legal marriages and extra-marital sexual affairs between Negro males and lighter females are commonplace occurrences in Itá. Nor do the stories told about the Negro serve the function of "proving [his] inferiority"; on the contrary, they have the function of proving a superior quality; namely, his craftiness. In Itá these stories are not told by a white caste about an inferior caste: they are stories told by people of various racial hues about their fellow citizens. In Itá the stereotypes held in regard to the Negro show him in a favorable light. To be sure, they show the Negro as inferior to the white, but he has many attributes which are highly valued in Itá society.

Yet at the same time people in Itá disparage the Negro in a rather warm and humorous manner. They know and make use of widespread Brazilianisms which disparage and belittle the Negro, such as, "If the Negro does not soil when he enters, he does when he leaves." But these sayings are apt to be used by pretos about themselves, and by people in a light joking manner to chide their intimate friends of obvious Negro ancestry. No one in Itá, to our knowledge, is ashamed of Negroid ancestry, and the prestige of the "old Negroes" is high in Itá tradition.

The stereotypes which the people of Itá hold regarding the *tapuia* or the caboclo (American Indian physical type), on the other hand, are not so favorable as those referring to the Negro. The caboclo appears as a good hunter and fisherman. He has a special sensitivity for the habits of animals and he knows almost instinctively where and how to hunt or fish. No one can remember a famous hunter who was not a "caboclo with but three hairs on his chin." Eneas Ramos was known in his earlier years as an excellent hunter. He was born and raised in the rural district near Itá where he learned very early to hunt, but people attribute his skill to the fact that "he is *tapuia*." These concepts are harmless enough, for skill at hunting is something useful and to be admired in Itá. Still caboclo and *tapuia* are used in a sense of dispraisal; people do not use them when speaking directly to people of Indian physical characteristics.

The term, as stated earlier, has a double meaning—one indicating low social status, and another indicating American Indian physical characteristics. Furthermore, most of the stereotypes associated with the caboclo or the *tapuia* are derogatory. The caboclo is considered lazy: "They do not plant gardens, but live from the sale of a little rubber and by fishing for their meals." The caboclo is thought to be timid because he lives isolated in the forest. "They prefer to live like animals, away from others, deep in the forest," one man said. The caboclo, however, is thought to be tricky and exceedingly suspicious. A popular local saying has it that "the suspicious caboclo hangs up his hammock and then sleeps under it." Commercial men say that the caboclo must be watched in any business deal; he will insert a rock in the core of a large ball of crude rubber to increase its weight when he sells it to the trader.

People of American Indian descent, unlike those of Negroid descent, do not like to be reminded of their Indian ancestry. The children playing in front of on Itá home were heard many times teasing the housewife of caboclo physical type. They called her *tapuia* and *índia,* and she would reply in anger, "Go away, your parents are Indians themselves." In the Amazon the Indian, even more often than the Negro, was the slave in colonial society. In the opinion of the European, the Indian was a nude barbarian and of less prestige than the more expensive African slave. Today, Indian physical characteristics are therefore a symbol not only of slave ancestry but also of a social origin in colonial times lower than the Negro's.

INDIA

By Thomas George Spear

THE CONTACT OF TWO RACES so dissimilar in character, in culture and in institutions as the English and the Indian raises the problem of the contact of cultures in its most acute form. Mutual influence is easiest when two cultures

From Thomas George Spear, *The Nabobs: A Study of the Social Life of the English in Eighteenth Century India* (London: Humphrey Milford, Oxford University Press, 1932), Ch. VIII. By permission.

are basically the same; radical difference tends either to mutual repulsion, or to absorption of one by the other. In the case of India easy contact was made more difficult by the institutions as well as by the character of the two peoples. There was first the difficulty of institutions, and secondly the difficulty of character. The Hindus were so used to foreign invasions and the sight of alien communities settled in their midst, that they had become perhaps the most tolerant people upon earth; a man was accepted as a part of India so long as he did not attempt to interfere with others, and was indeed expected to conform to his own rather than any other communities' customs. But the defensive and microscopic division of society into castes, whose life was their religion, and religion their life, at the same time made Hinduism as socially exclusive as it was communally tolerant. Foreign communities could be amongst, but not of the Hindus. Added to this there was the insularity of the English character, as marked in the eighteenth century as to-day, which made the English persist in their customs and habits of life even in most unfavourable circumstances. Count Keyserling's verdict on the modern Englishman finds a clear echo in Maria Graham's description of the English at the Cape: "They live like the English everywhere, as much in the manner they would do at home as circumstances permit."

Politically the English love of liberty, sharpened on the whetstone of the struggle with the Stuarts, encountered a universal despotism; morally the still lingering puritanism met an immense and complicated polytheism; and socially their convivial habits and meat-eating tastes, the very characteristics which in Europe would have formed bridges of fellowship with other nations, aroused only the disgust of the Brahmin and the bania. With the Mussulman, these inhibitions indeed did not apply, but relations with them were soured beforehand by the tradition of hostility and bigotry which had descended from the days of the Crusades. Finally the contact of peoples so dissimilar was further complicated by political factors, such as the earlier pomp and later insignificance of the Moghul Court. Men's opinions of each other are influenced more than they know by irrelevant factors like power, prosperity and prestige, as modern Japan well illustrates. Over such chasms had the bridge of understanding to be thrown.

At the beginning of the eighteenth century the English merchants still lived in [trading] factories under the discipline of the President, and dined at a common table. They received goods from up-country and despatched them to Europe, but they went little abroad from their own settlements except from one factory to another and as occasional ambassadors to the Moghul Court. They had in consequence little social intercourse with Indians as equals. . . . The Company's servants were frequently ignorant of the country languages, and the debased Portuguese which was the *lingua franca* of the coast was all that most of them acquired; complaints were made from time to time of loss and inconvenience caused by the factors' ignorance, and a chaplain was on one occasion proposed as an envoy to the Moghul Court because 'he was well versed in the Persian tongue.' What social intercourse there was took place, therefore, between the Company's servants, the dubashes and the banians. . . .

On the west coast of India, however, conditions were different. In Bombay the initial poverty of the island, the necessity of attracting Indian merchants, and the competition of Surat made the Company much more dependent on

Indian goodwill, and in the Parsis the English found a race much closer to them in temperament than either Hindus or Mohammedans. At Surat the English merchants were in the midst of a populous city under a foreign government, and only one among several European competitors. Here the English were the weaker party, trading by the grace of the Moghuls; Indians and English were on an equality, and it is not surprising to find that there was more in the way of real intercourse here than anywhere else. The English lived in a factory as elsewhere, it is true, but this did not prevent them from dining out and from entertaining strangers and the Moghul magnates were the most welcome guests with their common hunting and drinking tastes. . . .

The banians were held in considerable respect by the Europeans as astute and honest traders, and friendly intercourse went to the length of practical jokes by young factors, who pretended to shoot birds near the banians' gardens in order to see them come out and pray them not to take life. Finally the Company's chapel was bare of all images, in order not to offend Mussulman puritanism. There is no other instance of such regard for Indian susceptibilities by any but missionaries for many a year afterwards. Apart from Surat, therefore, the English were quite separate in ideas as well as in social intercourse. As far as they thought at all, they thought of Mohammedans as profligate and of Hindus as superstitious, and of both as quite incomprehensible. The Indians on their side considered all Europeans in general and the English in particular to be winebibers. . . . The one thing in which the English were unique was their lack of religious observance. The Portuguese, the French and the Dutch all made much of their priests and ministers; the English alone neglected them. . . .

In thought and opinion there was separation and disapproval without contempt. The difference between European and Hindu outlook was too great, the prejudices of Mussulmans were too deep, for either race to have any great attraction for the other, but there was in it no trace of racial feeling or talk of inferiority. Francisco Pelsaert disapproved of the extravagent waste of the Moghuls, Bernier and Manucci exposed the weakness of their armies, but none of them objected to living amongst, or even serving under, the Moghuls. Many of Shah Jehan's artillerymen were Europeans, . . . and the early embassies of the eighteenth century still show the greatest respect. Even down to 1760 a European servant like Macdonald, with more than the ordinary servant's self-respect and all his pride of race, could work and mix familiarly with Portuguese, Parsi and Mussulman servants. There was no 'European Third' in the eighteenth century. The mutual opinions of Indians and English in the early years were largely compounded of ignorance and prejudice, but they contained in them little trace of racial bias. Europeans and Indians disapproved of each other's social systems, but they had not yet the tolerant pity which comes of a sense of inborn superiority. Pride had not yet been sanctified by science; patriotism still meant belief in one's own country as the best, but not the conviction that all other countries were inevitably inferior.

When the position of the East India Company changed towards the middle of the century, the character of racial relations changed also. On the one hand the old merchants occupied new positions, on the other the supply of Englishmen greatly increased, first as soldiers and then as administrators and traders. The result was to set in motion a double current, of increasing contact and knowledge of Indian life, and of increasing contempt of everything Indian as irrational, superstitious, barbaric and typical of an inferior civilization. The first was bred of contact with the Hindu and Mussulman aristocracy, the second with the servant class of the Presidency towns; the first was typical of the period between 1760 and the return of Hastings in 1785; the second perhaps reaches its zenith in Macaulay's famous description of Sanskrit and Persian literature. As the Anglo-Indian function developed from trade to empire, from embassies to administration, the criterion of judgment swung round from the naïvely patriotic belief that one's own customs are necessarily the best, to the equally naive idea that the strongest is necessarily the best. But before the political change was complete there was a period of political equality, when the East India Company was one of the chief powers in India without yet becoming the paramount power. The old traders had become diplomatists—and often financiers—and had not yet been ousted by the soldier turned empire-builder, the Dundas recruit from Scotland, or aristocratic governors from England. There was not only opportunity but necessity for intimate acquaintance with Indian manners and customs, and most government officials were thrown back by their work to a large extent on Indian society. The Indian Princes on their side had quite ceased to regard the Company as troublesome traders, and were displaying an increasing interest in European methods in order to discover the secret of European success. For the present, then, the tide of racialism was quite unperceived in the cross-current of mutual contact and interest, and there ensued a period of cosmopolitan intercourse. It was the Golden Age of the adventurer and the diplomatist.

This new social intercourse was more marked with Mussulmans and Parsis than with Hindus, owing to the caste difficulty of interdining. It had its centre at Madras, where the Nawab held his court in the Chepauk Palace, in Bombay, where the relations of Europeans with Parsis had long been closer than with any other communities, and at towns like Lucknow and Murshidabad where English residents were stationed at Indian courts. . . .

Very scrupulous and very European was the cultured Serfagi, Rajah of Tanjore, who was educated by the missionary Swartz, in whose memory he wrote the first example of English verse by an Indian. He became a student of English science and literature as well as a patron of Indian art, and was English enough in his manners to give a banquet in the English style at his accession.

The Nawab of Arcot was only the first and most long-lived example of such social and convivial intercourse. "Nabobs and Soubahs throughout India," wrote the authors of The European in India in 1800, "are in the habit of giving public breakfasts, and of occasionally inviting all the European gentry in their vicinity to grand dinners, nautches or dances, and other entertainments." On both sides there was much give-and-take; the English had long acquired a taste for nautches, and developed new ones for elephant fights and hookah smoking; the nawabs on their part experimented with English food and drink. "Many excellent Mussulmans," say the same authors, "are above prejudice, and often eat substantial slices of ham under the designation of Belatty Heron or English venison." Salabat Jung, chief of Ellichpur and a tributary of the Nizam, entertained the officers of several regiments to dinner during the Maratha war and attended the dinner himself, an action which was favourably contrasted with the conduct of Hindu and Maratha chiefs. Before the coming of Cornwallis many Indians were still in positions of authority in British India, and reciprocal entertainments were common. After the dinner or the breakfast there were usually entertainments, the chief being cock and elephant fights, nautches and occasionally plays.

In the north the two chief centres of social intercourse were the Palace of Mubarak-ad-daula, the Nawab of Bengal at Murshidabad, and the court of the Nawab Wazir of Oudh. Significantly enough no memories of the Black Hole prevented European intercourse with the Mussulman princes; wherever they were assured of a luxurious and hospitable welcome they gathered like flies to the honey-pot. The same rule applied to the "East Indians," at that time segregated from English society; "anyone of this class," says F. J. Shore, "whose circumstances will allow him to give good entertainments, will not find the English (in Bengal at least) at all backward in partaking of them." At Mursh- idabad there was, from the time that the Company "stood forth as dewan," a resident at the court of the fainéant nawab, and Europeans in his bodyguard; the office of Resident was considered so lucrative that great sums were ex- pended in order to obtain it. The friends of the Resident were entertained in the European manner by the Nawab, and amused themselves with purdah inter- views with the Begams. This went on until Cornwallis laid the axe to the tree in 1787, and withdrew all the officers under the suspicion of deriving "unjustifiable advantages.". . . The Resident was the permanent head of this society. The nawabs on their part, from the time of Asaf-ad-daula showed a lively interest in things European. They were fond of giving public breakfasts, sometimes with elephant fights to follow, and not infrequently entertained the whole Euro- pean community to dinner. . . .

In the upper provinces further amusement was provided by the recurrent appearance of fugitive Moghul princes like that of Shah Alam in Allahabad from 1767 to 1770, and of his son Mohammad Bakht in Oudh in 1784. Even the Emperor at Delhi habitually granted interviews to every casual traveller who penetrated thither. In Hindustan this social intercourse reached its fullest development with military adventurers like the Comte de Boigne, General Perron, George Thomas and Colonel Skinner, who spent their lives in the service of Indian Courts or as independent adventurers among Indian princes. Social intercourse was constant and unrestrained, and the manner of life as much Indian as English.

The intercourse of Mussulmans with Europeans did not extend to European ladies as yet. The difficulty was Indian rather than English, for the English ladies did not share the scruples of later generations about mixing with men whose wives remained in purdah. Warren Hastings related to his wife his mistake in allowing the Nawab Wazir to see two English ladies, and his efforts to assure him that they were by no means representative of English beauty; and Lord Valentia recorded the disgust of the Wazir's son at the appearance of two English ladies who insisted on attending a joint dinner at Lucknow. In both instances the initiative came from the English side, the moral recoil from the Indian, and in both cases English public opinion sympathized with the Mussulman feelings. In this particular matter the freedom of the eighteenth century woman went too far, but on the other hand her lack of Victorian tastes and taboos removed one of the greatest obstacles to cordial racial relations.

They had no objection to the hookah, and occasionally smoked it themselves; they freely attended and enjoyed nautches; they adopted the fashion of the turban and carried it to London. Society at that time was predominantly masculine and the women had perforce to accept the masculine point of view; but the later change in their outlook was perhaps as much due to the increasing regard for propriety and sober deportment, the incipient spirit of Victorianism which the Evangelical Revival fostered among the fashionable in London and Calcutta, as to a mere increase in numbers and a higher standard of refinement. It is one of the misfortunes of the history of racial relations in India that as soon as Mussulman society began to rid itself of its traditional feelings about the unveiled woman, European society imported a fresh stock of prejudices about the veiled woman of the purdah, the joint product of the evangelical missionary and of new-born racial pride.

In Hindustan and Bengal the intercourse between Europeans and Mussulmans was almost entirely with princes and nobles. They had in a sense common trades as soldiers, as diplomatists, as members of a governing class, and common tastes in hunting, feasting, wine and nautches. The prestige of military success had given every European an entry into aristocratic Indian society, while the cancer of racial pride had not yet destroyed his enjoyment of it. But with the merchants and bankers of Bengal there was little intercourse at any time; the temperament of Bengali banians was too antipathetic to that of English adventurers for contact ever to advance beyond occasional formal dinners. In Bombay, however, it was otherwise; into the relations between English and Parsi merchants crept something of the cordiality that existed between English and Muslim lords in Hindustan. At the beginning of the century, the Parsis still kept their own customs. In 1770 the cheerful Macdonald was treating two Parsis in a "Roman Catholic" tavern; by this time the Parsis had many Englishmen in their employ as ships' captains, and social intercourse was frequent. They often borrowed carriages from the English for their weddings ("which were lent with great good humor"), and invited them to their feasts. At this time men and women were still segregated, but by the end of the century they had become largely Europeanized in their manners as well as in their feasts. Their dinners were now complete with tables and chairs, the rooms with mirrors and prints; and what entitled them to even more respect, they owned "nearly all Bombay." Much wine, "specially Madeira," flowed at these gatherings. They kept their own carriages and horses now and had two or three houses each; their westernization was already largely complete except for their adherence to early marriage and their failure to educate their women. The same social intercourse also extended to Mussulman merchants of Bombay; one "jovial, hearty fellow" named Chillabie, "broke through the rites of his religion to have company with the English gentlemen and to drink wine" as early as 1772. The difference between this and the aristocratic intercourse of the upper provinces was that, while the one continued to develop into the modern Bombay cosmopolitanism, the other after a brief period of brilliance faded away into the drab hues of racial and social exclusiveness.

With the Hindus there is not so much evidence of extensive social intercourse. Of the Hindu princes, the Rajputs were too distant to come into contact with the English, and the Marathas too independent and suspicious to encourage very cordial relations. Officers attending a durbar of the Peishwa had to remove their boots until the nineteenth century, when their wounded feelings found vent in an arrangement by which uncovering the head was considered an equivalent; and they generally considered the Mussulman princes far more 'courteous and free' than the Marathas.

But the seal of social intercourse is personal friendship, and this, too, had its place in the life of the eighteenth century. At that time the best of the Company's officials were acquainted with Persian and many of them became genuinely interested in Persian literature. This is seen at its best in the encouragement given by Hastings to Oriental studies, in the enthusiasm of Sir William Jones, Wilkins and Colebrooke, and in its popular and vulgarized form in the songs first learned from the nautch girls and translated into popular drinking songs. Such knowledge and such tastes gave them common interests with the Vakils, Nawabs and Rajahs whom they met, and intimate friendships resulted. Beneram Pandit, the Vakil of Scindia, was intimate with Hastings, General Palmer and Chapman; Hastings in recording a meeting with him at Benares writes of him to his wife as "one whom you know I reckon among my first friends." With the Nawab Asaf-ad-daula of Lucknow he had also a close friendship, though there was in it a note more of admiration of a younger for an elder than the equal relationship of scholars which existed between him and Beneram. Nor did these friendships cease with absence or with Hastings' departure to England. As late as 1802 the Nawab Wazir offered him through Palmer a pension to tide over financial difficulties, and Palmer in his periodical letters to Hastings frequently mentions the 'anxious inquiries' of his old Indian friends. Beneram's brother Bissambu Pandit, Ganga Gobind Singh, Ali Ibrahim Khan, the incorruptible judge of Benares whom Cornwallis refused to supersede, and his son were others in the Hastings circle. Charles Turner, Chapman and Scrofton wrote about them in the same way. Faizulli Khan, wrote Turner in 1799, was learning Greek from the Armenian Padre Parthenio. In 1789 Palmer forwarded a letter from "that excellent man Tufferzul Hussain Khan" who "is respected and admired by all who know him." Chapman wrote of "my friend and fellow traveller," Bissambu Pandit, than whom, wrote Thompson, "none is more sincere in his devotion." In 1801 Palmer lamented the loss "of that excellent man Taffazul Hussain Khan and with him all that was wise and good among the Mussulmans." This is the language of friends and of intimates, untainted by any breath of patronage or racial pride. They appear in private letters between intimates where no possible motives for tact or circumlocution would operate. All the Indians concerned, it will also be noticed, with the exception of the Nawab Wazir, were officials or Mussulman gentry; men of culture, but not men of princely rank who might enjoy the free-masonry of aristocratic feeling. The Englishman did not yet wait for the Indian to learn English before he would talk to him, but learned himself Persian instead; he did not demand a complete 'western education' before a man could be considered completely civilized, but enjoyed and himself composed Persian poetry. Hastings, in public the Hastin Bahadur of pomp and occasional high-handedness, was in private the most unassuming and friendly of men. This is the reason that he was 'anxiously enquired for' twenty years after he had left India forever, and that his name became a legend.

But as the century drew to its close, a change in the social atmosphere gradually came about. The frequency of grand dinners and 'reciprocal entertainments' decreased, the formation of intimate friendship with Indians ceased, except in obscure corners of the country where administrators like Sir Thomas Munro or diplomatists like Colonel Tod or land settlement officers were thrown back upon Indian society. The higher posts of the Government were filled with appointments from England, its designs became more imperial and its attitude more haughty and aloof. The gulf which Mussulman Nawabs and English *bon viveurs,* diplomatic pandits and English scholars had for a time bridged over began ominously to widen again. With it the attitude of the average English-man changed also from one of disapproval of Hindu 'superstition' and Mus-sulman 'bigotry' or philosophic interest in Hindu mythology and the Golden Age and the histories of Moghul glory, into one of contempt for an inferior and conquered people. A 'superiority complex' was forming which regarded India not only as a country whose institutions were bad and people corrupted, but one which was by its nature incapable of ever becoming any better. An attitude of superiority requires not only that a people and its institutions should be bad but also that they should be incapable of improvement, and for this reason expressions of pity, of patronage or of "long-suffering understanding" are often more expressive of that attitude of mind than the most full-blooded denunciations. Many hard sayings inspired by the heat of a temporary irritation can be forgiven, but it is the polite disdain which founds its tolerance on the basis of necessitarianism, that rankles in the mind like a festering sore. It is one of the ironies of Indo-European relations in India, that the purging of the administration coincided with the widening of the racial gulf. Cornwallis not only made a new aristocracy by the Permanent Settlement, he also made a new governing class by his exclusion of all Indians from the higher governmental posts. . . . Corruption was stamped out at the cost of equality and co-operation. In his own mind, as in the commonly accepted view, there was a necessary connexion between the two measures; "every native of Hindustan," he said, "I verily believe, is corrupt." As with the land question, he found an intricate problem and honestly attempted to solve it, and as with the land question his solution had a fallacious simplicity which gave it an illusion of success. He thought English corruption could be solved by reasonable salaries, and did not stop to consider that the advantage of Indian goodwill made it at least worth trying as a remedy for Indian corruption also. He never thought of creating an Indian imperial bureaucracy on the model of Akbar's mansabdars, which by special training, proper salaries and the encouragement of equal treatment, promotion and honours, might have been bound to the Company as the Moghul officials were bound to the Emperor. His honesty enabled him to appreciate single-mindedness when he found it in individuals, as in the case of Ali Ibrahim Khan, but his knowledge of the country was not wide enough or his insight into character deep enough to enable him to perceive the great reservoir of loyalty and devoted service which might have been tapped to fertilize the parched garden of Bengal administration. So the garden was watered by thin sprays of efficiency from small watering-cans of duty instead of by the streams and fountains of co-operation and common ideals, until in our own days, instead of the rose trees and lotus flowers that had been looked for, came up stubborn cactuses of criticism and bitterness. Then as now first-class character was no substitute for third-class brains, nor did innocency of intention mitigate the effect of the blunders of ignorance.

This change in the social atmosphere was subtle in its effects and slow in its operation. The first step was the arrival of Cornwallis, who came as a reformer of abuses with plenary powers, and brought with him the view-point of the India House and Whitehall, no previous knowledge of the country, and a lack of that imaginative sympathy which would have made up for his ignorance. He lived simply and hated ostentation, but the atmosphere of the Governor-General's house became inevitably more English and more Olympian; he had no close contact with Indians and did not notice their gradually increasing estrangement. As his intentions became better known, distrust changed to respect, but the social estrangement continued unchecked. . . . Measures like that of withdrawing all Europeans except the Resident from Murshidabad, while fully justified by the facts, had the further effect of tending to separate the two races. Finally came the limitation of the higher government ranks to Europeans only. In 1790 the Nizamat courts with their criminal jurisdiction were abolished, and in the Zillah courts Europeans presided with Indian assessors. . . . The old princely ceremonial was modified at the same time, no nazars were to be presented to princes in person except to the house of Timur; the Shahzada was informed that the customary honours paid to Moghul princes would not be provided if he visited Calcutta; Sa'adat Ali of Lucknow and the Nawab Mubarak-ad-daula on similar visits were refused the usual royal honours, and no one was appointed to welcome them. The warmth of geniality and the punctilio of etiquette, so essential to friendly social relations, were now lacking; every Indian felt that he was no longer a *persona grata* at the Government House. The effect of the closing of the avenues of official and especially legal appointments was to drive the old governing classes into seclusion and to leave none but the clerk, the banian and the shroff to represent Indian character and culture to the average Englishman.

To Cornwallis succeeded Sir John Shore, whose rigid views nullified the advantage which his knowledge of the country gave him. With Wellesley the process proceeded apace. He habitually adopted towards princes like the Nawab of Arcot and the Nawab Wazir of Oudh the tone of a hectoring schoolmaster, and could hardly be expected to notice at all the existence of those of lesser rank. By him Indians were excluded along with Anglo-Indians from the regular entertainments at Government House. . . . With him the habit of speaking or writing of Indians as of some strange order of beings unaccountable in their constitutions and actions, to be dazzled by ostentation and to be impressed by invincible power, from being the custom of the Calcutta class of 'low European' became the fashionable and dominant attitude. . . .

This change of feeling and attitude is confirmed from other sources, which provide many details to illustrate the general attitude. "Europeans," wrote Captain Williamson in 1810 with twenty years' experience of the country, "have little connexion with natives of either religions," except for business. No Hindus and few Mussulmans would eat with Europeans; they would not join the occasional nautches, wild-beast shows or feasts to which they still asked Europeans. Mrs. Graham, visiting Calcutta in 1810 after living in Bombay and staying in Madras, deplored that "the distance kept up between the Europeans and the natives, both here and at Madras, is such that I have not been able to get acquainted with any native family as I did in Bombay. . . . This mixture of nations ought, I think, to weaken national prejudices, but among the English at least, the effect seems to be diametrically opposite. Every Briton appears to pride himself on being outrageously a John Bull." Amongst the Europeans the feeling was strong that Indians should always be subordinated to Europeans. The maintenance of "prestige" had now become a dominant factor of policy, and as usual in such cases, was most piously believed in by those who had very little prestige to lose. The necessity "of upholding the British character" was now so well understood that "nothing short of absolute compulsion would actuate a magistrate to commit a European woman on a charge for neglect of duty, inebriety, insolence or other such impropriety." In such an atmosphere there was no room for the breath of social intercourse. As the new century advanced, things grew worse rather than better, until the time of Bentinck, who achieved fame by permitting Indians to drive to the Governor-General's house in carriages. By that time, in contrast with their attitude to the feasts of Warren Hastings' days, Mussulmans considered dining with Europeans degrading. On going to a station no Englishman thought of calling on the notables of the district, as was once done as a matter of course; instead certificates of respectability were required of the notables before they could be guaranteed a chair when they visited the officer. In the courts no sitting accommodation whatever was provided for spectators or for any officials of the court except the judge. In Calcutta many writers expected every Indian to salute them, and many, it is said, were so ignorant of Hindustani that after several years they could not count beyond twenty. . . .

One of the more fundamental causes of this social estrangement is to be found in the increasing number of women in the settlements. By another irony the same influence which improved the morals of the settlers increased the widening racial gulf. As women went out in large numbers, they brought with them their insular whims and prejudices, which no official contact with Indians or iron compulsion of loneliness ever tempted them to abandon. Too insular in most cases to interest themselves in alien culture and life for its own sake, they either found society and a house amongst their own people, or in the last resort returned single and disconsolate to Europe. The average Anglo-Indian was equally insular, and his contact had usually first been established by the tyranny of solitude and in time sanctified by custom and tradition. So with the advent of women in large numbers a new standard was introduced, one set of customs and traditions died out, and another equally rigid and not necessarily better took its place. A woman's reaction to strange conditions was instinctive rather than rational, but rationalization quickly followed. The attitude of airy disdain and flippant contempt had the background of fear which an unknown and incalculable environment inevitably excites in everyone, but above all in the ignorant and the emotional. For the men the establishment of English homes in place of the prevalent zenanas withdrew them still more from Indian ways of thought and living, and the acquisition of homes and families gave them something to lose which they had never had before, and thus made them the victims of the same fear. It is this which accounts for the strange panics which from time to time agitate European communities in the east, and for their apparently unaccountable ferocity at times of crisis. This change of attitude did not pass unnoticed at the time and is thus rather crudely described.

Every youth, who is able to maintain a wife, marries. The conjugal pair become a bundle of English prejudices and hate the country, the natives and everything belonging to them. If the man has, by chance, a share of philosophy and reflection, the woman is sure to have none. The 'odious blacks', the 'nasty heathen wretches', the 'filthy creatures' are the shrill echoes of the 'black brutes', the 'black vermin' of the husband. The children catch up this strain. I have heard one, five years old, call the man who was taking care of him a 'black brute'. Not that the English generally behave with cruelty, but they make no scruple of expressing their anger and contempt by the most opprobrious epithets, that the language affords. Those specially who, while young, are thrown much among natives, become haughty, overbearing and demi-Asiatic in their manners.

Another contributory factor to this growing racial estrangement was the influence of the evangelical missionaries and chaplains. While their personal relations with Indians—at any rate in the case of the missionaries—were usually on terms of equality, their repugnance to Hinduism and Islam and all the 'abominations of heathenism' was so great, and their denunciations of them so violent, that they propagated the idea of Indian society as irredeemably corrupt and degraded. Henry Martyn, the most violent of them all, lived the simplest of lives and frequently courted European censure by mixing with Maulvis and Pandits and by such little acts as walking about in the evening instead of riding and driving; at the same time the violence of his denunciations confirmed the Europeans in their belief that few Indians were fit to associate with, that it was a waste of time to mix with them, and that the merit of missionaries consisted not in giving their lives to the service of India, but in condescending so far and giving up the privileges of a gentleman. The attitude of Brown who "never permitted the heathen to obtrude their abominations on Europeans if he could prevent it," of the Lutheran Kiernander by his tacit abandonment of work amongst the Bengalis for the more congenial employment of converting the Roman Catholic Eurasians, both had the same effect. Swartz of Tanjore and Carey of Serampore rose above this attitude, but the one was too remote from European settlements, the other too suspect for his anabaptism to have much influence....

But the principal cause was the simple though often neglected fact of the rapid increase of the European community after 1760. The influx was largely military, but also partly official and commercial. The soldiers consisted largely of royal troops serving in India for a few years only with a maximum of national pride and a minimum of desire to understand the country; the rest formed a nucleus of an English settlement in Calcutta and Madras, which lived its own life, ran its own shops and newspapers, entertained itself at balls and routs and concerts, admired or criticized itself on the Chowringhee Road and congratulated itself at the Governor-General's receptions. Except for the Rajahs and Nawabs who entertained officers and who declined in social importance as they decreased in power and political prestige, none of these often met Indians except as servants or on terms of business. The social ideal changed from a desire to live like a Nawab to a desire to make each settlement and cantonment down to the smallest station a replica of an English model. As the ideal and ambitions of the majority swung from India to England (powerfully aided as already noticed by feminine influence) there was no influence left to overcome the natural insularity and exclusiveness of a highly self-conscious and self-confident community. India became an unknown country to the English inhabitants of Calcutta and Madras, and what is unknown a natural conservatism will always condemn. So in 1827 "it was the extremity of bad taste to appear in anything of Indian manufacture—neither muslin, silk, flowers nor even ornaments however beautiful." The sentiment became general, which is still sometimes expressed, "How nice India would be if it wasn't for the Indians." Calcutta fixed its gaze on the pomp of Vauxhall and Brighton, and it had no time to perceive the treasures which lay at its feet.

Racial feeling assumes many forms. In its simplest form, there is pure colour prejudice, the repulsion felt by the sight of a man of strange colour. This is a temporary feeling which disappears on further acquaintance. So in the early days Indians were always called "blacks" by Europeans, but this did not affect their ordinary intercourse. But if the general condition of free intermixture is lacking, this colour sense may easily become a first barrier to intercourse, as in fact happened in the society of the later century. But since it depends on ignorance and novelty, it is comparatively of little importance.

The next variety is formed of a union of colour-feeling and the particularity which all nations have in varying degrees. Everything foreign or new is judged from the standpoint of familiar customs and condemned in proportion as it differs. This prejudice is strong enough amongst those of different nations in any circumstances, and it can therefore hardly be absent when those of different race make contact with each other. The man who calls the French frog-eaters and the Germans beer-swillers is likely to call the Italians dagoes, the Mussulmans "profligates" and Hindus "superstitious." This is specially characteristic of the uneducated, and in India it was particularly prevalent among the soldiers. But this general condemnation does not preclude individual intimacy, and so it was the same men of whose conduct Hindus most complained, the "low Europeans" of the records, who adopted the Indian mode of life most extensively and inter-married most freely.

Beyond this instinctive level comes the stage where moral judgments begin to be made. This is the special sphere of the half-educated who judge one culture from the standpoint of another and condemn it before they have ever understood it. As this reaction is more subtle, it is proportionately more difficult to combat, since the defects it points out are real, while the virtues which exist are omitted or glossed over. Indeed, the more one's view is limited to the values and standards of one's own culture, the more convinced will one become of the defects of other cultures. This attitude was, of course, very rife in the eighteenth century, the Hindus being condemned for superstition, exclusiveness, pacifism and divisions, the Mussulmans for bigotry, profligacy and intolerance.

But even such generalizations do not preclude appreciation of and friendly relations between individuals. The next stage in race feeling is where the individuals of a race, as well as its specific institutions, are held to be lacking in essential virtues. Here it is that race superiority as a doctrine and not as a blind instinct first emerges. In the eighteenth century it was sometimes sanctified by an exclusive type of Christianity which assumed in Christians a virtue denied to infidels, as in the twentieth it is dignified by the pseudo-science of writers of the type of Mr. Lothrop Stoddard under the catchword of racial characteristics. It found expression in the eighteenth century—more commonly at the end than at the beginning—in the description of all Hindus as effeminate and servile, and of Mussulmans as cruel and faithless. On the other hand, Indians returned the compliment by considering all Europeans to be winebibbers, proud, unscrupulous and licentious.

The last stage in the formation of a superiority complex is that which not only regards a people as inferior collectively and individually but also as one "on whose nature Nurture can never stick." To-day this sort of view has to seek what support it can get from science since it can get none from religion, but it has always been widely held under the name of "practical experience." It is the worst as it is the most subtle of these forms; it breeds a hopeless tolerance which is perhaps worse than the frank crudity of the colour maniac, it paralyzes and discourages all effort in the victims.

All these forms were present in varying degrees in India in the eighteenth century, but until the latter half never in so strong a form as to segregate completely the two races. Then what Cornwallis had unwittingly sown Wellesley and Lord Hastings reaped, and the separation which was already a fact became a dogma. Broadly speaking, race prejudice at the beginning of the century was instinctive and disappeared with time and better acquaintance; at the end it was doctrinal and precluded the acquaintance which might have removed it. India settled down to a period of social segregation and it was left for Ram Mohan Roy with his advocacy of western reforms and Bentinck with his greater sympathy towards India to lay the foundation of a new and better spirit.†

JAMAICA

*

By Leonard Broom‡

JAMAICA HAS LONG ATTRACTED the interest of American sociologists. Here a British colony, close to our shores, experienced color slavery and arrived at a kind of "race relations" different from that developed in the United States. Jamaica, passing through a brief stage termed "Apprenticeship," achieved emancipation of her slaves a third of a century earlier than did the United States, and without civil war. Her whites constitute a small minority.

The basic racial pattern of Jamaica was laid down in the eighteenth century.

---

†[Note on the meaning of some words used in this reading: dubash—the Governor's Tamil secretary, steward; banian—a Bengali Hindu of the commercial class and often a Brahmin, a steward or chief of an establishment; hookah—a curved implement or tube for smoking; jemadar—in charge of the palanquin bearers; nabob—an Anglo-Indian who has amassed wealth; palanquin—a hammoch-like conveyance, often enclosed, borne on the shoulders of men by poles; dewan—a native manager of a government establishment, a confidential servant; begam—a Hindu woman of rank; durbar—official reception: zenana—establishment for women, the East Indian harem; ghee—a solid white oil obtained from a tree of northern India; nautch—an entertainment the principle of which is dancing girls; nawab—a Moslem ruler or viceroy in India, by courtesy any person of rank and distinction.]

‡ Adapted from Leonard Broom, "The Social Differentiation of Jamaica," *American Sociological Review*, XIX (April, 1954), 115–124. With permission.

At the end of the seventeenth century there were an estimated ten thousand whites and forty thousand slaves, principally blacks. Less than a century later the whites numbered about eighteen thousand, but there were a quarter of a million slaves—an increase of over two hundred thousand. An additional increment of whites in the first quarter of the nineteenth century was followed by a decline after the Apprenticeship period. By 1844 there were less than sixteen thousand whites in the Island, and their number has since fluctuated little. The census of 1943 reported 13,400, hardly more than the white population of 1775. Meanwhile the colored (mixed bloods) increased from 68,500 in 1844 to 216,000 in 1943, and the black population increased from 293,000 in 1844 to nearly a million in 1943. The whites, barely maintaining their numbers, have steadily declined in proportion from about 4 per cent of the population in 1844 to 1 per cent a century later. Table 1 summarizes the changing racial composition of Jamaica.

Table 1. The Racial Composition of Jamaica, 1673–1943*

Year	Source[1]		Black	Colored	White	Chinese	East Indian	Total
1673	N	a	9.5		7.7			17.2
	per cent		55		45			100
1696	N	b	40.0		10.0			(47.4)[2]
	per cent		84		21			
1736	N	a	80.0		8.0			(94.2)
	per cent		85		8			
1775	N	a	200.0		12.7			(209.6)
	per cent		95		6			
1788	N	b	256.0		18.3			(291.4)
	per cent		88		6			
1793	N	c	261.4[3]		30.0			291.4
	per cent		90		10			100
1844	N	a	293.0	68.5	15.8			377.4
	per cent		78	18	4			100
1861	N	a	346.4	81.1	13.8			441.3
	per cent		79	18	3			100
1871	N	a	392.7	100.1	13.1			506.1
	per cent		78	20	2			100
1881	N	d	444.2	109.9	14.4	.1	11.0	580.8
	per cent		76	19	3	....	2	100
1891	N	d	488.6	121.9	14.7	.5	10.1	639.5
	per cent		76	19	2	....	2	100
1911	N	d	630.2	163.2	15.6	2.1	17.4	831.4
	per cent		76	20	2	....	2	100
1921	N	d	660.4	157.2	14.5	3.7	18.6	858.1
	per cent		77	18	2	....	2	100
1943	N	d	965.9	216.2	13.4	12.4	26.5	1237.1[4]
	per cent		78	18	1	1	2	100

* Frequencies are given in thousands; percentages are given to the nearest percent; . . . . signifies less than 1 percent.

[1] The sources follow. (a) W. J. Gardner, A History of Jamica, 2nd Ed., 1909, passim. (b) W. L. Burn, Emancipation and Apprenticeship in the British West Indies, 1937, passim. (c) Bryan Edwards, The History, Civil and Commercial, of the British Colonies in the West Indies, 1793, Vol. 1, p. 230. (d) Eighth Census of Jamaica, 1943, p. 93.

[2] Numbers in parentheses are census estimates which do not equal the sum of the racial components.

[3] This figure includes 1,400 Maroons, 250,000 Negro slaves and 10,000 "freed Negroes and people of colour," Edwards, loc. cit.

[4] Includes "Not otherwise specified."

Historians of the British Caribbean have amply documented the drain of white population out of the area. The high sugar prices in the latter half of the eighteenth century accelerated the movement, for the planters could live luxuriously in England on the returns from their holdings. According to Ragatz, "When the permanent decline in revenues from tropical American holdings . . . set in, overseas owners as a class failed to return, take personal possession and salvage what they might, but instead, after exhausting credit, they transferred their estates to holders of their paper, while planters actually in the West Indies, becoming hopelessly entangled in debt . . . forsook the colonies." The practice of sending the planters' children to England for their education, whence they often failed to return or returned miseducated for colonial life, reinforced this tendency. The consequence was a heavy drain of the trained talent out of the Island and an abdication of insular responsibilities to multiple office holders, agents, and mortgagees. In their turn the agents often departed. "Social stability was . . . far to seek; how far must be clear to anyone who cares to search among the names of the chief men in Jamaica in the eighteen-thirties . . . for the names of men who held . . . offices a hundred years before." The reasons for this discontinuity are to be found in vital as well as migratory causes. The sex ratio was heavily masculine, the life expectancy of the poorer immigrants, the clerks and overseers was exceedingly low, and the practice of concubinage reduced legitimate fertility.

Throughout Jamaican history the whites were thus drained off as fast as they arrived, and a vacuum was created in positions of intermediate responsibility. One segment of the population, the manumitted or free born colored, was always present to enter the vacuum. Many of these were children of the planters and their concubines. Some had European education, and even those less trained compared favorably enough with the impoverished, forgotten men of the plantation, the English clerks and indentured whites. *The precondition for the differentiation of the black and colored populations was then established,* just as it was in South Africa, Brazil, and the United States. But in Jamaica the lack of an adequate population of qualified whites, or indeed of unqualified whites, afforded the colored a greater opportunity to differentiate themselves from the blacks.

Spanish definitions of color long persisted in Jamaica, and in the eighteenth century the recognized gradations were black, mulatto, terceroon, quadroon, mustee, musteefino, and white. The child of a white and a musteefina (or mustee, or quadroon, according to various writers) was called "English, free of taint." Thus Edwards at the end of the eighteenth century wrote: "The children of a White and Quinteron consider themselves as free from all taint of the Negro race. Every person is so jealous of the order of their tribe or cast, that if, thru inadvertence, you call them by a degree lower than what they actually are, they are highly offended."

Lightness, valued as a promise of higher status, became valued for itself, and status became equated with lightness. The early literature often refers to colored free men but black slaves. Certainly the differential statuses, which are all too apparent in the 1943 census, are reinforced by the selective perception of census takers. For example, a phenotypically black civil servant of the upper categories is most likely to be classified as colored. A dark colored peasant is most likely to be classified black.

Differential manumission operated so that, according to Gardner, "the greatest portion of those fairer than the mulattoes were free" at the beginning of the nineteenth century, and the "creole distinction of brown lady, black woman was . . . strictly observed; and except in the smaller towns, different shades of color did not readily mingle." John Stewart reported in 1823 that 95 per cent of the white males had colored mistresses and that into the hands of their male children "much of the property of the country (was) fast falling," certainly an overstatement of the case. Polite society ruled by white women might admit a few highly educated and well-to-do colored men, but colored women were much more rigidly excluded. The distinction between the society of men and of women presumably was a by-product of concubinage, and its effects persist to this day.

If colored persons had little or no entree to high society, some were accumulating the necessary equipment for substantial middle class status as early as the 18th century. An Assembly inquiry in 1763 showed that property valued at 250,000 pounds sterling had been left to colored children. The list included four sugar estates and thirteen cattle pens. The legislature then passed a statute invalidating bequests by whites to non-whites in excess of 1,200 pounds. Subsequently by individual acts the Assembly from time to time permitted what it had expressly forbidden. Inheritance of property by colored persons from colored persons was unrestricted, so that the accumulation of wealth in the hands of the colored was only retarded.

The colored population made most general progress in the urban areas where they entered the professions, administrative jobs and trades. Even before Apprenticeship they comprised the majority of the voters in Kingston and in three of the parishes. Had they voted *en bloc,* they could have elected at least nine of the forty-five members of the Assembly, but prior to 1837, there were only three colored members. In 1837 eight were elected.

Here is a rough approximation of the status ladder as it appeared in the Island in the first quarter of the 19th century, before Apprenticeship and Emancipation:

(1) The invisible man, the absentee landlord; the executive; the resident creole planters and the top representatives of overseas companies—all whites.
(2) Estate attorneys and agents and well-to-do Scottish and Jewish merchants; some professionals—all whites.
(3) Other merchants and urban specialists, including some colored; a few colored planters and professionals.
(4) Colored artisans, tradesmen and semi-professionals.
(5) Brown slaves not in field labor.
(6) Black slaves working in the fields.

The first two categories were, of course, very small in numbers. The indicated correlation of color and status was not perfect. For example, blacks could be found in the levels immediately above field slavery, and there were some colored at the very bottom. An additional, I trust unnecessary, caution should be kept in mind: no interval values can be assigned to the several positions.

The avenues of vertical mobility and their categorical limitations have been indicated in the foregoing discussion. Colored slaves were manumitted more often than blacks; colored slaves were more often than blacks employed in domestic, urban, and entrepreneurial activities (e.g. as peddlers) where they could acquire the prerequisite skills for further mobility. For the first few steps up the ladder some training was more important than some land. At higher levels, although literacy and training in themselves had status value, the validation of high status rested on land ownership or, at least, its control.

After "the fall of the planter class" the merchants increased in relative importance and, as urban influences grew, the roles of Jews (see below) and the colored expanded. Some of those, e.g. Scots and Jews, who had achieved higher status in urban functions penetrated the planter group or emigrated to England, but the colored elements consolidated and developed their intermediate positions. This was done by further education, the acquisition of real estate especially in urban areas, intermarriage, and an expansion in trades and professions. All of these processes were retarded by the persistently low level of the Jamaican economy. Planter interests maintained their strong representation in the Assembly, and colored men who never comprised more than a third of its membership up to its dissolution in 1865, generally opposed the Country party, dominated by the English planters. The black and colored peasantry increased, and overseas companies tended to replace individual absentee landlords.

The varieties of colored employment are worth detailing. John Bigelow, proprietor and editor of the *New York Evening Post,* who visited Jamaica in 1850, reported that the pilot in Kingston harbor was a mulatto, that the revenue officers were mostly colored, that most of the eight hundred man police force were colored. In a visit to court he found two lawyers, all but one of the officers of the court, and most of the jurors colored. At this time Edward Jordan, a colored man, was public printer, editor of the *Kingston Morning Journal,* and leader of the Administration party. His is said to be the first portrait of a colored man to appear in the history gallery of the Institute of Jamaica.

Americans have been impressed with the permissiveness of Jamaican race relations for more than a century. Bigelow summarized the case as well as we could ask: ". . . one accustomed to the proscribed condition of the free black in the United States, will constantly be startled at the diminished importance attached here to the matter of complexion. Intermarriages are constantly occurring between the white and colored people, their families associate together within the ranks to which by wealth and color they respectively belong, and public opinion does not recognize any social distinctions based exclusively on color. Of course, cultivated or fashionable people will not receive colored persons of inferior culture and worldly resources, but the rule of discrimination is scarcely more rigorous against those than against whites. They are received at the 'King's House' . . . and they are invited to (the governor's) table with fastidious courtesy. The wife of the present mayor of Kingston is a 'brown' woman . . . so also is the wife of the Receiver General himself, an English gentleman, and one of the most exalted public functionaries upon the island. . . . One unacquainted with the extent to which the amalgamation of races has gone here, is constantly liable to drop remarks in the presence of white persons, which, in consequence of the mixture of blood that may take place in some branch of their families, are likely to be very offensive. I was only protected from frequent *contretemps* of this kind, by the timely caution of a lady, who in explaining its propriety, said that unless one knows the whole collateral kindred of a family in Jamaica, he is not safe in assuming that they have not some colored connections."

Social stratification in Jamaica cannot be understood as an uninterrupted continuum of status positions. No matter what empirical criteria are employed, gross discontinuities are to be found. Given the historical forces briefly reviewed, this fact should cause no surprise, but the extreme character of this status cleavage affects all facets of Jamaican society.

Table 2. Literacy and Education by Color and Ethnic Identity, Jamaica, 1943*

	Black	Colored	White	Chinese and Chinese Colored	East Indian and E. I. Colored	Syrian and Syrian Colored	Total[1]
Total population 7 yrs. & older	794,574	179,532	12,477	9,234	21,378	857	1,018,955
Per cent illiterate	28.1	13.8	3.8	13.9	48.6	5.6	25.6
Per cent literate (schooling)	71.9	86.2	96.2	86.1	51.4	94.4	74.4
Pre-prof. and professional	.3	1.3	13.1	.4	.2	1.9	.6
Secondary or practical	1.1	9.8	48.1	12.0	2.1	46.4	3.4
Elementary	70.5	75.1	35.0	73.6	49.1	46.1	70.4

* Computed from Eighth Census of Jamaica, 1943, Table 54, p. 108.
[1] Includes "Not otherwise specified."

As elsewhere in the Western World, literacy and education are preconditions to vertical mobility. In Table 2 are summarized the relevant statistics. A little over one per cent of the blacks have more than an elementary schooling and fully 28 per cent are illiterate. Only the East Indians show a higher rate of illiteracy. The colored and Chinese groups occupy an intermediate position, but both have substantial populations with more than elementary schooling. The whites and Syrians are far better off. Stated crudely, 96 per cent of the Jamaican population is an undifferentiated mass in regard to education, with elementary schooling or none. Combining illiterates with those having only elementary schooling, we find the groups have the following percentages of illiteracy: Blacks, 98.6; East Indians, 97.7; Colored, 88.9; Chinese, 87.5; Syrians, 51.7; Whites, 38.8. These figures are for the population seven years of age and older. The residual population of illiterates and those with limited education is subject to reduction for all groups, but disproportionately so for Syrians and whites.

The same relationships exist in the distribution of secondary schooling. The whites are five times better off than the colored, the colored ten times better off than the blacks. In this respect the Syrians approximate the other whites, the Chinese resemble the colored, and the East Indians again resemble the blacks. One qualification must be made to the statistical generalization about the educationally depressed characteristics of the Chinese. Their limited formal schooling is ameliorated by extensive *informal* practical training in small commercial enterprises, which is not revealed in Table 2. Effectively they are better educated than the Census records suggest.

The data on professional and pre-professional schooling are presented in the next section. Suffice it to say that the educational prerequisites for even modest vertical mobility are available for only a small part of the colored and for a very small proportion of blacks and East Indians.

Table 3 approaches the phenomenon of status cleavage with different data. About half the black and East Indian and about a third of the colored wage earners got ten shillings a week or less, an exchange value in 1943 of about two dollars in U.S. currency. This does not take into account a high rate of unemployment, which operates selectively against the low wage earners and reduces their mean earnings disproportionately. The heavy concentration of blacks and East Indians in agricultural labor largely contributes to their disadvantageous position. The better wage status of the colored is, on the other hand, probably related to their higher incidence of urban employment. The other color and ethnic groups had very small numbers in the lowest wage category.

Table 3. Wage Earnings by Color and Ethnic Identity, Jamaica, 1943*

	Black	Colored	White	Chinese and Chinese Colored	East Indian and E. I. Colored	Syrian and Syrian Colored	Jewish	Total
Total wage earners	151,101	33,630	2,990	1,526	4,770	163	233	194,458[1]
Per cent earning:								
More than 100s/wk.[2]	.3	5.6	41.5	5.0	.5	17.8	33.5	1.9
Less than 10s/wk.	58.4	32.1	2.1	6.1	49.8	2.5	1.7	52.2

* Computed from *Eighth Census of Jamaica*, 1943, Table 125, p. 220.
[1] Includes "Not otherwise specified."
[2] The shilling was then valued at about 20 cents U. S.

Jamaica has a predominantly agricultural economy. The size of farms operated may, therefore, be taken as another measure of the degree of differentiation of the several elements of its population. Table 4 shows that once again the blacks, East Indians, and colored are found in an inferior position. In this case the Chinese and Syrians resemble the undifferentiated groups, but their involvement in agriculture is small, and their poor agricultural status is, therefore, of little importance. The Census data do not permit us to treat separately the colored segments of the Chinese and Syrians, but we may guess that these elements constitute most of the small operators, grouped in their respective ethnic categories.

Table 4. Farm Land Tenure by Color and Ethnic Identity, Jamaica, 1943*

	Black	Colored	White	Chinese and Chinese Colored	East Indian and E. I. Colored	Syrian and Syrian Colored	Jewish	Total
Total farm operators	51,763	12,398	950	81	922	18	19	66,173[1]
Per cent operating:								
More than 100 acres	.7	4.9	43.3	3.7	2.2	5.5	52.6	2.1
Less than 10 acres	78.4	61.6	23.8	65.4	72.2	77.8	10.5	74.3

* Computed from *Eighth Census of Jamaica*, 1943, Table 200, p. 306.
[1] Includes "Not otherwise specified."

Three sets of data have thus been used to suggest the gross characteristics of Jamaican stratification. Each criterion—education, wage earnings, and farm land tenure—showed the blacks and the East Indians in a very disadvantageous position and the colored population only somewhat better off.

Further comment on the depressed elements of these populations should bear on the channels of mobility open to them rather than on additional stratification details. The available data will permit us only to suggest the broad outlines of such an analysis. Very large proportions of blacks and East Indians, and to a lesser extent the colored, are agricultural laborers or small peasants who lack the minimal educational skills. An expansion of the agricultural economy might incidentally improve their status by providing steadier employment at somewhat higher rates of pay or, in the case of peasants, by yielding better returns on crops. In other words, assuming continued agricultural functions, changes in their life chances lie in changes in the whole economy (except, of course, in the cases of the movement of unusually lucky or able individuals). In any event, the relative position of these groups in the economy would not be significantly altered. Given their lack of education and experience, urban employment can only offer unskilled work or the opportunity to acquire limited skills in such jobs as domestic service.

The depressed urban workers move in a more fluid and differentiated labor market in which some opportunities for upgrading are possible. Furthermore, insofar as they can combine a small capital accumulation with commercial or manual skills, they can make a shaky upward step as independent entrepreneurs. As we shall see below, however, these chances are severely limited. Lacking some dramatic expansion of the economy, the character of the status cleavage of Jamaica does not seem subject to drastic change.

Just as the status cleavage and mobility are the chief topics for studying the undifferentiated elements of the population, the proper study of the highly differentiated elements is function. Table 5 summarizes the color and ethnic identity of the population. In this population, predominantly African in origin, several groups are visible by racial characteristics, cultural characteristics, or simply social identity. This is important because, as we shall see, the more or less visible groups, although quite small, are the very ones which perform distinctive functions in the society.

Table 5. Color and Ethnic Identity of the Population, Jamaica, 1943

	Number*		Per cent[1]
Black	965,960		78.1
Colored	216,348		17.5
White (unlisted below)	12,550[2]		1.0
Jewish	1,259		.1
Chinese	6,879 }	12,394	1.0
Chinese colored	5,515 }		
East Indian	21,393 }	26,507	2.1
East Indian colored	5,114 }		
Syrian	834 }	1,005	.1
Syrian colored	171 }		
Others and unspecified	1,040		.1
Total	1,237,063		100.0

* Compiled from Census of Jamaica, 1943, Table 46, p. 92.
[1] Ibid., computed from Table 47, p. 92.
[2] Discrepancies in figures for whites in this table and in Table 1 derive from the detailed and summary tables of the Census, from which these data were summarized.

First, let us reexamine Tables 2, 3, and 4 to identify the highly differentiated groups. We note that the whites are educationally the most highly qualified group. Thirteen per cent of the whites had pre-professional or professional schooling, compared with 1.3 per cent of the colored and only .3 per cent of the blacks. To run the percentages the other way, although whites are about one per cent of the population, they account for almost one quarter of the highly educated group; the colored, who are about 18 per cent of the population, and the blacks, who make up 78 per cent, share equally in the remainder. This, however, puts an unduly favorable interpretation on the educational position of the blacks, for a large share of the blacks so classified are pre-professionals and clergymen.

Table 3 shows those wage earners getting more than 100 shillings per week (20 dollars U.S.), an income associated with good job stability. Less than two per cent of all wage earners received this amount, but two-fifths of the whites, one-third of the Jews, and almost one-fifth of the Syrians did. On the other hand, only a fraction of one per cent of East Indians and blacks earned as much as 100 shillings per week.

Table 4 tells the same story in the case of large farm operations. About two-fifths of white operators run large farms; indeed a summary of mean holdings would show them in a most advantageous position. One-twentieth of colored operators run large farms, and they account for about half of the larger holdings. Less than one per cent of black farm operators run large farms. The blacks who make up nearly four-fifths of all farm operators run only one-fourth of large farms.

Table 6 permits us to assess the differential positions of the several ethnic elements in commercial functions. To interpret these data fully we would need to classify by size and type of enterprise. Nevertheless, some clues may be noted —for one thing, the disproportionate representation of colored, whites, and Jews in the non-retail category. Only the blacks and East Indians have less than their "share" in this classification, which includes the strategic urban commercial functions.

Table 6. Male Owners, Managers, and Professionals, Jamaica, 1943*

		Black	Colored	White	Chinese and Chinese Colored	East Indian and E. I. Colored	Syrian and Syrian Colored	Jewish	Total[1]
Total managers and professionals	N	3,951	2,712	1,014	1,487	242	162	139	9,819
	per cent	40.2	27.6	10.3	15.1	2.6	1.6	1.4	100.0
Retail trade	N	2,549	1,103	94	1,310	194	124	28	5,429
	per cent	46.9	20.3	1.7	24.1	3.6	2.3	.5	100.0
Excluding retail trade	N	1,402	1,609	920	177	48	38	111	4,390
	per cent	31.9	36.6	21.0	4.0	1.1	.9	2.5	100.0

* Computed from *Eighth Census of Jamaica*, 1943, Table 92, pp. 179 ff. and unpublished census data. Includes: "Wage Earners and Unpaid Workers," "Own Account Workers," and "Employers." Excludes those engaged in agriculture.

[1] Includes "Not otherwise specified."

In the retail trade category the most striking fact is that the Chinese have a larger share than any other group except the blacks. Moreover, their occupational visibility is not merely statistical, for they are predominant in the retail grocery trade throughout the Island and are very important in the related food processing industry. The opportunity to develop a retail grocery trade lay fallow in the hands of the colored population until the latter 19th century when it was taken over by the Chinese with their greater entrepreneurial experience. It would be very difficult now, short of political interference, for the black or colored population to make much headway in this business. As a consequence of their semi-monopoly over the most conspicuous of businesses, the Chinese have come to occupy a difficult position. In scores of towns they stand as strangers who possess the goods most desired by the peasantry and small wage earners. They tend to be ethnically exclusive in their associations, perform few elite functions, and are fairly isolated from the blacks, colored, and the other ethnics. Their conspicuousness could easily be translated into vulnerability. This is suggested in an editorial in *Spotlight,* a Jamaican periodical:

If the Chinese in Jamaica don't do a *volte face* soon they are going to plunge the whole island into serious racial trouble. As one whose goodwill towards them is no secret, I feel duty-bound to give this note of warning—or these few words of advice. Jamaica's race relations record is too good to be spoilt. So I must warn now before it is too late.

I remember how bitterly they complained to the Moyne Commission of '38 that everybody was against them though they offended no one but merely minded their own business. I remember what wise old Lord Moyne told them. He said in effect: You people are not pulling your weight in the community. You build a wall around yourselves and live within it. People don't like walls, particularly if they get to thinking that what's within is inimical to them. Remove your wall. Integrate with the community, and stop giving the imperssion that you are only interested in grabbing and scraping all you can out of the island to take back to China. Forget about China. You are Jamaicans. Be Jamaicans—like the Jews, Syrians, Negroes and others whose ancestors also came from alien lands.

That was sound advice. But the Chinese haven't taken it. Instead, they have built a thicker and higher wall. Those who venture out and identify themselves with the rest of the Jamaican people are so few they are lost in the crowd.

The rest of Jamaicans are beginning to look at the Chinese wall. And it is not a friendly look; it is a look that bodes ill, a threat to the continuance of internal peace. If the Chinese keep piling up wealth and hate behind that wall, giving back nothing to the community, they may find it expedient to go back "home" sooner than they hope—if China is still home for any large numbers of Jamaican Chinese. . . .

They hate Negroes more than all ("Nigger" is their favourite word for anybody black), though they have bred more half-Negro children than any other group during the past 50 years. They ostracise any of their group who accept employment with Negro firms. There is the case of a Chinese girl who married a Negro some time ago. Her folks haven't spoken to her since. . . .

. . . The Chinese take full advantage of all the facilities the community offers, yet such facilities as they have as a group are reserved for Chinese only. Examples: only Chinese are employed in Chinese businesses; only Chinese kids are accepted in the Chinese public school; only Chinese are admitted to membership in the Chinese Athletic Club.

Few Chinese even bother to vote. Every public subscription list shows the same few names. . . .

Political control of Jamaica will ever remain in the hands of Negroes. Since it is too late to bar all Chinese—as some other Caribbean countries have done—it is not too late to enact the kind of legislation which will force the Chinese out from behind the wall. . . .

In contrast the Jews, Syrians, and other whites who also perform important commercial functions are involved in varied enterprises, chiefly concentrated in the urban areas. In their exchange functions they have less direct contact with the general public. Like the Chinese, the Syrians are concentrated in commercial activity. Unlike the Chinese, at the turn of the century they entered into competition with the relatively well established dry goods and wholesale firms run by creole whites and colored. In large part through the skill of a single family, the Syrians have become a major economic force, tightly integrated and with close ties to the Syrian community in North America and throughout the Caribbean.

Although a detailed discussion is impossible here, a word must be said about the Jews of Jamaica who have never exceeded a few hundreds. They were originally of Spanish and Portuguese origin and were important in the entrepot trade with the Spanish Caribbean. Along with the Scots, they dealt in plantation stores, a large scale business in which sales were made in bulk. In the 17th and early 18th centuries Jews suffered from discriminatory taxation and civil disabilities. The special taxes were rescinded first, and then, early in the 19th century they were relieved of the remaining impediments. As the colored population became urbanized and achieved some vertical mobility, intermarriage and concubinage with Jews as well as with other whites took place. It is not clear to what extent Jews left the Island for England, but they undoubtedly shared in this migration.

As has been indicated, Jews are widely distributed through the urban occupations. Of approximately 200 listed in the Jamaica *Who's Who* (1946), a very inclusive roster, nearly half are in business activities of one sort or another, and most of the remainder are in the free professions or the civil service.

There is not space to report here on current Jewish intermarriage and related problems. It would be safe to assert, however, that despite the observance of religious holidays by Jewish firms and the maintenance of a congregation, the group is the most fully integrated of all the ethnic minorities into Jamaican society. Like the colored, many of their number perform elite functions.

The other whites, especially the English and Jamaica creoles, control most of the largest estates, the finance and the shipping activities. Polite society is dominated by these whites, or more accurately, by the white wives of these men. There are also a number of cliques of high status centering on the colored professionals, but the town clubs, the yacht club, and the country clubs are not racially exclusive. Their memberships, of course, are disproportionately white and light colored as a consequence of the distribution of money, education, and occupation. Perhaps in the country parishes one or two clubs composed exclusively of creole whites might be found, but these are rural survivals of an earlier period.

* *

By T. S. Simey

THE MIDDLE CLASSES [among the so-called Jamaican coloured] are in a much more precarious position than the masses generally. In order to make their way upwards in the social scale, they have to adopt patterns of behaviour fundamentally different from those of the masses. They are driven to demonstrate their relative superiority by cutting themselves adrift from their own people, and identifying themselves with the white middle classes as far as possible. Middle-class culture tends to be a 'white' culture. The use of the local dialects is frowned on; remarkable instances of the rejection of the local surroundings can be seen in the art classes in the schools, where it is more usual to find paintings of European flowers (which the pupils have never seen) than of the West Indian country-side. All that is beautiful and attractive in West Indian life, social and other, is rejected in favour of a stilted imitation of a 'foreign' way of life. The Negro middle classes cut themselves adrift from society to a much more marked degree than is usual with middle classes generally, and a gulf between the classes comes into being which is a prominent fact in the lives of the individuals living on its sides. The gulf is so wide, indeed, that the West Indian middle classes have come to be astonishingly ignorant of the conditions and habits of life of the masses. They may think that they know a great deal about them, but their knowledge is largely composed of a series of beliefs whose function is to rationalize the situation in which they are placed. A representative of the West Indian middle classes, for instance, will tend to argue, quite sincerely, in one breath that the peasantry is industrious, thrifty, and responsible, and in another that it displays every social evil or shortcoming to an excessive degree. This ambivalence of attitude is due to the fact that whilst the middle classes wish to emphasize their equality with other peoples, they know that they cannot in fact cut themselves adrift from the masses of their own people, with which their future is closely identified. When therefore the idea of identification is uppermost in their minds, the virtues of the masses are stressed; when their own position in relation to the world at large is in question the tendency is to emphasize differences and adopt a highly critical attitude.

The general effect of this is that middle-class people feel themselves isolated from their fellow men, and adopt a highly dictatorial attitude to the masses below them, whom they may regard with contempt. Fear of identification with the masses is acute, and they may go to extreme lengths to avoid it. They are individualistic, made so by the constant struggle in which they have to take part to achieve a position in society, and maintain it after they have won what they desire. There is thus always a latent combativeness between man and man. A West Indian illustration, describing the competitiveness of the middle classes, likens them to crabs in a basket, which are supposed to allow one of their number to climb to the top, and then make a concerted rush to prevent the adventurer from getting out. The way of the pioneer is hard indeed, for he has

From T. S. Simey, *Welfare and Planning in the West Indies* (Oxford: At the Clarendon Press, 1946), pp. 101–105. With permission.

to sacrifice so much for gains which are often hard to demonstrate. Moreover, he may find himself rejected as a leader by the masses who, antagonized by the distinctions which the middle-class man is forced to make between himself and them, may either prefer a person who is, or professes to be, one of themselves, or reject him outright in favour of a member of the white upper caste.

The compelling social tendencies of the present age give as the dominant aim of modern society the acceptance of middle-class patterns of conduct by the whole population, and this is as true in the West Indies as anywhere else. There is no going back, no possibility of founding a new culture on working-class society alone. The burdens which the dynamic trends of modern culture impose on the middle classes are peculiarly cruel in the West Indies. The middle classes are certainly exceptions from the general rule that West Indians are even outwardly a happy people. From the point of view of the white middle and upper classes, as well as from that of the coloured middle classes, the world may well appear to be peopled with hostile individuals who seem to ring them round on every side. Their social superiority is a privilege which it is hard for them to carry with dignity, since it brings with it a wholly artificial position of power in the community. To take an outstanding example, the white or 'light' man can have his way with the women of the people, and he often does. He suffers from feelings of guilt, and even if he does not provoke envy and hatred in this way, as often happens, he will tend to fear those he has wronged, and assume that they are waiting for an opportunity to revenge themselves both on his own person and that of his relatives.

An extremely unstable emotional tension is generated in this and similar situations. The very fear of insurrection has on many occasions provoked insurrection, since measures taken to suppress smouldering discontent have fanned it into a blaze time after time. Some of these 'insurrections' were without doubt entirely imaginary, merely arising out of excessive fears in the minds of the slave-owners, or, more recently, of the upper classes, but the savagery of the measures taken to suppress them was none the less unrestrained. The cruelties practised by the upper classes in stamping out rebellion have only been equalled by those for which the slaves in revolt were responsible during the successful insurrection in Haiti. Repetitions of these events are still feared at the present time for the same psychological causes that operated in the more remote past. There is always a certain tension in the West Indian social atmosphere, and this accounts for the 'touchiness' of the West Indian peoples concerning the disturbances which are so common a feature of their contemporary social history.

The middle classes obviously suffer from a profound spiritual *malaise*, which not only embitters their lives but also prevents them from placing their undoubted abilities at the disposal of their communities in the way they would like to do. The strain of living bears particularly heavily on the young men and women of the middle classes, who find it hard to adjust themselves to the conflicting calls that are made on them. They need all the understanding and sympathy which the world can provide. Perhaps the most urgent of the social problems of the West Indies is, indeed, the winning of the confidence of young, intelligent, and well-educated people by the leaders of West Indian communities, and the enlisting of their energies in the task of rebuilding the societies in which they live.

SOUTHEAST ASIA

By Melvin Conant

THE OVERSEAS CHINESE in Southeast Asia, numbering some ten million, constitute a complex, important problem in human relations. In Burma, Thailand, Indochina, the Philippines and Borneo, Indonesia, Singapore and Malaya, overseas Chinese play an important and sometimes dominant economic role; their political allegiance to China and failure to become assimilated into the national life of Southeast Asian nations make them objects of suspicion. The overseas Chinese are frequently the object of legislation affecting licenses, trading permits, ownership of land and firms and the Chinese school systems created by overseas Chinese for the schooling of their children. These laws are opposed by the overseas Chinese for, if fully implemented, they would bring to an end much of their economic power and end the "isolation" of the Chinese communities. The overseas Chinese have on occasion asked for the support of whatever government occupies Peking in an effort to apply pressure on those governments passing oppressive legislation; these appeals for assistance have not always succeeded and they have inevitably increased resentment and suspicion of the loyalties of the overseas Chinese.

In most of the nations of Southeast Asia the number of overseas Chinese forms an important but not a sizable minority. The significance of these emigrant Chinese lies not in their numerical strength but in the very special economic role they play in the rural areas, in the cities and coastal trade; in banking, credit and international trade. Out of a population of eighteen million Burma has some 300,000 overseas Chinese. Thailand's population is estimated to be 18 million with 2.5 million Chinese included. Indochina has 900,000 Chinese with a total population of 28 million and Indonesia, with a population of some 75 million, contains only 1.5 million overseas Chinese. Based on these figures, Chinese do not constitute more than 5 per cent of the total population of Southeast Asia. In Malaya, however, the special economic position of the Chinese is given added importance by the fact that Chinese almost equal Malays, there are about 2.9 million Malays and some 2.6 million Chinese. Singapore, a British colony, is predominantly Chinese (80 per cent); but throughout most of Southeast Asia, overseas Chinese constitute a small minority in many nations.

Economic power accounts for the significance of these minorities, but politically they are also important because of their attachment to China and because, without particular political stakes in their "second home," they have not played an active part in the various nationalist movements that have swept nations in that part of Asia. This political passivity during wars for independence did not endear them to the nationalists who regarded the overseas Chinese' economic interests and security as dependent on the law and order of the colonial power—as they usually were. The "dual loyalties" of Chinese—their economic interests abroad and their political interests back home in China—have on occasion seen leaders of overseas communities play a key role in the

Written during the summer of 1954.

encouragement and financing of political, revolutionary movements, such as the effort by Sun Yat-sen, which the overseas Chinese hope will prove strong enough to protect their interests abroad. This is well known to other Asians. They ask themselves if the overseas Chinese in their midst will ever be fully loyal to Indonesian or Thai, Malay or Burman interests. The relations between the overseas communities and the nationals of the nation in which the Chinese reside are complex and frequently give rise to serious friction; riots and massacres are not unknown. The roots of the problem lie deep in the past.

About a thousand years ago, a few pilgrims and scholars and occasional tribute missions to Peking were the primary contacts between China and Kingdoms in Southeast Asia. As the years passed, Chinese from their southern coastal region began to travel farther South and established small trading centers in Malaya, Java and parts of Indochina. The value of these centers increased with the centuries as more and more Chinese left their homes for these overseas stations usually with the expectation of returning to their provinces in retirement. The coming of Western rule created a climate in which the Chinese could work to their best advantage. The Western powers created situations of law and order and also encouraged the importation of labor from China to work the estates and mines. The greatest period of Chinese emigration into Southeast Asia occurred in the 19th century and the first decades of the 20th. The Chinese were prepared to work at incredibly low wages with long hours of hard work; they saved diligently and opened small stores. Some accumulated more capital and continued to branch out. They often did this without competition from the native peoples who frequently lacked the experience necessary to compete but who more often did not share the value systems of the Chinese entrepeneur; in most areas the process of Chinese accumulation of economic power proceeded steadily until, today, a relatively few overseas Chinese have important economic control, sometimes national monopolies. There is this to their credit, at least: a considerable part of the economic development of Southeast Asia has been due to their constant efforts although Western enterprise is usually credited with most of the apparent progress evident in the region. This economic role aroused, not unexpectedly, envy on the part of other Asians and this attitude has been reinforced by the social and cultural isolation of most overseas Chinese.

Throughout Southeast Asia, wherever Chinese have constituted an overseas community, they have persistently resisted efforts to assimilate them to the national life. The overseas Chinese brought with them and maintained their own social customs, institutions and schools. They have sought to keep alive Chinese traditions and culture; they have rigorously encouraged the learning of Chinese and frequently ignored the national language of the country in which they reside. Support for the all-important Chinese schools has come from the overseas community but, in a significant amount, also from whatever government is in control in Peking. The Kuomintang and the Communists have been equally concerned over the status of these overseas schools for the same reason: as long as the Chinese have their own schools, encourage the teaching of Chinese and the practice of Chinese traditions, the overseas Chinese will be important "pockets" whose significance to China could be very great—in times of expansion, for example.

None of this has been lost on the other Asians who in every country in

Southeast Asia have sought to legislate or direct the private Chinese schools out of existence. Most nations in the area have various citizenship requirements which Chinese must meet if they are to remain in business, hold market and trade licenses, etc. While considerable effort is put into the fragmentation of these overseas communities, the license restrictions and citizenship regulations are not usually implemented in a positive fashion. Even those Chinese who decide that their future requires them to associate with the nations as citizens do not always find it easy to meet the rigorous and sometimes discriminatory acts of officials who seek only the disappearance of the overseas communities and not their integration into the national life with a continuation of their economic influence. This attitude forces the overseas Chinese to seek support from home and the cycle continues.

There is evidence that in certain nations, Thailand and Malaya, for example, a number of Chinese do pass out from the overseas community and meld into the national life. But these numbers have never been significant and in any case do not lessen the antagonisms expressed against the Chinese. Those who become part of the national life usually pass completely into the social and cultural and political life of the nation and do not form a "transition" group or bridge between the Chinese community and the nation as a whole. For the most part, the overseas Chinese community remains apart in its own settlement.

Perhaps the most acute problem of the relationship of Chinese communities with nationals exists in Malaya. The problem is particularly important because the Chinese hold great economic power, as elsewhere, and because the Chinese show signs of becoming the dominant political force in Malaya as they now are in the neighboring colony of Singapore. In most nations in Southeast Asia the size of the Chinese population is small in comparison with the total population but in Malaya the Chinese almost equal the Malays and the Malays see the Chinese dominant economically today and fear political domination in the near future.

There are some 2.9 million Malays in Malaya and 2.6 million Chinese. A number of the latter are "straits-born," in fact almost 60 per cent. Chinese emigration to Malaya began some five hundred years ago with the usual traders, coastal shippers and government expeditions. The coming of the British and their decision to exploit the natural advantages of the location of Singapore created a situation in which British order attracted large numbers of Chinese who sought economic opportunity in the peninsula. During the 19th and first half of the 20th century, Chinese immigrants poured into Singapore and the straits settlements to the North. The Chinese who arrived in the peninsula came as ordinary coolie laborers for the greatest part. They worked on the docks, railways, estates and mines. They began small farms and developed rural trade. By dint of hard labor and toleration of incredibly low living standards, the Chinese gradually worked their way out of the laborer class, began to peddle merchandise, open stalls, then small stores; branches were begun in other areas and finally the great business houses were developed. For every Chinese who began to improve his lot hundreds failed. Perseverance and the pressure of relatives left at home contributed to the never ending attempts to rise. Remittances home from the overseas Chinese in Malaya and Singapore were important—often vital—to one's family and the flow of money became a useful and important source of foreign exchange to the Chinese government. The impact of the British and Chinese traders is great on Malaya; both peoples have been entrepreneurs in Malaya and shared in the rapid economic and agricultural development, the building of roads and bridges and the development of Singapore as the great entrepot of the East. These changes occurred without the significant participation of Malays who remained for the most part in fishing and small-scale agriculture. Increasingly, as the influence of Chinese grew, the Malay sultans and their supporters became ever more conscious of their inability to compete with the foreigners and relied on keeping political control as their main defence against the Chinese tide. In the past, the British assisted the Malays in this respect partly because of treaty obligations and partly because the continuation of British rule in Malaya might well depend on the ability of the British to keep the Malays dominant politically as long as the Chinese were active economically; if immediate Chinese interests did not coincide with Malays' then the possibility of an active all-Malaya nationalist movement seemed remote. The British role in Malaya today reflects the acute problem of Chinese-Malay relationships; the British are essential in Malaya in order to provide some semblance of order—they are the police in the full sense of the word. Without British control the Chinese-Malay problem would almost certainly result in continuing riots, bloodshed and destruction. British economic interests in Malaya cannot be over-estimated—Malaya is one of the biggest dollar earners for the Commonwealth; the willingness of the British to play the "peace-maker" and the policemen stems largely from the enormous economic stake of Britain in Malayan rubber and tin.

In recent years, the British have encouraged efforts within Malaya which seek to end the bitter strife between the Malays and the Chinese. The serious and almost fatal problem of Communist terrorism throughout Malaya contributed to this change in British attitude. Most of the jungle terrorists are Chinese; the Chinese communities in Malaya, Singapore and Thailand have served as weapons and intelligence channels for the Communists. In 1949, as Chinese Communists succeeded in establishing rule over the homeland, their influence increased markedly particularly amongst the younger generation. The British believed that one way of preventing Malayan Chinese from going Communist completely was to work out some compromise—particularly on political grounds—whereby a degree of Malay-Chinese cooperation would lay the basis of a new kind of nationalism for Malaya. If the Chinese, so the theory ran, had a political stake in the future of Malaya they would be less likely to throw their full allegiance to Peking. The British have put pressure on the Malay sultans and the Malayan people to give more political rights to the Chinese in their midst, to offer Chinese citizenship and obtain their participation in political affairs. As can be imagined this British policy was not attractive to the Malays who saw their land being swallowed by the foreign Chinese. In the past several years, however, Malays have offered limited citizenship opportunities to the overseas Chinese; today some 30 per cent of the overseas Chinese have gained citizenship in the Malay states. This trend will accelerate, despite continuing opposition from Malays, as long as the British remain in Malaya.

British pressure on the Malays to relent in their opposition to the Chinese in their midst has been accompanied by heavy pressure on the Chinese communities. This has taken a number of forms but essentially the British have sought to weaken and eventually eradicate some of the institutional devices whereby the Chinese kept themselves isolated from a large part of Malayan life. The most important of these devices is the Chinese school system.

For many years the maintenance of a strong system of Chinese schools throughout Southeast Asia has been the key means of maintaining contact with the homeland, preserving a homogeneity amongst overseas Chinese and keeping alive the traditions and learning of China. The Kuomintang Government appreciated early the importance of ties with the overseas Chinese communities. Chiang Kai-shek kept close liaison with them as has Mao Tse-tung. As noted before, the overseas Chinese are regarded as a source of foreign exchange and, most importantly, as groups which might under certain circumstances facilitate the expansion of China. The British and Malays appreciate this but they are also aware of another facet: as long as the Chinese students continue to attend private Chinese schools not only is it difficult to know all of the curricula but the schools with their emphasis on things Chinese further isolate the Chinese from participation in any kind of "Malayan" life. For many years the British imposed stringent yet frequently uninforceable regulations on these schools. As long as the financial support of the schools comes from the communities and the national Chinese treasury, it is difficult to tax or license them out of existence. Recently, the British have examined with Chinese and Malays the possibility of developing an all-Malaya school system into which would go both Malays and Chinese. Since the majority of the Chinese would not go willingly, the British attempted to begin the integration by forbidding the teaching of Chinese alone in schools, by cutting down drastically on the external, foreign financial support, by far more rigid inspections of the schools and far higher standards, etc. This policy of developing a basic national school system strikes at the heart of the communal societies of Malaya and has not proceeded without many fights from all sides. The Chinese have responded most recently to this British pressure by creating a new university, primarily for Chinese, in opposition to the long-established University of Malaya. The Chinese assert that the British administrators and Malays in the University have failed to create adequate opportunities for students of Chinese background and that it has become necessary for them to have their own institution. The British have tried to delay this event but the Chinese have subscribed large amounts of money for their Nanyang University. (Other reasons have been advanced by the Chinese for the need of such an institution. A large number of overseas Chinese throughout Southeast Asia return to Communist China for their college and university years and the founders of the Nanyang University hope that the existence of a free university will attract many who would otherwise travel to Communist China.) The symbolic character of a Chinese university in a divided Malaya is important to the British, the Malays and the Chinese.

Not all efforts towards harmony have stemmed from the British. Several leaders in the Chinese communities and among the Malays have made periodic but still unsuccessful attempts to develop all-Malayan societies, political parties and community organizations. The Malayan-Chinese Association is an important example; unfortunately its original purpose was not that of the United Malays National Organization, a communal group, which did not seek to develop as an organization within which Chinese and Malays alike might participate. The MCA, despite its promising beginning, never succeeded in becoming a national organization and its Chinese character remains dominant.

While these efforts at creating Malay-Chinese harmony continue, it is unfortunately true that the unresolved communal problem in Malayan life today remains the paramount problem of the greatest importance to the future of the Malays and Chinese and of deep concern to others who see in the continued expansion of Communist China into Southeast Asia, the possibility of a new and critical role for many Chinese communities scattered throughout the area.

CANADA AND ITS JAPANESE

By Forrest E. LaViolette

STUDIES OF ETHNIC AND RACIAL GROUPS IN CANADA have been rather infrequent and few in number, although such groups have been of central importance in the building of the Dominion, and their acculturation problems have been significant in the formation of the national image. Somewhat understandably, through war and its consequences, we have more studies of the French-Canadians and Japanese than of others. The battle of the Plains of Abraham in 1759 resulted in the first becoming a conquered group, and eventually they were given constitutional rights of language and religion. Their institutional structures and informal controls in a single province, Quebec, had so developed by 1867 when the Dominion was formed, that they are most unlikely to disappear into the culture of English-speaking Canadians. The French do not intend to be assimilated; it is just as true that no one has a right to expect them to become so. Thus Canada, it appears, will remain a bi-cultural nation. In international affairs its biculturalism gives Canadians a distinctive orientation and an exemplary position. Since *La bonne entente* has been strained seriously only for two short periods during world war involvements, French-English accommodations give Canadians a claim to distinction in a world which has lost considerable of its racial or ethnic homogeneity and is having trouble finding a new basis for cooperation.

A second hard fact of Canadian national life from this perspective of intergroup relations is that the Dominion has developed historically with a Great Neighbor to the South. Living alongside the United States has not been easy even though the two countries are each others best customers. Until World War II Canadians had no satisfactory way of conceiving of themselves vis-a-vis the United States and other world powers. They rejected the conception of being a minority group among nations. Their role was too crucial, and their level of economic and political maturity seemed to them such that they were an independent nation in all respects but obviously a unique one, made so by geography and history. Hence when an eminent public servant, Mr. Lester B.

By Forrest E. LaViolette. A more detailed study of the Japanese problem of British Columbia is reported in the author's *Canadian Japanese and World War II* (Toronto: University of Toronto Press, 1948).

Pearson, referred to Canada as a "middle-sized nation," it was a felicitous symbol of identification in world affairs which Canadians seemed to need. It avoided a number of embarrassments since national power could not, with satisfaction, be scrutinized too closely. Furthermore, for national survival, it assisted in standing off the over-whelming power and pervasive cultural influence of the United States as the 1951 findings of the *Report,* published by the Royal Commission on National Development in the Arts, Letters and Sciences, so well demonstrates.

It is within this framework of two of the hardest facts of Canadian national history and life—that of biculturalism and a continuing struggle for identity—that one comes to understand more adequately immigration policy and the position of certain groups in the life of the Dominion today. Pre-war immigration policy was always highly selective, with first preference for British, then Americans and other Europeans. But even though immigrants were sought, population did not grow as rapidly as did the American, and many Canadians going to the States seemed to be almost an insult to national honor. Policy also favored certain occupational groups. And as is well known, it placed severe restrictions upon Asiatics even though they were members of the Empire as in the case of East Indians.

Settlement of the Canadian West and Pacific Coast has resulted in the emergence of a number of continuing ethnic and racial minorities. In turning directly to the Japanese in Canada, we leave aside several inviting opportunities for studying the origin of minorities, their position in the regional social structure which was developed, and how they have historically affected the national image in its formation. Then, too, of course there are other ethnically derived peoples of the Prairie Provinces where acculturation has taken place and assimilation has worked towards the conception of being Canadian. As intriguing as any of these may be for analysis, it is British Columbia which dramatically has demanded the attention of the Dominion, secured it on numerous occasions, and finally in a period of war denied emphatically its hystericism but still demanded the expulsion of about 22,000 people of Japanese descent.

Anti-Japanism in British Columbia became a public creed and doctrine. We shall interpret it as an aspect of the struggle to establish a stable social organization in a new area of settlement which was characterized by very rapid social change. The first phase of this struggle can well be termed the struggle to remain British. Major issues of this struggle were formulated in colonial days—some of them for only a short period after provincial status was achieved, but others, of interest to us here, were found lively even after World War II. The first of these issues was that of population.

When British Columbia became a province in 1871, it was indeed clear that available settlers, because of lines of communication, were chiefly in the United States or the Orient. To remain British necessitated changing lines of travel directly east to the Dominion and attempting to fill up the province with ethnics who could be trusted to remain or could become quickly loyal to the Crown. To help solve this and for economic development, Ottawa agreed to construct a railroad as a national project. But in solving problems of construction, Ottawa had to import Chinese and permit contractors to continue using Chinese labor in spite of strong opposition. Control of Oriental immigration early, became an issue with Ottawa. Other problems emerged, and legislative action became a characteristic means by which British Columbians at-tempted to solve their Oriental problems. For instance, in 1874 the Chinese were prohibited from voting; the same legislation was extended to the Japanese in 1895. Although the completion of the railroad in the 1880's opened the Prairie Provinces and accelerated the growth of the population on the coast, still in absolute numbers and in a large area with enormous potentials of wealth in mining, fishing, and lumbering, the numbers of people continued to be a problem. Just as importantly, perhaps, was the highly developed sensitivity generated by physical isolation; it is the only part of Canada which faces the Orient and is a long distance from the Maritimes and Central Canada. Funda-mental to a number of issues has been this peripheral position in the Dominion's geography. In this peripheral area, population, so far to this day, has grown chiefly by migration. Although it has not been said explicitly, it seems safe to infer that in this isolated area the British Columbians have always assumed that in a biological race for survival, they could not compete with the Orientals.

A second feature of the provincial population related to the formation of anti-Japanism was its colonial characteristics. A high proportion of early resi-dents were British-born, and it is they who dominated the colony and then the province in economic and political activities. It is not until after World War II that we find the colonial character of the population sufficiently reduced so that it is no longer a factor in the affairs of the province. During this almost century-long period of development and transition, British immigrants were like other ethnics away from their mother-land. They were highly defensive of their cultural origins. Furthermore, it is a period of British Empire expansion, and it is a period, 1865–1920, in the United States, which we know to have been full of talk about Anglo-Saxon superiority.

A third feature of the population has been its concentration within the southwest corner of the province. The whole province has been dominated by the urban areas of Victoria and Vancouver, the latter of course having been made more important by becoming the terminus of the two trans-Canada rail-ways. The significance of this concentration for our purpose is dual. First, the Japanese concentrated in this urban region, and of course within Little Tokyo in Vancouver. And secondly, Vancouver is the sensitive center of news—of rumor, as well as fact. Even with modern means of travel and communication, concentration continues around the southeast corner. As a metropolitan region its hinterland has clearly defined boundaries.

From the first it was assumed by Britishers that Orientals could not be assimilated. Furthermore, there was not the least notion that the immigrants from the Far East and their descendents could or would come to understand principles of British democracy and the social organization built upon them. Hence, the means to control Orientals was one which hoped for total exclusion. Since Dominion and Empire politics did not realize that wish in the case of the Japanese, regional demands for tighter restrictions prevailed until the annual quota was 150. Provincial efforts at control through the legislative assembly became set early in the history of the province but did not adjust themselves to the changing characteristics, especially the social characteristics, of Cana-dians derived from Oriental immigrants. We may attribute this rigidity to local efforts at regulating competition becoming political in character, to the con-sequences of provincial-Dominion relations, and to trends in international

affairs, especially the relations between Japan and Britain. For brevity it is
necessary to claim that these several complexes of relationships became integrated into a racial creed which, supported by statutory law and federal regulation, can be called a public doctrine. It is this racial creed and public doctrine
which formed what was known in Canada as the British Columbian problem.
At the time that war spread to the Pacific Basin, it was highly integrated, and
evidence indicates that there were no important prospects of changes at that
time. Changes might have emerged when the politicians had found that the
struggle to remain British was over and that Canada was an independent
country with its own North American adaptations of Anglo-Saxon traditions,
with its biculturalism, and with its continuing struggle for identity vis-a-vis the
United States.

There are three basic premises to the racial creed and doctrine which
emerge out of the history of British Columbia. All three fit together into a neat
logical relationship supporting each other, and later making the conclusion for
expulsion seem so natural and without any basis for challenge. The first of
these may be stated simply as the fact that the Japanese tolerated a low standard
of living. Westerners have always looked upon Orientals as simply getting along
on less. Differences in economic status within the Japanese group or differences
in the consequences of occupational discrimination as they affected families
were either unobserved or unknown by most non-Japanese. But the most
important aspect of this problem was the fact that it was defined as un-Canadian
to be poor, to tolerate low standards, standards which were in evidence in
Little Tokyo, in villages of fishermen, and in the "typical" Japanese farm house.
Actually obvious changes were taking place among the Japanese by 1938, but
by then international affairs were such that no correction of this conception to
fit more closely with objective evidence, could take place.

The earlier assumption of inassimilability persisted and as a second premise
it became integrated with the first. It started on the assumption of the desirability
of a homogeneous Caucasian population, preferably Anglo-Saxon. Hugh
McLennan, the novelist, has pointed out that even with British settlers, Canada
has tended to emphasize a continuation of the Old World culture. This, we
suppose, is no longer so, but it was effective in the formative years. The low
rate of intermarriage, the formation of Little Tokyo, the maintenance of
language schools, the differences in orientation towards the world, the frequent
visits to Japan—these were all argued to support the premise of inassimilability and to justify the continued exclusion from Canadian life, especially the
franchise. Contrary and obvious evidence to the argument was accumulating
as the shift from the generation of immigrants to the first generation of native
born was having some effects, such as the establishment of the *New Canadian*
in 1936. But again, occupational discrimination continued and the politicians
were able to appeal to the controlling group whose sentiments had not changed
significantly over many decades.

Finally, an alderman of Vancouver pointed out and named what the
Japanese in British Columbia were actually up to. It was "peaceful penetration." This pointed directly to efforts at illegal entries, at their interest in the
fishing industry, at their homes which were convenient points for observing
maritime activities, and at businesses and firms located in strategic areas. It
was known for certain that the Japanese had maintained a political loyalty to

the Emperor and were at the command of the Imperial Government of Japan. Thus, according to this premise, they were advance agents of a military invasion of, or smaller attack upon, British Columbia. Because of pressures from Ottawa, fishing licenses over the years had been reduced from fifty to twelve per cent of the total issued, but the stories and rumors of fishing boats carrying on marine surveying and planning work for invasion continued. Indian bitterness against fishing competitors had been acute for decades; problems of trade unionism in the industry deepened the lines between Japanese, Indians, and Whites. Although federal regulation had managed some of the problems, and Ottawa's investigations into illegal entries had satisfied responsible officials that the claims were invalid, none of these were satisfactory to British Columbians in the municipal and provincial governments or among provincial members of Parliament. Since immigration and regulation of fishing were under Dominion control, the Japanese question was one which was always watched carefully by Members of the House of Commons, and many pages of *Hansard* testify to how carefully provincial affairs, Dominion policy, and international developments were used to support the racial creed and to demonstrate that British Columbia was misunderstood by the rest of Canada.

In the development of this regional system of rejection and exclusion, there was no elaborate etiquette of race relations. It was first and foremost a system of control which was formal, based upon statutory regulation, and kept in effect largely by politicians and occupational discriminations. Through disfranchisement, many occupations could not be entered by Japanese because they were not on the provincial elections list. And so, also, they were disenfranchised for Dominion elections. At the time war started in the Pacific, there was no exclusion from public education on any level. It was, furthermore, appropriate for non-Japanese to attend church and community functions with Japanese, although residential and cultural selection based upon Little Tokyo did not make conditions easy for neighboring or fraternizing. But occupational discrimination was tight and so were the prospects for continuing the basis for exclusion from provincial and national life.

For decades, in fact for generations, provincial officials were prominent in actions against the Japanese. This role became more crucial in a war situation. When the press repeatedly called urgent attention to the delays of Ottawa in providing adequate defenses for the province, it was easy for the politicians and local officials to fall back upon the historically established conceptions of the Japanese in their midst, and it was to the premises of inassimilability and peaceful penetration that they turned to justify the necessity for expulsion as a defense measure. Anything Ottawa did was less than satisfactory, and it was not until partial evacuation was converted into complete removal that local officials seemed satisfied. But further than this, there is evidence to support the inference that they hoped for complete and permanent removal from the province. This in retrospect appears to the last period of the struggle to remain British, for in the post-war period with the Cooperative Commonwealth Federation as a political power in the province, some of the old planks of the Liberal Party and the Conservative Party have been abandoned and "pig-tail" legislation has gone. Even the native Indians were enfranchised in 1949.

Japanese removal involved the relocation of some 21,000 residents of the coastal defense zone. It was done as a wartime measure, and to the British

Columbians it was defined as a necessity. Ottawa was forced to reject the *nisei* for military service, for it would have automatically granted the franchise to some 2,500 Canadian-born Japanese in the postwar years. As in the United States, there was a demand for segregating those who were loyal to or wished to return to Japan. But Prime Minister King delayed this phase of the program so long that it did not become an effective part of the scheme of total removal from the province. In the census of 1951, it is reported that 33.1 per cent of the Japanese of Canada live in British Columbia as compared with about 95 per cent in 1941. Although the data are not available to indicate what provincials think the evacuation meant to them, at least in 1946 it was clear that except for the most devoted CCF'ers and some fair-minded people, the meaning was to be found in the three premises stated above, the desirability of breaking these down by distributing the Japanese throughout the Dominion, or sending the disloyal to Japan, and the necessity of doing it during war as a measure of national defense. Questions of constitutional and civil rights of citizens and legally resident immigrants are by no measure found in that period. The fact that removal may have been based upon a military misconception does not enter into the discussion.

For Eastern Canadians, particularly those in Manitoba, Ontario, and Quebec, it was even during the war and in the immediate postwar period that an entirely different interpretation was formulated. It was true that eastern journalists had helped stir up the regional demand. And it is true that, given the history of anti-Japanism in the province and the condition of war, it seemed sensible to remove them from the coastal zone. But as removal took effect and easterners became acquainted with the Japanese, the premise of tolerating a low standard of living, of being inassimilable, and of their engaging in peaceful penetration could not be accepted. There were rejections here and there. But as has been shown by research in the Chicago area, and undoubtedly the findings are valid in Canada, the Japanese, both foreign and native-born, appear to have many attributes of character which employers admire. Furthermore, eastern pressure groups interested in the national life of Canada were concerned with more than the labor which the evacuees could provide. Strong pressures from church groups, political opponents in Parliament, and from civil liberties committees all held in check the effort on the part of British Columbian officials to achieve total expulsion. Although the Supreme Court of Canada and the Privy Council in London upheld the right of the federal government to repatriate Canadian citizens, this case was unpopular with public opinion. Furthermore, war in the Pacific was over, the political "hot potato" had been deftly handed by Mr. King to the Privy Council, and Canada was well on it way to exploiting a postwar posterity instead of grinding through a depression as had been anticipated.

Finally we may indicate that the meaning of evacuation for the national life can be seen in the handling of the Citizenship Bill in 1946 and 1947. Prior to this, there was no legal category designated as Canadian. Legislation was in process. Members of Parliament from British Columbia attempted to secure exclusion of the Japanese, but this was not permitted. We would suppose that the transition from the struggle to remain British to that of Canadian identity had on the level of national life become fully completed with the passage of that act. In the province of British Columbia, we suspect its development was lagging; not until the C.C.F. came into power shortly thereafter would we suspect that British Columbia had become fully Canadian.

In 1951 there were only 21,663 Canadians of Japanese origin, of which just 6,293 were foreign-born, and of this number 80 per cent had become nationalized citizens. It is seldom in history that such a small group, for in 1941 there were only a few more in the Dominion, plays such an important role in forming, in testing, and in validating a national self-conception. This no longer is an issue; many comments in the *New Canadian* indicate that war and evacuation were the hard ways to become Canadian. Although they knew that they did not want a low standard of living, that they were assimilable, and that peaceful penetration was not for them, they had no way to prove it. In any case, objective proof was not what British Columbians wanted. It required partial removal and eastern Canada to demonstrate to the provincials that the region was part of the nation and that the beliefs of earlier decades may have been useful but were no longer valid, or possibly we should say sufficiently valid, for a province which has lost its frontier and has developed a somewhat more stable social organization.

SOUTHERN UNITED STATES

*

By U. B. Phillips

AN OHIO RIVER FERRYMAN has a stock remark when approaching the right bank: "We are nearing the American shore." A thousand times has he said it with a gratifying repercussion from among his passengers; for its implications are a little startling. The northern shore is American without question; the southern is American with a difference. Kentucky had by slender pretense a star in the Confederate flag; for a time she was officially neutral; for all time her citizens have been self-consciously Kentuckians, a distinctive people. They are Southerners in main sentiment, and so are Marylanders and Missourians.

Southernism did not arise from any selectiveness of migration, for the sort of people who went to Virginia, Maryland, or Carolina were not as a group different from those who went to Pennsylvania or the West Indies. It does not lie in religion or language. It was not created by one-crop tillage, nor did agriculture in the large tend to produce a Southern scheme of life and thought. The Mohawk valley was for decades as rural as that of the Roanoke; wheat is as dominant in Dakota as cotton has ever been in Alabama; tobacco is as much a staple along the Ontario shore of Lake Erie as in the Kentucky pennyroyal; and the growing of rice and cotton in California has not prevented Los Angeles from

From U. B. Phillips, "The Central Theme in Southern History," *The American Historical Review*, XXXIV (October, 1928), 30–31. With permission.

being in a sense the capital of Iowa. On the other hand the rise of mill towns in the Carolina Piedmont and the growth of manufacturing at Richmond and Birmingham have not made these communities Northern. It may be admitted, however, that Miami, Palm Beach, and Coral Gables are Southern only in latitude. They were vacant wastes until Flagler, Fifth Avenue, and the realtors discovered and subdivided them.

The South has never had a focus. New York has plied as much of its trade as Baltimore or New Orleans; and White Sulphur Springs did not quite eclipse all other mountain and coast resorts for vacation patronage. The lack of a metropolis was lamented in 1857 by an advocate of Southern independence, as lack of an essential for shaping and radiating a coherent philosophy to fit the prevailing conditions of life. But without a consolidating press or pulpit or other definite apparatus the South has maintained a considerable solidarity through thick and thin, through peace and war and peace again. What is its essence? Not states rights—Calhoun himself was for years a nationalist, and some advocates of independence hoped for a complete merging of the several states into a unitary Southern republic; not free trade—sugar and hemp growers have ever been protectionists; not slavery—in the eighteenth century this was of continental legality, and in the twentieth it is legal nowhere; not Democracy—there were many Federalists in Washington's day and many Whigs in Clay's; not party predominance by any name, for Virginia, Georgia, and Mississippi were "doubtful states" from Jackson's time to Buchanan's. It is not the land of cotton alone or of plantations alone; and it has not always been the land of "Dixie," for before its ecstatic adoption in 1861 that spine-tingling tune was a mere "walkaround" of Christie's minstrels. Yet it is a land with a unity despite its diversity, with a people having common joys and common sorrows, and, above all, as to the white folk a people with a common resolve indomitably maintained—that it shall be and remain a white man's country. The consciousness of a function in these premises, whether expressed with the frenzy of a demagogue or maintained with a patrician's quietude, is the cardinal test of a Southerner and the central theme of Southern history.

* *

By V. O. Key, Jr.

THE SOUTH MAY NOT BE THE NATION'S number one political problem, as some northerners assert, but politics is the South's number one problem.

From afar, outlanders regard southern politics as a comic opera staged on a grand scale for the amusement of the nation. They roared when Texans elected "Ma" Ferguson as their governor to serve as proxy for her husband,

Reprinted from *Southern Politics in State and Nation*, pp. 3–11, by V. O. Key, Jr., by permission of Alfred A. Knopf, Inc. Copyright 1949 by Alfred A. Knopf, Inc.

barred from office by an earlier impeachment and conviction. They shuddered when Louisiana was ruled by Huey Long, a flamboyant advocate of the subversive doctrine of "Every Man A King." Yet he put on a good show. The connoisseurs of rabble-rousing relished the performance of Gene Talmadge, he of the "red galluses" and the persuasive way with the wool-hat boys. Bilbo's artistry in demagoguery excited, if not admiration, attention from beyond the hills of Mississippi. Alabama's "Big Jim" Folsom, the "kissing governor," Texas' W. Lee O'Daniel, flour salesman and hillbilly bandsman, South Carolina's "Cotton Ed" Smith, eloquent exponent of the virtues of southern womanhood, and other fabulous characters have trod the southern political stage to the accompaniment of hilarity—often derisive—from the other side of the Mason and Dixon line.

But southern politics is no comic opera. It is deadly serious business that is sometimes carried on behind a droll façade. By the process of politics we determine who governs and in whose interests the government is run. Politics embraces far more than campaigns and elections. Actions by legislature, by governors, and by all agencies of government between campaigns are readings of the balance in a continuous competition for power and advantage. The management of government is as much a part of politics as is campaign oratory. Moreover, the political process extends beyond the operation of those formal mechanisms that we usually call government. Custom, the organization of the economic system, and, now and then, private violence have a role in determining who governs and who gets what.

In its grand outlines the politics of the South revolves around the position of the Negro. It is at times interpreted as a politics of cotton, as a politics of free trade, as a politics of agrarian poverty, or as a politics of planter and plutocrat. Although such interpretations have a superficial validity, in the last analysis the major peculiarities of southern politics go back to the Negro. Whatever phase of the southern political process one seeks to understand, sooner or later the trail of inquiry leads to the Negro.

Yet it is far from the truth to paint a picture of southern politics as being chiefly concerned with the maintenance of the supremacy of white over black. That dominance is an outcome, but the observer must look more closely to determine which whites and which blacks give southern politics its individuality. The hard core of the political South—and the backbone of southern political unity—is made up of those counties and sections of the southern states in which Negroes constitute a substantial proportion of the population. In these areas a real problem of politics, broadly considered, is the maintenance of control by a white minority. The situation resembles fundamentally that of the Dutch in the East Indies or the former position of the British in India. Here, in the southern black belts, the problem of governance is similarly one of the control by a small, white minority of a huge, retarded, colored population. And, as in the case of the colonials, that white minority can maintain its position only with the support, and by the tolerance, of those outside—in the home country or in the rest of the United States.

It is the whites of the black belts who have the deepest and most immediate concern about the maintenance of white supremacy. Those whites who live in counties with populations 40, 50, 60, and even 80 per cent Negro share a common attitude toward the Negro. Moreover, it is generally in these counties that large-scale plantation of multiple-unit agriculture prevails. Here are located most of the large agricultural operators who supervise the work of many tenants, sharecroppers, and laborers, most of whom are colored. As large operators they lean generally in a conservative direction in their political views.

If the whites of the black belts give the South its dominant political tone, the character of the politics of individual states will vary roughly with the Negro proportion of the population. The truth of that proposition will be abundantly illustrated as the story progresses. At this point it is only necessary to call attention to the marked differences in the composition of the population of the southern states. Over a third of all Mississippi whites live in counties over half Negro, while only 2.4 per cent of Florida whites reside in such counties. Equally striking differences prevail between the two states in their politics.

The black belts make up only a small part of the area of the South and—depending on how one defines black belt—account for an even smaller part of the white population of the South. Yet if the politics of the South revolves around any single theme, it is that of the role of the black belts. Although the whites of the black belts are few in number, their unity and their political skill have enabled them to run a shoestring into decisive power at critical junctures in southern political history.

Two great crises have left their imprint on southern political behavior: The War of the 'sixties and the Populist revolt of the 'nineties. Both these social convulsions had an impact on political habit whose influence has not worn away even yet, and in both of them the black-belt whites played a determining role. In the maneuvers leading to The War those with most at stake—the owners of large numbers of slaves—were to be found roughly in the same areas as present-day black belts. They recruited allies wherever they could find them; their allies were fewest in the regions of few Negroes. Opposition to The War was most intense in the highlands and in the upcountry, where the soil would not support a plantation economy and where independent yeomanry had no overwhelming desire to take up arms to defend the slave property of the lowland planters.

The impressive—and unfortunate—political victory of the large slave-holders came in their success, despite their small numbers, in carrying their states for war. Within the South the scars of the dispute over whether to go to war remain in persistent Republican enclaves in the highlands of eastern Tennessee, western North Carolina, northern Georgia, northern Alabama, and in isolated pockets elsewhere over the region. West Virginia, which was torn away from the Commonwealth, stands as an even more impressive reminder of the lack of unanimity within the South over a policy of war. Yet even more significant for the practical politics of the South of today is the fact that The War left a far higher degree of southern unity against the rest of the world than had prevailed before. Internal differences that had expressed themselves in sharp political competition were weakened—if not blotted out—by the common experiences of The War and Reconstruction. And, however unreasonable it may seem, it follows—as even a sophomore can see from observing the European scene—that a people ruled by a military government will retain an antipathy toward the occupying power.

In the second great crisis whose influence persists—the Populist revolt—political cleavages often fell along the same lines as in the dispute leading to The War. The details of the pattern differed, of course, from state to state as did the timing of the great upsurge of agrarian radicalism. Yet everywhere the most consistent, the most intense rural resistance to Populists and like radicals of the day came from the black-belt whites. They had valiant allies in the merchants and bankers of the towns and in the new industrialists. Against these defenders of the status quo were arrayed the upcountrymen, the small farmers of the highlands and other areas where there were few Negroes and where there was no basis for a plantation economy. And they were joined by many of the workers of the cities which were beginning to grow, as well as by many poor white farmers of other regions.

The black-belt whites, the townsmen, and all the allied forces of conservatism staved off radical agrarianism, although not without leaving a residue of a belligerent attitude that for decades found expression in support for leaders who at least talked, if they did not always act, against the "interests." And in crucial campaigns even now the counties of several states divide about as they did in the elections of the agrarian uprising.

The battle of Populism left a habit of radicalism in the upland areas; fortuitously it also strengthened the position of the black-belt whites. Intense agitation over Negro voting came as an aftermath of the Populist crisis. In some states the Negro had been disposed to go along with the coalition of upcountry white Democrats and Republicans under the Populist or fusion banner. Everywhere the plantation counties were most intense in their opposition to Negro voting; they raised a deafening hue and cry about the dangers to white supremacy implicit in a Negro balance of power. The Populists, with the death of their party on the national scene, dispiritedly returned to the Democratic party which offered them more than the party of McKinley and Hanna. And in the disillusionment brought about by Populist defeat, the black belts were able to recruit enough upcountry support to adopt poll taxes, literacy tests, and other instruments to disfranchise the Negro. Even on Negro disfranchisement, however, almost everywhere the battle was close. While the upcountryman had no love for the Negro he suspected, at times rightly, that the black belt was trying to disfranchise him as well as the black man.

In the fight against Populism and in the subsequent agitation about the place of the Negro, the black belts strengthened their position by reenforcing the South's attachment to the Democratic party. The raising of a fearful specter of Negro rule and the ruthless application of social pressures against those who treasonably fused with the Republicans under Populist leadership put down for decades the threat of the revival of two-party competition.

Two-party competition would have been fatal to the status of black-belt whites. It would have meant in the 'nineties an appeal to the Negro vote and it would have meant (and did for a time) Negro rule in some black-belt counties. From another standpoint, two-party competition would have meant the destruction of southern solidarity in national politics—in presidential elections and in the halls of Congress. Unity on the national scene was essential in order that the largest possible bloc could be mobilized to resist any national move toward interference with southern authority to deal with the race question as was desired locally. And the threat of Federal intervention remained, as the furore over the Lodge force bill of 1890 demonstrated.

This sketch of the broad outlines of the foundations of southern politics points to an extraordinary achievement of a relatively small minority—the whites of the areas of heavy Negro population—which persuaded the entire South that it should fight to protect slave property. Later, with allies from conservatives generally, substantially the same group put down a radical movement welling up from the sections dominated by the poorer whites. And by the propagation of a doctrine about the status of the Negro, it impressed on an entire region a philosophy agreeable to its necessities and succeeded for many decades in maintaining a regional unity in national politics to defend those necessities.

If the interpretation is correct—and there are many deviations in detail—the political prowess of the black belts must be rated high. The thesis, however, runs counter to the idea that many top-drawer southerners firmly believe, viz., that the poor white is at the bottom of all the trouble about the Negro. The planter may often be kind, even benevolent, towards his Negroes, and the upcountryman may be, as the Negroes say, "mean"; yet when the political chips are down, the whites of the black belts by their voting demonstrate that they are most ardent in the faith of white supremacy as, indeed, would naturally be expected. The whites of the regions with few Negroes have a less direct concern over the maintenance of white rule, whereas the whites of the black belts operate an economic and social system based on subordinate, black labor.

The critical element in the structure of black-belt power has been the southern Senator and his actual, if not formal, right to veto proposals of national intervention to protect Negro rights. The black belts have had nothing to fear from state governments on the race question, although control of state governments by hill people with their Populist notions might mean heavier taxation for schools and other governmental services. On the fundamental issue, only the Federal Government was to be feared. The black belts became bulwarks of Democratic strength. Their common attachment to the Democratic party gave them security of sorts against Republican meddling in the South. In the great apostasy of 1928 it was not the black belts that went Republican; they stood stalwart in the Democratic ranks. By the same logic, in 1948, after the Democratic party had abandoned the black belts, it was not the South as a whole that deserted the party. The seat of rebellion was the delta of Mississippi, the home of great planters, few whites, and many Negroes, as well as the last vestige of ante-bellum civilization. In the Dixiecrat standard-bearers, Governor Thurmond of South Carolina and Governor Wright of Mississippi, there was neatly symbolized the roots of a southern solidarity that was in process of erosion. As chief executives of the two states with the highest proportions of Negroes in their population, they spoke fundamentally for the whites of the black belt and little more, at least if one disregards their entourage of professional Ku Kluxers, antediluvian reactionaries, and malodorous opportunists.

Perhaps 1948 marked the beginning of an even sharper rate of descent in the long curve recording the decline in the power of black-belt whites. Yet their success—in conspiracy with the grand accidents of history—in cementing the South to the Democratic party will for a long time exert a profound influence on the politics of the South. Attachments to partisan labels live long beyond events that gave them birth.

If the critical element in the southern political system has been solidarity in national politics, there is logic in defining the political South—as it is here defined—in terms of consistency of attachment to the Democratic party nationally.

Eleven states and only eleven did not go Republican more than twice in the presidential elections from 1876 to 1944 (both inclusive). These states constitute the South for the purposes of this study. They are: Alabama, Arkansas, Florida, Georgia, Louisiana, Mississippi, North Carolina, South Carolina, Tennessee, Texas, and Virginia. Of these states only two went Republican twice in the period 1876–1944: Florida in 1876 and 1928 and Tennessee in 1920 and 1928. Five went Republican only once: South Carolina and Louisiana in the disputed election of 1876 and North Carolina, Texas, and Virginia in 1928. Alabama, Arkansas, Georgia, and Mississippi maintained an unbroken record of Democratic loyalty.

A high percentage of Negro population is associated with the Democratic voting tradition of those states we call "the South." In nine of them one-fourth or more of the population was Negro in 1940. Tennessee and Texas are marginal to "the South" by the criterion of Negro population. Tennessee in 1940 was 17.4 per cent Negro and Texas, 14.4. Maryland, which we exclude from the South, was 16.6 per cent Negro, but its voting habits diverged markedly from those of Tennessee and Texas. The range of Negro population—from 49.2 per cent in Mississippi to 14.4 in Texas—suggests that even "the South" is by no means homogeneous and that if the Negro influences the politics of the South, there ought to be wide variations in political practices from state to state.

Much labor could be expended on a definition of the South. Indices of illiteracy, maps of the distribution of cotton production, averages of per-capita income, and scores of other statistical measures could be used to delimit the region. Some writers have tried to delimit the South in terms of psychological attitude and have spoken of "the mind" and "the spirit" of the South. For the immediate purpose no better delimitation can be devised than one based on political behavior. And it can be contended, of course, that the regional cast of political attitude has a reality and a being over and beyond all the underlying social and economic characteristics that can be pictured in endless tabulations, correlations, and graphic representations.

Incidentally—and not without importance—it may be noted that the eleven states that meet the test of partisan consistency also are the eleven states that seceded to form the Confederacy.

PART III

The Ecology

of Race Relations

INTRODUCTION

WE SHOULD NOW HAVE IN MIND a very general map of the world in which there
are a number of race relations "regions." The distinguishing characteristics of
each of these regions have to be studied and understood in terms of its own
special historical experiences.

Race relations regions are not necessarily coextensive with existing administrative or governmental units; they may occupy only portions of such areas or
they may extend beyond them. A region like "the South" has had a more or less
independent existence between the State on the one hand and the United States
on the other. South Africa as a race relations region seems to be extending itself
northward beyond the legal borders of the Union of South Africa. To the extent
that such natural regions or areas, if we may so characterize them, have been
differentiated out of an evolving world community they also may be studied
independently of geography and history, that is, they may be studied ecologi-
cally.

"We must not deal with states, nations and empires as primary things which
have to be reconciled and welded together," is the way H. G. Wells put it. "We
must deal with these divisions as secondary things which have appeared and disappeared almost incidentally in the course of a larger and longer biological
adventure." In this "larger and longer biological adventure" should we regard
race as a primary or as a secondary thing?

The fundamental and elemental human group consists of the people of the
earth, a mere aggregation which has no form. With migration and competition

individuals and groups begin to move into place and this amorphous aggregation takes on form, that is, it becomes a community. Smaller communities become parts of an ever-enlarging world community. Human ecology approaches the study of the human community from much the same standpoint as plant ecology approaches the study of the plant community, that is, as a competitive and cooperative arrangement stripped of all those qualities considered cultural and social. Actually, however, it is impossible to attain such a level of abstraction in human ecology since social and cultural factors are always re-entering the competitive relations between human beings to effect changes in their spatial and economic relationships with each other.

Is there such a thing as an "ecology of race relations?" What light do ecological findings throw upon the origin and nature of race and of race relations? What appears to be the connection between the biological struggle for existence and an existing ecological order? What breaks up an ecological order? Is racial competition identical with biological competition? If not, what is the difference? At what point does the struggle for existence become social and racial? Does it appear that the idea of race itself enters the biological struggle for existence as a factor changing the nature and outcome of that struggle?

What is succession? Does succession imply the proposition that the groups successively occupying the same space are "different" racial or ethnic groups? What do you understand by a "survival system?" The great Bantu people of South Africa are not following what an Australian governor once called "the natural progress of the aboriginal race toward extinction." How would you account for this? Jews have learned how to live and survive in cities. Other urban groups have to maintain their numbers by a continuous process of recruitment from the countryside. What is involved in learning biologically how to live in cities? Is it necessary for existing racial stocks to mix and produce new specimens of mankind in order to adapt to radically new conditions? When we speak of racial survival just what is it that survives?

What is segregation and how would you distinguish between segregation and discrimination? How is segregation related to succession? When do cities offer an escape from racial classification and when do they contribute to its continuation through the existence of racial ghettos? What is the significance of segregation for racial survival? What would constitute indexes of segregation?

What is a racial division of labor? Distinguish between the racial division of labor as 1) a stereotype, and 2) a skewed occupational distribution. How can the existence of a racial division be established as a fact? To what extent does the ordinary division of labor and laborers in a society enter into the differentiation of different groups and into the definition of those groups as racial groups? Distinguish between the racial division of labor as 1) an economic fact and 2) as a moral fact. What is a criminal tribe and what do you know about the so-called criminal tribes of India? To what extent is it true that the "other race" is always a sort of criminal tribe? What parallels, if any, exist between economic divisions of labor by sex and economic divisions of labor by race? Does there appear to be any historical connection between the two? What connection is there, if any, between the racial division of labor or occupation and the taboo against racial intermarriage in a society? What is the importance of the racial division of labor in the formation, the integration and the maintenance of the human community?

How does the urban or the rural (frontier) location of industry, both agricultural and manufacturing industry, affect the process of racial stereotyping? How does the type of commercial and industrial entrepreneurship affect the form and content of social relationships defined as racial? Do these relationships and definitions seem to vary as between plantation, mine, farm, commercial company, and manufacturing industry? How? When is industry a breeder of racial stereotypes and doctrines? When is it a dissolver of such stereotypes and doctrines? How does the idea of race enter into the proletarianization of labor?

MIGRATION ETERNAL AND UNIVERSAL

By Ellen C. Semple

EVERY COUNTRY WHOSE HISTORY WE EXAMINE proves the recipient of successive streams of humanity. Even sea-girt England has received various intruding peoples, from the Roman occupation to the recent influx of Russian Jews. In prehistoric times it combined several elements in its population, as the discovery of the "long barrow" men and "round barrow" men by archaeologists and the identification of a surviving Iberian or Mediterranean strain by ethnologists go to prove. Egypt, Mesopotamia, and India tell the same story, whether in their recorded or unrecorded history. Tropical Africa lacks a history; but all that has been pieced together by ethnologists and anthropologists, in an effort to reconstruct its past, shows incessant movement—growth, expansion, and short-lived conquest, followed by shrinkage, expulsion, or absorption by another invader. To this constant shifting of races and peoples the name of historical movement has been given, because it underlies most of written history and constitutes the major part of unwritten history, especially that of savage and nomadic tribes.

Among primitive peoples this movement is simple and monotonous. It involves all members of the tribe, either in pursuit of game or following the herd over the tribal territory, or in migrations seeking more and better land. Among civilized peoples it assumes various forms and especially is differentiated for different members of the social group. The civilized state develops specialized frontiers—men, armies, explorers, maritime traders, colonists, and missionaries, who keep a part of the people constantly moving and directing external expansion, while the mass of the population converts the force once expended in the migrant food-quest into internal activity. Here we come upon a paradox. The nation as a whole, with the development of sedentary life, increases its population and therewith its need for external movements; it widens its national area and its circle of contact with other lands, enlarges its geographical horizon, and improves its internal communication over a growing territory; it evolves a greater mobility within and without, which attaches, however, to certain classes of society, not to the entire social group. This mobility becomes the outward expression of a whole complex of economic wants, intellectual needs, and political ambitions. It is embodied in the conquests which build up empires, in the colonization which develops new lands, in the world-wide exchange of commodities and ideas which lifts the level of civilization till this movement of peoples becomes a fundamental fact of history.

Otis Mason finds that the life of a social group involves a variety of movements characterized by different ranges or scopes: (1) The daily round from bed to bed. (2) The annual round from year to year, like that of the Tunguse Orochon of Siberia who, in pursuit of various fish and game, change their residence within their territory from month to month, or the pastoral nomads who move with the seasons from pasture to pasture. (3) Less systematic outside movements covering the tribal sphere of influence, such as journeys or voyages to remote hunting or fishing grounds, forays or piratical descents upon neighboring lands, eventuating usually in conquest, expansion into border regions for occasional occupation, or colonization. (4) Participation in streams of barter or commerce. (5) And, at a higher stage, in the great currents of human intercourse, experience, and ideas, which finally compass the world. In all this series the narrower movement prepares for the broader, of which it constitutes at once an impulse and a part.

Civilized man is at once more and less mobile than his primitive brother. Every advance in civilization multiplies and tightens the bonds uniting him with his soil, makes him a sedentary instead of a migratory being. On the other hand, every advance in civilization is attended by the rapid clearing of the forests, by the construction of bridges and interlacing roads, the invention of more effective vehicles for transportation whereby intercourse increases, and the improvement of navigation to the same end. Civilized man progressively modifies the land which he occupies, removes or reduces obstacles to intercourse, and thereby approximates it to the open plain. Thus far he facilitates movements. But while doing this he also places upon the land a dense population, closely attached to the soil, strong to resist incursion, and for economic reasons inhospitable to any marked accession of population from without. Herein lies the great difference between migration in empty or sparsely inhabited regions, such as predominated when the world was young, and in the densely populated countries of our era. As the earth grew old and humanity multiplied, peoples themselves became the greatest barriers to any massive migrations, till in certain countries of Europe and Asia the historical movement has been reduced to a continual pressure, resulting in compression of population here, repression there. Hence, though political boundaries may shift, ethnic boundaries scarcely budge. The greatest wars of modern Europe have hardly left a trace upon the distribution of its peoples. Only in the Balkan Peninsula, as the frontiers of the Turkish Empire have been forced back from the Danube, the alien Turks have withdrawn to the shrinking territory of the Sultan and especially to Asia Minor.

Where a population too great to be dislodged occupies the land, conquest results in the eventual absorption of the victors and their civilization by the native folk, as happened to the Lombards in Italy, the Vandals in Africa, and the Normans in England. Where the invaders are markedly superior in culture, though numerically weak, conquest results in the gradual permeation of the conquered with the religion, economic methods, language, and customs of the newcomers. The latter process, too, is always attended by some intermixture of blood, where no race repulsion exists, but this is small in comparison to the diffusion of civilization. This was the method by which Greek traders and colonists Hellenized the countries about the eastern Mediterranean and spread their culture far back from the shores which their settlements had appropriated. In this way Saracen armies, soon after the death of Mohammed, Arabized the whole eastern and southern sides of the Mediterranean from Syria to Spain, and Arab merchants set the stamp of their language and religion on the coasts of East Africa as far as Mozambique. The handful of Spanish adventurers who came upon the relatively dense populations of Mexico and Peru left among them a civilization essentially European, but only a thin strain of Castilian blood. Thus the immigration of small bands of people sufficed to influence the culture of that big territory known as Latin America.

Throughout the life of any people, from its fetal period in some small locality to its well-rounded adult era marked by the occupation and organization of a wide national territory, gradations in area mark gradations of development. And this is true, whether we consider the compass of their commercial exchanges, the scope of their maritime ventures, the extent of their linguistic area, the measure of their territorial ambitions, or the range of their intellectual interests and human sympathies. From land to ethics, the rule holds good. Peoples in the lower stages of civilization have contracted spatial ideas, desire and need at a given time only a limited territory, though they may change that territory often; they think in small linear terms, have a small horizon, a small circle of contact with others, a small range of influence, only tribal sympathies; they have an exaggerated conception of their own size and importance, because their basis of comparison is fatally limited. With a mature, widespread people like the English or French, all this is different; they have made the earth their own, so far as possible.

Just because of this universal tendency toward the occupation of ever larger areas and the formation of vaster political aggregates, in making a sociological or political estimate of different peoples, we should never lose sight of the fact that all racial and national characteristics which operate toward the absorption of more land and impel to political expansion are of fundamental value. A ship of state manned by such a crew has its sails set to catch the winds of the world.

Territorial expansion is always preceded by an extension of the circle of influence which a people exerts through its traders, its deep-sea fishermen, its picturesque marauders and more respectable missionaries, and earlier still by a widening of its mere geographical horizon through fortuitous or systematic exploration.

MOTIVES, MIGRATION AND SETTLEMENT

By Edgar T. Thompson

IT IS NOT ENOUGH to break down the expansion of Europe into the national divisions that took part in the settlement of overseas areas. It is of course true that the competition between Portugal, Spain, France, Holland, England, and later Germany led to important differences between these states in settlement policy and consequence, but it also is true that national rivalry was not the only complicating factor. Within the various colonizing nations there existed the rivalry of different elements variously motivated. Commercial interests in competition with each other were also in opposition to organized philanthropic, educational, governmental, and religious forces which in their turn were often at cross purpose with each other. We cannot treat any migrating and colonial group *en bloc* from the standpoint of national heritage. The British planters in the New World had, in all probability, more in common with the French and Portuguese planters than they had with British missionaries and British Puritans.

When the comparative consideration of migration and settlement is carried far enough it appears that national culture as a whole is not sufficiently elementary to account for variations in colonial development. Of more tangible importance in the actual course of settlement were the differences in motives that mobilized factions within national groups into various action patterns, and in the colonizing activities of the nations of Europe these different motives of special interest groups have worked themselves out into a variety of patterns.

Migrating groups variously motivated present themselves in a wide range of styles but in general they seem to fall into two broad types. In the first place, there are those whose members, possessing a sense of difference from others in political or religious faith, seek to withdraw and to segregate themselves from the world. Such migrations as the Pilgrams who went to New England, the Germans who went to Pennsylvania, and the Mormons who went to Utah, represent cultural migrations. Members of religious groups, trying to determine what the proper ends of life are, look for secluded spots where they can get possession of their own souls and direct their own lives within some scheme or system of beliefs. They migrate and settle as a community and they are concerned to maintain their institutions, including their agricultural practices, intact. They tend to reproduce, so far as circumstances allow, the folk agriculture of the lands from whence they came.

In the second place, there are those whose members seem possessed with a "will to power" and who move out into the world with a sense of expansion and conquest. They conceive of themselves as extending the frontiers of the world and of advancing their own status in it. They are adventurers, soldiers of fortune, traders, missionaries, planters, and administrators. The special purposes of

Adapted from Edgar T. Thompson, "Purpose and Tradition in Southern Rural Society: A Point of View for Research," *Social Forces*, XXV (March, 1947), 274–279; copyright 1947 by the Williams and Wilkins Company, Baltimore, Md., for the University of North Carolina Press and used with the kind permission of the publishers.

these men may differ widely, and with vastly different consequences, but they all operate on the fringe of change, "somewhere east of Suez," and they seek to adapt that change to their own interests.

Those who came to the tidewater of colonial Virginia fell into this latter class of settlers. They came from England, but the motives which dominated the particular segment of the English population which they represented did not originate in England. The history of their purpose is far older than England. Just where and when the motive of trade and production for trade originated need not concern us here. The story of its development, however, would have to include the long episode of the trading factory, an institution which went back to the Hanseatic League, the Italian *fondaco,* and beyond that to the Phoenician trading colony. The trading factory represents the original pattern of relations between overseas peoples of unequal economic development. Consequently the enterprising peoples have to maintain the trading terminus at each end. When the English, along with the Portuguese, the French, and the Dutch, adopted the pattern of the trading factory from the Italian and the Hanseatic merchants, they were, as were their predecessors, more concerned with trading facilities and the establishment of fortified harbors and stations than with command over the territory of the peoples with whom they traded. In the Orient, where the pattern of the trading factory took form, this simple commercial policy became a territorial policy when the factories of the English came into competition with those of other European nationals. But a territorial policy in the Orient did not require any wholesale migration of Englishmen to make it effective. The production of goods remained in the hands of natives. It was sufficient for the Europeans if the natives under their own rajas and sultans brought down the produce of spices, textiles, and tin to the factories in the seaports to be shipped to Europe and sold at extravagant prices.

It seems probable that the English establishment at Jamestown was founded on the model of the trading factory. Like the heads of English factories in India and elsewhere the head of the establishment at Jamestown was given the title of "president." The common store or magazine found in the factories of the Orient, the Levant, and the Baltic was reproduced at Jamestown. Again, those sent to early Jamestown by the Virginia Company were evidently not selected with reference to their fitness as farmers. But the New World situation turned out to be an entirely different kind of situation from that in which the trading factory had functioned successfully. There were no towns or cities in which to locate. The native population was not familiar with the practice of trade and, save for a few minor commodities, did not produce the goods required and were not disposed to do so. Under the circumstances men who went to trade remained to produce for trade and the trading factory evolved into the industrial planation.

The plantation became an organization for the accommodation of men of diverse class and race to each other in the production of an agricultural staple. But it did much more than define the pattern of race relations. It embodied an agricultural tradition, a tradition of exploitative farming. Tradition, however, is not something disembodied. Its operation in the various segments of our population is revealed in the different ways in which the members of those segments define situations and act these definitions out. The detailed analysis of the present and historical South from this point of view would, I am sure, throw a great deal of light upon southern culture. What follows is a bare outline of the role of the planter class, the poor white class, and the Negro class when seen in relation to the plantation tradition.

The motive of the trader or factor, modified by experience, became the motive of the planter, and the agricultural traditions which accumulated in the South originated in this modification. The life-organization of the planter was formed by his purpose and his ambition. The land passed into his hands as part of the new industrial purpose and he undertook to produce for the market an agricultural commodity which was entirely outside the traditional and folk agriculture of England. In Virginia this was tobacco. He might just as readily have planted opium poppies had there been any profit in them. The Indian was no longer looked upon as a customer but as a potential laborer. But the Indian was as worthless as a laborer as he was as a customer or independent producer and it became obvious that Virginia and the South would have to be settled by a new population willing to work or capable of being forced to work. Accordingly, an industrial army of occupation was moved into the area consisting first of white indentured servants and later of Negro slaves. Thus there grew up around the activities of the planter on the southern frontier a kind of camp agriculture which came to be known as plantation agriculture.

The purpose of the planter required the subordination of land and labor alike to the production of the crop. Land was tamed, not domesticated. One English traveller observed that "every planter considers himself only a temporary occupant on the plantation on which he is settled. He therefore goes on from year to year 'racking it out,' making it yield as much cotton and corn as he can without considering the future. He is always ready to sell out and travel further west." Similarly, labor, white or Negro, was regarded mainly as instrumental to the end of staple crop production.

The purpose of the planter was incorporated into the structure of the plantation, but the purpose of the institution as a whole did not thereby become the purpose of all its members. By some the pattern of waste and the exploitation of natural resources were adopted and transmitted to later generations but with the incentive to profit in wealth and status from that exploitation left out. Here is where the southern poor whites and Negroes enter the story. Almost universal in the descriptive literature on the poor whites is the emphasis upon the "void of pointless leisure" in which their lives are lived. What happened to the strong purpose which motivated their ancestors to come to America?

The act of quitting a familiar life in England and Europe for a strange and perilous one in America in an age when travel and communication were slow and difficult must have been motivated by deeply-set purposes and a great determination to realize them. It would be difficult to overemphasize the strength of purpose on the part of men who voluntarily sailed from England to the wilderness of the New World frontier. It was so with those planted on these shores by the Virginia Company and who became the "ancient planters," and it was just as true of those who came later as indentured servants pledged to work for five or seven years for a master in return for the cost of their passage. Some of these servants, possessed of some capital or with access to the capital of English investors, served out their time and became planters, but the opportunity to realize their intentions never came to most of them. In the competition for the status of planter relatively few were successful. The greater number failed and became the social ancestors of the present day "poor whites." Professor Abernethy suggests that the Scotch-Irish and German Protestants who flowed down the Valley of Virginia from Pennsylvania contributed mostly to the yeomanry of the South, whereas those who drifted west from the seaboard became the landless poor, the squatters and poor whites.

Those whites who were unable to maintain purpose, and who therefore lost it, were at a competitive disadvantage with those whites who could and did maintain it. They were subsequently defined as a class by their Negro slave competitors. Both John Fisk and T. J. Wertenbaker noticed that the appearance of Negro laborers in Virginia also marked the appearance of a class of mean whites. They had lived and worked as servants alongside Negro servants and slaves on the estates of the planters, but gradually they had been edged off the plantations and subjected to a process of natural segregation as they drifted together, intermarried, and locked themselves off from the plantation world. There was even some cultural reversion toward the level of the Indians. The isolation in which they were confined was not only spatial but temporal; it has extended itself to successive generations. In isolation other traditions were generated but the pattern of wasteful exploitation minus the motive of cumulative gain has persisted through the years more or less independently of the rest of the community.

The story of the Negro is very different. As Booker T. Washington was fond of saying, he is the only one of our citizens whose ancestors came to these shores by special invitation. In contrast to the marked strength of purpose animating the original white settlers from Europe, the dominating will that brought the Negro here was not his own. We are accustomed to attribute the difference between the progress of whites and Negroes in America to differences in race and culture, but it is entirely reasonable to suppose that, had there been no original differences in race and culture, the sheer presence of purpose in one group and its absence in the other would in time have accounted for at least a part of the difference in progress made by whites as compared to the Negroes. Added to this original difference in purpose was one hundred and fifty years of slavery which effectively blocked the acquisition by Negroes of the American tradition of achievement and material progress.

The contrast between poor whites and Negroes must not, of course, be exaggerated. The masses of southern Negroes, like the masses of southern whites, are impoverished both materially and spiritually. The great majority of Negroes face, in addition to problems purely racial, the same problems which confront the under-privileged white people of the South. But the general conclusion is, in my opinion, inescapable: the poor whites somewhere along the line suffered a failure of nerve and lost purpose; Negroes, on the contrary, came without purpose but are gaining it. The Negro is today mobilizing behind what is for him a great cause, the cause of interracial democracy. The poor white has no cause except the negative one of maintaining a precarious hold upon his position as a white man. Both Negroes and poor whites in the plantation areas of the South are caught in the same economic and social system so that the effort of one to rise invariably involves the other, but of the two the Negroes are in some respects the better off.

ECONOMIC SUCCESSION AND RACIAL INVASION IN HAWAII

By Andrew W. Lind

AS FAR AS THE WESTERN WORLD IS CONCERNED, the Hawaiian Islands began to rise out of the Pacific Ocean in the latter decades of the eighteenth century. Navigators and geographers have established their location on the map in mid-Pacific, near the northern edge of the tropics, and extending from the eighteenth to the twenty-second degrees of North latitude and from the 154th to 160th degrees of West longitude.

While this location, measured in terms of miles or degrees of latitude and longitude, is the same today as in the eighteenth century when Hawaii existed only for a few Polynesians scattered over the Islands of the South Pacific, for all practical purposes the water barriers have greatly diminished in this period. Geographical distances concern us only as they measure economic and finally social distances between individuals and groups.

The western sailing vessel was, of course, a vast improvement over the Hawaiian outrigger canoe as a medium of rapid and safe travel, and its introduction marks the initial shift in Hawaii's position. Judged by modern standards of communication, it still left the Islands largely isolated. James Hunnewell required a period of nine months and one day to make the sea voyage from the Atlantic coast to Honolulu in 1826, and the five months of sea travel by the *Thaddeus* carrying the first contingent of missionaries to the Islands in 1820 was not regarded as excessive. Sailing vessels, plying between Hawaii and China in the fur trade, could complete the voyage in from five and a half to seven and a half weeks. Of 85 voyages between San Francisco and Hawaii during 1850 and 1851, the median time required was seventeen days, the most rapid time being twelve days.

These distances have been greatly reduced through the introduction of mechanical devices of transportation. The following table of time distances of Pacific travel at various periods prior to modern air transport serves to indicate the degree to which Hawaii's position with reference to the rest of the world changed between 1780 and 1930.

Mechanical improvements in transportation are, however, the function and index of profound economic changes even more significant. The effective shifting of Hawaii's position in the Pacific is to be attributed primarily to its absorption within the streams of world trade and commerce. Our statements thus far have been concerned primarily with the limits set by Hawaii's geographical position and man's inventive genius to the contacts between these Islands and the rest of the world. The intensity of contacts, however, is even more dependent upon the establishment of bonds of economic interrelationship such as those which now knit the world into what McKenzie calls "a single complex of vital interdependence."

Adapted from Andrew W. Lind, *Economic Succession and Racial Invasion in Hawaii*, Abstract of Dissertation distributed by the University of Chicago Libraries, 1936. By permission of the author.

Time Distances between Honolulu and World Ports between 1780 and 1930

	Distance in Miles	1780–1850 Sailing Average No. of Days	1850–1930 Steam Average No. of Days
San Francisco	2,100	20	6
Puget Sound	2,400	25	7
Yokohama	3,440	..	10
Hongkong	4,900	60	13
Sydney	4,484	84	14
New Zealand	3,810	44	12
Manila	4,778	75	14
New York	7,668	146	11
London	10,525	159	13+
Bremen	11,233	172	14+

The factors which held these Islands captive in a waterbound isolation lasting for centuries are in many essentials the same as those which so long effectively prevented the white man from invading Java, India, the Philippines and Africa. The lack of contacts was due not so much to physical and psychological barriers to communication as it was to the absence of effective incentives to contacts. Hawaii had not acquired a position for itself in the widening web of trade relationships. And in an evolving world economy, this position must inevitably fluctuate according to conditions primarily economic which are quite as much determined outside the Islands as within.

During the era from 1876 on Hawaii was to be integrated within the expanding complex of world trade, within which physical distance, measured in terms of miles, would be superseded by distance, measured in time and cost units. Not only was a further important reduction of Hawaii's physical isolation to be effected through the spanning of the Pacific by fast traveling steamships and airplanes, but even more indissoluble ties of financial investments and credit were to be imposed.

The advantage of geographic proximity to Hawaii which mainland United States enjoys over its competitors became apparent in the early sandal-wood and whaling trade; and the years since 1876 have witnessed only a further development of the dominance of the United States, and particularly California, in the foreign contacts of Hawaii. By 1850 over 62 per cent of Hawaii's import trade was with the United States, chiefly California, and the Reciprocity Treaty of 1876 served to further guarantee the dominant control which they already possessed. Hawaii's exports, which increased so markedly in the ten years following Reciprocity was even more exclusively confined to the California markets. In 1884, for example, the United States, through its California ports, received 71,000 tons, or over 99 per cent of all Hawaii's foreign exports of sugar. The total exports of sugar increased from 13,000 tons in 1876 to 925,000 tons in 1929, of which almost the entire amount was shipped to San Francisco. The currents of stimulation measured by the value of import and export trade, between Hawaii and California, have been greatly intensified since Sugar became King in Hawaii.

The extensive commercial contacts with the outside world through such commodities as sugar, pineapples, rice, coffee, and tourists have stimulated commercial and trade relationships particularly with the United States, but in a degree with almost every section of the world. They have transformed these Islands from a primitive Polynesian commonwealth, into a highly specialized agricultural and industrial unit within the world complex of trade.

Diversification and uncertainty in trading contacts have been followed by specialization and regularity. The casual and tenuous ties established by tramp traders between the Sandal-wood Isles and Cathay, Siberia, the Pacific Northwest, California, Mexico, South America, and the islands of the South Pacific are replaced by the strong, yet pliable cables of the sugar and pineapple trade. Two hundred million dollars in import and export values between Hawaii and the United States now bind the Territory to the American mainland with a tenacity which the sinking of the Islands into the sea alone could destroy. The geographic proximity to the mainland has been vastly accentuated by a commerce which now dominates Island life.

Hawaii's position with reference to other regions about the Pacific basin has, on the other hand, been rendered more remote than formerly. The early contacts with Siberia, Alaska, and Mexico have almost totally disappeared; while trade relationships with British Columbia, South America, Japan, China, the Philippines, New Zealand, Australia, and Europe have assumed a very specialized nature within the Island economy. Hawaii is bound to one as a market for its crops, to another for its production commodities, and to others for consumption goods, but rarely to any one region for all these services. This dominating function is alone served by the United States. South America provides Hawaii with its fertilizers, New Zealand and Australia with a portion of its food; while Germany, China, and Japan now figure largely as sources for the consumption goods which their emigrants in Hawaii utilize. Thus, with the partial exception of the United States, considerations other than that of geographic distance determine the position of the Islands with reference to the rest of the world.

We have conceived the changing ecological position of Hawaii as the most abstract index of the entire Island epic. Each successive shift in Hawaii's relationship to the world community has produced and reflected profound economic and cultural reverberations throughout the Islands. It is assumed that one may ultimately correlate a large proportion of the personal experiences of the Hawaiian population, including attitudes and opinions, with these changes in the Island position.

During the 150 years since the discovery of Hawaii by Captain Cook, three major economies, corresponding closely to the three eras of Hawaiian-world contacts, have successively occupied the dominant role as the agencies for the exploitation of the region's resources and the securing of a livelihood for its population. The orderly sequence of economies—the one not only preceding in time but preparing the way for its successor—may conveniently be denoted by the term economic succession. Succession is the most abstract term used to designate the process by which one type of social organization follows another in orderly sequence. Succession is to be distinguished from the mere historical sequence of events, in that it takes account of the factors which condition the transition from one stage to another. In the final analysis succession is concerned with, and is reflected in, the changes of position of individuals and groups. The description of this process in Hawaii involves some discussion of the factors operating to effect the passing of one economy and the appearance of the next.

The three economies which have thus far occupied the Hawaiian stage—the native economy, the pioneer or intermediary economy, and the present plantation economy—may be presumed to mark the universal pattern of development in regions similarly situated, i.e., insular regions located in the tropics, already occupied by a primitive culture, but possessing what Nieboer calls "open resources." An examination of the history of the West Indies, Java, Sumatra, Ceylon, the Philippines, and the Islands of the South Seas would probably reveal a highly similar pattern of economic development.

The native economy of early Hawaii was maintained some years after western civilization had made its initial impact. It involved an organization of the productive processes effectively designed to exploit the indigeneous resources according to the rather simple and fixed demands of the native population. The occupation of the soil, its cultivation, division and tenure, and the orientation of the ceremonial and religious life of the people were of a sort to effectively sustain the underlying fish and *poi* economy. Even the feudal character of the social organization, with its hierarchy of office and privilege, was closely integrated with the existing economy. Such a regime was obviously self-sufficing, and trading contacts within the Islands were almost lacking, while those with the outside world were nil.

Almost coincidentally with the initial shift in Hawaii's position due to its discovery by the English explorers, the native economy began to decline, and its rival and successor, the western pioneer economy, sank its first roots into Island soil. The impersonal struggle between the rival economies was protracted and bitter, and the dominance of the invading system was hardly established before it was, in turn, threatened by the emerging plantation economy. The period of transition between the native and pioneer economies witnessed the gradual abandonment of the system of native agriculture and the diversion of Hawaiian energies to the satisfying of the demands of the invading traders for sandal-wood, specialized food supplies, timber, and for native labor. Agricultural lands in certain regions were abandoned; local economic self-sufficiency was greatly diminished; foreign commodities displaced local manufactures for native consumption; population began to concentrate in the emerging seaport towns; and a widespread social disorganization ensued. Many of these changes are susceptible of quantitative statement.

The pioneer economy may be conceived as fulfilling an intermediary function between the native and climax plantation economies, a fact which is reflected in the brevity of its span of dominance. This era was initiated by a lengthy period of experimentation and transitory contacts. For approximately a half century after Captain Cooks' discovery, the western pioneer economy maintained its foothold upon Hawaiian soil by means of casual, highly speculative, and short-lived trading relationships with the natives. The settled foreign population during this early period was very meager and of uncertain origin and status; and the native population and the natural resources functioned largely as raw materials to be exploited by the foreigners as rapidly and extensively as possible. During this period the invading economy began its inroads upon the indigenous culture and established for itself certain economic claims upon the Islands which have persisted and expanded to the present day. The latter half of this era witnessed the establishment of a considerable settled foreign population in Hawaii as resident cultivators and traders. During this period an approximation to the American homestead system enjoyed a rather precarious existence for a number of years, and the initial plantation experiments were made.

Indicative of the underlying shifts in Hawaii's position relative to the world at this time (1830–1860), and the emergence of the pioneer economy as dominant in the region is the rise of the town as the organizing center of the new regime. Foreign capital began to seek investment in Hawaii; and trade, as a legitimate and permanent function of the community, was established through the seaport centers. Specialization of function, the division of labor, and the integration of Island life through the deepening channels of communication and transportation between the dominant centers and the periphery, provide additional indices of the evolving economy.

The climax period in the economic succession in Hawaii was finally established only after a lengthy struggle extending over a half century, in which the advance of the invading economy was contested not only by its predecessors in the series, but even more by the rival plantation systems in foreign lands. The field of contest was, in part, removed from Hawaii to the world exchanges of sugar, coffee, and pineapples, and to the council chambers on tariffs, embargoes, and immigration. When "sugar became king" in Hawaii, the last important alteration in the position of the Islands in the world community occurred. Hawaii became oriented to the world markets and eventually epitomized in its most advanced form the science and technological achievement of the western world.

The bases for the final ascendancy of the plantation system must be sought in a variety of factors, most of which are operative in all agricultural regions within the tropic and subtropic zones. Keller, Nieboer, and others have analyzed the rise of the plantation system, and Hawaii appears to conform quite closely to the general pattern—an abundance of arable land in the tropics with a geographic and cultural setting which prevents the use of white labor, the specialized and extensive cultivation of one or two stable crops, the resort to force as a device to secure native labor, the importation of cheap labor likewise subjected to some type of compulsion to guarantee continuity of service. Hawaii moreover illustrates the role of large bodies of capital, organized for large scale production and cooperative enterprise, in the dominance of the plantation regime. The gradual perfection and development of this system, in response to the pressure exerted by the world market, has resulted in an organization of the processes of agricultural production which is perhaps without peer in the western world; the resources of science and technical skill have been mobilized for the assistance of industry on a mammoth scale and at tremendous expense. The plantation system in Hawaii, with its organization of all the factors of production, including land, labor and capital, and the entire community itself, for the maximum of economic efficiency, probably marks the crowning achievement of western capitalism in this field.

Correlative to and implicit in the economic succession briefly sketched, has been a series of ethnic labor invasions and occupational displacements in Hawaii, which have had profound social implications. These extensive population movements fortunately lend themselves to quantitative analysis and thus provide another basis for comparison with the changing ecological position of the Islands. The more dramatic and doubtless the most significant of these movements have been initiated and controlled by the plantation system and are thus confined in point of time to this latter period. The cultivation of the soil under Caucasian control in Hawaii, as elsewhere in the tropics, has been conducive to the establishment of a highly stratified society. Judged both by the wage received and the social status achieved, the rise of a distinct cleavage between the plantation laborer and the rest of society is clearly marked; and equally evident is the tendency for the laborer to escape from this category as rapidly as the opportunity presents itself.

The natural consequence has been the continuous cycle of (1) labor importation, (2) its exploitation for a few years, and (3) the plantation exodus. This fundamental pattern, with minor variations, seems to persist throughout the plantation system, in spite of governmental interference, strikes, excessive shipping costs, and foreign proscriptions. When one source of supply fails, another is soon discovered to provide this labor juggernaut with fresh material; when Chinese threatened the scheme through sheer numbers, Japanese were used to checkmate, and when these latter proved onerous in their demands, Portuguese, Koreans, Porto Ricans, Spanish, and Filipinos relieved the situation. With but slight and infrequent interruptions, the flow of population into the plantation hopper and later out into the Hawaiian non-plantation receptacles, to the United States, or back to the country of origin goes on unceasingly.

Each new supply has left its special imprint upon the Hawaiian social system, varying in its intensity and significance according to the size of the invading group, its age and sex composition, and the pattern of culture. The ever changing hues of Hawaii's polyglot and polychrome population and the warp and woof of its perplexing interracial problems are largely to be traced in the flux and flow of its ethnic labor groups.

Another series of significant ecological movements, correlated with the underlying economic pattern and the changing role of Hawaii in the world trade streams, relates to the shifting positions of each of the immigrant groups along the economic and social ladder in Hawaii. As the laborers effect a release from the plantation system, each ethnic group characteristically follows a given set of patterns in becoming accommodated occupationally to non-plantation life. The nature of the accommodation varies in part with the date and order of arrival in Hawaii of the particular group among the rest, the occupational experience and tradition of the group in the old country, the vested interests of the dominant group in the specific occupation, as well as the capacity of the occupations to absorb additional units.

Primary in its influence upon the rate of the vertical movement of the immigrants and their children is the pressure exerted through the population at the lower levels of society. The principal forces initiating this upward movement of population are the pressure of the natural increase of population, the negative influence of the plantation, the superior standard of living which the Hawaiian environment affords to the immigrant, as well as the freedom to compete for a more desirable position.

FROM INDIAN TO NEGRO IN THE
COLOMBIAN CHOCÓ

By Robert Cushman Murphy

THE GREATER PART OF THE PACIFIC SEABOARD from Panama to western Ecuador was never effectively occupied by the Spaniards. To this day, indeed, the rain-forest area between shore line and Andes remains a region of sparse human population, as well as one in which the original armed contest between white and red men has been succeeded by a struggle, biological rather than warlike, in which red and black peoples are the chief competitors. As Eder has written, large parts of Colombia once overrun by conquistadors and missionaries have ever since remained all but untraveled by white men. In this second phase, however, the native Indian of the Chocó has become a steady loser to the introduced African, and the ultimate inequality is likely to prove more marked than that of the earlier and overt conflict between aborigines and Caucasians.

Various fates overtook the groups of Indians with whom the Spanish conquerors came in contact in the Caribbean, Panama, and northern Colombia. Caribs and Chibchas, for example, were exterminated, either in warfare or in subsequent enslavement. The Cuna, on the other hand, successfully resisted encroachment from the beginning and, after conclusion of a large-scale migration from the Pacific to the Atlantic side of Darien, have maintained both independence and racial integrity to the present day. The Chocó tribes, of the Pacific watershed and the San Juan-Atrato Valley, at first resisted; next, in the latter part of the seventeenth century, they partly capitulated, mainly as a result of the enmity between themselves and the Cuna; but subsequently, in 1726, they violently threw off the Spanish yoke that threatened complete subjugation. After that date the Chocó peoples retained a large measure of security, from aloofness even more than from combativeness, until a new source of danger appeared in a negro population capable of outbreeding them in their own territory. . . .

At the delta of the San Juan River, Colombia, the first Spanish visitors found platformed villages of impressive size, and the coastal population of the Bay of Chocó (Buenaventura) remained relatively large and hostile at least into the eighteenth century. It has been a subject for marvel in both early and recent times that the drier, more healthful segments of alluring aspect along the western slopes of the Baudó mountains harbored few indigenes, whereas their number abruptly increased between Cabita Bay, Colombia, and Cape San Francisco, Ecuador, a stretch marked by maximum heat and rainfall and bordered almost uninterruptedly with *manglares*. The low-gradient rivers mentioned above of course supply the answer. The Chocó Indians were and are a riverine people; with them, as with their successors, a canoe was the place in which a man spent the greater part of his life.

Adapted from Robert Cushman Murphy, "Racial Succession in the Colombian Chocó," *The Geographical Review*, XXIX (July, 1939), 461–471; copyright 1939 by the American Geographical Society of New York and used with the kind permission of the publisher.

Chocó, or Emperá, is the general term for all the Indians of the Pacific drainage area since the emigration of the Cuna. The population is divided into two linguistic subgroups, the Nonamá-Chocó, of the San Juan tributaries, and the "true Chocó," who inhabit the valley of the River Baudó and regions south of Buenaventura. The Indians usually call themselves *cholos,* in contradistinction to negroes and whites. According to Wassén, the Chocó have a very close affinity both in blood and in culture with the natives of northwestern Amazonia, on the other side of the Andes, rather than with those of the Isthmus of Panama and the Gulf of Darien. For centuries Chocó and Cuna have lived side by side without mingling, one of the genetic evidences of this fact being that albinos are apparently unknown among the Chocó though notoriously common among the Cuna. . . .

Wassén, Nordenskiöld, and other anthropologists are at pains to point out that the Chocó have always been predominantly an inland people, a circumstance no doubt connected with their origin. In addition to the fact that they dwell at present along the middle and upper reaches of Colombian rivers, there is the curious linguistic evidence that these Indians today possess no native words for marine animals and attributes; for the whole category of maritime nouns, indeed, they seem to have adopted a Spanish vocabulary. This raises the unsolved problem of the date at which the Cuna first began their historic evacuation from the Pacific coast, perhaps in the face of a gradual invasion of alien stock from somewhere beyond the mountains to the southeast.

Wassén's Chocó guides informed him of a tradition that the Cuna (meaning, as he then supposed, merely an enemy people) formerly dwelt on Gorgona, an island that has certainly supported no aboriginal population since the date of its discovery by Pizarro. The Swedish scholar was inclined to discount this tradition, believing that Gorgona was unsuited for permanent occupation and that artifacts had never been found there. Ten years earlier, however, Hornell had reported on important archeological finds made at Gorgona during the *St. George* expedition of 1924. Various neolithic implements, together with sculptured boulders depicting animals and deities, an abundance of potsherds under 12 to 18 inches of soil close to the shore of the island, fragments of large stone troughs, and clear indications of ancient pile dwellings showed beyond a doubt that Gorgona had once been the home of large numbers of Indians. Even earlier than Hornell, Father Merizalde del Carmen had written of ancient fishhooks and bracelets of gold and pottery jugs obtained along the narrow channel that separates Gorgona Island from its southern outlier, Gorgonilla.

It thus seems likely that in some era before the arrival of the first Spaniards emigration and other circumstances had already brought about a marked diminution in the aboriginal population along parts of the Pacific coast between Panama and Esmeraldas. We shall now turn to the changes of the subsequent historical period. Throughout the seaboard between the Isthmus and Buenaventura there are at present relatively few human beings other than negroes and mulattoes, a condition that holds likewise along the coast southwest of Buenaventura. It is certain, moreover, that the white population of Tumaco and of the recent and subsidized settlement at Solano Bay is making scant headway. Elsewhere in the Chocó the "new population of hardy and enterprising foreigners" predicted by Trautwine as not far distant has never materialized.

Cieza de Leon gives a passing picture of the prompt extermination of the

Indians on the readily accessible Pearl Islands very soon after the founding of Panama. Dampier, during a visit made more than a century and a half later, found that in 1685 this archipelago was not inhabited by any whites but that the gentlemen of Panama maintained negroes there to cultivate the plantations. Furthermore, the larger forested islands of the group sheltered at that date great numbers of runaway slaves, who hid in the woods by day and pillaged the crops and stock at night. De Viana speaks in some detail of the wholly black population, slave and free, in 1791.

Concerning a similar direct extermination of Indians by whites southward from the Gulf of Panama along the continental coast we have less information. It is evident, as was noted above, that during the sixteenth century the population density increased in that direction; for the first voyagers found few Indians near Piñas Bay, more near Point Marzo and the Gulf of Cupica, still more about the mouths of the San Juan, and so very many near Cape San Francisco, Ecuador, that, as Prescott cites from the chronicles, "ten thousand warriors" mustered to oppose the march of Pizarro. Setting aside later changes in racial composition, the distribution of population has retained a similar arrangement up to our own day.

When Woodes Rogers cruised along Pacific Colombia in the first decade of the eighteenth century, the Chocó coast was still inhabited by Indians who, he wrote, "make War and Peace with one another at discretion" and who were prompt to man canoes in order to attack any ship that seemed to be in difficulty offshore. The Bay of Buenaventura, in particular, was then "all round inhabited by warlike *Indians.*"

In Tecames Road (i.e. the Esmeraldas River, Ecuador) Rogers also found numbers of still savage Indians on August 26, 1709. At this date there were a few resident Spanish priests distributed through the country, and also a large number of negroes, but the conspicuous element in the population still consisted of more or less naked and painted indigenes.

Another century passed, and Mollien could write that the villages of the Chocó were "inhabited for the most part by negroes, people of colour and some Indians." The early Spaniards had, of course, brought in negro slaves to work the mines and to undertake various domestic labors. Moreover, there was doubtless a continuous sequence of escape from Panama down this lost coast. Enactment of legislation in Colombia providing that all slaves born after July 16, 1821, should be liberated when they attained their eighteenth year practically ended organization and facilitated dispersal of the negroes through the wilderness.

There are abundant indications that the first black *cimarrones* to come among the Chocó were hospitably received, doubtless because of common enmity toward the Spanish slaveholders, and that a mixture of blood occurred to a degree never known among the Cuna. Later, however, the Chocó developed so strong a sentiment against miscegenation that they became intolerant of association with either negroes or zambo half-breeds. Anthropologists who have visited them agree in emphasizing this trait. When Captain Allan Hancock's yacht *Velero III* visited Puerto Utria in January, 1935, the party found that a small community of primitive and painted Chocó kept aloof from near-by negro or negroid families. It thus appears that in present-day competition between black man and red the latter is being forced back rather than absorbed.

In the account of the cruise of H.M.S. *Pandora* and *Herald,* during which Puerto Utria was discovered, in 1848, Seemann refers to the Colombian coast from the vicinity of Punta Quemado northward to Piñas Bay as unchanged from its pristine condition except for the disappearance of the bulk of the aborigines. In December, when his vessel was lying off Ardita Bay, a canoe came out from shore with four Indians and two negroes. Today the whole crew of such a craft would assuredly be negroes. When the *Pandora* entered Cupica Bay on December 28, 1847, the alcalde of the district was an Indian, as were all the inhabitants of the little village near the mouth of the Cupica River.

Selfridge visited Cupica Bay in March, 1871, or about a quarter of a century after Seemann. The inhabitants of the village then numbered a hundred, mostly negroes, though Selfridge refers to two or three neighboring families of Chocó Indians, the remnant of a once numerous tribe. At the date of my call at this same harbor, on September 11, 1937, several negro youths who visited my launch informed us that the residents of the community were now all blacks and that Indians were rarely met anywhere in the coastal neighborhood. Restrepo corroborates this and states that two hundred colored people occupy the thirty thatched huts of Cupica.

Michler, who preceded Selfridge by more than a decade, had already found that in 1858 the Humboldt Bay region was devoid of resident Indians of pure blood, though the nomadic Chocó of the inland rivers occasionally made trips to this part of the ocean front for coconuts, from the shells of which they manufactured cups and other utensils. The contemporary inhabitants of the Bahia Ensenada, or Kelley's Inlet (a part of the bight known as Humboldt Bay), were principally zambos, together with many renegade negroes from Panama and Jamaica and a few white outcasts. The assemblage was described by the engineers of the interoceanic-canal survey as composed of thieves, wreckers, sharpers, ex-pirates, and escaped convicts. The chief interest of such epithets is that they indicate the open and yet obscure path extending southward from the Isthmus for individuals who had a desire to disappear. . . .

Whether or not the Chocó were the Indians who inhabited the Pacific coast four centuries ago, they are now almost exclusively an inland people. But even in the interior the expanding negro population has had the effect of pushing them everywhere farther and farther upstream, and the numerical relationship between the races is shifting steadily in favor of the blacks. Merizalde del Carmen estimated in 1921 that the human population in the part of the Colombian Chocó that lies between the Naya River and the Ecuadorian border totaled 7000, of whom 80 per cent were negroes, 18 per cent mulattoes, 1½ per cent whites, and ½ per cent Indians. This is a ratio of 160 pure blacks to one Indian! The decimation of the southern Indians is ascribed by this author to epidemic and other disease as the immediate cause. Both he and Aubert de la Rüe list at length the fevers, skin maladies, ectoparasites, and other evils that afflict the entire region.

Farther north in the Chocó, particularly along the River Baudó, the tributaries of the San Juan, and the River Jaqué in Darien, the Indians have persisted to a greater extent; but even here the Chocó families residing in the marginal zone frequently change their abodes in order to get out of the way of the oncrowding negroes. Because of the distinctive architectural motif of each people, it is easy for even the hurried traveler to recognize the respective territories of Indian and black and to observe the transitory intermingling near their borders.

The San Juan River itself has become wholly dominated by negro settlement, as is true also of the lower reaches of its western affluent, the Docordó. According to Wassén, the middle and upper reaches of the Docordó are at present the main headquarters of the Nonamá-Chocó. That there are still unknown centers of Indian population in the vast and poorly explored region between the San Juan-Atrato axis and the sea may be taken for granted. Mr. G. William Bylander, Swedish consul at Buenaventura, who is extremely conversant with the Chocó Indians, has orally informed me that itinerant Jesuit priests discovered in 1937 two hitherto completely unsuspected primitive Indian settlements on the upper Baudó and that one of these was a community of no fewer than 2000 persons. Aubert de la Rüe writes of the *bravos* of the upper Yurumangui Valley, with whom no white man has yet established contact in their own territory but whose existence is known by the *jai* or boat-model offerings they send down on the current of the river at certain seasons. As Nordenskiöld has said, the Indians seek the parts of the country in which they believe they may be left alone as much and as long as possible.

A number of authors have touched casually on various aspects of the interracial competition in which the Indian is proving the consistent loser, but the whole subject is worthy of further consideration. Initially, of course, the negro enjoyed the prestige that pertained to his association with the white conquerors. He had the white man's language; he inevitably shared the attitude of the Spaniard toward the Indian; and he has remained to this day the confidant of the white rather than of the Indian. In other words, the negro is a Colombian, the Chocó Indian a savage. Many examples of this psychological relationship are to be found in recent anthropological literature dealing with the region.

Then there is the matter of purely physical attributes, such as stature and weight, which would be likely to have both direct and indirect effects. The native Indians of the western Colombian rain forest, like their Amazonian relatives, are a small people. Trautwine found in the middle of the last century that most of the Baudó men were less than five feet five inches in height. The Chocó negroes, on the other hand, are notably large and powerfully built. . . .

The slowly changing basis of food supply in the Chocó has undoubtedly had a more detrimental effect on the Indian than on the negro. Despite the vast expanse of wilderness and the relatively low density of human population, game has tended to become scarce over large areas. In the forests on and about the "inland island" of Munguidó, or elsewhere in the periodically flooded territory of the lower San Juan river system, an Indian may now have to hunt all day before finding the spoor of one of the two kinds of peccaries, of deer, agouti, or smaller game. Working with this is the fact that pressure of the negroes has driven the Indians into areas less suited to the cultivation of simple agricultural crops than their former downstream holdings. The concentration of the Indians along the higher stretches of the rivers, where rapids are numerous and the volume of water least, also tends toward a quick depletion of edible fish and other stream resources. In the Chocó the height of the river floods comes in November, the period of lowest water in January. In the latter season the Indians take a heavy toll of fish from pools near the headwaters of the rivers through the use of a vegetable poison. All such factors make the Indian, who formerly relied chiefly on the chase, more and more dependent on cultivated crops and domesticated animals, while at the same time the territory he has come to occupy becomes less and less suited to both. Archer says:

> Many days the family has no meat because the hunter has returned empty-handed after a long hunt, and at times like this they simply eat more rice or boiled plantains. The parrots are now wary and fly too high to be shot; the monkeys no longer frequent the haunts of man. It is a hard struggle indeed to wrest a living in competition with the increasing Negro population.

The African is unquestionably better acclimated, or congenitally more resistant to the historic maladies of the white man, than the Indian is. It is fair also to speculate as to whether the proverbial "million years" of selective evolution in the hot and humid Congo has not adapted the negro to the Chocó environment to a degree nearer perfection than the autochthonous Indian. The racial occupancy of the Indian is perhaps to be measured by at most some tens of thousands of years, and he seems less fitted to his habitat than the interloper. Bates, indeed, published more than sixty years ago certain cogent observations in support of this thesis:

> I have already remarked on the different way in which the climate of this equatorial region affects Indians and negroes. No one could live long amongst the Indians of the Upper Amazons, without being struck with their constitutional dislike to the heat. . . . No Indian resident of Ega can be induced to stay in the village (where the heat is felt more than in the forest or on the river) for many days together. They bathe many times a day . . . They are restless and discontented in fine dry weather, but cheerful in cool days, when the rain is pouring down on their naked backs. . . . They are very subject to disorders of the liver, dysentery, and other diseases of hot climates; and when any epidemic is about, they fall ill quicker, and suffer more than negroes or even whites. How different all this is with the negro, the true child of tropical climes! The impression gradually forced itself on my mind that the red Indian lives as a stranger or immigrant in these hot regions, and that his constitution was not originally adapted, and has not since become perfectly adapted, to the climate.

Concomitant effects of the interracial struggle in the Chocó have saturated the ideology of both Indians and negroes. The magic power of the negro is held in universal awe by the Indians, as Wassén reports. Many negroes are *brujos,* or wizards; many of both sexes possess the evil eye. They are credited with an ability to kill fish merely by looking at them, or by means of a glance to cause children to develop boils or to fall ill in other ways. Already, after less than four centuries of association, one of the most horrific demons in Chocó mythology has assumed the guise of a negro. The racial superstitions are to a certain extent mutual, as Nordenskiöld reports, and the blacks stand in great dread of the Indians' knowledge of vegetal and animal poisons and of their ability to handle deadly snakes and to "plant" them where they are likely to do vengeful harm. Nevertheless, even the part of the competition that pertains chiefly to a psychic plane works out far more to the disadvantage of the Indian than of the negro.

The ultimate conclusion in the sphere of human geography would seem to be that the negro is the fittest heir of the Chocó. He enjoys the typical "pre-adaptations" of Cuénot, which imply that an organism wins out if it possesses traits that particularly suit it to a given environment or that enable it to find a new environment where such traits confer relative advantages. Transplanted from Africa, the negro has become, as regards survival, a "native" superior to his predecessor, even over the obstacle of a greatly inferior sanitary code. Like many elements of the humid-tropical Caribbean biota, he has succeeded willy-nilly in breaking through to the Pacific seaboard at the weakest point in the continental barrier, which is the Isthmus, and has spread thence into all rain-forest terrain that attains no great altitude. In the mountain regions, or wherever aridity begins at sea level, as in both Mexico and Peru, his numbers decrease and the Indian more nearly holds his own, with whites rather than blacks as competitors. But in the Chocó the negro has won a secure footing among a large number of West Indian coastal organisms that accomplished still earlier invasions of the Pacific littoral. To this same "West Indian" category, indeed, the black man might secondarily be regarded as belonging.

IMPERSONAL ASPECTS OF RACE RELATIONS

By Edward B. Reuter

THE CONTACTS of culturally advanced and simple peoples have been studied in much detail; the processes are well defined and the outcome is predictable. The first trader who exchanges items of European manufacture for goods of native origin initiates a struggle for survival that moves irresistably to a displacement of the native culture and a destruction of the native people. The facts are too familiar and the cases too numerous to require extended documentation.

The European infiltration into a virgin area is characterized by the introduction of various articles superior to corresponding items of indigenous origin. The trader's whiskey, fire arms, metal tools, woven cloth, and other goods have obvious advantages; their acceptance and use is a commonsense procedure. The articles are eagerly sought in exchange for local products and presently they replace articles of native manufacture. By degrees, the indigenous arts are neglected and the skills are presently forgotten. The foreign goods become necessities; the natives become increasingly dependent on trade and increasingly obligated to furnish goods or labor in exchange. There is an insidious disorganization of native life and economy which results presently in a more or less complete ecological displacement—a substitution of foreign for native goods. The unsuspecting natives are thus brought into the orbit of the European economy.

From Edward B. Reuter, "Culture Contacts in Puerto Rico," *The American Journal of Sociology*, LII (September, 1946), 91–93.

The process of succession is always concealed in a great mass of concrete historical detail which varies in character with the size of the native population, the power and social organization of the native people, the products of the area, and other matters of local incidence. But whether the contacts are in America or Australia, Hawaii or the Caribbean, the general movement is a progressive displacement of the native culture and the simpler people.

One conceives the process in wholly impersonal terms. It is of course true that, in many areas, the contacts of the European and native peoples have been marked by ruthless mistreatment of defenseless people. It is equally true that, in other areas, the contacts of advanced and backward peoples have been characterized by paternal attitudes and by kindly and sympathetic personal relations. In a moral context the concrete relations, whether monstrous or humane, are matters of prime importance; in analytical study they are, at most, of incidental concern: they do not affect the end results. The real struggle is one of values. When stone and metal tools come into competition, the stone items, with the people who struggle for their retention, become museum pieces while the metal items come into general use and their users inherit the earth. The competition of the bow and the rifle, the ox-cart and the motorized truck, magic and science, Choctaw and English have but one possible end: the replacement of the less by the more efficient is inevitable; the people are pawns, they assimilate or they disappear.

In the present-day world, the primitives no longer have a place; in large part they are already gone, even in the more remote areas they are going. We may regret the disappearance of the quaint and curious customs of another era and of peoples uncorrupted by the inhuman folkways of the urbanized and industrialized West, or we may rejoice at the disappearance of the forms of misery, squalor, filth, and brutality that are inseparable parts of the primitive way of life. But, aside from our emotional reactions, we know that the primitive peoples and their way of life are to be displaced. We are permitted to hope that the displacement will be merciful; we know that it is inevitable.

But there are other millions who are not primitive but whose future seems to depend upon factors over which they have only limited control. There are many areas, large and small, of backward or divergent culture; and there are numerous minorities, nationalities, and racial groups of precarious status in a rapidly changing world. These excluded peoples and folk cultures are largely outside the orbit of European knowledge, but they are not outside the orbit of European influence. If the world is one, as scholars have long known and as politicians are beginning to discover, these cultural islands will presently lose their isolation and cultural autonomy. They will, inevitably, come within the world market; somehow they will be integrated into the economic and cultural world of the future.

Exactly what happens, in concrete detail, in the contact of European and folk culture, we do not know. Certain aspects of cultures are curiously tenacious of life. We are continually confronted, in our scientific and technological world, with magical practices, folk beliefs, types of mind, and other reminders that we are not as far removed as we would like to think from our primitive and folk ancestry. We are all painfully aware, for example, that our educational system is as much traditional as it is rational, that it is encumbered with survivals from earlier eras, that its content is often a body of pre-scientific lore, that its methods are antiquated, that its personnel is sometimes closer to the medieval monastery than to the scientific laboratory. And in other areas of life, social and intellectual vestiges are even more numerous; sometimes they are the prevailing patterns of thought that resist displacement and seek to dominate the way of life. In addition to the intellectual lag, the persistence of the medieval in the modern world, in spite of the educational machinery, or because the educational machinery has remained so largely medieval, every nation has a varied assortment of nationalistic and other groups emotionally wedded to special values and inefficient ways of life that insure their social exclusion and cultural retardation.

Aside from the racial and cultural islands within the dominant culture areas, there are numerous regions, often of considerable population, on the byways of European expansion. Some are colonies, or areas otherwise protected and controlled by major powers; some are independent or semi-independent regions. Because of their isolation these areas are, from the urban point of view of Western civilization, culturally backward. In a more leisurely and less crowded world, the isolated lands and peoples remained undisturbed and developed indigenous economies and value systems reasonably suited to their needs. They were self-centered and often self-satisfied; commonly they were proud of their provincial differences and jealous of their values. But the isolation of these islands is being broken; they are coming increasingly into the world market, under foreign political and military direction and control, and into contact and competition with Western science and technology.

The social scholars concerned with racial realities are interested to describe the natural history of contacts where peoples of folk, retarded, or divergent culture meet the peoples of industrial civilization. They wish to define the sequence of growth steps in the transition from the folk status to civilization, from the traditional culture to the world in which they must learn to live. This, I assume, is our scholarly interest in the various African districts, Haiti, Puerto Rico, the Virgin Islands, the Caribbean generally, and other areas of folk or deviate culture that are due to undergo rapid and perhaps catastrophic changes.

It is important, from a practical point of view, that such study be advanced rapidly and extensively. The contacts of Western culture are of real concern in the present and in the future; an understanding of the processes of fusion and displacement is important to the peoples themselves and to the administrators who will increasingly administer the areas. It is essential to know what can and what cannot be done in order to avoid action programs that are wasteful or impossible of accomplishment. Intelligent behavior in the contact of peoples requires a scientific understanding of the processes involved.

The Caribbean chain of islands, and each island separately, is an ideal laboratory for fundamental racial and cultural research. The data are numerous and diverse. The islands are variable in terrain, rainfall, fertility, products, racial composition, population density, historic experience, cultural heritage, social tradition, economic possibility, language, political aspiration, and in other respects. Each island is distinctive in traits and in its combination of traits, but they have a common cultural future; no island individually nor the chain of islands collectively is a self contained unit. Inevitably the islands must become an integral part of a major economic and cultural unit; the alternative, if there be an alternative, is an increasingly decadent and miserable existence on the outer fringe of the cultural world.

ON THE CHANCES OF BEING BORN WHITE

By Stringfellow Barr

I BELIEVE there is a trick by which we Americans can understand these two billion men, women, and children scattered all over the globe. Will the reader play "Let's pretend" with me, the way children do? Let's pretend that you have not yet been born but will be born this year, somewhere on the planet, somewhere in this Mighty Neighborhood. And let's try to estimate your chances of living a happy, healthy, decent, and useful life.

If you are born this year (1950), then on the same day more than 200,000 other babies will be born, all over the world.

You will have less than one chance in twenty of being born in the United States. Your chance of being born in the Soviet Union will be not much better. These countries may be heavily armed, but most people just don't live in them.

You will probably be colored. Remember that you and the 200,000 other squawking brats who will be the day's baby crop are going to be born all over the planet and that there are just not many openings in the places where the white race lives. You must take your chances with the other babies. And the chances are, you will be colored—colored black, or colored brown, or colored yellow.

Your chances of being born white this year are not more than one in three. Your chances of being Chinese are one in four; of being born in India, better than one in nine.

If you are born colored, you will probably be born either among people who have recently revolted and thrown out the white folks who used to govern them or else in a country that is still trying to throw the white folks out. If you are born in Africa, you are likely to learn the maxim: "Never trust a white man."

You have only about one chance in four of being born a Christian. It is far more likely that you will be born a Confucian or a Buddhist, a Mohammedan or a Taoist.

If you are born in the United States—and, remember, that's quite an *if*—you will probably live longer than a year. But if you are born in India, which is more likely, you have only a little better than a one-to-four chance of living more than a year. But cheer up! your chances in some places would be worse; and, besides, even if you survive babyhood in India, you have only a fifty-fifty chance of growing to maturity.

If you are born colored, the chances are overwhelming that you will be chronically sick all your life—from malaria, or intestinal parasites, or tuberculosis, or maybe even leprosy. And even if you are not chronically sick, you are likely to be weak from hunger. You have about a two-to-one chance of suffering from malnutrition, either from too little food or from food that is not a

Reprinted from Stringfellow Barr, *Let's Join the Human Race* (Chicago: University of Chicago Press, 1950), Sections 3 and 4; copyright 1950 by the University of Chicago and used with the kind permission of the publisher.

balanced or nourishing diet. You have a reasonably good chance of experiencing real famine—to the point where you will be glad to eat the bark off a tree. But this chance is extremely hard to calculate.

Again, if you are born colored, you have only a one-to-four chance of learning to read. And since you almost certainly will not own a radio, you will be pretty well cut off from that part of the human family that has enough to eat and that is reasonably healthy. You will most likely live in a mud hut, with a dirt floor and no chimney, its roof thatched with straw. You will almost certainly work on the land, and most of what you raise will go to the landlord. In addition, you are likely to be deeply in debt to the local moneylender, and you may have to pay him annual interest of anywhere from 30 to 100 per cent.

RACIAL IMMUNITY TO DISEASE

By Hans Zinsser et al

WE HAVE DEALT at some length with the experimental aspects of inherited resistance, since here seems to lie the most trustworthy evidence which we possess at present for regarding it as a real phenomenon. In man, the many reported differences between races or groups are much more difficult to analyze. Indeed, most of these can usually be traced to factors that do not constitute true racial immunity, such as diet, poor living conditions, isolation from contact with certain agents of disease, social and religious habits—all of which are hard to appraise. For example, it has frequently been remarked that the greater susceptibility of the Negro in the United States compared with that of the white races to tuberculosis may depend upon genetic factors peculiar to the former race. But one can urge with equal cogency that this well-established fact may be attributed to adverse environmental conditions or that both sets of factors are concerned. In this connection, the results of the recent survey carried out by Kahn among the Bush Negroes of Dutch Guiana are of interest, since they show that although opportunity for infection is present, this is very infrequent, as revealed by the extremely low rate of positive tuberculin tests, and the great rarity of clinically recognizable disease. The isolation of the group which have lived under the natural conditions to which they were accustomed in Africa before transportation as slaves to America may account in part for these unusual findings. Kahn, however, suggests that the favorable circumstances of their life may be of considerable importance in bringing about this unusual situation.

The reputed racial resistance of Negroes to yellow fever is without much

Reprinted from Hans Zinsser, John F. Enders, and Leroy D. Fothergill, *Immunity: Principles and Application in Medicine and Public Health* (5th ed., New York: Macmillan Co., 1939), pp. 110–112; copyright by the Macmillan Co., 1939 and used with the kind permission of the publishers.

doubt due to mild childhood disease. This point of view has been maintained in the past by Hahn and others and is confirmed by the recent epidemiological studies summarized by Sawyer and carried out by members of the International Health Division of the Rockefeller Foundation in areas where yellow fever is endemic, using the mouse protection test as an index of previous infection. Similarly, the resistance of Negroes to malaria and of Mexicans to smallpox and typhus fever are likewise in all probability due to unrecorded attacks of the disease sustained at any early age.

On the other hand, it is possible that the extraordinary susceptibility of various aboriginal peoples to such newly introduced diseases as measles, syphilis, and tuberculosis may be due to the fact that no opportunity has arisen for the natural selection of more resistant individuals to take place through the weeding out of the most susceptible by death from the disease. Thus various authors have surmised that the constant decline in morbidity and mortality rates of tuberculosis in the United States and elsewhere that has obtained during the last fifty years or more may be partly conditioned by selection of this sort with the emergence of a genetically more resistant stock. It has been suggested that the decline of leprosy in Europe from its high incidence in the Middle Ages to its almost complete disappearance at the present time may be due to the operation of the same process. Certainly this disease exhibits a marked tendency to appear in a number of individuals of the same family. Hopkins has studied the occurrence of leprosy from the familial point of view and concludes that his data suggest a hereditary lack of resistance. The fact that he found only a small number of cases in husband and wife, whereas blood relatives revealed a high incidence in leprous families, supports his findings. Hopkins' analyses of the cases of leprosy at the National Leprosarium at Carville, Louisiana, also point to a racial susceptibility of Mexicans compared with Americans of European origin, whereas the Negroes of Louisiana would seem to be more resistant than either of these other races.

Surveys carried out by means of the Wassermann and Kahn tests by Shattuck and his associates among the Maya Indians of Yucatan and Guatemala show that although infection with syphilis is present, the clinical manifestations of the disease even in the absence of modern methods of treatment are usually extremely mild. Shattuck raises the question as to whether this enhanced resistance may not be attributed to a long process of selection.

It has been rather generally held that the white races are refractory to yaws, at least to the disease in its typical form. Cases of infection have, however, been reported in whites, although they are admittedly rare. Since there is a very close relationship between yaws and syphilis and considerable evidence which points to a cross-immunization effect, it is difficult to be entirely certain concerning the greater susceptibility of dark-skinned races, although this seems quite probable.

From the foregoing considerations, it is manifest that racial immunity among human beings is certainly attributable to acquired resistance in most instances. But the possibility exists none the less that genetic factors may be occasionally involved. Moreover, it is extremely difficult even under the conditions of animal experimentation to determine in any given case which type of immunity is responsible for the observed results. Still more uncertain is the nature of the mechanism underlying innate resistance.

COMPETITIVE BREEDING

By Ruth Allen

IF THE MIGRATION of a people is to be effective, it must be a migration of families. Because it is such a movement of families, the penetration of Texas by the Mexican peon is effective and, shall we say, fear inspiring. The Mexican woman has been taught as her guide to conduct, the vow of the Moabitess, "Where thou goest, I will go." Up and down the road she follows the men of her family, sleeping in the open, cooking by the side of the highway. She gives birth to her children, cares for her sick, and buries her dead as she makes her passage. She brings with her across the Rio Grande, traditions of feminine subservience which seem strange in twentieth century America. And here, these habits are probably strengthened, for a period at least, for she has fewer contacts with the new civilization than the male members of the family and her ignorance of the English language is greater. Consequently, fear borne of ignorance makes her more dependent upon husband or father than she would be in a familiar situation. The modern Woman Movement, and demands for economic independence have left her untouched. Uncomplainingly, she labors in the field for months at a time and receives as a reward from the head of the family, some gew-gaw from the five and ten cent store, or, at best, a new dress. The supremacy of the male is seldom disputed. First her father, then her husband, or, if she becomes a widow, her son, receive her unquestioning service.

In a recent survey of the industrial and economic position of the farm women in five central Texas counties, 294 Mexican women were included; and the facts given in this paper are a condensation of some of the findings of that study. The economic struggle between groups of unskilled laborers will be, for a time at least, a contest between standards of living. This standard is judged, in the main, from that part of the family economy which is most under the control of the women of the group. Some of the facts brought out show clearly that the Mexican woman who comes to the farms of central Texas, asks little, for she brings from the past a condition of rural living to which the poorest Negro tenant rarely ever sinks. In the process of displacement taking place steadily and surely in the farm tenancy of the state, this attitude of the woman plays a part, it is possible, a decisive part. Many landlords and employers of farm labor say frankly that the Mexican is not "always wanting something" as is the American or even the Negro and, therefore, they like him better. An analysis of the work and the conditions of work and living of the Mexican woman will throw some light upon this preference.

Of the 294 women covered in the survey, 269 lived on farms. Eighty-seven per cent of this number were members of the families of tenants, the large majority, of the families of "croppers" or "halvers." The other 13.0 per cent were members of families of wage laborers who lived on the farm throughout the year. None was in the family of a land owner. Since no attempt was made to

Reprinted from Ruth Allen, "Mexican Peon Women in Texas," *Sociology and Social Research*, XVI (November-December, 1931), 131–142, with the kind permission of the author and the publisher.

select either individuals or communities, it seems sound to assume that this economic status is typical of the Mexican farming family in the section. One hundred fifty-six of these women were born in Mexico and the others were natives of Texas. Eighty-eight, almost one-third, were unmarried.

In order that the living on the farm shall be wholesome and comfortable, the farm home must produce much in goods and services. It seems almost trite to suggest that the amount of human welfare and family prosperity found in the individual home, will vary almost directly with the amount of home production carried on. This fact the Mexican, in either theory or practice, has failed to grasp. The Mexican woman on the central Texas farms is unproductive in any economic sense, and, consequently, the home over which she presides is unproductive. Of the 269 women who lived on farms, only eight did any canning or preserving of food and no one of these did an amount that an American housewife would consider worthy of note. But the lack goes even further for they had nothing to preserve. Two hundred and five had no garden and not one had an orchard. Two hundred and ten women had no cow. Seventy-eight raised no chickens and only seventeen had flocks of more than fifty. It must be kept in mind that these figures relate to individual women; but, if the families from which they come were considered, the proportion would probably be greater, for the families with several mature members are usually better off. Home production for the typical Mexican farm wife consists of inexhaustible supplies of tortillas, when the ingredients are available; peppers from her little patch dried for the winter, and some making of clothes.

In addition, the Mexican woman asks few conveniences in order to accomplish the work which she does. Though there were, as a rule, large groups to be clothed, 124 had no sewing machine. Clothes, such as they had, were bought ready made or sewed by hand. Even cleanness of garments was secured only with great effort. Ninety-three women had all water hauled; and, even then, much of it was not such as would conduce to whiteness of garments. The mud tank upon which both stock and people depend, was, in most cases, the source of supply. Some hauled from creeks and a few from wells. Most of those who did not haul water carried it from long distances. Thirty-five women had not even a flat iron to smoothe their garments. The amenities of existence find still less place in their lives. Only four had a telephone and a few more than half of the total owned an automobile. Only 24 had a magazine or paper of any sort either English or Spanish. Eighty-five per cent had no books of any sort. But 64 had a musical instrument in their homes, and this fact is not without significance. It is certain that many more had some method of getting music which could not be reported in cut and dried figures. The French harp plays its part, and it is to be regretted that the accordion has ceased to be for them a real musical instrument. Very few of these Mexican farmers are within even a few miles of a church to which they belong and the women are losing what must have been a great stabilizing force in their lives. Whether the loss tends to better or to worse, we cannot here discuss but, to the women, it is cause for regret. Only 69 of the women visited went to church at all regularly, that is, as often as once a month. For social life, the women are dependent upon those of their own group who live near.

These women need not, however, travel over much space in order to accomplish their work. Only twelve had to keep as much as one room for each person living in the house. Twenty-two kept house where there were ten or more persons to a room. One hundred and ninety-four lived where there were two or more persons to a room. It may be necessary to insist that they lived, not in city tenements, but in the rural districts of Texas where the population per square mile is approximately twenty-one persons.

But, it is not in such groups as the Mexican peons or the Texas tenant farmers, that leisure women are found. Since the Mexican woman does not produce services in the home, she must find another method of adding to the economic welfare of the family. Two courses are open. She may bring children into the world and rear them to an age at which they may aid in the production of a money crop, or she herself may go into the fields. It is a generally accepted principle, that a woman must either do field work herself or produce workers to take her place. Of the 269 women living on the farm, 152 worked in the field for two months or more a year. The latter group comprised all save eight of the unmarried women and 74 of the married. The figures in regard to the comparative number of children of the two groups of married women are rather revealing. Of those doing field work, one-sixth have no children, while of those staying in the house, less than one-twenty-first have no children. Of those not doing field work, one-eighth have nine or more children while of the other group one-twenty-fourth have families of nine or more. The arithmetic average of the number of children borne by women who stay at home is 4.8 as compared with an average for the field workers of 3.7. The average for those having children is 5.1 and 4.4 for the two groups respectively. The Mexican mother of a large family meets the inquiry as to whether she does field work with an almost unconscious bridling and air of superiority: "Oh, no. I have plenty children to work in field." That the exemption from field work is a reward of merit rather than a recognition that the woman may have enough to do at home, is indicated by the fact that the women who do not work in the fields have on an average 2.4 children under 15 years of age while the women who do field work consistently have an average of 2.6.

In spite of the fact that the bearing of children is considered a necessary service, little care is taken that the physical strain upon the mother shall be as low as possible. Ninety-seven of the 165 mothers had only midwives in attendance at each confinement. The midwives are women who have little preparation for their work save the act of declaring themselves specialists in caring for expectant mothers. Quite often a woman is attended by her mother or an older relative. Forty women had a doctor only in attendance at each birth. The others had sometimes one and sometimes the other, or it may be both, the doctor for one visit and the midwife for a week. Seldom does the Mexican peon woman take longer than a week for the process of bringing a child into the world. Three days of confinement and rest is commonly considered necessary. The term "no good" is often used in speaking of a woman who seems not able to stand the strain and still be fit for work. It is little wonder that the Mexican woman of thirty-five thinks herself old.

The field working woman does not punch the timeclock; therefore the amount of work done is an estimate on the part of the interviewed and the interviewer. It is not likely that the figures are much overestimated, for, if she chops cotton, hoes corn, and picks cotton whenever it is done, the work will last for at least five or six months of the year. During this time she must hold herself in readiness to go to the field whenever the weather permits. The working day may be taken as eight hours and the week as five days. The figures given relate to the year 1928, when there was a "bumper" cotton crop in the section. The size of the crop in any year will have a marked effect upon the proportion of work done for hire, but it will not affect greatly the total amount of work done. One hundred and ten of these women work for their families only with no definite remuneration. Nine women whose families were tenants worked for hire after their own crop was gathered. This group seems rather small but the Mexican who has a settled location objects, as much, or probably more than the American of the same economic level, to working for wages on the part of the women of his family. Thirty-three of the women were in the families of casual laborers who worked no land for themselves.

Of these 152 women who worked regularly in the field, 63.5 per cent worked for four months or over. Thirteen and two-tenths per cent worked for eight months or longer. Since only 42 worked for hire, and nine of these worked for their families so long as there was work to be done, it follows that most of the work was unpaid. Not a single woman of the 110 reported that there was any arrangement to pay for her labor. When the income of the tenant farmer is considered, it becomes evident that this labor is given in return for a livelihood, and, as appears from facts already given, a miserable one at that. But even when the woman becomes a hired laborer she has no individual economic existence. Her husband, father, or brother handles the financial affairs. She does not collect her own money; she does not know how much is paid for her services; she seldom knows how much cotton she picks a day or how many acres she chops. The wage paid is a family wage and the family is distinctly patriarchal in its organization. When family groups of from ten to twenty members may be secured to pick cotton, and the women keep house in the open air or in disreputable shacks, there is all the advantage of group living and the employer profits therefrom. What effect would be had upon the cost of production of cotton, if the price of picking were set for the individual laborer rather than for the group? How long would the group system continue, if the women refused to practise their sphere under existing conditions?

The women who work for hire are of two classes: first, are those already mentioned who live on a farm but in the families of wage workers. These women, in the main, work in their own communities and do not travel great distances. The large part of the work is done on the farms on which their husbands are employed. The other class belongs to families whose male members are not regularly employed on a farm. Their homes are in town and they travel for six to eight months, coming back for a brief rest before starting again upon their round. For some of these the living conditions are indescribable. Houses which have been abandoned as unfit for human habitation, outhouses which have no preparation for housekeeping are their homes. The congestion of living quarters reaches almost the saturation point. In one instance, thirty people lived in four rooms, without a stick of furniture save a stove and it was unusable. In another instance, twelve people lived in two rooms and took six young men boarders. In still another, fifteen people including five married couples and one other woman lived in two rooms. It boots nothing to say that these are only temporary quarters. They are, but they will be exchanged for other quarters no better, and it may be worse. The filth due, partly at least, to lack of toilet facilities and the difficulty of securing water, is at times almost revolting. On the Western Plains with the weather at freezing temperature, they live in tents, in smokehouses, and in cars. There is no evidence that these conditions are harder upon the women than upon the men, but the babies pay a heavy tribute to King Cotton.

That the Mexican women are not perfectly adjusted to the condition in which they find themselves is suggested by the fact that three-tenths of the women are unmarried. Nine of these are more than twenty-five years of age, and thirty-three are more than twenty. Marriage at rather an early age was an almost inevitable step in the old home; but now it seems not only evitable but, it may be, almost impossible because of the new social conditions. The unmarried woman does not, however, leave home. She lives under a tradition which sends the son forth to seek his fortune but requires the girl to wait under the paternal roof. It may be of considerable significance to note that 27 of these girls, all save one of those over twenty-five, are found in ten families and that these families averaged nine children apiece, most of them small. It is possible that these girls remain unmarried because their work is necessary to eke out the family existence, for grown unmarried sons living at home are comparatively rare. Another element which enters in is probably the scarcity of eligible men in the rural community. The father and mother are very careful of their daughters and they do not marry strange men. An interesting comment is that of a young man who had married one of five sisters. The four couples with the girls' parents were together. Referring to the unmarried state of the youngest sister, he remarked, "She ain't got no pretty clothes and men will not marry girls without pretty clothes. We all going together this cotton picking and buy her clothes and she be married in about three weeks."

Yet even marriage has ceased to bring to the Mexican woman the stability and security of the past. The Mexican man asserting his masculine right to greater freedom, is becoming impatient of the ties of marriage and of family. This new world gives him opportunities to make money and have a good time which have never before been offered. But these cannot be enjoyed if they must be shared with a wornout wife and six children. The deserted wife is becoming a pathetic and surprisingly common figure among the Mexicans. She is at a disadvantage as compared with the Negro woman who has commonly found the Negro man an undependable source of financial support, for she lacks the Negro's physical strength and ability to care for herself and her offspring. There comes to mind a frail slip of a woman with five young children, whose husband had left her several months before. "He said she couldn't do nothing but have children." The group was trying to pick cotton but the mother's lack of strength and the ages of the children made it impossible for them to cover even present expenses. They had, of course, been absorbed by the mother's family, but that meant the dividing of a bare subsistence among a larger group. More pathetic is a young wife with eight small children. She had left her family across the River to follow her husband into the new home. But he loved music and he loved to dance. And now he is gone, leaving her almost hopeless. She has to leave her home because a woman with small children cannot farm—and what is she to do?

After the rather depressing picture of the Mexican woman in her home surroundings, one is tempted to ask: Has she anything to add to this civilization into which she has projected herself and of which she bids fair to become a component part? It is probable that she has one real contribution. Seldom is there a Mexican home so mean that it has not its spot of beauty. It may be a tiny flower garden protected by wires and sticks; it may be some colored handwork on the table or the chair; or, it may be the shrine in the corner where bits of color, bright pictures, and cheap images and trinkets are gathered. The visitor has the feeling that here are people who never forget that hyacinths are as necessary as bread to human life. A rather significant observation is that the Mexican woman, seldom, if ever papers her house with newspapers as is commonly done by the Negro and the white tenants. She demands something more ornamental and so beautifies her walls with pictures. Some rooms stand out vividly in the mind. For one, jewelry catalogues had been robbed of their treasures and adorned the walls—not without method. One side was covered with clocks and another with silver goblets. Picture the result if you can, but the room was at least interesting. Another home had three rooms papered with some kind of bank statement divided with blue lines. Each piece was exactly fitted to each adjoining piece and there were hundreds of them. The effect was rather blue and somewhat dizzying, but it did have color. Along the same line, the writer recalls a home in which she was given a bucket of coals over which to warm her fingers, while the girls entertained her with music from the victrola. And who shall say that victrolas do not make for fuller living than furnace heat? If the Mexican woman can take with her to a higher standard of living, her love of color, her desire for beauty, she may be able to give to one of the drabbest spots in American civilization, the Texas tenant farm, some little touch of joy.

But from another angle, what does Texas hold in store for this dark-eyed, quiet woman? If she raise her standard of living, which is her only course unless she is to be, even more than in the present, the lowermost boundary of the competitive realm, she will cease to be an incomparable asset to the farm economy. Her daughter, following the American and the Negro girl, will go to the town where she will receive for a day's work, if not a day's pay, at least some definite remuneration. In the town, she will join the ranks of unskilled workers, for education and training will not be available for two or three generations at best. Barriers of racial prejudice will hem her in: she herself refusing equality with the Negro and the American refusing equality to her. Severed from her family as she must be perforce if she delays or refuses marriage, yet hardly fitted for a life of independence, it is rather staggering to think of her helplessness in a world of individualistic competition. And in the process of adjustment, she will have weight to drag with her all women and all men who work for wages in the industrial life which she touches.

THE CYCLE OF RACIAL COMPETITION IN COLONIAL TERRITORY

By G. Mesnard

IF, IN THE WORLD as a whole, the populations of a purely industrial type of civilization (wrongly called European or Occidental) are in demographic decline either actually, potentially or immanently—actually as in France and Austria which are in a phase of depopulation by excess of deaths over births, potentially as in Germany and England where there has been a decrease in the annual number of births and immanently as in Roumania and Japan where the apparent and real birthrates have decreased—then it cannot be expected that this phenomenon should have spared 'European' populations which have come in contact with populations of a (from the industrial point of view) half-civilized type, whether these have been numerically superior or inferior.

Be it in the United States (Negroes), in New Zealand (Maoris), or even in South Africa where the most tenacious European colony in the world is to be found, the more civilized population is decreasing as a proportion of the total. It gives way numerically before the less civilized, just as in an economy bad money crowds out good money.

This phenomenon can naturally be explained by the fact that the races which we call inferior profit at the present moment to the full from the material benefits of our civilization, while we ourselves are suffering from its excess (socialism, materialism, etc.).

Thus, far from the European tidal wave submerging the world, as one formerly thought and with reason, this wave is thrown back by another which is now much stronger.

Yet, undoubtedly, these races who are in full increase now will become 'civilized' in their turn and, following our example and that of all preceding civilizations, will perish in their turn for the same eternal reasons.

Let us take an example which is of special interest to us Frenchmen, that of our colonies in North Africa.

While it is still true that, thanks to continued European immigration, the European populations of Tunisia and Morocco still maintain their proportion in the total, this is no longer true of our oldest colony in Africa, Algeria.

For Algeria the decline has already begun:

5,233,000 natives and 833,000 Europeans in 1926
6,249,000 natives and 973,000 Europeans in 1936

That is, 13.7 per cent Europeans in the total population in 1926 and only 13 per cent in 1936.

Still, it has been known for a long time that censuses, even when exact—

Adapted from G. Mesnard, "La régression relative des Européens en Algérie." Congrès International de la Population, Paris, 1937. VI *Démographie de la France D'Outremer* (Paris: Hermann et Cie, Editeurs, 1938). Translated by Everett C. Hughes.

which is not always the case even in the most civilized countries—can give only a static picture of demographic phenomena. Figures of demographic *movement* give a more dynamic view of the situation; they are therefore of more interest and are in general also closer to the truth.

Here they are for Algeria:

TABLE I

	BIRTHS		DEATHS		INCREASE	
	natives	Europeans	natives	Europeans	natives	Europeans
1922	129	21	104	14	15	7
1926	147	21	82	13	65	8
1930	168	22	79	13	89	9
1935	214	20	106	13	108	7

Thus it would seem that the European population of Algeria was "stable" since the absolute figures of births and deaths, and excess of birth over death, are practically constant. But this is not so, for it is only when relative figures are stable that a population is stable. The very fact that these absolute figures are constant shows that the population is actually declining, as is shown by the following rates:

TABLE II

(rates per thousand)

	1922	1926	1930	1935
Birth rate	28	25	25	21
Death rate	19	16	15	14
Increase	9	9	10	7

Thus, if as a consequence of the present world increase in life expectancy the mortality has declined five points, or 21 per cent—a decrease which is a passing phenomenon, since the rate of mortality corresponding to the average life expectancy of the Europeans in Algeria is 17 to 18 per cent—the increase has diminished by two points, or 22 per cent, and the birth rate, the only factor which ultimately counts, has dropped seven points or 25 per cent in a period of 13 years, which contains a complete cycle of prosperity and crises.

The rates of the native part of the population are as follows:

TABLE III

(rates per thousand)

	1922	1926	1930	1935
Birth rate	25	28	30	35
Death rate	21	16	14	18
Increase	4	12	16	17

This table is exactly the opposite of the other. Mortality has declined, to become, at one point, even less than that of the more aged European population. Increase has jumped to the enormous figure of 17. And as to the birth rate, it has continually increased to the very high figure of 35.

The result of this is that the present European population of Algeria is in decline not only in relation to itself, but it is in even greater decline in relation to the native population which is increasing prodigiously.

In fact, an indigenous population only ⅙ of the population of France (which includes many foreigners and also many Algerians) and six times more important than the European colony that shares its territory, has a number of births equal to that of France itself and ten times more important than that of the Algerian colonial French population. It increases each year by more than 100,000 individuals, while that of France diminishes by on the average 30,000 (virtually 300,000) and that of the French colony increases not even by a tenth, the increase of the latter (which will still for some time remain positive) being less than a half of that of the natives.

Will France be conquered, demographically speaking, by her own conquest?

WHAT IS IT THAT SURVIVES?

By George Henry Lane-Fox Pitt-Rivers

SO LONG AS THE DECLINE of race and the decline of population are confused the facts will never be clearly recognized. The infiltration of alien stock may check the decline of the total population, while, at the same time, the racial elements of the original population continue to decline. That is to say, races die out in localities where the populations are actually increasing. If, however, we are able to distinguish the different ethnic elements in a population, the whole of which may be, and probably are, subject to the same environmental factors, we discover that the unmixed racial elements that formerly thrived under the old environmental conditions are disappearing as the new or miscegenated elements are surviving in increasing numbers. Thus, in the process of an adaptable population gradually being substituted for an unadaptable population a "race" becomes extinct. The effect of outbreeding or mixing has here stimulated population growth, not because outbreeding is *per se* more favourable to survival than *inbreeding,* but because outbreeding has been the means of introducing a new racial element in the mixed stock more adaptable to new conditions of environment, the new miscegenated stock becoming more generalized by the gradual infiltration of foreign blood also becomes better adapted. But the mixed-blood stock would not have competed favourably for survival with the full-blood stock unless the old conditions adapted to the needs of the specialized stock had changed. As an illustration of this might be mentioned the superior survival-value of the more inbred elements among the Navaho Indians, themselves the most free of alien blood of all the North American Indians, whose nomadic life and environmental conditions in Arizona have been least affected by European contact.

From George Henry Lane-Fox Pitt-Rivers, *The Clash of Culture and the Contact of Races* (London: George Routledge and Sons, 1927), pp. 102–103.

Where the aboriginal population fails to mix its blood sufficiently with the immigrant invaders its extinction is more evident and has the appearance of being more rapid.

The looseness with which the term "race" is used still helps to obscure the processes of race extinction and substitution that are taking place wherever races or ethnic groups are not segregated or endogamous. "C'est par un vice de langage, qui a causé les plus grand maux à l'humanité," observes Comte de Laponge, "que le nom de race a été donné aussi à des groupements humain caractérisés par une certaine communauté de langues, de religions et de coutumes." Mr. Hocart protests that the confusion which used to exist in the use of the words Aryan, Indo-European, Celtic, etc., which were applied to languages or groups of languages as well as to the people who spoke them, still prevails to a great extent in the use of other ethnic terms such as Melanesian; we speak of a Melanesian race, found chiefly in the islands of Melanesia, and also of Melanesian languages, but all Melanesian-speaking people do not belong to the Melanesian group of races, and all Melanesians do not speak Melanesian tongues; while it is probable that the so-called Melanesian type originally adopted its languages from a proto-Malayo-Polynesian people.

INTERINDIVIDUAL AND INTERGROUP COMPETITION

By Amos H. Hawley

BASIC IN ALL INSTANCES of race conflict, and perhaps of majority-minority group conflict in general, is the fact of intergroup competition. The specific criteria by which the dominant and the subordinate groups are distinguished are themselves of incidental significance. What is important is that two such populations represent rival claimants to local resources or alternative labor supplies. The rôle of the contests between colonial and native peoples and of labor conflicts in shaping our patterns of race relations is too well known to require review here.

The particular status of the population at a disadvantage takes form as members of the dominant group seek to narrow the sphere of competition by excluding from free participation in common activities all individuals who conform to a certain definition. Conceivably, discriminatory action may be directed toward any definable segment of the population. Usually, of course, it centers upon a recognized minority which happens to be conspicuous as a result of its physical peculiarities, its segregated existence, its unique historic past, or all

Reprinted from Amos H. Hawley, "Dispersion versus Segregation," *Papers of the Michigan Academy of Science, Arts and Letters*, XXX (1944), 667–674, with the kind permission of The University of Michigan Press.

taken together. Exclusion finds justification in the majority group on the score of an alleged inferiority of ability and general social worth inherent in members of the lesser group. Hence the position of the latter becomes circumscribed by numerous prejudicial practices and fictions aimed at isolating it from all claims to equality in community life.

To be sure, a group may contribute to its own segregation. Voluntary or "accidental" segregation frequently occurs. Cultural enclaves are formed by immigrants because of their inability to effect an immediate transition to the mode of life in the new area, and by religious sectarians who wish to foster a peculiar pattern of living. On the other hand, a group confronted with discrimination is awakened to self-consciousness and strives defensively to create a society of its own. The compensatory reaction often entails a more complete withdrawal into a restricted area and type of life than conditions warrant. In all such instances the group assumes the risk of incurring discrimination or increased discrimination.

Systematic discrimination against a racial or minority group is visible in segregation, which may appear in manifold forms. Residential restrictions, confinement to certain occupations, exclusion from use of public facilities, denial of the franchise and of access to courts of law, charges of moral and intellectual ineptitude, these and other manifestations of segregation operate in various combinations. The subordinate status of the group may be read from the modes of segregation to which it is subjected. There is little question but that segregation is the root of the problem viewed from the standpoint of the minority population.

Now, though an imposed segregation is expressed in many ways, it seems that the most fundamental form is spatial or residential. The function of all restrictions of this order is obviously to protect a competitive advantage for the dominant group. Spatial segregation, however, contributes to this end more directly and effectively than does any other type of circumscription. It is the fullest practicable attainment of exclusion and isolation. The physical separation of the opposed groups is in itself a barrier to participation by one in the affairs of the other. But it also has the effect of throwing into sharp focus the differences between the groups; in fact, it accentuates those differences through heightening the visibility of the minority population. In exaggerating the illusion of homogeneity and, at the same time, obscuring the reality of individual variation spatial segregation provides support for prevailing stereotypes. Prejudicial beliefs are further reinforced by the aspect of concreteness which is lent thereby to social distance. In short, spatial segregation keeps the interracial issue in the foreground of attention, clearly defines the accepted interrelations, and simplifies the problem of control. Separation in space is probably an indispensable condition of subordinate status applied to a group as a whole. A fair generalization from history would seem to be that no minority group—racial, ethnic, religious, or political—may long exist without some degree of physical isolation.

Given the hypothesis of a necessary dependence of subordinate group status upon spatial segregation, it follows that a breakdown of the isolation and a scattering of the group is the essential first step in obviating the position of inferiority. Redistribution of the members of the subjugated group to approximate the same pattern of territorial spread characterizing the dominant population would, by this reasoning, reduce the competitive threat felt in any one area or sector of the economy, differentiate the minority so fully as to prevent its appearing as a homogeneous mass, and eliminate the identity of the group. The group would thus be absorbed in the general population. These are inferences which must be examined more carefully.

Competition is a function of the ratio of resources to population. Its intensity rises and falls as the relative value of the denominator in the fraction increases or decreases. But where the population is subdivided into groups competition tends to shift from an interindividual to an intergroup basis. When this occurs the fundamental competitive issue is altered; to the problem of how much each individual competitor will be able to obtain is added the problem of how many individuals from each group will have opportunity to enter into the competition. An unknown factor in this connection concerns the limits of tolerance in one group for competitors of a second group: At what point in the changing numerical balance, that is, does competition shift from an interindividual to an intergroup basis? Though this question is not answerable at present, it is nevertheless clear that, when Group A comprises the overwhelming majority of the individuals involved in competition, the relationship tends to remain on an interindividual basis. But as Group B increases proportionally to Group A, competition may be expected to assume more of an intergroup aspect.

It is common knowledge, for example, that representatives of alien groups living among a native population experience few, if any, restrictions so long as their numbers are small. The Jews remaining in Spain after the great expulsion in the sixteenth century enjoyed the same privileges that were accorded the gentile population. Likewise, Jews born and raised in small American towns where their numbers are slight are often unfamiliar with practices of anti-Semitism. They are accepted and frequently are so assimilated to the life of the community as to be scarcely aware of themselves as in any way different from their fellow citizens. Essentially similar experiences have been had by early migrants from Europe, by Orientals in the United States, and by Negroes when they are thinly scattered among the white population. The small numbers of Negroes living in Northern states had, prior to the Negro migrations of 1916- 19, an enviable freedom of activity and opportunity by contrast with their coracialists in the South. In Iowa, to cite but one instance, in the years during World War I Negro labor was solicited, paid the same wages as white labor, admitted to skilled employment in all industries, and subjected to no discrimination. The Negro population of Iowa at the time was less than one per cent of the total.

When, however, the size of an alien or a subordinate group begins to increase relative to the native or dominant group and to loom progressively larger as a competitive force, tensions develop, restrictions accumulate, and the minority is more and more suppressed. Traditionally minority peoples are well aware of this. Descendants of early Jewish settlers in the United States looked with dismay upon the large influx of Russian and Polish Jews in the latter part of the nineteenth century. They made an unsuccessful attempt to colonize the newcomers in the less densely settled agricultural areas of the country. Similarly, Northern Negroes feared the northward migrations of Southern Negroes. Events confirmed their apprehensions. Wherever in the North migration brought an appreciable increase in the Negro population, the behavior of the white population underwent a marked chanage. Northern whites became aware of a race problem. The free access to stores, schools, churches, and employment opportunities which the old Negro populations in Chicago, Dayton, Detroit, Philadelphia, and other cities had enjoyed was gradually withdrawn. Differentiation and segregation became more rigorous and were applied alike to the old residents and the new arrivals.

It is of interest to note, parenthetically, that the response of Southern whites to the exodus of Negroes was an attempt to arrest the movement. Finding that licensing of labor recruiters at exorbitant fees, interference with the mail, violent attacks upon migrating Negroes, and other negative measures failed, the South resorted to more persuasive and positive steps. As a result, some improvements were made in Negro-white relations. Wage differentials were reduced, short-weighting and cheating in stores and commissaries were stopped in many localities, working conditions generally were improved, inequalities in education were partially removed, and a number of minor changes were brought about.

The phenomenon of increasing strain with increasing numbers has been observed in other connections. The Chinese, who at first were welcomed to the Pacific Coast as "ideal" citizens and workmen, were abruptly made the butt of hostilities when, in the period 1869–85, as the transcontinental railroads were completed, they were dumped upon the labor markets of western cities. At a later date Japanese immigrants passed through the same cycle of welcome and opposition as the mounting competition of their growing numbers began to be felt. An Asiatic Exclusion League, formed to press for legal exclusion of the Oriental immigrant, was constituted by 238 member associations, 202 of which were labor organizations. The series of events which led to Oriental debarment was, however, but a phase in a larger development aimed at the immigration of aliens in general. Southeastern Europeans, finding no free land available, crowded into the cities of the East and the Middle West in search of industrial employment. Their competition gave rise to the hue and cry "the new immigration." Finally, the traditional policy of the United States encouraging immigration was reversed in the quota enactments. In the East, as in the West, organized labor assumed the leadership in securing immigration restriction.

Related to the influence of numbers through their bearing upon competition in affecting subordinate-group status is the quality of homogeneity in the group concerned. An important feature of discriminatory and segregative practices is their categorical character; they imply that the population upon which they are directed is an undifferentiated mass, each individual being just as inferior as the next. Despite the manifest error in such an implication, it contains an element of truth. A spatially segregated group not only appears to be but is actually homogeneous in certain general respects as, for example, its qualifications for employment in the institutions controlled by the dominant group. Segregation, whether voluntary or involuntary, is a restriction of opportunity; it hampers the flow of knowledge and experience and thus impedes diversification of interests and occupations. Migrants settling in a new and strange community are for the most part fitted for only the least specialized functions. And to the extent that they establish a segregated existence in the new community the alien individuals tend to retain their uniformity. Spatial segregation, therefore, operates in two ways to preserve a minority status. In that it causes the group's peculiarities to stand out in clear contrast to the traits of the majority, it emphasizes the uniformity within the group. Thus the group is exposed to categorical definitions of one kind and another. But spatial segregation also imposes a certain limitation of opportunity which interferes with the differentiation of individuals composing the group.

The redistribution of a segregated population may be expected to dissolve the attribute of homogeneity, both apparent and actual. The departure from the norm evident in the peculiar traits possessed by members of the minority group loses its massive character as the individuals separate and scatter over a wide area. Individual variants are expected and tolerated in local situations. Moreover, since the individual who is removed from his group cannot easily be viewed against the background of his racial or ethnic fellows, he tends to be regarded less as a representative of a type and more as an individual. Furthermore, a group whose members become widely distributed sooner or later loses its ability to act in concert and hence its identity as a group. It may possibly be reconstructed as a statistical class, but it cannot be regarded as a group in the sociological sense.

The histories of various European nationality groups settling in the United States are illustrative. So long as they remained compact units they kept their national traits and group structures. Under such circumstances they were also subject to attacks and subordination by the native population. On various occasions the Irish, Greeks, Italians, Poles, and many others have known the meaning of minority status. The progeny of immigrants, however, drift away from the foreign settlement and merge with the general population. Eventually the group itself disappears unless it is replenished by fresh immigration.

Colored populations, of course, have greater difficulty in losing themselves in the white group. Even so, the principle of small numbers seems to operate in their case as in the others, as has already been indicated. Any one who has observed the behavior of experienced Negroes in formal public gatherings in which whites are numerically predominant has noted that, instead of congregating, they disperse and keep apart from one another. Color is not so foreboding in an individual as in a mass of individuals. It is not unlikely that the redistribution of Japanese-Americans in rural areas, villages, and cities throughout the nation, being carried on at present by the War Relocation Authority, will end that problem and culminate in their final acceptance on an equal footing in American society.

The actual differentiation of the group is of greater importance. Migration, we know, is an educative experience; it opens new vistas and provides a basis for comparison and criticism of the familiar. It expands the scope of one's knowledge and action and thus stimulates the development of latent potentialities. Relocation in a new geographical and social context requires, in fact, readaptation of the migrant's behavior. Old habits must be modified and novel patterns of behavior must be acquired in order to deal successfully with the new habitat. It is not surprising, therefore, that migration almost invariably involves a change of type of occupation. The extensive occupational diversification of the Negro population occurred with, if not as a result of, its large-scale movement from the South to the North and from rural to urban areas in the South. But the still considerable concentration of Negroes in a few types of employment is evidence of the continuing segregation of the group, in the Southern region primarily, though also in restricted zones in cities.

RACIAL SEGREGATION IN THE CITY

By Louis Wirth

FOR THE PAST five hundred years the Jewish settlements in the Western world have been known as ghettos. The modern ghetto, some evidence of which is found in every city of even moderate size, traces its ancestry back to the medieval European urban institution by means of which the Jews were segregated from the rest of the population. In the East, until recently, the ghetto took the form of the "pale" of settlement, which represents a ghetto within a ghetto. The ghetto is no longer the place of officially regulated settlement of the Jews, but rather a local cultural area which has arisen quite informally. In the American cities the name "ghetto" applies particularly to those areas where the poorest and most backward groups of the Jewish population, usually the recently arrived immigrants, find their home.

From the standpoint of the sociologist the ghetto as an institution is of interest first of all because it represents a prolonged case study in isolation. It may be regarded as a form of accommodation through which a minority has effectually been subordinated to a dominant group. The ghetto exhibits at least one historical form of dealing with a dissenting minority within a larger population, and as such has served as an instrument of control. At the same time the ghetto represents a form of toleration through which a *modus vivendi* is established between groups that are in conflict with each other on fundamental issues. Some of these functions are still served by the modern ghetto, which, in other respects, has a character quite distinct from that of the medieval institution. In Western Europe and America, however, it is of primary interest because it shows the actual processes of distribution and grouping of the population in urban communities. It indicates the ways in which cultural groups give expression to their heritages when transplanted to a strange habitat; it evidences the constant sifting and resifting that goes on in a population, the factors that are operative in assigning locations to each section, and the forces through which the community maintains its integrity and continuity. Finally, it demonstrates the subtle ways in which this cultural community is transformed by degrees until it blends with the larger community about it, meanwhile reappearing in various altered guises of its old and unmistakable atmosphere.

From Louis Wirth, "The Ghetto," *The American Journal of Sociology*, XXXIII (July, 1927), 57–71.

This paper concerns itself, not with the history of the ghetto, but with its natural history. Viewed from this angle the study of the ghetto is likely to throw light on a number of related phenomena, such as the origin of segregated areas and the development of local communities in general; for, while the ghetto is, strictly speaking, a Jewish institution, there are forms of ghettos that concern not merely Jews. Our cities contain Little Sicilies, Little Polands, Chinatowns, and Black Belts. There are Bohemias and Hobohemias, slums and Gold Coasts, vice areas and Rialtos in every metropolitan community. The forces that underlie the formation and development of these areas bear a close resemblance to those at work in the ghetto. These forms of community life are likely to become more intelligible if we know something of the Jewish ghetto.

The concentration of the Jews into segregated local areas in the medieval cities did not originate with any formal edict of church or state. The ghetto was not, as is sometimes mistakenly believed, the arbitrary creation of the authorities, designed to deal with an alien people. The ghetto was not the product of design on the part of anyone, but rather the unwitting crystallization of needs and practices rooted in the customs and heritages, religious and secular, of the Jews themselves. Long before it was made compulsory the Jews lived in separate parts of the cities in the Western lands of their own accord. The Jews drifted into separate cultural areas, not by external pressure or by deliberate design. The factors that operated toward the founding of locally separated communities by the Jews are to be sought in the character of Jewish traditions, in the habits and customs, not only of the Jews themselves, but of the medieval town-dweller in general. To the Jews the spatially separated and socially isolated community seemed to offer the best opportunity for following their religious precepts, their established ritual and diet, and the numerous functions which tied the individual to familial and communal institutions. In some instances it was the fear of the remainder of the population, no doubt, which induced them to seek each other's company, or the ruler under whose protection they stood found it desirable, for purposes of revenue and control, to grant them a separate quarter. The general tenor of medieval life no doubt played an important rôle, for it was customary for members of the same occupational group to live in the same locality, and the Jews, forming, as a whole, a separate vocational class and having a distinct economic status, were merely falling in line, therefore, with the framework of medieval society, in which everyone was tied to some locality. In addition, there were the numerous ties of kinship and acquaintanceship which developed an *esprit de corps* as a significant factor in community life. There was the item of a common language, of community of ideas and interests, and the mere congeniality that arises even between strangers who, coming from the same locality, meet in a strange place. Finally, the segregation of the Jews in ghettos is identical in many respects with the development of segregated areas in general. The tolerance that strange modes of life need and find in immigrant settlements, in Latin quarters, in vice districts, and in racial colonies is a powerful factor in the sifting of the urban population and its allocation in separate local areas where one obtains freedom from hostile criticism and the backing of a group of kindred spirits.

Corresponding to the local separateness of the Jew from his Christian neighbors there is to be noted the functional separation of the two groups. Just as the world beyond the ghetto wall was external to the life within the ghetto, so the personal relationships between Jews and non-Jews were those of externality and utility. The Jews supplemented the economic complex of medieval European life. They served a number of functions which the inhabitants of the town were incapable of exercising. The Jews were allowed to trade and engage in exchange, occupations which the church did not permit Christians to engage in. Besides, the Jews were valuable taxable property and could be relied on to furnish much-needed revenue. On the other hand, the Jews, too, regarded the Christian population as a means to an end, as a utility. The Christians could perform functions such as eating the hind quarter of beef, and could purchase the commodities that the Jews had for sale; they could borrow money from the Jew, and pay interest; they could perform innumerable services for him which he could not perform himself. In the rigid structure of medieval life the Jews found a strategic place. The attitude of the medieval church had coupled trade and finance with sin. The Jews were free from this taboo, which made the occupation of merchant and banker seem undesirable to the Christian population. The Christian churchmen were not troubled about the "perils of the Jewish soul," for, so far as they knew, he had no soul to be saved. What made the trade relation possible, however, was not merely the fact that it was mutually advantageous, but the fact that trade relationships are possible when no other form of contact between two peoples can take place. The Jew, being a stranger, and belonging, as he did, to a separate and distinct class, was admirably fitted to become the merchant and banker. He drifted to the towns and cities where trade was possible and profitable. Here he could utilize all the distant contacts that he had developed in the course of his wandering. His attachment to the community at large was slight, and when necessity demanded it he could migrate to a locality where opportunities were greater. He owned no real property to which he was tied, nor was he the serf of a feudal lord. His mobility in turn developed versatility. He saw opportunities in places where no native could see them. While the ghetto was never more than a temporary stopping-place, the Jew was never a hobo, for he had an aim, a destination, and his community went with him in his migrations.

While the Jew's contacts with the outside world were categorical and abstract, within his own community he was at home. Here he could relax from etiquette and formalism. His contacts with his fellow-Jews were warm, intimate, and free. Especially was this true of his family life, within the inner circle of which he received that appreciation and sympathetic understanding which the larger world could not offer. In his own community, which was based upon the solidarity of the families that composed it, he was a person with status. Whenever he returned from a journey to a distant market, or from his daily work, he came back to the family fold, there to be recreated and reaffirmed as a man and as a Jew. Even when he was far removed from his kin, he lived his real inner life in his dreams and hopes with them. He could converse with his own kind in that familiar tongue which the rest of the world could not understand. He was bound by common troubles, by numerous ceremonies and sentiments to his small group that lived its own life oblivious of the world beyond the confines of the ghetto. Without the backing of his group, without the security that he enjoyed in his inner circle of friends and countrymen, life would have been intolerable.

Through the instrumentality of the ghetto there gradually developed that social distance which effectually isolated the Jew from the remainder of the population. These barriers did not completely inhibit contact, but they reduced it to the type of relationships which were of a secondary and formal nature. As these barriers crystallized and his life was lived more and more removed from the rest of the world, the solidarity of his own little community was enhanced until it became strictly divorced from the larger world without.

The forms of community life that had arisen naturally and spontaneously in the course of the attempt of the Jews to adapt themselves to their surroundings gradually became formalized in custom and precedent, and finally crystallized into legal enactment. What the Jews had sought as a privilege was soon to be imposed upon them by law. As the Jews had come to occupy a more important position in medieval economy, and as the church at about the time of the Crusades became more militant, there set in a period of active regulation. The ghetto became compulsory. But the institution of the ghetto had by this time become firmly rooted in the habits and attitudes of the Jews. The historians of the ghetto are usually inclined to overemphasize the confining effect of the barriers that were set up around the Jew, and the provincial and stagnant character of ghetto existance. They forget that there was nevertheless a teeming life within the ghetto which was probably more active than life outside.

The laws that came to regulate the conduct of the Jews and Christians were merely the formal expressions of social distances that had already been ingrained in the people. While on the one hand the Jew was coming to be more and more a member of a class—an abstraction—on the other hand there persisted the tendency to react to him as a human being. The ghetto made the Jew self-conscious. Life in the ghetto was bearable only because there was a larger world outside, of which many Jews often got more than a passing glimpse. As a result they often lived on the fringe of two worlds. There was always some movement to get out of the ghetto on the part of those who were attracted by the wide world that lay beyond the horizon of the ghetto walls and who were cramped by the seemingly narrow life within. Sometimes a Jew would leave the ghetto and become converted; and sometimes these converts, broken and humiliated, would return to the ghetto to taste again of the warm, intimate, tribal life that was to be found nowhere but among their people. On such occasions the romance of the renegade would be told in the ghetto streets, and the whole community would thereby be welded into a solid mass amid the solemn ceremonies by which the stray member was reincorporated into the community.

The inner solidarity of the ghetto community always lay in the ties of family life, and through the organization in the synagogue these families gained status within a community. Confined as the province of the ghetto was, there was ample opportunity for the display of capacity for leadership. The ghetto community was minutely specialized and highly integrated. There were probably more distinct types of personality and institutions within the narrow ghetto streets than in the larger world outside.

The typical ghetto is a densely populated, walled-in area usually found near the arteries of commerce or in the vicinity of a market. The Jewish quarter, even before the days of the compulsory ghetto, seems to have grown up round the synagogue, which was the center of Jewish life, locally as well as religiously.

A common feature of all ghettos was also the cemetery, which was a communal responsibility and to which unusual sentimental interest was attached. There were a number of educational, recreational, and hygienic institutions, such as a school for the young, a bath, a slaughter house, a bakehouse, and a dance hall. In the close life within the ghetto walls almost nothing was left to the devices of the individual. Life was well organized, and custom and ritual played an institutionalizing rôle which still accounts for the high degree of organization of Jewish communities, often verging on overorganization. These institutions did not arise ready made. They represent what life always is, an adaptation to the physical and social needs of a people. In this case particularly, those institutions that had to deal with the conflict and disorder within the group and the pressure from without were the characteristic form of accommodation to the isolation which the ghetto symbolized and enforced. This holds good not merely for the institutions of the ghetto, but for the functionaries and personalities that center around them. The Jews as a race as we know them today are themselves a product of the ghetto.

The ghetto, from the standpoint of biology, was a closely inbreeding, self-perpetuating group to such an extent that it may properly be called a closed community. Not that there was no intermarriage, but these mixed marriages as a rule were lost to the ghetto. The Jews have frequently and rightly been pointed out as the classic example of the great force of religious and racial prejudices, of segregation and isolation, in giving rise to distinct physical and social types. These types persist roughly to the extent that ghetto life and its effects have continued relatively unchanged, which is most true of Eastern Europe and the Orient. The difference in community life accounts in large part for the differences between various local groupings within the Jewish population.

The Russian, Polish, and in part the Roumanian, Jews differ from those of Western Europe—the German, French, Dutch, and English Jews—in several fundamental respects. For a long period the Jews of the East were merely a cultural dependency—an outpost—of Western Jewry. When an independent cultural life did develop in Russia, Poland, and Lithuania, it was self-sufficient and self-contained, set apart from the larger world. Not so with the Jews of Western Europe. They were never quite impervious to the currents of thought and the social changes that characterized the life of Europe since the Renaissance. While the Jews of the East lived in large part in rural communities, in a village world, those of the West were predominantly a city people, in touch with the centers of trade and finance near and far, and in touch at least for some time with the pulsating intellectual life of the world. While the Jews of the Rhine cities were associating with men of thought and of affairs, their brethren in Russia were dealing with peasants and an uncultured, decadent, feudal nobility. When the Jewries of the West were already seething with modernist religious, political, and social movements, those of the East were still steeped in mysticism and medieval ritual. While the Western Jews were moving along with the tide of progress, those of the East were still sharing the backwardness and isolation of the gentile world of villagers and peasants. Although until the middle of the last century the Jews of the East were never quite so confined in their physical movements as were the ghetto Jews of the West, the former lived in a smaller world, a world characterized by rigidity and stability; and when they were herded into cities, in which they constituted the preponderant bulk of the total population, they merely turned these cities into large villages that had little in common with the urban centers of the West. Many features of local life in the modern Jewish community bear the imprint of the successive waves of immigrants first from the West and then from the East.

The formal enactments that made the ghetto the legal dwellingplace of the Jews were abolished toward the middle of the last century in most of the countries of the world. Strangely enough, the abolition of the legal ghetto was opposed by a great portion of Jews as late as a hundred years ago, for they had a premonition that the leveling of the ghetto walls would mean the wiping out of separate community life, which the formal ghetto rules merely symbolized. Those who saw in the new freedom the waning influence of the Jewish religion and the ultimate dissolution of Jewish life in separate communities had two things left to console them: (1) the formal equality decreed by law did not at once gain for the Jew ready acceptance and a parallel social status among his fellow-citizens; and (2) although Western Jewry seemed to be crumbling, there were approximately six millions of Jews left on the other side of the Vistula who were still clinging to the old bonds that exclusion and oppression had fashioned. . . .

Just as the ghetto arose before formal decrees forced the Jews into segregated areas, so the ghetto persists after these decrees have been annulled.

Mr. Zangwill has said: "People who have been living in a ghetto for a couple of centuries are not able to step outside merely because the gates are thrown down, nor to efface the brands on their souls by putting off their yellow badges. The isolation from without will have come to seem the law of their being."

The formal abolition of the ghetto and the granting of citizenship did for the Jews about what the emancipation proclamation did for the Negro. Slavery was more than a mere legal relationship, and the ghetto was more than a statute. It had become an institution. Though the physical walls of the ghetto have been torn down, an invisible wall of isolation still maintains the distance between the Jew and his neighbors.

Even in towns containing only a handful of Jews, there will be found in all parts of the world some more or less definitely organized community. The ecological factors that enter into its development are essentially those of the medieval ghetto. There are several items besides the continuity of traditions from within and prejudice from without that account for the persistence of the modern ghetto, particularly in American cities. One of these is the colonization movement among the Jews, by which Old World communities are sometimes kept intact in the New World. But even where no such organized effort exists, it is remarkable to what extent the Jewish community tends to perpetuate its old surroundings. . . .

In countries where the contact between Jew and non-Jew has been continued for a few generations, and where no new immigration from other countries in which the Jews retained their old status has taken place, the ghetto has to a large extent disintegrated. Under these circumstances, not only does the ghetto tend to disappear, but the race tends to disappear with it. Contact with the world through education, commerce, and the arts tends to bring about a substitution of the cultural values of the world at large for those of the ghetto. This contact, moreover, frequently brings about intermarriage, which is most frequent in those localities where intercourse between Jew and Gentile is least restricted. It is safe to say that the present fifteen and a half million Jews in the world constitute only a small proportion of the living descendants of the original Jewish settlers in the Western world at the beginning of the Christian era. They are merely the residue of a much larger group whose Jewish identity has been lost in the general stream of population. What has happened in the case of the Jews is essentially what has happened in all minority groups in recent times. As the barriers of isolation have receded, social intercourse and interbreeding have decimated the size of the group and leveled its distinguishing characteristics to those of the milieu.

A Jewish community may in some respects be said to exist after the obstacles to ready intercourse with the world outside have been removed, but it tends to become a nondescript community. Where, however, as is the case in most large cities of Western Europe and especially the United States, a steady influx of new immigrants has replenished the disintegrating community, there a ghetto, with all the characteristic local color, has grown up and maintains itself. It is with such a community, as found in the Chicago ghetto, that this study has dealt.

Western ghettos differ from those of the East in that the former comprise at least two sections, the native and the foreign. The native section lives in some sort of concentration within convenient distance from the communal institutions. A rise in material prosperity is generally followed by a removal to a better district, where a new Jewish area is created, but one less distinguished from its environment by external tokens. The foreign section, however, lives in a state of dense concentration. Their poverty makes them settle in the poor quarter of the town, where they reproduce the social conditions in which they have been born and bred, so far as the new environment will allow. The ghetto in the East may be a symbol of political bondage; but in the West the only bondage that it typifies is that exercised by economic status, by sentiment and tradition.

If you would know what kind of Jew a man is, ask him where he lives; for no single factor indicates as much about the character of the Jew as the area in which he lives. It is an index not only to his economic status, his occupation, his religion, but to his politics and his outlook on life, and the stage in the assimilative process that he has reached.

West of the Chicago River, in the shadow of the central business district, lies a densely populated rectangle of crowded tenements representing the greater part of Chicago's immigrant colonies, among them the ghetto. It contains the most varied assortment of people to be found in any similar area of the world. This area has been the stamping-ground of virtually every immigrant group that has come to Chicago. The occupation of this area by the Jews is, it seems, merely a passing phase of a long process of succession in which one population group has been crowded out by another. There is, however, an unmistakable regularity in this process. In the course of the growth of the city and the invasion of the slums by new groups of immigrants there has resulted a constancy of association between Jews and other ethnic groups. Each racial and cultural group tends to settle in that part of the city which, from the point of view of rents, standards of living, accessibility, and tolerance, makes the reproduction of the Old World life easiest. In the course of the invasion of these tides of immigrants the ghetto has become converted from the outskirts of an over-grown village to the slum of a great city in little more than one generation. The Jews have successfully displaced the Germans, the Irish, and the Bohemians, and have themselves been displaced by the Poles and Lithuanians, the Italians, the Greeks, and Turks, and finally the Negro. The Poles and Jews detest each other thoroughly, but they can trade with each other very successfully. They have transferred the accommodation to each other from the Old World to the New. The latest invasion of the ghetto by the Negro is of more than passing interest. The Negro, like the immigrant, is segregated in the city into a racial colony; economic factors, race prejudice, and cultural differences combine to set him apart. The Negro has drifted to the abandoned sections of the ghetto for precisely the same reasons that the Jews and the Italians came there. Unlike the white landlords and residents of former days and in other parts of the city, the Jews have offered no appreciable resistance to the invasion of the Negroes. The Negroes pay good rent and spend their money readily. Many of the immigrants of the ghetto have not as yet discovered the color line.

The transition and deterioration of the ghetto has been proceeding at such speed that the complexion of the area changes from day to day. Dilapidated structures that a decade ago were Lutheran and Catholic churches have since become synagogues, and have now been turned into African M. E. Churches. Under the latest coat of paint of a store-front colored mission there are vestiges of signs reading "Kosher Butchershop" and "Deutsche Apotheke."

True to the ancient pattern, the most colorful and active section of the ghetto is the street market, which resembles a medieval fair more than the shopping district of a modern city. But this institution, together with the rest of ghetto culture, is fast declining. The life of the immigrants in the ghetto is so circumscribed and they are so integrally a part of it that they are unaware of its existence. It is the children of the immigrant who discover the ghetto and then . . . flee. What a few years ago was a steady but slow outward movement has now developed into a veritable stampede to get out of the ghetto; for, with all its varied activities, and its colorful atmosphere, the ghetto nevertheless is a small world. It throbs with a life which is provincial and sectarian. Its successes are measured on a small scale, and its range of expression is limited.

Not until the immigrant leaves the ghetto does he become fully conscious of himself and his status. He feels a sense of personal freedom and expansion as he takes up his residence in the more modern and less Jewish area of second settlement. As late as twenty years ago, when the first Jewish fugitives from the ghetto invaded Lawndale, an area about two miles west, which in Chicago represents the area of second settlement, they came into collision with the Irish and the Germans, who had turned what was recently a prairie into something like a park. It took the Jews about ten years to convert it into a densely settled apartment-house area. At first they could not rent. Experience in the ghetto from which the Irish and Germans had been displaced had given these residents a vision of what was in store for their homes. But this time the Jews could afford to buy, and they bought in blocks. By 1910 Lawndale had become a second ghetto. Its synagogues were a little more modern than those of Maxwell street; the beards of the Lawndale Jews were a little trimmer, and their coats a little shorter, than in the original ghetto; but Lawndale had become Jewish. Those residents of the ghetto who stayed behind derisively called Lawndale "Deutschland," and its inhabitants "Deutschuks," because they were affecting German ways.

But the Lawndale Jews found little rest and satisfaction. Their erstwhile neighbors, impelled by identical motives—to flee from their fellow-Jews, and be less Jewish—had given Lawndale a new complexion, unmistakably Jewish, though not quite as genuine as that of the ghetto itself.

In their attempt to flee from the ghetto, the partially assimilated Jews have found that the ghetto has followed them, and a new exodus sets in. The plans of those who fled from the ghetto in order to obtain status as human beings—as successful business or professional men, rather than as Jews—have been frustrated by the similar plans of others. So it is with the third settlement in the fashionable apartment hotels and the suburbs. As the area becomes predominantly Jewish, the non-Jewish settlers move, and the Jews begin the pursuit anew. Scarcely does the Jew get a glimpse of the freer world that looms beyond the ghetto when he becomes irritated by the presence of his fellow-Jews, more Jewish than himself; he is bored, disgusted, and resumes his flight.

In the process he changes his character and his institution. But what has held the community together in spite of all disintegrating forces from within and without is not only the replenishment of the ghetto by new immigrants—for this is a waning factor—but rather the return to the ghetto of those who have fled but have been disappointed and disillusioned about the results of their flight. They have found the outside world cold and unresponsive to their claims, and return to the warmth and the intimacy of the ghetto. Finally, the Jewish community has been kept intact by the fact that the outside world has treated it as an entity. The Jewish problem, if there be one, consists in the fact that the ghetto persists in spite of the attempt of so many to flee. As long as the nucleus remains, it will serve as a symbol of community life to which even those who are far removed in space and in sympathies belong and by which they are identified.

The Jews as individuals do not always find the way to assimilation blocked. They make friends as well as enemies. The contacts between cultural and racial groups inevitably produce harmony as well as friction; and the one cannot be promoted nor the other prevented by nostrums and ready-made programs and administrative devices. Interaction is life, and life is a growth which defies attempts at control and direction, however rational they may be, that do not take account of this dynamic process. In the struggle for status, personality arises. The Jew, like every other human being, owes his unique character to this struggle, and that character will change and perhaps disappear as the struggle changes or subsides.

What makes the Jewish community—composed as it is of heterogeneous cultural elements and distributed in separate areas of our cities—a community is its capacity to act corporately. It is a cultural community and constitutes as near an approach to communal life as the modern city has to offer. The ghetto, be it Chinese, Negro, Sicilian, or Jewish, can be completely understood only if it is viewed as a socio-psychological, as well as an ecological, phenomenon; for it is not merely a physical fact, but also a state of mind.

WHITE MAN'S COUNTRY

*

By Robert E. Park

ANALYSIS REVEALS THE FACT THAT the race problem is a question of latitudes. It assumes a different shape in the United States and in the West Indies; in the northern and in the southern states. In Central Africa and on the West Coast the problem is that of the white man in a black man's country; in South Africa it is that of the black man in the white man's country.

A white man's country is any part of the world in which the white man can live; a black man's country is any part of the world in which the white man can't live and the black man can. It is in this sense that, although the population is overwhelmingly black, South Africa is still a white man's land.

The similarity between the racial situation in the southern states and in South Africa is due to the fact that, in both instances, the black man is living or seeking to live in a white man's world.

"Notwithstanding the markedly different experiences through which each country has gone since European settlement first began, the visitor from South Africa to the southern states sees much that is familiar." There are differences but they are less than the resemblances. "In essence the problem is the same for both of us."

Not latitude alone but numbers are factors in the racial situation. In South Africa the Negro population is vastly larger and is increasing more rapidly than the white. In this country the reverse is true.

The author believes that "the genius of the European peoples concerned will probably enable them to govern their tropical dependencies with justice and consideration, and adjust their methods to suit the development and changing needs of the governed. . . . In South Africa and the United States," however, "the problem is much more complex and difficult." In the tropics the white man is a mere sojourner. Here and in South Africa the races live permanently side by side. It is the problem of the twentieth century to discover a basis of adjustment.

Robert E. Park, from his review of Maurice S. Evans' *Black and White in the Southern States: A Study of the Race Problem in the United States from a South African Point of View* (London: Longmans, Green & Co., 1915), in *The American Journal of Sociology*, XXI (March, 1916), 696–697.

* *

By William E. Hocking†

You GET THIS IDEAL of guidance only where the contact between white and black is restricted to that of missionary and administrator giving their best to the black man without thought of permanent residence or settlement in his midst. This is the important point: missionary and administrator, say in Tanganyika or in West Africa, are temporary sojourners, looking forward when their work is done to well-earned retirement in Europe. Hence their attitude towards the blacks is purely professional and in that sense unselfish: they are there to do the best they know for the blacks, and then retire. The trouble begins when you get the white settler, who comes to stay, to make his home, to leave his progeny. Then you begin to hear of making the land a 'white man's country,' which—as the blacks cannot be exterminated and replaced by whites, and are moreover wanted for the sake of their cheap labor—means 'a country fit for the white man to live in,' which in turn means a country in which the white man is permanently and exclusively boss not merely because he is at present the more civilized, but simply because he is white. The talk is of maintaining 'white civilization,' and undeniably at present the white man is the repository of that civilization. But the actual aim is not to maintain that civilization by communicating it as fully and rapidly as possible to the blacks: the aim is to maintain the social, economic, political predominance of the white people, by erecting every sort of barrier, legal, economic, social, to their advancement, i.e., to their becoming civilized to the point where they might claim those fundamental rights due to all civilized men, which rights are part of the definition of being civilized.

NEGRO-PYGMY RELATIONS IN THE ITURI FOREST

By Patrick Putnam‡

THIS FOREST IS INHABITED BY TWO KINDS OF PEOPLE, Negroes and pygmies, who maintain an almost symbiotic relationship, based on trade. A Negro village may own approximately 100 square miles of forest territory. In this territory are the Negro village and pygmy village. The former is permanent,

† From William Ernest Hocking, *The Spirit of World Politics* (New York: The Macmillan Company, 1932), pp. 416–417, by permission of the author.

‡ Adapted from Patrick Putnam, "The Pygmies of the Ituri Forest," in Carleton Coon (ed.), *A Reader in General Anthropology*, by permission of Henry Holt & Co., copyright 1948.

in a clearing; the latter is temporary, under the forest trees. In maintaining their relationship, it is the pygmies' job to take in honey and meat, while the Negroes' obligation is to give them plantains. In addition, the pygmies may bring in a certain amount of wild baselli fruit in season, or roofing leaves, or rattan and fibers for net making; in return they may acquire ax blades, knives, and arrowheads from the Negroes.

There is no strict process of barter involved, and no accounting kept, other than through general observation. If the pygmies are stingy, their Negroes will hold back their bananas. If the Negroes are stingy, the pygmies will leave the territory and go to live with other pygmies serving other Negro hosts.

This relationship is interfamilial, between a pygmy family and a Negro family. It is a matter of close personal relations, inherited, on both sides, from father to son. These alliances may change from time to time, but when they do there are usually hard feelings; if a man's pygmy leaves him to serve another host it is a kind of divorce. In the old days, a frequent cause of intervillage warfare among the Negroes was the luring away of each other's pygmies.

Before the Belgians stopped intervillage and intertribal warfare, the most important single duty of the pygmy was to act as scout and intelligence agent in the forest. As soon as he became aware of a raiding party crossing the boundary of his host's territory he would hotfoot it to the village to give warning. This eternal vigilance on the part of the pygmy was probably of more value to his hosts than the meat that he brought in. Now that the need of this has ceased he is fulfilling only half of his contract; the Negro, who still provides plantains and manufactured objects, is still fulfilling all of his. Still both are satisfied.

Ordinarily, the pygmy keeps inside the territory of his Negro hosts. Individuals and small family groups may go outside to visit relatives in other bands, but this causes no disturbance because the visitors turn in their game to the hosts of the kinsmen whom they are visiting. This constant milling about evens up on the whole, and the number of pygmies in any band at any one time is about the same. There are occasions, however, when the hunters of a band may have a strong reason to pass beyond the landmarks which designate their hosts' territorial boundaries. If there is a lot of game just over the border and no pygmies there to catch it, the pygmies will tell their Negroes, who tell the Negroes owning that part of the forest. An agreement will be made between the two groups of Negroes, and the pygmies will be allowed to take the game, provided that they pay a part of it to the owners of the forest, and another part to their own hosts. This kind of economic treaty, therefore, brings the pygmies of a given band into contact with two groups of Negroes, and may initiate new relationships.

When the pygmy camp is close to the Negro village, some of the pygmies may come in every evening. They will leave a couple of old men to stay behind in the camp as guards, smoking hashish, and the rest will go into the village, usually around four o'clock in the afternoon, after the day's hunting is over. From then until dark a few pygmies are usually to be seen hanging about the women's quarters. If a white man arrives, however, they quickly disappear, through fear that he will confiscate their antelope, or any other game that they may have brought with them.

These mass visits are made particularly if it is going to be a moonlit night and if wine drinking is going on. If there is a moon they will stay and dance; if not, they will come home at dark. The Negroes give them wine in a condescending way, and the pygmies put on what the Negroes consider to be wild, barbaric dances.

Sometimes the pygmy camp is as much as two days' journey from the village. In this case, the pygmies go in seldom, and browbeat their wives to make them go in to get plantains.

A visitor to a Negro village can nearly always see bunches of plantains lying around on the ground; they have been placed there for the pygmies, who pick them up and carry them home. There is no need for any special bargaining or designation; the pygmies know which bunches are for them.

The pygmies consider themselves inseparably attached to their hosts and think it their duty to provide them with meat. Although they feel that they are supposed to turn over all honey and elephant meat, in each case they eat all they can before taking it into the village. They never preserve or store any food. Their duty of feeding the Negroes meat is therefore regarded as somewhat of a nuisance. On the other hand, when the pygmy wants something from a Negro, he wheedles and "begs" for it. He may thus "borrow" a mortar, a skin-headed drum for dancing, etc., and will not return it until the Negro comes after it or sends for it. He will not put any of these things under cover, or care for them; he leaves them out in the rain to mildew and rot. The owner has to see that his property is cared for, and this forms a subject on which the Negro can make fun of the pygmy.

The form of this relationship is therefore a grudging duty in the case of giving, and a wheedling begging in the case of receiving. These outer forms fail to reveal the inner feeling of loyalty and affection between the parties concerned, but rather symbolize the existing situation in which the Negro is at the top of the scale and the pygmy at the bottom.

The Negroes distinguish four ranks or orders of living beings: people, pygmies, chimpanzees, and other animals. The pygmies are thus considered a species apart, neither human nor animal, but in between. The main point of distinction lies not in their size or physique, but in the fact that the pygmies do no cultivation.

The Negroes think of their pygmies as barbaric and uncultured, but at the same time they are often fond of them. A Negro may occasionally marry a pygmy woman, and the children are considered real children, complete human beings; they are brought up with the Negro's other children. The Negroes say that pygmy women are good in bed, cheap, and prolific, but that they are useless for women's work—cultivation and cooking. For a pygmy woman it is a great rise in the scale of living to marry a Negro as his second or third wife, despite the fact that pygmy wives are usually the butt of humor from the Negro wives. This is, however, a one-way process; no Negress could endure the pygmy way of living, and none of them ever marry pygmies.

The interplay between Negroes and pygmies may be illustrated by a number of examples in which they disagree on historical facts. The Negroes say that the pygmies once went naked, like animals. The pygmies hotly deny this, and assert that they always wore loin cloths. The Negroes admit that they themselves were once cannibals, but say that the pygmies ate more human flesh than they did.

This too the pygmies deny; they claim that they never ate human flesh except when the Negroes gave it to them.

In addition to the exchange of food and, formerly, protection, which form the basis for Negro-pygmy interaction, there is another activity which helps to cement their relationship. The Negroes have a circumcision school, of the usual Negro variety. This school is held about once in four or five years. There is no specific interval; it is probably that they wait until there are enough boys ready to form a class of the right size. These boys are anywhere from nine to fourteen years of age. Now the pygmies associated with these Negroes may send their boys through this same school with the sons of their hosts. Thus, the pygmy boys are away from home several months, are in close association with the Negro boys, and are taught the same secrets that the Negro boys learn. At the end they are all circumcised together, and their parents come to the Negro village to dance and get drunk with the parents of the Negro boys.

The keynote to the simple and specialized pygmy technology is the fact that they do not have to make any of their basic tools, but instead obtain effective iron cutting tools from their Negro hosts. This eliminates much work and the need for much skill in toolmaking, and provides them with more efficient instruments than they could possibly make for themselves at a food-gathering level of technology.

Hunting is the principal occupation of the pygmies; it is their principal reason for being able to maintain their relationship with their Negro hosts. Although between themselves the pygmies have little division of labor, in another sense they are all specialists in hunting, and the division of labor is between them and the Negroes. In this sense the pygmies form an ethnic caste, a genetically and occupationally segregated segment of a larger economic entity.

This does not mean that the Negro does no hunting. However, the pygmy spends all of his time hunting, the Negro only a portion of his. The pygmy depends largely on his ability to move noiselessly and swiftly about the forest, and to climb trees. The Negro depends on his greater patience and mechanical ingenuity, for he hunts largely by means of elaborate traps, deadfalls, pits, weighted spears dangled over elephant paths, and other deadly devices. The pygmy could never be induced to dig a pit; it is too much work, takes too long, and takes too much concentration and persistence. Nor do they ever use traps.

Throughout the pygmy country, the pygmies can be classified either as net hunters or non-net hunters, depending on whether they habitually practice big community hunts, driving animals into nets, or depend entirely on individual stalking as a means of securing game. They may also be classified by whether or not they use bows and arrows. In both net hunting and the use of the bow and arrow, the pygmies follow the lead of the Negroes among whom they live. Where the Negroes have nets, the pygmies have nets; where the Negroes have bows, the pygmies have bows. This is easily understood, since the Negroes make both the nets and the arrowheads. Presumably, the bowless pygmies are net hunters, for otherwise they could not live.

THE ECONOMIC ROLE OF THE ARABS IN INDONESIA

By Justus M. van der Kroef

FOR CENTURIES THE ARABS IN INDONESIA have fulfilled an indispensable role in Indonesian economy as middlemen, traders, and money lenders. Before the colonial period, their economic life, like that of other Oriental minorities, probably concerned itself with the purchase and sale of the luxury items on which the peddlers' trade of Southeast Asian antiquity depended. They may also have become involved in the trade in spices if they were pecunious enough. Since the nineteenth century however their economic activities have primarily been confined to overseas commerce in certain agricultural exports (rubber, sugar, and tea) cultivated by the Indonesian population and to the extension of credit both in cities and in the rural areas.

The inroads of Western estate enterprise, the opening of the village society to foreign, and frequently disrupting, influences, the introduction of money taxes and the ever-increasing cash needs of the Javanese peasant, all provided the setting for the Arab's economic function. It is significant that Arab immigration to Java takes such a big flight in the second half of the nineteenth century, precisely the era when Java and soon the other Indonesian islands, were opened up by the colonial government to private Western enterprise. The Javanese peasant, hitherto secure in the subsistence and cooperative structure of his village economy, was drawn ever more rapidly within the orbit of the modern, internationally oriented market economy. At the same time, the colonial government in the latter half of the nineteenth and early twentieth centuries, initiated a formidable array of emancipation schemes, which further had the effect of loosening the ancient communal bonds of the village and destroying its self-containing and self-sufficient character. However, the Javanese peasant found himself generally unable to cope with all these far-reaching changes in his life. On the one hand he persistently clung to the protective support of his village, on the other hand new monetary needs and also a widening of his wants forced him to earn more than his traditional food crop had provided him with. As a link between the villager and the outside world the Arab in Indonesia saw his golden opportunity.

In forging this link, the Arab like the Chinese, first of all began to buy up the extra crop, which the peasant periodically needed to sell. Travelling from village to village, usually in a definite territory (as in the environs of Djakarta or in the village society around Rembang and Tegal in central Java) the Arab made his contacts, and agreed to purchase surplus crops, even in advance of the harvest. When the peasant began to cultivate cash crops (i.e. rubber, sugar cane, tea, tobacco or coffee) in addition to his rice and maize in order to increase his earnings, the Arab expanded the scope of his middleman operations also. Aware of the peasant's chronic money shortages, his undeveloped habits

Reprinted from Justus M. van der Kroef, "The Arabs in Indonesia," *Middle East Journal*, VII (Summer, 1953), 311–317; copyright 1953 by The Middle East Institute, Washington D.C., and used with the kind permission of the publisher.

of saving and his fatalistic attitude toward the future, the Arab very early turned to money lending, advancing cash on an as yet unharvested crop, on cattle or heirlooms as collateral with the right to impound them, and also on land pawned to him by the villager.

Despite efforts by the colonial government to combat the usurious practices of the Arab moneylender and notwithstanding great progress in the establishment of village banks and government credit institutions in the past forty years, it would appear that the Indonesian seems to prefer to borrow from money lenders notwithstanding their exorbitant interest rates. This preference is due to a variety of reasons. First of all the villager may be quite some distance away from a government lending agency, whereas the Arab or Chinese lender may be a village fixture, living on the edge of the community. Secondly the lender is in a position to vary his lending rates and his amounts to a far greater degree than official banks, and thus more easily satisfies the incredible variety of the peasant's cash needs. Thirdly, the lender demands no formalities, can be reached at any time of day or night and helps without delay. Fourthly, the lender has no objection to accumulation of debt—rather the reverse—and is prepared to take considerable risks, particularly in connection with loans made in advance of the harvest. Finally, and perhaps most important, the lender is in many cases a familiar figure in the community, known to all and in many cases a part of the "village family"; his is not the impersonal, detached aura of the government loan agency or popular credit bank. The Arab lender *knows* his creditors, their personal and family problems, is familiar with the periodic money needs which may arise during birth and marriage ceremonies, circumcision rites and a host of other traditional culture patterns, the importance of which even today supersede mere economic desiderata in the peasant society. Since traditionally money is an alien, and often unaccepted element in rural life, the Arab middleman-lender makes superfluous the cumbersome money transactions which the villager dislikes. The lender has in fact been known to act as the villager's personal "agent," buying part of his crop, going to town to pay the villager's taxes and with the remainder buying for him in town the few commodities that he may desire. Is it any wonder that one expert, J. H. Boeke, has called the lender the "indispensable guide through the labyrinth of the money economy" of the Indonesian peasant?

It is against this background that the usurious practices of the Arab lender must be viewed. However there can be little question that his predatory interest rates kept thousands of Indonesian peasants in a state approaching debtor bondage. A few examples should suffice. In Djember, East Java, one Arab had lent 200 guilders, but the borrower agreed to repay 500 guilders after 10 months; a loan of 20 guilders was to be repaid with 35 guilders after 4 months; on a loan of 1000 guilders an interest of no less than 700 guilders was due after about 6 months! Over the entire district of Pekalongan, Java, Arab lenders, united in their own protective association, operated. Heads of the association resided in Tegal, long the center of Arab lending activities. There they advanced money to their more impecunious countrymen who roamed the countryside seeking to lure the peasantry into debt. Rates of 200% interest a year are regarded as "reasonable" among these Arab lenders, according to one informant. The size of some Arab money lenders' "investments" is well illustrated by the case of a lender in the Bangil region of East Java, who in one large village alone had lent out a total of 300,000 guilders. In Cheribon, West Java, many cases of Arab usury are on record, particularly in connection with those borrowers who had to default on one of their payments. A typical example was that of a European who had borrowed 200 guilders, but had agreed to repay 320 guilders in 8 monthly installments of 40 guilders. When after 4 months he had to ask for a temporary extension on the fifth payment, his Arab creditor agreed only on the condition that henceforth his monthly payments would be 48 guilders. According to the report of one lender, the common rate prevailing among Arabs was: 100 guilders borrowed, 200 guilders to be repaid in 10 monthly payments of 20 guilders. Yet in the course of his long experience this Arab lender had found that only 1.2% of the total amount lent out was not or could not be collected.

The brazenness and unscrupulousness of Arab lenders in seeking victims was proverbial in some areas of Indonesia. In the vicinity of Tegal, Central Java, Arabs not only roamed the countryside, but also had numerous dealings in the towns, especially where no popular credit banks were in existence. If during a public sale a prospective buyer did not have sufficient funds, "two or three Arabs together" offered to act as co-signers. In the afternoon, after the sale, the victim was then visited by his Arab creditors who forced a note on him, of at least one and a half times the price of the purchased goods. Especially among gamblers does the Arab lender find fertile territory. "It is widely known here," thus one government report concerning Arab lenders in Tegal, "that when a gambler has lost his money in the middle of the night, he simply rouses an Arab lender. The gambler merely has to sign a note for twice the amount borrowed and he can quietly continue his game." Often, too, Arabs visited houses during working hours, attempting to force a loan on housewives. The above-mentioned report described as "everyday scenes" the laying in wait of creditors on a Saturday afternoon in front of shops and plants and on the first of the month in front of government and other offices, accosting women on the streets, and even the forced and illegal searching of the houses of those unable to pay. In the same area the number of the lenders' victims, especially among members of the Indonesian civil service, but also among Eurasians and Europeans, seems to have been extremely high.

Two obstacles are placed in the Arab lenders' way in connection with his lending activities. One is the *riba* (interest) prohibition in the Koran, the other is the government's measures against usury. It is evident that the Arab has been able to circumvent both. Ways to get around the *riba* prohibition include the "renting" of money and the fictitious sale of goods. The *"sewa oewang,"* renting of money, means that the Arab "leases," say, a rix-dollar (about $1) to his victim for three or four cents a day, just as if the rix-dollar were an object and not a coin. Or the Arab may sell a group of sarongs with a value of 55 guilders for 90 guilders. The "purchaser" (really borrower) signs a note for 90 guilders, and verbally agrees to make monthly payment of from 10 to 18 guilders. The Arab thereupon immediately buys back the sarongs for 50 guilders cash. The pseudo-sale thus is in fact a loan of 50 guilders, but 90 guilders must be repaid by the borrower in the agreed monthly installments. In the course of time the government has provided the citizen with the assistance of usury legislation but the debtor is generally not anxious to bring his case to court, for in so doing his most flexible and most ready source of credit may be permanently cut off.

Furthermore, the Arab lenders know how to protect themselves in cases where the law requires written proof of a loan. The custom is to write a note which does not list the interest rate separately, but rather states the full amount to be repaid, including the interest, while the initial amount borrowed is never indicated. Between what is written and what is previously agreed to orally by the lender and his victim, is generally a vast difference.

Along with Chinese, Arab interests have also gone out to the rural industry in Java. This kind of industry centers around a typical village workshop owned and managed in most cases by a Chinese or Arab and it is concerned with the manufacture of inexpensive consumer goods of imperfect quality such as umbrellas, muslin jackets and other textiles, native cigarettes (the so-called *krètèk*), matches, sandals and even flashlight batteries. In the vicinity of Surabaya, on the road to Sidoardjo, the author recently noted quite a number of these small-scale enterprises, mainly operated by Arabs, and with a highly flexible labor force, mostly composed of women and children. This kind of small-scale industry—the shop rarely has more than from ten to twenty laborers —is essentially the consequence of chronic and periodic money shortages among the rural population. But not only because they provide an opportunity to meet the periodic cash needs of the peasant are these workshops important. They are also channels of broadening the manufactured needs of the Indonesian, and they are significant because they give some direction to the want-creating process which is so indispensable to a modern industrial society. It is apparent however that conditions in these shops are often deplorable. Women have been known to hire themselves out for as much as three years at a time, in return for the payment of 30 guilders cash, board and room, and the right to some new clothing once a year. Because of increasing indebtedness the laborers' term of work may be extended and they may sink into a state of permanent debtor bondage, being at the complete mercy of the owner. Flagrant abuses, involving both Arab and Chinese operators were brought to light in the course of the first two decades of the present century. Fortunately the situation has much improved in recent times.

THE RACIAL DIVISION OF LABOR VERSUS SEGREGATION

By Albion Ross

THE GOVERNMENT IS DISCOVERING that South African housewives will not do their own housework.

This issue is beginning to play a considerable role in the growing city resistance to the pending urban-areas bill, which is similar to national legislation being pushed through now to separate the white and black races.

By Albion Ross, Special to the New York *Times* from Capetown, South Africa, March 7, 1954. The New York *Times*, March 8, 1954, p. 3, with the kind permission of the publisher.

Women do not intend to be separated from their Negro servants. Because of this, the Government is in trouble with the feminine part of city populations, notably in Johannesburg, the biggest city in the country.

A woman representative of the South African Institute of Race Relations here, discussing the amendment bill, referred to the presence of Negro servants as a "part of the South African way of life." This aspect of the situation is beginning to make increasing difficulties.

The South African way of life, as practiced by a large part of the white population, does not mean being waited on hand and foot. However, the Government's efforts to separate the Negro and white affects even stenographers and the wives of many workers.

Housework, in the sense that it is understood in the United States and Europe, is not a part of the South African way of life. To a great extent it is "kaffirs' work," the term for work customarily done for white housewives by Negroes.

A Dutch girl attending the University of Capetown found her student friends to be astounded because she cooked her own meals. She said many girls had confessed that they knew nothing about cooking. To learn to cook anything but a few specialties is held "unnecessary."

The issue is nearing a climax in connection with provisions in the urban-areas bill for cleaning out the "slums in the sky." These are the roofs of city apartment houses on which live the Negroes who do the housework for the dwellings beneath.

The bill provides that no more than five natives may live in any building in white city areas. This is enough for the building maintenance staff, but it means the servants will have to go to Negro areas outside the cities.

This threatens one of the most prized amenities of South African life. The Negro servant, costing a few dollars a month, hands you your cup of tea or coffee early in the morning at bedside. This is the first of a series of tea, coffee and lemonade servings that continue in the home or office all day long.

It remains to be seen whether any South African government will prove strong enough to get the housewife out of bed to make her own cup of tea.

In the large cities such as Johannesburg the situation is more serious. It is noted that because of the distance of the Negro areas from the city and inadequate transportation facilities, housewives will find themselves preparing breakfast.

At night the Negro servant will have to hurry home. Consequently, housewives may be forced also to get supper for the family.

All this suggests a profounder ideological significance than appears on the surface. The doctrine of apartheid, or separation of races, is running into a fact that now is being expressed more openly.

The apartheid group in power contends that racial segregation or separation, an essence of the South African way of life, is being disputed. However, there is a growing recognition that this way of life is not so much racial segregation, but what is known here as "baaskap." This is the Afrikaner term for "being the boss," or white supremacy.

A large section of both the Afrikaner and English-speaking population is swinging to the conviction that apartheid is nonsense, and that the real issue is the preservation of white supremacy.

INDUSTRY

By Everett C. Hughes

ONE OF THE MANY DRAMAS OF MODERN INDUSTRY is that of the meeting and of the working together of people unlike each other in race, nationality, and religion. Wherever it has gone—and industry is always moving into new parts of the world—it has put some new combination of the peoples of the earth at work together. The industrial revolution in England mixed the peoples of the South with those of the North and Irishmen with Englishmen. The Protestants of North Germany established industries in the Rhine; Catholic peasants of the region came to work in them. In the cotton mills of India, Hindus of various castes are herded together with their fellow Indians of other religions. Chinese city workers, driven from the urban East to the rural interior of their country by the Japanese invasion, even now find themselves making electrical equipment for war alongside rustics, also Chinese, who speak strange dialects and who until yesterday knew no tools more complicated than the sickle and the hammer.

In our own country, immigrants from the back provinces of all the countries of Europe have met each other in the steel mill, the mine, the packing house and in the loft where ladies' handkerchiefs are made. Recently, they have been joined by a new wave of rural Americans, some of them as uninitiated to industry as any European peasant who ever landed on Ellis Island, but English of tongue, bred in the most indigenous American traditions of religion, folklore, humor, fighting and rugged individualism, and physically of the purest Anglo-Saxon stock, or of one of the combinations of African with Indian, Spanish, French, or Anglo-Saxon that we call "Negro" in this country.

Although each of the combinations of peoples thus brought together is unique, there is likeness in their meeting and its consequences. Wherever strange peoples have met to work in industry, some have been more initiated in its ways and have possessed more tools and technical knowledge than others. The new have always had to learn not merely how to use their hands and heads at new tasks but also how to live by a new calendar and by the clock, how to deal with new kinds of people in unaccustomed relations to each other, how to use money as their main source of income, and how to order their lives to a new set of contingencies. In nearly all cases, those older and better placed in industry have attributed the newcomer's lack of skill and of the industrial frame of mind to their inherent nature, without being too clear as to whether this nature is a matter of genes or of nurture. The newcomers sooner or later reorganize their ways and their wishes about the new order of things, and become aware of the opinions that their industrial superiors, both workers and employers, have of them. A difference of industrial status that they once accepted as in the nature of things they now question. They speak of discrimination. They act as self-conscious minorities, discontented with their status, always act. To compare these processes, as they have occurred in various places and with various human ingredients, is an intriguing enterprise. We leave it for another day, reminding ourselves only that the races, the nations, and the religions have met again and again in industry, that they will so meet again and again; that they can and do work together, although not always in harmony; and that the groups now oldest in industry learned their industrial lessons from ethnic strangers who considered them poor pupils until they became effective competitors or respected fellow workers. Thus do race relations in industry look in the world-wide, generations-long perspective.

Our special concern, however, is with the relations of Negroes with other persons in American industry at the present time. This requires other perspectives. For, while the Negroes are presently in a phase through which numerous other groups have passed, their situation in American life is unique. It is so in this respect, that the relations of Negro to white Americans have been crystallized into a body of practice enforced upon both races, but more especially upon the Negro, by social pressure, economic sanction, and even by physical force. White Americans have elaborated and then worked deep into their very bones a body of belief about what Negroes are and ought to be like, as well as a complex of fears of what would happen if the practices and beliefs were to change.

Beliefs and fears concerning the Negro as an economic being are interwoven with those concerning him as a citizen, neighbor, and companion. In white American thought, furthermore, strong belief that the Negro is different from other kinds of people is mixed in about equal proportions with fear that he is just like the rest of us. And here lies the essence of the race problem in America; we fear in the Negro those very human qualities that American social philosophy encourages in others. We stubbornly wish that the Negro should be unique. Race relations in American industry must be seen from this perspective also. The danger, however, is not that we should overlook the uniqueness of the relations between Negro and white Americans but that we should magnify it. We cannot avoid the race problem in this country, although many people, especially in the North, would like to. All of us, Negro and white, are a part of the problem. It therefore behooves us to act as intelligently as possible. To do so, we must balance the unique features of the problem against its many likenesses with others. And we must see race relations in all the social matrices in which they occur.

One such matrix is industrial organization, considered as a system of human relations. And if I may present the conclusion of this chapter so near its beginning, that conclusion is not much more than the statement that "in industry" is the important term in the phrase, "race relations in industry." To know about race relations in industry, and to deal with them, one must look upon them as being of the same general order as other relations of people at work, requiring the same kinds of thinking and analysis, demanding the same understanding and skills; and, on the other hand, as little capable of settlement, once and for all, by some sleight-of-hand trick as other human problems in industry, and yet as amenable as others to those tentative, constantly repeated, never perfect, but often successful, decisions and actions by which a working organization is kept going to the moderate satisfaction of most people concerned.

THE PLANTATION

By Edgar T. Thompson

IN A VERY GENERAL WAY the South may be regarded as that part of the United States where the planter has been the chief history-making personality— as that part of the Nation where the planter has most powerfully impressed himself upon the form of society. The planter is a representative of that class of individuals who historically have possessed the land as an incident of some form of conquest and put themselves at the head of political institutions based upon the exploitation of the land. The plantation arises as the personal "possession" of the planter, and it is from the standpoint of his interests that the course of its development is directed. It is first of all a unit of authority over people which comes to be defined and expressed in terms of territory. Hence the plantation is commonly understood as a relatively large landed estate.

Plantations have never physically occupied the entire extent of the area known as the South, but in point of territory covered, the plantation society of the South is undoubtedly the largest the world has ever known. In addition to many other factors which have shaped the history of this society, the factor of sheer size alone has been a highly important one. The plantation society of the South has been big enough to have weight and mass and stability and to permit the development of a plantation "system" whose parts cooperated to maintain a certain type of agricultural economy and social organization. All other institutions within the South, like the family, the church, the school, and the state became parts of this system and supported it. Millions of people grew up within the system and accepted it because they knew no other and rarely if ever came into contact with ideas inconsistent with it.

The South has not been alone in its plantation experience, but most of its students and writers appear to have written and spoken as if it had. Southern writers and spokesmen have been concerned chiefly with issues over which the South has been in conflict with the North and West. They have for this reason been led to contrast the institutions of the South with those of other sections of the United States to the point of acute consciousness of differences. An inevitable consequence of contrast is a heightened sensitiveness to outside criticism and an attitude of justification and of defense.

The existence of the plantation in other times and places, however, provides a basis for comparative study which should immeasurably increase our knowledge not only of the institution itself but of similar societies which have been based upon it.

Historically, there have been at least three important plantation epochs. The first was the ancient Carthago-Roman system which developed around the production of oil and wine. Labor was supplied by slaves captured in war. The second developed in connection with the colonization and exploitation of the New World. It witnessed a rise of great tobacco, rice, sugar, indigo, and cotton

Adapted from Edgar T. Thompson, "The Climatic Theory of the Plantation," *Agricultural History*, XV (January, 1941), 49–60.

plantations. These were based upon Negro slave labor imported from Africa. The third and contemporary plantation development has centered in the countries bordering the Indian Ocean and in many of the islands of the Pacific. The plantations in this area are manned by cheap coolie labor recruited from regions of closed economic resources in the Orient. These huge enterprises have brought plantation agriculture to a point of efficiency and importance not hitherto known.

Aside from the plantation areas of the South the institution today controls the lives and destinies of millions of people in many other parts of the world. In the West Indies the remnants of an old colonial plantation system exist alongside the new and highly efficient plantations organized by American capital. In the Yucatan peninsula and throughout Mexico plantation estates are being broken down into small farms by the policy of the Cardenas government. The old coffee plantations of the highlands and the newer banana plantations of the lowlands give several of the Central American states dual plantation societies in many respects very different from each other. The "mass agriculture" of the banana industry has in recent years transformed primeval jungles into active and thrifty plantation communities. In South America the Guianas, Venezuela, Colombia, Ecuador, and Peru each have plantation areas proximate to their coasts. Brazil witnessed the rise of the first plantation society in the New World, a society based upon the cultivation of sugar cane by means of Negro slave labor. Today, however, it is the coffee *fazenda* of southern Brazil which gives that country what is probably the second largest plantation area in the world.

There are many important plantations in West Africa, notably in Liberia, but the outstanding plantation societies of that continent range from north to south in the eastern half, in Natal, Mozambique, Zanzibar, Tanganyika, Kenya, and Anglo-Egyptian Sudan. About each of these societies there are special points of interest which would repay comparative study. Kenya, especially since the first World War, has witnessed the rapid rise of an aristocracy of European landowners and the proletarianization of the native population. In Natal, an English planter class has developed the cultivation of sugar cane on large estates by the use of East Indian indentured labor and Bantu native labor. The clove plantations of Zanzibar are nominally owned by the once wealthy and all-powerful Arab planters.

In Asia there are several very important plantation societies with commercial outlets on the Indian Ocean. Perhaps the oldest of these is found in the island of Ceylon where on several occasions the estates have had to respond to drastic changes in world market conditions by shifting to different agricultural staples. The tea plantation society of Assam also has had a very interesting and somewhat unusual history. One of the most important plantation developments of modern times is that connected with the production of rubber in the Malay Peninsula. When it was discovered in the first decade of the present century that this long, narrow tongue of land was excellently suited to the production of rubber, the jungle was quickly converted into industrialized forests of disciplined rubber trees. The estates of European planters and companies became points where many peoples of diverse race and culture came together. No less important are the plantations in the Dutch islands of Java and Sumatra. Between the plantations of these two islands there are interesting and significant points of comparison and contrast. In the Philippines, American capital has developed sugar plantations while the Japanese have organized the sugar industry of Taiwan into large-scale producing units to meet domestic needs. Queensland, Australia, Fiji, and Hawaii are or have been the scenes of extensive sugar plantation enterprises. The plantation industry of Hawaii is especially significant for it has given the Territory one of the most heterogeneous populations in the world.

It is obvious from this incomplete and hurried review of plantation societies throughout the world that they are numerous enough to provide the materials for a comparative and scientific account of the institution and of the societies founded upon it. Naturally we are most interested in the South, but it is a frequent experience of science that insight into the problems of a given situation is gained only by going outside that immediate situation, and the widest and seemingly most irrelevant excursions are frequently the source of the most illuminating insights. It may be that the more we learn about other plantation societies directly the more we shall learn about Southern society indirectly.

Insofar as general theories of the plantation have been attempted, they have come, for the most part, from students of colonization and colonies. The reason for this is apparent. The study of colonies, as distinct from the study of a colony, invites comparison and classification. The most obvious characteristic of colonies lending itself to comparison is the economic basis of community life and, as Albert Galloway Keller, has said:

agriculture is the only important primary form of the industrial organization common to colonies of all latitudes and altitudes, and so the only criterion of classification of adequate generality, not to mention importance.

Some colonies are so conspicuously dominated by plantation agriculture and others by small-scale farming that a classification on this basis follows naturally. Keller has mentioned other students of colonization besides himself who recognized at least these two types of colonies. Keller believes, however, that the postulation of other types requires a shift to criteria of discrimination which are not common to all colonies.

The principal interest in the writings of these students of colonization is not so much in the fact that they agree in recognizing the plantation and farm colonies as two fundamental types as it is in the theory which they claim accounts for the determination of the situation in which each type is likely to arise. The explanation implicit, if not explicit, in the works of most of these men is that climate is the determining factor in the situation. This explanation is either stated or assumed in the writings of such men as A. H. L. Heeren and Wilhelm Roscher in Germany, Paul Leroy-Beaulieu in France, and H. E. Egerton and Benjamin Kidd in England. The most explicit statement of this point of view is by Keller:

colonies are, at least in their beginnings, societies of relative simplicity, as yet unendowed with that accumulation of relationships, institutions, and so on, through which older human groups appear to have rendered themselves, to some extent, independent of natural conditions. If this is admitted, either through conviction or as a working hypothesis, then it should be possible to construct a useful classification of colonial societies upon the broader variations of the natural conditions to which they are or have been exposed.

Of these conditions climate is, in the present case at least, the vital and determining one. It is usually so, carrying with it, as it does, so many other factors whose variations are correlated with its own; for instance, flora and fauna, including among the latter the microscopic fauna of disease. Climate, though itself varying in accordance with several factors, and though it evades classification except by type, may still, for the purpose in hand, be broadly divided into *tropical* and *temperate*. But this distinction would be of no utility in classifying colonies, because too general, if these distinct types of climate did not condition the human struggle for existence in a manner so vital as to determine two distinct types of industrial organization, upon which in turn, as what follows is designed to show, there would regularly be developed two distinctly variant types of human society. Thus the classification based upon climate and attendant influences may be shifted over into a classification based upon the type of the industrial organization. Anticipating what is to follow, we should then distinguish the tropical and the temperate colony upon the ground of their common and basic occupation, agriculture, and might name them respectively the *plantation colony* and the *farm colony*.

The temperate-zone farm colony is marked by economic and administrative independence. Since its products are likely to compete with those of the mother country, it tends toward local diversified self-sufficiency. The soil is intensively cultivated and care is given to its conservation. The unit of social organization is the family, and the population is fairly well divided between the two sexes. Hence there is little mixing with natives and no large mixed-blood population. Its democratic society is characterized by free labor.

The tropical plantation colony presents a marked contrast to the farm colony in almost every respect. Tropical products rank as luxury goods in the mother country, and the plantation colony tends to specialize in the production of one or more of them. Cultivation is extensive and exploitative. The colonists are predominantly males, and the racial unit is the individual and not the family. Consequently, relations with native women produce a mixed population. Since "Vital conditions do not permit of the accomplishment of plantation labors at the hands of an unacclimatized race," laborers must be imported from other tropical regions if the natives cannot be coerced.

Keller apparently thinks of the physical and meteorological environment as giving rise to local survival forms which in turn elaborate secondary social and political forms of higher complexity. The differences between the plantation colony and the farm colony grow out of differences in climate. Adjustment to varying climatic conditions along the colonial frontier results in two fundamentally different labor economies and social organizations. These statements seem to summarize the climatic theory of the plantation and the society based upon it as formulated by Keller.

In spite of the fact that most of the plantation societies in the present world community are grouped in or near the tropics, the theory is subject to some very great difficulties. In the first place, it does not account for the existence of plantation societies in areas of temperate climate. In Rhode Island, for example, after about 1650, the Narragansett planters developed "an industrial system which may fairly be compared with that of the Southern colonies." The situation in eastern Germany seems to be another exception to the theory. Although the lowlands of this area have an inhospitable climate with long, severe winters, after the twelfth century this frontier developed a system of large estates which seems to conform to the plantation pattern and which has been maintained for over six hundred years.

The climatic theory also fails to explain the existence of tropical colonies where small farming characterizes the agricultural economy. Saba Island in the Dutch West Indies seems to illustrate such a situation. Costa Rica in Central America apparently is another exception. It is a tropical country with a native-born white population of small farmers. Originally whites of Spanish origin settled the land in family groups and today "of 58,976 real estate holdings Costa Ricans hold legal title to 47,000." However, after several hundred years of existence as a small farm society the banana plantation with Negro labor is now beginning to make inroads.

A third objection to the climatic theory is that it does not account for the very great and significant differences between plantation societies. They establish themselves in a variety of ways and vary greatly from place to place and from time to time. The differences between any two plantation societies may be as great as the contrasts between a plantation society and a small-farm society. James G. Leyburn evidently believes that the differences between what he calls the "settlement-plantation" society and the "exploitative plantation" society are very great. He recognizes these, not as sub-types of plantation society generally, but as full types of frontier societies along with the farm type and the ranching type.

Perhaps the most serious shortcoming of the climatic theory is its failure to account for the transition from plantation to farm, or *vice versa,* in a single area where the climatic factor remains stable. The same area and climate maintains itself through kaleidoscopic changes in economic and social life. Vincent T. Harlow has described a change in Barbados from a colony of small farms operated by white owners to a colony of large plantations operated by Negro slave labor. On the other hand, according to Avery Craven, Virginia and Maryland had by 1860 "come largely to the small farm and the small farmer." By that time the Governor of Virginia was advertising her agriculture as no longer characterized by "the large plantation system" but one of "smaller horticultural and aboricultural farming."

The fact that in the present world community plantation societies are grouped in or near the tropics, which at first seems to support the theory, may be accounted for on other than climatic grounds. It is obvious that, because of climatic conditions, most of the agricultural products characteristic of the tropics cannot be grown elsewhere. Some, like cane sugar, can be produced in temperate zone areas, but the costs are materially higher when production is attempted outside the areas of optimum natural conditions. Bananas, for example, can be grown under hothouse conditions in Canada, but they can be grown profitably only in the tropics. For this reason banana plantations are found in the tropics and nowhere else. They are located by the nature of the major crop. Bananas need not be grown only on a plantation basis; they may be, and frequently are, grown and marketed by peasant farmers. In the latter case the small banana farm is also necessarily restricted to areas of tropical climate.

Although the natural distribution of particular plantation staples is determined or limited by climatic factors, it does not follow that the plantation institution itself is so determined. Plantations are largely concentrated in the tropics, not because of climate, but because, in the present world community, tropical regions constitute a highly important and accessible trade and agricultural frontier, and the plantation is always an institution of the frontier. The tropics constitute a frontier where there are exploitable agricultural resources attractive to capital and which are nearer to consuming centers in terms of transportation costs than are the vast areas of sparsely peopled but potential agricultural lands in the temperate zones. Plantations have developed along nontropical frontiers in the past and conceivably may in the future.

For these several reasons, therefore, the limitations of the climatic theory seem to be more important than its applications. It does not provide a satisfactory basis for research upon the nature and problems of plantation society. Dissatisfaction arises when an effort is made to use it. Of possible significance in this connection is the fact that after elaborating the climatic theory of plantation and farm colonies in the first chapter of his *Colonization,* Keller made very little actual use of it in the following chapters which deal with particular colonies.

The question raised by a climatic theory of the plantation is really part of the larger and more fundamental question of acclimatization. The acclimatization of human beings usually is discussed in connection with white settlement in equatorial regions. Many writers believe that the acclimatization of white settlers in the tropics is constitutionally impossible. Thus Benjamin Kidd is well known for his opinion that "in the tropics the white man lives and works only as a diver lives and works under water. . . . Neither physically, morally, nor politically, can he be acclimatized in the tropics." Ellsworth Huntington has argued that in the tropics the white man loses his will power and gives himself up to idleness, displays of temper, drunkenness, and sexual overindulgence. Madison Grant has conceded that the "Nordic race can exist outside of its native environment as landowning aristocrats who are not required to do manual labor in the fields under a blazing sun" but not if its members are compelled to support themselves by their own labor. The logical consequence of such views is expressed in the conclusion of William Z. Ripley that "a colonial policy in the tropics means a permanent servile native population, which is manifestly inconsistent with political independence, or with any approach to republican institutions."

It has long been assumed both in the North and in the South, that cultural differences between these two sections of the United States derive from climatic differences. Many if not most students of Southern society have made this assumption. Ulrich B. Phillips, for example, began his important work on *Life and Labor in the Old South* with the statement: "Let us begin by discussing the weather, for that has been the chief agency in making the South distinctive," but he recognized the fact that "The South is nowhere tropical except at the tip of Florida." More recently Clarence Cason in his study of Southern society insisted that the summer heat was and is the basic factor in all Southern culture. Conducive to inactivity under the Mississippi dictum that "only mules and black men can face the sun in July," the heat, he thought, created in the South a serenity for which all men strive.

Involved in all these opinions concerning the impossibility of white acclimatization in the tropics as well as those concerning the connection between Southern civilization and the climate of the South has been the assumption that only the Negro and other nonwhite peoples were capable of doing the work necessary for agricultural production under the conditions imposed by a tropical or semitropical climate. This assumption was in large measure the economic justification for Negro slavery in the South before the Civil War. Dr. Thomas Cooper, president of South Carolina College, probably stated the opinion of most white Southerners of the period when he said: "Nothing will justify slave labour in point of economy, but the nature of the soil and climate which incapacitates a white man from labouring in the summer time."

Public statements alleging a superior tolerance on the part of the Negro to the climate of the South are heard less frequently since the Civil War, but the opinion, nevertheless, is still widely held. However, the gradual realization that there are now more white than Negro tenants and sharecroppers on Southern plantations seems to have been accompanied by a tendency to shift the explanation from the climate to hookworm in order to account for the inefficiency and low status of agricultural labor. However, many upper-class Southerners seem to assume that hookworm is only a polite name for laziness which in turn goes back to an innate mental and moral inferiority.

Popular opinion regarding the acclimatization of man has been, for the most part, based upon two assumptions: first, that the different races of mankind are distinct species, each sprung from a separate origin in its own native habitat, and second, that climate is the principal factor in limiting or regulating the distribution of species. It is significant that the various climatic theories of human society, from Aristotle to Huntington, are closely associated with the various racial theories of society. "These two theories," according to Robert E. Park, "have this in common, namely, that they both conceive civilization and society to be the result of evolutionary processes—processes by which man has acquired new inheritable traits—rather than processes by which new relations have been established between men." The climatic theories support the view that social distinctions are biological and constitutional in origin rather than the result of history and circumstances.

Tested scientific knowledge concerning acclimatization is limited and the data are very inadequate. With respect to the acclimatization of human beings, cultural factors have never been taken fully into account. Complicating factors which have to be eliminated before the single factor of climate can be isolated and its effect upon human settlement in new areas determined, include such matters as the persistence of personal habits, diet, immunity or susceptibility to disease, and race mixture. Also climate itself has to be broken down into its separate elements of temperature, humidity, monotony or variety, the chemical rays of the sun, and various other factors. The writer is not competent to discuss these complicating factors, but one consideration relative to the climatic theory of the plantation may be pointed out. The problem of acclimatization is something more than the physiological problem of the conditions that control the birth, health, and growth of individuals. It is more than a matter of the optimal and limiting temperatures, humidities, etc., for this bare physiological process. It is rather a problem of the capacity of the individual, the group, or the race to maintain itself in the struggle for numerical supremacy against others. It is the problem of the importance of a single factor, climate, as it affects an individual or a group in relation to other individuals or groups. The importance of this factor of climate is directly proportional to its selective action. Acclimatization, therefore, is fundamentally a problem of competition—of biological competition.

Acclimatization involves not merely living away from a homeland; it also involves competing successfully with the natives or with other invaders of the new area. It is a process of adjustment to a different climatic situation, but it is measured in terms of success or failure in the competition with others in the same territory, and highly important in determining the outcome is the matter of just who the others are. A European group, for example, might successfully settle a new area when its competitors are, say, Indians, but not when its competitors are Negroes or Javanese. Acclimatization is a relative matter.

It is relative because the social forces operative in a given situation at a given place and time are relative, and social forces determine to a large extent how biological forces act. The acclimatization of man is influenced by a variety of cultural factors which are nonexistent in animals below man; it is conditioned by many factors which are not included in the struggle for existence among the animals and plants. The kind of human beings which tends to prevail in an area may, for instance, be determined in large part by the general conception of their status. It is reasonable to suppose that an important factor in the failure of the white man to become acclimatized to a tropical or semitropical climate is his unwillingness to compete with the natives or with the darker races on terms necessary to success. As Earl Hanson has said: "In New York and London and on our Western plains a man is allowed to be himself and to do and live about as he pleases. In the tropics he must above all be a white man and maintain the superiority of the white race, largely by a careful refusal to do any work." One of the factors which help to determine how biological forces work is a code which expressly forbids the white man in the tropics to do agricultural labor.

Another historical and social factor which influences the operation of biological forces is the practice of slavery. American slavery was to a very high degree a noncompetitive status which gave the Negro a place on the land without the necessity of competing for it. Slavery likewise is a social arrangement which operates somewhat like domestication in the relations between men and animals. Slaves and domesticated animals are naturally protected against a competition which otherwise might eliminate them. Slavery does not allow full biological competition between the races inhabiting an area, although all are exposed to the same climatic environment.

There seems, therefore, to be nothing in the facts of acclimatization, so far as we know them, to support the climatic theory of the plantation. Acclimatization, and biological competition generally, is fundamentally important in altering populations and institutions in any part of the world, but the alteration may take opposite directions in two tropical colonies or in two temperate-zone colonies. Because of its tendency over a period of time to produce a homogeneous population the process of biological competition would tend normally to establish the small family-sized farm. The plantation, on the other hand, represents an intruding force from without which is political in character. It arises as a regulator of population movements and racial contacts in the interest of a planter in connection with the exploitation of agricultural resources for market.

The contrast between plantation and farm is an aspect of the contrast between estate agriculture and peasant agriculture throughout the world generally. In many countries the latter two represent distinct and competing systems of agriculture within the same climatic area with now one, now the other, dominant. In the South the plantation and the small farm with its self-directing labor have, since the days of original settlement, existed side by side. According to W. M. Daniels, the competition between them

epitomizes the greater part of the *ante-bellum* industrial history of the South. The struggle moreover was an oft-renewed fight, and not a single pitched battle. In the same territory, as, for example, in seaboard Virginia, the early supremacy of the plantation yielded later, when the soil's pristine fertility had been exhausted, to the farm. And in general, while the superior efficiency of the plantation for the raising of staples vanquished the farm system in the short run, Providence for once fought against the "big battalions" and was bent on according the final victory to the smaller contestant.

The plantation is not to be accounted for by climate. It is a political institution, and has to be accounted for as the state and other political institutions based upon the authority principle are accounted for, and these institutions have never been restricted to any one climatic situation. On the contrary, they have ranged from Egypt to Iceland.

A conclusion suggested by these considerations is that the climatic theory of the plantation in its popular signification is an element in the resistance to social change. It is part of an ideology which rationalizes and naturalizes an existing social and economic order, and this everywhere seems to be an order in which there is a race problem. Popular interest in acclimatization and in the question of climatic determinism does not seem to arise except in interracial situations, and it arises in these situations as the political or conflict expression of an underlying economic and biological competition between the races involved.

A theory which makes the plantation depend upon something outside the processes of human interaction, that is, a theory which makes the plantation depend upon a fixed and static something like climate, is a theory which operates to justify an existing social order and the vested interests connected with that order. Under such a conception the problems of a plantation society can be looked upon as concerning only God who alone can control the climate, and the climatic theory turns out to be really a sort of divine-right theory of the plantation. Actually, however, the theory, like other sentiments, beliefs, and attitudes connected with the plantation system, must be understood as a product of forces working within the system itself, as an important part of that system but not as an explanation of it.

PART IV

The Idea of Race

INTRODUCTION

THE ECOLOGICAL ORDER, about which questions were raised in the previous chapter, is logically a pre-racial and even a pre-social order. It is the result of a process of competition, tempered by cooperation, which goes on beneath the level of public consciousness. The ecological process is a sort of stage-setting process, and, depending upon the way in which it arranges people and their institutions into spatial and sustenance patterns against the earth, it appears to determine, or at least to strongly influence, the sort of political and social relations which subsequently will develop. If people are not ordinarily aware of the ecological process of what are they aware?

In this chapter and in the chapter to follow we shall raise questions concerning the significance for race of the general theory of in-group out-group systems. These systems arise and take form out of conflict, and of conflict people are very conscious, often acutely conscious. Indeed, it is conflict which may be said to produce the fact of both individual and group consciousness.

Just what is it, however, that determines any particular in-group out-group *gestalt?* Obviously there are any number of potential lines of discrimination between groups, but some overall idea must exist to make any given distinction significant to those who make it. While acutely aware of the conflict, the adversary-defining idea behind it may be completely taken for granted by those most concerned. To view the idea in this way is to view it, not as a logical construct, but as a thing, as an integral part of the social structure and as a phase of culture.

Now race is only one such idea. It is by no means present in all situations of conflict. Where it exists, however, it appears as a constant in human belief which reaches an exceptionally high level of regularity and recurrence. The avenues of thought of those possessed by it are race-bound in some high degree. The idea seems to have an autonomy of its own, and where it appears the

[235]

structure of society is given a rigidity it would not otherwise have. It would seem, therefore, that before we can understand race conflict and the nature of interracial society we must better understand, or at least appreciate, the nature and history of the idea of race and of the kinds of situations in which it appears and functions.

It was suggested in the Introduction that the race problem is, fundamentally, the problem of understanding and dealing with the idea of race. The idea is such a force in the relations between individuals and groups that alone it can break up a friendship, a marriage, a neighborhood, a community or even a nation. When possessed by it people can hate, denounce, and even kill one another. Does it follow, then, that it is something which a swift act of good-will could eradicate even if the act could be forthcoming? Do people actually exist as Negroes or "Natives," as Jews, or as Caucasians in their own right, or is it the judgement of a society that creates such distinctions? What is the actual source of the racial image which is pinned onto particular individuals?

Consider, for instance, what is in the minds of people when they speak of a certain kind of marriage as an "interracial marriage." Is there really any such thing as an interracial marriage? If so, to whom is it interracial? What is the conception of the marriage to those who marry? What is the conception of the marriage to those who call it interracial? What social values does racial endogamy seek to isolate and to protect? Is the case against miscegenation and intermarriage really that the mixing is biologically or morally bad, or is it that it tends to destroy the identity of the group regarded by its members as the superior race? Why are certain individuals designated as "mixed bloods" in some societies while other individuals of much the same type and degree of mixture in other societies are not so designated? Can a race line divide the members of a single family or any other primary group? When such a line appears is it any longer a family? What is the significance of the fact that most if not all peoples locally designated as mixed-bloods are at least nominally Christian in religion? What is the significance of the fact that ordinarily they speak by preference a European language? To what extent is the practice of "passing" present and significant only when the idea of race is present and significant? How does passing differ from 1) conversion, and 2) assimilation?

What is the difference between the epistemology and the sociology of ideas? How would you distinguish between the idea of race and the concept of race? Do ideas have histories? What do you know or what can you find out about the history of the idea of race? Consider the relative importance of the following as factors in the genesis and development of the idea: 1) the myth of the existence of fabulous peoples, 2) the conception of certain peoples as heathen, pagan or "lost souls," 3) Calvinistic predestination, 4) the expansion of Europe and the sudden contact with overseas peoples, 5) the image of the "native," 6) democratic and Christian egalitarianism, 7) European imperialism, 8) the doctrine of organic evolution, 9) skin color and other physical differences.

Race has been 1) damned as a conspiracy, and 2) dismissed as a mere superstition. Is the idea of race either one of these, or something else? Is the idea ever subject to deliberate manipulation? What is meant by the description of the idea of race as a political idea? Does there not seem to have operated in every society destined to become an interracial society a dialectial process whereby certain protagonists and antagonists, dominated by the same idea, built up social contrast effects and created each other into race and counter-race? In this connection what do you know of the history of *limpieza de sangre* in Spain? And what do you make of the plaintive question of a Jewish writer who asked, "Why are Jews more rejected and resented than other people plainly their inferiors?"

What do you understand by a social situation? What is meant by a race-making situation? What seem to be the invariable and constant factors in the existence of an interracial situation? What is a frontier? What is a race frontier? Are there types of race frontiers? What seems to be the difference in race relations when 1) race frontiers correspond with national frontiers, and 2) when they fall *within* countries? Frontiers seem not only to generate or utilize ideas but also to destroy them. What sort of frontier situations appear hostile to the idea of race? As a race frontier ceases to be a frontier what happens to the idea of race?

Ideas not only exist but they appear to work in behalf of a way of life. What are the functions of the idea of race, that is, what does the idea of race do? What is an ideology? What is the nature and function of a racial ideology?

THE IDEA OF RACE AS A "NOBLE LIE"

Excerpt From the Republic of Plato

NOW, SAID I, can we devise something in the way of those convenient fictions we spoke of earlier, a single bold flight of invention, which we may induce the community in general, and if possible the Rulers themselves, to accept?

What kind of fiction?

Nothing new; something like an Eastern tale of what, according to the poets, has happened before now in more than one part of the world. The poets have been believed; but the thing has not happened in our day, and it would be hard to persuade anyone that it could ever happen again.

You seem rather shy of telling this story of yours.

With good reason, as you will see when I have told it.

Out with it; don't be afraid.

Well, here it is; though I hardly know how to find the courage or the words to express it. I shall try to convince, first the Rulers and the soldiers, and then the whole community, that all that nurture and education which we gave them was only something they seemed to experience as it were in a dream. In reality they were the whole time down inside the earth, being moulded and fostered

From *The Republic of Plato,* translated with introduction and notes by Francis Macdonald Cornford, 1945, pp. 106–107. Reprinted by permission of Oxford University Press, Inc.

while their arms and all their equipment were being fashioned also; and at last, when they were complete, the earth sent them up from her womb into the light of day. So now they must think of the land they dwell in as a mother and nurse, whom they must take thought for and defend against any attack, and of their fellow citizens as brothers born of the same soil.

You might well be bashful about coming out with your fiction.

No doubt; but still you must hear the rest of the story. It is true, we shall tell our people in this fable, that all of you in this land are brothers; but the god who fashioned you mixed gold in the composition of those among you who are fit to rule, so that they are of the most precious quality; and he put silver in the Auxiliaries, and iron and brass in the farmers and craftsmen. Now, since you are all of one stock, although your children will generally be like their parents, sometimes a golden parent may have a silver child or a silver parent a golden one, and so on with all the other combinations. So the first and chief injunction laid by heaven upon the Rulers is that, among all the things of which they must show themselves good guardians, there is none that needs to be so carefully watched as the mixture of metals in the souls of the children. If a child of their own is born with an alloy of iron or brass, they must, without the smallest pity, assign him the station proper to his nature and thrust him out among the craftsmen or the farmers. If, on the contrary, these classes produce a child with gold or silver in his composition, they will promote him, according to his value, to be a Guardian or an Auxiliary. They will appeal to a prophecy that ruin will come upon the state when it passes into the keeping of a man of iron or brass. Such is the story; can you think of any device to make them believe it?

Not in the first generation; but their sons and descendants might believe it, and finally the rest of mankind.

Well, said I, even so it might have a good effect in making them care more for the commonwealth and for one another; for I think I see what you mean.

THE FABULOUS RACES

By Herbert Collins

To THE GALLERY of grotesqueries and caricatures all peoples have contributed. Since antiquity marvelous people have been created as symbols of prowess, beauty, or evil to instruct and entertain. For speculative lands like the Antipodes, prodigious people have been conveniently fashioned who were deformed enough to be different but were not absolutely dehumanized. Idols, masks, and costumes have been invented in order to impersonate imaginary creatures with the result that any individual or deity could be transformed into a monstrous or sublime figure. Sometimes, as was the case with Hellenistic and

Medieval mechanicians, poets and philosophers, clocks and automata have served as models for mechanicomorphic conceptions of human beings. But the most numerous of fabulous people are the strangers encountered by credulous travellers and explorers.

Towards the end of the Fifteenth Century voyages of discovery without parallel since Greek and Roman explorations occurred in the Western World. A thousand years of literary travel based on Classical remnants and Scripture were terminated, but not before old judgments were applied to new circumstances. So extensive was the scale of discovery, and the peoples encountered so unexpected, that no available preconceptions could sufficiently account for the findings. But Europeans were no less impoverished of beliefs about what to expect than their predecessors were in comparable circumstances. Furthermore, they were willing to reconcile what they found with their inheritance of myths and legendary histories. The Classical inheritance, grown marvelous through the glosses of Medieval commentary, supplied some of the assumptions with which Europeans accounted for the strangers they discovered.

With a zest for the exotic and the remote, the Greek and Roman explorers, and especially their popularizers, had repeatedly discovered savages and prodigies. Remote populations served to account for the origins of organized life, to point up the moral of either the degradation or superiority of civilization, or to explain the varieties of mankind. Diet, climate, manners, and customs were accepted as determiners of physical differences. When these factors least resembled what the discoverers admired or expected, they became the causes for all manner of physical features which grew marvelous with the least prodding. It was during these formative centuries of travel and discovery that the fabulous races were bred.

The fabulous races have had a host of special creators among whom Herodotus, Ctesias, Megasthenes, Strabo, Pliny the Elder, Solinus, and later Isidore of Seville, Cantimpre, Bartholomew the Englishman, and Sir John Mandeville were the most prolific. They synthesized the reports of travelers, soldiers, sailors, and explorers, or borrowed from their literary predecessors. A rudimentary Ethnology resulted which became bookish and fanciful under the guidance of Medieval geographers. Even Marco Polo, who broke with tradition to journey into unknown lands, on one occasion heard that beyond the island of Madagascar Negroes go naked and wrote that they have "large mouths, their noses turn up towards the forehead, their ears are long, and their eyes have the aspects of demons."

But long before Geography and Anthropology became stale in the absence of new discoveries, a four-fold classification based on diet, climate, customs, and physical appearance had become established. On the evidence of diet alone extensive populations were discovered. The Ichthyophagi ate fish, the Hippemolgi drank milk, the Lotophagi consumed the lotus plants, and the Rhizophagi ate roots. Mouthless men known as Gangines lived on the smell of roast meat and the scent of fruits and flowers. There were elephants, locusts, turtles, monkeys, and reptiles in the diets of other peoples. The Anthropophagi were considered the most savage of men for they feasted on human flesh.

Although the naming of some people was made easy by reference to their diet, others were classified by their manners and customs. The Hyperboreans were considered free from disease, and they terminated old age in a blissful suicide. The Atlantes had no proper names and had no dreams. The Troglodytes had no voices, lived in caves, and drank blood. A people known as Choromandae dwelled in the woods, had no speech except a horrible scream, and were most likely monkeys. The Scythian Massagetae and Issedonians were reputed fabulous because they ate their aged relatives, or so the Greeks liked to believe. Not only were the Amazonians described, but they were geographically located.

Among the pre-Renaissance explorers and travelers the array of customs and manners in domestic life, raiment, worship, and industry of remote people such as Ethiopians, Scythians, Germans, and Tartars frequently became racial characteristics. According to Isidore of Seville, the Scythians were nomads, and some "are monstrous and savage, and live on human flesh and blood." At a later date the Tartars appeared to Matthew Paris as "inhuman and beastly, rather monsters than men." They were without "human laws, know no comforts, and know no other language than their own." Not until the religious and commercial travelers, commencing with Carpini, Rubruck, and Marco Polo, do the accounts of remote people contain increasingly accurate reports. Marignoli, a traveler to Cathay, demolished the unexamined legend of one-footed men.

There are no people who have but one foot, which they use to shade themselves withal. But as all the Indians commonly go naked, they are in the habit of carrying a thing like a tent roof on the cane handle, which they open at will as a protection against sun or rain . . . this the poets have converted into a foot.

The rarities most proper to remote regions and the choicest specimens of the fabulous races were the monstrosities and deformities that survived intact until the Age of Discovery when credulous travelers sometimes claimed actually to have found corroborative evidence for their mental baggage. What appear simply to be physical features such as eyes, nose, hair, lips, and skin color were transformed into the weirdest stories. Pliny, for example, attributed various physical features to equatorial heat "which is the great agent in imparting various forms and shapes to bodies." Giraldus the Welshman went so far as to affirm that the character of different people varies with the different climatic conditions. These ideas persisted. Buffon, having learned that there was little variation of physical types in America, accounted for the new evidence with the claim that the Indians had not long enough been exposed to the "circumstances by which varieties are produced." At any rate, the encyclopedias, maps, books of travels, and stories of marvels available before the modern voyages of discovery were replete with all the cyclopic versions of race.

There were one-eyed Arimaspians who were perpetually at war with the gold-guarding Griffins; flat-nosed Ethiopians; and Fanesi with enormous ears suitable to clothe their nakedness. The Astomi had no mouths and lived on the air they breathed. Other people such as the Blemmyae were believed to have their eyes and mouths in their chests. The Schiopodes were swift with their one foot which also served as an umbrella. Tailed men were found in India, Formosa, and the East Indies. Dog-headed and monkey-headed populations as well as Macrocephali, whose heads were disfigured for esthetic reasons, abounded in Africa and India. An earless people known as Presumbani were also admitted to exist. And this does not by any means exhaust the gallery of monstrosities, for there were men with enormous lips, others with reversed gaits, and even bisexual Androgyni. This is a phantasmorgia that is incomplete without the geneologies of Noah's sons, since the descendants of Ham and Japhet became the Huns, Scythians, Tartars, and all manner of monsters among whom Gog and Magog were the most notorious.

When almost on the verge of discovering new lands, Europeans possessed expectations that were derived from the past and eagerly projected them into the present. On the Walsperger Map of 1448 many fabulous races of memorable lineage were delineated repeating the cosmography of the Hereford Map. The *Nuremburg Chronicle,* which appeared in 1493, contained plates of the most renowned of fabulous races. The early printed editions of Sir John Mandeville's *Travels* were never lacking in illustrations of the deformities enumerated in the twenty-second chapter of that literary fabrication. John van Doesborgh's book concerning the discoveries, brought out in 1519, contained a plate depicting a fabulous race with one eye centered in the forehead and a vivid scene of Anthropophagi feasting on human limbs. Sebastian Munster's *Cosmographia Universalis* carried the graphic representation of marvelous people as far as 1574. According to Lynn Thorndike, fabulous races were mentioned by Frisius in 1530, and Aldrovandi, a Sixteenth Century naturalist, devoted a whole volume to monsters. The Jesuit Eusebius even located in California natives with ears drooping almost to the ground, and for other early popularizers Virginia was a convenient place to locate hermaphrodites.

It was not unusual that during the Fifteenth and Sixteenth Centuries regions that were inhabited by undocumented people and stocked with resources not mentioned in any Bestiary, Herbal, or Lapidary were treated with hackneyed notions and distorted transcripts of reality. Anthropological, as well as botanical and anatomical descriptions, were so burdened by an accumulation of the fabulous that such men as Theodore de Bry, Otto von Brunfels, and Andreas Vesalius tried to combat unexamined legends by means of naturalistic illustrations to accompany their treatises. The same conditions that were congenial to the fabulous and the fantastic in human geography were, on the other hand, also hospitable to Francois Rabelais when he wrote *Gargantua and Pantagruel* as well as to Hieronymous Bosch when he painted his fantasy pictures. It is also noteworthy that this age of travel and exploration also witnessed the appearance of utopian literature and the beginnings of mechanical and experimental science. Whether it was ethnology, satire, utopia, or science which was occupying the labors of men of thought, the place of fact and fancy in human life was being avidly examined.

The stunned travelers from Europe "ascribed the many new kinds and colors of men to a series of separate creations in other Edens" which Scripture failed to mention. Evidence that had previously invalidated the existence of Antipodeans—mirthful, dancing, and multidigital—was conveniently employed to appraise other strange people. The difficulties involved in fitting newly discovered people into the popular ethnology were recognized by the Eighteenth Century Scottish historian William Robertson. In his *History of America* he observed that "The first appearance of the inhabitants of the New World filled the discoverers with such astonishment that they were apt to imagine them a race of men different from those of the other hemisphere."

The Spanish colonial administration became involved in the complicated issue of whether the Indians were rational or brutes. In the ensuing theological and legal disputes Bartholomew Las Casas contended that "all the peoples of the world are men," and argued somewhat successfully for a humanitarian approach to the Indians. The position that the Indians were "little men" was argued by Juan de Sepulveda. He maintained that the Indians were contaminated with "so many impieties and obscenities" that prudence dictated their enslavement. To the North, John Eliot and other likeminded men had also to decide whether the Indians could be christianized and educated as well as dealt with in diplomatic matters. Their languages, customs, and religions provoked speculations concerning the Scythian, Moorish, or Israelite origin of the Indians. "But the difficulty still remains," Daniel Gookin wrote, "whence all these Americans had their first original, and from which of the sons of Noah they descended, and how they first came into these parts."

It must have been a strain to describe new peoples with any complete avoidance of old analogies. Paradise, the Isles of the Blessed, giants, Anthropophagi, featureless and beardless people were easy to find. The inhabitants of Patagonia were alternately giants or ordinary human beings depending on the credulity of their visitors. Newness was passed off as ugliness; mutilations were considered hereditary; unfamiliar habits were interpreted as laziness. And some people were mistaken for the masks they wore. Captain Frobisher was a typical source of exotic information. To demonstrate that there were strange people whose likeness was never seen, read, nor heard before, he carried an Eskimo back to England in 1576 only to have "this new prey" die at the end of the voyage. Other explorers such as Cartwright and Fourneaux did succeed in capturing remote people. The dispatch of such victims to Europe contributed to the interest in "wild men" among philosophers, ethnologists, and circus-goers. In such people Buffon believed a philosopher "might be able to ascertain the force of natural appetites" and see "the mind undisguised." But Buffon embraced the traditional primitivistic doctrine "that virtue belongs more to the savage than to the civilized men, and that vice owes its birth to society."

The Noble Savage was found in all his exemplary ways. From Montaigne to Rousseau a host of writers sought and found in the New World the reincarnation of the Golden Race of antiquity. New speculations concerning the nature of man and new poetic imagery were found in the reports of voyagers. In Captain Thomas Cook's estimation the natives of New Holland were happy in not knowing the use of civilized conveniences. "They live in a tranquility," he wrote in his Journal, "which is not disturbed by the inequality of condition." The Tahitians of Diderot and the Hurons of Voltaire were actually the counterparts of the Hyperboreans: literary creatures of social criticism. The colonists, however, were not dealing with paper men, but with Indians, Negroes, and enslaved peoples. Shortly, European settlers were going to substitute biological for mythical analogies in their conceptualizations of imputedly inferior peoples.

The evaluation and classification of the rich lore concerning new peoples was not easily performed. Buffon, who observed this process, reported that Indians were often assumed to have necks so short, and shoulders so elevated, that their eyes appeared to be upon the latter and their mouths in the chest. In other words, the Blemmyae were found in the New World. He rejected such tales on the grounds of esthetic and ceremonial disfigurement and tailoring. One entry in Captain Cook's Journal recorded the custom of certain Alaskan Indians to mutilate the upper part of the lip with an incision to form a second "mouth." Other Pacific coast Indians regaled themselves in ceremonial masks impersonating beasts. Credulous observers would have been deceived, the Captain wrote, "and in their relations would have attempted to make others believe" that there were men with two mouths or that there existed "a race of beings partaking of the nature of man and beast." The same fables that were current in Europe, William Robertson critically observed, "have been revived with respect to the New World, and America too has been peopled with human beings of monstrous and fantastic appearance."

Christopher Columbus perhaps better than any other traveler epitomized the anthropological revolution ushered in by the voyages of discovery. He sometimes wavered before the reports of men with one eye, others with tails, giants, and Amazons. Like Herodotus, Columbus was somewhat amazed to find beardless men. Yet on one occasion he wrote that "Down to the present, I have not found in those islands any monstrous men, as many expected."

THE CONTRIBUTION OF THOMAS HOBBES

By Hannah Arendt

THE PHILOSOPHY OF HOBBES contains nothing of modern race doctrines, which not only stir up the mob, but in their totalitarian form outline very clearly the forms of organization through which humanity could carry the endless process of capital and power accumulation through to its logical end in self-destruction. But Hobbes at least provided political thought with the prerequisite for all race doctrines, that is, the exclusion in principle of the idea of humanity which constitutes the sole regulating idea of international law. With the assumption that foreign politics is necessarily outside of the human contract, engaged in the perpetual war of all against all, which is the law of the "state of nature," Hobbes affords the best possible theoretical foundation for those naturalistic ideologies which hold nations to be tribes, separated from each other by nature, without any connection whatever, unconscious of the solidarity of mankind and having in common only the instinct for self-preservation which man shares with the animal world. If the idea of humanity, of which the most conclusive symbol is the common origin of the human species, is no longer valid, then nothing is more plausible than a theory according to which brown, yellow, or black races are descended from some other species of apes than the white race, and that all together are predestined by nature to war against each other until they have disappeared from the face of the earth.

If it should prove to be true that we are imprisoned in Hobbes's endless process of power accumulation, then the organization of the mob will inevitably take the form of transformation of nations into races, for there is, under the conditions of an accumulating society, no other unifying bond available between individuals who in the very process of power accumulation and expansion are losing all natural connections with their fellowmen.

Racism may indeed carry out the doom of the Western world and, for that matter, of the whole of human civilization. When Russians have become Slavs, when Frenchmen have assumed the role of commanders of a *force noire,* when Englishmen have turned into "white men," as already for a disastrous spell all Germans became Aryans, then this change will itself signify the end of Western man. For no matter what learned scientists may say, race is, politically speaking, not the beginning of humanity but its end, not the origin of peoples but their decay, not the natural birth of man but his unnatural death.

THE MYTH OF BLOOD

By M. F. Ashley Montagu

THERE ARE MANY WORDS in the vocabulary of Western man which are characterized by an exaggerated emotional content; that is to say, such words are distinguished by a high emotional and a low rational, or reasonable, quality. Race is such a word, blood is another. Race is a word which has assumed a high emotional content in relatively recent times, blood, on the other hand, is a word which, from the beginning of recorded history, has always possessed a high emotional content.

That blood is the most immediately important constituent of the human body must have been remarked by men at a very early period in their cultural development. The weakening effect, or actual death, produced by an appreciable loss of blood can hardly have escaped their notice. Hence, the identification of blood as a vital principle of life, and its endowment with special strength-giving qualities must have been almost inevitable steps in the process of endowing this red fluid with a meaning. Among all primitive peoples blood is regarded as a most powerful element possessed of the most varied and potent qualities. To enumerate these, and the functions they are believed able to perform, would alone fill a volume.

In the cultural dynamics of Western civilization the concept of blood has played a significant and important rôle. From the earliest times it has been regarded as that most quintessential element of the body which carries, and through which is transmitted, the hereditary qualities of the stock. Thus, all

By M. F. Ashley Montagu, "The Myth of Blood." Reprinted by permission of The William Alanson White Psychiatric Foundation, Inc., from *Psychiatry* (1943), 6:15–19. Copyright, 1943, by The William Alanson White Psychiatric Foundation, Inc.

persons of the same family stock were regarded as of the same blood. In a community which mostly consisted of family lines whose members had, over many generations, intermarried with one another, it is easy to understand how, with such a concept of blood, the community or nation would come to regard itself as of one blood, distinct, *by blood,* from all other communities or nations. This, indeed, is the popular conception of blood which prevails at the present day. Thus, for example, if one turns to the *Oxford Dictionary* and looks under "blood," the following statement is found:

Blood is popularly treated as the typical part of the body which children inherit from their parents and ancestors; hence that of parents and children, and of the members of a family or race, is spoken of as identical, and as being distinct from that of other families or races.

It is this conception of blood as the carrier of the heritable qualities of the family, race, or nation, which has led to its application in such extended meanings as are implied in terms like blue blood, blood royal, pure blood, full blood, half blood, good blood, blood tie, or blood relationship, and consanguinity. Putative racial and national differences are, of course, recognized in such terms as German blood, English blood, Jewish blood, and Negro blood; so that today the words race and blood have come to be used as synonyms.

When the meaning of these terms is analyzed the manner in which the general conception of "blood" operates may be more clearly perceived. Thus, the term *blue blood* which refers to a presumed special kind of blood supposed to flow in the veins of ancient and aristocratic families, actually represents a translation from the Spanish *sangre azul,* the blue blood attributed to some of the oldest and proudest families of Castile, who claimed never to have been contaminated by foreign blood. Many of these families were of fair complexion, hence in members of these families the veins would, in comparison with those in the members of the predominatingly dark-complexioned population, appear strikingly blue. Hence, the difference between an aristocrat and a commoner could be easily recognized as a difference in blood; one was a blue blood and the other was not.

The expression blood royal refers to the generally accepted notion that only such persons as are of royal ancestry have the blood of kings flowing in their veins. No person, however noble his ancestry may be, can be of the blood royal unless he has the blood of kingly ancestors in his veins. Thus, kings are held to belong to a special class of mankind principally in virtue of the supposed unique characters of their blood. In order to keep the blood of the royal house pure, marriages are arranged exclusively between those who are of the royal blood. In England, for example, no member of the royal family who stands in direct line of succession to the throne may marry anyone but a member of another royal house. The most recent example of the consequence of disobeying this rule is, of course, the case of the present Duke of Windsor, who was forced to abdicate his succession to the throne of England because of his declared intention to marry a person who was not of royal blood.

In common parlance, and in the loose usage of many who should know better, terms like *full-blood* or *pure-blood,* and *half-blood,* very clearly illustrate the supposed hereditary character of the blood and the manner in which, by simple arithmetical division, it may be diluted. Thus, *full-blood* or *pure-*

blood are expressions which are alleged to define the supposed fact that a person is of unadulterated blood, that is, he is a person whose particular ancestors have undergone no admixture of blood with members of another race. Within the last century these terms have come to be applied almost exclusively to persons who are not of the white race, to persons, in short, who are alleged to belong to the supposed inferior rungs of the racial ladder. It is possible that this restricted usage has been determined by the fact that these expressions have generally done most service in the description of native peoples or of slaves, as in full-blooded Negro, pure-blood Indian, or merely full-blood, or pure-blood. Such an unedifying association would be sufficient to secure the non-application of the term to any member of the superior races.

A half-blood, in contradistinction to a full-blood or a pure-blood is a person whose blood is half that of one race and half that of another, for example, the off-spring of an Indian and a white. What is actually implied is that while a *full-blood* or *pure-blood* may claim relationship through both parents, a *half-blood* may claim relationship through one parent only. For example, a mulatto, that is, the offspring of a white and a Negro, is for all *practical* purposes classed with the group to which the Negro parent belongs, and his white ancestry is, for the same purposes, ignored. In practice, it often works out that the *half-blood* is not fully accepted by either of the parental stocks, because of his adulterated blood, and he becomes in the true sense of the expression half caste, belonging neither to the one caste nor to the other; for in Western society the so-called different races are in reality treated as if they were different castes.

A person is said to be of good or gentle blood if he is of noble or gentle birth, or of good family. Here the assumed biological determinance of social status, by blood is clearly exhibited, that is to say, a person's rank in society is assumed to be determined by his blood, when, in fact, it is in reality the other way round, that is to say, blood is actually determined by rank. The ancestors of all noblemen were once common people, plebians, it was not a sudden metamorphosis in the composition of their blood which caused them to become noble; it was rather an elevation in social status which endowed them with supposed superior qualities. Such supposed superior qualities are not biological in any sense whatsoever, and belong purely to the ascriptive variety of things. That is to say, they have no real but a purely imagined existence.

The statement that a person is of bad blood, in the sense that he is of common or inferior character or status, is rarely encountered, for the reason, presumably, that those who use such terms have not considered the blood of such people worth mentioning at all. Thus, for example, while there is an entry in the *Oxford Dictionary* for "Blood worth mention," there is none for blood *not* worth mention. In the sense in which blood is considered as the seat of emotion, bad blood is taken to be the physiological equivalent of ill-feeling. In this sense, of course, bad blood may be created between persons of good blood.

The term *blood-relationship,* and its anglicized Latin equivalent *consanguinity,* meaning the condition of being of the same blood, or relationship by descent from a common ancestor, enshrines the belief that all biological relationships are reflected in, and are to a large extent, determined by the character of the blood. This venerable error, along with others, requires correction.

This brief analysis of the variety of ways in which blood is used and understood in the English language, and in Western civilization in general, renders it sufficiently clear that most people believe that blood is equivalent to heredity, and that blood, therefore, is that part of the organism which determines the quality of the person. By extension it is further generally believed that the social as well as the biological status of the person is determined by the kind of blood he has inherited. These beliefs concerning blood are probably among the oldest of those surviving from the earliest days of mankind. Certainly they are found to be almost universally distributed among the peoples of the earth in very much the same forms, and their antiquity is sufficiently attested by the fact that in the graves of prehistoric men red pigments are frequently found in association with the remains. These pigments were, most probably, used to represent the blood as the symbol of life and humanity, a belief enshrined in the expression "he is flesh and blood," to signify humanity as opposed to deity or disembodied spirit. There in the grave was the flesh, and the pigment was introduced to represent the blood.

As an example of a myth grown hoary with the ages for which there is not the slightest justification in scientific fact, the popular conception of blood is outstanding. Were it not for the fact that it is a bad myth, harmful in its effect, and dangerous in its possible consequences, it might well be allowed to persist; but since great harm has already been done, and will increasingly continue to be done, unless this myth is exposed for what it is—one of the most grievous errors of thought ever perpetrated by mankind—it is today more than ever necessary to set out the facts about blood as science knows them.

In the first place let it be stated at once that blood is in no way connected with the transmission of hereditary characters. The transmitters of hereditary characters are the genes which lie in the chromosomes of the germ cells represented by the spermatozoa of the father and the ova of the mother, *and nothing else*. These genes, carried in the chromosomes of a single spermatazoön and a single ovum, are the *only* parts of the organism which transmit and determine the hereditary characters. Blood has nothing whatever to do with heredity, either biologically, socially, or in any other manner whatsoever.

The belief that the blood of the mother is transmitted to the child, and hence becomes a part of the child, is an ancient but completely erroneous one. Scientific knowledge of the processes of pregnancy have long ago made it perfectly clear that there is no actual passage of blood from mother to child. The developing child manufactures its own blood, and the character of its various blood cells is demonstrably different from that of either of its parents. The mother does not contribute blood to the fœtus. This fact should for ever dispose of the ancient notion, which is so characteristically found among primitive peoples, that the blood of the mother is continuous with that of the child. The same belief is to be found in the works of Aristotle on generation. Aristotle held that the monthly periods, which do not appear during pregnancy, contribute to the formation of the child's body. Modern scientific knowledge shows that this notion is quite false, and thus completely disposes of the idea of a blood-tie between any two persons whether they be mother or child, or even identical twins. Hence, any claims to kinship based on the tie of blood can have no scientific foundation whatever. Nor can claims of group consciousness based on blood be anything but fictitious, since the character of the blood of all human beings is determined not by their membership in any group or nation but by the fact that they are human beings.

The blood of all human beings is in every respect the same. To this there is only one exception, and that is in the agglutinating properties of the blood, which yields the four blood groups. But these four blood groups are present in all varieties of men, and in different groups differ only in their statistical distribution. This distribution is not a matter of quality but of quantity. There are no demonstrable or known differences in the character of the blood of different peoples. In that sense the biblical *obiter dictum* that the Lord "hath made of one blood all nations of men to dwell on the face of the earth" is literally true.

Scientists have for many years attempted to discover whether or not any differences exist in the blood of different peoples, but the results of such investigations have always been the same—*no difference is to be discovered*. In short, it cannot be too emphatically, or too often, repeated that in every respect the blood of all human beings is identical, no matter what class, group, nation, or 'race' they belong to.

Obviously then, since all people are of one blood, such differences as may exist between them can have absolutely no connection with blood.

Such facts, however, do not in the least deter Nazi propagandists from continuing to use the blood myth to set people against one another. The prevailing official Nazi view of the matter was presented to the Congress of the Nazi party at Nuremberg exactly six years before the invasion of Poland by the official Nazi distorter of the truth—who, for some mysterious reason, is called a philosopher—Arthur Rosenberg.

"A nation," he said, "is constituted by the predominance of a definite character formed by its blood, also by language, geographical environment, and the sense of a united political destiny. These last constituents are not, however, definitive; the decisive element in a nation is its blood. In the first awakening of a people, great poets and heroes disclose themselves to us as the incorporation of the eternal values of a particular blood soul. I believe that this recognition of the profound significance of blood is now mysteriously encircling our planet, irresistibly gripping one nation after another."

The extravagant and utterly preposterous claims which the Nazis have been able to make on the basis of the blood myth are only equalled by the superstitions which prevail among others in the same connection. These were recently given much publicity when the Red Cross segregated the blood of Negroes for the purposes of transfusion. In other words, the myth of blood seems almost as strongly entrenched here as among the Nazis. It will be generally admitted that this is an undesirable and dangerous situation, and that the sooner the facts about blood are made known the better.

The astonishing thing about the objection to Negro blood is not so much that it is based upon a misconception, but that the same person who refuses to accept Negro blood may at the same time be perfectly willing to have his children suckled by a Negro wet-nurse! The same person will be ready to submit to an injection of serum derived from a horse or cow or some other animal, and while he himself may have been suckled by a Negro wet-nurse, and even entertain the greatest affection for Negroes, he will violently object to any pollution of his blood by the injection of Negro blood into his own.

Quite clearly this is a false belief, a superstition, for which there is no ground in fact but plenty in traditional belief. In actual fact the blood of the Negro is identical with that of all other human beings, so that for the purposes of transfusion, or any other purposes, it is as good as any other blood.

The objection to Negro blood is, of course, based upon the antique misconception that the blood is the carrier of hereditary characters, and since the Negro is regarded as possessing racially inferior characters, it is feared that these may be transmitted to the recipient of the transfusion. Both prejudices are groundless.

What modern science has revealed about blood, then, renders all such words as blood royal, half-blood, full-blood, blood-relationship, and the others to which reference has been made utterly meaningless in point of fact, and dangerously meaningful in the superstitious social sense.

THE IDEA AS THE GROUP'S CONCEPTION OF ITSELF

By Alfred Fouillée

IN DISCUSSIONS OF THE RACE PROBLEM there is one factor of supreme importance which has been so far disregarded—to wit, the opinion or *idea* which a race has of itself and the influence exerted by this idea. It is a view I have long been contending for, namely, that every idea is the conscious form in which feelings and impulses are cast. Thus every idea contains within it not merely an intellectual act, but also a certain orientation of sensibility and of will. Consequently every idea is a force which tends to realise its own object more and more fully. This is true of the idea of race, just as it is true of the idea of nation. Hence we have (1) a certain self-consciousness in a race, imparting to each of its members a kind of racial personality; (2) a tendency to affirm this personality more and more strongly, to oppose it to other racial types and secure its predominance. In other words, the race-idea includes within it a race-consciousness. It is certain, for instance, that a white man shares the idea and the will of his race—a result the more inevitable inasmuch as he has but to open his eyes in order to distinguish white from yellow or black. Frenchmen or Russians may not be able to recognize one another at sight, but there can be no confusing blacks and whites. Colour is a visible and immediate bond between men of white, black, or yellow race. Even among white men certain types lend themselves to easy recognition and the setting up of a tie between men who share certain typical features. Take, for instance, the dark dolichocephalic Arab type, or the dark brachycephalic Turkish, and compare either with the fair dolichocephalic English type.

If an ethnic consciousness gives a race greater solidarity and inward unity, it has, on the other hand, the disadvantage of culminating nearly always in an

From Alfred Fouillée, "Race From the Sociological Standpoint," in G. Spiller (ed.), *Inter-Racial Problems* (London: P. S. King and Sons, 1911), pp. 24–25, with permission of Staples Press Ltd., successors to P. S. King and Sons.

assumption of *superiority* and, for that very reason, in a feeling of natural
hostility. The yellow man thinks himself no less superior to the white than the
white man believes himself superior to the yellow. At all events, he believes
himself to be very different, and from the conviction of difference to that of
enmity there is only a step.

Differences of language and custom—and, above all, of religion—serve to
intensify the hostility. All religion is sociological in character, and expresses
symbolically the conditions native to the life or progress of a given society. The
religion of a race converts it into a huge society animated by the same beliefs
and the same aspirations. Moreover, all religion is intolerant, and hostile to
other religions. It believes itself to be the truth, and thus seeks to universalize
that which is only the particular spirit of one race or one nation—*e.g.*, the
Jewish spirit, the Christian spirit, the Mahommedan spirit. When, then, the
ethnic consciousness becomes at the same time a religious consciousness, the
assertion of the individuality of a race implies a counter-assertion to the individuality of other races. It is hidden warfare, passing over at the very first
opportunity into open warfare.

THE IDEA OF RACE AS A POLITICAL
IDEA

By Eric Voegelin

THE RACE PROBLEM is branching out today into so many fields that a
preliminary understanding becomes necessary as to the special topic with which
the present paper is concerned. Let us first make it clear negatively that the
question of the classification of the human races does not come within the scope
of this inquiry. The race idea should be distinguished from the race concept
which is used in natural science. Furthermore, we are not concerned with the
improvement of a given human population through eugenic measures. And,
finally we do not intend to deal with the problem of political and social relations between the white and the colored races. When we speak of the race
idea we have in mind chiefly the idea as it is used by modern creeds, of the type
of National Socialism, in order to integrate a community spiritually and
politically.

An adequate understanding of the problems involved in the functioning
of the race idea, in the sense just outlined, still meets with certain difficulties.
They have their origin in the readiness of many people to adopt a partisan
stand on the race question. It is widely believed that the assertions of race
theorists in the political field have to be either true or false; and we see on the

Reprinted from Eric Voegelin, "The Growth of the Race Idea," *The Review of Politics,* II
(July, 1940), 283–286. This valuable article continues through p. 317. It should be read in its
entirety if the original is available.

one hand the convinced believers in the all-importance of racial differences, and on the other hand the equally convinced disbelievers, inclined to stigmatize the race idea as a mad illusion without solid foundation in fact.

As a matter of fact, the race idea with its implications is not a body of knowledge organized in systematic form, but a political idea in the technical sense of the word. A political idea does not attempt to describe social reality as it is, but it sets up symbols, be they single language units or more elaborate dogmas, which have the function of creating the image of a group as a unit. The life of a social group in general, and of a political group in particular, when understood in behavioristic terms, dissolves itself into individuals, their actions, and the purposes and motives of such actions. The group as a unit is not found on this level of observation. What welds the diffuse mass of individual life into a group unit are the symbolic beliefs entertained by the members of a group. Every group has its symbols which permit of concentrating into an emotional and volitional substance that which, if viewed empirically, is a stream of human action, articulated by behavior patterns and purposes, of highly questionable unity. A symbolic idea like the race idea is not a theory in the strict sense of the word. And it is beside the mark to criticize a symbol, or a set of dogmas, because they are not empirically verifiable. While such criticism is correct, it is without meaning, because it is not the function of an idea to describe social reality, but to assist in its constitution. An idea is always "wrong" in the epistemological sense, but this relation to reality is its very principle, and there is no point in proving it for every single instance. (This, however, should not be misunderstood as a relativistic attitude towards ideas. I fully recognize the differences of ethical and metaphysical values between ideas. But the ethical or metaphysical value of an idea does not depend upon its correctness as a picture of social reality.)

A political idea is not an instrument of cognition. But this does not mean that it has no relation to reality, or that any product of a fertile imagination can serve as a political symbol. History shows that social symbols, even when they move very far away from empirical reality, have at least their starting point in it, and that the link to reality cannot be broken without their function being destroyed. And history also shows that not just any part of reality will be used for the development of symbols but that certain basic universal experiences regularly tend to become the material starting point from which the transformation into a symbol begins. It is impossible here to enter upon a systematic survey of such basic experiences, and it is equally impossible to discuss in detail the process of creation of symbols. One example, leading up to the special problem of the race idea, will have to suffice for an illustration of the question involved.

Man belonging biologically to the animal realm, his procreative functions form a large reservoir of elemental data which may be transformed into unifying social symbols. The most obvious of the symbolic uses is the interpretation of a group as a biological unit by descent. The symbol of blood relation is so powerful that it is frequently forgotten that even when the symbol comes closest to reality, *i.e.,* when it is applied to the family consisting of parents and children, even in this case the unit includes normally at least two persons who are not blood relatives—I mean the parents. This point will be sufficient both to make clear the discrepancy between the biological reality and the political nomenclature and to justify our reference to the latter as symbolic language destined to function as a unifying instrument of group life. As soon as the idea of the blood unit goes beyond one generation, including grandchildren and further descent, the function of the blood symbolism becomes more apparent because the departure from reality grows wider. The ancestors of any given individual go back in time indefinitely, increasing in number with every generation by powers of two. No simple principle of order can be derived from this pattern of reality. In order to organize this collective as a unit, simplifying symbolic lines are drawn, the most important of them being the father line and the mother line, concepts responsible respectively for the patriarchal and matriarchal symbolisms. There is no biological reason why the line going back to the father, the father's father, etc., or to the mother, the mother's mother etc., should be distinguished from any zig-zag line drawn at random across the genealogical table. And there is no biological reason why any one of the 64 males in the seventh ancestor generation, or any one of the 128 males in the eighth generation, etc., should be distinguished as *the* forefather from the rest. The father and the mother, as the immediate progenitors, are the simplest elements of biological reality to serve as the unifying group symbols.

These simple considerations show the nature of the relation between a symbol and reality. The symbol is based on an element of reality, but it does not describe reality. It uses the datum in order to represent by means of that single, comparatively simple element a diffuse field of reality as a unit. As a consequence, heated argument is possible about the merits of any symbol. Those who belong to the social group and believe in its existence will always be able to point to the element of reality which is contained in their group symbols, and to prove that their social group is *really* a unit. Those who are politically opposed to the group in question will always be able to point out the discrepancy between the symbol and the reality which it represents. And, according to their temper and intellectual sophistication, they will stigmatize it as hypocritical, as an ideology, a myth, or an invention of a ruling class to deceive a guileless people. A scientific analysis has to keep clear of both of these fallacies, and to describe realistically the growth and function of the symbol.

THE DOCTRINE OF RACE

By Houston Stewart Chamberlain

RANKE HAD PROPHESIED that our century would be a century of nationality; that was a correct political prognostic, for never before have the nations stood opposed to each other so clearly and definitely as antagonistic unities. It has, however, also become a century of races, and that indeed is in

Adapted from Houston Stewart Chamberlain, *Foundations of the Nineteenth Century*, tr. by John Lees (New York: John Lane Co., Ltd., 1913), Vol. 1, pp. xciii–xciv, 257, 260–263, 269–271.

the first instance a necessary and direct consequence of science and scientific thinking. I have already said at the beginning of this introduction that science does not unite but dissects. That statement has not contradicted itself here. Scientific anatomy has furnished such conclusive proofs of the existence of physical characteristics distinguishing the races from each other that they can no longer be denied; scientific philology has discovered between the various languages fundamental differences which cannot be bridged over; the scientific study of history in its various branches has brought about similar results, especially by the exact determination of the religious history of each race, in which only the most general of general ideas can raise the illusion of similarity, while the further development has always followed and still follows definite, sharply divergent lines. The so-called unity of the human race is indeed still honoured as a hypothesis, but only as a personal, subjective conviction lacking every material foundation. The ideas of the eighteenth century with regard to the brotherhood of nations were certainly very noble but purely sentimental in their origin; and in contrast to these ideas to which the Socialists still cling, limping on like reserves in the battle, stern reality has gradually asserted itself as the necessary result of the events and investigations of our time.

I understand by "Teutonic peoples" the different North-European races, which appear in history as Celts, Teutons (Germanen) and Slavs, and from whom—mostly by indeterminable mingling—the peoples of modern Europe are descended. It is certain that they belonged originally to a single family, as I shall prove in the sixth chapter; but the Teuton in the narrower Tacitean sense of the word has proved himself so intellectually, morally and physically pre-eminent among his kinsmen, that we are entitled to make his name summarily represent the whole family. The Teuton is the soul of our culture. Europe of to-day, with its many branches over the whole world, represents the chequered result of an infinitely manifold mingling of races: what binds us all together and makes an organic unity of us is "Teutonic" blood. If we look around, we see that the importance of each nation as a living power to-day is dependent upon the proportion of genuinely Teutonic blood in its population. Only Teutons sit on the thrones of Europe.—What preceded in the history of the world we may regard as Prolegomena; true history, the history which still controls the rhythm of our hearts and circulates in our veins, inspiring us to new hope and new creation, begins at the moment when the Teuton with his masterful hand lays his grip upon the legacy of antiquity.

Not a year passes without our being assured at international congresses, by authoritative national economists, ministers, bishops, natural scientists, that there is no difference and no inequality between nations. Teutons, who emphasise the importance of race-relationship, Jews, who do not feel at ease among us and long to get back to their Asiatic home, are by none so slightingly and scornfully spoken of as by men of science. Professor Virchow, for instance, says that the stirrings of consciousness of race among us are only to be explained by the "loss of sound common sense": moreover, that it is "all a riddle to us, and no one knows what it really means in this age of equal rights." Nevertheless, this learned man closes his address with the expression of a desire for "beautiful self-dependent personalities." As if all history were not there to show us how personality and race are most closely connected, how the nature of the personality is determined by the nature of its race, and the power of the personality dependent upon certain conditions of its blood! And as if the scientific rearing of animals and plants did not afford us an extremely rich and reliable material, whereby we may become acquainted not only with the conditions but with the importance of "race"! Are the so-called (and rightly so-called) "noble" animal races, the draught-horses of Limousin, the American trotter, the Irish hunter, the absolutely reliable sporting dogs, produced by chance and promiscuity? Do we get them by giving the animals equality of rights, by throwing the same food to them and whipping them with the same whip? No, they are produced by artificial selection and strict maintenance of the purity of the race. Horses and especially dogs give us every chance of observing that the intellectual gifts go hand in hand with the physical; this is specially true of the moral qualities: a mongrel is frequently very clever, but never reliable; morally he is always a weed. Continual promiscuity between two pre-eminent animal races leads without exception to the destruction of the pre-eminent characteristics of both. Why should the human race form an exception? In spite of the broad common foundation, the human races are, in reality, as different from one another in character, qualities, and above all, in the degree of their individual capacities, as greyhound, bulldog, poodle and Newfoundland dog. Inequality is a state towards which nature inclines in all spheres; nothing extraordinary is produced without "specialisation"; in the case of man, as of animals, it is this specialisation that produces noble races; history and ethnology reveal this secret to the dullest eye. Has not every genuine race its own glorious, incomparable physiognomy? How could Hellenic art have arisen without Hellenes?

If the men who should be the most competent to pronounce an opinion on the essence and significance of Race show such an incredible lack of judgment —if in dealing with a subject where wide experience is necessary for sure perception, they bring to bear upon it nothing but hollow political phrases—how can we wonder that the unlearned should talk nonsense even when their instinct points out the true path? For the subject has in these days aroused interest in widely various strata of society, and where the learned refuse to teach, the unlearned must shift for themselves. When in the fifties Count Gobineau published his brilliant work on the inequality of the races of mankind, it passed unnoticed: no one seemed to know what it all meant. Like poor Virchow men stood puzzled before a riddle. Now that the Century has come to an end things have changed: the more passionate, more impulsive element in the nations pays great and direct attention to this question.

Nothing is so convincing as the consciousness of the possession of Race. The man who belongs to a distinct, pure race, never loses the sense of it. The guardian angel of his lineage is ever at his side, supporting him where he loses his foothold, warning him like the Socratic Daemon where he is in danger of going astray, compelling obedience, and forcing him to undertakings which, deeming them impossible, he would never have dared to attempt. Weak and erring like all that is human, a man of this stamp recognises himself, as others recognise him, by the sureness of his character, and by the fact that his actions are marked by a certain simple and peculiar greatness, which finds its explanation in his distinctly typical and super-personal qualities. Race lifts a man above himself: it endows him with extraordinary—I might almost say supernatural— powers, so entirely does it distinguish him from the individual who springs from the chaotic jumble of peoples drawn from all parts of the world: and should this man of pure origin be perchance gifted above his fellows, then the fact of Race strengthens and elevates him on every hand, and he becomes a genius towering over the rest of mankind, not because he has been thrown upon the earth like a flaming meteor by a freak of nature, but because he soars heavenward like some strong and stately tree, nourished by thousands and thousands of roots—no solitary individual, but the living sum of untold souls striving for the same goal. He who has eyes to see at once detects Race in animals. It shows itself in the whole habit of the beast, and proclaims itself in a hundred peculiarities which defy analysis: nay more, it proves itself by achievements, for its possession invariably leads to something excessive and out of the common— even to that which is exaggerated and not free from bias. Goethe's dictum, "only that which is extravagant (*überschwänglich*) makes greatness," is well known. That is the very quality which a thoroughbred race reared from superior materials bestows upon its individual descendants—something "extravagant"— and, indeed, what we learn from every racehorse, every thoroughbred foxterrier, every Cochin China fowl, is the very lesson which the history of mankind so eloquently teaches us! Is not the Greek in the fulness of his glory an unparalleled example of this "extravagance"? And do we not see this "extravagance" first make its appearance when immigration from the North has ceased, and the various strong breeds of men, isolated on the peninsula once for all, begin to fuse into a new race, brighter and more brilliant, where, as in Athens, the racial blood flows from many sources—simpler and more resisting where, as in Lacedaemon, even this mixture of blood had been barred out. Is the race not as it were extinguished, as soon as fate wrests the land from its proud exclusiveness and incorporates it in a greater whole? Does not Rome teach us the same lesson? Has not in this case also a special mixture of blood produced an absolutely new race, similar in qualities and capacities to no later one, endowed with exuberant power? And does not victory in this case effect what disaster did in that, but only much more quickly? Like a cataract the stream of strange blood overflooded the almost depopulated Rome and at once the Romans ceased to be. Would one small tribe from among all the Semites have become a world-embracing power had it not made "purity of race" its inflexible fundamental law? In days when so much nonsense is talked concerning this question, let Disraeli teach us that the whole significance of Judaism lies in its purity of race, that this alone gives it power and duration, and just as it has outlived the people of antiquity, so, thanks to its knowledge of this law of nature, will it outlive the constantly mingling races of to-day.

What is the use of detailed scientific investigations as to whether there are distinguishable races? whether race has a worth? how this is possible? and so on. We turn the tables and say: it is evident that there are such races: it is a fact of direct experience that the quality of the race is of vital importance; your province is only to find out the how and the wherefore, not to deny the facts themselves in order to indulge your ignorance.

VIRGINIA

By Edgar T. Thompson

THE EXPERIMENTAL STAGE in the development of American slavery, so far as the South is concerned, belongs to the history of Virginia. The story begins with the English folkway of apprenticeship which paved the way for white indentured servitude in the colonies. Indentured servitude, in turn, was the historic base upon which Negro slavery was constructed. Apprenticeship is a system of industrial education, generally for minors. In Elizabethan England custom and law bound the apprentice to a master for a period of service generally seven years in length. The master was one skilled in a craft, a trade, or a profession. He was given authority over the apprentice, with power of corporal punishment, to aid in imparting his skill. Customary guild regulations and previous enactments were codified in the Statute of Artificers in 1562, which put a premium upon agricultural apprenticeship. The statute required a written contract between master and apprentice, a contract binding both parties, but one which apparently operated to the special advantage of the master. Justices of the peace and officers of the towns were later empowered to bind out unemployed minors to masters under certain conditions. In this way apprenticeship became a part of the system of poor relief. This was the status of apprenticeship at the time of the plantation of America.

The word *plantation* originally had reference to an organized and controlled migration. Plantation was a method of moving and settling labor, especially in overseas territory, where it was needed and where it might be profitable. World changes incident to the discovery of new lands and to the shift in the routes and commodities of trade brought about in England an agrarian revolution. The reorganization of manorial estates, in order to supply rising urban markets, resulted in the uprooting of thousands of people who filled the highways and crowded the towns and cities. England regarded itself as overpopulated, and for the first time the nation officially realized that it had a problem of the poor. The poor laws and vagrancy laws, which were enacted during the first half of the sixteenth century, sought to restore the lost social equilibrium by re-establishing geographical and social stability.

Now the thinning-out of the rural population of England and the plantation of newly discovered lands abroad with new populations were both parts of the same fundamental and necessary process of population redistribution in an evolving world-economy. England was assuming a central position in this enlarging world-community. Plantation was an expression of an expanding overseas trade, and especially of trade which required the production of goods in overseas territory by European enterprise and management. It therefore involved the migration of European capital and European management. But it was where native people could not be brought under control as laborers, at

Reprinted from Edgar T. Thompson, "The Natural History of Agricultural Labor in the South," in David K. Jackson (ed.), *American Studies in Honor of W. K. Boyd* (Durham: Duke University Press, 1940), pp. 127–145; copyright 1940 by Duke University Press and used with the kind permission of the publisher.

least in sufficient number, and where a labor migration from Europe had therefore to be organized that the real nature of plantation was revealed. It was essentially an industrial army of occupation.

Plantation originally was transplantation, and the capitalist sponsors of the enterprise resided in England. Upon the rise of the planter resident in Virginia, an independent but responsible agent for the employment of English capital, migration changed to emigration and immigration. With a demand for labor on the part of the colonies, and with an oversupply in England, emigration to the colonies was a natural consequence. But the mechanism through which the new migration took place had to be different from that employed in plantation proper. It was no longer by means of an individual of wealth or a company transplanting or "planting" people in a wilderness. It now became a problem of delivering a potential laborer in England to a potential employer in America. It was a problem of how to transport the laborer since transportation was expensive and ordinarily quite beyond his means. A modification of the system of apprenticeship proved to be the solution. The laborer in return for the cost of his transportation voluntarily bound himself, or involuntarily was bound, to work for a master in the colonies for a specified period of years. Variations of this practice developed in time, but it remained the basic pattern during the period of indentured servitude.

"Indentured servitude was thus the Colonial analogue of the agricultural apprenticeship provided by the Statute of Artificers," says Douglas, "and as such flourished chiefly in the great agricultural areas of the South." But apprenticeship and indentured servitude, originally very similar, quickly developed some very important differences. In the first place, the apprentice was generally a minor, while the status of indentured servant came to be held, usually, by an adult man or woman. In the second place, indentured servitude soon lost the educational function which was the essential mark of apprenticeship. Tobacco as then cultivated in Virginia required a good deal of hard labor but demanded no special skill on the part of anyone. The planter as entrepreneur was likely to be the only member of the plantation able to envisage the whole market situation, a situation more or less outside the view of the servant, and in this capacity his function was indispensable. But as master his knowledge of the art of cultivating tobacco probably did not long remain much greater than that of the servant. Or certainly he did not need seven years to teach the servant all he knew. The word *master* ceased to mean a man who was master of his craft and came to mean a man who was master of others. The element of skill dropped out, but the element of authority and discipline remained and became, in fact, stronger as time went on. This change operated to degrade the status of the servant, and later on, of course, of the slave, to a position much lower than that of the apprentice.

These and other differences between apprenticeship and indentured servitude developed from the fact that the latter was to function in a social and economic situation entirely unlike that in which apprenticeship functioned. It was again a difference between a situation of open and a situation of closed resources. For indentured servitude in the colonies served the double function of a system of labor recruitment and control and a means of promoting immigration. In its latter function it served also, in theory at least, as a principle regulating the alienation and acquisition of land. Through the "headright" system planters were in part compensated by the community for the expense to which they were put in bringing over servants. Servants, in turn, in some of the colonies, were given grants of land upon completion of their terms of service.

As property classes developed in such a colony as that of Virginia, where insurrectionary plots on the part of servants were discovered, the increased exercise of authority on the part of the planter was demanded by the community. The harsh vagrancy laws of England furnished precedents for the intervention of the public in the contractural relations between master and servant. Such public coercion, as distinguished from the enforcement of contracts, was supposedly in the interest of the public, but it also coincided with the interest of the planter. The vagrancy laws upon which public coercion was based were the legal sources of the harsher features of Colonial servitude and of slavery.

From the planter's point of view indentured servitude had an essential disadvantage in that, having been paid in advance, the servant had little inducement to work hard or to perform his work with care. Judged by the uncomplimentary remarks so frequently made by planters, he was inclined to work about as little as he could. Under the circumstances, punishment for breach of contract or for offenses against the interest of the planter could hardly take the form of dismissal. Such an action on the part of the planter would have been equivalent to throwing the rabbit into the briar patch. Neither could punishment take the form of a fine in money since the servant had generally no means wherewith to remit a fine. Many of the incidents which further differentiated indentured servitude from apprenticeship and prepared the way for slavery developed from the resort to apparently necessary alternative forms of punishment. The alternative forms were of two general types: (1) corporal punishment and (2) the lengthening of the period of servitude.

The offenses which ordinarily required punishment were, in general, those which violated the planter's right to the full time and service of the servant under the terms of the indenture. Idleness was a common complaint, but running away was, perhaps, the most frequent offense. Even when the servant was recovered, the loss of time and expense were serious to the planter. Offenses that partook more directly of infringements against the peace and order of the community, as well as against the interests of the planter, included robbery, rebellion, and crimes of violence.

In Virginia corporal punishment for these and other offenses was provided for in a law of 1619 which read, "If a servant wilfully neglect his master's commands he shall suffer bodily punishment." There was ample precedent for this in apprenticeship. Until 1662 the right of punishment was in the hands of the Assembly and the courts only, but undoubtedly it was exercised also by planters without legal right. Before the end of the seventeenth century corporal punishment had been extended to cover offenses against the dignity and status of the planter as well as offences against his interests. Further control by the planter over the servant's person and liberty of action was granted after the discovery of a plot of servants in 1663. The great alarm led to the strict regulation of such liberties as leaving the plantation and assembling.

Punishment by means of extension of time had its beginnings in Virginia in 1619, when the first General Assembly ordered servitude for wages as a penalty for "idlers and renegades." This was to be service to the colony in public works and meant, of course, service in addition to the term of the contract. "In this," says Ballagh, "we have the germ of additions of time, a practice which later became the occasion of a very serious abuse of the servant's rights by the addition of terms altogether incommensurate with the offenses for which they were imposed."

The offenses which made the servant liable to corporal punishment were also those which led to punishment by the addition of time. Often both punishments were inflicted. Offenses especially punishable by addition of time, however, seem to have been those involving relations between the sexes, e.g., marriage without the consent of the planter, fornication, and bearing bastard children. For these and other offenses "additions of time frequently amounted to as much as four or five years, or even seven years in some cases, and were often more than the original term of servitude." Second and third offenses, of course, brought the addition of even more time so that we read of servants for twenty-five years, servants for forty years, and servants for life.

Not only were servants given additional time for offenses committed by them, but even when not guilty of offense they often were sold or held for periods longer than their indentures called for. A large number of suits for freedom came before the courts. With labor so greatly in demand the offenses were not all on the side of the servant.

It is easy to see that slavery was on the way, but the displacement of servitude by slavery was also to involve the displacement of white labor by Negro labor on the plantations.

In the narrative of Master John Rolfe we are told that "about the last of August [1619] came in a Dutch Man of Warre that sold us twenty negars." In this sentence Rolfe noted the entrance into Virginia of a new group different in skin color, language, and religion. The members of this group did not voluntarily break the home ties of Africa and set out for a land of opportunity in America. Neither were they motivated by the land hunger which induced many a white servant to bind himself voluntarily to several years of hard labor. They were transported against their will. In America all Englishmen might hope to become "gentlemen" because all might hope with good chance of success to possess land, and in England the possession of land had carried that coveted status. But Negroes were not motivated by this particular tradition and purpose. They therefore were placed at a competitive disadvantage with white servants who shared in the European tradition of their masters.

Perhaps because John Rolfe used the word *sold* in his journal, and because Negro slaves later were sold, it has been assumed that complete slavery was introduced into Virginia in 1619. To be sure, white servants who waited until they had reached Virginia to find their masters frequently were sold to the planters by ship captains, but it was their time only which was sold, not their persons, in order to meet the cost of passage. Hence, as Russell says, "an inference that these twenty negroes were slaves, drawn from the fact that they were sold to the colony or to the planters would not be justified." Mr. J. C. Ballagh in his *A History of Slavery in Virginia* was the first to call attention to the fact that Negroes were not originally introduced into that colony as slaves. His investigations seem to have established the proposition that "servitude . . . was the historic base upon which slavery, by the extension and addition of incidents, was constructed."

In 1619 there was little in the mores of the English settlers in Virginia to countenance actual slavery. These Englishmen had had no previous contact with Negroes and they had no traditional prejudice against them. The Negro was not a white man, and this difference must have been immediately felt, but there was no crystallized objection to him on the score of race. Antipathies based upon olfactory and hygienic objections, and prejudices based upon the fact that the black people were heathen, seem to have existed, but Negroes were not marked off as a distinct racial group. Indeed, between them and the white servants laboring at the same tasks on the plantations there existed for a while a spirit of camaraderie. Many masters held both the Negro and the white servant in equal contempt.

Negroes introduced into Virginia in 1619 and many years thereafter seem to have taken their places in the colony as indentured servants with all the rights and liberties of indentured servants. A census taken in 1624–25 enumerated twenty-three Negroes all listed as "servants." Two Negroes, Anthony Johnson and Mary, his wife, both probably members of the original party of twenty, had not only served out their terms of servitude and become free, but a land patent of 1651 shows Johnson to have been the owner of 250 acres of land assigned to him in fee simple. In 1651 Richard Johnson came in either as a free Negro or as a servant. Only three years later he was given 100 acres of land for importing two other persons.

Hence it appears that Negroes in early Virginia had taken their places as servants along with white servants, and upon completion of their terms of service they received the freedom dues to which servants were entitled. They themselves became landholders and masters of servants. It is even possible that for a time they held white servants, since a measure subsequently enacted forbade the holding of Christian, i.e., white, servants by Negro masters. In at least one instance white servants on a plantation worked under the direction of a Negro overseer.

But Negro servants could not escape the operation of forces which, as we have seen, were forcing indentured servants generally into positions of more complete subordination. Not only did Negro servants not escape them, but because of the special disabilities under which they labored they were more easily victimized than were the white servants. Three servants of Hugh Gwyn, a white planter, two of them white and the third a Negro, ran away from the plantation of their master. Apprehended and brought back for trial, each received a flogging by order of the court. In addition, the two white servants were given an extra year of servitude, but "the third, being a negro . . . shall serve his said master or his assigns for the term of his natural life." "Being a negro" was beginning to have its effect.

It is interesting to note, however, that Negro as well as white masters took advantage of Negro servants. Of course, there were only a few Negroes who were masters of servants, but these few responded to the situation very much as did the white masters. One especially interesting illustration of this is the case of Anthony Johnson, to whom reference already has been made. Johnson was the defendant in a suit brought against him by another Negro, John Casor, for his freedom. From the court records of Northampton County, Russell presents the following facts regarding the case:

According to the records made of the case, John Casor set up the claim in 1653 "Yt hee came unto Virginia for seaven or eight years of Indenture, yt hee had demanded his freedom of Anth. Johnson his Mayster; & further sd yt hee had kept him his serv[an]t seaven years longer than hee should or ought." Casor appealed to Captain Samuel Goldsmith to see that he was accorded his rights. Goldsmith demanded of Johnson the servant negro's indenture, and was told by Johnson that the latter had never seen any indenture, and "yt hee had ye Negro for his life." Casor stood firmly by his assertion that when he came in he had an indenture, and Messrs. Robert and George Parker confirmed his declaration, saying that "they knewe that ye sd Negro had an Indenture in one Mr. [Sandys] hand, on ye other side of ye Baye & . . . if the sd Anth. Johnson did not let ye negro go free the said negro Jno. Casor would recover most of his Cows from him ye sd Johnson" in compensation for service rendered which was not due. Whereupon Anthony Johnson "was in a great feare" and his "sonne in Law, his wife, & his own two sonnes persuaded the old negro Anth. Johnson to let the sd. Jno. Casor free."

The case would be interesting enough and very instructive if it had ended here, but the sequel is more interesting still. Upon more mature deliberation Anthony Johnson determined to make complaint in court "against Mr. Robert Parker that hee detayneth one Jno. Casor a negro the plaintiff's Serv[an]t under pretense yt the sd Jno. Casor is a freeman." His complaint was received, and the court "seriously considering & weighing ye premises," rendered the following verdict, than which there are none stranger on record: "The court . . . doe fynd that ye sd Mr. Robert Parker most unrightly keepeth ye sd Negro John Casor from his r[igh]t Mayster Anthony Johnson & . . . Be it therefore ye Judgment of ye court & ordered that ye sd Jno. Casor negro shall forthwith return into ye service of his sd Mayster Anthony Johnson and that the sd Mr. Robert Parker make payment of all charges in the suite and execution."

A Negro master is successful in his suit against a white master and wins the right to hold his Negro servant for life! "Thus was rendered," Charles Johnson comments on this case, "in strange and fateful irony, the first legal decision involving the right to the perpetual services of a Negro. The decision was obviously not made on racial grounds, as the chance position and relationship of the litigants in the suit well establishes."

For about fifteen years before the passage of the first acts of the Virginia slave code, Negro servants were being recorded as servants for life. Such servants "are call'd Slaves," said Beverly, "in respect of the time of their Servitude, because it is for Life." They were servants against whom the usual punishments by addition of time could not hold. Slavery was therefore fast becoming established in custom, and it was only a question of time before it would receive the sanction of law.

In the decade 1660–70 various statutes were enacted affording this sanction and effecting the legal transition from servitude to slavery. In 1661 an act to punish "English running away with negroes" who were "incapable of making satisfaction by addition of time" was passed. Servitude for life, however, was not yet actual slavery, but with it came a problem, the practical solution of which was the final step in the transition to that condition. This was the problem of the status of the offspring of servants who were "incapable of making satisfaction by addition of time" because they were servants for life. "It was evident," says Ballagh, "that parents under an obligation of life service could make no valid provision for the support of their offspring, and that a just title to the service of the child might rest on the master's maintenance."

Where both parents were servants for life the question of the disposition of the legitimate offspring was no very great problem since there was no difficulty in defining the status of the offspring. Custom already had assigned to them the status of the parents. But illegitimacy and miscegenation had complicated the matter enough to require the formal establishment of some "principle of heredity." Illegitimacy without miscegenation was difficult enough since the instability and change of frontier life made the determination of parenthood on the male side more uncertain than is the case in stable communities. Notwithstanding the rule of English common law that the child should follow the condition of the father the opposite principle that the condition of the mother determined the status of the offspring was adopted in Virginia and in all the other colonies except Maryland. This was in keeping with the idea prevailing at the time expressed in the saying that "Motherhood is a matter of fact, but fatherhood is a matter of opinion."

Miscegenation complicated the matter further by raising the question of the definition of a Negro. Where both parents were known to be Negroes there was no doubt as to the status of the offspring. But there were serious doubts as to the position of mixed-bloods, and many, if not most, of the illegitimate children of female Negro servants for life were mulattoes. Peter Fontaine may have exaggerated when he said that the country swarmed with mulatto bastards, but undoubtedly there were many.

The problem of interracial sexual contacts and illegitimacy was one of the most stubborn to confront the colony. Although the white planter class was not free from such contacts, the greatest amount of irregularity in the first century of settlement seems to have developed between white and Negro servants. These probably began shortly after the introduction of the first Negroes, for in 1630 the court entered an order of punishment for the offense. From this time on the assembly, the courts, and the church wrestled with the problem without success. It was one of a series of legislative acts dealing with the problem which became the means of finally and legally establishing complete slavery in Virginia. The act of 1662 reads as follows: "Whereas some doubts have arisen whether children got by any Englishman upon a negro woman should be slave or free, be it therefore enacted and declared by this present grand assembly, that all children borne in this country shall be held bond or free only according to the condition of the mother."

The "principle of heredity" laid down in this act "was wholly foreign at that time to the condition of servitude, and broadly differentiated it from the system which resulted." The term *slave* was used without definition of any kind, for the act was not intended to create a race of slaves but to settle a question which had arisen in the operation of a custom and to prevent sexual irregularities and race mixture. "Notwithstanding its effect it is clear that the purpose of the act of 1662 was primarily punitory." Hereditary slavery grew directly out of the problem of the mulatto.

Negro slavery was thus a response to a situation whereby the planter got laborers to cultivate his tobacco and the Negro got someone who was responsible for his sustenance as a minimum consideration. It was the sort of labor desirable for tobacco-growing under frontier conditions. It involved certain relative advantages over white servitude since the tasks to which the Negro was put involved mainly routine manual labor and little use of machinery, tools, and techniques outside the culture of natives of Africa. Negro slavery assured the planter a more or less long-time and stable supply of labor.

In addition to dependability it was necessary, also, that labor for the production of agricultural staples on the Southern frontier be movable. In the absence of cheap fertilizers, planters found it necessary after a few years of cultivation of particular tracts of land to move to virgin fertile soil. This is one reason why primogeniture and entail failed to secure a foothold in the transmission of landed estates through inheritance. The incidents through which indentured servitude and slavery developed were those which had survival value for a type of controlled labor highly mobile in character. American slavery reproduced, or tended to reproduce, the personal rights and obligations of European feudalism and serfdom but with the laborer's right to a secure place on the land left out. It was the personal and legal attachment to a master, wherever he might go, rather than to a lord as landlord, that characterized American slavery.

Behind all these formal and legal facts in the development of American slavery were others of a more intangible sort. These were the facts of human nature, the sort of facts which, once grasped, makes any historical situation intelligible because it can then be measured against contemporary experiences and observations. The economic and legal systems in which men live are of great consequence to their actions, but these systems do not determine human relations entirely. The same human nature is present in any and every social system, and occasionally through the pages of history one gets a glimpse of it as something that illuminates and makes intelligible a situation whether one approves of that situation or not.

On the side of human nature the relations which took shape under the influence of daily contact and which eventuated in slavery, grew out of a community of interest in the production of a crop on an isolated plantation, and it would be difficult to exaggerate the extent of this isolation. In the wilderness of the forested Southern frontier master and man were subject to the law announced by Candide at the close of his unfortunate wanderings—they had to cultivate a garden together. Men of very different race and culture were associated together to make a living in accordance with the purposes of the planter and with the means at hand. Men who have to act together in any sort of capacity and for whatever purpose come to know what to expect of each other, and it would have been very strange indeed if between master and man a considerable degree of mutual confidence had not been established. Under the circumstances the relationship between them became, in all probability, a very comfortable one for both. It was something like a family relation; the master felt more secure and had a sense of added dignity and power because he had the permanent support and assistance of his man, particularly in trying times. In early Virginia the idea of a slave was, as we have seen, that of a servant for life, and slavery was, for the most part, a domestic relationship. It is necessary here to return to the subject of indentured servitude in order to see how the forces of human nature operated to effect the transition to slavery.

The servant, male or female, white or Negro, was usually a familyless individual living in close relation to the family of the master. It is a natural thing for a familyless man and especially a familyless woman to attach himself or herself to a family to which they render service and from the members of which they receive support and affection. Where the planter, his sons, and his servants worked together in the fields there could evolve very naturally a relationship which, when taken advantage of, might easily be made permanent.

The servant was an adult when he came to Virginia and began to serve out an indenture for perhaps five years or more. Five years of servitude in the isolation of the rural plantation would naturally build up habits of work and dependence and attitudes of subordination which would be well established when the day of freedom came. If for some delinquency the period of service is extended for perhaps five years longer, he would find it even more difficult suddenly to terminate old associations and go out on his own. Perhaps he is no longer a young man when his term of service is over, and advancing years have rendered him even more dependent upon the master and his family. It is easy to see why many such servants would rather remain and continue to perform accustomed work for an accustomed master than to go elsewhere.

The relationships of indentured servitude must undoubtedly have lent themselves to the building up of a state of moral insolvency among servants, a state of mind which would involve a tendency toward a dependence upon the master for protection and maintenance with a consequent surrender of responsibility for themselves. This human attitude is easily understood. Perhaps such an attitude induces many men to go into the army where one is assured of food, shelter, and clothing, and where someone else does the worrying. It is not unlike the religious attitude of surrender. In such circumstances what is demanded of the servant, the soldier, and the faithful is not merely service but loyalty.

Thus the master and servant relationship, embedded as it was in attitude and custom, and reinforced by the economic demand for labor, tended to lengthen itself into additional years without necessarily calling in the power of the law to achieve that end. In the case of Negro servants, and especially Negro female servants, where it might be expected that social dependence would be stronger, the lengthening of the relationship into slavery followed without difficulty. Such relationships made possible new plantation settlements on the frontier in a manner analogous to that of any pioneer family settling in the forest, making a clearing, and planting a crop. The forest might seem to invite escape, but few think of escaping, for few brood over their fate and the fact of bondage is not ordinarily reflected upon.

Slavery and the forms of discipline that went with it thus grew up in Virginia as a set of customary relations to meet the needs and exigencies of an agricultural situation of a certain kind. But it grew up, as we have seen, within the traditional and legal system of contract labor as it was known in England at the time. Apprenticeship and indentured servitude were legally sanctioned and enforced means of regulating labor. Two incidents of indentured servitude, corporal punishment and addition to the time of service, proved to be highly important in the evolution of slavery as a domestic relation. Still another incident in the legal evolution of indentured servitude which was transmitted to slavery and which promoted an opposite and harsher set of relations was that of the alienation of the servant or slave by sale or will.

One of the earliest legal questions in connection with indentured servitude to arise in Virginia concerned the right of the master to assign his servant's contract. The courts recognized this right whether the servant gave his consent or not. The result was more and more a disposition in the law to regard the servant and the slave as chattel property.

The problem which this presents in understanding the history of American slavery is the fundamental and ancient one of social form and social content, the problem of determining just how the formal and legal and conventional develop out of the simply natural. In the transmission of a habit or custom from one people to another, or from one generation to another, some of the meaning falls out and the practice inevitably undergoes some change. Under certain conditions of change, form and content tend to fall apart. Now with respect to slavery as it developed in Virginia, the individual who bought, inherited, or hired the slave as property would, of course, rarely maintain the original content of personal and shared experiences in which the slavery was embedded. On the plantations slavery developed as a domestic relation, but in the slave trade it tended to become an abstraction divested of all its human association, restraints, and inhibitions. In this latter form it was recognized in the law and maintained by public authority. Hence in the slave trade the most ruthless aspects of the system came to the fore, where, indeed, "ruthlessness was the law." Even the intimate relations of the slave family could not withstand the separating effects of the slave trade.

SOUTH AFRICA

By I. D. MacCrone

THE RACE ATTITUDES which were characteristic of South African frontier society towards the end of the eighteenth and the beginning of the nineteenth century, cannot be fully appreciated until they are brought into relation with the whole spirit and outlook of that society as determined by its historical evolution. Once we take into consideration the circumstances of time and place under which social development and race contacts took shape on the frontier, then its race attitudes appear in a new light as one of the very foundations upon which the whole society rested. The existence of frontier society was, in a very real sense, bound up with those attitudes since they helped to provide it with those qualities of group unity, cohesion and self-consciousness and those powers of group resistance and persistence without which it could not have survived to overcome its difficulties or to maintain its integrity.

Under frontier conditions every society is engaged in a more intense struggle either against the forces of nature or of man or of both than is usually the case

From I. D. MacCrone, *Race Attitudes in South Africa* (London: Oxford University Press, 1937), pp. 125–136. By permission of the Registar, University of the Witwatersrand, Johannesburg, South Africa. Revised and adapted by I. D. MacCrone.

with a more firmly established society; and the "atmosphere of war" so engendered must affect to a greater or less degree the individual expression of attitude. In such an atmosphere the attitudes that are brought into play readily tend to assume extreme and even violent forms of expression as a means of coping with and, if possible, ending the conflict. The insecurity which infects the whole of frontier life only serves to strengthen the attitude in the individual, to iron out individual differences and to stamp it in more firmly, as a means of defending the society against the threat from without. Hence we do not expect to find the operation of group attitudes, particularly race attitudes, qualified by other considerations and, least of all, by any consideration for the opposing group. The absence of recognised status relationships between groups such as exist in a more firmly established society will, under the unsettled conditions of frontier life, necessarily involve the dominant group or group that seeks to dominate in conflict with the other group or groups with which it comes into contact. Passive resistance, even if it merely takes the form of a failure to comply on the part of the latter, is sufficient to render more intolerant the attitudes of the dominant group while hostile action or counter-aggressiveness will make them more violent and embittered.

Since the race attitudes are only one element in a pattern of group attitudes we find that all the attitudes of the group, racial, religious, social, economic and political, come into play in a mutually supplementary way. In the inter-group conflict situation, therefore, in which race attitudes play the major part, no intra-group conflict between these attitudes and the other attitudes of the group can be tolerated since such an internal conflict can only be a source of weakness within the group itself. And of all the elements of the total attitude pattern or culture of our frontier society, race and religious attitudes were most closely and intimately associated with one another. The term "Christian" which in this context meant, in the first place, that the individual to whom it applied had been accepted and was recognised as a member of a group professing a particular religion, was universally used as synonymous with the terms "European" and "white man." The great importance attached to the profession of Christianity was very largely a persistence of the attitude brought by the first Europeans to the Cape at the time of its settlement in 1652. Generations of contact with non-Christian natives and heathen had only served to enhance that attitude and to give it a more vigorous exclusiveness. A generation later at the time of the mass exodus of pastoral farmers from the frontier districts, we find it being given explicit formulation by Anna Steenkamp, sister of the famous Voortrekker leader, Piet Retief, in a letter to her relatives at the Cape in which she gives two main reasons for the Great Trek of 1836–1837. The second reason is stated in the following terms:

the shameful and unjust proceedings with reference to the freedom of our slaves: and yet it is not their freedom that drove us to such lengths, as their being placed on an equal footing with Christians, contrary to the laws of God and the natural distinction of race and religion, so that it was intolerable for any decent Christian to bow down beneath such a yoke; wherefore we rather withdrew in order to preserve our doctrines in purity.

Of all the elements in his social heritage there was none to which the European of the frontier clung with greater fervour or which he prized so highly as

his religion. Although he might have lost touch with the main stream of contemporary European culture, the isolated frontier farmer or "Boer" still retained the peculiar tradition of his seventeenth century background in its
original form. It was that tradition strengthened during the course of more
than a century by the vicissitudes of race contacts on a steadily expanding
frontier, that played a fundamental part in making him race conscious and
determining his race attitudes since membership of his religious group was an
exclusive privilege which distinguished and separated him by an immeasurable
distance from those who did not share it with him. In the absence of any kind of
opportunity for public worship the religious exercises of the head of the household took on an added significance, and even in the poorest or most remote
homes of the frontier the Bible was to be found occupying the place of honour.
Thus in an account of the journey of the Governor van Plettenberg to the distant
frontier region of the Sneeuwberg in 1778 we read that:

in this poverty-stricken condition it was found that the households were provided
with such books as enabled them, in the absence of the opportunity for public
worship, to carry out religious exercises among themselves in their own families;
for the most part they were well behaved, reasonably well informed and strongly
desirous of a minister of religion.

To be able to write and to read the Bible comprised the extent of most frontier
education. The family Bible as the centre of family worship and as the register
that contained the records of the family births and deaths was an object of the
strongest sentiments. But its symbolic value was even stronger than these since
it was the outward and visible sign of that which was the most cherished
spiritual possession of the group.

For the frontier farmer, then, his religion was, first and foremost, a social
fact and a jealously guarded group privilege. By virtue of his religion he justified his right to dominate the heathen by whom he was surrounded. They fell
outside the pale and their claims, therefore, could never compete on equal
terms with those of the Christian group. The idea that Christian and non-
Christian were in any sense equal even before the law or that an offence against
the person or property of a non-Christian should be taken as seriously or be
dealt with as rigorously as a similar offence by a non-Christian, was entirely
foreign to frontier mentality. When the revolutionary doctrines of liberty,
equality and fraternity arrived on the frontier towards the end of the eighteenth
century they were warmly welcomed, not merely because they served to justify
the repudiation of the Dutch East India Company's rule but also because they
were a genuine reflection of the democratic spirit of frontier society. But outside the closed circle of that society they abruptly ceased to have any validity—
a limitation which in view of the relations obtaining with those to whom these
doctrines were not considered to apply, appeared as a paradox even to contemporary observers. But from the point of view of the frontier farmer there
was no real inconsistency in his attitude. In fact, to have taken up any other
attitude would have been tantamount to undermining the whole foundation
upon which his society rested. It would have been equivalent to a defeat, the
reversal of a tendency that had been steadily developing for generations. Under
the circumstances in which he was placed and with the whole weight of his
social heritage upon him, the frontier farmer was literally coerced into adopting

the attitude which he did to those who fell outside his group. The inconsistency lay rather on the side of those who, failing to appreciate the total situation to which his attitude was the appropriate response, attempted to apply standards of social behaviour which would have appeared to him to make his continued existence on the frontier impossible.

The implications of the religious and social elements in the race attitudes of the frontier farmer are well illustrated by the manner in which all attempts at regularizing or improving the state of existing interracial relations were received. Since such attempts invariably appeared as a threat against the principles of group privilege and of race inequality, they necessarily excited reactions of suspicion and hostility. The experiences of the liberal-minded General Janssens, governor at the Cape (1803–1806) during the short-lived regime of the Batavian Republic in Holland, were an indication of what lay in store for similar attempts at reform on the part of the British government and officials who would come after him. After the second British occupation in 1806 when the Cape finally passed under British rule, the chronic unrest particularly on the Eastern frontier became progressively aggravated not merely by the presence of an alien government at Cape Town but by the presence of a government which was determined and which at the same time possessed the means to enforce some degree of law and order in what otherwise threatened to become an anarchic situation. The efforts of successive British governors, for example, to bring the relations between European farmers and detribalised Hottentots who for the most part had been reduced to a servile status, under the rule of law were resented by many as "contrary to the laws of God and the natural distinction of race and religion"; not to speak of their being a wholly unwarranted interference with the prevailing practice "sanctioned since time immemorial" according to which persons of colour and more particularly Hottentots were destined to be the servants of the white man or European—a practice, moreover, that could readily be justified by an appeal to the Bible.

An even worse reception, it need hardly be said, awaited the efforts of the early missionaries who arrived on the frontier towards the end of the eighteenth century, since these men were actually trying to impart to the heathen the very special and exclusive possession which had hitherto marked off the group from all those by whom it was surrounded. Thus we find the eccentric but redoubtable Dr. van der Kemp whose name as a missionary has become a byword in South African history textbooks, recording in his journal (1801):

They (some farmers who were in revolt) complained that government protected the Hottentots and Caffrees, and encouraged them to rob and murder the Colonists; that they were instructed by us in reading, writing and religion, and thereby put on an equal footing with the Christians; especially that they were admitted in the church of Graaff Reinet, and that we kept meetings with them every evening in that place; and that they intended to fall upon Graaff Reinet and to force the Commissioner to put a stop to these proceedings.

The comparative failure of these early missionary efforts was regarded as a proof that such people were not fitted for Christianity while the actions of men like van der Kemp and Read who married women of colour were an awful example of the social consequences that would follow from the breaking down of the religious barrier.

The negative aspects of the Calvinistic creed as professed by the colonists, its doctrine of predestination, its emphasis upon the community of the elect, the exclusive twist that could be given to its teachings, were all perfectly adapted to the interracial situation of the frontier. The conclusion was readily drawn, and applied, that the heathen fell outside the scheme of salvation. Attempts at christianizing them were not merely not sanctioned by, but actually contrary to, the teachings of the Bible. Even the long-suffering Janssens whose sympathy with the efforts of the missionaries at the mission station of Bethelsdorp (which soon came to be known locally as "Bedelaarsdorp" or "Village of Beggars"), though genuine was restrained, felt compelled to write:

Instruction! Instruction! is what they lack above all else; they call themselves men and Christians, the Kaffirs and Hottentots heathen, and for this reason they believe that they are permitted everything. A brother of Thomas Ferreira who pretends to have some literature, has made the discovery that the Hottentots are the descendants of the accursed race of Ham, and consequently are condemned by God Almighty to servitude and ill-treatment.

Hendrik Swellengrebel, son of a former Cape governor, writing at a time when the contacts between the Europeans and the Bantu tribesmen were still at a tentative stage, remarks:

Our countrymen in question gave an unfavourable account of the Kaffirs, whom they described as extremely treacherous. Preening themselves on their Christianity, the others were merely black crafty heathen whose only intention was to destroy the Christians. As a result of this belief their treatment of this nation was also fairly harsh and offensive, a matter about which I had frequent arguments with them.

Under such circumstances the intense and exclusive group consciousness of the European inhabitants of the frontier found expression in a consciousness of race and social supremacy which coincided almost uniformly with the distinctions based upon creed and colour. Christianity and skin-colour became so closely associated with one another that any one by itself could serve as a criterion of group membership and of social superiority. And, conversely, the absence of any one of these carried with it the stigma of religious, social and racial inferiority which almost automatically excluded the individual so distinguished from membership of the group. The group had, in fact, become to all intents and purposes a kind of colour-caste or closed group into which the individual was born or from which he was excluded as the result of the same accident. It would appear also that as a result of this increasing emphasis upon a rigid ingroup-outgroup distinction, individuals of the group in question had begun to acquire that particular quality of ethnocentrism according to which only members of their own group in their role of "men and Christians" could be truly regarded as human beings.

Of the two criteria that of skin-colour was the more pervasive and the more consistent in its operation. In spite of the fact that an individual, especially if he were light skinned, might achieve some kind of religious, racial or social equality which would enable him to secure admission into the colour-caste group, inferiority was always found associated with a dark or black skin but never with a white skin which, on the contrary, was everywhere associated with religious and social superiority. And since differences of skin-colour are so obvious and easily identifiable, they can, more readily than any other physical difference, become attached by a process of conditioning to the prevailing social attitudes of the group. When once such a colour difference comes to serve as the sign of a distinction which either includes or excludes and as the mark on which discrimination against a group is based, the result is a group-colour prejudice.

Although colour prejudice as such was not so rigidly exclusive in its operation as it has since become, there is some contemporary evidence to show that it was already firmly established before the end of the eighteenth century. Distinctions of colour even when they came into conflict with those other distinctions with which they usually coincided and to which they originally owed their existence, were certainly by now and probably had been for some time, more important than any other criterion as a means of group inclusion or exclusion. Since colour prejudice as a social attitude on the part of the individual can have no reality apart from the existence of the group, much of its operation in the individual will depend upon the circumstances in which the group has developed and the conditions under which social contacts take place. On the frontier, as we have seen, contacts with other groups were more or less of the anarchical kind that is characteristic of frontier conditions. Under such circumstances group attitudes were more violent, more intense, and brought into play the more hostile and aggressive tendencies as the result of the local situation. In the older, more settled parts of the country such as the predominantly slave-owning agricultural districts of the western Cape, where social contacts were to a much greater extent regularized by status, and where relations on that basis were on the whole of a far friendlier and more intimate kind, distinctions based upon differences in social status or class associated with differences in skin-colour were likely to be more conspicuous than distinctions based upon differences in race or religion.

The position occupied by the free burgher in the community which had been steadily developing at the Cape during the eighteenth century is well brought out by the following contemporary account:

Accustomed from youth to command slaves, he believes himself to be exalted over all others and obeys with an ill grace. This conceit of himself has a result that even a farmer would not exchange his position for that of anyone else. He is proud of the name of African; Cape Burgher appears to him a grand title. This overweening pride gives rise to indolence. Few whites will lend a hand in agriculture or roll up their sleeves in the warehouse; it is the work of slaves! what are slaves for? is the reply.

For more than a generation this same burgher, both in the town and in the country, had been living under conditions that strongly favoured the growth of a sense of assured social superiority not only over other classes in the community but over strangers as well. The rising standards of life and of civilization were reflected in the domestic architecture of town and country houses and by the generous scale on which some of the wealthier landowning farmers lived—"these planters so proud of their colour" as they were described by the French traveller le Vaillant. It is not surprising that members of this class attached a great deal of importance to the rights and privileges of burgher to which they were entitled. The distinction between burgher and non-burgher had become of much greater importance than it had been in the early days of the colony. To have been baptized was no longer even sufficient as a claim to freedom from servile status and, therefore, still less for admission to burgher status as it had been in the past. One had to be born free, of free-born parents who were themselves of Christian, that is, of pure European descent in order to be accepted as a fully qualified burgher on an equal social footing with other members of the same class. Significantly enough, one of the earliest cases of overt colour prejudice on record is an incident that occurred in the agricultural district of Stellenbosch and which is described as follows:

That the burghers Daniel Bosman, Hermanus Bosman the Younger, and Pieter Daniel de Villiers, of whom the first named had acted as spokesman, on the 30th October (1788) even before the Company in question was drawn up in readiness to move off to the field of drill, had approached him (the Landdrost) and in their own name as well as in the name of their fellow burghers who were enrolled in the said Company, had declared that they were not willing to serve together with the Burgher Johannes Hartog the Younger who they had discovered for the first time on that day had been appointed to the effective rank of corporal, though they would serve with him as a common soldier, on the ground that he was of a Black Colour and descended from Heathen (vermits denselven Swartagtig van Couleur, en van Heydenen afkomstig zou zyn).

The foregoing incident shows plainly enough the direction in which group sentiment was developing with regard to skin-colour, and how firmly it had become associated with an inferior or servile status in the community as well as with a "Heydensche afkomst". Whereas formerly persons of colour had been freely admitted into the European or Christian community on the ground that they were of mixed parentage in addition to having been baptized, they were now, more and more, being excluded on the very same ground even in spite of having been baptized. Thus, ever since slavery had been introduced during the first decade of the settlement at the Cape, it had been taken for granted that a baptized slave could claim his freedom. The inevitable result in time was:

that the children born in slavery are neither baptized nor given any religious instruction. There is a common and well-grounded belief that Christians must not be held in bondage; hence only such children as are intended for emancipation, are baptized.

When, in 1792, the question was explicitly raised by the Church Council of Stellenbosch whether owners who permitted or encouraged their slaves to be baptized would be obliged to emancipate them, the matter was referred to the Church Council of Capetown for its opinion. That body replied that neither the law of the land nor the law of the church prohibited the retention of baptized persons in slavery while local custom strongly supported the custom, and added:

that it would contribute in no small measure to the obstruction of the progress of Christianity if in this matter a stipulation were made to the effect that no one should be permitted to allow his slaves to be baptized upon confession of faith unless he himself were held bound to emancipate the same.

Our historical study of the changes in race attitudes on the part of the European may appropriately be brought to a close at this stage in their development. If we have succeeded in showing that the race attitudes which the first Europeans brought with them to the Cape had undergone a radical alteration, and if our account of the factors which contributed to this result is at all convincing, then the original aim of this historical survey has been accomplished. For we have now reached familiar ground since the attitudes themselves, in so far as we have succeeded in identifying them, are very similar to those which we find displayed on all sides at the present time. The changes that have taken place in them since the close of our period may be important but they are hardly comparable with the changes that took place during that period. For what has changed is not so much the attitudes themselves as the grounds on which they are rationalized as the result of the shift of emphasis from the Christian and his "religion" to the White man and his "civilization." And those same attitudes, more particularly in the form in which they had developed on the frontier, were to be one of the decisive factors in shaping the course of nineteenth-century history in South Africa.

The first half of that century was to witness some startling developments in the history of race contacts which are still very much alive in the hearts of the descendants of those who took part in them and of those who share their outlook. Fortunately for us, we are relieved by the limited aim of this investigation from having to undertake a further inquiry into the extremely complicated interracial situation which arose on the frontier between Boer and Bantu and which was made still more complicated by the arrival of the Briton, whether as government official or as missionary or even as settler, upon the scene. The history of those days is the stuff of the present-day politics of the Union since the same issues are at stake to-day which came to the forefront at the time of the Great Trek of the frontiersmen, exactly a century ago.

The Great Trek itself has been rightly described as the central event in South African history—a kind of historical water-shed which has ever since determined the flow of South African events—while its more or less immediate causes have been pretty thoroughly thrashed out in the textbooks. But its roots are without a doubt to be found in the history of race contacts and the developments of race attitudes during and up to the close of the eighteenth century before ever the Kaffir or the Englishman had appeared upon the boards. It is unfortunate, therefore, that the exciting and in many ways heroic and moving episodes that constitute for most minds the history of the Great Trek, should be allowed to obscure the importance of the eighteenth century as the formative period of those race attitudes on the part of the European which make an adjustment, satisfactory to both White and Black races, the most difficult problem of twentieth-century South Africa.

NORTHWESTERN EUROPE

By Christen T. Johassen

THAT THE MAIN THESIS OF RACISM has been proven false by scholars and scientists does not alter its effectiveness or importance as a world force; on the contrary, it raises questions as to why it has persisted though shown to be without validity. And as Scheler points out, "the sociology of knowledge is not concerned merely with tracing the existential basis of truth, but also of social illusions, superstitions, and socially conditioned errors and forms of deception."

The peoples of northwestern Europe and the United States have always been very conscious of the culture which they inherited from the classic civilizations of the Mediterranean basin; indeed, in common language "culture" is usually used to describe those parts of our culture which were acquired from Greece and Rome. We are perhaps less conscious of how much of our cultural heritage, our habits, and values were acquired from the ancient peoples of the North Sea basin. These cultural factors are less dramatic and evident because they are acquired in the subtle process of socialization, rather than through a foreign language or a formal educational institution, and have in this way endured through the ages passed from generation to generation. Thus past events are encysted in the social attitudes of today, and these events cannot be fully understood without reference to their origins and developmental history, for the present attitude represents merely the latest or contemporary phase of the total genetic process.

Barzun has pointed out the apparent paradox that modern, Nordic, racial ideology has originated in the writings of Latins such as Tacitus, Bougainville, and de Gobineau, these authors really used the Nordics as Samuel Johnson used the Chinese, or More the Utopians, to create invidious comparisons as a critique of their own society. It is significant that these doctrines did not become very important in the ideology and politics of the Latin countries where many of them originated, but did achieve much greater influence in some northern European countries. This is understandable when it is realized that cultural diffusion is selective and that the culture of the ancient peoples of the North Sea Basin contained a rather complete racist theory which was integrated with their mythology and their total value system, and which in most respects paralleled the myths of modern racist dogma.

The *Rigsthula* is a cultural poem which describes the racial make-up, the functions and relationships of social classes in Viking society, and explains the origins of these classes and their function on a mythological basis. According to this poem it was the god Rig who created the different classes of society. Thrael, of the lowest class, is described as black-haired with wrinkled skin, rough hands and knotted knuckles, thick fingers, ugly face, twisted back, and big heels. Thrael's wife would hardly win any beauty contest either since she had, accord-

Reprinted from Christen T. Johassen, "Some Historical and Theoretical Bases of Racism in Northwestern Europe," *Social Forces*, XXX (December, 1951), 156–160; copyright 1951 by the Williams and Wilkins Company, Baltimore, Md., for the University of North Carolina Press.

ing to this account, crooked legs, stained feet, sunburned arms, and a flat nose. Their function as described by this work was to carry burdens all day, dig turf, spread dung, and herd swine and goats.

Karl, the yeoman, however, is pictured as sturdy and strong with a ruddy face and flashing eyes. It was his duty to manage the farm, build houses, and fashion other artifacts.

Mothir, the woman of the noble class, is described as having bright brows, a shining breast, and a neck "whiter than the new fallen snow." And her son, Jarl, by the god Rig, is portrayed in these words, "Blond he was, and bright his cheeks, grim as a snake's were his glowing eyes." Jarl's function as a warrior and ruler is described in detail; he, unlike either Thrael or Karl, is taught runes.

This poem like the rest of Norse mythology may be looked upon as a mental production which gave the Vikings explanations about nature, society, and themselves, gave them answers to questions they could answer in no other way, and therefore helped them to solve problems arising out of activity in these spheres of life.

The thralls found in Scandinavia at the opening of the Viking Age were probably to a large extent descendants of the short, brunette, brachycephalic race which the tall, blond, long-headed Norse had conquered when they moved into Scandinavia. The Vikings, as they conducted their raiding and conquest expeditions to England, Ireland, and Continental Europe would bring back captives which were made slaves. These were for the most part shorter and darker than their captors. Thus certain racial characteristics such as short stature, dark hair and skin, and a flat nose became associated with inferior social status, and inferiority in general; while blondness, light skin, and certain facial features became connected with superiority. These ideas were supported by mythology and tended to persist even though a certain amount of race mixture went on generation after generation.

It is certain that much of the cultural mass, such as aspects of laws, language, values, usages, etc., of the modern nations of the North Sea basin can be traced to the culture described by Norse Sagas and other documents which have survived. It is therefore reasonable to hypothesize that the values regarding racial characteristics, social status, inferiority and superiority survived along with other elements and formed a fertile mental atamosphere in which racism could grow and achieve its rankest flowering in the age of Hitler.

There is considerable evidence to support this point of view. Of all the purveyors of Aryanism and its various forms, Arthur de Gobineau must be given the dubious honor of being the most important. It was he who with subtlety and brillance fused the scattered racist ideas of philosophers, ethnologists, and the musings and exuberances of the poets into a coherent intellectual whole, and in striking prose gave life to the dry scholarship of the linguistic paleontologist that preceded him. His abilities as a synthesizer and a writer surmounted the many errors of his ideas and the falsity of his basic premise, and helped make racism one of the most influential ideas of the Nineteenth and Twentieth centuries. In many respects de Gobineau is to racism what Adam Smith is to capitalism. It was de Gobineau who turned the "Aryan Controversy," chiefly concerned with the location of the homeland of the Aryan language and people by philology and anthropology, into an ideology of racial superiority and inferiority that was to have such portentous consequences for the history of our times. Although de Gobineau used "Aryan" to describe his chosen people it is clear that he meant Nordic in the restricted sense. It was essentially his work which crystallized the Nordic myth and gave it the present form and direction. Those who followed him, Houston Stewart Chamberlain and Hans F. K. Günther in Germany, and Madison Grant and Lothrop Stoddard in the United States developed and elaborated what he had started.

De Gobineau's central thesis that race and aristocracy are the most important elements in civilization and that the hope of the world has always been the fair-haired Aryan or Nordic was proposed in a four volume work, *Essai sur l'inégalité des races humaines* (1853–1855). Later (1879) he published *Histoire d'Ottar Jarl, Pirate Norvégien conquerant du pays de Bray en Normandie, et de sa descendance.* And it is significant for this paper that in a letter to Mm. Wagner he stated that the *Essai* was written in consequence of research begun on the history of his family and that it was written in part to prove scientifically the superiority of his own race. He believed that he was a direct descendant through Norman stock of Ottar Jarl, a Viking hero of ancient Norway. Furthermore, in a passage in *Ottar Jarl* he states that this book continues his *Essai* and his *Histoire des Perses* which were written only to serve as prefaces. Certainly de Gobineau in his research for *Ottar Jarl* must have come in contact with the values and ideas about race and aristocracy expressed in the *Rigsthula*.

One of the great intellectual movements of the Nineteenth Century, Romanticism, helped to make the peoples of Scandinavia, Germany, England, and America conscious of their Norse heritage. In his rejection of neo-classical themes the Romanticist sought inspiration in other directions, one of these sources being ancient Norse sagas and Teutonic ideas. Norse and Anglo-Saxon themes are important aspects of the Romantic movement in Scandinavia, England, and the United States. The same was true of Germany and it was no accident that Houston Stewart Chamberlain, disciple of de Gobineau, who elaborated and popularized Gobinism, was an enthusiastic admirer of Richard Wagner who perhaps better then anyone resurrected and dramatized old Nordic myths in his *The Ring of the Niebelungen.* Wagner and Gobineau were good friends and the German master found great pleasure in being told that the *Ring* embodied the quintessence of de Gobineau's principles of German race superiority. Chamberlain's marriage to Wagner's daughter joined individuals who were already intimately spiritually related. That Hitler should find both Wagner's operas and the present Wagner family worthy of his intense patronage is therefore understandable.

It should appear then that the central ideas of racism had been part of the intellectual atmosphere of northwestern Europe since the beginning of historical times and most probably long before, and that the Romantic movement created a renaissance and dramatization of Norse ideals in the Nineteenth Century. In fact, de Gobinau himself was essentially and typically a romanticist.

Though some forms of racist ideas were present in Spain, Portugal, and particularly France, racism never took root and grew to such virulent proportions in these countries even though their exploitation of colonial peoples created a situation in which one could expect such ideas to flourish. However, religious traditions, and the traditions of the Inquisition were strong in these countries and it was to this type of mental productions that the Spaniards and

Portuguese turned for their rationalizations. The exploitation by the Latin colonial powers of the natives was no less brutal than that practiced by the colonizers from northwestern Europe, but it was justified by different premises. The Spaniards, for example, justified their exploitation of native peoples on the basis that these people were pagans and therefore outside the pale of Christian ethics and consideration. It might be argued that, since the result was the same, whether exploitation was justified on a racial or religious basis had no significance. But this difference was to be of tremendous significance for the modern world. The difference of religion could be overcome by conversion, and in Spanish, Portuguese, and French colonies amalgamation was often accepted and even encouraged, while in English and Dutch colonies where racist ideas predominated amalgamation was usually strongly discouraged and proscribed, and intermarriage was the exception rather than the rule. This is one of the important facts which explains why the race problem is being solved through amalgamation in such countries as Brazil, while it is perhaps more acute than ever today in such countries as South Africa where English value systems predominate.

On the other hand, not all the countries of northwestern Europe whose culture can be traced back to Norse and Teutonic origins have elaborated racism intellectually, nor has it found expression in political movements. The Scandinavians like other peoples have not been free from chauvinism, ethnocentrism, and extreme nationalism, but it appears to be correct to state that in modern times racism, so prevalent in Germany, Great Britain, and the United States, has not appeared here. For example, Penka's thesis that Scandinavia was the cradle of the Aryans, which was popularized in England by G. H. Randall's *The Cradle of the Aryans* (1887), received little notice in Scandinavia, and the Scandinavian anthropologists Montilius and Sophus Muller did not assent. And even under the Nazi occupation of Norway and Denmark when espousal of Nordicism had immediate and tangible rewards the doctrine gathered comparatively few adherents. Thus in Scandinavia where the old Norse ideas of race and aristocracy should certainly be as strong as anywhere, significant ideological and political movements based on racism are conspicuously absent.

It would appear, therefore, that other factors besides the presence of racist traditions must be invoked to explain the apparent contradiction.

The other factor, which was present in Germany, Great Britain, and the United States and not in Scandinavia, was the historical situations in which the former countries became involved. Racism in Germany as an intellectual movement developed concomitantly with the strong drive for nationhood which culminated in the unification of Germany in 1871. It was given further impetus by German imperialism and reached its climax of development under Hitler who found it an effective weapon in his drive to recreate German power and self-respect after the disastrous defeat of World War I. It is probable that imperialism rather than nationalism was the dominant situational factor in Great Britain. And in the United States the presence of a large slave population in a society ideologically committed to liberty, equality, and Christian ethics played a decisive role. It is significant in this regard that the first English translation of de Gobineau was by H. Hotz of Montgomery, Alabama, whose labor of love was undertaken as a piece of pro-slavery propaganda. Furthermore, the people of the United States were engaged in the conquest and consolidation of a continental nation which involved the liquidation, removal, or forcible segregation of the original inhabitants who differed from themselves both racially and culturally.

These situational factors were not present in modern Scandinavia. Scandinavian countries were not engaged in imperialistic enterprises and the national states of Denmark and Sweden had been established for a long time. And Norway's nationalism, though not regained fully before 1905, was realized in a struggle where the contestants were fellow Scandinavians, very much alike in both culture and race. In other words, though the ideology of racism was readily available the logical and psychological necessity for it was lacking. In Germany, Great Britain, and the United States, however, both the cultural tradition and the historical situation created a favorable climate for racism to develop.

NEW GUINEA

By Stephen W. Reed

THE GREAT BIRD-SHAPED ISLAND OF NEW GUINEA, which stretches east and west for more than fifteen hundred miles between the equator and the Australian continent, is one of the last large areas in our contracting world to be brought within the orbit of Western enterprise and control. The political dependency of this island derives primarily from the fact that New Guinea has been a supine land of open resources whose infinitely fragmented aboriginal population has been powerless to prevent the loss of its autonomy in the face of organized European force. It also has been a territorial prize of growing importance in two world wars, but in none of these decisive events have its native peoples had an effective voice. Given the low levels of social organization and cultural achievement which have prevailed in New Guinea time out of mind, it is difficult to imagine how European contact in the nineteenth and twentieth centuries could have resulted in anything other than the typical colonial polity which has been the country's fate.

Inhabited by countless small tribal groups and discrete communities of Oceanic Negroids, New Guinea has ever been and yet remains a prototypical region of underdevelopment in virtually every sense of that word. Its native peoples have never known social, political, or racial solidarity in any form; and nationalism exists only as a small cloud on the horizon. Although they share in a number of common cultural similarities and a uniform physical heritage—testifying to their probable common origins and centuries of internal contact

---

A more detailed account of culture contact and the development of caste in New Guinea is reported in the author's *The Making of Modern New Guinea* (Philadelphia: American Philosophical Society, 1943).

and contagion—their poverty in goods and techniques, their rudimentary social and political structures, and the unresolved babel of their many local tongues all evidence the pervasive "primitiveness" of the whole island.

Commencing about eighty years ago the impact of Western enterprise and exploitation began to be felt in the peripheries of the island. Starting slowly, but gaining momentum decade by decade, this impact has wrought radical changes in native life and outlook. Gradual European penetration during most of this period has been dramatically quickened by the events of two world wars, especially the most recent. Western economic, political, and missionary enterprise in particular have weakened if they have not destroyed the original ubiquitous tribalism of the entire area. Economic self-sufficiency, once known to virtually every local community, is now a thing of the past in all but the most remote settlements; local autonomy in the social order, formerly universal in the essentially chiefless proto-democracy of the village, is now hedged around by codified rules and legal sanctions of imposed European administrations; and social relations between the aboriginal peoples and their new overlords have developed along the fundamental fault-line of racial and cultural cleavage which divides the plural society of modern New Guinea. The purpose of this brief sketch is not to attempt a summary of all the changes which have occurred in native and European life on this latter-day frontier, but rather to explore the patterned relationships which have developed between members of the two major racial groups in this contact situation. Race relations, of course, are never isolable from the major aspects of institutional life; and consequently behavior labeled "racial" can only be seen in the context of concrete cultural situations and activities. Such facts and generalizations as are presented here will pertain to situations and events in the Australian, or eastern, half of the island only. The Western half, title to which is currently in dispute between the Netherlands and the Republic of Indonesia, can offer many instructive parallels; but owing to the extreme dearth of contacts and communications between east and west, Western New Guinea might almost be considered a separate island.

With the exception of its coastal fringe and the smaller islands of the Bismarck Archipelago lying to the eastward, New Guinea was known only to a handful of explorers and cartographers until well into the nineteenth century. This very failure of the region to arouse the cupidity of individuals and nations until the rest of the world had been partitioned among European powers was unquestionably an undisguised blessing. It meant that New Guinea was spared many of the destructive influences which decimated aboriginal populations in the Pacific and elsewhere—European diseases, firearms, and alcohol were never introduced in such lethal quantities as proved fatal to many other island dwellers. Nor did the rapacious whalingmen and sandalwood traders make the New Guinea region a focus of their devastating operations and recreations. The lateness of European entry into New Guinea meant also that improvements in the conventional treatment of native peoples which had taken centuries to achieve on other continents could become operative from the start when this island was at last opened to the West.

Not until the 1870s did European traders, missionaries, and planters first begin to establish permanent footholds in the islands of eastern New Guinea and thus to pave the way for colonial accession. And while these men were primarily individual entrepreneurs or representatives of private organizations in Australia and Europe—such as trading firms and mission societies—there were also in the area a few official agents of European powers who, in a casual manner, looked after the interests of the native peoples. Thus the labor-recruiting custom known as "blackbirding," which often amounted to no more than kidnapping of Pacific Islanders for plantation labor in Queensland and Fiji, was never pushed very far into the New Guinea area. And the practice was legally abolished as soon as Germany and Great Britain respectively laid their claims to the northeast and southeast sections of the great island.

During this first, pre-governmental, period in the history of modern New Guinea, a period of virtually uncontrolled free enterprise which lasted until the annexations of 1884, the Europeans permanently settled in the area were never more than a score or two in number and their contacts with natives were restricted to a relatively small circle of coastal communities in the Bismarck Archipelago. Census figures were non-existent at the time, but it would seem safe to infer that the population ratio then would be of the order of one European to one or two hundred natives. The gradual growth of the European population to its present eight to ten thousand, accompanied by the steady expansion of its influence over a broader native population base in inland New Guinea, has resulted in the persistence of this same kind of ratio. This is a fact of great significance in the relations between the two groups, as will be shown presently.

The trader, the missionary, and the planter each in his own way developed by trial and error a *modus vivendi* in this alien environment which aimed to insure successful operations vis-à-vis the native peoples. Traders were concerned only to establish a regular, short-run system of profitable barter in local products. Economic opportunism was their guiding value, and friendly intercourse was fostered only because it insured profitable trade relations. Traders' "factories" usually were located outside of native settlements where their recruited private police could prevent attack and help to control the barter system. Missionaries needed to enter into far more intimate and lasting contact with the native, for their concern to change his way of life, and even his mode of thought, demanded continuous application to the social order in the villages. They took a long-range view which was alien to the trader. Planters also took liens on the future when, with recruited native labor, they cleared and laid out their cultivated tracts of coconut palms and other crops. To them the native population provided the indispensable reservoir of cheap labor without which commercial agriculture would be an impossibility. A steady, docile labor force was therefore their chief desideratum.

The annexation of northeastern New Guinea and the Bismarcks by Germany and the Territory of Papua by Great Britain in 1884 introduced the fourth major component of European interest and intent—territorial government and white administration of native affairs. Since then the country has experienced several phases of foreign rule: under a German chartered company, German and British colonial offices, Australian military and civil administrations, and a brief period of Japanese military occupation. After the first World War the former German sector came within the League of Nations mandate system, and after the second the United Nations trusteeship agreements prevailed—both under the auspices of the Australian government. Yet despite the changing status of New Guinea in international affairs which accompanied these several historic shifts, one cannot fail to note the remarkable continuity which has obtained throughout in the handling of native affairs. The Germans, to be sure, prior to the loss of their territory in 1914, looked upon colonial administration as merely a means or adjunct to economic development of their possession. They were little concerned with problems of native welfare and desires. As one observer has stated, "a remarkable fact about German colonial administration is the conspicuous absence of slogans about the high moral purposes informing colonial policies."

The views of succeeding Australian administrations, and of some segments of the non-official population, stand in marked contrast in this matter. Sworn to honor the idealistic statements of the League mandate and the UN trusteeship agreement which advance the natives' rights and interests, Australian territorial administrations have constantly reiterated the high purposes of native welfare and development which stem from these charters. But at the same time, the brief Australian experience in colonial rule has brought into operation in New Guinea many of the Anglo-Saxon racial attitudes and values which impede if they do not negate these goals. In general, then, it may be said that while Australian officialdom has paid lip-service to this newer complex of humanitarian ideals that were never formally recognized or advanced by the Germans, their actual handling of native affairs down to World War II has been essentially a continuation of earlier colonial practices aiming to insure an unchallenged paramountcy of European status and interests. The administration has acted as a strong countervailing force toward the exploitation of native society by the other agencies of trader, planter, and missionary; and it has invested the indigenous peoples with an increasing number of specific legal rights and safeguards. But as a positive and constructive agency in the modernization of native life its accomplishments have been meager. This does not mean that the will has been lacking to help the natives learn to stand on their own feet. Rather does it reflect the financial stringency which has faced the territory—all capital development having to be paid for out of local revenues and very modest subventions from the Australian government—and reliance on European private enterprise for the economic development of the area.

It is not possible to reconstruct in all its probable shadings a full picture of the earliest native reactions to the demands of white-skinned foreigners in their land. But if the native mind of these early years remains inscrutable, some of his recorded behavior is well known. Instances of violent and murderous attack on lone Europeans and on isolated patrols and outposts have occurred in every decade, if not annually, right down to the present. Such extremes of violence represent one end of the spectrum of race relations which can never be ignored nor totally forgotten. The murder of one European by men of a single tribe or village is never regarded as an isolated case with its own unique background of causes, even though full investigation of such occurrences in recent years has shown time and again that natives have acted under what was, in their own eyes, adequate local provocation. Aware of their vast numerical inferiority, Europeans have been haunted by the spectre of what a dozen tribes or a hundred villages acting in concert might do to the entire European community. Whether real or not, this constant felt threat to their property, their physical security, and their very lives has acted as a powerful force in preserving a united European front.

Europeans in every calling—traders, labor recruiters, missionaries, and government officers—have on occasion fallen to the spears and arrows of dissident native individuals and groups. But in all of these bloody reprisals racial hatred has never loomed as a significant motivating factor. This can be seen from the fact that other New Guinea natives in the employ of Europeans have normally been fair game, too, and many of them have suffered the same fate as their masters. If there existed any mature sense of racial solidarity among the native population as a whole one would scarcely expect to find such an absence of discrimination. Aggression which has resulted in bloodshed between the two racial groups normally has arisen over differences in concepts and behavior which have not yet been linked to doctrines of race.

A less violent but far more widespread native reaction to the presence of demanding foreigners occurs in the form of chronic grumbling and verbal expressions of the desire to see the departure of all Europeans from the island. It is easy to gather evidence of such latent animosity, which runs the gamut from mild criticism to sullen obstruction—but how to interpret it is a more difficult matter. European lack of understanding of and insensitivity to native cultures and behavior has been proverbial. It required an anthropologist to point out that the Melanesian Pidgin expression for white man, *bum bum,* is literally translated "stinking wild man." The recurrent nativistic movements during the last half century, such as the Vailala madness and the more recent Cargo cult which have arisen in numerous widely separated localities in the wake of European contact, are examples of an organized yearning to speed the departure of Europeans from the land. This has been a constant theme of these relatively passive protest movements. Yet even in such manifestations one can detect an unresolved ambivalence—a nostalgic yearning for the lost freedoms of an idealized past, together with a desire to have and enjoy more of the material goods from Europe whose very possession has cost them an important part of those freedoms. Obviously, too, European administration provides a convenient scapegoat for any or all of the normal frustrations of village life; and New Guinea natives would be something less than human if they failed to vent their spleen on the government for both real and fancied wrongs.

Over against these dramatic negative reactions to the European impact, one must align the infinitely larger body of positive evidence of tolerance, accommodation, and adjustment which has been the normal situation in this land. For the most part, natives have behaved as though their relationships with Europeans were advantageous. The great majority of native communities has always been more willing than not to barter for European goods, to provide indentured labor in European enterprises, and passively to accept the imposed rule and taxation of an external governmental authority. The desire for European tools and goods was perhaps the strongest solvent to feelings of intransigent hostility; and the intelligent application of a policy of controlled gradualism in the opening of new territory has paved the way for closer union and understanding between the two groups.

Eighty years ago the widest conceivable gap—racial, linguistic, and cultural—separated the white immigrants from the native population. The racial, and to a lesser degree the linguistic schisms still remain: miscegenation has been virtually nil, and except for some thousand-odd Chinese all Asiatics who were introduced by the Germans have been repatriated by the Australians; and the indispensable trade jargon of Melanesian Pidgin, which has arisen as the major means of intercommunication in eastern New Guinea, is a volatile and makeshift speech. But the interaction and coöperation between the two groups in economic, political, and social life has produced a new cultural entity which is a unique result of the contact process. Instead of the original dual division, New Guinea society today consists of three distinct cultural strains—aboriginal, European, and a new composite variety which may be called *Kanaka* culture. Rising out of the juxtaposition and mutual adjustments of two such widely divergent groups, this new cultural product is the result of an endless series of trials and errors.

Present participants in this composite, still largely amorphous culture include the few thousand race-conscious, politically dominant Europeans on the one hand, and a million and more natives of eastern New Guinea who vary widely in their experience and acceptance of new ways of life on the other. The latter group, though indispensable in the island's agricultural, mining, and commercial economy, forms a definitely inferior caste. It is the native, for instance, who has ever borne the greater burden of adjustment; for superiority in force, techniques, and organizing ability rest exclusively in the hands of Europeans. European adjustments to the land and its people have been required, of course, but these have rarely been of so fundamental a kind as radically to alter the basic institutions and values of the white men. They appear rather as concessions or indulgences which the whites have employed in order to maintain good will and profitable relationships with native societies. The social self-sufficiency of the white men as a group is a characteristic of tropical frontiers generally.

Germs of what was to become a rigid caste system were sown in the pioneering days at the end of the nineteenth century. Differences between European and native in skin color and physique, in tools and material goods, and in traditional values established a towering wall of demarcation between them. From the very beginning the whites constituted a superior caste in their own eyes, and they quickly came to insist upon patterns of native behavior which would symbolize and magnify such status differentiation. For their part, the natives had to *learn* that their new position was universally inferior because the caste concept was rarely found to exist in aboriginal value systems here. Broadly viewed, the development of caste stratification in modern New Guinea has been one of the major structural consequences of European immigration.

The Germans, in their time, laid the foundations of the present caste structure, just as they also established methods of native administration and schemes of colonial economy which, with inevitable modifications, have persisted down to the present. To them the servile status of all natives was perfectly normal and in no wise a source of ethical doubt. They held and ruled the island at a period when modern notions of humanitarianism and self-determination of subject races were rarely heard. Far-reaching shifts in world opinion have since forced the Australians to move with greater circumspection in the field of native affairs lest adverse sentiments be aroused at home and abroad. Principles of democratic egalitarianism in colonial rule have been forcefully advanced in both the Mandate clauses and the Trusteeship agreements; and current administrative activities are more strictly judged in terms of fair play and welfare considerations than ever before. Inevitably, therefore, there must be a greater discrepancy between Australian claims and practice than ever existed in German times. The Australians pay formal homage to a more generous set of ideals, but they are forced to achieve their mundane purposes by giving with one hand what they take away with the other. Cloaked in undefined slogans and expedient rationalizations, social discrimination based on caste has become as prominent a feature of contemporary life in New Guinea as it ever was in the past.

"White prestige" is the doctrinaire device capping the caste structure in modern New Guinea; any behavior or attitude judged as tending to lower the self-ascribed status of Europeans in the eyes of natives is regarded as a peril to white supremacy. So long as European domination rested exclusively upon armed guards and European weapons, no threat to the white man's position was envisaged. But now that rights have been more liberally assigned to natives, and the use of naked force is limited to extreme emergencies, the European resorts to a complex of caste rules—taboos, proscriptions, and legal sanctions— to insure his continuing superiority. The stock conceit of the colonial who dresses for dinner each night in the heart of the bush is a manifest absurdity. Nevertheless, this caricature does symbolize a vital characteristic of Anglo-Saxon culture, namely, its extreme ethnocentrism in the presence of foreign, and especially "inferior," cultures. Few overseers, managers, and the like in New Guinea bother to change into fresh "whites" after a long day's work. They do, however, symbolize their cultural integrity and superiority in other ways that are no less apparent.

One must visit the larger centers of contact in New Guinea to see the caste system operating in its most highly developed form. It functions on out-stations, missions, and plantations also, but not with the same intensity. It is only fair to add that many Europeans of all classes in New Guinea are as free of racial prejudice and consciousness of caste as it is possible to be: missionaries and government officials are less seldom found among the ranks of upholders of white supremacy, but for this very reason they are condemned by the majority. In centers of white population—Wau, Madang, Kavieng, and Rabaul—the "native problem" as verbalized in European conversation means the problem of keeping the natives in a servile position. Any behavior of natives capable of being interpreted as overstepping caste lines is labeled "cheekiness." Individual Europeans differ widely in their interpretation of what constitutes "cheeky" conduct, but it factors down to any word, action, or demeanor which fails to connote an unquestioning respect for white prestige. Although the law wisely refrains from treating with cases of *lèse majesté,* any native who talks back to a white man or otherwise assumes an "insolent" manner in areas of long European contact is considered dangerous. At the least, he will be kept under careful surveillance in his relations with whites.

In the European towns the castes never mingle socially except by reason of their formal institutional relationships. Natives never enter white stores except on errands for their masters. When they do, they must use special entrances. There is contact, of course, between personal servants and their employers in the intimacy of white homes, but even in these close associations Europeans seldom joke with their servants or seek to cultivate any close familiarity. Addressing a native woman on the street would bring a European under suspicion of having an affair with her. It is interesting to note that patterns of white supremacy are consciously inculcated not only in European children, but even in their dogs. Dogs owned by Europeans are ordinarily trained not to tolerate natives, thus making them valuable as watchdogs to keep prowling natives away from European homes. If a dog does become friendly with natives, its owner will say, "Yes, Rover was a good pooch, until he went *kanaka*."

Always in the development of any pattern of race relations, certain codes of conduct for the subject people gradually take on an identifiable form. The "black code" of New Guinea is still in process of formulation, and, as noted above, new factors have been introduced in island life which suggest that further change rather than crystallization is yet to come. But prior to the last war the code was sufficiently integrated and well known to embrace most of the communities which had had contact with Europeans. In newly-opened areas and at governmental base camps raw natives could observe and imitate the deferential behavior of police boys and personal servants toward the white man. Bush natives who were too forward in their approach to the European might receive a warning kick or a slap in the face from the latter's servants, or they might be laughed out of countenance by the more sophisticated work boys and police.

The black code is complemented by a corresponding code of white behavior, and newcomers to the territory learn it rapidly. Some white men, aware of the complexities of the problem, may counsel caution and tolerance, but these can hardly make themselves heard above the chorus of the prejudiced majority who feel that they know all the answers. The Rabaul *Times,* a local newspaper founded in 1925, and the *Pacific Islands Monthly,* an Australian journal written for the commercial interests, in Oceania have both served as sounding boards for all shades of opinion on the "native question." Their columns throw considerable light on the nature of the white code and the pressure to conformity which it entails. In a *Times* editorial entitled "Beer, Brawls, and Prestige," we read:

There have been several boats lately in our port, and there have been several encounters in the precincts of Chinatown between various members of ships' crews, which have resulted in much gore being strewed over the cement floors, to the amusement of the native witnesses. . . . For the sake of the white man, who lives in a black man's country, such public exhibitions of the low down traits of character of such a class of whites should be eliminated. The white man's most valuable possession in this country is the prestige of the white race.

It was a most disgusting sight to see a number of men fraternizing with coloured men emanating from some [other] islands in the Pacific. . . . The whites concerned evidently did not think it beneath their dignity to personally serve them with drink, and, to cap it all, danced and sang freely with them. Heaven knows our prestige is low enough. Why are these Pacific Islanders allowed in a public bar?—because they are American subjects? The colour line must be drawn somewhere.

So the comments run. "Why cannot the nations of this world understand that for the majority of the coloured races there is only one law which the masses understand—the law of the clenched fist?" asks the *Pacific Islands Monthly.* When not criticising the natives for lack of respect, they stress the point that whites cannot expect to merit that respect unless they truly earn it. A more serious interpretation of the matter was well presented by a New Guinea planter who wrote as follows:

The only logical solution of the native problem is that, being unable to alter the type of kanaka available, improvement can only be effected by altering the type of white overseer. . . . Too often we get the white man who is ashamed to be seen caring for natives in a human way lest he be mistaken for a "missionary" or be accused of being a "kanaka man."

At the present time many undesirable types are employed to supervise labor, not necessarily bad men, often merely unsuitable men. There is, for instance, the nervous type who is often unnecessarily cruel because he is actually afraid. Believing himself to be isolated in a lonely spot amongst savages, he tries to be the "strong man," which by nature he is not.

We have also, the man who will not allow his boys to chew betelnut, or to paint themselves, or to put flowers in their hair. Or the man who cannot stand the sound of "kundus" [drums] at night. Such men are not interested in the cause or necessity for such customs. If the thing annoys them the natives must be made to give it up.

[There is also] . . . the self-indulgent overseer (unfortunately all too common) who gets drunk and neglects his labour for days at a time. Finally, there is the type of young man who cannot be bothered with natives and thinks it "infra dig" to dress a festering wound or to see that each boy gets his issue of food.

Economic factors are clearly the major source of this constant endeavor among the European community to protect and magnify its superior status. Commercial success and profitable economic development have ever been the principle reason for the Europeans being here at all: even the missions have had to operate as commercial enterprises in order to underwrite their evangelical works. And the success of every industrial venture has been predicated on the use of "cheap" labor which local males can provide. Modern systems of cost accounting raise serious doubts about just how much is saved with this cheap and inefficient labor force; but such systems are a rarity among New Guinea enterprises, and Australian immigration laws prohibit the importation of any other labor. The result of these conditions is an occupational structure consisting of European executives and managers at the top, unskilled native workers at the bottom, and an impassable gap in between. So long as the natives are restricted by law and custom to their caste occupations, are not directed toward the development of their own possibly competing enterprises, are denied technical and academic education, and are prevented from acquiring "radical notions" about their personal and social self-improvement, there can be no real threat to European dominance in the corporate life of this new society. Native advancement is therefore most strongly resisted among the commercial interests in New Guinea because of their fear that it would jeopardize their firm control of the economic structure.

Caste conflict thus stems ultimately from the innate inequalities of territorial economic life, inequalities which have persisted since the arrival of the first Europeans. But more recently this conflict has taken on a morbid sexual coloration as well which lends powerful emotional support to the prestige symbol. The growing stability of the colonial system during the inter-war years induced more and more Europeans to bring their wives and families to New Guinea, and the tendency toward balance of the European sex ratio added a new dimension to the inter-racial codes. In particular, "the alarming increase of crime by natives against European women" during the mid-'thirties caused a wave of near-hysteria in the towns and led the administration to provide "boy-proofed" sleeping rooms, enclosed by heavy chicken wire, in European house-holds where women resided. This was done in response to a series of sexual attacks by natives on white women in the larger towns. The system of native employment which concentrated large numbers of young male workers in sexually maladjusted labor lines had deprived them of their normal village life and their own sexual partners; and it is perhaps not surprising that such attacks should have occurred. But these attacks were magnified by frightened Euro-peans to the point where they were made to appear as assaults on white woman-hood in general—in fact, on the white race itself. Public opinion in the Euro-pean community was mobilized by a citizens' association to press for a more stringent native policy which would incorporate added safeguards to white prestige. The non-official majority believed that the problem of sexual aggres-sion against their womenfolk, indeed, the problem of all caste offences by natives, could only be solved by a harsher system of punishment. They felt that government officers, for example, should be granted liberal discretionary powers to flog, without trial, any native who was insolent or who gave offence. It is clear that this group, which was so largely responsible for the economic health of the territory, believed that existing laws and regulations governing native behavior were quite inadequate to enforce the caste rules exclusively in the European interest.

In World War I the Australians had supplanted the Germans with scarcely an interruption in native administration or in the economic life of the territory. But in 1942 there was a complete break in both administration and commerce while the Japanese were filling the vacuum left by the Australian retreat. The incredibly hard campaign to win back the abandoned territory exacted a heavy toll among the natives no less than among the Allied forces themselves. For the better part of two years in some areas, longer in others, most of the natives adopted a passive attitude of watchful waiting toward the change in rulers. Some "collaborated" with the Japanese, others remained "loyal"; but the ma-jority, by their behavior, seem to have preferred to sit it out.

One can only speculate on the possible effect on the native mind caused by the initial defeat of Australians by Asiatic troops. Elsewhere in the Far East, we are told, such reversals stoked the fires of anti-colonialism. But in the light of the rudimentary development of racial consciousness in the New Guinea popu-lation such effects must here have been minimal. It is certain that the harsh treatment meted out by the Japanese very quickly antagonized the New Guinea villagers who experienced their occupation and made them ready to welcome the Australians when they fought their way back. The formation of the Aus-tralian New Guinea Administrative Unit (ANGAU) within the Australian Imperial Forces was an important factor in the reconquest of native New Guinea. Organized for purposes of recruiting native labor for combat units dur-ing the fighting, bringing reconquered areas back into effective production, and administering the rewon territory, ANGAU insured some measure of continuity in administration and the re-establishment of civil order at the earliest practi-cable moment. Staffed in part by civilians and officers who had lived and worked in the territory before the war, ANGAU also helped to keep alive the spirit of caste superiority and the same kind of master-servant relationships prevailing in the inter-war years. Through personal behavior and official directives the unit strove to revert to the *status quo ante* and to hermetically seal off the natives from contact with non-colonial troops who might spread "dangerous thoughts" among them. By use of derogatory forms of address—"boy," "coon," "boong"—by the whole armory of segregational practices, and by illegal but customary forms of physical chastisement—in all of these ways did members of ANGAU hope to re-establish the prestige and unchallenged authority of European colonialism.

The war itself looms already as a kind of watershed in the development of race relations in New Guinea. The military defeat of Europeans, the loss of life and property among natives under Allied saturation bombing, the heavy conscription of natives to serve as carriers and food-providers, and the violent inflation in money wages—these were some of the conditions which accompanied an extreme crisis in the economic life and served as an impetus to a reassessment of caste relations. One of the most decisive events in this social ferment was the contact between natives and a new type of European—the Australian soldier. "The xenophobia which is normally regarded as characteristic of Australians," says Hogbin, "is bound up with the protection of living standards, and if these are not threatened there is frequently an impulse to champion the underdog." ANGAU personnel with stakes in the territory valued white prestige because it exemplified their economic dominance over the teeming native population. The average "Aussie" soldier, on the other hand, was only an unwilling visitor in the island who could approach these exotic people without stereotypes or suspicion. Whatever they made of it, this distinction between Australians of different types was not lost on the natives. Although the presence of Negro troops among the American units in New Guinea was immensely important in widening the native horizons of thought, most of the natives' direct contacts were with Australian soldiers. The glimpses of a brighter future for themselves which dance before the natives' eyes today—a future in which education, rising wages, better health, and a larger measure of control over their own destiny loom large—will probably stem in large part from their learning experience during the war years. It seems certain that the present stirrings toward greater independence, as witnessed in a plea for fair shares put to a visiting United Nations mission, have broken the spell of supine acceptance of a universally ordained inferiority.

A FRAGMENT FROM HAWAII

By Lucy G. Thurston

Kailua, October 28, 1835.

DEAR MRS. HOMES:

Sixteen eventful years have run their round since that interesting period, in which we threw a die, which can be equaled only by that which is thrown for eternity. Oft as the mind reverts to those scenes, your home and its hospitalities ever come up with vivid interest before the mind. Since that period new relations have arisen in our family; father and mother, son and daughter, brother and sister. We behold ourselves multiplied to six, a number still unbroken, either by death or separation.

A gentleman who visited us from Boston, told me that a lady from that place wished him to ascertain whether the missionaries kept *servants* in their families. She had heard so by way of a young lady who had visited the Islands, but "could hardly believe it." In our own house we have the various classes of master and mistress, of children, and of household natives. There is a native family attached to our establishment, whose home is a distinct house in our common yard. They give us their services. One man simply cultivates taro, two miles up the country, and weekly brings down a supply of the staff of life for ourselves and our dependants. Another man every week goes up the mountain to do our washing. Frequently he finds water within two miles. Often he is obliged to go five, sometimes ten miles. He likewise brings fresh water for the daily use of our family, from like distances,—brings it (over the rugged way, overspread with lava,) in large gourd shells suspended at the two ends of a strong stick, the heavy weight resting upon his shoulder. In like manner a third man brings brackish water from a distance of half a mile, to be used in household purposes. He, too, is master of the cookhouse, a thatched roof, with the bare ground for the feet, with simply stones laid up in the middle for a fire place. No chimney, no oven, no cooking stove. But there are the facilities of a baking kettle, a frying pan, a pot, and a saucepan. He, who under the old dispensation, officiated as priest to one of their gods, now, under a new dispensation with commendable humility, officiates as cook to a priest and his family. Then, aid in the care of the house, of sewing, and of baby-hood, devolves on female hands.

We commenced mission life with other ideas. Native youth resided in our families, and so far as was consistent, we granted them all the privileges of companions and of children. Not many years rolled on, and our eyes were opened to behold the moral pollution which, unchecked had here been accumulated for ages. I saw, but it was parental responsibilities which made me so emphatically *feel* the horrors of a heathen land. I had it ever in my heart, the shafts of sin flying from every direction are liable to pierce the vitals of my children. It was in these circumstances that I met with an account of the celebrated Mrs. Fry's first visiting the wretched inhabitants of a prison. The jailer, after

From Lucy Thurston, *Life and Times of Lucy G. Thurston* (Ann Arbor, Michigan: S. C. Andrews, 1882), pp. 125–131. By permission of the Executive Committee of the Hawaiian Evangelical Association. Letter to Mrs. Isabella Homes, Boston, Mass.

vainly endeavoring to dissuade her from a step so perilous, said: "At least leave your watch behind." Mrs. Fry left for a few hours her well ordered home. But had she taken her children with her, and there patiently set down to the formation of their characters, beneath the influence of prison inmates, she might have found in her path some such trials as fall to a mother's lot in the early years of a mission.

In looking at my own situation, no comparison seemed to my mind as just and vivid, as the necessity of walking unhurt, in the midst of red-hot ploughshares. Here it was, that I found myself soiled with the filth of the slough of despond. I reviewed the ground on which I stood. The heathen world were to be converted. But by what means? Are missionaries with their eyes open to the dangers of their situation, to sit conscientiously down to the labor of bringing back a revolted race to the service of Jehovah, and in so doing practically give over their own children to Satan? If children must be sacrificed, better a thousand times leave ignorant mortals to do it, than for us who know our Lord's will. In investigating this subject in the heart of a heathen land, I could see no alternative but that a mother go to work, and here form a moral atmosphere in which her children can live and move without inhaling the infection of moral death. As Jews can educate children to be Jews among Gentiles, and Roman Catholics can educate children to be Roman Catholics among Protestants, so let Christian Parents educate children to be Christians among the Heathen. Some decisive steps must be taken or the appalling vices of the heathen will become inwrought in the very texture of our children's characters. The first important measure was to prohibit them altogether the use of the Hawaiian language, thus cutting off all intercourse between them and the heathen. This, of course, led to the family regulation, that no child might speak to a native, and no native might speak to a child, babyhood excepted. This led to another arrangement, that of having separate rooms and yards for children, and separate rooms and yards for natives. The reason of this separation, and this nonintercourse was distinctly stated to household natives, and to native visitors. We are willing to come and live among you, that you may be taught the good way; but it would break our hearts to see our children rise up and be like the children of Hawaii, and they will be no better if exposed to the same influences. The heathen could see that it was such evidence of parental faithfulness and love, as was not known among them, and looked on with interest and amazement to see how it was that children could be trained to habits of obedience, a thing they never heard of. But if I wished to make trial, they would not be in the way. Indeed, they would like to see the experiment tried. I have often seen them shed tears while contrasting our children with their own degenerate offspring. When in the dining room and kitchen, attended by my children, nothing was uttered in the Hawaiian language but by way of giving or receiving directions in the most concise terms. When the hour for instruction came, and I left my children behind me, I could sit down with the same circle, and the restraint was removed. Thus they learned that in the presence of my children I was the the mother, and that when alone in their own presence, I was the companion and the teacher. Thus they were situated, attached to our household, but excluded the privileges of children. To me, it appeared no more in the light of affecting ease and style, than does the conduct of Elijah, fleeing from the anger of Ahab, to be fed twice a day by unclean birds.

I had experienced the debilitating effects of this long summer, commenced in 1820; I had felt disease so invade my frame as for years to render domestic aid essential to my very existence. During this season of adversity, far away from the comforts and aid of civilized man, far from that medical skill which visits the couch of suffering humanity to alleviate distress, and to raise from debility, my reliance was my husband. The responsible office of the physician, the tender duties of the nurse, and the menial services of the kitchen, have all been his. But how can an individual give efficiency to public labors, when from hour to hour, from day to day, from week to week, and from year to year, his attention is divided between the cook-room and the nursery. In these helpless circumstances I have been thankful for the imperfect services of natives, even though their entrance into our family caused apprehensions and mental sufferings, which have often excited reflections like this. Crucifixion is the *torture of days*. These maternal anxieties which hourly prey upon the heart, and produce so many sleepless nights, is the *anguish of years*.

But why do I dwell on conflicts, when I am allowed to sing of victory. Our two oldest children opened their eyes when thick darkness was still brooding over this polluted land. Without being left to stumble on the dark mountains, they have been borne along the tide of life, till at the age of twelve and thirteen years, they came to the same fountain for cleansing as is opened for the poor natives to wash in. So well established are their christian habits and principles, that we have, of late, allowed them free access to all our Hawaiian books, and to listen to preaching, besides to each a class of little girls, whom they every day meet for instruction under school regulations. But the restriction of non-intercourse among the natives is not removed.

Dear Mrs. Bishop, who was laid in her grave six weeks before the arrival of the reinforcement, longed exceedingly to see and give them a charge from her sick couch. The purport of it was this: "Do not be devoted to domestic duties. Trust to natives, however imperfect their services, and preserve your constitutions." I needed no such warning, for I had learned the lesson by my own sad experience, and when, after years of prostration, I was again permitted to enjoy comfortable *health,* I availed myself of the aid of natives for the accomplishment of such domestic services as they were capable of rendering. I found that the duties of the housekeeper, of the mother, of the teacher of our children, of day schools and weekly meetings, among the natives, often drew me down to the couch. For as one of our physicians told me, "You may as well talk of *perpetual motion,* as to think of performing as much labor here as you could have done by remaining in America."

I have spoken simply of our own domestic arrangement; but all our mission families are regulated much on the same plan; and were our patrons, or our husbands, now to say, "Look to New England for examples: there ladies of intelligence and refinement, holding superior stations in life, often sustain, unaided, the labors of their own families,—go thou and do likewise,"—it would be one of the most effectual means that could be taken to send the sisters of this mission either *down* to their *graves,* or *home* to *America.*

As to the effects produced upon natives thus employed in our families, they have more intelligence, more of the good things of this life, more influence among their fellows than they could otherwise possess; and numbers of them, I doubt not, will be added to that great company, which no man can number, redeemed out of every kindred, and tongue, and people, and nation.

This letter far exceeds the limits I prescribed to myself when taking the pen. But knowing that heavy oars are plied on that side of the waters for the benefit of those who are here your servants for Christ's sake, I thought good to spread before you our situation and principles of action.

Yours affectionately,

LUCY G. THURSTON

NATIVES: THOSE EXPLOITED IN THEIR OWN HOMELANDS

*

By Arnold J. Toynbee

WHEN WE WESTERNERS call people 'Natives' we implicitly take the cultural colour out of our perceptions of them. We see them as trees walking, or as wild animals infesting the country in which we happen to come across them. In fact, we see them as part of the local flora and fauna, and not as men of like passions with ourselves; and, seeing them thus as something infra-human, we feel entitled to treat them as though they did not possess ordinary human rights. They are merely natives of the lands which they occupy; and no term of occupancy can be long enough to confer any prescriptive right. Their tenure is as provisional and precarious as that of the forest trees which the Western pioneer fells or that of the big game which he shoots down. And how shall the 'civilized' Lords of Creation treat the human game, when in their own good time they come to take possession of the land which, by right of eminent domain, is indefeasibly their own? Shall they treat these 'Natives' as vermin to be exterminated, or as domesticable animals to be turned into hewers of wood and drawers of water? No other alternative need be considered, if 'niggers have no souls'. All this is implicit in the word 'Natives', as we have come to use it in the English language in our time. Evidently the word is not a scientific term but an instrument of action: an *a priori* justification for a plan of campaign. It belongs to the realm of Western practice and not of Western theory; and this explains the paradox that a classificatory-minded society has not hestitated to apply the name indiscriminately to the countrymen of a Gandhi and a Bose and a Rabindranath Tagore, as well as to 'primitives' of the lowest degree of culture, such as the Andaman Islanders and the Australian Blackfellows. For the theoretical purpose of objective description, this sweeping use of the word

Reprinted from Arnold J. Toynbee, *A Study of History* (London: Oxford University Press, 1936), I, 152–153; by permission of Oxford University Press and The Royal Institute of International Affairs.

makes sheer nonsense. For the practical purpose of asserting the claim that our Western Civilization is the only civilization in the World, the usage is a militant gesture. It signalizes the fact that all the non-Western societies which are alive in the World today, from the lowest to the highest, have been swept up into our economic net, and it postulates the contention that this common predicament is the only important fact about any of them. In short, the word 'Natives' is like a piece of smoked glass which modern Western observers hold in front of their eyes when they look abroad upon the World, in order that the gratifying spectacle of a 'Westernized' surface may not be disturbed by any perception of the native fires which are still blazing underneath.

* *

By Hannah Arendt

MANKIND REMEMBERS the history of peoples but has only legendary knowledge of prehistoric tribes. The word "race" has a precise meaning only when and where peoples are confronted with such tribes of which they have no historical record and which do not know any history of their own. Whether these represent "prehistoric man," the accidentally surviving specimens of the first forms of human life on earth, or whether they are the "posthistoric" survivors of some unknown disaster which ended a civilization we do not know. They certainly appeared rather like the survivors of one great catastrophe which might have been followed by smaller disasters until catastrophic monotony seemed to be a natural condition of human life. At any rate, races in this sense were found only in regions where nature was particularly hostile. What made them different from other human beings was not at all the color of their skin but the fact that they behaved like a part of nature, that they treated nature as their undisputed master, that they had not created a human world, a human reality, and that therefore nature had remained, in all its majesty, the only overwhelming reality—compared to which they appeared to be phantoms, unreal and ghostlike. They were, as it were, "natural" human beings who lacked the specifically human character, the specifically human reality, so that when European men massacred them they somehow were not aware that they had committed murder.

From Hannah Arendt, *The Origins of Totalitarianism* (New York: Harcourt, Brace and Company, 1951), p. 192; published in Great Britain under the title, *The Burden of Our Time*. By permission of Harcourt, Brace and Company and Martin Secker and Warburg Ltd.

SLAVERY: WHERE THE RACE PROBLEM
AND THE LABOR PROBLEM MEET

By Frank Tannenbaum

PROFESSOR WILLIAM L. WESTERMANN in a conversation with me has pointed out that when the definition of slavery was symbolized by the Negro, it spelled the death knell of slavery itself within the European cultural area. Slavery is an ancient and universal institution in human experience. It was an accepted, even if not an honored, way of life. The slave was always legally at the bottom of the scale. He had the least claims upon consideration and the fewest prerogatives among living men. But the slave's inferiority was largely legal rather than moral. Certainly that was true in the Greek city-state period and in the ancient world after the days of the Middle Stoic group and the early Christians fathers. Anyone might become a slave—the accidents of war or poverty might force even the best men into the position of belonging to another, either temporarily or permanently. It was a misfortune when it occurred. It was not an evidence of baseness, except in cases where men were made slaves as a punishment for crime. But, in any case, slavery was of a nature that was independent of race, or even of class, for a soldier belonging to the "best family" might be taken in war and enslaved.

Slavery had no identification until modern time with any one race. As a general rule in antiquity it did not involve the assumption of congenital or racial inferiority. But when, as a result of the discovery of the Western World, the people out of Africa were forced to migrate to the other side of the Atlantic by many millions, slavery and the Negro came to be synonymous. The Negro became the slave. The Indian, except under very restricted circumstances, and only for a very few years, was also a slave, but for all practical purposes the slave and the black man were identifiable in the minds of the Europeans and people of European culture.

The results of this change were unexpected. For one thing, slavery became a moral issue, something it had never been before. If only the Negro could be a slave—only the Negro and no one else—the question soon arose: why the Negro? A whole series of explanations was soon devised to justify slavery for the Negro. The justifications were numerous and many-sided, finding support in Biblical as well as presumably scientific sources. But the mere fact that slavery had to be justified left the question open to doubt. Men began to ask, why the Negro? On what grounds and for what reasons? If slavery is just, then it must include other peoples as well; otherwise it was not acceptable to the conscience of Europe, at least to the extent of fully quieting Europe's conscience on the matter. And if reasons could be adduced on one side, they could also be adduced on the other. The entire question of slavery itself as a moral institution came to be questioned and finally repudiated. As long as slavery was something that anyone might suffer, then it could be looked upon as a

From *Slave and Citizen: The Negro in the Americas* by Frank Tannenbaum, pp. 110–112. By permission of Alfred A. Knopf, Inc. Copyright, 1947 by Alfred A. Knopf, Inc.

misfortune. When it became identified solely with the Negro, then it became a matter of doubt whether any man ought to be permitted to suffer it. Interestingly enough, the Negro himself became a party to the argument and denied the imputation that he, of all people, had been selected to be the eternal pariah of the race. Educated Negroes in some countries became important in the agitation against slavery. Slavery was therefore finally abolished for the Negro, within the European frame of reference, on moral grounds, because it was unjust that any one race should be so singled out. When Negro slavery was abolished, slavery was abolished. The issue had been so stated during the agitation over Negro slavery that by implication all slavery had become unjust.

DO RACIAL DIFFERENCES ADVANCE AS CULTURAL DIFFERENCES RECEDE?

By John Gillin

THE GENERAL CHARACTER of "race" relations in Latin America is probably known well enough to readers of this *Journal* to require no extended treatment. Lord Bryce summed the matter up thirty-five years ago when he wrote: "The distinction between the races is in Spanish America a distinction of rank or class rather than color." Speaking in general of the Indians, he continued: "They are not actively hostile to the white people, and, indeed, get on better with their landlords than some European peasantries have done with theirs. But they live apart, inside the nation, but not of it." It is the contact between "races" without conflict which I wish to discuss in this paper, taking as the point of departure field studies made in one community in Guatemala by my associates and me.

The community to which I refer is San Luis Jilotepeque in the Department of Jalapa, eastern Guatemala. . . . San Luis is a town of between three thousand and thirty-five hundred population and the center of a township with a total population of about seventy-five hundred. About one-third of the population is *ladino;* the remainder are Indians of the Pokomám branch of the Maya stock. . . . With respect to western Guatemala, Redfield reports a situation somewhat like that of San Luis. "Neither Indians nor *ladinos* [these rural agricultural *ladinos*] express fear, hatred or contempt of the other," he says, and there is no open conflict between the two social categories. In San Luis there is likewise no overt conflict, but, as we shall see, there is a good deal of "contempt" expressed by *ladinos* for the Indians and a constant use of symbols calculated to bolster the idea of *ladino* social "superiority."

From John Gillin, " 'Race' Relations Without Conflict: A Guatemalan Town," *The American Journal of Sociology*, LIII (March, 1948), 337–343.

The Indians and *ladinos* in San Luis are distinct social categories and even practice distinct culture side by side. The *ladinos* are in the minority yet maintain a superordinate social position. In order that this situation be maintained, two things are primarily necessary. In the first place, the groups must be distinguishable one from the other, and the differences must be fairly obvious. This is accomplished mainly by the use of certain symbols. Second, the superordination of one group over the other must involve an unequal distribution of privileges in favor of the upper group. This means that there must be an agreement between the two groups on the value or desirability of certain goals but that access to and achievement of these goals are rendered easier to members of one group than to those of the other. Let us examine briefly the ways in which these requirements are met.

First is the matter of mantaining social distinctiveness between the two groups. Although there are a few blond *ladinos,* many of the upper caste are dark and scarcely distinguishable from recognized Indians by hereditary features alone. Thus hereditary traits are not reliable as caste symbols. Furthermore, residential segregation is not found, as it is in North America, as a device for keeping the social categories separate. Although the *ladino* houses tend to cluster about the plaza and the Indian dwellings are more numerous toward the outskirts of the town, there is no absolute rule regulating residence. Except on the plaza itself, the houses of the two groups are sprinkled more or less indiscriminately throughout the town. The fact that *ladinos* often occupy more desirable sites (such as street corners) is due to the fact that they have more money and are economically more able to acquire these sites than are the Indians.

The following are the principal symbols of distinction. First, a caste relationship is maintained in that, although sexual exploitation of Indian women by *ladino* men is permitted clandestinely, socially recognized marriage between the two groups is prohibited. Informal unions do occur, however. One of our informants was an Indian man who was living with a *ladina* woman. Their two children were taken to be reared by the mother's family after the man's death and are considered *ladinos.* Several other *ladinos* are known to have had one Indian parent. The offspring of such unions are known as *cruzados* ("crossed"). It is a social dictum that *cruzados* may be *ladinos* but that "pure Indians" may not be so considered. However, this is not strictly followed in practice, although it is true that an uncrossed Indian stands a better chance of being accepted as a *ladino* if he moves to another community. In the second place, the Indians wear a special costume. The dress of Indian women is radically different from that of the *ladina* women and consists of a picturesque wrap-around skirt of cloth woven by Indians in the west, and embroidered blouse, many strings of bright beads, and a flowing cloth head shawl. Indian women always go barefoot and when working about their houses, along the river, or in the fields are often unclothed above the waist, a custom never practiced by *ladina* women. Indian men wear for work the typical Spanish-American peon costume, consisting of short-tailed white shirt and loose white trousers hanging slightly below the knee. *Ladino* men never wear these garments. For dress occasions, however, Indian men wear garments of modern European design. On such occasions the caste symbol is the fact that they never wear shoes; they are either barefoot or, more often, shod in sandals. On dress occasions *ladino* men always wear shoes, even though they have no socks. Likewise Indians never wear neckties, although *ladinos* usually do on festive occasions. Moreover, Indians are bilingual, whereas *ladinos* speak only Spanish.

Values in the two cultures differ in many respects, but it is true that both Indians and *ladinos* agree that the following goals are desirable: money, ownership of land, political power, and social prestige of certain types. *Ladinos* get more of all these things.

The Indians have been thoroughly conditioned to the instrumental value of money and have developed wants which can be satisfied only with money—manufactured articles like clothing, beads, knives, containers, etc.; religious sacraments and fiestas involving services of an ordained priest; land and cattle. The *ladinos,* however, have monopolized most of the business, other than trading in the semiweekly markets, and the *ladinos* control the price of labor which, in 1942, was ten cents per day and, in 1946, thirty cents per day. A few Indians have managed to accumulate wealth; one is a fairly large landowner and another a successful trader, who operates, however, in other towns. The obstacles to accumulating wealth are considerably greater for the Indians, and it is the exceptional Indian who is able to accumulate more than small amounts of money. In 1942 in a sample of sixteen Indian families, the average cash expenditure per year was a little over twenty-five dollars.

Both Indians and *ladinos* are passionately interested in owning or controlling land, but for somewhat different reasons. To the *ladino* land is a source of income which one may enjoy without labor. To the Indian land is a mystical as well as an economic source of security, which one tends lovingly with his own hands. This is not a region of large haciendas, but the *ladinos* have monopolized about 70 per cent of the useful land. These tracts are organized into relatively moderate-sized holdings called *fincas;* the manual labor is done by *peones,* usually Indians. At present, it is almost impossible for the Indian group to increase its holdings by purchase. . . .

Customs favoring the *ladinos* have been traditionally enforced. For example, a *ladino* may drop into an Indian house and be served a meal with the family. This is supposed to be an "honor" for the Indians. But a *ladino* would not consider inviting an Indian to his table for a meal. Indians are supposed to enter *ladino* houses only by the back door and after receiving permission. Indians are expected to tip their hats, to get off the sidewalk into the street, and to use the word "Señor" when meeting *ladinos*—forms of etiquette which are not reciprocated by the *ladinos*. I have never heard a *ladino* address an Indian as "Señor" except in satirical manner, although a respected Indian man will be called "Don," a more familiar form of respectful address.

There are various types of amusements which are exclusively reserved for *ladinos,* more or less on the basis of prestige. Indians are not permitted inside the two local pool parlors, although they may watch the play through the windows. There is a basketball court on one side of the plaza, but even small children are forcibly expelled from it if they are Indians. The "lower" race is not invited to social functions, such as dances, amateur theatricals, and drinking parties given by the *ladinos,* although the *ladinos* come uninvited to the social affairs of the Indians, and their presence is supposed to be an honor calling for special deference on the part of the hosts.

This situation is obviously "unfair" to the Indian majority of the population. Yet up to the present only one violent reaction by the lower race has been recorded. This developed during the revolution of 1944, when the dictator Ubico was overthrown. A mob of Indians armed with machetes attacked a *ladino* druggist, who was also a landowner, former mayor, and a representative of the "conservative" faction among the *ladinos*. This demonstration, however, was inspired by a *ladino* politician of the opposite faction, who stimulated his Indian followers with liquor. Yet that such a demonstration occurred at all indicates that sentiments of aggression exist in the Indian, even though excitement and liquor are required to bring them out.

The fact is, however, that the Indians of San Luis are not seething with smoldering resentment. Few symptoms of suppressed aggression are to be found. Even in 1946, when alcoholic liquor was more freely obtainable than formerly, I never saw an Indian grow aggressive toward *ladinos* while under its influence. In the great periodic Indian fiestas aggression is noticeably absent; Dionysiac release of any sort is practically unknown. Rorschach tests on thirty Indians showed aggression in only 6.7 per cent, although 30 per cent of the thirty *ladinos* tested showed signs of a small degree of aggression. Our conclusion at present is that the Indian group does not *feel* excessively frustrated. How is this to be explained?

The easy "explanation" is to say that the Indians have become "accustomed" to the situation. But to say that a situation is the result of custom is not to explain it. The total system of customs must, in principle, afford satisfactions which are not immediately apparent, if latent and active aggressiveness is absent.

The dominant position of the *ladinos* and the presence of certain customs which support their superior status undoubtedly date back to the colonial era and were probably established and maintained for a long time by force, either actual or threatened. This is the method of conquerors everywhere. Force alone, however, has never been known to stabilize a situation of this kind over the centuries.

The answer for the time being seems to be that the lower group—the Indians—have developed and maintained a fairly satisfying culture of their own and that the *ladino* pressure is not felt to be onerous or unendurable. In the first place, the Indians here are actually and theoretically free. Possibly due to the absence of a developed hacienda system, there are few Indian families bound to the land of any *ladino* master. It may be argued that the majority of Indians are held in virtual economic thrall in one way or other by the *ladinos,* but this thralldom is neither obvious nor uncomfortable. The average Indian is a free agent, even though he may have to rent a milpa on shares from a *ladino* or work for wages, either of which arrangement may be to the advantage of the *ladino*. If trouble and poverty come, however, the situation is so phrased by the Indians that the primary blame is not placed on the *ladinos,* either as a class or as individuals. If one is poor and unfortunate, according to statements in the great majority of confidential and informal interviews, it is because the individual or the community has failed to follow the word of God, or has been lazy or negligent, or, occasionally, because of "conditions" blamed on the central government. Among the latter is the present high valuation of the currency as compared with that of pre-Ubico times. This is regarded as due to something done by the government in Guatemala City, but it is not blamed on the local *ladinos* of San Luis, who, indeed, have nothing to do with it.

A second circumstance of perhaps as great importance is the fact that the Indians have maintained a culture of their own distinct from but parallel to that of the *ladinos*. The persistence in function of the separate, rather independent Indian culture has had an important bearing upon the mitigation of so-called race tensions.

The Indian culture in San Luis is not, of course, a purely aboriginal one; it has incorporated many elements originally derived from the European tradition. But it is distinct from the culture of the *ladinos*. This is particularly important in respect to many of its mental patterns, that is, cultural patterns of value and attitude. The local *ladinos* affect to deprecate many of the Indian customs, but on the whole they do not interfere with them. It is implicitly held that the Indians have a right to their own customs, strange or barbarous as they may be from the point of view of the "enlightened" *ladinos*. In short, there is a mutual tolerance of each other's mode of life by the two groups, at least up to a certain point.

Now every culture, if it persists, is a mechanism for providing certain satisfactions for the people. They are, of course, connected with the drives, wants, or desires of the group which practices the culture. Many such desires or wants—of the type called "secondary drives"—are generated in the members of the group or category through the operation of the culture itself. If there is one thing we know about culture it is that, once the universal species needs are satisfied by the operation of a system of custom, it does not matter very much what the other wants are, so long as the culture tends to satisfy them. In such a case the people will be to a degree contented, other things being equal.

The Indian culture of San Luis provides a number of satisfactions quite independently of the *ladinos*. In some respects it would seem to be more satisfying to be an Indian than a *ladino*. Social security and a sense of belonging are provided by the Pokomám kinship system. This is a partially classificatory system which connects the individual with a large and ramifying group of kinsmen by reciprocal rights and duties. The Spanish system of the *ladinos* is neither so extensive nor so tightly knit in terms of behavior patterns. Religion is deeper-seated and more meaningful in the everyday life of the Indians than of the *ladinos*. To be sure, both groups are nominally Catholic. But the Indian religion contains this and something more. Rain-making ceremonies, planting and harvest ceremonies, apparently incorporating certain aboriginal elements, are practiced exclusively by the Indians. The cult of the saints is in their hands. The only significant *cofradías* or laymen's clubs are Indian. A great variety of superstitions and beliefs regarding nature, the weather, personal health, and destiny are part of the Indian culture. Although this system of beliefs may not be "enlightened" in the estimation of the *ladinos,* it does give an orderliness to the Indian Weltanschauung; and the customs connected with the beliefs provide cultural means for reducing anxieties and worries. The Indian system of magical curing, for example, may not prevent death, but it at least permits the patient to die in peace of mind.

Ladino prestige is largely measured in terms of money and wealth and things which money will buy; Indian prestige is gained by character, experience, and wisdom. These qualities cannot be bought. The few men of wealth in the

Indian group are not the most respected. Prestige does not come by externals which can be added to the core of the self. . . .

In the Indian culture work on the land is honorable. In fact, a man who has no land, either rented or owned, which he can work with his own hands feels himself somewhat less than a man. During the agricultural season scarcely any reward will induce an Indian to leave his milpa, but a *ladino* considers such work degrading. Furthermore, the Indians have preserved a number of handicrafts. These perhaps are not so much practiced for the inherent satisfaction they provide, as in the case of agriculture, as for the cash which they produce. Yet pride of workmanship attaches to such work, whereas there is almost no customary activity of this sort to give satisfaction to a *ladino*. Indian men plait straw hats, net bags, and fishnets; they make grinding-stones and waterfilters. Indian women make beautiful red-and-black water jars which their husbands peddle in distant towns. As a result of all these activities, boredom and idle time are practically unknown among the Indians. whereas they are a major problem among the *ladinos*.

In a word, then, Indian patterns provide satisfactions which tend to blot out the frustrations inherent in the situation. Also they require an output of energy which might otherwise be diverted to aggressive activity.

It goes without saying that a situation of this sort can and probably will, in the course of time, be changed. If the Indians should become literate and acquainted with the materialistic goals of the average man in modern Western civilization, it seems inevitable that they will develop a sense of frustration and dissatisfaction. However, individuals who wish to make the effort can move away from San Luis and become accepted as *ladinos* in some other community.

The mode of life of the *ladinos* is essentially that of Western man in general, in a rustic and rather poverty-stricken form. They are aware of the alleged delights of the great world beyond San Luis, but they lack the means to gratify the wants stimulated by reading about them in the illustrated magazines. Most of the *ladinos* are vaguely discontented and bored. Their continual plaint is that life is so *triste,* by which they mean that it is so uninteresting and unexciting. If a leader or a movement should arise which succeeded in convincing the *ladinos* that the cause of their discontent was the Indians, one could foresee conflict.

In summary, San Luis Jilotepeque provides one example of racial adjustment as we find it in Latin America. How general this situation may be it is impossible to say at present for lack of sufficient studies. At any rate, we see a stabilized situation in San Luis in which the so-called "races" or "castes" live side by side without conflict. The situation is frankly without "racial problems" as they are usually described either in terms of physical anthropology or in terms of sociology. Problems of social and cultural adjustment of course exist, but they do not revolve about the mutual relations of the two major elements of the population. As in Latin America generally we see that the two alleged races are not radically distinguished by physical features and that the definition of status is phrased primarily in cultural rather than biological terms. Although the *ladinos* or mestizos claim and obtain superior rewards in money, land-ownership, political power, and certain aspects of social prestige and etiquette, their activities are not injurious to the satisfaction of the basic animal drives of the Indians. The *ladinos* do not as a rule inflict pain, starvation, and other forms

of severe punishment upon the Indians. Likewise each group tolerates the culture of the other. Thus aggression and frustration are in large measure avoided,
and satisfactions are provided for wants as created and defined by the two cultures. A certain stability and amiability are achieved without strict segregation
and in the presence of a good deal of miscegenation.

It should be made clear that the "solution" of the "race" problem fortuitously and perhaps temporarily achieved in a place like San Luis is not one which
can be applied under present conditions in the United States. In the first place,
social segregation is not an essential part of the Latin-American pattern. "Jim
Crow" is unknown to most mestizos; there is no segregation in stores, in residential districts, and in buses. Segregation in jobs, recreational privileges,
and economic opportunity is of course practiced. However, it seems to me
that the important thing in Latin America is that mestizos and Indians are
segregated *culturally* rather than *physically*. In North America, on the other
hand, the segregation is *physical* rather than *cultural*. That is to say that, among
ourselves, members of the colored groups share with the whites the same
cultural patterns, which also means the same culturally induced wants, desires,
and goals, but are physically excluded from participation with the whites. In
both instances a "problem" is present. The solution in each case may be accelerated by an understanding of the variety of forms which such "problems"
may take.

THE ROLE OF THE PORTUGUESE AS A
CATALYTIC AGENT IN RACE
RELATIONS

*

By Sir Hugh Wyndham

PORTUGAL WAS WELL SITUATED to be the pioneer of the impact of
Europe on Africa. Her ships on leaving port sailed into more generally favorable
conditions of wind and of current than did those of her more northerly neigh-
bours. She officially divided the new world with Spain, and the west coast of
Africa and Brazil fell to her lot. She was able, therefore, to establish a self-
contained imperial Atlantic system based on a circular route. Her caravels
after leaving Lisbon could load cargoes of slaves in Africa, being helped on
their course by the Guinea current. The South-East trade winds and the South-

Reprinted from Sir Hugh Wyndham, *The Atlantic and Slavery* (London: Oxford University
Press, 1935), pp. 8–14; by permission of Oxford University Press and The Royal Institute of
International Affairs.

East Equatorial Current took them across to Brazil, where they delivered their slaves, and then returned home loaded with Brazilian products. Her position was further strengthened by her island possessions on the west coast being convenient bases for her operations on the mainland. Madeira was a settlement colony assimilated both culturally and politically to the mother-country. The Cape Verde islands formed a slave-labour colony whose government was more military and, therefore, more suited to be the supporter of Portuguese influence in Nigritia; and the inhabitants were granted the privilege of trading direct with it without having to apply to Lisbon for licences. The island of San Thome was also a slave-labour colony with a military governor. It was the base for the great proselytizing, trading, and civilizing adventure in the kingdom of Kongo; until experience proved it to be inadequate for the purpose and Loanda took its place. It was also the centre of the Portuguese slave-trade on the Slave Coast, which began early in the sixteenth century. Elmina, their fortress on the Gold Coast, at first exported only gold; and after it had been captured by the Dutch the importance of San Thome became all the greater.

Portugal had more than a century to complete these arrangements before competition on the west coast became acute, and before her absorption by Spain attracted the full force of Protestantism against her. But her most potent weapon for establishing herself was not her command of the sea, nor her fortresses. It was rather her peculiar methods of assimilation, by which whenever any individual adopted a standard of civilization, which was neither inconveniently high nor exclusive, he was accepted into the European fold and enjoyed equal opportunities of advancement. Miscegenation, which was the rule, and which was not always illegitimate, worked to the same end. Mulattoes frequently rose to high positions. They were decorated with the Order of Christ. They commanded Portuguese ships. They became interpreters and advisors to native chiefs and to resident Europeans. They generally claimed to be Christians, although many of them were unbaptized. From them were recruited most of the priests and the itinerant missionaries, some of whom rose to be dignitories of the Church, who evolved and fostered a Christianity which was distinctively African-Colonial. They became brokers, middlemen, and merchants, at times handling considerable capital, and securing so firm a hold over the trade of a place that their co-operation was essential in any transaction. Portuguese became the lingua franca of commerce, and no merchant could compete who was ignorant of it.

The process of building up this tradition began when Portuguese settled along the coast of Nigritia, between Cape Verde and Sierra Leone, which soon became impregnated with it. The individuals upholding it might be white or Mulatto, or as black as any Native; they might even be domestic slaves, but they formed a separate extra-tribal element in the communities in which they lived. Their pride of acquired position and race protected them from absorption, and they maintained their traditions for generations even where the infusion of fresh Portuguese blood from Europe ceased.

Their descendants on the Gambia, in the seventeenth century, after it had fallen under the dominance of England and of France, are examples. They lived together in little groups, employing themselves in trade, and clinging with 'a kind of affectionate zeal' to the Portuguese language, and to their claim to be Christians. They took it in great disdain 'be they never so black' to be called

Negroes, and carefully maintained the use of the Portuguese language. In the next century their position remained unchanged. A Mulatto priest from the Cape Verde Islands visited them annually, christened and married the accumulations of the previous twelve months, and said Mass in a small church at Tancrowell. They reckoned themselves to be whites because they were Christians, and most remarkable of all, made some pretence of observing the canons of Christian continence.

They were equally prominent in the eighteenth century. 'The only brisk trader on the Gambia' in 1730 was Senhór Valentine Menendes, a Portuguese with whom the Royal African Company of England was happy to make a contract for the supply of slaves at fifteen bars a head. Senhór Antonio Vos was almost as formidable, but was less punctual in his payment. There was general complaint on this score. The Portuguese were 'difficult to manage', being ready borrowers, and 'but indifferent paymasters'; and the Company was obliged to warn its agents against giving them credit. And yet their co-operation in trade was essential; and to antagonize them was fatal. Captain Dear found this out to his cost in 1730. He had so mean an opinion of Portuguese in general, and of Black Portuguese in particular, that he could not forbear letting them know what he thought of them. He was sent to Cacheu on a trading voyage, with Simon Menendes as his supercargo. He treated him no better than the rest. He refused to allow him to have anything to do with the trading; and the venture was in consequence a complete failure, much to the disquiet of the English agents on the Gambia, who were afraid it would alienate Valentine Menendes.

After losing control of the Gambia the Portuguese Government concentrated on the Cacheu and Geba rivers, and established the present-day Portuguese Guinea. They erected a fort at Cacheu, and another at Farim a hundred leagues inland. They did the same on the Geba, and thereby secured control over the neighbouring country and, according to Barbot, avoided having to pay rents to the native chiefs. They did not, however, depend for their defence mainly on the military prowess of their garrisons, which, being composed of deported criminals who subsisted mainly on robbery, were a menace only to those whom they were supposed to protect. They established themselves in their usual way. At the end of the seventeenth century Cacheu contained about three hundred houses, which were mostly inhabited by Mulattoes. Their parish church was served by a curate, and by an occasional visitor from the Bishop of Santiago. They 'traded where they listed', and penetrating overland to the Gambia outflanked the monopoly of its exports to which the English and the French aspired.

A still more remarkable, albeit somewhat apocryphal, example of the potency of the Portuguese tradition is the history of the village of Guianala on the north bank of the Rio Grande. During the seventeenth century its native inhabitants were reputed to be of Portuguese extraction, but as having renounced Christianity and civilization, and as having reverted to barbarism. In the meantime the French had turned their attention to the island of Bissao, and had traded with its Natives. André Brue went there in 1700, and obtained permission to open a factory. He also landed on the island of Bulama and explored it. Alarmed by these activities the Portuguese re-established themselves at Guinala. At once the place regained its former reputation, and was reported to be 'inhabited only by Portuguese who had been there from father to son for a long time'. The same phrase, but now dated 1778, was quoted by President Grant in his award of the island of Bulama to Portugal in 1870 as against the treaties by which the British Bulama Association claimed to have acquired it in 1792. The President regarded the historical continuity of the Portuguese tradition as the decisive factor.

The position at Sierra Leone and at Sherboro was the same as on the Gambia. The co-operation of White, Mulatto, and Black Portuguese was essential to successful trading, although larger profits could be made by dealing direct with the Natives. In the hope of undermining their influence the Agent of the Royal African Company at Sierra Leone suggested, in 1679, that forty or fifty Barbadoes Negroes, who could speak nothing but English, should be imported. With their assistance, he declared, 'we should be more formidable than all the Portuguese in the country'.

This Portuguese penetration stretched as far south as the limits of discovery during the lifetime of Prince Henry the Navigator. After his death Alfonso V farmed out the Guinea trade to Fernando Gomez for an annual rent of 500 ducats, on condition that he extended the discovery of the coast by 500 leagues. He fulfilled his contract, but his methods had not the assimilative effects which were apparent further north. On the contrary, he laid the foundations of a permanently more hostile and suspicious attitude on the part of the Natives, particularly of the Ivory Coast, who had not the natural aptitude for trade which others had, and whose memories of kidnapping atrocities were inconveniently retentive. He did not establish nurseries for the production of Portuguese Africans. The aridity of the coast, the Guinea current, and the prevailing wind, were hindrances to easy marine intercourse. Moreover, his ships were poorly equipped, and his crews meanly attired. They approached trading places with scant ceremony, and pressed to complete their lading in order to get back to Portugal as soon as possible.

The old policy was revived, however, by John II establishing a settlement on the Gold Coast. The site chosen for it was under the jurisdiction of a chief named Karamansa whose relations with the Portuguese had been friendly. He had made a commercial treaty with Fernando Gomez for whose vessels he had always done his best to secure a quick lading, and whom he permitted to open a gold-mine in the neighbourhood. He deprecated a departure from these old and tried methods of intercourse, and suspected that more intimate relations might lead to a lessening of friendship. Eventually he was persuaded to give his consent, in consideration of an annual payment or rent for the ground on which the fort was erected. The 'Note' which embodied this arrangement, afterwards got into the hands of the Denkeras and then into the possession of the Ashantis, and was looked upon as the title-deed proving its possessor to be the landlord of the occupiers of Elmina. The fort was the first to be erected by the Portuguese south of Goree. But in addition to a fortress a civilian community surrounding and dependent upon it to serve as an island of Portuguese influence was essential. It was soon developed. The Elminas became a community of Natives living apart from their original tribal relationships, and under European control and protection. They fought for the Portuguese, defeating the first Dutch attack in 1625. Their town was endowed with the privileges and immunities of a European city. Its Governor was appointed triennially by the King of Portugal. Its native citizens evolved a political organization of their own which survived into the nineteenth century. They were at first divided into three companies each under a chief, who was directly responsible to the Governor. Later on this elementary constitution assumed a more democratic form and each district was governed by a 'Brasso', an 'Assistant Caboceer' (adapted from the Portuguese and meaning Headman or Chief) and other inferior officers, all of whom, meeting together in each Brasso's house alternately, formed 'the regency of this little republic', which was responsible for the government of the native town and for the administration of its justice, subject, of course, to the veto of the Governor, which was rarely exercised.

Naturally, Mulatto families soon became prominent. Like their brethren of Nigritia, they claimed to be Christians with no greater visible justification than answering, fairly pertinently, questions relating to the Faith. They emphasized the extra-tribalism of the inhabitants, who earned the reputation of being the most civilized on the Gold Coast owing to their long relationship with Europeans. They clung pertinaciously to their political privileges, as the Dutch afterwards discovered.

The difference between their position and that of the coast communities in Nigritia, outside Portuguese Guinea, was that it was extraterritorial as well as being extra-tribal. They had their own system of justice, and their own government, whereas the Portuguese in Nigritia outside Portuguese Guinea had neither. Although socially distinct, they were in Nigritia juridically subject to the local chiefs to whom they paid dues and taxes, by whose 'safe-conduct and permission' they traded, and who seized their property when they died, reducing their children to destitution. The Elminas suffered from none of these indignities. On the other hand, the ground on which Elmina stood was leased. The title of the Portuguese to it was therefore weaker than was their tenure in Portuguese Guinea, where they freed themselves of their obligation to pay rent.

* *

By The Rev. R. Walsh

IN THE EVENING we arrived at Confisco, where we proposed to stop for the night, as the rain, with its usual accompaniments, had set in very violently.

This place, which is a solitary mansion in the wilderness, consisted of a long edifice, having a venda, with a quarto attached, and at some distance a large rancho. It is situated on a small plain, under the ridge of a wooded hill, with a grass lawn, skirted with thicket in front, and a clear broad stream, tumbling over a pebbled bed, bounding it on one side. The house, which was neatly kept, had a broad portico, supported on rustic pillars; and the whole, though wild and solitary, was exceedingly romantic and pretty. My host was a white

From the Rev. R. Walsh, *Notices of Brazil in 1828 and 1829* (London: Frederick Westley and A. H. Davis, 1830), II, 242–244.

Brazilian, more pleasing in his aspect and manners than most others I had met with. He showed me into a comfortable quarto, newly plastered with white clay, with beds and mats of green bamboo, which were fresh and fragant, and formed a strong contrast with the mouldering filth I had left. When supper was ready, he took me kindly and courteously by the hand, to an apartment where it was laid out on a clean cloth, and well and neatly dressed, a stewed fowl with pão de trigo, accompanied by green vegetables—a species of brassica which he cultivated.

When I had finished, he invited me to his porch, where he brought me some excellent coffee, and set a mulatto of his establishment on an opposite bench, to play on the guitar for my amusement. He then called forth and introduced me to his whole family. This consisted of two mothers, a black and a white, and twelve children, of all sizes, sexes, and colours; some with woolly hair and dusky faces, some with sallow skins and long black tresses. In a short time, they made up a ball, and began to dance. It was opened by the youngest, Luzia, a child about four years old, with dark eyes, and coal-black hair. She was presently joined by a little black sister, and they commenced with a movement, resembling a Spanish bollero, imitating admirably well the castanets with their fingers and thumbs. The movement of the dance was not very delicate; and the children, when they began, showed a certain timidity and innate consciousness that they were exhibiting before a stranger, what was not proper; but by degrees they were joined in succession by all the children, boys and girls, up to the age of seventeen and eighteen, and finally by the two mothers of the progeny. I never saw such a scene. It was realizing what I had heard of the state of families in the midst of woods, shut out from intercourse with all other society, and forming promiscuous connexions with one another, as if they were in an early age of the world, and had no other human beings to attach themselves to. I had personally known some, and I had heard of others, brothers and sisters, who without scruple or sense of shame, lived together, supporting in other respects the decencies of life; but here it was carried beyond what I could have supposed possible, and this precocious family displayed among themselves dances, resembling what we have heard of the Otaheitan Timordee. I soon retired, but the sound of the guitar continued a long time after.

THE PROTESTANT BACKGROUND OF
MODERN WESTERN RACE
FEELING

*

By Arnold J. Toynbee

IN OUR WESTERN HISTORY, the Protestant movement started immediately before the movement of overseas settlement; and, in the eighteenth century of our era, the competition between the peoples of Western Europe for the command of the overseas world ended in the victory of the English-speaking Protestants, who secured for themselves the lion's share of those overseas countries, inhabited by primitive peoples, that were suitable for settlement by Europeans, as well as the lion's share of the countries inhabited by adherents of the living non-Western civilizations who were incapable at the time of resisting Western conquest and domination. The outcome of the Seven Years' War decided that the whole of North America, from the Arctic Circle to the Rio Grande, should be populated by new nations of European origin whose cultural background was the Western Civilization in its English Protestant version, and that a Government instituted by English Protestants and informed with their ideas should become paramount over the whole of Continental India. Thus the race-feeling engendered by the English Protestant version of our Western culture became the determining factor in the development of race-feeling in our Western Society as a whole.

This has been a misfortune for Mankind, for the Protestant temper and attitude and conduct in regard to Race, as in many other vital issues, is inspired largely by the Old Testament; and in matters of Race the promptings of this old-fashioned Syriac oracle are very clear and very savage. The 'Bible Christian' of European origin and race who has settled among peoples of non-European race overseas has inevitably identified himself with Israel obeying the will of Jehovah and doing the Lord's work by taking possession of the Promised Land, while he has identified the non-Europeans who have crossed his path with the Canaanites whom the Lord has delivered into the hand of his Chosen People to be destroyed or subjugated. Under this inspiration, the English-speaking Protestant settlers in the New World exterminated the North American Indian, as well as the bison, from coast to coast of the Continent, whereas the Spanish Catholics only exterminated the Indian in the Caribbean Islands and were content, on the Continent, to step into the shoes of the Aztecs and the Incas—sparing the conquered in order to rule them as subject populations, converting their subjects to their own religion, and inter-breeding with their converts.

Again, the English Protestants took up the trade in negro slaves from Africa to the New World and afterwards obtained the monopoly of this trade

Reprinted from Arnold J. Toynbee, *A Study of History* (London: Oxford University Press, 1936), I, 211–216; by permission of Oxford University Press and The Royal Institute of International Affairs.

as one of the perquisites in the Peace Settlement at Utrecht (A.D. 1713). The Spanish and Portuguese Catholic settlers bought the human merchandise which the Protestant slave-traders offered them; but the Spanish and Portuguese Empires and the 'successor-states' which eventually took their place as independent states members of the Western Society were not the fields in which the institution of plantation slavery, which had thus been introduced into the New World, struck deepest root and grew to the most formidable proportions. The stage on which the tragedy of negro slavery in the New World was played out on the grand scale was an English-speaking Protestant country: the United States.

Finally, in Continental India, where the English could not think of supplanting the conquered 'natives' as they had supplanted them in North America, but could only impose their rule on them as the Spaniards had imposed theirs on the 'Natives' of Mexico and Peru, the sequel was not the same as it had been in the Spanish Indies. In British India, unlike Spanish America, only a negligible number of the 'Natives' were converted to the religion of the ruling race or were physically assimilated to it by interbreeding. For good or evil, the English Protestant rulers of India have distinguished themselves from all other contemporary Western rulers over non-Western peoples by the rigidity with which they have held aloof from their subjects. They took to the Hindu institution of caste as readily as if they had not found it established in India when they came but had invented it for their own convenience.

Of course the fanaticism and ferocity of the race-feeling which the Old Testament once instilled into Protestant souls have both considerably abated as Protestantism itself has evolved through Rationalism towards Agnosticism. First the traffic in negro slaves, and finally the very institution of negro slavery in the New World, have been abolished by the English-speaking peoples themselves under the promptings of their own consciences and at the price of their own blood and treasure; and the attitude of the Englishman in India towards the people of India is no longer the attitude of unmitigated aloofness and superiority that it used to be. The improvement in feeling and conduct has certainly been very great. Yet even now this improvement is only partial and is still precarious.

The slavery once imposed nakedly on uprooted and transplanted Black Men by immigrant White Men of English speech and Protestant faith in the New World will be imposed under camouflage, in our generation, on other Black Men in the homeland of the Black Race by the Dutch and English settlers in South and East Africa, if these settlers once obtain a free hand to deal with the native African peoples at their discretion; and this revival of negro slavery— this time on the negro's native continent—will not be the less pernicious for being hypocritically disguised. The battle over negro slavery, which was fought out in the NewWorld during the century ending with the end of the American Civil War, may have to be fought out in Africa once again; and even if Light discomfits Darkness for the second time, the sequel to the American battle over this issue shows how hard it is for the Light to drive the Darkness altogether off the field. In the United States, where negro slavery has been abolished at so great a cost, race-feeling remains to perpetuate the social evils of racial inequality and racial segregation. We can foresee that in Africa, too, the sequel, at the best, will be the same. The young communities of English-speaking White people in the United States and in the Union of South Africa and in Kenya Colony, upon whose future the more distant prospects of our 'Anglo-Saxon' version of Western culture very largely depend, are already in the grip of the paralysing institution of Caste.

Meanwhile, the successive phases of Protestant race-feeling have left their mark on our Western thought in the form of various race-theories, as a slowly dying volcano leaves a record of successive eruptions in the petrified streams of lava that permanently disfigure its flanks.

Among English-speaking Protestants there are still to be found some 'Fundamentalists' who believe themselves to be 'the Chosen People' in the literal sense of the term as it is used in the Old Testament. This 'British Israel' confidently traces its physical descent from the lost Ten Tribes. We may leave it to dispute its claim to the title with the rival claimants, the most redoubtable of whom are the Afghans and the Abyssinians.

There are other English-speaking Protestants—or ex-Protestants, for these would count themselves among the number of the intellectually emancipated—who hold the doctrine of 'British Israel' in a figurative or metaphorical sense. Without contending that the English-speaking peoples of the White Race are descended from the Children of Israel after the flesh, these transcendentalist 'British Israelites' do maintain that they have succeeded to the Israelites' role of being 'the Chosen People' in a spiritual sense—that the mantle of Elijah has fallen upon Elisha, whether by some divine sleight of hand or by the accident of which way the wind blew when the mantle was in the air. However it may have happened, the English-speaking peoples have become (on this view) the Heirs of the Kingdom, the depositories of the hopes and capacities of Mankind, the chosen vessels through whose instrumentality the Human Race is destined to attain to the goal of its endeavours. This doctrine is resonantly enunciated in Mr. Rudyard Kipling's *Recessional*.

THE TRADER VERSUS THE FARMER IN
RACE CONTACTS

By William C. McLeod

RACE MIXTURE BETWEEN red man and white in North America never took place on a large scale in colonial days. The traders, both French and British, invariably took Indian wives. An Indian wife was an asset to a trader among the Indians. But the agricultural settlers, both French and British, did not want Indian women as wives. Farmers needed wives who knew the ways of European housekeeping and husbandry, who knew how to milk cows, fry eggs, and so on. Indian women would not do. The farmer, even in Virginia, so late as 1632, often preferred to pay the expense of importing women of ques-

---

Reprinted from *The American Indian Frontier* by William C. McLeod, pp. 359–361, by permission of Alfred A. Knopf, Inc. Copyright 1928 by Alfred A. Knopf, Inc.

tionable repute from the European cities, at considerable cost, than to take Indian women who would be helpless on a farmer's homestead. Champlain offered one hundred and fifty francs as a dowry to each French-Canadian farmer who would marry an Indian girl, but his offer was in vain.

The writers of popular texts have insisted that there was a difference in race between the Nordic and the Latin races which manifested itself in a difference in personal relations with the Indian. In contrasting the French and the English they make the cardinal error of comparing French traders not with British traders but with British agriculturists; and the needs of a French colonial régime which never developed to the point where the trading interests lost control with the needs of dominantly agricultural British settlements. French and British traders alike married Indian women and gave rise to numbers of half-breeds; and both groups were able to adapt themselves to Indian ways of life and the Indian manner of thinking.

And as for the Spanish and Portuguese—no one is more capable of the development of intense "race" prejudice than the Iberian. But the Iberian peoples have always understood the social nature of their group hostilities. The Moor and the Jew in Spain and Portugal were hated only so long as they refused to become Christians; Christianized they were racially absorbed by both the aristocratic and the commoner strata of the population.

In the Americas the early Spanish settlers interested in agriculture and industry preferred to import European wives. It was largely the military who initiated the development of an important half-breed stock which, because of the civilizing nature of the Indian policies pursued, became of social, political, and economic importance and served as a link between the wholly red and the wholly white elements in the population. This is in contrast with the fate of the half-breeds in North America, who were dragged away from civilization by the fur-trading interest, and absorbed largely into the native population, sharing its fate.

SEX RATIO, MISCEGENATION AND RACE RELATIONS

By Herbert Moller

IN THE EARLIER STAGES of colonial life and on the frontier the scarcity of women resulted in a readiness to accept culturally inferior women as life companions. The tendency to racial miscegenation can be observed in all those regions, and again among those social groups, which had an extremely high sex ratio.

Reprinted from Herbert Moller, "Sex Composition and Correlated Culture Patterns of Colonial America," *The William and Mary College Quarterly*, II (April, 1945), 131–137.

The greater extent of racial miscegenation in Spanish and Portuguese America cannot be attributed to an inherently different attitude on the part of the Latin peoples in their relations with the natives. The development of race relations in New France would disprove this assumption at once. During the latter half of the seventeenth century, when the early French colonists had an exceedingly high sex ratio, there was no prejudice against alliances with Indian women. Though only four marriages between Frenchmen and Indians were recorded, left-handed marriages are known to have been frequent. From lack of new immigrants, however, the sex ratio of the eastern parts of Canada was fairly balanced at the turn of the century, and thereafter mixed marriages fell out of favor. Quite otherwise were conditions in the strongly masculine settlements in the west of Canada and in Louisiana. There concubinage with young Indian squaws was the rule through the eighteenth century. As a report has it: *Chaque garçon a des sauvagesses, les soldats comme les autres;* and even "officers, who wore the sword and the plume, had children by Indian females."

Similarly in the British colonies miscegenation was practiced wherever white women were extremely rare and where current moral ideas were not yet influenced by the presence of a considerable number of white women. Among the Puritans of New England such a condition never existed. There a strong racial repugnance was prevalent from the very beginning of the settlements. In contrast to their French neighbors of Acadia, many of whom "turned Indian" and became "squaw-men," the Puritans loathed any fraternizing. As early as 1627, when Thomas Morton and his party of male servants "set up a May-pole, drinking and dancing aboute it many days together, inviting the Indien women, for their consorts, dancing and frisking together, (like so many fairies or furies rather,) and worse practices," the Puritan community shuddered with disgust. There were, of course, some individuals who did not entertain any scruples with regard to social intercourse with the Indians. As in the other colonies, they were found particularly in the servant class which always had a higher sex ratio than the upper strata. Such persons, however, were kept under close surveillance from the earliest times.

It has been suggested that the aversion to race intermixture with the Indians originated in the bad feelings engendered by the bitter Indian wars. But in New England at least it did not wait for that; and historical experience all over the world shows that warfare as such, no matter how sanguinary, does not prevent the mingling of the nations involved. In fact, intermarriage between whites and Indians was most frequent in the frontier areas and in Indian territory. The custom among travelers of taking Indian women as temporary wives was of lasting importance only through the half-breed offspring they left behind. But apart from the itinerants there were many hunters, trappers, traders, and adventurers who came to live in these outlying regions. In a frontier account such as Pickett's *History of Alabama* one meets a great number of so-called "Indian countrymen" and mixed breeds, many of whom were extraordinary men. There were in those regions Scotch, French, British, Jews, Dutchmen, and American-born; the latter were mostly of Scotch-Irish descent; "many of them were men of some education; all of them were married to Indian wives, and some of them had intelligent and handsome children." In 1799, when John Pierce established the first American school in Alabama, "the pupils were strangely mixed in blood, and their color was of every hue." The farthermost frontier, however, did not set the pattern for American society. In contrast to the custom in the Spanish colonies, Indian wives were not acceptable to the compact white settlements of the East. Traders returning thither used to send their Indian wives and mixed-breed children back to the Indian camp from fear of being ostracized. Many of the mixed-breeds, therefore, became leaders of the Indians, particularly in the wars from 1812 to 1814.

Racial repugnance, however, had been absent also in the middle and southern seaboard settlements as long as their sex composition remained extremely unbalanced. Among the Dutch settlers of the New Netherlands who were largely unaccompanied by Dutch women "there was a continuous illicit intercourse which affected the formation of society as it did on the English frontiers." Domine Megapolensis stated in his treatise on the Mohawks that "Dutchmen run . . . very much" after the Indian women. The earliest occurrence of racial mingling between British settlers and American aborigines was the intermarriage of the lost settlers of Roanoke and the Croatan Indians. In early seventeenth-century Virginia there was no feeling against mixed marriages. "The natives and the colonists mingled freely and it was anticipated that this social mingling would continue until the natives were assimilated to European culture. Indians came and went in and out of the villages of the settlers and the chiefs were frequent guests in the homes of the colonists. There was occasional intermarriage." Besides the well-known union of Pocahontas to John Rolfe, several later cases are on record.

During the last half and particularly towards the end of the seventeenth century, when racial antipathies were taking root, the Indian population was steadily being pushed back. The feeling of racial aversion now was directed mainly against the Negroes who were imported in ever-increasing numbers. Miscegenation between whites and Negroes occurred on a large scale from Pennsylvania to Georgia and in the West Indies through the seventeenth and eighteenth centuries. Prior to 1691 only a very few white men were penalized in Virginia on account of "fornication" with Negro women. Prohibitive legislation to disqualify Negroes for marrying whites was enacted only when public opinion had become emotionally ripe for it. This stage was indicated by the substitution of the doctrine of racial inferiority for the weaker ideology of religious disqualification.

It has often been noted that the racial purity laws were defied most frequently by lower-class whites and in particular by the indentured servants and the convicts, those social groups which had a higher sex ratio than the rest of the population. "Mingling of races in Maryland continued during the eighteenth century, in spite of all laws against it." It also appears to have been frequent in eighteenth-century Pennsylvania, here apparently due to the continual influx of Germans and Scotch-Irish. Regular mixed marriages were frequent in Pennsylvania. A prohibitory law was enacted in 1725, but it seems not to have been strictly enforced and later was repealed altogether. In 1780 twenty per cent of the slave population of Chester County were registered as mulattoes. The evidence of the court records of the South to the effect that the offenders were "almost always of the lower classes" is no doubt partly attributable to the fact that slave owners were rarely brought into court for cohabitation with women of colored races. But it is certainly also indicative of different moral ideas among the heavily male immigrant groups and among the well-established part of the population which insisted on the racial purity legislation.

With regard to regions as well as to social classes there appears to have been a coincidence of a balanced sex ratio and aversion to miscegenation which suggests a causal relationship between these two factors. Racial antipathies were practically non-existent in seventeenth- and eighteenth-century Europe. They originated in the American scene. The most plausible explanation, so far, for the increasing avoidance of interracial marriage in the British colonies has been the need of agriculturists and tradesmen for wives "who knew the ways of European housekeeping and husbandry," whereas traders, both French and British, could afford to marry Indian women. If this economic factor accounts for the *disinterestedness* of the seaboard settlements in Indian wives and in women of African origin, it fails to explain the growth of racial *repugnance* heavily charged with emotions of horror and disgust. The emergence of an attitude of moral indignation can psychologically be explained, however, by the presence and influence of white women. As a matter of fact, only a very few cases are on record of a white women brought into court for illicit relations with a Negro. On the other hand the number of male offenders was large; and when not restrained by laws and public sentiment, men also of British stock had no scruples about intimacies with colored women. Mary Rowlandson's story of her Indian captivity, first published in 1682, was one of the earliest and most popular narratives dictated by a sense of disgust; and her attitude towards the Indians, "those black creatures," "such atheistical, proud, wild, cruel, barbarous, brutish, (in one word) diabolical creatures," was produced by emotional aversion as much as by anything she actually suffered. Women, as a rule, refrain from matrimonial and social relations with men of a social and cultural stratum lower than their own. The vast majority of women persist in this attitude even if the alternative is celibacy; and whenever there was a surplus of women in the upper or middle classes of Europe, fathers faced the problem of how to provide for their unmarried daughters. Women, as a rule, want to identify themselves completely with their husbands or lovers, while men do not share this urge to any similar degree. Aversion to so-called "hypogamy" is considered a normal trait of feminine psychology and its existence can be taken for granted in any stratified society. Whereas in Europe this feminine attitude prevented women from marrying beneath their social status, it worked in America against their marrying into culturally and socially inferior races. Moreover, through their enhanced influence on family and community life, women became more or less unintentionally the foremost agents in the establishment of racial barriers. Thus the development of aversion to racial miscegenation in the thirteen colonies can be traced to the invasion of feminine sentiments into colonial society.

PART V

Race Conflict

INTRODUCTION

"To UNDERSTAND RACE CONFLICT," Ruth Benedict said, "we need fundamentally to understand *conflict* and not *race*." This remark suggests that the conflict is there first. Out of conflict are differentiated and defined groups whose members are especially indoctrinated, trained and disciplined to carry on the struggle. They are, in other words, conflict groups. The race group is just one form of such a militant grouping. Like every in-group it takes form and develops rapport, discipline and self-consciousness because of its relation to an out-group or counter-race. In conflict, as contrasted with competition, the other group is specifically recognized and identified as an opponent. What appears to be the role of "unfair" competition between peoples of different physical marks and unequal standards of living in bringing about racial recognition and conflict?

It is a commonplace observation that new groups are always forming and re-forming around some axis or mode of group alignment. The idea of race is one such axis around which the groups of a society may form themselves. Its special importance appears to lie in the fact that, unlike most other principles of group alignment, the principle of race is highly persistent and enduring. But, as in all in-group versus out-group systems, competition, conflict and cooperation in an interracial society are complexly intertangled so that, almost like a machine, it shakes and vibrates as a whole. To the extent that the struggle between the groups is over values and interests actually common to all, the effect is to establish a society, a "group of groups," in which the member groups or races are at once separated from each other and integrated into each other. The very struggle of race against race gives an impetus to the unification of the society. The constituent races come to possess, up to a point, an indivisible social and cultural inheritance, and it may be that this is the most important fact about race relations and race conflict. If so, why? Check these statements

[313]

against the facts from such an interethnic society as the Jewish-Gentile society of Germany, the Negro-white society in the South, the Hindu-Moslem society in India, the English-French society in Canada, or any other.

In a well-known poem Kipling said that "the things you will learn from the Yellow and Brown, they'll 'elp you a lot with the White." If this is true it also may be true that the better Whites understand themselves, the better will they be able to understand the Yellows, the Browns, the Blacks, and all other peoples. Would it contribute anything to our better understanding of interracial society if we altered one of Mead's statements to read: "We cannot attain interracial-mindedness until we have attained a higher degree of racial-mindedness than we possess at present"? Can we profitably relate racial-mindedness and inter-racial-mindedness in a manner analogous to Mead's analysis of national-mindedness and international-mindedness?

Is the statement from Ruth Benedict, quoted above, entirely true? What does the widespread opinion that the race problem is essentially an insoluble one suggest about the nature of *race* conflict? Is it true that conflict between peoples identified as racially different tends to take on a dimension not present in other forms of group conflict, a dimension which transforms "problem" into "tragedy"? What do you know of the history and meaning of the phrase "war of the races"? How does it compare with Sorel's myth of the general strike? Has there ever been an organized war between two distinct racial groups? Or is it that groups already at war tend to define each other as racially different? Why is race conflict so often associated with the sense of a peculiar sort of danger, as a "peril"? What is a civil war? At what point does a war cease to be a civil war and become an international or interethnic war?

How is race conflict actually experienced by individuals? Does race conflict ever express itself in a form unique to itself? When and under what conditions do insurrections, rebellions, strikes, riots, lynchings, pogroms, feuds, and other forms of group conflict become forms of race conflict? When they become expressions of race conflict what changes, if any, are brought about in them? What do you understand by racial politics and how important a role does it play in American politics generally? What do you understand by geopolitics and what part do allegedly racial groups play in it?

An incident of race conflict is race consciousness. Without consciousness, Heraclitus told the Greeks, men act as men asleep; with consciousness, they act as men awake. The idea of consciousness evokes the image of being awake, of being aware. How does race consciousness differ from other forms of group consciousness? Is there a significant distinction between consciousness of race, race consciousness, and racial self-consciousness? What difference might the presence of race consciousness in an individual make in his actual behavior? Under what circumstances is a person likely to feel proud of his race? Ashamed of his race? Under what circumstances will an individual say "we Smiths," "we Methodists," "we Americans," "we Whites"? How do we know who "we" are? In what way or ways, if any, do pan-racial movements differ from ordinary race consciousness? What is the evidence, if any, for the proposition that among the non-white peoples of the modern world there has been a progressive development from race consciousness to pan-racial consciousness to pan-colored (non-white) consciousness?

Is it true that every "we," no matter how innocently used, contains the germ of the idea of superiority? Is the group's conception of its own superiority over other groups the chief end in view, or does such a conception function as a means to other ends? If so, what other ends? In other words, what is the function of the idea of race superiority? What is a "race" leader? What types of race leaders are there?

SOCIETY AS A GROUP OF GROUPS

By Edgar T. Thompson

SUMNER'S CONCEPTION OF SOCIETY AS A "group of groups" affords a useful and illuminating point of view for the organization and analysis of interracial as well as other types of societies. In the following paragraphs quoted from *Folkways* Sumner states his conception in connection with primitive society but it is no less useful when applied to modern or civilized society. He says:

The conception of "primitive society" which we ought to form is that of small groups scattered over a territory. . . . A group of groups may have some relation to each other (kin, neighborhood, alliance, connubium and commercium) which draws them together and differentiates them from others. Thus a differentiation arises between ourselves, the we-group, or in-group, and everybody else, or the others-groups, out-groups. The insiders in a we-group are in a relation of peace, order, law, government, and industry, to each other. Their relation to all outsiders, or others-groups, is one of war and plunder, except so far as agreements have modified it. . . .

The relation of comradeship and peace in the we-group and that of hostility and war toward others-groups are correlative to each other. The exigencies of war with outsiders are what make peace inside, lest internal discord should weaken the we-group for war. These exigencies also make government and law in the in-group, in order to prevent quarrels and enforce discipline. Thus war and peace have reacted on each other and developed each other, one within the group, the other in the intergroup relation. The closer the neighbors, and the stronger they are, the intenser is the warfare, and then the intenser is the internal organization and discipline of each. Sentiments are produced to correspond. Loyalty to the group, sacrifice for it, hatred and contempt for outsiders, brotherhood within, warlikeness without—all grow together, common products of the same situation.

A society is a group within which smaller groups are in a continuous state of interaction. Thus there is not one but many societies and the concept "society" becomes a highly relative one varying from a group of neighboring families on up to a group of nations. The condition of competition, conflict and

Adapted from Edgar T. Thompson, "Race Relations in the Modern World," *The Journal of Negro Education*, XIII (Summer, 1944), 273–279, with the kind permission of the publisher. Howard University, Washington, D.C.

rivalry between the groups of which a society is composed tends to increase the solidarity of each "in" or we-group. It is this conflict which turns an aggregation of individuals into a group whose members are conscious of membership in it. "We" expresses this consciousness but in the course of a single conversation a modern man may use "we" in several different societal contexts. Thus in "we Smiths" the "others" obviously are other families and the society is a group of families, whereas in "we Negroes" the others are other race groups and the society is a group of racial groups. What is not so clear is the source of the ideas which bring about the realignment of individuals into new and different "we" groups as time passes. Race is one of these relatively new alignments.

Because each group is bound to be more controlled and guided by its own experiences than by the experiences of other people it either becomes more or less ethnocentric or it ceases to be a group. The disposition to evaluate the strange in terms of the known converts the realization of difference into a moral judgment. We judge ourselves by our best traits and others by their worst, and our best traits include practically all the traits we have; virtue is defined by the qualities we attribute to ourselves. Thus Houston Stewart Chamberlain speaks of "a certain noble striving for property" which he finds among the Aryans, while among the Jews this same tendency is referred to as "the most despicable usury." Ethnocentrism is rooted in the division between friend and foe but it transforms this division into one between good and bad.

To Sumner "primitive society" is composed of "small groups scattered over a territory." It is a territorial society, but the member groups are not intermixed upon the territory. There is a sort of "no man's land" between them so that the cultural distinctiveness of each is obvious. Ethnocentrism therefore needs no great transcendental myth, for spacial distance is sufficient to protect the exclusiveness of the tribe or clan. But when conquest, immigration, and trade intermix men of different complexion and culture on soil which all may claim as a common social if not legal inheritance there is a tendency to seek or to create some principle for maintaining social distance. When society becomes a congeries of groups and the members of one group cannot put physical distance between themselves and the others, a principle like language, religion, nationality, or race may be employed to effect separation.

With the intermixing of groups upon the same soil comes the state, and states lie alongside each other with no "no man's land" between. Boundaries become sharp and sensitive lines of demarcation as relations of trade and war effect a new and larger intergroup or society. Such a society was Europe where the idea of nationality was evolved to serve as a basis for state rivalries and for claims to territories and populations lying within other states. The idea of nationality is closely related to the idea of race.

The series of changes which began in the period of the Great Discoveries and which led to, and followed, the Industrial Revolution resulted in an ever widening circle of political and economic relations. This series of changes might be described as a revolution in distance since it greatly increased control over a larger part of the physical world by making the resources of every part more available to other parts. One of the first effects of the revolution in distance was the transformation of the Atlantic into an inland sea. The Atlantic became an area of interaction, an interaction which continually changed the character of all the peoples on both sides of it and tended to give them a common European culture. To this new and larger society Ramsay Traquair has given the name the Commonwealth of the Atlantic.

The expansion of Europe and the opening up of overseas areas for trade and settlement involved a change whereby native and non-European peoples, many of them at any rate, gradually became integral parts of the white man's economic order. This was less true of North America where the Indian was pushed aside. He was culturally distinct and highly "visible," but his group has never become an integral member of the Atlantic group of groups. Hence the attitude toward him has settled down into one of relative indifference. It is significant that he has posed no serious race problem. Rather it was in connection with the incorporation of the Negro into this society that racial ideas became useful. The idea of race developed as a working element in colonial areas as a means of effecting control over the Negro's labor and of fixing him in a permanent caste position.

For a long time certain hermit nations like Japan continued to remain outside the family of nations. They possessed little or no national or racial consciousness since they were not concerned about their status in a society of which they were not members. But advances in cheaper and faster means of transportation and communication continued to reduce the size of the planet and to bring all peoples living on it closer together. Their very differences made them useful to one another and customers of one another. When Japan, for example, began to trade with the rest of the world her people began to expand out over the Pacific. The Pacific became a commonwealth of nations as the Atlantic had become earlier. It was in Hawaii, in California, in Australia, and in Malaya that Japanese became conscious of the low place assigned their country by the other nationals. People who have known defeat and that "sickening sense of inferiority" are the people who discover their souls, and so it is too with nations. When the Japanese became group conscious and involved themselves in a struggle to improve their status their membership in the family of nations became a fact.

The Great Society, as Graham Wallas calls it, has become a fact too. The struggle for status between races and nations has become world-wide; the subject peoples are struggling to be free and the sovereign states are struggling to maintain or to raise their prestige. It is significant that in their fight for places in the sun the two Axis partners, Germany in Europe and Japan in Asia, should both base their claims upon the principle of race. But they are not employing the principle in exactly the same way.

Thus the member groups of a society are at once separated from each other and integrated into a common community. Each has to live in a common space or environment with the others so that "to live" necessarily means "to live with" the rest. The competition, rivalry or prejudice between the constituent groups is not a denial of societal unity but rather an affirmation of it. Men do not compete or fight for ends which all do not prize. Competitition and conflict therefore inevitably go on within a circle of common values and interests, or values and interests held in common up to a point. This is why society is a "group of groups."

The fact that a group within a society is in conflict with other groups to whom it nevertheless is bound suggests why European immigrants in American cities so frequently settle down alongside their hereditary enemies. It would seem that they have to stick together in order to stay apart, for the image which a group forms of itself is bound up with the way the other groups within the same society regard it. It follows that if a group wishes to maintain its values, its historical memories, and, in general, its conception of itself it has some need for the constant reminders provided by its enemies.

Common interests and common societal values are required to point up the issues for conflict, and the more the member groups of a society hold in common the intenser the conflict. It is well known that there is no fight like a family fight, not only because those who are presumed to love each other have the power to hurt each other most, but also because they share experiences from which it is impossible for each member to free himself. Great bitterness also is observed in religious sectarian conflict and in intra-trade union and political party fights. Feuds between mountain families inhabiting the same cove are particularly uncompromising and long-lasting. Civil wars have the reputation of being bitterer than international wars. Antisemitism in Christian lands is surely connected with the fact that both Jew and Gentile have "prayed to the same God, preached more or less the same morals, feared the same evils, and hoped for the same heaven." Similarly, Southern whites and Negroes have more interests in common with one another than either has with any group outside the South, but in the economy which they pursue together the competition and conflict between them are constant. On a larger scale, whites and Negroes in the United States have more in common than either group has with any group outside the United States.

Here is the paradox: it is precisely because the members of both groups profess belief in the ethics of the Sermon on the Mount, in the principles of the Declaration of Independence, and in the doctrines of a trial by a jury of one's peers and no taxation without representation that there is racial prejudice and conflict. Without these common beliefs and ideals there could be no basis for claiming rights and duties and there could be nothing to point up these claims into issues. Neither group can advance by asserting its own interests against the interests of the whole; each must state and argue its case in terms of the values accepted by all. Minority and subordinate groups fighting for democracy and justice and freedom for themselves find it necessary to wage the fight in behalf of all.

When we look beyond the borders of American society out to the competitions and rivalries of the nations and races composing the Great Society what we have to observe is something very similar. The nations are in that society because they have some measure of common interests and common values. Beyond that measure their interests and values are uniquely their own. But in their common society they accuse each other of breaking the peace, of restricting trade, and of destroying civilization. In the fight arising from the accusations and counter-accusations in which we presently are engaged, the freedom for which we fight will have to be won, as Pearl Buck has somewhere said, not race by race, or nation by nation, but as a human essence.

INTERGROUP RELATIONS IN
NEW YORK CITY

By Konrad Bercovici

NEW YORK, like no other city, offers the best study of the nations of the world, samples of each being centered in different sections within easy reach of one another. You can go into the Spanish quarter and forget easily you are in Anglo-Saxon country. More than that, you can be in different provinces of Spain; for the people of these different provinces, on coming here, gather and form folds of their own, until the Spanish district forms in itself a copy of Spain. The people of each province live in the same proximity to one another as they do in their own country.

You can go into the French district, and live in France while you are there, with Parisians clustering by themselves nearer to where there is light and gaiety, and the Normans further away on the side streets, withdrawing within themselves as northern people are wont to do. The Bretons, frugal and sober, keep to themselves. The southern Frenchmen from Marseilles and Orleans and Tours gather in their own cafés and restaurants to discuss and talk about their gardens at home across the waters, and to sing their own songs, their own provincial love-songs.

If you go further, into the Italian colonies, for there are many in the city, you will see the streets of Naples, the sidewalks littered with fruit- and vegetable-stands of all kinds; and the gay Neapolitan call of the fishermen on Mulberry Street is the same gay call of the fishmonger of the Neopolitan Strada. And there is the same antagonism between the northern Italian and the southern one. There is the big, bellowing Calabrian who detests his smaller-sized brother from Sicily, and the Roman-born who has contempt for both of them. The Milanese and Tuscanese consider themselves so far above the other Italians they disdain living in their neighborhood, and have their own quarters elsewhere.

There is the Russian district, with moody Slavs worrying themselves, torturing themselves about this and that and the eternal question. Big, heavy-boned, broad-shouldered, sunken-eyed Slavs with a mixture of Tarta blood, colorful in their barbaric emotions, powerful in their inert solidarity, more daring because less flighty, more influential because of their resolute steadiness. It was among them here that the overthrow of Russia's old régime was planned. And living close to them their gay and lighter cousin, the Czechs and the Croatians and the Slovenes, dancing to lighter tunes and singing lighter songs, ready to sacrifice all their worldly goods to an ideal, carrying their patriotism further than any other nation, further even than the Poles, their immediate neighbors in the city.

And what is one to say about the Hungarian quarter? Where the children of Attila have kept their own tongue so pure that not a single Anglo-Saxon word has penetrated their speech. You can see them daily. Their homes, in crowded tenement quarters, still retain that individuality which is their own. The color schemes of their decorations and the manner of arranging their furniture and the relation between the older and the younger element, and their quick reactions, stamp them as a kind apart in this maelstrom.

Further below them is the Rumanian quarter, a race of men considering themselves superior to all others of the Balkan states because they are the descendants of the old Romans. Their own Gipsies live among them, despised and loved by them; hard-working peasants vainly trying to adapt themselves to a different life, disliking the Hungarians, suspecting the Russians, neighbors at home across the Carpathians and the Pruth, neighbors here across a dividing sidewalk.

The great German population of the city, divided and subdivided when there is peace on the other side, is united when its integrity is attacked or endangered. Slow, careful artisans; slow, careful merchants, with the same *Gemütlichkeit* as at home, still reading their home papers to their wives and children, still leaning back in their soft, comfortable chairs, in their immaculately clean homes. Neighborhoods may change and switch about them, but they remain where they have once settled.

And there are Danish and Finnish, and Norwegian and Serbians, and Slovak and Swedish quarters, each one with its own life, guarding jealously its national characteristics. There is the Syrian district with one principal street and several side streets, one of the oldest streets in the city, with the houses built a hundred years ago.

The Greeks live in close quarters in proximity with peoples near which they live at home, as if New York were a reproduction of some old Levantine city, Alexandria or Saloniki, with a dash of Stamboul on Madison Street, a block from Washington's first home in this city.

A map of Europe superposed upon the map of New York would prove that the different foreign sections of the city live in the same proximity to one another as in Europe: the Spanish near the French, the French near the Germans, the Germans near the Austrians, the Russians and the Rumanians near the Hungarians, and the Greeks behind the Italians. People of western Europe live in the western side of the city. People of eastern Europe live in the eastern side of the city. Northerners live in the northern part of the city and southerners in the southern part. Those who have lived on the other side near the sea or a river have the tendency here to live as near the sea or the river as possible. The English, islanders, living on the other side of the Hudson as if the river were the channel that separates them from the rest of Europe.

A reformation of the same grouping takes place every time the city expands. If the Italians move further up Harlem, the Greeks follow them, the Spaniards join them, with the French always lagging behind and the Germans expanding eastward. And yet these people hate one another as only neighbors can hate one another. It is not love that attracts them to where the others are. Hatred proves a more potent element of attraction than love.

JEW AND GENTILE IN MEDIEVAL
GERMANY AS A SOCIAL PAIR

By Marvin Lowenthal

NO QUARREL CAN BE SO BITTER as a family feud. When the Jew first opposed the Christian, which he did long before the pagans were hardly aware of a difference between them, he employed all the fury of a man fighting his brother; and the Christian, far from turning his cheek, never forgot or forgave this initial onslaught; the memory of it colors both the Gospels and the Acts. The Christians, moreover, had suffered a bitter disappointment. Their way to salvation had been offered "to the Jew first" (Romans I.16), and he had refused it. Again, Jewish scriptures and their promises furnished the basis of Christian belief; and as long as the Jews, who were the acknowledged guardians of these scriptures and presumably an authority on them, denied that the promises had been fulfilled by Christianity, they proved a painful and potentially fatal embarrassment. Then, too, Christians and Jews were for some centuries missionary rivals over half the globe. Finally, as Christian dogma shaped itself—wherein the persistent and annoying denials of the Jews were explained away through the claim that the Jews by their own prophecies were doomed to reject the Messiah—and as the hope of winning over the Jews waned and as the prospect of capturing the Romans grew more flattering, the Church flung off its troublesome family connections with the Synagogue by enthroning the Jew as its pre-destined hereditary foe. It was clever theology, it was cleverer politics, even if it was questionable history, to assert that the Jews, and not the Romans, killed Jesus.

This simple assertion, based on an obscure and uncertain police incident in a remote provincial capital, was to prove another determining factor in the ensuing centuries of Jewish history.

The fence the Jew staked about his home—the Talmud—was not meant, like monastery walls, to be a rampart against life. Indeed, it had been raised to ward off the enemies of life. Historically the talmudic discipline had been a defense against Rome—we need only remember Johanan ben Zakkai and the school of Jabneh. Later it rendered a similar service against the heirs of Rome: the Holy Roman Empire and the Roman Catholic Church. Within the shade of the thorny hedge planted at Jabneh and re-planted along the Rhine, the Jew cultivated his garden.

But his security had a broader base. He not only had a home in the universe, but he lived in the same universe as his medieval neighbors, whether friends or foes. Their houses all stood up the same street. Church, mosque, and synagogue prayed to ostensibly the same God, preached more or less the same morals, feared the same evils, and hoped for the same heaven. Paradise, the

Adapted from Marvin Lowenthal, *The Jews Of Germany: A Study of Sixteen Centuries* (Philadelphia: The Jewish Publication Society of America, 1936), pp. 9–10, 100–107; copyright 1936 by the Jewish Publication Society of America and used with the kind permission of the publisher.

Garden of Allah, and *Gan 'Eden* were geographically one. Conversion, repent-
ance, *teshubah,* the road to the garden, traveled the same route. The very things
the medievals fought about—the nature of God and the way to salvation—
they largely held in common. The bitterness of the battle testified that though
their language differed, they agreed in their knowledge, or presumed knowledge, of what they were fighting about—a world and goal as real and familiar
to one combatant as another. No one on that street ever spoiled its violent
blood-stained harmony by asserting there was no God, there was no salvation,
by suggesting they were pursuing figments, and cracking skulls for the sake of
shadows. So firm were their common religious convictions that no one—except
in Heine's imagination—dreamed of disarming priest and rabbi, or rabbi and
iman, with the summary judgment: *sie alle beide stinken.*

And, finally, in that medieval street—with God at one end and the Devil
at the other—the Jew, by an unwelcome but general consent, was recognized
to be the oldest inhabitant. The synagogue might be a drab cell compared to
the cathedral of Cologne, the Jew might be insignificant in numbers and his
house sequestered and spat upon, but he enjoyed all the pride, the inner dignity
and strength, of a first settler.

The stiff-neck of the Jew—a stumbling-block to the German moralists
and missionaries—was partly the stubbornness of an oak aware of its gnarled
centuries. The refusal of the Jew to commit an act which, though innocent
in itself, might injure the good repute of Israel and thereby cast a reflection
on God—"profane," as he said, "the Holy Name"—a naive and sublime impudence—was the last word in *noblesse oblige.* "Jews," reads the *Book of the
Pious,* "shall not indulge in pleasures from which Christians hold aloof—if
a Jew sees a Christian about to do wrong, he shall make every effort to dissuade
him—else the Name of God be profaned." These are the maxims of aristocrats.
When we remember that the men who preached them had every incentive to
lose themselves in hatred and malice—to rejoice in pleasures denied their
enemies or triumph in a Christian's fall from grace—we may well call them
the aristocrats of God. Their refusal, to be sure, had a practical bearing. When
the incautious act of an individual Jew might literally plunge his family and the
community in blood, the "profanation of the Name" was more than a theological
delicacy. But for all that, the sense of communal responsibility—certainly the
strength and tone of it—issued in part from a well of ancestral pride, from the
consciousness of a tradition which, as the Jews believed, harked back to the
dawn of the world. A first family keeps more than wine in its cellar to fortify
its long thin line.

But the parallels go further. The Christians had their *Ordo Vagorum,*
wandering scholars, hundreds of them, who tramped (and studied) from school
to school. So did the Jews. For every *Bachante* sleeping on straw and copying
the words of a *Meister* in the cold of the morning, there was a *Bahur* at the
feet of his *Rab;* and often enough rabbi and disciple were compelled to flee
along the roads in search of a new asylum of learning. Coming closer to the
life of the masses—the flirting with magic and devils, the homely wisdom of
housewife and husbandman as well as in the fancies of the learned—we find
the superstition of the Jew going hand in hand with the German. Fables, folk-
medicine, amulets and incantations, symbols and omens had no respect for
church bans or ghetto regulations. There, at the lowest rung, in the things

people lived by, not under the cloak of eternity, but from hour to hour, the Jew was at one with his world.

There is no need to talk of influence, borrowing, or plagiary. Jewish *Geist* moved with the *Zeitgeist*. Common views and common visions were plucked from the common air. The ghetto walls were porous. On double-hinges its gates swung both ways.

HINDU AND MOSLEM IN INDIA

By K. T. Behanan

RELIGION IS BOTH a cementing and divisive force. Religion (the Latin root is "religare" which means "to bind fast") cements and strengthens the bonds of oneness and brotherhood among its adherents, but it also generates animosity and hatred toward out-groupers generally and toward adherents of other religions.

For an illustration of this dual cementing-divisive function we have only to look at the Hindu-Muslim relations in the past thirty years. From the very beginning, the Indian national movement leaned heavily on Hindu culture and history for its dynamism and spiritual strength. Its symbols, its songs, including the national anthem, and its flag are all of the warp and woof of Hindu culture which in turn is enveloped in religon. It should be borne in mind that a secular culture divorced from religion, which even in the West is a comparatively recent development, is unknown in India either among the Hindus or Muslims. The national movement, because it has its roots in the predominantly religious Hindu culture, gathered incredible momentum in the course of a few years. It unified and aroused the Hindus as no other movement in Indian history has yet succeeded in doing. Its sheer irresistibility forced the mighty British to come to terms.

But the movement has been like a twin-clock with springs that work in opposing directions. As the Hindus were being wound up in one direction against the British, the Muslims automatically wound themselves in the opposite direction. They were as much opposed to the potentially dominant Hindus and their religion as to the British. Perhaps the entire development was historically inevitable. The Hindu Congress leaders may have had no conscious design to dominate all of India, although some Muslim leaders see a deliberate attempt to enslave them in a free India. In the absence of a secular culture, in which both communities could have participated on equal terms, the Hindus,

Adapted from K. T. Behanan, "Cultural Diversity and World Peace," in Wayne Dennis (ed.), *Current Trends in Social Psychology* (Pittsburgh: University of Pittsburgh Press, 1948), pp. 56–63; copyright 1948 by University of Pittsburgh Press and used with the kind permission of the publisher.

who are educationally and economically far more advanced than the Muslims, rooted the nationalist movement in their own religious culture. It is well known, of course, that any nationalist movement must appeal to the particular traditions and tribulations of the people, and the Hindus and Muslims had little in common except submission to an outsider. Their cultures and habits were immersed in mutual distrust and hate, engendered by the nature of their religions. Since the Hindus are more politically advanced than the Muslims, it was inevitable that they should have taken the lead in the nationalist movement; and since the Hindu rallying point was religion, and not any secular appeal, it was inevitable that hatred of the Muslim should be a factor in the movement. As with Ireland and Italy, the appeals were rooted deep in the war cries of past glories. In the case of the Hindus one of the most glorious war cries, for instance, was an anti-Muslim song composed by a Bengalee novelist. The song was taken from one of his novels which deals with Muslim invasion of Bengal in the pre-British period. In the early years of the nationalist movement many Muslim leaders protested against the use of this song in a movement that was intended to bring the two communities together against the British. Muslim protests fell on deaf ears, and the song has now become the national anthem of a predominantly Hindu, not a united India.

In actual fact, very few Indian leaders seemed to have anticipated the consequences of their nationalist policies. Of the most influential Hindu leaders with whom I have spoken, not a handful were able to see, either at the outset or in retrospect, that the present communal tension is a result of nurturing the nationalist movement within the exclusive confines of Hindu culture. With emotional intensity they pursued their goals, and they can see nothing but the "natural evils" of the Muslim viewpoint as the explanation for the present conflict. The thousand-year-old bitterness between the two communities had been semidormant under the superior physical force of the British, whose religious tolerance made it convenient to do no more than suppress actual fighting. The internal strife which Britain had found convenient for the purposes of ruling the country was fanned to life in recent years by the aggressive Hindu nationalism and the resulting Muslim fears. Both communities wanted political freedom, but freedom had a different meaning to each. To the Hindus it meant freedom from the British, and to the Muslims it meant freedom from both the British and the Hindus. Freedom has dawned, but on a divided country. And the communal conflict continues.

Westerners who have had no personal experience with the high degree of antagonism that cultural differences centered around religion can arouse, might wonder why other and nonreligious differences do not engender the same degree of persistent and continued hostility between communities. My explanation is that the intensity of ingroup-outgroup feeling induced by mores and taboos that have a supernatural or religious sanction is greater than the corresponding feeling produced by mores that have no supernatural sanction.

The vast majority of Muslims in India and Pakistan are converts from Hinduism and racially in the same stock as the latter. Stripped of their sartorial and tonsorial differences, which the two cultures have forced on their adherents, it would be impossible to distinguish a Hindu from a Muslim. Despite the common racial origins and the fact that the two cultures have existed side by side for nearly a thousand years, and despite the fact that for the past 200 years both groups were ruled by a racially different foreign power, intermarriage between the two communities was very rare. The few men and women who did intermarry were generally members of the far-left political parties—men and women who had broken away from the main stream of their own traditional culture. I am convinced from personal experience that there have been more intermarriages between Hindus and Westerners on the one hand, and between Muslims and Westerners on the other, than between Hindus and Muslims.

Situations where Hindus and Muslims dine together, no doubt, are more frequent than intermarriage, but are still confined to that small segment of modernized men and women who live in the larger cities. Ordinarily every city and town has its separate Hindu and Muslim restaurants. Water served to the passengers in the trains of the country is labeled "Hindu water" and "Muslim water." The large mass of Hindus would not think of being served by a Muslim because this would cause a form of pollution. While Islam does not prohibit dining with other groups, the caste Hindu social attitude toward Muslims has, especially in recent years, developed a negative counterreaction. Now, the Muslims frown upon dining with other groups.

In the general antipathy between these two cultures, two specific differences directly rooted in religion have made the antagonism almost irreconcilable. The monotheism of Islam brooks no compromise with any form of creed or worship other than its own. Hindu doctrinal laxity, on the other hand, has led to tolerance toward the *metaphysical* beliefs of all other religions. On the doctrinal side, it is the aggression and intolerance of the Muslim that has brought about counter-aggression in the Hindu to whom it is a matter of no importance whether God is 1 or 2 or 3.5. On the other hand, the caste system which is an integral part—perhaps the social core—of Hinduism, brooks no compromise with the democratic outlook of Islam. The Hindu sees a threat to his caste system in the relatively democratic or noncaste culture of Islam.

While Islam in India, like every other culture in the world, has certain class lines, these lines by no means approach the sharpness of the *fellah-effendi* class distinctions observed in Islamic countries which were under Turkish rule until recently. The Muslim society is both relatively and potentially a social democracy.

One might say, therefore, that the Muslim is socially tolerant but doctrinally intolerant, while the Hindu is doctrinally tolerant but socially intolerant. These fundamental differences, among many others, have throughout the centuries continued to generate intense fear and hostility.

THE PLANTATION AS A FORM OF
INTERRACIAL SOCIETY

By Edgar T. Thompson

BEFORE THE CIVIL WAR, according to an old story, variations of which are even now occasionally heard in the South, a white gentleman owned a plantation; but, unable to make a living from it, he began the practice of the law and became a very successful lawyer. On his plantation he possessed a large and beautiful mansion, a number of race horses, and more than a hundred Negro slaves. But instead of being supported by the plantation, he and the law supported the plantation. He rode the circuit, defended criminals, established titles, argued cases, and otherwise worked very hard in order to maintain his estate.

One afternoon he returned from a hard days' work to find the mules idle in the stable, the cotton in the grass, and his Negroes asleep in the barn. He shouted angrily. The Negroes scrambled to their feet and began their excuses. But the master, shaking with anger, announced his most awful verdict: "I'm going to quit practicing law and let you lazy niggers starve to death."

Of course, this is a white man's story. On the other side is a story told somewhere by Booker Washington. In a certain small Southern town an immigration agent addressed a meeting of whites. An aged Negro stopped to listen as the agent's work was under discussion.

"Boss," he finally inquired of a white man, "who is dis here emmygration man and what is dis here emmygration?"

It was explained that the agent was an employee of a railroad company trying to induce more white people to locate in the South.

"But Cap'n," said the Negro, "us niggers has got mo' white folks around here now dan us kin take kere of."

Negroes and whites have always been tightly interlocked in the economic and social order of the South. Whatever the white man may think he thinks about Negroes, and whatever the Negro may think he thinks about whites, one fact is certain and that is that they are highly interdependent members of the same society. Each has played a very important part in the life of this society, and each, in its own opinion, has played a more important part in the life of the other than the other has played in its own life. Hence the stories in each group expressing belief in the almost complete dependence upon it of the other.

The existence of a color line may and does involve the isolation of whites and Negroes, and members of each racial group may and do live in separate social worlds from which the others are, in varying degree, excluded. Nevertheless, between them there is a bond resulting from a common way of life and

Reprinted from Edgar T. Thompson, "The Plantation: The Physical Basis of Traditional Race Relations," in Edgar T. Thompson (ed.), *Race Relations and the Race Problem* (Durham: Duke University Press, 1939), pp. 180–183; copyright 1939 by The Duke University Press and used with the kind permission of the publisher.

an intertwined experience. Even conflict has established the inter-human ties more closely. For society reposes upon the fact of interlacing expectations and obligations, and the differentiation of the people of the South into two great racial "moities" has had the effect of setting up a basis for reciprocal services and obligations. Paradoxically, the very cleavage between the ruling and servant classes in the South, based to a large extent upon race, has constituted the bond which has held them together. Back of the divisions and the competitions of race are the common values of a common community.

This common society of whites and blacks, this "Southern" society, is, like every other society, a product of collective action. Individual members of the two races have found ways and means of effecting various practical working arrangements. A Negro informant told Dollard that "one of the few things Negro and white men do together is to hunt," but this statement ignores the countless number of occasions when "we" is used to refer to activities and achievements in which members of both races share. Many like Huckleberry Finn and Negro Jim have shared the same crusts, smoked together, fished off the same log, and lied and stolen together in the common cause of self-preservation. Even sharecropping, in spite of its present bad reputation, is not all cropping. At its worst there is sharing not only of the crop after it has been gathered but of the equipment, the work, and the risk involved in making it.

But interracial cooperation in the South is and has been much more important and far more extensive than these statements would indicate. It was from the very beginning one of the terms of his residence in America that the Negro become a party to various schemes of cooperation for the econmic exploitation of the country's resources. To be sure, "cooperation" was forced upon him, but without some sort of division of labor two peoples as different in physical appearance and in tradition as whites and Negroes originally were, would not, in all probability, have remained to live together on the land as neighbors. It was said of the Chinese coolies who were imported into the Transvaal that there were only two possible places for them, the mine and the prison. In the South, for a long period in its history at least, it is very near the truth to say that a Negro who was not on a plantation doing the kind of work he was expected to do, and having the sort of relations with whites he was expected to have, was under suspicion if not actually in prison.

The most important *modus vivendi* of interracial cooperation in the South developed in connection with the production of agricultural staples like tobacco, rice, indigo, cotton, hemp, and cane sugar for the market. Agricultural production and race relations became institutionalized in the plantation.

The plantation is basic in any analysis of race relations in the South for several reasons. Its wide distribution from Maryland to Texas has served to characterize and define a whole region and not merely a small locality. It emphasizes the connection between the economic and the political aspects of race relations. It is a unit of collective activity and hence also a unit of human relations ordinarily involving members of both races. It thus serves to center attention upon the *relation* between whites and Negroes rather than upon these two races separately. The plantation brings these relations to a focus in an elementary cell-like unit. Finally, the plantation has set the cultural norm of race relations and defined what constitutes conformity and non-conformity, racial orthodoxy and heterodoxy.

THE RISK IN CLOSE ACQUAINTANCE

By G. M. Stratton

VON HUMBOLDT FELT that the hostility among many of the peoples of the New World was largely due to the physical barriers which prevented their intercourse. And today it is often said that nations need only to be acquainted with one another to become friendly. The familiar story of Lamb is tellingly used to enforce this. For when he expressed dislike of a certain person, and a friend protested that Lamb didn't know him, Lamb expressed amazement that he should be expected to dislike anyone that he *did* know!

And so some persons see in the new means of communication an end of international enmities. Nothing more is needed, they believe, than to allow the increasing intercourse to bring its sure result. International friendliness and law and orderly behavior will come by steamship, railway, automobile, and airplane; by newspapers, mails, telegraph, telephone, and by wired and wireless communication. These for the first time in all history are bringing the ends of the earth to know one another, and those who know one another are friends.

We find, in consequence of this belief, an effort to facilitate mutual acquaintance. International visits by bar associations, medical associations, chambers of commerce, advertising men; an exchange of professors, especially of those engaged in research and teaching in the field of intercourse between States; special scholarships and fellowships for travel and study in foreign countries; these may be intended at times only for breadth of personal learning, but often they look also toward closer ties between particular countries—as when Cecil Rhodes provided for the coming to Oxford of Americans, Germans, and Colonial British; and when Emperor Wilhelm and President Roosevelt encouraged an exchange of professors between Germany and the United States. Still oftener the aim is to bring all peoples into friendly relations by making them familiar with one another.

And since language is the great means of acquaintance, language is looked to by many who hope for good will by intercourse. Here is the one sure way to know a people, it is held; here is the talisman against misunderstanding. The possession of the same mother tongue by two nations, it is felt, gives almost a guarantee of peace between them; but next to a common mother tongue comes the acquiring of a common tongue. In consequence some have the hope that all peoples will learn the same additional language to supplement their own—English, or French, or something made out of hand, like Esperanto. Mutual understanding is the very substance of right social conduct, it would appear, and language is the key to understanding.

Now nothing could be further from my thought than to belittle all or any of these attempts at a freer intercourse. There should be more and not less of them; and public-minded wealth, let us hope, will bring their increase. But we may with all sympathy look steadily at them, asking ourselves whether the faith just described is entirely sound, whether nothing more is needed to rid the international world of enmity and injustice than for the nations to become acquainted.

And with a word further about language, the belief in its efficacy to relieve international tension is in part because suspicious or warring nations usually speak different tongues, as France and Germany, Italy and Greece, the United States and Spain, Russia and Japan, England and the Transvaal. But we must remember that nations so generally speak languages different from one another that no strong inference can come of that; if they fight at all, they can hardly choose but fight a people of foreign tongue. To counterweight whatever of gravity is in this ill will between countries divided by language, one must take due account of the wars between peoples speaking the same language: Prussia and Austria, England and Ireland, Spain and her colonies, England and her colonies, England and the United States, the German states with one another, the Italian states with one another, the Ancient Greek states with one another, the English-speaking American states, the Spanish-speaking American states with one another. And we must take account also of the opposite type of fact— the long success in avoiding war where the language is not the same, as between Holland and Denmark, Holland and England, Holland and Belgium, Belguim and England. To these and scores more should be added the success of the French and English in Canada, of the Flemings and Walloons in Belguim, and of the French-speaking, German-speaking, and Italian-speaking cantons of Switzerland. From such evidence must we not conclude that while speech is important, it is by no means of the first importance. It creates neither war nor peace. Deeper than the verbal expression is the spirit to be expressed, which if generous and intelligent can be perceived through a fairly opaque medium, and if narrow and nettling is all the more clearly understood when done by those who use the same words for their ill will.

Doubt is awakened in our minds by nations that know each other most, and like each other least. The Chinese and the Japanese are close together in blood and culture and place of living; Buddhism and Confucianism are bonds between them; they can read each other's written language; each people probably understands the other better than it understands any other people. And yet of Japan's two modern wars, one has been with China; and there has been earlier hostility, and the feeling is hardly cordial now. The French and the Germans likewise are close to each other in blood and territory, and they have had a growing knowledge of each other for centuries and indeed for thousands of years, from a time before the coming of Caesar among them. Every educated German knows something of the French language, and looks wistfully at the urbanity of the French; Geothe pleased the Saxons by saying that one of their cities was a miniature Paris and made its people cultured:

> Mein Leipzig lob' ich mir!
> Es is ein klein Paris und bildet seine Leute.

The French, even if they do not care greatly to know well any foreign people, have been forced to pay attention, century after century, to their neighbors northeast of them. And yet war after war has been fought between them, and they probably will long remain for each other the arch objects of distrust. England's sea power in Elizabeth's reign made that country know—and hate— Spain as she then knew and hated no other nation. Again, the French and

English have but a thread of water between their coasts and yet, when not busy fighting each other, they have eyed each other with unusual suspicion. And certainly the English colonists of America in the eighteenth century knew England as they knew nothing else. Yet then and for a century afterward, they felt perhaps more friendly toward the French. Feeling turned its back on all the old familiarities which grew out of language, literature, law, and religion, and took its own headstrong course to fight two wars with the mother country. And there was also the antipathy among the American states themselves, after their union; between North and South, between sections of a people who had come to know each other better even than they knew the English, having struggled in common for liberty and for a new government and against all the hardships of the frontier.

Indeed the conditions which make for acquaintance are among the most powerful to make for enmity. Neighborhood is one of the most dangerous of international situations. The neighboring and acquainted states of Germany when they were not held together by strong political union quarreled with one another. Machiavelli depicts for us no happy family of the Italian states of his time. The Greek states in snug Hellas found implacable enemies in one another. War does not select the countries in greatest ignorance of each other, but rather the reverse.

Indeed intercourse is as important for enmity as for friendship. The idea is without scientific warrant, as we may later see, that men are hostile by nature and with no outward cause, while friendliness requires care and cultivation. Each of these responses comes of meeting and contact; being equally natural and equally cultivated; and whether there shall be friendliness or enmity depends upon the quality of this meeting. Acquaintance, intercourse, are essential to enmity, bringing occasions of "misunderstanding," which is not so much a defect of acquaintance as it is a failure of adjustment. And with nations a failure of adjustment is easier to compass than successful adjustment. With nations, therefore, Lamb's happy remark could be used either in the form he gave it or in an opposite form: they cannot be expected to dislike each other until they meet. For with contact come conflicts of interest, and rarely a settlement that satifies all. Lean grudges remain to be fed; and as the attention becomes fixed upon unsatisfied desires and upon the hopeless moral inferiority of all one's neighbors, the relations are not eased but are heavier-laden.

And yet while acquaintance is the way to enmity, it is the way and the only way to lasting friendship. It is through the perilous gate which opens into discord that nations must arrive at enmity. The nations that are fast enemies consequently are not the only ones that are well acquainted. Great Britain and the United States of recent decades, the United States and Canada, the Scandinavian nations, could hardly have attained what degree they have of mutual good will if there had been no long familiarity. Passing attraction may spring up overnight when stranger-nations face suddenly a common danger: Napolean's armies trampling over Europe brought together countries as separated as Austria and Britain; the fear of Russia has been more than once a bond between Turkey and Britain; the late Alliance in Central Europe finally gathered against itself the ends of the earth. It would not be true that nothing lasts of all this association. The enlarged acquaintance, the experience of actual cooperation among those that did cooperate, has made possible a new web of relations among them. The crust of habit has been broken, and these countries can never again be quite so startled by the idea of cooperation, nor require quite so intense a stimulus to make them fellow-workers.

A large part of the fallacy that acquaintance always leads to friendliness is perhaps due to the two meanings in "understanding." We quite correctly say that war grows out of misunderstanding. And then nothing seems more reasonable than that all hostility can be prevented merely by knowing one another.

But what is needed is not alone such understanding as a skilled huntsman has of his quarry; who knows the animals' feeding time and place, the timidities, the keenness of sense, the "spoor," the vital spot for his bullet. Knowing more of this than perhaps does any scientist, he brings down his game.

A larger kind of understanding is necessary, where tolerance and appreciation are fused with the knowledge, as in the understanding between a man and his dog, or between friends, where the knowledge is no less than with the hunter, but with something added to transform the whole. That the higher form of understanding can easily be changed into the lower and then be restored, is evident from playmates or friends who may fall out and fall in again, or in courtship with its transient misunderstandings. The misunderstanding here is not equivalent to a decrease of knowledge; no facts need be forgotten that were known before. What is said in ill temper is not unintelligible; it is only too intelligible: But the attitude has changed.

The sources of friendliness and of hostility, then, are somewhat larger than those of intelligence merely, of acquaintance with fact. The mutual attitude, the use to which the knowledge of each other is put, the breadth of purpose behind the acquaintance—these are the fateful additions. Such a vital thing as good will can somehow be present even with considerable ignorance, and be missing even where there is fair degree of knowledge.

The practical question, therefore, is not whether we shall have mutual acquaintance, but what we shall do with it, and whether we shall rely upon it alone. We may or may not wish it, yet acquaintance is upon us; the hidden corners of the earth now find themselves on the highways of land and water and air. Invisible, inaudible messages are throbbing across deserts and mountain chains and oceans. But the easy confidence that all these things will of themselves bring friendliness is misplaced. The almost unbroken contact, the readier intercourse, the fuller acquaintance prepares almost indifferently for either an increased good will among nations or an increased danger and mistrust. Indeed the intimacy of relations, if nothing additional and constructive is done regarding it, is apt to bring trouble rather than freedom from trouble. The new annulling of space, the knocking-out of partitions, means a universal surprised confronting, with all the novel problems and risks which come with such proximity.

SOCIETY AND THE SELF

By George Herbert Mead

IN THE YEAR 1910, in an article entitled, "The Moral Equivalent of War," William James stated the anomaly of war in the following sentences: "There is something highly paradoxical in the modern man's relation to war. Ask our millions, north and south, whether they would vote now (were such a thing possible) to have our war for the Union expunged from history, and the record of a peaceful transition to the present time substituted for that of its marches and battles, and probably hardly a handful of eccentrics would say yes. Those ancestors, those efforts, those memories and legends, are the most ideal part of what we now own together, a sacred spiritual possession worth more than all the blood poured out. Yet ask those same people whether they would be willing in cold blood to start another civil war now to gain another similar possession, and not one man or woman would vote for the proposition."

This was written for the Association for International Conciliation and was published four years before the beginnng of the Great War. If the same proposition were offered to the voters of the nations who fought through that war, I doubt if there would not be as unanimous a consensus of opinion in favor of expunging that war from history and replacing it by a peaceful advance toward our present day, though there might be a tough-minded group in the community who would insist that there had been gained in the awful conflict a lesson that could never have been learned in any less terrible an experience. And that lesson they would say was the duty that lies upon the society of the human race of doing away with war. We are in no mood to cover up the criminal ineptitude of warfare by the heroisms which it displays or the ideals which it may consecrate. Yet we have not become noncombatants. The country would arm to a man in a genuine war of self-defense, but the doctrine of the recently solemnized Pact of Peace, that war as a legimate measure of public policy has been forever damned, has the full-hearted support of the communities of the Western world. And I do not think that it is the horror of human suffering, even on the colossal scale of the Great War, that has been the controlling sentiment in this almost unanimous consensus of the communities of the world. We have learned more from the published archives of Foreign Offices than we have from the records of battlefields and atrocities.

We have learned that those who controlled public policies and finally mobilized armies were utilizing fears and hatreds and cupidities and individual greeds and jealousies which were far from representing issues over which the communities themselves wished to fight or thought they were fighting. We know that even in this day a war may arise between self-governing communities, but we know also that the issues that would lead up to this war, if they could be intelligently presented to the peoples involved, would never be left to the arbitrament of the god of battles. Even national cupidity, if it exists,

Reprinted from George Herbert Mead, "National-Mindedness and International-Mindedness." *The International Journal of Ethics*, XXXIX (July, 1929), 385–407, by permission of the University of Chicago Press.

realizes that under present conditions a so-called sucessful war will cost more than it can profit. Warfare is an utterly stupid method of settling differences of interest between different nations.

Professor James's position is this, that no people would enter upon a war for the sake of that very ideal heritage, which they would not be willing to sacrifice after the war was fought. He did not believe that in prospect any community would regard war as a spiritually profitable undertaking. The belief I have expressed is that as regards the Great War no nation in retrospect regards the spiritual results of fighting it as a sufficient price to pay for having undergone its evils. Having stated his paradox, that while a war in retrospect may have paid a spiritual dividend which renders it a great national blessing, no war in prospect can be so assessed, Professor James advances to the explanation of war's continued existence, for we do not now maintain armies and navies for the sake of "battles long ago" but in preparation for those which may be just around the corner. I am using the word spiritual as the opposite of material. It covers every value that we cannot put into economic form.

Let us be quite clear upon the issue under discussion. It is conceded by everyone that any war but a genuinely defensive war is a prospective evil which intelligent communities will avoid. We are not entering into the contentious question whether offense is not the best method of defense, nor are we, at present, undertaking to define the field which a genuinely defensive war will defend, whether this field will include national honor and peculiar interests. We will assume that these questions have been decided in a common agreement to the satisfaction of all civilized communities. It is evident that if this fortunate position were ever attained, intelligent statesmanship would without difficulty eliminate war.

And Professor James goes on to point out the spiritual losses which society will suffer if war goes. First of all come "those ancestors, those memories and legends—the ideal part of what we now own together," the spiritual heritage from war. But it is not upon this that Professor James insists, for he admits that we cannot deliberately shape our conduct to reach these results. We cannot plan wars to obtain spiritual heritages. The important spiritual values that he spreads out which come to us from war are the hardihood of body and mind, the willingness to pay to the uttermost for a supreme value, the ability to get out of our lesser selves, the acceptance of a supreme discipline which consistently subordinates minor ends to an ultimate end, the sense of at-oneness with all others in the community in the great enterprise, that exaltation of spirit which we all know is the loftiest experience and is so rare of attainment. For these war is in some sense a school. Professor James does not discuss the seamy side of this schooling and the immense spiritual frustrations which it involves. And indeed he is not called upon to do so, since he was a pacifist and was seeking for the moral equivalent which he thought we should provide if we abandon this schooling, however costly and unintelligent it may be. For there is in his opinion nothing in an industrial civilization, which is organized for profit and comfort, whose springs of action are competition and our efforts to get ahead of our fellows, and whose great social organizations fail to sweep the individual into emotional realization of his identity with the community—nothing indeed in such a civilization that does or can provide this schooling. We conduct our government only by the use of political partisanship. The church anxiously avoids the major issues of the community. Loyalities to family, business, or schools, the more intense they are, the more exclusive are they.

Professor James's suggestion is that the youth of the country should be conscripted for useful labor, in which they would get the hardihood of body and mind which military training gives. It would be essential to the accomplishment of the purpose which Professor James had in mind that this labor should be felt by the conscripted youth to be necessary to the life of the community. They would have to feel that they were identified with the community in what they did, if they were to reach that emotional fusion which war under favorable conditions induces.

I do not think that Professor James regarded his suggestion so much as an immediately practicable undertaking as an illustration of the type of experience which society in some fashion must bring into the lives of citizens if they are to get the qualities and training which war gives however imperfectly. What he insists upon is that the social ends and values are there and that they should enter the lives of our citizens, and that society has within its power to work out in some fashion practicable ways in which this can be accomplished. His scheme of conscription to community labor was a striking and picturesque manner of presenting what ought to be a logical part of a pacifist program.

Nearly twenty years have passed since Professor James wrote "The Moral Equivalent of War," and within those years the Great War has been fought, and has brought forth the League of Nations, the most serious undertaking to end war which international society has ever made. The attention of the pacifist is upon other things than the "moral equivalent of war." A hopeful project has been put into actual operation, and the relations of nations have been subject to a publicity and a sort of criticism which are novel in history. We have remained outside of the League of Nations because in our history we have been largely outside of the political life of Europe that led to the great catastrophe. We have been and are unwilling to enter into that complex of national, racial, and economic problems which are so foreign to us. But the outcome of the war has none the less brought us into more intimate human and economic relations with European peoples than we have occupied in the past, and the absence of imperialism in our history and our fundamental dislike of militarism inevitably arouse a sympathy with the great experiment that is being tried out at Geneva. The pacifist has a text to preach from that that he never had before and a practical program that was inconceivable twenty years ago. The somewhat embarrassing challenge which the great psychologist put up to him, he has pushed one side in the press of more practicable undertakings. Indeed, one re-reads the essay today with a certain sense of unreality.

Following this essay in *Memories and Studies* is an after-dinner address given by Professor James at a peace banquet. There is there the same account of human nature, bred through long centuries to fight, the same emphasis upon the failure of the pacifists' program to come to terms with the exigencies of life, and there is the same sense of the strength of the enemy—the rooted bellicosity of human nature and its demand for the thrill of battle. Said Professor James, "A deadly listlessness would come over most men's imagination of the future if they could seriously be brought to believe that never again in *saecula saeculorum* would a war trouble human history. In such a stagnant summer afternoon of a world, where would be the zest or interest?" We have had a surfeit of those thrills and have counted their costs, says the pacifist. It is not necessary to see the good in fighting any longer. The task of getting rid of it is too insistent when we have seen it and lived through it on the grand scale. There is the Peace Pact and there is the World Court, the very inception of which was American. For us to remain out of it is a scandal. In the midst of such activities why should the pacifist stop to consider the psychology of fighting? But the challenge is still there, and it may be that the pacifist is not wisely pushing it one side, in the press of his immediately practicable undertakings. He might get a deeper insight into their import.

Let us consider the spiritual values in which war may school men and women, however costly the schooling may be. The hardihood of body and mind—the opposite of the nature of Roosevelt's "molly-coddle"—can conceivably be secured without the expense of warfare. The program suggests that of Charles Lamb, burning down the house to get a roast pig, but it points out sharply the criticism upon the present order of society. Our insistent motives to strenuous conduct are personal and individualistic, those of success in the competitions of business, the professions, and the social struggle. The effective public ideals are those of well-being, comfort, and that condition of body and mind in which men can enjoy life. Our social programs look to the removal of evils, sickness, misery, and drudgery. As Frederick Harrison said of the ideal of the utilitarians, they look toward a world in which everyone could be sure of smacking his lips over a good breakfast of ham and eggs. The strenuousness of life seizes upon the individual in the struggle for the means of living and competitive success, but it does not inexorably involve his public interest, until the existence of his society is threatened, and when a man becomes altruistically interested in public ends, these ends appear as the alleviation of suffering and attained enjoyments rather than as his own achievements—the concentrated interest in mastering and controlling his world.

The other values that war may foster—willingness to pay to the uttermost for supreme goods, the rising above our lower selves, the acceptance of a discipline which subordinates minor ends to ultimate ends, and the exaltation that rises from identification of one's self with all who are with him in the great enterprise—that we should look away from civil life to war to arouse these is but a further reflection upon the conscious motivation of that civil life. War presents common goods in an imperative mood, which they will not assume in peaceful times, and therefore gives them a hold upon us which they never secure in philanthropic undertakings.

Professor James, however, has painted a picture of men who enjoy fighting immediately and have the zest of violent adventure in their blood through a long physiological and social heritage—the immanent bellicosity of human nature—which I think he has overdrawn. The average man does not want to fight for the sake of fighting. Threaten him and what is precious to him and the fighting complex is indeed ready to blaze out. His interest in violent adventure is easily satisfied by the movie, the detective tale, and the dramas of literature and history. Professor James was himself sympathetic with the revulsion to violence from drudgery and ennui. There is a story current that after a two days' session at a Chautauqua he exclaimed, "O, for an Armenian massacre!" But I do not think that in the interests of peace we have to combat a fundamental instinct of bloodshed. If the bare interest in slaughtering our fellows were so immediate, the campaigns of Army and Navy Leagues would be much simpler and much less expensive. The case for war does not lie in the fighting itself, but in that for which war compels us to fight. . . .

In a word we make the public good our immediate interest when it arouses the fighting spirit. Otherwise it is apt to be a philanthropic good, to reach which we must put one side our private interests. To be interested in the public good we must be disinterested, that is, not interested in goods in which our personal selves are wrapped up. In wartime we identify ourselves with the nation, and its interests are the interests of our primal selves. And in the fighting mood we find that we are in sympathetic accord with all others who are fighting for the same cause. Then we experience the thrill of marching in common enthusiasm with all those who in daily life are our competitors, our possible rivals, and opponents. The barriers are down which we erect against our neighbors and business associates. In daily life they may be hostile to our interests. We proceed warily. We protect ourselves even against our partners, associates, and employees with contracts and agreements defended with penalties. Even our good manners are means of keeping possible bores at a distance. It is sound sense to regard everyone as a possible enemy. In wartime these barriers are down. We need to feel the support of our fellows in the struggle and we grapple them to ourselves. The great issue itself is hallowed by the sense of at-oneness of a vast multitude.

It is easy to study this in everyday situations. Gather ten or fifteen of your acquaintances and make the subject of your conversation the admirable qualities and services of some one known to all. Then change the subject of converse to someone for whom all have a common dislike, and note how much warmer is the sense of at-oneness of those who are engaged in common disparagement than in encomium. The hostile attitude is peculiarly favorable to social cohesion. The solid South is the product of common hostility to the negro as a social equal. The Ku Klux Klan is a deliberate manufacture of compact groups by the use of racial and religious antipathies. I think it is worth our while to make some inquiry into this cohesive power, which the hostile impulse in human nature exercises with such absolute authority.

We have long known that behind the spiritual exaltation of wartime patriotism and the irresponsibility of mob-consciousness lies the same psychological mechanism. And this fact is a ground neither for extrolling it nor for damning it. It is just a psychological mechanism which like other mechanisms has served both fine and ignoble ends. It is equally inept to define, with Dr. Johnson, patriotism as the last refuge of the scoundrel, and to exalt Judge Lynch as the embodiment of social justice. But it is both apt and obligatory upon us to examine this mechanism when we are not caught in its meshes, and are free to comprehend it; for when we are involved in it, it is next to impossible to approach it with impartial consideration. Neither the patriot in his moment of exaltation nor the member of the blind mob in his unrestrained ferocity is capable of following the dictum: Know thyself. He may conceivably get outside of his intoxication, but he is then engaged in controlling his passionate impulses. He is in no mood to understand them.

I have already indicated the character of this mechanism. The hostile impulse unites us against the common enemy, because it has force enough to break down customary social textures, by which we hold others at a distance from our inexpugnable selves. But it was this social structure by which we realized ourselves. Our rights and our privileges, our distinctions of capacity and skill, our superiorities and our inferiorities, our social positions and prestige, our manners and our foibles not only distinguish and separate us from others but they constitute us what we are to ourselves. They constitute our individualities, the selves that we recognize, when we thank God that we are not as other men are, and when we determine upon what terms we can live and work with members of our families, with our neighbors and our countrymen. If these are in any degree broken down we are no longer the same individuals that we were. To join ourselves with others in the common assault upon the common foe we have become more than allies, we have joined a clan, have different souls, and have the exuberant feeling of being at one with this community.

There lie in all of us both of these attitudes. It is only in our common interests and our identities with others that there is found the stuff out of which social selves are made—and it is only in distinguishing and protecting these selves from others that we exercise the self-consciousness that makes us responsible and rational beings.

But even the apparatus of this self-consciousness we have borrowed from the community. What are our rights in which we defend ourselves against all comers, but the rights which we recognize in others, that ours may be recognized by others? What are our peculiar powers and capacities but the facilities by which we perform our parts in common undertakings, and where would they be if others did not recognize them and depend upon them? The proudest assertion of independent selfhood is but the affirmation of a unique capacity to fill some social role. Even the man who haughtily withdraws himself from the crowd, thinks of himself in terms of an ideal community which is but a refinement of the world in which he lives. It is by assuming the common attitudes to each other, which an organized community makes possible, that we are able to address ourselves in the inner forum of our thoughts and private purposes. A self is a composite or interaction of these two parts of our natures—the fundamental impulses which make us co-operating neighbors and friends, lovers and parents and children, and rivals, competitors, and enemies; on the other side the evocation of this self which we achieve when we address ourselves in the language which is the common speech of those about us. We talk to ourselves, ask ourselves what we will do under certain conditions, criticize and approve of our own suggestions and ideas, and in taking the organized attitudes of those engaged in common undertakings we direct our own impulses. These two parts are the matter and the form of the self, if I may use Aristotelian phraseology. The one is the stuff of social impulses and the other is the power which language has conferred upon us, of not only seeing ourselves as others see us but also of addressing ourselves in terms of the common ideas and functions which an organized society makes possible. We import the conversation of the group into our inner sessions and debate with ourselves. But the concatenated concepts which we use are ours because we are speaking in the language of the outer universe of discourse, the organized human world to which we belong.

In the sophisticated field of self-consciousness we control our conduct. We place ourselves over against other selves and determine what we want to do, what we have a right to do, and what other people may do. Here we assert ourselves and maintain ourselves by recognized rights and accorded privileges. In the field of the stuff—the matter—of personality we have no such power. We are born with our fundamental impulses. We choose our business associates and the members of our clubs and the guests at our dinner parties, but we *fall in* love, and whatever action we take upon this primal premise, it is not a matter of our own choice. We say that we instinctively help a child who has fallen down, and our immediate attitudes toward puppies, kittens, and little pigs are different from those we take toward dogs, cats, and hogs, and the impulse to helpfulness is just as much an endowment as the impulse of hostility. This primal stuff of which we are made up is not under our direct control. The primitive sexual, parental, hostile, and co-operative impulses out of which our social selves are built up are few—but they get an almost infinite field of varied application in society, and with every development of means of intercourse, with every invention they find new opportunities of expression. Here by taking thought we can add to our social stature. But we have no direct control over our loves and our hates, our likes and our dislikes, and for this reason we are relatively helpless when a common enemy fuses us all into a common patriotic pack or stampedes us under the influence of sympathetic terror.

This, then, is the stuff out of which human social selves are made up, their primal stuff or matter of social impulses, and the form of sophisticated self-consciousness. But society is the interaction of these selves, and an interaction that is only possible if out of their diversity unity arises. We are indefinitely different from each other, but our differences make interaction possible. Society is unity in diversity. However, there is always present the danger of its miscarriage. There are the two sources of its unity—the unity arising from the interconnection of all the different selves in their self-conscious diversity and that arising from the identity of common impulses; the unity, for example, of the members of a great highly organized industrial concern or of the faculties and the students of a great university and the unity of a crowd that rushes to save a child in danger of its life. By these two principles of unity society is maintained; but there is an ever present risk of failure. Every society has it at the back of its mind. We want security and we distrust it. Society in every period of its history has presented to itself that danger in one form or another. Today we dread the Bolsheviki. At another time it has been the "interests"; at times the mob, and at other times the arbitrary power of a monarch.

We come back to our original question. How shall we get and maintain that unity of society in which alone we can exist? The ever present method of creating cohesion from below, from the impulses, is found in the common hostile impulse. The criticisms which are exercised upon the civil motives are but illustrations of this. Government is by partisanship. We can bring the voters to the polls only through their hostility to opposite parties. A campaign for a community chest is quickened by competitive teams. The great days of the religions have been the days of hostility, between the religions, between the Church and the sects, or between different churches. The fight with the devil and all his angels united men whom a common hope of salvation left untouched. More evident still is the need of the fighting attitude when a large community with varied groups and opposing interests is to be brought into a self-conscious whole. The antagonism of the Chinese to the Japanese and the English did more than anything else to awaken a Chinese national spirit. In our Civil War slavery was the issue, because it divided the nation. Men of the North fought for the Union and in fighting for it they felt it. The readiest way of arousing an emotional appreciation of a common issue is to fight together for that issue, and until we have other means of attaining it we can hardly abandon war.

It is not a question of thrills nor a satisfying a deep-seated bellicosity in the human animal. It is a question of making ourselves actually feel the values that are wrapped up in the community. While war was still a possible national adventure, there was a certain rough psychological justification for the dictum, that at least one war in a generation was essential for the spiritual hygiene of the nation. The toleration of secret diplomacy, the cherishing of national honor and peculiar interests as lying outside the field of negotiation had behind it an obscure but profound feeling that in national honor and in these peculiar interests were symbolized a national unity which could be made precious by the arbitrament of war.

What better illustration of this can be found than in the Monroe Doctrine? None are agreed upon what the doctrine is. The nations of South and Central America in whose interests it was inaugurated with one voice denounce it. It is absurd to say that we can find an issue in the threatened neighborhood on this hemisphere of European powers, when our continent-wide, unfortified Canadian frontier, within the century and more since it was established, is almost the only frontier in the whole wide world that has not been crossed by belligerent forces. No, it is something—no matter what it is—for which we will *fight*. To think of it in these terms is to feel that there is a nation back of it. The more unintelligble the issue is, the more it emphasizes the unanimity of the community. It is an issue that cannot be discussed for we cannot in cold blood find out what the issue is. We must be of one mind about it, for it is impossible to have different minds about that which no one can comprehend. The only issue involved in the Monroe Doctrine is this, are you a patriot, are you a red-blooded American, or are you a mollycoddle. Let us get down to real reasons and abandon good reasons. Even when we hope that there may be no future wars, we feel that we should keep certain issues which can arouse the fighting spirit, for the sake of their effect in drawing men together in a fashion which cannot be achieved by public interests, which are after all so divisive.

I take it that this is the real question that is put up to us by Professor James's moral equivalent of war. Can we find outside of the fighting spirit that unifying power which presents a supreme issue to which all others are subordinated, which will harden us to undergo everything, and unite us in the enthusiasm of a common end?

> When I have borne in memory what has tamed
> Great Nations, how ennobling thoughts depart
> When men change swords for ledgers, and desert
> The student's bower for gold, some fears unnamed
> I had, my Country—am I to be blamed?

There is nothing in the history of human society nor in present-day experience which encourages us to look to the primal impulse of neighborliness for such cohesive power. The love of ones' neighbor cannot be made into a common consuming passion. The great religions that have sought to embody it when they have dominated society have appeared as the Church militant. . . . There is, to be sure, no falling off in numbers of those who identify themselves with different Christian sects in the Western world, but there never was a time when the churches have had less power in organizing the community into common action. We can unite with common zeal to aid the victims of famines, of earthquakes, and of conflagrations, but we do not go into nor come out of such common undertakings with a sense of the supremacy of the nation or society that holds us together. The passion of love between the sexes isolates those whom it consumes, and family life segregates us. The positive social impulses exhibit no forces that bind us immediately together in conscious devotion to the complex community out of which our sophisticated selves arise. They have their place in the cults, mores, and customs that form the tissues of human society, but they do not flame out into a patriotism that can fuse men in the devotion to the fatherland.

The Great War has presented not a theory but a condition. If war were a possible measure of public policy, it might be kept for the sake of social cohesion, even if the ends for which wars are ostensibly fought were illusory and inadequate. But the Great War has made this no longer possible. Every war if allowed to go the accustomed way of wars will become a world war, and every war pursued uncompromisingly and intelligently must take as its objective the destruction not of hostile forces but of enemy nations in their entirety. It has become unthinkable as a policy for adjudicating national differences. It has become logically impossible. This is not to say that it may not arise. Another catastrophe may be necessary before we have cast off the cult of warfare, but we cannot any longer *think* our international life in terms of warfare. It follows that if we do *think* our national and international life, we can no longer depend upon war for the fusion of disparate and opposing elements in the nation. We are compelled to reach a sense of being a nation by means of rational self-consciousness. We must *think* ourselves in terms of the great community to which we belong. We cannot depend upon feeling ourselves at one with our compatriots, because the only effective feeling of unity springs from our common response against the common enemy. No other social emotion will melt us into one. Instead of depending upon a national soul we must achieve national-mindedness. . . . Let me repeat if we surrender war there is no way of maintaining national unity except in discovering that unity in the midst of the diversity of individual concerns. There *is* a common good in which we are involved, and if society is still to exist we must discover it with our heads. We cannot depend upon our diaphragms and the visceral responses which a fight sets in operation.

There is something profoundly pathetic in the situation of great peoples, that have been struggling up through long centuries of fighting and its attendant miseries, coming closer and closer to each other in their daily life, fashioning unwittingly larger racial, lingual, liturgical, confessional, political, and economic communities, and realizing only intermittently the spiritual life which this larger community confers upon them, and realizing it only when they could fight for it. The pathos comes out most vividly in the nationalisms of the nineteenth and twentieth centuries. These nationalisms have meant the sudden realization that men belonged to communities that transcended their groups, families, and clans. They had attained selves through which they entered into relation with their common nationals, and the only way in which they could seize upon and enjoy this new spiritual experience was in the fight for its symbols, their common language and literature, and their common political organizations. The pathos lies in the inability to feel the new unity with the nation except in the union of arms. It is not that men love fighting for its own sake, but they undergo its rigors for the sake of conjunction with all those who are fighting in the same cause. There is only one solution for the problem and that is in finding the intelligible common objects, the objects of industry and commerce, the common values in literature, art, and science, the common human interests which political mechanisms define and protect and foster. But all these values are at first divisive. They appear at first as individual and class interests and at first one fights for them and against others who threaten them. The rational attitude is to find what common values lie back of the divisions and competitions. Within our communities the process of civilization is the discovery of these common ends which are the bases of social organizations. In social organization they come to mean not opposition but diverse occupations and activities. Difference of function takes the place of hostility of interest. The hard task is the realization of the common value in the experience of conflicting groups and indviduals. It is the only substitute. In civilized communities while individuals and classes continue to contend, as they do, with each other, it is with the consciousness of common interests that are the bases both for their contentions and their solutions. The state is the guardian of these common interests, and its authority lies in the universal interest of all in their maintenance. The measure of civilization is found in the intelligence and will of the community in making these common interests the means and the reason for converting diversities into social organization.

The Great War has posed the problem before contending nations of carrying civilization into the community of nations; that is, it has left us with the demand for international-mindedness. The moral equivalent of war is found in the intelligence and the will both to discover these common interests between contending nations and to make them the basis for the solution of the existing differences and for the common life which they will make possible. . . .

What I am seeking to bring out is that the chief difficulty in attaining international-mindedness does not lie in the clash of international interests but in the deep-seated need which nations feel of being ready to fight, not for ostensible ends but for the sake of the sense of national unity, of self-determination, of national self-respect that they can achieve in no other way so easily as in the readiness to fight.

National-mindedness and international-mindedness are inextricably involved in each other. Stable nations do not feel the need in any such degree as those that are seeking stability. . . . Self-defense remains a permissible ground for fighting, but with no war of offense there would be none of defense, and wars would vanish with the development of adequate means of negotiation, but we are not willing to have the readiness to fight disappear. So we retain national honor and peculiar interests. Why cannot these be adjudicated as well? Because these touch the sense of national self-respect. As long as we have these provisos, we have the proud sense of being willing to fight—to stake everything upon the assertion of national selfhood. It was this sense which

President Wilson's unfortunate phrase offended—being too proud to fight. It was seemingly a phrase that contained a contradiction in terms. Pride predicates a fighting-spirit.

Now, if I am not mistaken such an attitude at the present period in human history is a revelation of an uncertainty of national selfhood and a grasping after the approved means of securing it—the wartime spirit. For at this period of the world's history there is no point of national honor and peculiar interest which is not as open to reasonable negotiation in a community of self-respecting nations as any of the so-called justiciable and negotiable issues, if we were sure of ourselves. But we are not sure of our national selves, and a certain amount of national psychoanalysis would be very valuable if not very probable. One thing, however, is clear, that we cannot attain international-mindedness until we have attained a higher degree of national-mindedness than we possess at present; and a rough gauge of it will be found in the necessity of retaining national honor and peculiar interests as *causae belli*.

Such a formulation seems to imply that if we were willing to get down to real reasons and abandon good reasons, if we were willing to be really reasonable we could immediately banish the threat of war from our international and our national life. I do not believe that this is the case. Civilization is not an affair of reasonableness; it is an affair of social organization. The selfhood of a community depends upon such an organization that common goods do become the ends of the individuals of the community. We know that these common goods are there, and in some considerable degree we can and do make them our individual ends and purposes, to such a degree that we have largely banished private warfare from the recognized methods of maintaining self-respect in civil conflicts. But there are still great gaps in our social organization, notably between our producers and the social service which they perform. Here there are groups that have to assure themselves of their self-respect by fighting on occasions. The labor unions and the employers as well preserve their solidarity, that is their sense of common selfhood, by the mechanism of hostility, that is by the threats of strikes and lockouts. Back of it lies the inability of the laborer to realize himself in the social process in which he is engaged. Where such a situation becomes acute, men, if they can, will always bind themselves together by hostile organizations to realize their common purposes and ends and thus assure themselves the selfhood which society denies them. . . . We will get rid of the mechanism of warfare only as our common life permits the individual to identify his own ends and purposes with those of the community of which he is a part and which has endowed him with a self.

"WE AND THEY"

By Rudyard Kipling

Father, Mother, and Me,
    Sister and Auntie say
All the people like us are We,
    And every one else is They.
And They live over the sea,
    While We live over the way,
But—would you believe it?—They look upon We
    As only a sort of They!

We eat pork and beef
    With cow-horn-handled knives.
They who gobble Their rice off a leaf,
    Are horrified out of Their lives;
And They who live up a tree,
    And feast on grubs and clay,
(Isn't it scandalous?) look upon We
    As a simply disgusting They!

We shoot birds with a gun.
    They stick lions with spears.
Their full-dress is un—.
    We dress up to Our ears.
They like Their friends for tea.
    We like Our friends to stay;
And, after all that, They look upon We
    As an utterly ignorant They!

We eat kitcheny food.
    We have doors that latch.
They drink milk or blood,
    Under an open thatch.
We have Doctors to fee.
    They have Wizards to pay.
And (impudent heathen!) They look upon We
    As a quite impossible They!

All good people agree,
    And all good people say,
All nice people, like Us, are We
    And every one else is They:
But if you cross over the sea,
    Instead of over the way,
You may end by (think of it!) looking on We
    As only a sort of They!

By Rudyard Kipling, *Debits and Credits* (London: Macmillan and Company, 1926), pp. 327–328.

THE NATURE OF RACE CONSCIOUSNESS

By William O. Brown

RACE CONSCIOUSNESS is a major form of group consciousness. In this paper it is defined as the tendency towards sentimental and ideological identification with a racial group. For the individually race conscious the race becomes an object of loyalty, devotion, and pride. By virtue of this fact it becomes an entity, a collective representation. The race becomes a fiction, a stereotype which to the race conscious is a reality.

H. A. Miller has indicated that a class, a nationality or a race aware of its status in relation to a dominant class, nationality or race with which it is in conflict tends to develop what he aptly terms an "oppression psychosis." Certainly this is true in the case of racial groups. Thus at the present time the ideology of the oppressed is developing among the natives of Africa, especially those of white-controlled South Africa. And the Negro in the United States gives frequent and eloquent expression to this type of sentiment. The following poem by James D. Corrothers is a typical expression of this feeling of self-pity and oppression:

> To be a Negro in a day like this
> Demands forgiveness; bruised with blow on blow
> Betrayed like him whose woe dimmed eyes gave bliss
> Still one must succor those who brought one low,
> To be a Negro in a day like this.
>
> To be a Negro in a day like this
> Demands rare patience—patience that can wait
> In utter darkness. 'Tis the path to miss,
> And knock unheeded at an iron gate,
> To be a Negro in a day like this.
>
> To be a Negro in a day like this
> Demands strange loyalty. We serve a flag
> Which is to us white freedom's emphasis
> And one must love when truth and justice lag,
> To be a Negro in a day like this.
>
> To be a Negro in a day like this—
> Alas! Lord God what have we done?
> Still shines the gate all gold and amethyst,
> But I pass by the glorious goal unwon,
> To be a Negro in a day like this.

The race conscious Negro reflecting on his sorrowful lot pities his poor race. Speaking of Armistice Day a Negro writer is unable to see anything joyous in it for the Negro:

Adapted from William O. Brown, "The Nature of Race Consciousness," *Social Forces*, X (October, 1931), 90–97.

So this is Armistice Day. We stand today at another milestone. Our feet are tired, for they have been bruised by our walks along the way. Somehow our burdens have become very heavy, and we have grown, O so weary.

Not always is this self-pity of the despairing type. At times it is cool and detached. In the case of the Negro this type of attitude is expressed in the writing of some of the younger Negroes such as Hughes and Cullen. Notice, for example, this neat little turn from Hughes:

> I do not hate you,
> For your faces are beautiful, too.
> I do not hate you,
> Your faces are whirling lights of loveliness, too.
> Yet why do you torture me,
> O white strong ones,
> Why do you torture me?

The race conscious may realize their dilemma, pity their race, and yet be determined to take their punishment standing up. This sentiment is frequently expressed, for example, in the poetry of the Negro, the editorial page of the Negro press and in the spoken word. Self-pity may be dignified, accompanied by courage. A Zionistic Jew, Maurice Samuel, ends one of his books, *You Gentiles,* with a sentence that epitomizes this reaction. Says he, "Whatever we do we are damned—and I would rather be damned standing up than lying down."

Closely associated with the oppression psychosis of the race conscious is their excessive sensitivity. Since the race conscious identify their personal status with that of their race any attack on the race is taken personally. The race conscious are ware of their status in relation to their race. They become "touchy" or supersensitive. To demean the race they feel is to demean every member of it. Naturally, derogatory pictures of their race are resented. Speaking of this racial hypersensitiveness among Negroes, Miller says,

Supersensitiveness to insult is becoming characteristic of the Negroes. This is merely the oppression psychosis in action. The Negro is merely becoming racially self-conscious.

Since the race conscious are sensitive they naturally resent anything that impugns the status of their race. Hence they protest vehemently against the notion of their inferiority as a race. Any definition of status for the race that implies subordination angers and hurts them. And any type of behavior on the part of members of their race that implies the subservient attitude to other races they condemn. For example, Negroes, deplore the "Uncle Tom" type of Negro, the name "Uncle Tom" becoming an epithet that stings. The race conscious Negroes demand that the group as a whole give up its "tin cup" habit of asking for money for churches and other institutions, such a practise being regarded as lowering. Racial status becomes a precious possession to the race conscious.

Among the race conscious their race is reacted to as a social object. It becomes a fiction, a mental stereotype. To it one writes poems. One praises it and becomes eloquent about its achievements, virtues or qualities. The race is personalized. It is an object of feeling, sentiment, and thought. This selection from Helen Johnson, a Negro writer, illustrates the point.

> Ah my race
> Hungry race,
> Throbbing and young—
> Ah my race,
> Wonder race,
> Sobbing with song—
> Ah my race,
> Laughing race,
> Careless in mirth—
> Ah my veiled
> Unformed race
> Fumbling in birth.

The race conscious posit their race as an entity to which they have obligations. They have a conscience about this race. They must serve it, fight for it, be loyal to it. To the outsider the race of the race conscious may appear to be an imaginative construction but to the initiated this race is a reality, in a sense, a personal experience.

Race pride is an aspect of race consciousness. It implies the tendency to place highly one's race, to exalt its virtues, to take pride in its past, its great men, its achievements. The racially proud express what Sumner has termed ethnocentrism. Their race becomes the measure of all things. It becomes the central, pivotal human grouping. Invariably race pride tends to be an expression of the sentiment of racial superiority. This is even true of subordinate racial groups such as the Negro in the United States or the natives of South Africa. Such a belief gives support to race conscious individuals. It bolsters their self-respect, exalts their conception of themselves and inures them against the pain incident to a low status. The race consciousness of a subordinate racial group is apt to be more defensive than is true of that of a dominant racial group. Psychologically its utility is probably greater for the former than for the latter, though to the statusless in the dominant racial group it proves a great boon, giving them a sense of their value that is out of proportion to reality.

This race pride is expressed in several forms. Thus racial achievements are magnified. In the case of racial groups of an inferior status memory of racial achievements compensates for the tribulations of subordination. Stress placed on the achievements of the race represents an attempt to effect a more favorable impression of the race both by its members and by outsiders. This manifestation of racial pride is a defensive gesture, being an attempt to bolster one's conception of one's race. And thus the race conscious individual, contemplating his great racial past, is secured in his sense of personal worth.

Glorification of the individually great of the race is another expression of the pride of the race conscious. The great man of the race becomes a symbol. His achievements typify the possibilities of the race. This great man, in the ideology of the race conscious, tends to become a mythological figure. Through him they vicariously achieve status. This fact is very well exemplified in the following glorification by Countee Cullen of three of the Negro great.

These men were kings albeit they were black;
Touissaint and Dessalines and L'Ouverture;
Their majesty has made me turn my back
Upon a plaint I once shaped to endure.

These men were black, I say, but they were crowned
And purple-clad, however brief their time.
Stifle your agony, let grief be drowned:
We know joy had a day once and had a clime.

Dark gutter snipe, black sprawlers-in-the-mud,
A thing men did a man may do again;
What answer filters through your sluggish blood
To those dark ghosts who knew so bright a rein?
"Lo, I am dark, but comely," Sheba sings;
"And we were black," three shades reply, "but
    kings."

This idealization of the great men of the race is a means of glorifying the race as a whole. It exalts the race in the eyes of its race conscious members. As a result the race conscious themselves are exalted. The psychological states of depression, sense of inferiority and humility give way to those of a feeling of personal worth and pride.

Correlating with those traits of race consciousness previously discussed is race prejudice. Race prejudice seems to be an inevitable accompaniment of race consciousness. This is true whether the race consciousness is that of dominant or dominated races. Consciousness of race implies awareness of difference. It effects the division of the racial world into "out" and "in" races. It results in stereotypes of the "out" race. Thus to the race conscious white man all Orientals are alike, as are Mexicans or Negroes. His reaction to them is defined in terms of a derogatory picture or stereotype of them. The native in South Africa or the Negro in the United States who is racially conscious reacts the same way to the oppressing white man. In fact probably the race prejudice among the race conscious of the dominated racial groups is more bitter and potent than is true of that among the dominant races. The contemplation of what the "superior" race has done to the subordinate race naturally breeds hatred. The race conscious of the low status group are aware of past and present exploitation. They recall with bitterness the limitation of their freedom and their debasement. Grievances are formulated, becoming a part of their ideology. The Negro poet, Claude McKay, gives eloquent expression to the prejudice of the race conscious in the following poem.

Oh, when I think of my long-suffering race,
For weary centuries despised, oppressed,
Enslaved and lynched, denied a human place
In the great life line of the Christian West;
And in the Black Land disinherited,
Robbed in the ancient country of its birth,
My heart grows sick with hate, becomes as lead,
For this my race that has no home on earth.
Then from the dark depths of my soul I cry

To the avenging angels to consume
The white man's world of wonders utterly:
Let it be swallowed up in earth's vast womb,
Or upward roll as a sacrificial smoke
To liberate my people from its yoke!

The race conscious easily believe in a portentous destiny for their race. The race conscious among the "superior" races are aware of the "burdens," duties and obligations of their race to "uplift," Christianize or "civilize" the "backward" races. This is their mission and their destiny. But it is not only the race conscious of the dominant races who have a sense of mission. The race conscious children of the "backward" and "inferior" races are likewise aware of a future and a mission. They have faith, a faith that is often naive, tinged with the messianic element. The following profession of faith by a follower of Garvey is typical in this respect.

Garvey taught us six great truths. First, this is not our country and we are not to remain here and become a part of this nation. Second, we have no constitutional rights. Having been unable to force them in the constitution—they were put there as a free gift to be withdrawn at will—we now have no power to compel their enforcement. Third, politics, religion, and education cannot solve the Negro problem; nothing but a government owned by Negroes will solve it. Fourth, begging and pleading will not get for us what other races have had to use force to obtain. Fifth, Africa is the natural home of the black man and will remain so when these countries where white men live become too crowded. It is our duty to carry our education to the native African, teach him the ways of civilization as we know it, and become great men of the world in and among our own people. Sixth, Africa must be redeemed. The alien race will give back Africa as soon as they know that all of the four hundred million Negroes want it. These are the ideals Garvey followers look to for salvation and whether Garvey be dead or alive, we will follow them to victory or eternal defeat.

No race conscious member of a subordinate group can believe that his race is to suffer forever the status of an outcaste. There will come a time when his race shall "enter the kingdom." Notice this element in the poem quoted below from the pen of Countee Cullen.

We shall not always plant while others reap
The golden increment of bursting fruit,
Nor always countenance, abject and mute,
That lesser men should hold their brothers cheap;
Nor everlastingly while others sleep
Shall we beguile their limbs with mellow flute,
Nor always bend to some more subtle brute;
We were not made eternally to weep.

The night, whose sable breast relieves the stark,
White stars, is no less lovely being dark,
And there are buds that cannot bloom at all
In light, but crumble, piteous and fall.
So in the dark we hide the heart that bleeds,
And wait and tend our agonizing seeds.

In the hope for a better future the proscribed and race conscious can "fight with faces set, still visioning the stars."

The race conscious of the dominant group do not monopolize the notion of being "a light to the Gentiles." Their brethren of the "inferior" races tend also to develop the ideology of saviors. They are apt to feel that their suffering has refined and spiritualized them, making them superior to their gross natured persecutors. A delicious sense of moral superiority is achieved. Witness the following sample from J. S. Cotter:

> Brother, come!
> And let us go unto one God,
> And when we stand before Him
> I shall say—
> "Lord, I do not hate,
> I am hated.
> I scourge no one,
> I am scourged.
> I covet no lands,
> My lands are coveted.
> I mock no people,
> I am mocked."
> And Brother, what shall you say?

The Suffering Servant idea is implicit often in the race consciousness of the proscribed races. To fight with gross, material weapons would reflect on their moral character. Hence the race bides its time, hoping that the example set of suffering and moral fortitude will soften the stony hearts of the tormentors. McKay has expressed this sentiment well, speaking of the Negro.

> Think you that I am not fiend and savage too?
> Think you that I could not arm me with a gun
> And shoot down ten of you for every one
> Of my black brothers burnt by you?
> Be not deceived for every deed you do,
> I could match—outmatch; am I not Africa's son,
> Black of the black land where black deeds are done?

> But the Almighty from the darkness drew
> My soul and said: even thou shall be a light
> Always to burn on the benighted earth,
> The dusky face I set among the whites
> For these to prove thyself of highest worth;
> Before the world is swallowed up in night,
> To show thy little lamp: go forth, go forth!

For the race conscious among the races of low status to believe in a better future is essential. Race consciousness otherwise would atrophy and die. Hope is essential to its vitality. And to be able to believe that while they suffer and "envision the stars" they are at the same time performing a mission satisfies the human need for the feelings of worth and superiority.

Up to now there is probably little or none of the sentiment of solidarity among the various dominant races. A community of feeling has not as yet developed, though certain ideologists agitate for such a sentiment. Incompatibility of national and regional interests and values prevent this development. But the opposite is the case among the proscribed races of the world. Thus the Negro in the United States who is assimilated to the ideology of race consciousness sympathizes with the struggles of the African natives, protests against the imperialism of the United States in the Caribbean, appreciates the nationalism of the Indians and Chinese and is sympathetic generally with struggling minorities. The race conscious who belong to proscribed groups sense a spiritual unity and are aware of a common cause. At the Brussels conference of oppressed races and nationalities a young African is reported to have said:

Ah you Chinamen among my auditors here, I embrace you as comrades. You are setting a grand example of revolt for all the oppressed colonial peoples. I only hope that they will catch the inspiration from you.

In the modern world the oppressed races have a common foe, the white peoples of Western Europe and their cousins of the United States. This isolable and convenient enemy makes the emergence of sentimental solidarity among the oppressed easy. The mechanisms of modern communication aid in the diffusion of this feeling to all the oppressed children of men. The oppressed have common experiences, face the same problems, those involving racial status, and hence speak a common language, ideologically speaking. Each oppressed group is strengthened by this realization. The cause of race consciousness takes on a wider meaning and importance.

SOCIAL MOVEMENTS INVOLVING RACIAL GROUPS

By Clarence E. Glick

I PROPOSE TO POINT OUT SOME PHASES of collective behavior theory which may be derived from analysis of social change in interracial situations, particularly with regard to the role of social movements in social change. More specifically, I would like to indicate how we may improve our frame of reference for analyzing social change through social movements by considering social movements in the field of race relations.

At the outset, three kinds of social movements involving persons of different racial origins must be distinguished: *racial* movements, *interracial* movements, and *non-racial* movements. These movements should be considered with refer-

Reprinted from Clarence E. Glick, "Collective Behavior in Race Relations," *American Sociological Review*, XIII (June, 1948), 288–294. By permission.

ence to the typical sequence of changes which occur once different racial groups come into contact with one another. These three kinds of movements should be regarded as arbitrary divisions of what is actually a continuous series. As relationships between racial groups develop, some aspects of this series become predominant; certain types of social movements particularly relevant to the current hase of the social change sequence successively assume larger proportion in the configuration of collective actions.

Racial movements draw their participants from *one* of the racial groups involved in relations with one another. Racial movements may develop either in the group with dominant or subordinate status. The African Colonization Society among ante-bellum whites, which was interested in eliminating the "race problem" in America by returning the Negroes to Africa, illustrates a racial movement among the dominant group while the Garvey Movement and most "native movements" or nationalistic, independence movements are examples of those among subordinated groups. Either implicitly or explicitly, the objectives of most racial movements involve changes which would widen the social distance and even limit the physical contacts between the racial groups, at least temporarily. As the racial groups strive to retain or regain their social and cultural identities, political dominance or independence, or economic ascendance, the emphasis is upon inner cohesion of the racial group at the expense of contacts and association with other racial groups in a unified social life.

Interracial movements differ from racial movements in the origins of their participants and in their objectives. They draw members from both the dominant and the subordinate racial groups. More important, their activities are directed toward objectives which, if attained, would promote social change toward further integration of the different races into a common social system on a "non-racial" basis. Interracial movements, of course, vary widely in the rate of speed that integration is sought or in the extent of social integration that is tolerated and worked for. As in racial movements, attitudes of race-consciousness are present among the participants, but here "hostilities" and "resentments" are likely to be more covert, less openly expressed, than in racial movements since members of both racial groups are acting co-operatively, with personal contacts, toward shared objectives. These objectives typically have to do with improvement of living conditions and status opportunities of persons in the subordinate racial group. Those who participate in the movement do so as "race members" and with full awareness of the racial identity of the other participants. The National Urban League, the National Association for the Advancement of Colored People, dozens of the interracial committees formed in cities of the United States during the recent war are examples of interracial movements.

Non-racial movements, like interracial movements, draw their participants from various racial groups but are distinguished from interracial movements in that the fact of racial affiliation is only an incidental element in the membership. The objectives of non-racial movements are not primarily concerned with the welfare of a subordinated racial group or with altering the nature or conditions of relationships between racial groups. Non-racial movements are directed toward types of social change which would affect the whole society, or any part of it, without reference to racial factors. Achievement of these objectives would, in many cases, affect the interracial pattern, but this would be an indirect effect of the social action rather than the motivation for such action. The objectives of non-racial movements appeal to certain individuals of various racial origins but do not attract all individuals of any particular racial group. Non-racial movements occur in a society composed of people of divergent racial origins who are becoming or have become socially integrated into a common status system, at least to the point where racial identity may be subordinated in certain situations to other factors. Race consciousness, in this instance, diminishes until it largely or completely disappears. Physical divergencies related to various racial origins play little more part in interpersonal relations within non-racial movements than unusual stature or a disposition toward baldheadedness. Each participant interacts with the others as a "person" with likable and disliked characteristics. In Hawaii the participation of individuals of Chinese, Japanese, Hawaiian, Portuguese, and *haole* ("North European") ancestries in the organization of a union of plantation workers, and the participation of other individuals of the same diverse ancestries in the promotion of the cause of an international "Federal Union" represent movements in "Hawaiian society" which are *non-racial* in character.

The order in which these types of movements has been presented here is the order in which they may be expected to appear in a typical race relations sequence. Comparative studies of interracial situations indicate that as contacts develop between races who initially are culturally as well as physically divergent from one another and as the groups are drawn into increasingly continuous association on various levels, there tends to be a typical series of transitions involving conflict and accommodation before assimilation dissolves group barriers and incorporates all of the population elements into a more or less unified society. Before this sequence is completed some forms of all three of these types of social movements will almost certainly have emerged. The predominance of one or another of these types of social movements may serve as an index to each phase of the sequence. Racial movements, which tend to polarize the groups, are most characteristic of those phases in which conflict is most intense. Interracial movements occur when some sort of status system has been worked out and conflict has been reduced to the extent that antagonisms between the groups can be subordinated to the achievement of objectives representing an area of agreement. The appearance of non-racial movements is incontrovertible evidence of extensive assimilation of at least some proportion of the different groups into an emerging unified society. It must be emphasized, however, that in a complex society different phases of the sequence may exist cotemporaneously in different geographic areas, on different status levels, and in different specialized fields of activity. It follows that differnt forms of each of these three types of movements may be going on simultaneously. The research student interested in trends in race relations, therefore, might find significant evidence in the relative importance of these types of movements and the proportionate support which they receive from possible participants.

It was stated above that the types of social movements which have been characterized should be regarded as divisions of a continuous series. Further consideration of racial and interracial movements in relation to changes in race relations indicates that each of these may be considered with respect to another axis definable in any given situation. This axis may be referred to as a collective action continuum. It represents another continuous series concerned with the scope and direction of the social change felt to be needed and the speed with which the changes are to be inaugurated. Arbitrary divisions of this continuum, from "right" to "left," might be called "reactionary," "status quo," "conservative reform," "liberal reform," "radical reform," and "revolutionary." The South presents a type-situation admirably suited to a consideration of racial and interracial movements with respect to this collective action continuum. In this type-situation contacts between racial groups have brought acculturation to the point where both groups are culturally capable of participating in a common social system. No barriers to social integration exist as far as language and the general institutional complex is concerned, apart from those phases which involve racial attitudes and practices. These attitudes and practices have become organized in a pattern of racial accommodation commonly referred to as a caste system. We have excellent studies of the structure, contours, public practices and ideologies of this system. We have relatively little theoretical analysis of what happens as this racial accommodation breaks down. The place and interrelation of collective behavior phenomena in the dynamic phases of racial interaction call for at least as much analysis as have the more static aspects of accommodative patterns.

Collective behavior theory would lead us to anticipate that social movements are not the first social and collective phenomena to emerge as opposition to traditional racial accommodations develops. It is more likely that there will be individual protests by members of the subordinate group, reflecting their personal dissatisfactions with the status quo. Organized opposition to the existing system does not appear as soon as these individual dissatisfactions are felt. Protest feelings find expression in more or less subtle acts of aggression, some directed toward members of the dominant group, others expressed within the subordinate group itself. But while the acts themselves provide immediate satisfactions for the self, they are not concerted steps toward social change and are far from a frontal attack upon the structure of interracial accommodation.

The tension underlying these protest acts, however, almost inevitably takes on a collective character within the isolated confines of the subordinate racial group as the acts are talked about, taught to others, tolerated, approved, or encouraged. Individual tension becomes transformed into racial tension as there comes about a mutual realization of feelings of unrest and dissatisfaction among in-group members. This tension mounts when it is realized that a corresponding, but counter, tension exists in the dominant group. In this situation some collective outburst may occur. Generally this is of a violent nature and gives vent to the individual feelings of a number of persons. Such outbursts are usually soon quelled. Even if they run their course they bring no immediate improvement in the situation since they usually lack any well-defined objectives. But they do have an indirect function in social change in that they provide temporary emotional outlets and thus help the irreconcilables of the subordinate group to maintain organized personalities. The feelings of racial tension which produce and are in turn stimulated by such temporary phenomena are an asset in any effective mobilization of the dissatisfied into organized racial or interracial movements which do have a more rationally planned program for social change.

Also the more dramatic collective outbursts, such as race riots, attract attention from members of the dominant group, and some of these, for various reasons, become drawn into collective action that is concerned with race problems. The forms of collective action to which they are attracted may be racial movements rather than interracial ones—that is, the members of the dominant group may think of the problem of dealing with the racial situation as "their" problem—they control the social order and they expect to take whatever action is necessary to make it run smoothly. There is not, however, unanimity as to what the appropriate action is to be. Three main types within this division of the "collective action continuum," as it appears in the dominant group, may be distinguished: the *reactionary,* the *status quo,* and the *conservative reform*.

The *reactionary* type includes those whose pattern of ideas may be constructed as follows: the traditional pattern of interracial accomodation was satisfactory and workable; the subordinate group no longer accepts it; the existing authorities do not impose it, at least with enough rigor; it is necessary for the participants in this movement to take action to re-impose the traditional pattern.

The ideas underlying the *status quo* group differ from those of the reactionary movement in that there is recognition that changes are actually taking place which make the traditional pattern of interracial accommodation no longer realistically possible. But it is felt that the subordinate group wants to change things too fast and is getting out of hand; the community gets unfavorable publicity from such outbursts, which is undesirable from business and other points of view; there is local criticism of the administration in power, which threatens its tenure; there is a desire for immediate action which will calm the current disturbance and a hope for some techniques for more effective suppression of future disturbances. The "committee of citizens" formed at a time of crisis or incipient crisis may represent this type of movement, but its nature is likely to be sporadic rather than continuous. Members of such a commitee are likely to be drawn from the upper strata of the dominant racial group. They are not genuinely concerned with basic conditions underlying interracial violence and the breakdown of racial accommodation or instituting forms of action which would affect these basic conditions. Neither do they wish to revert to older patterns which may have worked in the past. Not "back to the past" but "back to normal" is the characteristic wish of this group.

Farther along on the continuum is the *conservative reform* movement. Here the configuration of ideas is somewhat as follows: the reactions of the subordinate racial group indicate that the social system is not functioning properly; their reactions are at least partially justified and the conduct of individuals of the dominant group participating in violence is deplorable; the existing political administration is inadequate; improvement of the efficiency and quality of administration is to be sought through reform; to the extent that reforms in administrative policy and procedure are achieved the obvious sources of immediate irritation underlying unrest in the subordinate group will be reduced. This movement is likely to include those in the dominant group who are the "socially conscious elite": persons who themselves are in socially and economically secure positions and are able and willing to recognize shortcomings in existing policy and actual practice. Their interest in administrative reform is sincere and the activities of the organization that may be formally established will continue long after public tension related to violence has died down. It is to be emphasized, however, that in this group there is little reconsideration of the social ends or values that are implicit in the social system. The objectives may include an improvement, perhaps a more humane organization, of the means of control; they may even include an increase in public facilities and services for the subordinate group. There may be a recognition that a "separate but equal" policy for dominant and subordinate racial groups is, in practice, more "separate" than "equal" and that it is desirable to work toward achieving the "equal" facilities. While this does not involve any alteration of the *ideal* public policy, it does mean change of *actual* policy and practice. Such change, if initiated, may not produce many immediate, observable changes in the relations between the races but will actually initiate fundamental changes in the long run.

When racial accommodation in the type-situation which has been considered here is in the process of breaking down, there emerge forms of collective action, primarily types of social movements, which ultimately involve persons from most segments of the class structure of both the dominant and subordinate groups. In addition to the three types of collective action among dominant group members discussed above, there can develop, and probably will, both *interracial* and *non-racial* movements, promoting objectives which directly or indirectly will produce social change in race relations. However, these movements are more likely to fall into those parts of the collective action continuum which we have identified as "conservative reform," "liberal reform," "radical reform," and "revolutionary." There is not time to describe the configuration of ideas and objectives associated with each of these, as was done in the preceding section for the "reactionary," "status quo," and "conservative reform" movements within a racial group. In the time that remains, it will be possible to touch upon only a few additional features of the collective behavior phenomena relating to the interracial movements that develop.

Interracial movements are fundamentally concerned with the social consequences of the incomplete merger of two societies. These two societies are traceable, historically, to the coming together of two racial groups possessing different cultures. Within the region where they have finally come into contact, they live under a common economic, political, and cultural order which has given relative positions to members of the two groups without fusing them into a unified society. Interracial movements, by the fact that they involve the cooperative efforts of members of both groups toward attaining shared goals, project the possibility of further social integration. But the interracial movements may vary greatly from one another with respect to the extent to which the recognized objectives include the possibility of complete social integration on a non-racial basis and also with respect to the speed which such an eventuality, if visualized, is to be directly attempted.

Each interracial movement is composed of different combinations of persons of the two groups. Persons in one interracial movement may be willing to subscribe to a program of social change that is similar to that of the "conservative reform" racial movement, with the difference that they would be willing to work *with,* as well as *for,* members of the subordinate group in carrying out the program. In another interracial movement, departing farther from a status quo position on the collective action continuum, the members may take the view that nothing short of complete integration on a "non-racial," non-seg-regated basis will be acceptable. There may, of course, be many shades of viewpoint represented by as many different interracial movements, each attract-ing its distinctive combination of persons from the two groups.

The co-existence of several interracial movements with different orienta-tions introduces new axes of inter-group conflict in race relations. The lines of conflict between the dominant and subordinate racial groups become blurred as clashes develop between the interracial movements themselves, since the membership of each of the latter is interracial. People in movements varying greatly with respect to the scope of social change desired may not only regard one another as "conservatives" and "radicals," but also divert much energy to conflict against each other. Even more important conflict may develop be-tween one of the interracial movements—particularly if it is regarded as "radi-cal"—and organizations from the dominant group which are nearer the "status quo" or "reactionary" positions on the collective action continuum.

The *kind* of action to be taken, as well as the scope and speed of the action, may be another source of disagreement between particular interracial move-ments. In general, the tactics, paralleling closely the conservative-to-radical objectives, range from quiet conciliation to openly defiant, militant action. An organization using the former method may work informally among the con-trolling personnel of the conventional institutions, attempting to bring about change by gaining a series of minor concessions related to a major objective. This action will be little publicized lest resistance be aroused and further prog-ress be blocked. On the other hand, the militant interracial movements may marshal every available instrument of communication in order to focus public attention, even if the desired immediate action is not expected. The "gradual-ists" may resent such methods on the basis that their own efforts are made more difficult by the militant group, while the militant group may feel that the gain-ing of minor concessions is simply a delaying action.

An additional factor in the conflict between interracial movements may be associated with the temporal sequence in which the movements develop and their subsequent rivalry for status as organizations. It is probable that the "more conservative" ones will come into existence at a time when racial ac-commodations are breaking down but the dominant group controls are so strong that more aggressive movements would not be tolerated. Later, as these con-trols become weaker, more militant, "radical reform" movements may be organized but they have to compete for membership with the older movements. In doing so, they may take a more extreme position than might otherwise be the case. They may even develop out of a schism in an older movement as more ag-gressive collective action is demanded. Those who have roles in the older move-ments may resent the rise of new movements and thus hinder adjustment of their own organizations to changes which are actually taking place. At the same time effective co-ordination of the efforts of all interracial movements toward a common, broad objective is made impossible.

In the perspective of collective behavior theory, it can be seen that these interracial movements which develop rivalry and conflict among themselves, actually at the same time are mutually beneficial to one another and the very fact of their co-existence is an element in the social change process. For one thing, as has been pointed out, the co-existence of action groups with varying degrees of conservatism, liberalism, and radicalism, but all oriented toward social change, makes it possible to draw into collective action a great variety of persons who might not find a place in the dichotomous situation of either the "status quo" or "a particular program of social change." And, paradoxically, the activities of the more extreme "radical reform" movements in the community may actually serve to draw persons into participation in the conservative reform movements who might otherwise not act at all. The "radical" activities draw the attention of many persons to questions which had hitherto been of little concern, at the same time arousing defense reactions from many other persons. Some of the former group may be motivated to join a conservative reform or even a liberal reform interracial movement in order to meet the challenge presented by the "radicals." The very existence of the radical reform movement makes the others seem less radical than they would appear if they were the most extreme group in the collective action continuum. But participation in any social action program in a particular situation gives persons experiences and contacts not only within the movement but with participants in other movements to the "right" or to the "left." This may change their orientation and may lead them to participate in movements which they would not have initially entered. Shifts in membership from movement to movement over time need to be studied within this framework.

RACIAL MESSIAHS

By Justus M. van der Kroef

ONE OF THE MORE NOTEWORTHY ASPECTS of the social and cultural patterns of the divers peoples of the Southern Pacific islands is the unique element of Messianism. From the mainland of Southeast Asia eastward to the New Hebrides many cultural traditions appear to revolve around a cataclysmic view of history, a day of reckoning and a millennium, in which the community, led by some savior, or supplied with unbounded material wealth, will be able to overthrow the shackles of foreign control and reach a state of blessedness on earth. The importance of these Messianic traditions for the development of nationalism and contemporary Communism in continental Southeast Asia and adjacent islands is tremendous. In the case of Indonesia, for example, a country which only recently won its independence, Messianic traditions played a role in the development of nationalistic fervor as it was projected against Dutch overlordship. In Melanesia, a region still under the dominance of the various metro-

Revision and extension by Justus M. van der Kroef of his article, "The Messiah in Indonesia and Melanesia," which appeared originally in *The Scientific Monthly*, LXXV (September, 1952), 161–165; copyright 1952 by American Association for the Advancement of Science and used with the kind permission of the publisher.

politan powers, such traditions have also been considered as precursory manifestations of a new and unsettling spirit of nationalism.

In Java, Messianic traditions appear to have been influenced by the Hindu
concept of the four periods of world history, in which the oldest and most nearly
perfect, the "Golden Age" of antiquity, gradually has disintegrated but will be
re-established after a period of chaos, and by the Islamic *mahdi* ("Messiah")
expectation. Among the oldest Messianic prophecies in Java are those attributed
to Jayabhaya, ruler of the East Javanese kingdom of Kadiri (1130–60), although little evidence exists that the prophecies connected with this name are
actually his. According to Jayabhaya, Java—or perhaps all of Indonesia—
would be free after a period of domination by a "yellow" race. The length of
corn and rice stalks would signify a coming liberation from foreign rule, and
Indonesia would re-enter the lost "Golden Age." The Jayabhaya myth, in a
sense forms a connection with other apocalyptic expectations among the Javanese, particularly those which explained the advent of the Javanese empire of
Mataram, governed by a pure "definitive" dynasty, as opposed to the older and
"impure" dynasty of Madjapahit. So strong was this concept of a millennium,
that when the Dutch succeeded in establishing a permanent foothold in the
Indies, Javanese historians fostered a new myth and a new apocalypse. This
time, the leader of the Dutch, "Djankoeng," was described—and popularly regarded—as a descendant of Sakènder, i.e. Alexander the Great! But "Djankoeng's" dynasty was but a continuation of that older, and "impure house" that
ruled Java before the rise of Mataram, and hence "Djankoeng"—and the
Dutch—would be ultimately doomed.

Another variant of the Jayabhaya myth, and one which also had considerable popularity among the Javanese, holds that after the Dutch seemingly destroy Mataram, a just and avenging prince will arise, one Si Tandjoeng Poetih,
who hails from Mecca and who, in a "democratic" uprising will drive the Dutch
out. One of Poetih's successors, Prince Eru Tjakra, is even today among the
simple village folk, the hero of the millennium, who will bring the golden future.
It is therefore hardly any wonder that later Javanese rebels, like Diponegoro
assumed Eru Tjakra's name to add to their prestige.

During the Japanese occupation of Indonesia in the second world war such
prophecies had an immense popularity and led to a confident expectation in
many circles of complete independence after the Japanese regime had ended.
In the period of Dutch colonial control the *ratu adil* idea gained ground. *Ratu
adil* was generally understood to be some benevolent and just ruler—possibly
reflecting a Christian influence—who would end the present hard times and
restore the greatness and tranquillity of the past. Throughout colonial history
a number of demagogues appearing as the *ratu adil* kept the countryside aroused
from time to time. In the nineteenth century, especially, Muslim Messianism
appears to have been prominent in Java. The influx of a number of Muslim
mystics from the Near East and India, the Islamic *réveil* caused by the Java War
(1825–30), and the activities of Diponegoro seem to have made the times ripe
for political agitation of a mystic-religious cast. Notable examples are such
mystics as Kjai Hasan Maulani, who was exiled from Java by the Dutch in 1842
after having kept Western Java in unrest with his Messianic prophecies of an
impending cataclysm and a "liberation" of all the faithful from infidel rule, and
Mas Malangjoeda, who met a similar fate because of his incendiary prophecies

in 1887. Messianic prophecies also appear to have emanated from Prince Diponegoro, the leader of the Javanese rebellion against the Dutch known as the Java War. Diponegoro believed it to be his mission to cleanse the island from all foreign contamination and to restore the religious and moral purity that had characterized ancient Javanese civilization. The immense veneration among contemporary Indonesian nationalists for Diponegoro, and his designation as "Prince Liberator" and "Hero of Freedom," indicate the great popularity of these Messianic traditions in Java today.

In the present century Islamic Messianism has manifested itself in such groups as the Hizbul Waton and the Sabillera, Muslim fanatics led by mosque officials, mystics, or fanatics, who made common cause with the disorganized units of the Indonesian Republican Army in its struggle against the Dutch. A near-berserker fury was unleashed by these bands against European and Chinese minorities, who were regarded as the fitting objects of the *perang sabil* ("holy war"). In numerous massacres, especially in Malang (East Java), circumcision was practiced on the Chinese and European victims before they were killed. Islamic Messianism has continued until very recent times. For example, for the past three years the government of the Indonesian Republic has struggled to subdue the Da'rul Islam movement in West Java, which seeks to establish the long-heralded Islamic theocracy along the lines suggested by numerous *mahdis* in Indonesia in bygone years.

As is also evident from the so-called cargo cults in Melanesia, the Messianic element appears to flourish in those areas where a relatively secluded and homogeneous population is suddenly subjected to an incisive process of culture change, enforced from without. An example is the "Samin movement" in Java before, during, and after the period of the first world war. This was an era of a growing administrative supervision and centralization of the government on all political and social levels, even the remotest villages. Tax assessors, agricultural agents, and a host of other public servants descended upon the village society, which was thus drawn almost perforce within a Western orbit. In a small village in Eastern Java there lived around 1920 a simple pious peasant, Samin by name, who because of his austere life and devotional habits was regarded as a saint by his fellows. Samin had a small number of pupils, to whom he confided a simple, pacifist, and fatalistic philosophy of life, which stressed complete submission to the order of the cosmos. With the advent of the government's administrative and technical reforms in Samin's village, his outlook began to change. Resentment in the community over the forceful alteration of customs and traditions made Samin a champion of the village folk, who opposed further Dutch innovations. Into Samin's preaching crept a note of prophetic warning that a day of reckoning was at hand, in which the white man would be overthrown, and a new golden age of peace and tranquillity would come into being. The Samin movement spread into neighboring districts, and Communist agitators were quick to seize the opportunity to utilize the popular discontent for their own objectives. With the capture and deportation of Samin and the influx of more cautious civil administrators, the movement collapsed. But in other areas of Java, notably in Bantam, Indonesian resentment toward Dutch administrative reforms led to similar outbreaks.

Messianic concepts and traditions have been noted on other islands of Indonesia. On Borneo the *njuli* movement, and in the Minehassa region of Celebes the *mejapi* movement, are cases in point. The basis of the *njuli* movement is the expectation of resurrection after death, including the return of the communal ancestors, the restoration of the lost "Golden Age," the preservation of ancient laws and the driving out of all innovations. The *njuli* cult entails a secret terrorist fraternity under the autocratic leadership of a village elder, who sends out "apostles" to spread the doctrine. It is almost certain that the *njuli* cult began as a result of the conflicting and unsettling influences of Islam, Christianity and government introduced innovations in the Daya communities of Southeastern Borneo.

The *mejapi* movement may have been influenced by Christian traditions of Jesus as the Savior; the religious element is much stronger here than in the *njuli* movement, and at the same time it is more active politically. The same is perhaps true of the *parhu damdam* movement among the Bataks of Sumatra. Both the *mejapi* and the *parhu damdam* movements are concerned with the preparation for a millennium by some savior or liberator, whose ancestry is linked with traditional deities, and whose love for an especially "chosen people" is woven into folkways and legend.

Messianic traditions in Indonesia are extremely diverse, but those that have been studied in Melanesia appear to be rather uniform in pattern. It is in this area that the popular desire to reach a status equal to that of the European or to enjoy the European's material achievements has given birth to so-called cargo cults, most of them movements of very recent origin. The central theme is that someday the ancestors of the community will bring in a "cargo" on a ship, and that this cargo will contain the goods or techniques that will give the community equal standing with the Europeans. In some areas it is believed that these ancestors will be white, like the Europeans, so that there is a suggestion of a priori genealogical equality. Probably one of the first occurrences of such a cargo cult was the one noted by F. E. Williams in the Gulf Division of Papua in New Guinea. The chief features of this "Vailala madness" were the expectation of a cargo, in a ship manned by white ancestors, communal meals in honor of the dead, and divination rites and trances. In subsequent years similar expectations and practices began to be prevalent in northern New Guinea, in which a Messianic element forecasting a cataclysmic change in the subordinate status of the community to the white man predominated. Hanneman has noted how, immediately after the end of the second world war, the departure of the American military caused some native communities to re-create forcibly the setting of the advanced technology and the material goods with which they had come in contact during the war. Communities were organized in camps along the model of military barracks, discipline was imposed, teaching of English and of sexual continence was encouraged, and at the same time the villagers destroyed their gardens, food reserves, and killed their livestock in the hope of thus hastening the day of the coming of the new cargo, which would contain the material bountifulness that would at last strike a balance between the old and the new.

The departure of the Allied forces from Malaita Island in the Solomons similarly gave birth to a cargo cult, called *Masinga* ("fraternity") rule. Here the myth of the coming of the cargo was combined with demands for political self-determination, for education, and for higher wages. Military drill and the exacting of "voluntary" gifts of money from the inhabitants became the chief activities of those who participated in the *Masinga* movement. Despite arrests of the ringleaders and stringent measures against extortion, the cult continues; the expectation that native society will attain all the material benefits that characterize the Western world, and in particular such countries as the United States, seems too strong to be stamped out overnight. What is perhaps even more important is that the United States appears in some cults as the land of origin of the expected cargo, and that the ancestors of the aborigines who will bring the cargo are themselves Americans! An example of such a cult is the "John Frum" movement in Tanna in the southern New Hebrides, which began in 1940–41. The god Karaperamum, believed to be the single ancestor of all inhabitants of the island, and master of its highest mountain, was expected to reappear shortly in the form of the "King of America, John Frum." At first John Frum spoke directly to his people but later sent his orders through messengers. The Christian movement sank into disrepute; the people left churches and missions and went to live in small units in relative isolation in some of the more deserted sections of the island. Traditional practices, such as dances and the drinking of alcohol, which had been forbidden by some missionaries, were revived. A new currency, which had a coconut stamped on it, came into use. All the white man's money was spent, or sometimes even thrown into the sea, the theory being that when all the money was gone, the white traders could no longer make a living and would leave, thus hastening the coming of John Frum. The "King of America" would bring bountiful blessings to all, particularly the material goods in use among the Westerners. Some natives took to wearing imitation wrist watches made of bamboo, constantly shouting "the time" to their fellow-villagers. A number of John Frum's "messengers" have been arrested, among them one who had gone so far as to demand labor for the construction of an airport where American planes could land. Although missionary activity has been resumed, dancing and immoderate consumption of *kava* (an alcoholic beverage) go on as before. The John Frum movement has spilled over to other, neighboring islands. On the extreme north of Malekula, a cargo cult began in which one of the leaders indicated that a U. S. Army captain by the name of W. Otto had promised to send the "cargo" direct from America.

The ramifications of the cargo cult can be very wide. Propaganda on behalf of the organization of a native cooperative can be made in terms of an announcement of a future millennium. This occurred, for example, on Malekula when efforts were made to improve copra production through a co-operative movement, which also had as its objective the amelioration of the living standard of the community as a whole. Communist activity may be allied to a cargo cult. This occurred on Lifu, one of the Loyalty Islands, where money was collected for a ship, whose cargo—or so it was believed—would be made up of the material goods assembled by the Communist Party of France. The cargo cult here involved not only the expected material blessing and the hope of a coming millennium of freedom but also widespread Communist-inspired popular agitation for political liberty, which caused considerable concern among the authorities. Again, in some areas, the religious element seems to predominate in the cargo cult, and a factor of religious syncretism provides a new "mythical justification for the general wish to get rid of the white men and at the same time acquire their riches." An early example of the religious character of Messianism in Melanesia is the Tuka cult of Fiji, flourishing in the latter half of the last century. According to the followers of the Tuka, a prophet called Nava savaka dua ("he who speaks once") would arise, reverse the existing social and racial values, and make of the Christian God a lesser deity, subordinate to the local traditional gods. This cult seemed to have replaced the even older prophecy of the serpent god Ngendrei, who would one day return and restore the glory of his people over the whites. Elsewhere on Fiji, the tradition of the coming of a new and just king, apparently similar in function to the Javanese *ratu adil,* has recently gained new popularity, particularly with the sullen, though sporadic, resistance against the further inroads of Christian missionary activity that has characterized the islands of late. The new king is said to be a repository of traditional priestly power, and his religious might is expected to be so strong that all foreign gods will have to make way for him. Taking the religious characteristics as a focal point, it would appear that in this respect, too, the Melanesian exhibits a desire to "get even" with the Westerner. It would appear that the "cargo cult" is not necessarily the result of the impact of Western influence upon indigenous society alone. In the Eastern and Central Highlands of New Guinea it has been found, that a Messianic expectation may be born quite organically, i.e. mainly as the result of a sharp awareness on the part of the human group that its wants cannot be met by existing means of satisfaction, with the result that the community turns to wishfulfillment, and agitates itself with the hope of a coming abundance of food or weapons, brought by the ancestral spirits. In this part of New Guinea, destruction of property through war or through ruinous potlatch practices create an acute need for material goods, a need which if it remains unsatisfied "naturally" results in the belief in a coming "cargo." Nevertheless most of the cults seem to exhibit some Western impact.

The political factor is quite strong in many of these Melanesian cargo cults. Many have as their multiple objective liberation from white rule as well as sudden abundance and relief from what is felt to be the community's distress over alien influences in its life. It is of interest to note that the white man does not entirely play the role of the villain in the cargo cult. Berndt has noted that in some cargo cults it is firmly believed that the white men are the reincarnated ancestors, who have returned to bring abundant blessings upon society.

It is difficult to pronounce any general conclusions as to the various Messiahs and their respective movements, because of the immense diversity of cultural and social backgrounds against which they have arisen. From an anthropological point of view, however, it may be said that these apocalyptic tendencies are expressions of an incisive process of culture change, of a lack of balance in traditional society and of a gradual collapse of most cohesive elements of social organization. The projection of an element of cultural equality expressed primarily through material means or through some "white" racial strain parallels similar developments in other areas of the world that have come increasingly in contact with the West, notably Africa and the interior of Australia. The white skin color is traditionally a symbol of aristocratic family origin; among the Javanese kings and nobility a white or pale olive color supposedly denotes divine kinship. The significant role of the ancestors in the cargo cults and in some Messianic traditions in Indonesia is not accidental. The original humans who founded a given community were reputedly closest to the precepts of the divinely guided cosmos and social order; later generations of men are believed to have corrupted these precepts, and only a physical return of the founding ancestors can therefore bring the peace and prosperity of the old, lost, "Golden Age." It is possible that for this reason, in Indonesia as well as in Melanesia, the worship of the dead is one of the last remaining strongholds of traditional culture, and even in those areas where Christianity and Western civilization appear to have made the greatest gains, ancestor worship and veneration for the dead continue. During severe illness dead ancestors are supplicated to restore health; in communal meals the dead are still remembered. As Jean Guiart recently reported for New Caledonia: "I know a Catholic missionary, who, having permitted his flock to hold a recapitulative funeral feast in the traditional way, was worried to find small heaps of diminutive yams, which nobody seemed to care to take, and the presence of which nobody seemed willing to explain."

Finally, two other features of the Messianic cults may be noted: one that I would like to call their "positivistic" aspect, the other their "nihilistic" aspect. As has been noted for Southeast Asia in another connection, a significant feature of the outlook of many intellectuals in this area is their desire to adopt or emulate the technical or scientific achievements of the West without making a commensurate effort to analyze or to understand adequately those culture traits in Western life that have made the technology possible. Despite the desire to emulate the Westerner and his ways, many retain an inner seclusion, a cultural isolation, and appear to be willing only to adopt the outward phenomena or the scientific and technical achievements whereby the West has manifested itself to them. In Melanesia, and in the present state of development of Melanesian nationalism, of which the cargo cult is undoubtedly an important precursor, this tendency seems best illustrated by the very concept of the cargo itself, a concrete, almost "packaged," entity, representing techniques and material goods, which can somehow be acquired, applied, and reproduced without any understanding of the culture or even of the mechanical processes that underlie them. Rather, incipient nationalism in the cargo cults seems to be averse to the traditions of the Westerner, apart from his scientific achievements. The old gods and the old folkways reappear, in slightly modern dress, but little if any identification with Western culture traits appears to exist, even among those who have for reasons of expediency "adopted" Western manners.

The "nihilistic" aspect of the cargo cult and of Messianic movements in Indonesia seems apparent from the wanton destruction of food, livestock, and implements, from enforced sexual continence, and from the practice of abortion and infanticide. It is as if one wished to wipe the slate entirely clean, so that the coming of the cargo, the millennium, the literal "fresh start," will be hastened. Action for action's sake, discipline, even military drill, become characteristic features of this peculiar nihilistic tendency. One thinks in this connection of the sheer nihilistic spirit that motivated the guerrilla bands in the Indonesian revolution, their myth of invincibility, their belief in some talisman or other magical object, said to give them complete mastery over their enemies. One remembers the apparently senseless destruction perpetrated by these bands, perhaps motivated by the all-pervading Messianic urge that the day of reckoning was at last at hand, that a new beginning for all was now being made. This nihilistic character in association with certain Messianic traditions has earlier been noted in Indonesia in another connection. One is struck by similar features in the pre-nationalist cargo cults of Melanesia. Whether this nihilism is similar in both cases cannot of course be definitely ascertained, but the appearance of the phenomenon is worthy of some notice.

To the social scientist, both Indonesia and Melanesia offer the unusual opportunity of attempting to further analyze and possibly to channel these Messianic traditions and expectations along constructive lines and of bringing them into some semblance of harmony with the new culture traits of the changing societies in the Pacific area.

NEGRITUDE

*

By Georges Balandier

ANY STUDY OF THE MANIFESTATIONS of race relations must take account of both the relative *situation* of the various races (real or presumed) in contact within a society, and of the *cultural resources* available to each for expression of their reactions to the situation. The importance of the second varies directly as the extent to which cultural coincide with racial differences. For it is upon these differences that the dominant group bases its justification of unequal status and its doctrines advocating separate development of the races.

This explains the great variety of ways in which such differences can be, or must be handled in various situations. In some cases, the differences lead to attempts at complete, even physical, assimilation to the dominant group; i.e., to elimination of the differences themselves. A young essayist of the Antilles (F. Fanon in his book *Peau Noire, Masque Blancs*), analyzing the behavior of his most advanced compatriots, denounces them for their tendency to whiten themselves, to yield to a process of "lactification". And the sociologist, Bastide, writing of Brazil, shows the significance of such attempts to assimilate to the "race" enjoying superior status. In other cases, inversely, the fact of difference is exalted; the traits most peculiar to the race are considered the most desirable, and, in the extreme case, a sort of counter-racism is built up in response to the positive racism of the dominant group. The theory of *negritude,* which we are to discuss, lies on this line of exaltation of the essential traits of the "race" occupying an inferior position. One must, however, point out that these two types of extreme reaction are not mutually exclusive; the transition from the first to the second can, in proportion to experienced reverses, occur very suddenly.

These observations lead us to note both the role played by cultural facts and the changes which may affect their use in racial relations. They lead us

---

"La Theorie de la négritude: expression des rapports entre Noirs et Blancs," unpublished paper by Georges Balandier. Translated by Professor B. R. Jordan, Duke University.

also to note how strongly racial attitudes are affected by the irreducibility of specific racial traits combined with a wide cultural gap between the racial groups living in contact. One cannot overemphasize the role of this combination in the relations between Black and White in Africa. J. P. Sartre, in his essay, *Orphée Noir,* gives it particular importance: "A Jew, a white among whites, can deny that he is a Jew, declaring himself a man among men. The Negro cannot deny that he is a Negro and so claim for himself this abstract, colorless humanity. He is *black.*" It is by taking the most irreducible elements of his biological and cultural make-up as a starting point that the Black commences to express his reactions to inferiority. Sartre says of him: "With his back against the wall of hard reality, he proudly faces the white man and boasts of his blackness." Starting from this point, one can understand the construction of the theory of negritude.

One could not affirm, however, that there is *one* attitude common to all the Blacks who react to the pressures exerted by the dominant white groups (holding a superior position). The manner of affirming one's blackness varies according to the group, e.g., westernized elite, urban or rural proletariat; people closely bound to traditional cultures, or "exiled" from them. It varies also according to the norm which regulates, even amid unequal relationships, the connection between Blacks and Whites.

Recognition of these differences of the expression of reactions having fundamentally the same meaning is indispensable in the psycho-sociological frame of reference. Where Sartre stops in analyzing the movement which he qualified as the affirmation of negritude, there the investigator of racial relation begins. The negro laborer of Dakar or Elisabethville reacts as a laborer and first becomes conscious of his race where it is used to justify discrimination affecting him in his role of worker. His protest is given direction by his position as industrial wage-earner combined with his status in a dominated racial category. In the case of the black villager, the reaction is more determined by the alterations introduced into the socio-political and cultural systems to which he is traditionally ascribed. His racial reactions are part of his attempt to maintain the most specific cultural features and to recover a modicum of political autonomy. The prophetic religious movements, which have developed in broad regions of Christianized Africa, often show this triple character; the works of B. G. Sundkler (cf. *Bantu Prophets in South Africa*) and my own (*Messianismes et Nationalismes en Afrique Noire*) bring out the full significance of these new movements.

In the case of the elite groups, profoundly marked by the European cultures peculiar to the various imperial powers, the racial reaction is expressed in a less diffused manner. It is spelled out; it imparts energy to a number of contemporary cultural manifestations and leads to political claims. It is, however, characterized by a certain ambiguity, since, from the very outset, it must have recourse to a language and to symbols which are peculiar to the dominant European group against which the reaction is directed. J. P. Sartre notes forcibly this contradiction: "when the negro declares in French that he rejects French culture, he accepts with one hand what he rejects with the other." This ambiguity is all the more clear-cut in proportion as the policy of assimilation has been more completely developed. For a while such a policy may arouse the most vigorous negative reactions, it also imposes the most extensive use of the cultural equipment brought by the colonizer. The theory of negritude is doubly significant in this respect.

The notion of negritude, and its use to repudiate any system of race relations which relegates the Black to an inferior place, figures largely in the work of recent French-language writers in the West Indies and Africa. It inspired the outstanding creative literature of the early post-war period. This literature is the creation of authors who are also influential political leaders. It appears to be the poetic expression of a new self-consciousness which gives inspiration, at another level, to the movement for political emancipation.

This close connection appears clearly in the first poems of Aimé Césaire, West Indian writer and politician of whom it has been said "he reconciles the poet and the politician." In a long poem entitled *Notes on a Return to the Native Land,* this cultivated scholar undertakes to go back to the sources of African civilization, to return, in his own words, to his "Bambara ancestors." He creates then the term *negritude,* in extolling the wisdom and the "noble patience" of the African peasant in tune with the land which feeds him.

Such is the starting point of a theme which was to develop afterwards with surprising success. The expression permits the construction of a racial idealogy adopted (for a time) by a large part of the black intelligentsia of French culture. The subjective value of the word is undeniable but its meaning is hardly precise; it is above all the affirmation of modes of thought and conduct considered as *characteristic* of the Blacks. It stands for a recovery of initiative, in the sense that the Black affirms himself as such, proudly before the White. It reveals the birth of a movement of psychological liberation and the works that it inspires have thus, in the words of J. P. Sartre, the character of an "evangelical literature." He characterizes such a current of thought with felicity of expression when he gives to its creators the title of "black evangelists." The latter are the founders of a hope which is also found, formulated differently, active on other levels of socio-cultural reality and, on a broader scale, among those negro-african societies (which are) at present most active. They express in an explicit and symbolic manner changes characteristic of a large part of the black colonial world.

However, although this notion of negritude clearly reveals the relations between European colonizers and African colonials, at a certain phase of their history, it remains none the less imprecise: a "complex" which resists analysis. How is one to define it to start off? It is, first, a *critical attitude:* the calling up for judgment of a type of civilization (modern industrial) no longer accepted as plainly superior. It appears also as an act of accusation—the White has to justify the value of his civilization, and to explain the weakness they reveal and as a refusal. In a text entitled, "Prière d'un petit enfant Nègre," the Guadeloupian poet, G. Tyrolien, affirms this latter unequivocally: "Why must I learn things in books which speak to us of things which are not of our world . . . Lord, I do not want to go to their school anymore" (cf. Anthologie de la Nouvelle Poésie Nègre et Malgache, Paris, 1948).

The glorification of negritude appears, at a second stage, as the glorification of the most typically African ways. It puts in the foreground that conduct of the African which is least "artificial", most spontaneous, that which places the joy of living above the passion to act. It is with such a view that, A. Diop, editor of the review, *Présence Africaine,* contrasts the creative agitation of the

Europeans with enjoyment of "succulence" shown by the Africans. According to a phrase used by L. S. Senghor, "it is a matter of starting from the differences." The recourse to certain artistic and literary modes of expression thus becomes one of the principal manifestations of negritude; M. Senghor is not afraid to affirm "that what makes the negritude of a poem, is less the theme than the style, the emotional warmth which gives life to words." Negritude thus viewed resides less in the explicit utterance of opposition than in the manner, considered as typically negro, of expressing it. One can see then how undefined such a concept remains, how much the ideological creations induced by it, risk ending up in a vague glorification of black race and folklore; the latter may make one think of a modern use (with the purpose of stirring up a counter-racist movement) of old Utopias which contrast the excellence of "primitive" life with the disorder and the injustices brought by "civilization." In the thinking of many young Africans the concept has, above all, a symbolic value: it permits them easily to formulate claims which, although absolute, are none the less vague in character. It has more force of impact than of ideological content, but that is characteristic of every notion utilized in conflicts which involve racial relations.

This collection of observations is exemplified by the fact that the analysis of negritude is the work of a white philosopher, Sartre in his study, *Orphée Noir,* and is not that of a writer of African origin. The black leaders for themselves did not feel the need of such an investigation; they wanted above all to have an effective tool in hand.

J. P. Sartre's definition of negritude as "a certain quality common to the thinking and behavior of negroes," arouses no uncertainty. In another passage, he specifies: "negritude, to use the language of Heidegger, is the negro's 'being-in-the-world'." What does that mean? We encounter, in reading the analysis of Sartre, the themes that we have just set forth. The intensity of the man-nature relationship, as it emerges in the framework of negro-African civilizations, leads poets of *negritude* to extol the "proud" repudiation of technology; "what might pass for a shortcoming becomes a positive source of riches." Thus the work of these poets contrasts with European literary creations as "a poetry of farmers" contrasts with a "prose of engineers." This statement of the almost sexual harmony which man can maintain with nature represents the subjective aspect of negritude. The objective aspect resides in the experience of suffering and of servitude which the black men have acquired in the course of their history. Sartre insists on the role played by this theme in the creations of black writers; he emphasizes their import by pointing out: "it is by suffering that black self-consciousness is going to become historical." In thus extolling negritude, the writers mentioned realize a double advantage: the Black appears as the one who remains most capable of establishing fundamental harmony with nature (and by that very fact, the most capable of saving the European from the illness of technology); he is at the same time the one who has gone furthest in the experience of suffering and who has acquired, more than any other, "the sense of revolt." One experiences, in connection with this idealization of the Black, the impression of ambiguity pointed out elsewhere in this study. One understands that such a symbol is effective in the domain of conflicts created by unequal racial relations, but one can hardly see that the concept of negritude has been perfectly clarified.

Sartre poses the question at the end of his study: how is one to say what it is? It is not in specifying its content that he tries to describe it, but in defining the dialectic movement, the dynamic that such a concept reveals. He writes: "Negritude is dialectical; it is not only, nor especially, the unfolding of atavistic instincts; it represents the surmounting of a specific situation by free consciences." And in another passage, his analysis becomes much more explicit: "Negritude appears like the negative movement of a dialectic progression: the affirmation (theoretical and practical) of white supremacy is the thesis; the position of negritude as antithesis is the moment of negativity. But this negative moment has no self-sufficiency and the blacks who use it know that very well; they know that it aims to prepare the synthesis or realization of the human in a raceless society. Thus negritude is destined to destroy itself; it is transition and not a goal, means and not end." (Orphée Noir P. XLI)

One sees how Sartre insists on the fact that negritude represents only a "transition"; it creates an untenable position because it constitutes an ideology usable only for limited ends; it is connected with a recovery of initiative but does not contain enough constructive possibilities.

This notion of negritude quickly aroused severe criticisms. They are of two sorts. First are those which come from young writers who do not accept the racial implications of such a concept. It stems from the difficulty which Sartre approaches when he describes the situation of the "new negro" thus, "Since one oppresses him in his race and because of it, it is of his race that he has first of all to become conscious." And he solves this difficulty by a dialectic step: "this anti-racist racism is the only road which can lead to the abolition of differences in race". Is it really solved? F. Fanon, in his work already mentioned, does not accept this play of *black* racism in destroying *white* racism. He expresses, in the name of color, the right to recognition—a recognition which they would receive not as black men, but as *men,* without racial qualification. The objection is thus expressed from the point of view of an absolute humanity, capable of eliminating any specious subterfuge.

In another quarter, severe criticisms are formulated by Marxist writers and militants. They consider the theory of negritude as a hoax. One of them, in the review *Nouvelle Critique* (14 March 1950) condemns it radically in specifying that "it results in justifying escape into ecstatic contemplation." In course of general examination of characteristic cultural problems of present-day Black Africa, G. d'Arboussier, who was Secrétaire Général of the former African Democratic Congress, repudiates any analysis which makes of the racial element a dominant factor. He writes (revue *Europe,* special no. May-June 1949) of "the black nations." Going further and attacking the movement launched by the young African intellectuals and European scholars (with University connection or education), G. d'Arboussier rejects the idea of "African Renaissance." He justifies his criticism by showing that a similar orientation might tend to "advocate a cultural primitivism which would make of Black Africa a private hunting ground for ethnographers, and would end by disarming the Africans in their struggle for liberty and progress." The rejection of the concept of negritude is accompanied in this case by a rejection of the "return" to typical traditional civilizations.

These references are interesting for the investigator of racial relations. They show how much ideologies, utilized in this field of relations, *wear out* and lose their effectiveness as soon as the situation, which induced them, changes. The theory of negritude is, on one hand, a reaction to the policy of assimilation; assimilation which, in the mind of the typical colonial, could be only absolute —therefore, impossible or always deferred; the equality of rights was presented as conditioned by cultural indentity. But the significant progress achieved in the course of the last decade, tends to create this condition by the extension of "modernistic" elites. The typical colonials have then become the defenders of African cultural uniqueness, the partisans of radical differences which can permit the realization of radically different policies, accordingly as it is a question of the seats of empire or of territories beyond the sea. This uncertain element is added, in the case of the negritude concept, to all those we have already pointed out.

Another fact is to be noted. Certain of the black poets, creators of the notion of negritude, have tried to give it a broader significance. They have (A. Césaire for example) made of the Black the symbol of work, and have tried to bring out at the same time as the claims of the men of color those of the world proletariat. They have thus recovered one of the themes of Marxism-Leninism by defining its position with respect to colonial nations. And to the extent to which the theory of negritude remained vague, too imprecise to help to establish a policy, it is this latter which finally captured their support.

Thus the divergent orientations show up, starting from the same initial critical position of challenge to racism and colonialism. The antagonistic tendencies which we have just indicated have been the concern of only a restricted intellectual elite, but they had a wide repercussion up to about 1950. They are significant; for they show how much the reactions to colonization—total and fused at the start—tend to become differentiated. They reveal the hestitation between a movement related to diverse colonial nationalisms (which gets its energy from counter-racism at the same time as from an appeal to traditional values) and a progressivism of marxist spirit which places at the center of its argument the criticism of the colonial and capitalistic system more than racial glorification. These two acts are by no means peculiar to negro-African peoples. They show to what degree racial ideologies are fragile and how much reactions of a racial order are necessarily put down in a realm of deterministic operations in which race is only one of the operating factors.

**

By Aimé Césaire

Ceux qui n'ont inventé ni la poudre ni la boussole
ceux qui n'ont jamais su dompter la vapeur ni l'électricité
ceux qui n'ont exploré ni les mers ni le ciel
mais ceux sans qui la terre ne serait pas la terre
gibbosité d'autant plus bienfaisante que la terre déserte
davantage la terre

Extracted and reprinted from Aimé Césaire, "Cahiers d'un retour au pays natal," *Exchanges.* XXXI (Pentecote, 1957); permission to reprint has been given by *Présence Africaine: Revue Culturelle du Monde Noir*, Paris, France.

silo où se préserve et mûrit ce que la terre a de plus terre
ma négritude n'est pas une pierre, sa surdité ruée contre la clameur du jour
elle plonge dans la chair rouge du sol
elle plonge dans la chair ardente du soleil
elle troue l'accablement opaque de sa droite patience
Eia pour ceux qui n'ont jamais rien inventé
pour ceux qui n'ont jamais rien exploré
pour ceux qui n'ont jamais rien dompté
mais ils s'abandonnent, saisis à l'essence de toute chose
ignorants des surfaces, mais saisis par le mouvement de toute chose
insoucieux de dompter, mais jouant le jeu du monde
véritablement les fils aînés du monde
lit sans drain de toutes les eaux du monde
étincelle du feu sacré du monde
chair de la chair du monde palpitant du mouvement même du monde
sang! sang! tout notre sang ému par le cœur mâle du soleil
ceux qui savent la féminité de la lune au corps d'huile
l'exaltation réconciliée de l'antilope et de l'étoile
ceux dont la survie chemine en la germination de l'herbe.
Elia parfait cercle du monde et close concordance!

"TO MISS THE JOY IS TO MISS ALL"

By William James

OUR JUDGMENTS concerning the worth of things, big or little, depend on the *feelings* the things arouse in us. Where we judge a thing to be precious in consequence of the *idea* we frame of it, this is only because the idea is itself associated already with a feeling. If we were radically feelingless, and if ideas were the only things our mind could entertain, we should lose all our likes and dislikes at a stroke, and be unable to point to any one situation or experience in life more valuable or significant than any other.

Now the blindness in human beings, of which this discourse will treat, is the blindness with which we all are afflicted in regard to the feelings of creatures and people different from ourselves.

We are practical beings, each of us with limited functions and duties to perform. Each is bound to feel intensely the importance of his own duties and the significance of the situations that call these forth. But this feeling is in each of us a vital secret, for sympathy with which we vainly look to others. The others are too much absorbed in their own vital secrets to take an interest in ours.

By Williams James, "On a Certain Blindness in Human Beings," in *Talks to Teachers on Psychology and to Students on Some of Life's Ideals* (New York: Henry Holt and Company, 1912), pp. 229–242. By permission.

Hence the stupidity and injustice of our opinions, so far as they deal with the significance of alien lives. Hence the falsity of our judgments, so far as they presume to decide in an absolute way on the value of other persons' conditions or ideals.

Take our dogs and ourselves, connected as we are by a tie more intimate than most ties in this world; and yet, outside of that tie of friendly fondness, how insensible, each of us, to all that makes life significant for the other!—we to the rapture of bones under hedges, or smells of trees and lamp-posts, they to the delights of literature and art. As you sit reading the most moving romance you ever fell upon, what sort of a judge is your fox-terrier of your behavior? With all his good will toward you, the nature of your conduct is absolutely excluded from his comprehension. To sit there like a senseless statue, when you might be taking him to walk and throwing sticks for him to catch! What queer disease is this that comes over you every day, of holding things and staring at them like that for hours together, paralyzed of motion and vacant of all conscious life? The African savages came nearer the truth; but they, too, missed it, when they gathered wonderingly round one of our American travellers who, in the interior, had just come into possession of a stray copy of the New York *Commercial Advertiser,* and was devouring it column by column. When he got through, they offered him a high price for the mysterious object; and, being asked for what they wanted it, they said: "For an eye medicine,"—that being the only reason they could conceive of for the protracted bath which he had given his eyes upon its surface.

The spectator's judgment is sure to miss the root of the matter, and to possess no truth. The subject judged knows a part of the world of reality which the judging spectator fails to see, knows more while the spectator knows less; and, wherever there is conflict of opinion and difference of vision, we are bound to believe that the truer side is the side that feels the more, and not the side that feels the less.

Let me take a personal example of the kind that befalls each one of us daily:—

Some years ago, while journeying in the mountains of North Carolina, I passed by a large number of 'coves,' as they call them there, or heads of small valleys between the hills, which had been newly cleared and planted. The impression on my mind was one of unmitigated squalor. The settler had in every case cut down the more manageable trees, and left their charred stumps standing. The larger trees he had girdled and killed, in order that their foliage should not cast a shade. He had then built a log cabin, plastering its chinks with clay, and had set up a tall zigzag rail fence around the scene of his havoc, to keep the pigs and cattle out. Finally, he had irregularly planted the intervals between the stumps and trees with Indian corn, which grew among the chips; and there he dwelt with his wife and babes—an axe, a gun, a few utensils, and some pigs and chickens feeding in the woods, being the sum total of his possessions.

The forest had been destroyed; and what had 'improved' it out of existence was hideous, a sort of ulcer, without a single element of artificial grace to make up for the loss of Nature's beauty. Ugly, indeed, seemed the life of the squatter, scudding, as the sailors say, under bare poles, beginning again away back where our first ancestors started, and by hardly a single item the better off for all the achievements of the intervening generations.

Talk about going back to nature! I said to myself, oppressed by the dreariness, as I drove by. Talk of a country life for one's old age and for one's children! Never thus, with nothing but the bare ground and one's bare hands to fight the battle! Never, without the best spoils of culture woven in! The beauties and commodities gained by the centuries are sacred. They are our heritage and birthright. No modern person ought to be willing to live a day in such a state of rudimentariness and denudation.

Then I said to the mountaineer who was driving me, "What sort of people are they who have to make these new clearings?" "All of us," he replied. "Why, we ain't happy here, unless we are getting one of these coves under cultivation." I instantly felt that I had been losing the whole inward significance of the situation. Because to me the clearings spoke of naught but denudation, I thought that to those whose sturdy arms and obedient axes had made them they could tell no other story. But, when *they* looked on the hideous stumps, what they thought of was personal victory. The chips, the girdled trees, and the vile split rails spoke of honest sweat, persistent toil and final reward. The cabin was a warrant of safety for self and wife and babes. In short, the clearing, which to me was a mere ugly picture on the retina, was to them a symbol redolent with moral memories and sang a very paean of duty, struggle, and success.

I had been as blind to the peculiar ideality of their conditions as they certainly would also have been to the ideality of mine, had they had a peep at my strange indoor academic ways of life at Cambridge.

Wherever a process of life communicates an eagerness to him who lives it, there the life becomes genuinely significant. Sometimes the eagerness is more knit up with the motor activities, sometimes with the perceptions, sometimes with the imagination, sometimes with reflective thought. But, wherever it is found, there is the zest, the tingle, the excitement of reality; and there *is* 'importance' in the only real and positive sense in which importance ever anywhere can be.

Robert Louis Stevenson has illustrated this by a case, drawn from the sphere of the imagination, in an essay which I really think deserves to become immortal, both for the truth of its matter and the excellence of its form.

"Toward the end of September," Stevenson writes, "when school-time was drawing near, and the nights were already black, we would begin to sally from our respective villas, each equipped with a tin bull's-eye lantern. The thing was so well known that it had worn a rut in the commerce of Great Britain; and the grocers, about the due time, began to garnish their windows with our particular brand of luminary. We wore them buckled to the waist upon a cricket belt, and over them, such was the rigor of the game, a buttoned topcoat. They smelled noisomely of blistered tin. They never burned aright, though they would always burn our fingers. Their use was naught, the pleasure of them merely fanciful, and yet a boy with a bull's-eye under his top-coat asked for nothing more. The fishermen used lanterns about their boats, and it was from them, I suppose, that we had got the hint; but theirs were not bull's-eyes, nor did we ever play at being fishermen. The police carried them at their belts, and we had plainly copied them in that; yet we did not pretend to be policemen. Burglars, indeed, we may have had some haunting thought of; and we had certainly an eye to past ages when lanterns were more common, and to certain story-books in which we had found them to figure very largely. But take it for all in all, the pleasure of the thing was substantive; and to be a boy with a bull's-eye under his top-coat was good enough for us.

"When two of these asses met, there would be an anxious 'Have you got your lantern?' and a gratified 'Yes!' That was the shibboleth, and very needful, too; for, as it was the rule to keep our glory contained, none could recognize a lantern-bearer unless (like the polecat) by the smell. Four or five would sometimes climb into the belly of a ten-man lugger, with nothing but the thwarts above them,—for the cabin was usually locked,—or chose out some hollow of the links where the wind might whistle overhead. Then the coats would be unbuttoned, and the bull's-eyes discovered; and in the chequering glimmer, under the huge, windy hall of the night, and cheered by a rich steam of toasting tinware, these fortunate young gentlemen would crouch together in the cold sand of the links, or on the scaly bilges of the fishing-boat, and delight them with inappropriate talk. Woe is me that I cannot give some specimens! . . . But the talk was but a condiment, and these gatherings themselves only accidents in the career of the lantern-bearer. The essence of this bliss was to walk by yourself in the black night, the slide shut, the top-coat buttoned, not a ray escaping, whether to conduct your footsteps or to make your glory public,—a mere pillar of darkness in the dark; and all the while, deep down in the privacy of your fool's heart, to know you had a bull's-eye at your belt, and to exult and sing over the knowledge.

"It is said that a poet has died young in the breast of the most stolid. It may be contended rather that a (somewhat minor) bard in almost every case survives, and is the spice of life to his possessor. Justice is not done to the versatility and the unplumbed childishness of man's imagination. His life from without may seem but a rude mound of mud: there will be some golden chamber at the heart of it, in which he dwells delighted; and for as dark as his pathway seems to the observer, he will have some kind of bull's-eye at his belt.

. . . "There is one fable that touches very near the quick of life,—the fable of the monk who passed into the woods, heard a bird break into song, hearkened for a trill or two, and found himself at his return a stranger at his convent gates; for he had been absent fifty years, and of all his comrades there survived but one to recognize him. It is not only in the woods that this enchanter carols, though perhaps he is native there. He sings in the most doleful places. The miser hears him and chuckles, and his days are moments. With no more apparatus than an evil-smelling lantern, I have evoked him on the naked links. All life that is not merely mechanical is spun out of two strands,—seeking for that bird and hearing him. And it is just this that makes life so hard to value, and the delight of each so incommunicable. And it is just a knowledge of this, and a remembrance of those fortunate hours in which the bird *has* sung to *us,* that fills us with such wonder when we turn to the pages of the realist. There, to be sure, we find a picture of life in so far as it consists of mud and of old iron, cheap desires and cheap fears, that which we are ashamed to remember and that which we are careless whether we forget; but of the note of that time-devouring nightingale we hear no news.

. . . "Say that we came [in such a realistic romance] on some such business as that of my lantern-bearers on the links, and described the boys as very cold, spat upon by flurries of rain, and drearily surrounded, all of which they were; and their talk as silly and indecent, which it certainly was. To the eye of the observer they *are* wet and cold and drearily surrounded; but ask themselves, and they are in the heaven of a recondite pleasure, the ground of which is an ill-smelling lantern.

"For, to repeat, the ground of a man's joy is often hard to hit. It may hinge at times upon a mere accessory, like the lantern; it may reside in the mysterious inwards of psychology. . . . It has so little bond with externals . . . that it may even touch them not, and the man's true life, for which he consents to live, lie together in the field of fancy. . . . In such a case the poetry runs underground. The observer (poor soul, with his documents!) is all abroad. For to look at the man is but to court deception. We shall see the trunk from which he draws his nourishment; but he himself is above and abroad in the green dome of foliage, hummed through by winds and nested in by nightingales. And the true realism were that of the poets, to climb after him like a squirrel, and catch some glimpse of the heaven in which he lives. And the true realism, always and everywhere, is that of the poets: to find out where joy resides, and give it a voice for beyond singing.

"For to miss the joy is to miss all. In the joy of the actors lies the sense of any action. That is the explanation, that the excuse. To one who has not the secret of the lanterns the scene upon the links is meaningless. And hence the haunting and truly spectral unreality of realistic books. . . . In each we miss the personal poetry, the enchanted atmosphere, that rainbow work of fancy that clothes what is naked and seems to ennoble what is base; in each, life falls dead like dough, instead of soaring away like a balloon into the colors of the sunset; each is true, each inconceivable; for no man lives in the external truth among salts and acids, but in the warm, phantasmagoric chamber of his brain, with the painted windows and the storied wall."

These paragraphs are the best thing I know in all Stevenson. "To miss the joy is to miss all." Indeed, it is. Yet we are but finite, and each one of us has some single specialized vocation of his own. And it seems as if energy in the service of its particular duties might be got only by hardening the heart toward everything unlike them. Our deadness toward all but one particular kind of joy would thus be the price we inevitably have to pay for being practical creatures. Only in some pitiful dreamer, some philosopher, poet, or romancer, or when the common practical man becomes a lover, does the hard externality give way, and a gleam of insight into the ejective world, as Clifford called it, the vast world of inner life beyond us, so different from that of outer seeming, illuminate our mind. Then the whole scheme of our customary values gets confounded, then our self is riven and its narrow interests fly to pieces, then a new centre and a new perspective must be found.

The change is well described by my colleague, Josiah Royce:—

"What, then, is our neighbor? Thou hast regarded his thought, his feeling, as somehow different from thine. Thou has said, 'A pain in him is not like a pain in me, but something far easier to bear.' He seems to thee a little less living than thou; his life is dim, it is cold, it is a pale fire beside thy own burning desires. . . . So, dimly and by instinct hast thou lived with thy neighbor, and hast known him not, being blind. Thou hast made [of him] a thing, no Self at all. Have done with this illusion, and simply try to learn the truth. Pain is pain, joy is joy, everywhere, even as in thee. In all the songs of the forest birds; in all the cries of the wounded and dying, struggling in the captor's power; in the boundless sea where the myriads of water-creatures strive and die; amid all the countless hordes of savage men; in all sickness and sorrow; in all exultation and hope, everywhere, from the lowest to the noblest, the same conscious, burning, wilful life is found, endlessly manifold as the forms of the living creatures, unquenchable as the fires of the sun, real as these impulses that even now throb in thine own little selfish heart. Lift up thy eyes, behold that life, and then turn away, and forget it as thou canst; but, if thou hast *known* that, thou hast begun to know thy duty."

EPITHETS

By Wilmoth A. Carter

IF THE PRESENCE OF innumerable ethnic groups in America is sufficient to warrant her characterization as the great melting pot of the world, then the great variety of concepts which have served to nickname these groups might be taken as an index of the extent to which the ethnic population of the United States has actually affected the melting pot situation. If there is truth in the statement that America is a land of hybrids with the status of marginal men, then it is equally true that these groups have been the source of a functional language that tends toward a superabundance of hybrid synonyms used to designate such groups; one that is filled with visual concepts which seem to characterize particular groups: one that frequently gives evidence of both physiological and psychological attributes of racial groups; one which has been derived primarily from out-group relationships and has thus erected barriers to many inter-group relationships between American minorities.

Whether we regard the speech of the American people as indicative of degrees of adjustment to the minority pattern or not, the fact remains that some form of communication is necessary for transmitting the experiences of one group to another, and the language of a people seems the only means of achieving this end. Since America has become a great racial melting-pot she has seen the need for a common speech which guarantees participation of these groups in the community life of the nation. Even among people with a common speech, however, word connotations may vary according to the groups and situations in question. Thus, the participation of the many racial groups of America in the social life of the nation has necessitated a definition and often redefinition

Reprinted from Wilmoth A. Carter, "Nicknames and Minority Groups," *Phylon*, V (Third Quarter, 1944), 241–245; copyright 1944 by Atlanta University and used with the kind permission of the publisher.

of situations which have indicated the roles these groups have played on the stage of race relations, as well as fix the status of these groups within society. Is it any wonder that American minority groups—those that are designated as differing from the dominant social groups in race, nationality, attitudes, and general culture patterns—have acquired nicknames which have given them a fixed status in their relation to the majority or dominant group?

Status, as a factor in the process of social differentiation in America, has not only assorted the racial minorities into various singular categories but it has been the means for indiscriminately grouping numerous racial aggregates living in particular regional areas and designating them accordingly. Thus, Alabamians are called Yallerbones and Lizards; Virginians, Beagles; Oregonians, Webfooters and Beavers; Tennesseans, Wheeps, Big Benders, and Cotton manies; New Englanders, Blue-bellied Yankees; Delawareans, Blue Hens and Muskrats; Nebraskans, Bug eaters; South Dakotans, Coyotes; Louisianians, Pelicans and Cre-Owls; Floridians, Evergladers; Washingtonians, Evergreeners; North Dakotans, Flickertails; people of Maine, Foxes; Californians, Gold Hunters and Prune Pickers, Minnesotans, Gophers; Rhode Islanders, Gum Flints; people of Michigan, Wolverines and Lakers; Texans, Long Horns; Alaskans, Muskers; people of Connecticut, Nutmeggers; people of Massachusetts, Old Colonials; Marylanders, Old Liners; people of Omaha, Omahogs; West Virginians, Pandhandlers; Missourians, Pukes; Nebraskans, Sagebushers; New Jerseyans, Shamrods; New Mexico, Sunshiners; people of Oklahoma, Sooners; people of Illinois, Suckers; of Indiana, Weasels.

But what's in a name? What do nicknames mean? What is the role of the nickname in minority group relations? These questions are easily answered when one recalls that words symbolize ideas and express relationships between terms of thought, that names are descriptive qualifiers and semblances, and that nicknames serve both of these purposes in their description and replacement of actual or real appellations. Consequently, at the functional level in race relations, nicknames become symbols of social contact, social expressions, social experience, and social status. As mediums for the transmission of these contacts, expressions and experiences, nicknames likewise form the functional aspects of social interaction, through which processes nations and races seek adjustment to the total culture pattern. A glance at the material make-up of the racial melting-pot of America reveals that the racial groups which have been the source of origin for this novel language of nicknames are many. They include those who might be designated as English, Bohemian, Indian, Italian, Irish, German, Russian, Swiss, French, Scotch, Spanish, Jewish, Chinese, Japanese, Canadian, Mexican, Dutch, Danish, Finnish, Filipino, Norwegian, Scandinavian, Greek, Portuguese, Bulgarian, Belgian, Polish, Negro, White, and many others. Each of these groups within America has become highly visible as a result of significant nicknames whose diverse connotations are numberless.

Among the forces which have accounted for the high visibility of these groups, thereby resulting in the formulation of symbols and name calling, have been such factors as skin color, eye formation, texture of hair, mannerism in daily living habits, and adopted means of social control over other groups. Because some of these factors have been used repeatedly by anthropologists and ethnologists in their efforts to classify distinct races of man, it is not difficult to understand how similar features and characteristics have evoked appellations for differentiations between the racial groups. As by-products in the process of adjustment to a ready-made but ever-revolving culture pattern, the nicknames of America's melting-pot groups are little more than "collective representation which stands as symbols of the groups themselves." They are but criteria of the degrees of adjustment evident among the melting-pot groups.

Efforts at categorizing the many designations of American ethnic groups have prompted inquiry as to the underlying motives or basic ideas thereof. Careful analysis reveals several non-conventional trends in the development of such conceptual indices. In an attempt to satisfy the basic urges of the organism food becomes a significant item. Therefore, many of the nicknames of minority groups in America seem to have food as a pivotal nucleus for their origin, either because the group uses a particular food as a staple, because the economic life of the people is dependent thereon, or because the food is characteristic of the geographical area from which the people originally came. This is verified by the fact that a butterbox is a Dutchman; chili-eater, a Mexican; chili-picker, a Mexican peon; duck hustler, a white man; frogs and frog-eaters, Frenchmen; greaseball, a Greek; greaser, a native Spanish-American; bean-eaters, Mexicans; limey or lime juicer, an Englishman; herring choker, a Scandinavian; porker, a Jew; rice belly, a Chinaman; sausage, German; pea souper, French Canadian; spinacher, Spaniard; taffy, Welshman; herring punisher, Jew; pretzel, German; limberger, German; gin, Italian.

Aside from the economic factors and food habits of a racial group, there are other equally important means of characterization which have likewise been the result of the social adjustment processes. Such physical attributes as size, skin color, color and shape of eyes, head and nose, and head-dress or hair styles seem indicative of the fact that complete social adjustment is only possible where racial groups accept the names applied to them by other groups or become accommodated to the situation by creating contrast concepts for the latter. As evidence of names which have arisen because of the physical characteristics of racial groups, the following are of interest: birds eye maple—light mulatto girl; biddy—Irishwoman; buckra—whites; black ivory—Negro; blue nose—Canadian; buffalo—Negro; cotton top—whites; blue gum—Negro; half-whites —mulattoes; headlight—light mulatto girl; wrinkle face, leathernecks, pinks, parlor pinks, ofays, pales, pecks, red face pecks, peckerwood—whites; mustard, moon-eyed lepers, pigtail, yellow belly—Chinese; raghead—Indian; slant eye —Oriental; squarehead—German; flamed mouth—Irishman; pale sault—white woman; taffy tongue—Welsh; coal—Negro girl; coon, dark cloud, darky, dinge—Negro.

If words are the basis of ideation, then they are the epitome of characterization when particular traits, traditions, habits, aptitudes, attitudes, feelings, and historical occurrences are under consideration. When made applicable to racial groups these factors form the framework upon which functional language sets its stamp of names that are soon perpetuated into the culture. Thus, many racial groups are often more easily identifiable from the nicknames which denote behavior patterns than from the racial connotations themselves. Terms of this type characterize whites as "lynchers"; Jews as "Christ-killers," "suit and cloakers," "ready-to-wear-set"; Mongolians as "yellow perils"; Jews, "whipping boys of history"; Swiss, "yodelers"; Indians, "vanishing Americans"; Russians, "reds" and "Communists"; Swede, "Viking"; Jew, "swindler," "cheat," "moneylender," "chosen people," "refugees"; whites, "jig chasers"; Negro males, "lippie chasers"; West Indians, "monkey chasers"; whites, "cordwood crackers"; Negro, "eightball"; Italian, "ginney"; stupid Irishman, "harp"; Negro who could "pass," "kelt" or "keltch"; whites, "rosin chewers," "snuff-dippers," "gully diggers," "nigger lovers."

Due to the ecological distribution of the population many racial minority groups have become segregated into special residential areas, and as a result have often been designated by concepts which conform to the areas in which they live. Based upon areas in which they have voluntarily or involuntarily settled, Jews have become Ghetto Folks; Scotch—Highlanders; Whites—Mountaineers, Mountain Whoozies, Hill-billies, Saidy-fillers, Piney-wood Tackies, Piney-wood Roosters; and Negroes—Harlemites.

In many instances social adjustment demands that certain given and surnames become the specifications for particular racial groups in order to differentiate one group from the other, as well as afford a common name by which to maintain control over the group. Significant among such names are these: George, James, Sam, Sambo, Uncle Tom, Marcus, Garvey, Jim, Rastus—all applied to male Negroes; Aunt Jemima, Brown Sugar, Dark Meat, Shady Lady, Mandy, Mammy, Raven Beauty—female Negroes; John—a Chinaman; Dave, Ike, Sol—Jews; Mike, Pat—Irishmen.

Accommodation and adjustment in the realm of group relations tend to take the forms of superordination and subordination, or domination and submission. These usually have their prototypes in the wishes of the groups, which in turn seek expression through attitudes of one group toward another. Here again nicknames have been the motivating factors in exemplifying racial minority attitudes. This entire pattern is vividly portrayed in the pattern of Negro-white relations, where the dominant group has created attitudinal names for the subordinate group and the subordinate has retaliated by giving special names for the dominant group, thereby demonstrating the reciprocal relation between subordination and superordination. Names Negroes have for whites, as well as those whites have for Negroes, may be used to bear out this generalization. While whites have referred to Negroes as Ink Spitters, Skunks, Spades, Black, Negress, Nigger, Pickaninny, Bad Nigger and Boy, Negroes have called whites by such names as Buttermilk Swallowers, Hunkies, Hay Eaters, Hoe Sagers, Crackers, Poor whites, white trash, No count, Cap'n, Miss Annie, Mister Charlie, and many others.

One of the principal features of language which make social adjustment less difficult for many racial groups in constant contact with each other is the variety of meanings attached to one word. This has certainly assisted in the comprehension of the attributes, manners, customs of groups which, under other circumstances, might be difficult to characterize. In keeping with this trend—there have developed around American minority groups many general names which do not have one distinctive meaning but several general ones. Noteworthy among these are such names as Boche for German; Bohunk—Bohemian, Czech, Servian, Russian, Slav, and Moravian; Boy—Negro; Buccaneer—white; Heinie, Dutchie—German; Gringo—Mexican name for an American; Goo-goo and Gu-gu—Filipino; Dago, Wop—Italian; Hebe, Kike, Sheenie, Arab, Mockie—Jew; Hooch—Indian; Hunkie—Hungarian; Mick, Paddy, Tad,

Turk—Irishman; Skibby and Jap—Japanese; Canuck—Canadian; Celestian —Chinese; Bootchkey, Bohve, Bohick—Czech; Dee Donk—Frenchman; Doukhabors—Russian immigrants; Spick, Spiggoty—Latin American; Jick or Jickie—Portuguese name for an Englishman.

Such concepts as are noted herein, whether synonymous with naming, nick-naming, or misnaming, are products of a functional language that has become typical of the folkways and mores of American minority groups. The language has not always been consciously or intentionally formalized but, arising out of natural situations, it has become identified with the race relations pattern of the minority groups within America. It has aided in the interpretation of simple phenomena woven into the social pattern of racial groups; it has synthesized the group beliefs, habits, and attitudes; it has permitted an understanding of the process of culture diffusion; its structure and form have been determinants in the formulation of group philosophies—all of which are but indices of the fact that language has functioned as a medium of adjustment in the social relations of this nation's numerous minority groups.

THE PROTECTION OF GROUP VALUES:

ETIQUETTE

By C. A. Mace

WHEN WE REVIEW the conventions of address, the principles of etiquette and all the unformulated rules and customs which govern the be-havior of members of one social class in relation to members of another the impression is derived that these rules and conventions constitute an elaborate mechanism of defence against intrusion and intimacy—against *familiarity* when we use the word with a full consciousness of its etymological suggestions. These defences are erected not so much in the interests of the individual but in the interests of the family.

In his business affairs a man deals with others of differing social class with a relative absence of class consciousness. He will eat and drink with his social inferiors provided he is not called upon to present them at his family table. It is, perhaps, on account of the peculiar sanctity of the family circle that the status of the domestic servant is more affected by class considerations than is that of other workers of economically similar grade. The fact that class barriers are erected at the portals of the home engenders distinctive problems when cir-cumstances require that members of an inferior class should find a place within the domestic organization.

From C. A. Mace, "Beliefs and Attitudes in Class Relations," in T. H. Marshall (ed.), *Class Conflict and Social Stratification* (London: Le Play House Press, 1938), pp. 157–160. With per-mission of the publisher.

Defences against intrusion into the family circle are, of course, mainly in the interests of the younger generation in that circle. The chief danger against which provision must be made is the danger of the "injudicious" marriage. Broadly, we may say, that by the time a man has reached a position in which he has children approaching marriageable age his own social status is pretty definitely fixed. It will not be fundamentally affected by the achievement of a title—which merely accords social recognition to a status in principle established—or by the loss or gain of a fortune. Such changes, however, can affect the status of his children. Accordingly, so far as parents may have social ambitions, they are ambitious on behalf of their children, and so far as they have social anxieties they are anxieties regarding their children. Apart from the commission of crimes there are few things that are so *de-grading* as the inappropriate marriage. It is a much more serious matter if a youth marries out of his class than if he marries a woman of a different nationality or of a different religion.

If this analysis be correct, class consciousness is primarily a consciousness associated with a set of "avoidance reactions." A man who regards another as of an inferior social class is experiencing on grounds of cultural differences a disinclination to invite the other into his family circle. He is conscious of social inferiority in encountering similar resistances to intimacy in others.

How far, we may next inquire, are these avoidance reactions associated with specific positive attitudes to members of his own social class? How far do they involve a positive sentiment with regard to that class?

Here we must distinguish, even more sharply than elsewhere, between different social classes. There are many reasons why a sentiment for one's own class will differ at different levels in the social hierarchy.

Commonly the apex of the social pyramid is constituted by a relatively small group with distinctive characteristics, characteristics on the basis of which lay opinion will substitute in the place of the conception of a whole series of classes, the simple distinction between people who have "social standing" and those who have not. Probably every advanced nation has its "two hundred families" distinguished by the more or less long-standing enjoyment of power, united by continuous inter-familial association, and, still closer by intermarriage. Such conditions are conducive to the formation of a sentiment of typical constitution, a sentiment intermediate between patriotism and the sentiment for one's family or clan.

THE PROTECTION OF GROUP VALUES:
ENDOGAMY

*

By R. F. Alfred Hoernle

THERE HAS DEVELOPED in South Africa a race-attitude, or, better, group-attitude, of which the objection to race-mixture is the strongest expression. "Dit is die trots van die Afrikanervolk," writes one of my Afrikaans-speaking friends, "dat hy die enigste Europese volk is wat in 'n vreemde land, te midde van oorheersende getalle inboorlings, sy bloedsuiwerheid bewaar het . . ." (It is the pride of the Afrikaner people that it is the only European people which, in a foreign land, in the midst of overwhelming numbers of natives, has preserved its blood-purity . . .)

That the Afrikaans-speaking South Africans (to whom it is customary to refer as "Dutch" South Africans, although the majority of their family names would indicate a French Huguenot or German descent) especially in the two northern provinces maintain, both in theory and in practice, a more rigid barrier against race-mixture than do other sections of the South African population, at any rate until they, too, have come to share the Afrikaans' point of view, I do not wish to question. There are, no doubt, plenty of individual exceptions, as may be seen both from court-records of rape and seduction, and from Mr. Tielman Roos's "Immorality Act" of 1926. The fact remains that public opinion among "ware Afrikaners" is strong upon the point and does exercise powerful check even under conditions of living which favour laxity.

But it does concern us to discover more precisely just what is meant by "purity of blood" and "immorality" in this connection.

Purity of blood may mean either of two things. In the full sense it means complete avoidance of sexual relations with individuals of different blood, and, above all, avoidance of begetting and bearing half-caste children. In the more restricted sense, it means merely avoidance of intermarriage which would involve the incorporation of the half-caste children in the father's group. For, the father in the vast majority of interracial sex-relations being a white man, legal marriages with native women threaten to introduce mixed children as full members into the white group.

Now purity of blood in the first and full sense, however strong the feeling in its favour, has not been universally practised in the past by Afrikaans-speaking whites, nor is it universally being practised by them in the present. Hence, if Afrikaners pride themselves on purity of blood, it must be purity in the second and narrower sense, which keeps the blood of the group pure by avoidance of intermarriage, and, in any case, by the refusal to admit to membership of the group half-caste children, even though they be the offspring of legitimate marriage, and, with even less compunction, if they be the offspring of

From R. F. Alfred Hoernle, "Race Mixture and Native Policy in South Africa," in I. Schapera (ed.), *Western Civilization and the Natives of South Africa* (London: George Routledge and Sons, Ltd., 1934), pp. 274–276.

illicit unions. In line with this principle, one of General Hertzog's draft-bills on native policy proposed to count as a "native" any individual who has a native parent or grandparent. The touch of black blood excludes from the blood-pure group.

What we are dealing with here is, clearly, not a biological but a sociological phenomenon, parallel to the rules by which among the Royal Houses of Europe, though extramarital relations and even mesalliances on the part of their members are frequent, none the less the selection of mates from whom the legitimate heirs to the throne are to be born is narrowly restricted. In general, every self-conscious group seeks to perpetuate its own identity, and for this purpose lays down and defines conditions of membership. If the group happens to be a religious one, it will as a rule define its identity by the acceptance of a creed, and will then exclude from its ranks any member who refuses to accept, or insists on interpreting differently from the orthodox way, any article of its creed. Other groups lay down conditions of parentage as one of the qualifications for membership. Such a condition is the "bloedsuiwerheid" of the Afrikan-ervolk. It is not incompatible with interracial sex-relations as such, though it frowns upon them. But it is emphatically incompatible with race-mixture by way of intermarriage. Its principle is that white should marry white and beget white.

** **

By The Reverend Francis Ter Haar, C. SS. R.

IT IS AN INDUBITABLE FACT that mixed marriages are exceedingly harmful to the Church and to the souls of the faithful. . . . Pope Clement XIII was well aware of this fact when he said in 1763: "We consider such marriages to be very harmful to the Church." For this reason the Roman Pontiffs, the supreme pastors of the Church, have repeatedly stated that such marriages "must be entirely avoided," and have pronounced them to be "unlawful," "strictly forbidden," "wholly pernicious," "detestable," and have even said that the Church "abhors them." . . . As recently as the year 1922 the German Bishops asserted in their joint Pastoral letter: "Statistics have revealed that more souls are lost to the church annually through mixed marriages than are gained in the whole pagan world by the united efforts of missionaries." The same prelate added this striking assertion, regarding the offspring of these marriages: "We learn from accurate observation that usually the third generation is entirely Protestant." . . .

The most recent law of the Church about mixed marriages is set forth in

---

Adapted from the Reverend Francis Ter Haar, C.SS.R. *Mixed Marriages and Their Remedies,* Tr. from the Latin by the Reverend Aloysius Walter. (New York: Frederick Pustet Company, Inc., 1933). Pp. xiii–27. With permission.

the Code of the Canon Law, canon 1060: *"The Church most severely forbids everywhere marriages between two baptised persons, one of whom is a Catholic, and the other is a member of an heretical or schismatical sect; and if there is a danger of perversion of the Catholic party and of the offspring, such a union is also forbidden by the divine law itself."* . . .

Leo XIII confirmed this teaching in his famous encyclical "Arcanum," in which he writes: "Care must be taken that they do not easily contract marriage with those who are not Catholics, for when minds disagree about religious observances, it is scarcely possible to hope for agreement in other things. And the reason why persons should turn with dread from such unions is chiefly because they give occasion to a forbidden association and communion in religious matters, endanger the faith of the Catholic party, are a hindrance to the proper education of the children, and very often lead to the erroneous belief that one religion is as good as another, by confounding truth with falsehood. . . .

We take for granted that the non-Catholic party has seriously promised that the children will be brought up Catholics. But even then, the non-Catholic has parents and relatives who will use every means at their command to frustrate this promise. They will put forth reasons of love or of tender affection, reasons of honor and of fear. They will threaten to cut him or her off from the family with consequent temporal loss and serious disadvantages. Sometimes the non-Catholic husband is subject to masters or superiors in civil or military circles; these will make it difficult for him to gain promotion if he allows his children to be brought up as Catholics. Again, there are the ministers of religion who, with a zeal worthy of a better cause, purposely pay visits to such families. They try in every way to induce the non-Catholic to break his promise on the ground that it is not binding and even may not be kept with a good conscience. They will remind him of the faith in which he was baptized, of the dishonor he is bringing on the family and of the great pain he is causing his parents. It is quite probable that the non-Catholic will yield to these temptations and break his word. In the beginning perhaps, remembering his promise and desiring to please his spouse, he will allow the children, or at least some of them, to be baptized in the Catholic Church, but when the time has come for them to go to school, he will insist (and frequently have his way) that the school selected shall be a non-Catholic institution.

But take the case where the promises are kept and full permission is given for a Catholic education; even then this education, ordinarily speaking, will be very deficient and of little value. It must naturally lead to indifferentism. Clement XIII in his letter of November 16th, 1763 to the Bishop of Strassburg speaking of marriages in which the promises have been made, writes: "It is our opinion that such marriages will be very pernicious to the Church. If the mother who gives the first education is a non-Catholic have we not reason to fear for the religion of the children? In her motherly love she is anxious for their eternal salvation, and, convinced that her religion is the only true one, she will on every occasion instil it into their minds. And if, as will often happen, she scoffs at her husband, as if he were acting foolishly when he observes the days of fast and abstinence or when he goes to confession and Holy Communion, the children will little by little begin to despise the most sacred things. The first impressions of childhood are not easily erased in afterlife.

"On the other hand, if the mother is a Catholic, and the father, whose authority is respected by the children, ridicules in their hearing her religious sayings and actions, will they not begin to doubt the truth of their mother's religion? And what will happen if the parents begin seriously to discuss religion? The young mind is tossed to and fro and gradually becomes indifferent to every religion, which is the same as losing every religious conviction. Can there be anything more harmful and more likely to destroy religion?

"Again, should the Catholic parent die when the children are still very young, the non-Catholic will have full freedom to contaminate their minds with the poisonous principles of heresy. You can see, then, dearly beloved Son, what the Catholic Church may expect of the offspring of such marriages, and you can realize that we have reason to fear that far from propagating the Catholic faith, they will propagate heresy; nay, what is far worse, they will foster more and more a complete religious indifference which generally leads to ungodliness."

What we have said concerns the education in the home. The evil becomes worse when we consider the training given in school. The children of mixed marriages are not very often sent to a Catholic school, especially when they are being given a higher education. If the father is a Protestant, it often happens that, in spite of his promises, he will select a non-Catholic school. If the mother is a non-Catholic she will often procure the same type of education for the children by constant importunities, especially if the husband is not very religiously inclined.

The German Bishops in their Pastoral Letter of November 1922 to their flocks declare: "It is evident that mixed marriages remain a fruitful nursery for religious indifference, uncertainty and irreligion. What must the children think when their father makes the sign of the cross and their mother never does? When their father worships what their mother considers falsehood and superstition? It is impossible in such circumstances for their faith to remain firm and steadfast."

In some regions, in order that peace may be maintained between husband and wife in a mixed marriage, both agree, or at least the Catholic party tolerates, that the children be sent to what is called a public or neutral school. There, at least in theory, no religion is taught, but in practice the teaching will often be atheistic and infected with the modern errors of rationalism, religious scepticism and materialism, especially in the higher schools; at all events many things will be taught which are totally opposed to Catholic doctrine. When this educational course is completed, very often the children will be both in theory and in practice indifferent to every religion and their minds will be filled with false maxims. For this reason Pope Leo XIII wrote that marriages of this kind must be abhorred because "they are a hindrance to the proper education of the children and very often lead to the erroneous belief that one religion is as good as another by confounding truth with falsehood."

THE NATURE OF RACE CONFLICT

By James Darmesteter

"HISTORICAL SPIRIT" is a beautiful thing, but it is easier to abuse the term than to apply it properly. It takes a strange ignorance of facts, and a singular docility in regard to words, to make of the Jew the type of the Semite. Judaism is born in a Semitic medium, but it is the most absolute reaction imaginable against the religion, the manners, the traditions that prevailed in that medium; it is the living protest of broad humanity against the tribal idea. Here is revealed the social danger contained in this word "race," when it is snatched from the hands of science by the would-be men of affairs, and thrown out to the masses. Through it every struggle takes on a character of bitter and undying hatred, because the combatants are persuaded that there exists between them, not a momentary and accidental hostility, but an irretrievable and fatal one. War between these parties is supposed to be inevitable and eternal, since the cause is always present, and extends from the remote past to the distant future. Two organisms, two instincts, two irreconcilable souls, are supposed to be engaged in the struggle; not two men, but two vertebrates of a different order. Rapid or gradual extermination can alone put an end to the struggle. In the same way, during the War of Secession, the scholars of the South published "manuals of anthropology" in which the monkey occupied the intermediate place between the negro and man.

What is still stranger is that, in the bloody battle of words of the century, the scientific subdivision of races and racial instincts involves a subdivision of the hatreds and fatalities of war and destruction. The movement in Germany would prompt the Aryans to make an assault upon the Semitic world, but the Aryans are subdivided into secondary races which must in turn hate, fight, and exterminate each other by reason of the secondary hostility of their instincts,— the Germanic race against the Slavonic, the Germanic against the Latin. Humanity is merely a cruel and regular network of hatreds and sub-hatreds, interwoven with the hierarchy of races, and entangled by science and by war.

If the form of human thought in historical times was really an unchangeable expression of the first race, a permanent state of war, with no other outcome than extermination, would be the inevitable lot of humanity. Happily this is not the case, and among the infinite causes of the struggles that engage civilized nations,—struggles for outlets and for means of subsistence, clashings of pride, metaphysical quarrels,—the vague and obscure antipathies of race occupy the very lowest place. What is taken for them is merely the clash of colliding traditions. The clash of traditions, however ancient and deeply rooted, cannot produce a state of ceaseless warfare, since two opposing traditions, when brought into contact, end either by an adaptation of the one to the other, if they be equally strong and sound, or by the *conversion* of the one into the other. The law of the equilibrium of temperature reigns in the moral as well as in the physical world. The struggle of races can end only upon the battlefield and by

From Helen B. Jastrow (trans.) and Morris Jastrow, Jr. (ed.), *Selected Essays of James Darmesteter* (Boston: Houghton, Mifflin and Company, 1895), pp. 171–174. With permission.

extermination. The struggle of traditions, though carried to the battlefield, can find its definite solution only in the depths of thought and conscience. The extinction of a tradition does not involve the extinction of the race that possessed it, but its moral reconstruction, and generally the rejuvenation of its forces and of its aims.

THE CONFLICT OF COLORS

By W. E. B. DuBois

BUT WHAT OF THE DARKER WORLD THAT WATCHES? Most men belong to this world. With Negro and Negroid, East Indian, Chinese, and Japanese they form two-thirds of the population of the world. A belief in humanity is a belief in colored men. If the uplift of mankind must be done by men, then the destinies of this world will rest ultimately in the hands of darker nations.

What, then, is this dark world thinking? It is thinking that as wild and awful as this shameful war was, *it is nothing to compare with that fight for freedom which black and brown and yellow men must and will make unless their oppression and humiliation and insult at the hands of the White World cease. The Dark World is going to submit to its present treatment just as long as it must and not one moment longer.*

Let me say this again and emphasize it and leave no room for mistaken meaning: The World War was primarily the jealous and avaricious struggle for the largest share in exploiting darker races. As such it is and must be but the prelude to the armed and indignant protest of these despised and raped peoples. Today Japan is hammering on the door of justice, China is raising her half-manacled hands to knock next, India is writhing for the freedom to knock, Egypt is sullenly muttering, the Negroes of South and West Africa, of the West Indies, and of the United States are just awakening to their shameful slavery. Is, then, this war the end of wars? Can it be the end, so long as sits enthroned, even in the souls of those who cry peace, the despising and robbing of darker peoples? If Europe hugs this delusion, then this is not the end of world war,—it is but the beginning!

We see and hear Europe's greatest sin precisely where we found Africa's and Asia's,—in human hatred, the despising of men; with this difference, however: Europe has the awful lesson of the past before her, has the splendid results of widened areas of tolerance, sympathy, and love among men, and she faces a greater, an infinitely greater, world of men than any preceding civilization ever faced.

It is curious to see America, the United States, looking on herself, first, as a sort of natural peacemaker, then as a moral protagonist in this terrible time. No nation is less fitted for this rôle. For two or more centuries America has marched proudly in the van of human hatred,—making bonfires of human flesh and laughing at them hideously, and making the insulting of millions more than a matter of dislike,—rather a great religion, a world war-cry: Up white, down black; to your tents, O white folk, and world war with black and parti-colored mongrel beasts!

Instead of standing as a great example of the success of democracy and the possibility of human brotherhood America has taken her place as an awful example of its pitfalls and failures, so far as black and brown and yellow peoples are concerned. And this, too, in spite of the fact that there has been no actual failure; the Indian is not dying out, the Japanese and Chinese have not menaced the land, and the experiment of Negro suffrage has resulted in the uplift of twelve million people at a rate probably unparalleled in history. But what of this? America, Land of Democracy, wanted to believe in the failure of democracy so far as darker peoples were concerned. Absolutely without excuse she established a caste system, rushed into preparation for war, and conquered tropical colonies. She stands today shoulder to shoulder with Europe in Europe's worst sin against civilization. She aspires to sit among the great nations who arbitrate the fate of "lesser breeds without the law" and she is at times heartily ashamed even of the large number of "new" white people whom her democracy has admitted to place and power. Against this surging forward of Irish and German, of Russian Jew, Slav and "dago" her social bars have not availed, but against Negroes she can and does take her unflinching and im-movable stand, backed by this new public policy of Europe. She trains her immigrants to this despising of "niggers" from the day of their landing, and they carry and send the news back to the submerged classes in the fatherlands.

All this I see and hear up in my tower, above the thunder of the seven seas. From my narrowed windows I stare into the night that looms beneath the cloud-swept stars. Eastward and westward storms are breaking,—great, ugly whirl-winds of hatred and blood and cruelty. I will not believe them inevitable. I will not believe that all that was must be, that all the shameful drama of the past must be done again today before the sunlight sweeps the silver seas.

If I cry amid this roar of elemental forces, must my cry be in vain, because it is but a cry,—a small and human cry amid Promethean gloom?

Back beyond the world and swept by these wild, white faces of the awful dead, why will this Soul of White Folk,—this modern Prometheus,—hang bound by his own binding, tethered by a fable of the past? I hear his mighty cry reverberating through the world, "I am white!" Well and good, O Prometheus, divine thief! Is not the world wide enough for two colors, for many little shinings of the sun? Why, then, devour your own vitals if I answer even as proudly, "I am black!"

INCIDENT IN NEW ORLEANS

By Thomas Sancton

THIS INCIDENT OCCURRED at the end of a day which had begun like a youthful idyll. The time was late September. It was a cool, bright autumn day and whitecaps were gleaming on Lake Pontchartrain. A party of eight of my friends had met at a yacht club four miles above the city to go sailing. The club kept a fleet of little sloops which were rented to members for a dollar a day. We had done much sailing that summer. The feel of the thing was in us. We were tanned and our khaki trousers and dungarees were clean and faded. There were three girls with us, gay and beautiful in hair ribbons and lipstick and gaudy sweaters. Most of us had some connection with the university or the big morning newspaper and two of the girls were still attending school. Two older reporters with us had come along for a romp.

Almost every week-end that summer we had plowed up and down a staked-off racing course, whooping and arguing over two or three hundred yards of open water. After the race we took a swim in the lake and went to the Sail Inn tavern for drinks.

The tavern was a weather-beaten shack equipped with a bar, a music box, a couple of tables, and a carton or two of cigarettes. It was closer to the boat pen than the yacht club was, and it did a bigger business. The tavern was a great place to drink a beer or two between sailing and dinnertime. It was a bad place to be marooned for the length of a fine autumn day. We were to learn that.

A high wind was blowing and the yacht club manager had ruled out sailing for the morning. There was not a cloud in the sky, but the wind gage had climbed to the danger point. Lake Pontchartrain is peculiar. Its prevailing winds are erratic. We were always getting becalmed beneath a raw semitropical sun.

Against this eventuality we usually carried aboard a bucket of ice and a bottle of rum, or beer. We never regarded ourselves as heavy drinkers. But during the 1930's in New Orleans drinking was a part of life. We were restless and not very happy. Huey Long's thieves were plundering our city. Our decade was drifting inexorably toward the war. An evil, persistent wind blew into our faces, a wind from hell, and it withered the good things that were in us. We ducked into the taverns of our spirit and there, pouring tall ones, we waited.

It was nine or ten in the morning when we came out from the city. There was a chance that the noon sun would make the wind fall off, and then we could sail. So we went into the tavern for a drink. Someone took our little bottle of rum and made drinks for the eight of us. It wasn't much to go round. Yet as we held the icy liquor to the light there was amber fire in it and on this September day we were like tinder. A fresh wind blew through the open tavern door and outside we could see the whitecaps and the gulls. The rigging of the big boats cracked against the hollow masts. The salt smell of the Gulf of Mexico was in the air. There is an unforgettable quality about autumn days in the coastal South.

The wind blew so strong it became a joke to us. Someone would say, "Let

Thomas Sancton, "Race Clash," *Harper's Magazine*, CLXXXVIII (January, 1944), 135–140.

us go feel *of* the wind," and it began to seem very funny. We translated it into French and said it. We were feeling the warmth and intimacy of working in the same office, of having gone to school together. The girls were chattering and lovely. We teased them about all kinds of things. Lunchtime came and went. We devoured a sandwich in the tavern and went outside to feel of the wind again. But now we had almost forgotten that we had come to sail.

Our party developed into a real New Orleans breakdown. We kept the music box fed with nickels, beating out the jazz that had grown up almost within our memories in other taverns of our city. The round white Milneburg lighthouse, a famous landmark, stood in view only a short distance down the lake shore. The place had been given a kind of immortality (and a different spelling) in one of the earliest jazz classics, "The Milenberg Joys." Years ago there was a cheap resort town there, a place of bathhouses, fishing camps, and dancing pavilions, where the New Orleans Italians and Irish and *boogalie* French had gone to hold their picnics and fish frys; had caught heaping baskets of shrimp and crabs and brewed their fragrant gumbo soup; had got sunburned, drowned, drunk, quarrelsome and murdered; and had called for madder music. It was out of their hunger for laughing, gibbering horns and clarinets that New Orleans jazz was born. There is something in the air there.

So we danced, sang, laughed, and drank through all that day. At last we saw by the tavern clock that it was four in the afternoon, and three of us who had to go to work that night on the newspaper arose and declared the party at an end. I took a look at our rum bottles. There were six of them. The clear air blowing through the tavern, the absence of cigarette smoke, the atmosphere of relaxation had kept us clear-headed; yet it came over me that we must be faced with some sort of retribution.

Four of us got into a coupé owned by a young business man named Carter. We sped down the black-topped road toward the residential section of the city. The road paralleled a long navigation canal which had been dug in Reconstruction days from the lake to the heart of the city. Four miles inland from the yacht club the canal entered a fringe of the city's residential section. Here the road skirted the New Orleans country club and its lush green golf course. There was a short cut from the highway at the country club which we used to drive on, a narrow street which cut through a scraggly patch of Negro houses, crossed a drainage canal, and led through a mile of weed-grown barren lots to one of the principal streets of the uptown residential area.

The front seat of the coupé was badly crowded. There were Carter, Jeff (one of the older reporters), me, and one of the girls. We were still feeling buoyant. Carter turned into the short cut and shouted to friends sitting in parked automobiles by the swimming pool. We passed through the four or five blocks of Negro houses. They were tucked away along the banks of the drainage canal, back in the weeds, back in a bald and deserted section of the city where no one else particularly wanted to live.

As we passed through the Negro section and entered the open road again all of us sighted down it instinctively. It was a narrow, dangerous road. Two or three hundred yards ahead, a red delivery truck drove in from a dusty side street. In one voice we shouted to Carter. We had been singing a ballad about a clam digger. Carter shook his head from side to side and continued to shout the words. A reckless smile suddenly illuminated his face. He turned quickly to the left side of the road and shouted, "Out of my way!" and sped at the on-coming truck. Jeff and I lunged for the wheel. Carter blocked us with his shoul-der, laughing like a maniac. The big red truck loomed up before us. Suddenly I knew that six bottles of rum had done their work.

Carter was handsome, shrewd, and reckless, and on this September day he was well cast for the part he played.

The truck was driven by a Negro youth. He jammed on the brakes and brought the machine to a grinding stop and sat there, in a moment of terror I suppose, wondering if this fool of a white man was crashing deliberately head on. But no. At the last moment our brakes and tires shrieked and the shiny chromium bumper slid to a stop two feet from the motionless truck. Carter leaned out of the window and shouted again, "Out of my way!"

In my mind's eye I can still see this Negro. He wore a blue denim shirt with sleeves rolled above the elbows, exposing a pair of sturdy forearms. A black driver's cap with his trucking license sat on the back of his head. On his smooth chocolate face there was a look of humiliation and exasperation—and a wry acceptance of the event. Three centuries of slavery spoke to him in his blood. He sat there for a moment with a pained smile on his face. Carter kept whistling ominously and jerking his thumb to the other side of the road. Finally the Negro shifted to reverse and began to back slowly away to drive round us.

Ordinarily Carter would have let it go at that. But a devil had got inside him. This gag *had* to be played out to its wild, unpredictable end. He slammed the gears of his powerful automobile and followed the retreating truck. He crashed into the bumper and stepped on the gas, pushing the truck ahead of him down the road. The Negro applied the brakes. The two machines struggled to a stop.

"Get it out of the way," Carter cried, warming to the game. He stepped on the throttle again, the two bumpers groaned together, and the truck tires chirped and skidded ten feet down the road.

"Get it out of the way! Out of my way!"

Then the inevitable happened. The day reached a treacherous turning, and suddenly the imminence of violence and murder hung in the late red sunlight.

The groaning of motors had attracted a little group of Negroes, men and women, who came walking across the open lots from the houses back by the canal. Carter had forgotten that there was not another white man within half a mile of us. The Negroes stood on the sidewalk watching the truck and coupé buck it out. At first they stood in silence, beholding one more scene of an im-memorial humiliation. At first there had been only two, or three, or five, and we in the car had hardly been conscious of their presence. Suddenly there were more—twenty, perhaps thirty—and they were staring at us and muttering.

In another moment Carter doubtless would have backed, turned past the truck on the right-hand side of the road and driven off; and we should have talked about the incident for ten minutes and forgotten it forever. But suddenly a tall, bony, mean-faced Negro left the crowd and ran round the truck. The truck had no doors. He jumped on the running board and gave the chocolate-faced boy a contemptuous shove. The boy slid over instantly and a different kind of man was at the wheel. A third Negro youth jumped on the running board and sat beside them.

The driver ripped the gearshift into first and set the big Mack engine thun-dering. Carter did the same and the bumpers smashed and ground together.

Under this tremendous pressure something had to give. The front of Carter's lighter coupé lifted for a moment off the street and our bumper slid over the truck's thick, beveled bumper and locked behind two crosspins. The truck bumper ate into his grillwork and crumpled his fenders. Suddenly, with a feeling of disgust and fear, I realized that our car was trapped.

Carter pushed back at the truck for a few minutes, though there was no longer any point to it. The truck was fighting back, and it had the power. The Negroes were fighting back, and they had the numbers. Our tires began to burn on the asphalt. Finally he locked the emergency brake and it held. The machines came to a halt, like exhausted stags.

"God *damn!*" he muttered in disgust. We sat there for a moment in silence. The girl with us had courage. She said nothing, knowing we should have to work our way out of this jam as best we could. Carter got out of the car on one side and I on the other. If the three men in the truck had been white we should have expected to fight instantly. And what we would not have given then merely to be faced with the necessity of slugging it out with two or three husky Italian boys driving a produce truck from the farming section. We would have been licked no doubt, but a fist fight holds no terrors for the young. But we were faced with something different—a race clash—the Southern nightmare. White men and black men fight to kill. They use weapons: a stick of firewood, a garden spade, a heavy wrench, a knife. Suddenly I sensed the bitter knowledge that a thousand Negroes have died with—the feeling of being outnumbered.

And yet we were white men and this was still an advantage. It meant that a simple fist fight was impossible; but it meant also we were untouchable so long as the Negroes did not lose their heads. For death was in the offing for them too. They had only to plunge a knife or wield a jack handle, and there were six feet of hungry rope waiting in the Parish Prison. They had not yet forgotten that.

There we stood on this dirty New Orleans back street, only a mile from our homes, but in the heart of a savage land. A caste system had marooned this Negro settlement in white society. Now we were captives. But still we were white. It was a fearful thing to injure us. Scattered across the city were jails and firearms, nightsticks and shotguns, and all of it in the hands of white policemen.

Carter and I looked at the bumpers. The Negroes got out of the truck and watched us. I could see a gleam of burning excitement in the tall black driver's face. He was the one to watch. He was almost past the point of caring what happened. I was afraid of him.

Carter looked at the Negroes and said in an even voice, "Let's lift my bumper off."

"White son-of-a-bitch!" The Negro choked with rage.

"Nigger bastard! Wait till the cops come."

The Negro made no move. He stood looking at Carter. Behind me, I could hear Jeff opening the back compartment of the coupé. He was one of the older reporters, almost middle-aged, slender, tense. Heavy tools rattled. Jeff got in the car again and I heard the clunk of steel as he put them on the floor. He had got our weapons. In my mind's eye I could see them lying on the floor of the car: heavy wrenches, a hammer, a jack handle, a tire lever. I was afraid of the Negro. Man to man, no; but this was something different. I could see he was trying to make up his mind. What was passing behind those eyes? Was he trying to decide whether to go for his knife? He was standing on my side of the auto-mobile. I had it figured how to get a wrench in my hand. It would take him a few seconds to fumble in his pocket. Jeff had the door open. Before the Negro had his knife out I would have a plump, murderous wrench in my hand. So would Jeff. So would Carter. Then I wouldn't be afraid any more. Then there would be only one thing left in life for me to do: bring that iron crashing on Negro skulls.

I went back to the car. Jeff had an unconcerned look on his face. He looked and spoke as though we were still driving down the highway.

"You'd better call the cops," I said. "They know your name." He was a well-known reporter.

"Where?"

"We passed a little store a few blocks back."

He thought for a few moments and then grunted something indistinguish-able. I knew he didn't want to give the police his name. They would have some-thing on him. Finally he left and was gone ten minutes. Carter leaned on the opposite door and we talked a little with the girl. I looked at the tall Negro's face. He had heard me ask Jeff to call the police. The word hung heavy in the air.

Jeff came back and sat in the car. "They're coming," he said in a loud voice. There was a police station half a mile back toward the lake, across the boat canal. Several Negroes left the crowd and walked slowly through the weeds, pausing to look back over their shoulders. We waited for a long time; the police did not come. Carter and I went to the bumpers and began to jump on them.

"Leave it dere!" the Negro shouted instantly. "Leave de cops see it!" We ignored him.

"Leave it dere!" he shouted again and jumped out of the truck and walked up to us. My stomach was constricted in a tight knot. I wanted to lurch into him, smashing haymakers at his mean, skinny face. And yet—I was afraid of him. If this Negro fought a white man he could not count on surviving; and he would not let me count on it either. His knife would be out and he would try to "take me with him." That phrase had meaning. We stood there staring at each other, beneath the spell of the old Southern tragedy.

I walked to the little Negro grocery store—with eyes boring holes in my back—and called the chief dispatcher at police headquarters. I told him we were drinking and had driven on the wrong side of the road. I told him there would be a riot if the cops did not come. I had been a police reporter and I knew him.

"Jesus," he said, in the curious New Orleans accent. "Why didn't yez tell me. I couldn't make out what that other guy was talking about. He wouldn't give me his name."

I returned to the car feeling relieved and ashamed. The police would come quickly now. We had put down the rebellion. The light horse cavalry would top the hill and drive the Comanches from the wagon train. White blood had called to white blood. The native uprising was broken. I felt rotten.

I leaned on the door of the car and told Carter the police would come in a minute. The girl breathed a sigh of relief. Carter's face was flushed and his eyes bloodshot. Mine were too. The tension had sobered us, but we were tired. The red, swollen sun dipped toward the roofs. We were looking directly into it. This day that had been so cool and sweet had come to a shoddy end.

I was no longer worrying about the tall Negro, but instead I was mulling over the day's events. "This is wrong," I thought. "This is wrong." In a few minutes the police came. I watched the final scene as though I were not even a part of it.

The police came roaring down the little road, making a hellish racket. Two motorcycle cops and a long black patrol wagon drew up with sirens screaming. The motors and the wailing struck the fear of God into the Negroes on the sidewalk. In their wide-eyed faces I could see that most of them would like to run. It was too late. The law had arrived. Altogether there were eight burly cops. It was odd the way they came at us all in a bunch. Not one at a time, not by twos, not straggling. They converged on the scene all at once. It made them seem big and terrible, like giants. The motorcycle engines were thundering. Here indeed was frightfulness.

A police sergeant came to our car. "I phoned Charlie Boudreaux," I said. Carter told him we had hit a rock; that the brakes had thrown us to the left side of the road.

I will not forget the look on the Negro's face. He stood there in defeat, tall, silent, malevolent. He looked steadfastly at me and Carter as we told our lies. I believe he realized that he had really beaten us.

The sergeant said nothing to me or Carter. Charlie Boudreaux had told him to get us out of this jam and not to book us at the police station. The cop walked over to the Negroes.

"All right," he said ominously, "get these bumpers unhooked."

The chocolate-faced boy—the first driver—hopped to it. He must have been relieved to see the police. Now he knew where he stood. He had never wanted to fight with white men in the first place. Here at last was the law, telling him what to do.

"Come on, you niggers," the chocolate boy said. His voice was wheedling and melodious. "Git dis yere bumper *off* now!" He hunched his big shoulders over the bumper. For a long moment the tall Negro stood looking at us. Then he bent down slowly and went to work.

"All right," the sergeant said to us as the bumpers parted. "You boys watch yourselves. Drive it on off now."

"All right, you niggers," he said to the crowd. "Break it up now. Show's over. Go on home. Okay, boy, get this damned truck out the way. Go on with your delivering."

It was all over. Carter backed slowly from the truck, put the car in first, and we were away. He breathed a long sigh. "That's the stupidest thing I ever did," he said. We did not talk very much.

I went home and took a cold shower and put on clean clothes and went to work. Jeff was working also. We sat on a desk for a few moments talking. Then we got down to the night's routine. But the scene stayed in our thoughts, I cannot say how long.

RUMOR AND THE CHICAGO WHITE-NEGRO
RACE RIOT, 1919

*

By The Chicago Commission on Race Relations

RUMOR WAS OFTEN THE FIRST STEP in crowd formataion and often opened the way for the sharp transformation of a crowd into a mob. The circulation of rumors was partly due to natural repetition, often with increasing embellishment, by one person to another of what he had heard or read. The desire to tell a "big story" and create a sensation was no doubt an important factor. With so much bitter feeling there was also considerable conscious effort to provoke vengeful animosity by telling the worst that the teller had heard or could imagine about the doings of the opposite race. The latter type of rumor circulation especially fed the riot from the beginning to the final clash. It continues to be a constant menace to the friendly relations of the races.

Newspapers were often supplied a source of rumor material through mistake in fundamental facts, due either to misinformation or exaggeration.

Reports of numbers of dead and injured tended to produce a feeling that the score must be evened up on the basis of "an eye for an eye," a Negro for a white, or vice versa. A most unfortunate impression may be made upon an excited public, Negro and white, by such erroneous reporting as the following, in which newspapers, although they understated rather than exaggerated the number of injuries, reported that 6 per cent more whites were injured than Negroes, when the fact was that 28 per cent more Negroes were injured than whites.

The *Tribune* of July 29 in a news item said that before 3: A.M., July 29, twenty persons had been killed, of whom thirteen were white and seven colored. The truth was that of twenty killed, seven were white and thirteen colored.

The *Daily News* of July 29 gave the starting-point of the riot as the Angelus clash, referring to it as "the center of the trouble." The same item mentioned the spread to the Stock Yards district. The fact was that the assault upon street cars in the Stock Yards district Monday afternoon and rumors of further brutalities there helped to start the Angelus riot Monday evening.

The *Tribune* of July 30 stated that "the Black Belt continues to be the center of conflict." Up to July 30 the "Black Belt" had witnessed 120 injuries, while the district west of Wentworth Avenue had had 139. For the entire riot period the "Black Belt" furnished 34 per cent of the total number of injuries, and the district west of Wentworth Avenue 41 per cent.

Exaggeration in news reports, when popular excitement is at a high pitch, is peculiarly dangerous. For the very reason that the essential fact seems authenticated by the simultaneous appearance of the gist of the report in several papers, the individual reader is the more inclined to believe such exaggerations as may appear in his favorite journal.

Adapted from *The Negro in Chicago: A Study of Race Relations and a Race Riot* (Chicago: The University of Chicago Press, 1922), pp. 25–33.

Following are examples of rumors current during the riot and disseminated by the press and by word of mouth, grouped on the basis of the emotions which they aroused—vengeful animosity, fear, anger, and horror:

Daily News, July 30. Subheadline: "Alderman Jos. McDonough Tells How He Was Shot at on South Side Visit. Says Enough Ammunition in Section to Last for Years of Guerrilla Warfare":

> An alderman in an account of his adventures says the Mayor contemplates opening up 35th and 47th streets in order that colored people might get to their work. He thinks this would be most unwise for, he states, "They are armed and the white people are not. We must defend ourselves if the city authorities won't protect us." Continuing his story, he describes bombs going off, "I saw white men and women running through the streets dragging children by the hands and carrying babies in their arms. Frightened white men told me the police captains had just rushed through the district crying, 'For God's sake, arm. They are coming, we cannot hold them.' "

The point here is not whether the alderman was correctly quoted, but the effect on the public of such statements attributed to him. There is no record in any of the riot testimony in the coroner's office or in the state's attorney's office of any bombs exploded during the riot, nor of police captains warning white people to arm, nor of any fear on the part of whites of a Negro invasion.

Another type of fear-provoking rumor current in street crowds reported the force and the aggressive plans of the opposing race. Some of these rumors, current among Negro crowds, were to the effect that a white mob was gathering on Wentworth Avenue ready to break into the "Black Belt"; that a white mob was waiting to break through at Sixtieth and Ada streets; that a white mob was ready to advance upon Twenty-seventh and Dearborn streets. The first of these rumors had its effect upon the inception of the Angelus riot, and the second so aroused the fears of Negroes that when a white mob led by young white boys did step over the "dead-line" boundaries established by the police, guns were immediately turned upon them, and one of the invaders was killed. Of the third rumor, Police Lieutenant Burns said:

> . . . an old colored man came to me . . . and said that the colored people on Dearborn Street in the 2800 block were moving out in fear of a white mob coming from across the tracks from across Wentworth Avenue. . . . On the southwest corner of Twenty-eighth and Dearborn I found a number of colored men standing in front of a building there. They had pieces of brick and stone in their pockets and were peering around the corner west on Twenty-eighth Street apparently in great fear.

Among the whites fear was not so prevalent. A fear-producing rumor was revealed, however, in the examination of two deputy sheriffs who fired on a Negro. The deputies had heard that Negroes were going to burn up or blow up factories in the district which they were patrolling. When a dark form was seen in an alley, panic seized both deputies, and they emptied their revolvers at an innocent Negro who lived in the adjoining house.

Chief among the anger-provoking rumors were tales of injury done to women of the race circulating the rumor. The similarity of the stories and their persistence shows extraordinary credulity on the part of the public. For the most horrible of these rumors, telling of the brutal killing of a woman and baby (sometimes the story is told of a Negro woman, sometimes of a white) there was no foundation in fact. The story was circulated not only by the newspapers of both races, but was current always in the crowds on the streets. Here is the story as told in the white press:

Chicago Tribune, July 29:

There is an account of "two desperate revolver battles fought by the police with colored men alleged to have killed two white women and a white child."

It is reported that policemen saw two Negroes knock down a woman and child and kick them. The Negroes ran before the police could reach them.

Herald-Examiner, July 29:

Two white women, one of them with a baby in her arms, were attacked and wounded by Negro mobs firing on street cars. . . .

A colored woman with a baby in her arms was reported at the Deering Police Station, according to this item, to have been attacked by a mob of more than 100 white men. When the mob finally fled before the approach of a squad of police both the woman and child were lying in the street beaten to death, "it is said."

Daily News, July 29. Headline, given place of first importance in the pink section: "Women Shot as Riots Grow." Columns 7 and 8 of first-page white section are headed, "Attack White Women as Race Riots Grow. Death Roster Is 30."

The item reads: "Race rioters began to attack white women this afternoon according to report received at the Detective Bureau and the Stock Yards Police Station." The article continues, that Swift & Company had not received any such reports of attacks on their women employees. But farther on the item gives an account of a Swift & Company truck filled with girl employees fired upon by Negroes at Forty-seventh Street and the Panhandle railroad. The driver was reported killed and several of the girls injured.

The juxtaposition of "Death roster is 30" and "Attack white women" gives a wrong impression. The "several girls injured" at Forty-seventh Street evidently refers to the case of Mrs. Mary Kelly. The records of the state's attorney's office also show that Josephine Mansfield was supposed to have been wounded by Harris, *et al.,* but the charge was dropped. She was wounded in the shoulder, according to the police report.

Daily News, July 30:

Alderman McDonough described a raid into the white district the night before by a carload of colored men who passed Thirty-fifth Street and Wallace "shouting and shooting." The gunmen shot down a woman and a little boy who stood close by.

[Note.—No record of such a case.]

Here is the "injury done to women" story as it appeared in the Negro press:

Chicago Defender, August 2:

An unidentified young woman and three-months-old baby were found dead on the street at the intersection of Forty-seventh and Wentworth. She had attempted to board a car there when the mob seized her, beat her, slashed her body to ribbons, and beat the baby's brains out against a telegraph pole. Not satisfied with this one rioter severed her breasts and a white youngster bore it aloft on a pole triumphantly while the crowd hooted gleefully. The whole time this was happening several policemen were in the crowd but did not make any attempt to make a rescue until too late.

Concerning all of these stories it may be stated that the coroner had no cases of deaths of women and children brought before him. There was nothing in the police reports or the files of the state's attorney or hospital reports or the reports of Olivet Baptist Church, which would give any foundation for reports of the killing of a woman and child, white or Negro.

There were other rumors which had the same anger-producing effect as reports of attacks on women. A notable case of this kind was the fatal clash at the Angelus, an apartment house for white people at Thirty-fifth Street and Wabash Avenue, on Monday, July 28. The trouble here grew from four o'clock in the afternoon until it culminated in the shooting at 8:00 P.M. The excitement was stimulated by the rapid spread of various rumors. It was said that a white mob was gathering at Thirty-fifth Street and Wentworth Avenue, only a few blocks from the colored mob which was massed on Thirty-fifth Street from State Street to Wabash Avenue. The rumor was that the white men were armed and prepared to "clean up the 'Black Belt.' " Another rumor had it that a Negro's sister had been killed while coming home from the Stock Yards where she worked. Finally came the rumor that a white person had fired a shot from the Angelus building, wounding a colored boy. The rumor quickly went through the crowd swarming around the building, but no one heard or saw the shooting. A search of the building disclosed no firearms. Police Sergeant Middleton, Negro, described the situation as "everybody trying to tell you something and you couldn't get anything." Another Negro policeman said it was "just a rumor that went around through the crowd and everybody was saying, 'He shot from that window'; I would go to that window and the crowd would say, 'That is the window over there.' "

The anger-provoking power of rumor was seen in the ensuing clash. About 1,500 Negroes massed on one corner of Thirty-fifth Street and Wabash Avenue, and about 100 policemen grouped themselves at the intersection of the two streets. At the sight of a brick flying from the Negro mob the police fired a volley into the midst of the mob. More shots came quickly from both sides. Four Negroes were killed, and many were injured, among both the Negroes and the police.

The Angelus rumor appeared as follows in a Negro newspaper, the *Chicago Defender,* August 2: "White occupants of the Angelus apartments began firing shots and throwing missiles from their windows. One man was shot through the head but before his name could be secured he was spirited away."

In the case of Joseph Lovings, a Negro killed by an Italian mob, press reports that were entirely false tended strongly to provoke the anger of Negro mobs. For example:

Herald-Examiner, July 30: "He had been shot, stabbed and gasoline had been thrown on his body which had been set afire. The police extinguished the fire and took the body to the County Morgue."

Tribune, July 30: "This report says that he was stabbed and shot sixteen times, then his body saturated with gasoline and set afire."

The coroner's jury in commenting on this rumor said: "It gives us satisfaction to say that this rumor, from our investigation, is false and unsubstantiated."

Chief among horror rumors was the Bubbly Creek rumor, which took this form in the press:

Daily News, July 29. Subheadline: "Four Bodies in Bubbly Creek." The article does not give details but says, "Bodies of four colored men were taken today from Bubbly Creek in the Stock Yards district, it is reported."

This was one of the most persistent rumors of the riot, and intelligent men were found repeating it in half-credulous tones. A meat curer, talking in the superintendent's office of Swift & Company, said: "Well, I hear they did drag two or three out of Bubbly Creek. . . . Dead bodies, that is the report that came to the Yards, but personally I never got any positive evidence that there was any people who was found there."

A juror on the coroner's panel said: "A man told a friend of mine—I can furnish the name of that man—a man told him that he saw fifty-six bodies taken out of Bubbly Creek. They made a statement they used a net and seine to drag them out."

Mr. Williams, Negro attorney, said he was told that the bodies of 100 Negroes had been found in Bubbly Creek.

In its final report, the coroner's jury made this conclusive statement regarding the Bubbly Creek rumor:

Bubbly Creek has been the favorite cemetery for the undiscovered dead, and our inquiry has been partly directed to that stream. In our inquiry we have been assisted by the Stock Yards officials and workers, by adjacent property owners and residents, by private detective bureaus, the Police Department, Department of Health, State's Attorney's office, by observing and intelligent colored citizens, and by other agencies, and we are firmly of the opinion that these reports, so widely circulated, are erroneous, misleading, and without foundation in fact, the race riot victims numbering thirty-eight, and no more, nor are there any colored citizens reported to us as missing.

Rumor, fermenting in mobs, prepares the mob mind for the direct suggestion impelling otherwise law-abiding citizens to atrocities. Another more insidious and potentially more dangerous result is the slow accumulation of feeling which builds between the white and Negro the strongest barrier of race prejudice.

* *

By Robert E. Park

RUMOR, according to the authors of this voume, is an "irritating untruth." Rumor has been responsible, first and last, for a great deal of disorder in these United States. God only knows how many innocent victims we should have to charge to these "irritating untruths," if the whole truth were known. The Chicago race riot started in a rumor. The outbreak in Tulsa, on May 31,

Robert E. Park, review of *The Negro in Chicago,* by the Chicago Commission on Race Relations (Chicago: The University of Chicago Press, 1922), in *The New Republic,* XXXIV (April 11, 1923), 194, 196; copyright 1923 by *The New Republic* and used with the permission of the publisher.

1921, had a similar origin. In the Chicago riot thirty-eight people were killed and five hundred and thirty-seven injured. In the Tulsa disaster thirty people were killed, two hundred were injured, and more than a million and a half dollars' worth of property was destroyed.

A catastrophe of such proportions as these is not a mere breach of the peace. It has more the character of a great natural calamity; a sort of moral earthquake. There is something as inevitable about it as there is about any other part of the cosmic process. In a situation like this, in which we are, after all, so helpless, and where the possibility of fixing responsibility and securing justice is so slight, another sort of inquiry presents itself. Why in America, more than any other country, do we have race riots, mobs, lynchings, burnings and manhunts generally? What is there in the nature of our society, made up as it is of so many different racial and cultural groups, that subjects it to these sudden outbursts of the elemental passions? The thing is all the more inexplicable when we consider how tender hearted, humane and democratic we are!

Well, this is, as a matter of fact, precisely the question that the study of the Chicago race riot, which for the last three years and more has absorbed the attention of the Chicago Race Commission and a large staff of assistants, seeks to answer. In this report we have what is probably the first complete authentic and unbiased account of a race riot that has ever been written. But this volume is not merely a report; it goes further and seeks, not merely to state the facts, but to explain them. Here we have for the first time, I suspect, a study in mob psychology that traces to these sources the motives and the passions that find expression in these brutal orgies we call race riots. In this report, too, students of the mob will probably find the most important contribution to the psychology, and the sociology, of the mob that has yet been written.

Race riots—that is in substance what the report has to say about the matter —have their origin in a state of mind; in public opinion. It is one of the merits of this study that it has recognized this fact. The most unique, interesting and generally informing portion of the 700 pages of the report is that concerned with what is referred to as "public opinion in race relations."

There is no attempt in these chapters to correct, change, or argue with public opinion. Public opinion is a fact, a fact to be analyzed, dissected, studied. Quite as important for this study as public opinion, are the mechanisms by which public opinion is disseminated—for example the newspapers.

A very interesting chapter in this investigation is concerned with what is called the primary, that is to say the inherited and traditional attitudes, of white people toward colored. Actually this is a study of what we may call the "racial creed," which with differences of emphasis and of justification, seems to be about the same for all normal white Americans. Rumor, if unchecked, can do incalculable damage to race relations. Included under the term "rumor" are those unfounded tales, incorrectly deduced conclusions, partial statements of facts with significant content added by the narrator, all of which are given wide circulation and easy credence by the public. Other forms of rumor are tales of unheard-of brutality and of plots and plans which are either fabrications or partial statements of fact and serve only to stimulate resentment, fear, and a desire for retaliation. Of the rumors predicting riots, one example will illustrate: During the riot a white man was caught in the act of crawling beneath a house in which Negroes lived. In his pocket was found a bottle of kerosene.

He confessed that his mission was arson and justified his act by repeating to the police the current rumor that it was known that Negroes had set fire to the houses of whites "back of the Yards."

Starting with these premises it is not difficult for a white man to believe almost anything about a Negro, particularly if he is frightened or angry. It is when he is frightened or angry that rumor is so vastly devastating. Rumors, during the four days of the Chicago riot from September 27th to October 1st, "provoked many clashes" we are told.

Reports of the numbers of white and Negro dead tended to produce a feeling that the score must be kept even. Newspaper reports, for example, showed 6 percent more whites injured than Negroes. As a matter of fact there were 28 percent more Negroes injured than whites. *The Chicago Tribune* on July 29th reported twenty persons killed, of whom thirteen were white and seven colored. The true figures were exactly the opposite.

The study of public opinion, so far as it concerns the races, is mainly a study of rumor. What are those "primary opinions" to which we hold so devoutly, even when we are primarily interested, or believe we are, in the Negro's welfare? What are they but the crystallizations of anecdote, unauthenticated statements of fact and partial truths, all of them the naive interpretation of an ethnocentric imagination.

Mythical stories and anecdotes about Negroes, accepted by whites, are usually popular. Many of them have had a reasonable origin, but as a matter of fact have long outgrown it. So long as they are uncorrected they hold and exercise a marked degree of control over personal conduct.

Myth is distinguished in the report from rumor. "A myth," as here defined, "is usually an expression of a wish or a fear." This is to describe the myth in the same terms that Freud describes and explains dreams. A myth, in this sense, is a racial dream, expressing an unfulfilled fear or wish. Fear and wishes are the content of the myth, its form is rumor crystallized and become traditional.

One learns from this study, finally, what race riots are. They are not feuds, nor any other form of warfare, no matter how irregular, in which old grudges are revenged and certain personal and sentimental issues are settled. No, they are merely a kind of carnival in which lusty young bucks, "Ragen's Colts" for example, and young boys, cut loose and kill innocent and helpless people or wantonly destroy property, while a curious public, fearful but fascinated, turns out, as one stated it, "to see how it is done."

The crowds that turned out to see how it was done might include a reporter and a photographer. Some of the pictures in this report showing the mob in action were taken so close to the event that is perfectly possible to identify the participants.

This, as Mr. LeBon has said, is an age of crowds; an age in which the older order is in process of dissolution and the new order is not yet enthroned. In such an age and in such a time all the old bonds are loosened and the energies and passions they once held in check are released. These wild and savage outbursts of violence are, perhaps, but the playful antics of an emancipated youth seeking in this rude way an expression of its uncontrolled and lawless energies. . . .

One puts down the report with the conviction that man hunting is not, as has sometimes been assumed, a habit that we have inherited from the days when all America was a frontier; it is rather a part of the process by which America is now purging itself of its memories; memories which have lingered in the background of our national consciousness; memories which still control our thought and action, long after the world, to which belonged and of which they were a part, has disappeared.

What comes up in these irruptions we call race riots is old stuff, outworn ideas, ideas that belong to another age now dead and gone.

On the anniversary of the Coatesville, Pa., outbreak at which a Negro was slowly burned to death, John Jay Chapman went to Coatesville and held a prayer meeting. He said that he felt that the whole country would be better if one man did *something in penance!* There were only two persons at the prayer meeting beside himself, "and an anti-slavery negress lady" from Boston. But at this prayer meeting Mr. Chapman said some memorable things. He said:

"The subject we are dealing with is not local. The act, to be sure, took place at Coatesville and every one looked to Coatesville to follow it up. Some months ago I asked a friend who lives not far from here something about this case, and about the expected prosecutions, and he replied that 'it wasn't in his county'; and that made me wonder whose county it was in. And it seemed to be in my county. I live on the Hudson River; but I knew that this great wickedness that happened in Coatesville is not the wickedness of Coatesville nor of today. It is the wickedness of all America and of three hundred years—the wickedness of the slave trade. All of us are tinctured by it. No one place, no special persons are to blame. A nation cannot practice a course of inhuman crime for three hundred years and then suddenly throw off the effects of it." Less than fifty years ago domestic slavery was abolished among us; and in one way and another the marks of that vice are in our faces. There is no country in Europe where the Coatesville tragedy or anything remotely like it could have been enacted; probably in no country in the world, only in America. This, I think, is the moral, if there is a moral, of the report. It could only happen in America because public opinion is what it is. The people who are responsible for these outbreaks are the people who make public opinion. Let him who is without guilt among us throw the first stone.

PART VI

Status and Social Change

INTRODUCTION

STATUS IS A BROAD TERM FOR THE POSITION of a person or a group in a hierarchy of persons or groups. The struggle for higher status, "that great object which divides the wives of aldermen," said Adam Smith, "is the end of half the labors of human life." Robert E. Park added, "From this struggle no philosophy of life has yet discovered a refuge." Status is the nerve of the race problem as it probably is of every other social problem. If there is no issue of status there is no issue of race. It is in the effort to achieve or to maintain status that conflict arises. Does race conflict necessarily involve injustice and discrimination?

The result of status conflict is everywhere, even in communist society, what Boswell called the "grand scheme of subordination." The idea of race has implicated this scheme in another one, the "grand scheme of pigmentation" and other physical markings whereby men are rendered automatically and visibly superior or inferior. Where this is true popular interest can lead to the most minute grading of attention to particular individuals who exhibit even slight variations in physical trait and in behavior. Such detailed and personal attention to race is a reflection of the status sensibilities and aspirations of those who move in the common society.

What is the difference between a status and a "condition"? Why is it that efforts to improve the condition of disadvantaged people may meet with general approval while efforts to raise the status of the same people will meet with resistance? How do fluid statuses tend to get fixed? What actions or tricks do members of racial groups utilize to advertise or to conceal status? What is the effect of recording a racial status as in a census or a blue book? What is an "accursed" race and how does a group get to be one? What is the function of an accursed race in a society?

A society will normally have several status-ranking systems of which the

[403]

racial system may be only one. It is when the racial status system is inconsistent with, or contradicted by, other characteristics of the society which also have status-ranking value that there is a sense of comparison and grievance and problem. Consider this point in connection with the fact that, in America, the presumed equality of all citizens before the law exists alongside wide social and economic inequalities. What is the importance and significance of the fact that the scales of wealth and education in America are ceasing to coincide with the scale of race? How important in the changing picture of race relations in the United States has been the evolution of a Negro middle class? What do you understand by "social equality"? In the United States does it mean the same thing to whites and to Negroes? What do each of the different minority and racial groups in the United States, smarting under a sense of unequal treatment, appear to regard as the most effective "equalizer"—money, education, profession, office? Compare the effect on personaality of 1) rising status and 2) falling status. Is it possible that the race problem in certain race relations regions is in process of becoming a white rather than a colored problem?

How would you go about studying the process by which a racial order gets crystallized and fixed, the way it gets old? What are the sorts of things that must go on if a racial order is to remain approximately the same through time? What is the nature and extent of present findings on this subject and how would you go about advancing our knowledge on the subject? In the maintenance of a racial order the definition of the role of growing children of all groups is crucial. The definition of the roles of women also is crucial. Consider the parts played by conscious and unconscious patterning in the family, the neighborhood, the community, the institutions, the general economy and culture of a region in the perpetuation of a racial order.

What is the justification for linking the consideration of *status* and *change?* George Herbert Mead suggested that the central problem of society is that of achieving and preserving a balance between order and change. It is the problem of incorporating the principle of change and the methods of change into the order of society itself. Ordinarily order and change appear opposed to each other and each appears to be championed by different classes in the community. Aristotle, considering the matter from the practical standpoint of an Athenian aristocrat, laid it down that changes in an established order should be as few and as slight as possible. It seems that those who are best served by existing status distinctions are constantly seeking and discovering some principle of certainty which appears to make these distinctions permanent. When men come to abide in such an idea or principle they acquire an armor of belief which becomes part of their fighting apparatus; any attack against their status becomes an attack against the will of God, the order of nature, or against the nation's purposes, and the principle is used to fight back. What are, or have been, some of the ideas or principles which men have used or appealed to in an effort to freeze privileged positions in an existing social order? Consider the idea of race from this point of view. To what extent is its appearance in history bound up with periods of rapid social change or threatened change? What seem to be the advantages and disadvantages of race as a principle of certainty as compared with other ideas or principles similarly used?

What is the difference between change *and* race relations and change *in* race relations? Are the changes in race relations taking place in America today such as may be expected to effect alterations within the existing social structure merely, or do you foresee fundamental changes in the structure itself? What is the importance, if any, of the distinction? How would you design research intended to throw light upon this problem? What are some of the economic and ecological factors now at work changing the relations between the races in such a society as that of the United States? How are we to understand the place and effect of right-wing and left-wing action groups in changing race relations? Is it true that to resist change often effects the most radical change?

What constitutes progress in race relations? Can progress in race relations be measured?

STATUSLESS SOCIETY

By W. S. Gilbert

There lived a King, as I've been told,
In the wonder-working days of old,
When hearts were twice as good as gold,
    And twenty times as mellow.

Good-temper triumphed in his face,
And in his heart he found a place
For all the erring human race
    And every wretched fellow.

When he had Rhenish wine to drink
It made him very sad to think
That some, at junket or at jink,
    Must be content with toddy.

He wished all men as rich as he
(And he was rich as rich could be),
So to the top of every tree
    Promoted everybody.

Lord Chancellors were cheap as sprats,
And Bishops in their shovel hats
Were plentiful as tabby cats—
    In point of fact, too many.

From W. S. Gilbert's "The Gondoliers, or, The King of Barataria," in *The Mikado and Other Plays.*

Ambassadors cropped up like hay,
Prime Ministers and such as they
Grew like asparagus in May,
    And Dukes were three a penny.

On every side Field Marshals gleamed,
Small beer were Lords Lieutenant deemed
With Admirals the ocean teemed
    All round his wide dominions.

And party leaders you might meet
In twos and threes in every street
Maintaining, with no little heat,
    Their various opinions.

That King, although no one denies
His heart was of abnormal size,
Yet he'd have acted otherwise
    If he had been acuter.

The end is easily foretold,
When every blessed thing you hold
Is made of silver, or of gold,
    You long for simple pewter.

When you have nothing else to wear
But cloth of gold and satins rare,
For cloth of gold you cease to care—
    Up goes the price of shoddy.

In short, whoever you may be,
To this conclusion you'll agree,
When everyone is somebodee,
    Then no one's anybody.

STATUS ASPIRATIONS AND RACE CONFLICT

By R. H. Markham

THE RECENT REFUSAL of 54 Negro Wacs at Fort Devens in Massachusetts to obey Army orders, the subsequent trial of four of them for disobedience of a direct order, their condemnation to a year's imprisonment, and the voiding of the sentence have aroused much interest throughout the United States.

Reprinted from R. H. Markham, "The Case of the Negro Wacs," *The Christian Science Monitor*, (Boston) May 5, 1945; copyright 1945 by The Christian Science Publishing Society and used with the kind permission of the publisher.

Some Americans have looked upon these four young women as heroic warriors against injustice and as the sad victims of a ruthless military machine. Such admirers have even gone so far as to exalt the WAC mutineers as martyrs and to encourage them in defiance of their officers. In view of this interest and these conceptions, a dispassionate account of what took place may be useful.

Fort Devens is situated near Boston and is under the direction of the First Service Command, whose Commanding Officer is Maj. Gen. Sherman Miles. Late in 1944, a group of 103 Negro Wacs were sent to Lovell General Hospital, which is attached to Fort Devens and is under the same Service Command. At the time of the arrival of the Negro Wacs, the commanding officer of the hospital was Col. Walter Crandall of Maine.

About noon on March 9, Colonel Crandall informed General Miles's headquarters that 54 of the Negro Wacs had refused to continue with their work, thus defying military orders. The reason they gave for their insubordination was the claim they were being discriminated against and forced to do menial work from which white Wacs were relieved, and were not permitted to do more technical hospital work such as the white Wacs performed. They believed that by their mutiny they were striking a blow against racial discrimination.

General Miles informed the Colonel that he would immediately send Maj. Elizabeth Stearns and Col. Lawrence Wyant to help deal with the case. The Major was the Wacs' Director and the Colonel had been assigned to the First Service Command by the War Department as an expert on racial relations. Colonel Wyant was then at Amherst. He has much experience with Negro military units, has written a manual for them, and has commanded Negro troops with success.

On the morning of March 10, General Miles got in touch with the hospital and learned that nothing effective had been achieved and that there was no change in the situation. On learning this, he at once went to camp, taking with him the Judge Advocate and the Inspector General.

It is plain that the Commanding General had decided to put an immediate end to the mutiny, as any commander in his place would have done. Judging from the way he proceeded, one may be sure he had the following considerations in mind:

First, he was dealing with immature, inexperienced young women, who might not appreciate the gravity of their conduct and who might be acting under the influence of a rather widespread agitation regarding racial discrimination. In view of this emotionalism and the fact that the Wacs had not been long in the Army, the General wished to go to the utmost limits of leniency. He preferred, if possible, to handle the case as a misunderstanding rather than insubordination and to arouse in the young women a consciousness that they had displayed conduct unworthy of a soldier.

Secondly, it was desirable to avoid an open clash, whose repercussions would in any way discourage enlistment in the WAC or discourage white or Negro nurses from offering their services to the Army. The Commanding General wished, undoubtedly, to settle the matter in a way that would increase good will rather than intensify resentment.

Thirdly, the mutiny already had been going on for 24 hours, its cause was a racial complaint, there were 3,700 Negro troops at Fort Devens, and within a few hours, week-end leaves would take many of them into town. Plainly an immediate settlement of the matter was imperative. "Mutiny is notoriously contagious."

Finally and most important of all, the paramount duty of every commanding officer is to maintain discipline in the United States Army, in view of which mutiny cannot be tolerated, nor can officers argue with mutineers openly defying orders.

As the Army Manual for Courts-Martial defines it:

"Mutiny imports collective insubordination and necessarily includes some combination of two or more persons in resisting lawful military authority. The . . . insubordination . . . need not be active or violent. It may consist simply in a persistent and concerted refusal or omission to obey orders or to do duty with an insubordinate intent."

Also, it is certain that in considering the mutiny, General Miles and all the other authorities had in mind the interests of the thousands of patients in the hospital. Every ward was full of men needing constant care. Service of every kind was urgently needed and most helpers in the hospital were overburdened. Yet in the face of that, 54 Wacs walked out on their colleagues in service and on the wounded white and Negro soldiers.

After arriving at camp March 10, the General learned that Colonel Crandall had met with the 54 mutineers in a two-hour session, which had ended only in bitterness. The Wacs were convinced the Colonel was prejudiced against them, resented some of his remarks, and refused to change their decision.

After that, Major Stearns, a white woman staff officer, in charge of the Wacs, went to the WAC orderly room and sent word to the mutineers that they might come and see her. They sent back word they were in the day room across the street and if she wished to see them she could come over. Later they changed their minds, came to see her and a long, sharp meeting was held. The Major told the Wacs a continuation of the mutiny would not be tolerated and that they must return to work immediately, and, if they did, none would be punished. The mutineers continued in their defiant insubordination.

Following this unsuccessful meeting, Colonel Wyant was sent in to see the young women, accompanied by a Negro Captain and a Negro lieutenant. The Colonel was authorized again to inform the mutineers that all their complaints would be heard later, and if wrongs were found they would be righted. At that meeting, however, complaints were not in order, because the Wacs were out of court as mutineers. Again they were to be told that if they immediately returned to work they would not be punished. The Colonel was instructed that this meeting was not to last more than three quarters of an hour.

But after it had continued 1½ hours, the General telephoned the Colonel instructing him to report. The Colonel appeared and said that nothing had been accomplished. None of the young women had agreed to return to work.

On the failure of all these attempts to make the Wacs see their grave mistake, General Miles decided to take immediate final action. He called all the mutineers into a room before himself and his staff officers. And in a formal, military manner the Judge Advocate read the 64th Article of War, regarding punishment for disobedience to a direct order.

When this was completed and the Wacs showed that they understood its meaning, the General told them in a formal statement that all their complaints would be investigated by the Inspector General, there present, after they had returned to work. Then he read a direct order commanding the Wacs to "fall out" and to "fall in" at a different place, for work.

Every one of the 54 mutineers obeyed. However, three other young women failed to fall out and fall in. They remained by themselves as though persisting in disobedience. But it turned out that one of them was in the category of an innocent bystander or spectator, who had just "dropped in." The two others were Wacs whose transfer to another post had been arranged and was under way. These girls later said they had no intention of breaking Army orders and they had no work to go back to. They were detained for investigation and subsequently released. The mutiny was ended.

But within an hour, one of the original mutineers reported to her officer that she refused to go back to work. In the course of the same afternoon, two other mutineers also reported that they would not return to work. On the following Monday morning, these three were joined by a fourth. She was placed in a somewhat different legal category from the first three and charged not with defying an order of General Miles but of her superior, Lieutenant Victoria Lawson. All four were detained for court-martial and the army set up a defense council to defend them.

The President of the Boston branch of the National Association for the Advancement of Colored People, Julian D. Steele, was informed of developments, and General Miles accepted his offer to provide a lawyer for the four young women. The attorney designated by the Association was Julian D. Rainey of Boston, who took up the case with enthusiasm.

Three days later, Mr. Steele and six other officials of the Association signed a public statement containing the following paragraph: "We deplore the action of the colored Wacs in refusing to report for duty at Lovell General Hospital last week. We recognize that there is no right to strike in the armed services and that regular procedure has been established by the Army for reporting grievances and securing their correction. We also oppose the policy of the armed forces in segregating Negro service men and women. This policy frequently works serious hardships and injustices on individual colored personnel. It is deeply resented by most of them and is a source of frequent humiliation. Whether or not these young women were provoked into taking this action as a result of this policy, the action was regretable. We are certain that the splendid record which colored Wacs have made in this war will not be blemished by the misguided actions of these young women."

It is significant that the Boston Chronicle, the leading Boston Negro paper, wrote in its leading editorial April 7: "Two main issues were involved. . . . First the paramount problem of military discipline, which the girls had violated, and, second, the probable discrimination which motivated their ill advised action. . . .

"Like all other patriotic citizens, Negroes are indeed aware that sitdown strikes or other interference with the efficient military operation of the war effort cannot ever be condoned.

"The flouting of discipline, disobedience to duly constituted authority, cannot be countenanced for any reason in time of war, even for just grievances."

The trial was held March 19 before seven judges, of whom two were white WAC officers and two were Negro Army Officers. It was open to the press and was freely reported. Actually, the only question at issue was whether or not the defendants had refused to obey the orders of a superior. This fact was not disputed by anyone. Nevertheless, the young womens' attorney was permitted to take up the wide question of racial injustices. His plea was that because of discrimination practiced in the United States Army the girls were in an abnormal state of mind and so not morally responsible for their acts. In support of this point Mr. Rainey had testimony presented to the effect that the commanding officer had made offensive remarks about Negroes and had said Negro Wacs could do only menial work. The attorney was given much latitude beyond the specific question and publicly declared the trial was fairly conducted. The four girls who had defied orders were sentenced to a year at hard labor, dishonorable discharge, and loss of pay, which was exactly the same sentence that had been pronounced on a white Wac for a similar offense.

Two weeks later the office of the Judge Advocate General in Washington voided the sentence on the ground that the Commanding General was the accuser in the case and thus not competent to set up a court. The young women were released April 3 and sent back to work.

One of the four Wacs brought before the court was Private Mary Magdalen Green, 21 years old, from Houston, Texas. She has finished eight years of grammar school and one year of high school. She had been a general maid and nursemaid.

A second young woman was Private Anna Collins Morrison, 22 years old, from Dayton, Ohio. She has had eight years of grammar school and in civilian life was a maid. A third Wac was Private Johnnie Murphy, who is 21 years old, has finished grammar school and high school and had one year of study in office practice. Her civilian occupation was homemaker. The fourth member of the group was Private Alice E. Young, 23 years old, of Washington, D. C. She has finished grammar school and high school and studied one year at Freedman's Hospital.

Of these four girls, only one had had any real experience except in domestic work, and only one had any qualifications to do hospital work. The aptitude and classification scores of two of them were low and of two were fairly good. Two of the girls would seem to be promising material. All were privates. All entered the hospital at the end of October. Two had been punished for serious infraction of discipline prior to the mutiny.

These girls had enlisted with high hopes, and came to Fort Devens with bright dreams. All had been maids, their way upward seemed closed or at least very difficult, they had interpreted the words of recruiting officers as assurances of rosy prospects, and they hoped, on entering the Army, to become somebodies. It was a pleasant moment in their lives, and this writer admires their desire to get ahead. He wishes their dreams had come true.

But they didn't. The young women passed through no golden gate and found no "brave new world." As civilians they had performed dull, dirty work, and as soldiers they had to do about the same. The military uniform proved to be no fairy wand. These young women learned what about 8,000,000 other Americans have learned, namely that an army is full of disappointments. And they did not react as "good soldiers."

Now all interested persons will ask: Were the Negro Wacs really thrown into the midst of discriminations? Before taking up that question, I should like to emphasize that this study deals only with the case in hand and not with the general question of discrimination against Negroes in the armed forces. One must regretfully admit that there is discrimination on racial grounds in the United States Army. Since I have learned, after much experience, that there is no slick and simple cure for deep-seated prejudices, I could not glibly say how one should deal with every such case. But I do believe that the whole system of racial discrimination in an army fighting for democracy is a grave anonymity and that sincere white people will work unceasingly, urgently, and energetically with the Negro race to end it.

This is a paramount task for both races. Since the chief blame and shame for the wrong rests upon the white people, they should be most active in struggling to remove it. But I am sure the cause will not be helped by mutinies in military hospitals nor by the fomenting of race hatred on either side.

Therefore, without taking up the general question, let us return to Fort Devens and examine conditions there. The reader himself may be the judge. I visited Lovell General Hospital, where the Negro Wacs work, and was permitted to go, unhampered, wherever I wished. During this visit, I observed that Negro and white Wacs work in the motor pool under identical conditions, Negro and white soldiers, serving as technical helpers, work side by side. Negro and white patients share the same wards, Negro and white nurses serve together at identical tasks, Negro and white patients play games at the same card tables, Negro and white men and women eat at the same mess, sitting on the same benches, with the same food before them, Negro and white officers use the same club.

Should not these Wacs have received nicer jobs before? That is what every soldier in the Army asks about himself—and then having asked goes on doing dirty work. I believe that most people in the Army think they should advance more rapidly than they do. Promotions are very slow for all members of the armed forces except combat soldiers—and even sadly slow for them. There are not many generals in an army, at least not in a good army. Every day in the week, including Sunday, a visitor would see regular white soldiers sweeping floors, washing windows and tidying up at Lovell General. They do that side by side with the Wacs, working much harder and doing far more drudgery. And without promotion.

I saw a corporal who had been an expert mechanic in a number of textile factories. As a civilian he had supervised hundreds of workers. But at Fort Devens he is doing drudgery month after month and with no promotion.

Do Negro Wacs do disagreeable tasks that white Wacs do not do? No. Every Wac begins at the same place. But the last group of white Wacs had moved up a little, as the Negro Wacs came in. Consequently, for the moment, most of the drudgery fell to the newcomers. That is the situation in every institution on earth. Freshmen are always freshmen.

Is there then no discrimination? There is always and everywhere some discrimination. Mrs. Smythe, an estimable white matron, has resigned from a voluntary job in a Boston canteen. She wanted to sell at a counter, but the superintendent would not let her, because she was too short. That was discrimination in favor of the taller. Some of us always get less than others because we come late or have not qualifications or are bashful. Also, in every Army hospital, civilian help get better conditions than members of the armed forces.

The Wacs deeply resent this—white as well as Negro—but the difference is unavoidable.

Some people in all ranks of life say disagreeable things about milkmen, taxi drivers, bankers, maids, Britishers, Negroes and others. Some people in the hospital have been discourteous to the Negro Wacs and some Negro Wacs have also been discourteous. I am convinced one of the officers said things he ought not to have said.

The acting commanding officer of the hospital has long been a helpful and responsible white member of the N. A. A. C. P. and is undoubtedly one of the fairest, most considerate men in the country, Col. (Dr.) Julien E. Benjamin. Living requires much give and take. Half the people in Lovell Hospital have personal grievances, most of all, the wounded veterans lying week in and week out, month in and month out, in every sort of position, braced by every sort of contrivance. But most of them take it as good soldiers helping one another. On the whole, there is less institutional discrimination there than in most other places in the United States. It is one of the very hopeful places in our land.

For that reason, the way in which some Negro leaders have tried to arouse race hatred over this incident is regrettable. Here are samples of some of the things that have been written:

"Four Negro Wacs . . . Courtmartialed for mutiny, seen as martyrs to a cause. They represent the 'New Negro,' who is ready to fight and pay the price. . . . The dreary argument that Army orders must be obeyed . . . are to be dismissed with patience. Our people . . . who are wholly Negro in their thought . . . are tired of being delayed by professional race problem solvers, who take the white man's gold to keep us quiet. . . ."

"For the last 20 years a new kind of Negro has been swarming onto the scene. . . ."

"They are minus the traditional fear of the white man that was peculiar to other generations of Negroes."

"The girls are freed because they never should have been tried in the first place."

"We have won a point. . . . Let's . . . use the advantages gained for new and harder charges against the enemy."

"When Negro women stand up and fight back as did the four Wacs a rainbow appears. . . ."

"Whether these girls did right in refusing to obey orders is secondary. . . . They had sufficient cause not to obey those orders."

The same Negro papers from which the above paragraphs are taken also report that "the Boston ministers (Negro) assail" the moderate action of the N. A. A. C. P. and ask, "Has the organization gone white? Some of our leaders are downtown, hobnobbing with big folks."

I do not believe that a majority of Boston's Negro leaders hold such views. These appeals to mutiny and to a purely racial fight will not aid the cause of racial understanding in America. Rabid race haters on both sides make the work of us who believe in brotherhood more difficult.

On April 20, the Executive Committee of the N. A. A. C. P. supported the earlier statement of its officers, saying "there can be no question as to its appropriateness nor as to the integrity or motive of its signers. The Committee deplored "the unjust criticism and personal attacks" on Mr. Steele and its officials, "the effect of which was to attempt to create disunity and lack of confidence when all of our energies need to be directed into constructive channels."

Now we may ask, Was the voiding of the verdict against the four mutineers a good thing? It was good for one reason and bad for two. It indicated that the United States Government is so desirous of showing good will to all citizens and leniency toward the upword-striving underprivileged that it abolished the penalty for this flagrant military insubordination. Every display of good will is commendable. But the decision was also bad, in that it embarrassed a Commanding General who deserved only commendation, and established a special situation in camp by granting favors to recalcitrants.

For the moment, at least, there is a tendency on the part of the hospital personnel to look upon the group of rebels as "the girls who couldn't take it." Their status as good soldiers is compromised among the other soldiers, and their loyalty to their country is questioned. One sincerely hopes they will take advantage of this second chance to remove all such doubts.

Most Americans agree that our heroic and victorious Army, made up of men and women who do their duty even unto the supreme sacrifice, is not the final type of our democratic social order. And while I say emphatically that the Negro girls who mutinied and then persisted in disobedience performed a very grave disservice to their nation and their race, I do not intend to intimate that mere obedience is what is chiefly expected from any American citizen, white or Negro.

We know that after the war there will be a higher duty than fulfilling a superior's order; it will be loyalty to the supreme imperative, "Love thy neighbor as thyself." If a better "new Negro" is emerging, America will rejoice, and hopes that a better new white is evolving, too. We hope that the democratic and brotherly on both sides will work unremittingly together to reduce all kinds of discriminations to a minimum and establish a society in which we may live side by side as free American citizens mutually respecting and helping one another.

WHEN RACE COMES SUDDENLY

By Harnett T. Kane

WITHOUT ITS PEOPLE of African descent, the Delta scene would lack something of its gaiety and its warm humors. It would also miss a portion of its sadness. The darker Deltan knows laughter, and he knows tragedy as well, the tragedy that comes of racial minority and also of countless uncertain gradations between two colors.

Reprinted from Harnett T. Kane, *Deep Delta Country* (New York: Duell, Sloan and Pearce, 1944), pp. 214–220 by permission of the publishers, Duell, Sloan and Pearce, Inc. Copyright 1944 by Duell, Sloan and Pearce, Inc.

Many of his fellows have a skin that seems jet-black and shadowless; others show so fair a complexion that none but a neighbor would say that they were of the Negro race. The rest are of every intervening hue, tawny, brown, mahogany, and others. Though most speak English, some know nothing but French. A few use Spanish, and a number of them, like the whites, command something of the three tongues with an occasional smattering of additional ones. And though traditionally they have been Catholics, a large element have become Protestants, "Bab-teestes" in particular, even when they talk French in the pews and bring beads and rosaries with them. Whatever their shadings, these Deltans have exercised a quiet, unending, largely unperceived influence on those about them.

They stem from several groups. Some are descendants of slaves who spoke the language of their Latin owners; others are grandchildren of Negroes brought from the Atlantic seaboard by their Anglo-Saxon masters, who took up only a few words of Delta French. But many of the lighter-skinned ones declare with flashing eye that their people were "free—never slaves, no!" In Louisiana, or in Cuba or the West Indies, these ancestors had achieved freedom and then maintained themselves by their skills.

In the Delta of pre-Civil War days there appeared several planters of mixed blood, whose mothers had usually been mistresses of white men. Acquiring holdings and slaves of their own, such growers led circumspect lives that had rewards but also limitations. In matters pertaining to plantation management, they approached their white neighbors on approximately equal footing. Able in money affairs, they were careful to meet their business obligations; their accounts were kept in scrupulous order. Otherwise, they held to themselves. Their intimates, if they had any, must be of their own mulatto blood. Old parish records show a surprising number of slave owners whose names are followed by the notation, "free man of color" or "free woman of color."

An Orleanian made a number of business calls in the Delta one day during the last century. In each case, as the agent of a merchants' group, he was received with courtesy; he was impressed in particular with the last place at which he stopped. The French-speaking master, white-haired, goateed, met him at the door with easy grace, and escorted him into a drawing room of velvet elegance. A clap of the hands—a chair for the guest, Emilie. Another signal and a second servant appeared—a glass of water now, vite, vite! Still a third servant came with sherry—or would monsieur prefer brandy, perhaps? The visitor finished his transaction and left. That night at a public meeting of the sugar men, in connection with the tariff, he saw all of the owners of estates whom he had met except the final one. He turned to the chairman: Why wasn't Mr. ——— here? The chairman was surprised. The man he mentioned, sir, had colored blood. The Orleanian said then, and says now, "I would never have guessed."

Little by little the mulatto planters disappeared. Some of their children went back to New Orleans or New York or Paris, where they had been educated. Others took small houses along the river, becoming farmers and tenants, or opened stores. After the Civil War, other divisions by shadings occurred. Of those who remained in the Delta, the darker ones stayed in the upper, more settled places, closer to the city, often in the old plantation quarters. The lighter ones filtered into the lower stretches. They spoke French, sometimes Spanish;

they had a background of greater experience in fending for themselves than did the former slaves. Toward the Gulf, in the half-agricultural, half-aquatic life of the narrow fringes, no great holdings had ever existed. They found themselves not a rigidly restricted class but one of several varied elements: French, Spanish, Tocko, Filipino, all working at much the same tasks, fishing, trapping, raising rice and a few vegetables.

Here rose casual friendship rather than sharp resentment and division. In most frontiers, the settlers manage among themselves. Along the cut-off reaches few came to point a finger and raise questions about the exact status of this or that family whose wharf was next to another's. The lighter-colored people took to the waters, thatched their roofs with palmettos and sang lively French songs to their children in the purple twilights. When their homes were threatened, all of the lower Deltans fought together against water and storm. And in some cases, as elsewhere, further intermarriage occurred. A number of the lighter-skinned, by industrious application, achieved a fair economic success, building larger homes for themselves, prospering with expanded markets.

But new forces, reaching the Delta in the present century, brought new issues and social crises. The mass-scaled industries introduced their rules: Jobs for the whites, none for the Negroes. Such had been the regulations in other parts of the South; such they would be here. Men who, in the marsh, had labored side by side to support their children, could no longer work together. The lower Delta was being shaped by outside influences into a different pattern.

When centralized schools were set up, officials met and lists of prospective pupils were canvassed. This one, to whom was she related? What did that family do for a living? Would these be inclined to fight back? Such questions were not always asked in words. A quick glance, silence . . . a point was raised and settled. Ensuing scenes were tearful. Non, Monsieur, I am Spanish, I swear it. . . . A whitefaced boy, fist clenched in his pocket, maintained that his family was part Indian, part French. Everybody knew that, oui. You just come and ask at where we live. . . . A hysterical woman beat her hands on a table. It was just those people down the road. They had a fight with us over some duck', and it was their way to get back. An' don' you remember, Julien, the time my grandpère saved your uncle? Is this a way to pay back our family, ahn?

New bitternesses were aroused. Children whispered that this or that one was "dipped." In a school yard a taunt was passed: "You got a spot!" The usual retaliation was to pick up an oyster shell and throw it at the tormentor's head. Year after year the teachers were to receive anonymous notes: Did they know that so-and-so was not white? In at least one case, the word carried a threat. The parent of one girl sent a message claiming that she could prove another to be "tainted." She had just learned that the child in dispute was about to be graduated with first honors, while her own daughter was second. Now was that right, Mamzelle? The implication was clear. After long thought, the instructor gave the honors to the second pupil. "It seemed, all considered, the kinder thing to do," she said.

For the first time, the Delta saw the phenomenon known as a "color trial." Suits were threatened, and sometimes brought and won. Weeping parents faced each other before judges, and the shouted accusations and whispered denials went into the record. Damages were awarded, and decisions issued that this or that one was, without question, white. The aroused racial hatreds did not die.

Further differences grew, with gradations of caste based on varying hues. (These were not entirely new, but in later years they have strengthened.) On one side were the whites; opposite them, the dark; between them, the middle shades. The whites felt superior to the light-skinned; the light-skinned looked down on the blacks or near-blacks. In meeting places, and especially in churches, three divisions rose—a kind of layer cake of color, whites in the center, blacks to one side, middle-hued to the other. No member of one element could move under any circumstances to an empty place among the next. There would be mutterings, and a fight after or during Mass.

One mulatto group has resented its classification as "Negro" and refused to send its children to the same school as the darker ones. Bitterly, persistently, it has maintained its position against those only a shade too dark skinned. In a community in which the lighter-colored group predominates, the children drive away the slightly darker ones; those must go to a "nigger" school. When a darker teacher is sent to conduct a class for light-skinned, revolts break out. Parents will not permit their children to attend; lines of shadings have been set up for instructors as well as for students. A religious organization made a promising start toward Negro education in the Delta a few years ago; against the inner barriers of color, the effort collapsed.

A single-storied movie house thrived with a three-section division. Its manager decided to expand, to a more elaborate establishment of two levels. The whites would be downstairs, the others would divide the upper floor, each taking half. Both darker groups resented this; many of the middle element would not be "put up there with the black." The ambitious owner lost much of his trade.

The darker Negro, an earthier fellow, scorns such mulattoes. "Mules, neither one thing or nothing," and he spits when he says it. A mulatto declares with assurance, "But we have good blood, some of the best, n'est-ce pas?" When a mulatto child was born in the earlier day, as the tradition has it, the family inspected closely: "Not a bad lip. . . ." "*Good* hair, yes. . . . " "A nice nose, wouldn't you say?" In certain of the quadroon families of the Delta, a girl knew from her childhood that she must "proteck her skin." She and her sisters wore sunbonnets whenever they left the house, or when they sat on the gallery where the glare was strong. Never were they permitted to go barefoot; they donned long stockings as well as shoes, regardless of the status of the family. Over their arms they drew gloves against the sun. One who saw them walking about in summer with throats well covered by scarves did not conclude that they suffered from colds. When their brothers had hair that was not straight, they cut it short, kept it short, and wore hats whenever they could. All of this, pathetic or diverting as it might be to outsiders, was of course a conforming to the rule of caste that had been ordained by the society about them.

Deltans have charged that numerous light-skinned colored have left the Delta to be accepted elsewhere as white. The stories on the subject are doubtless exaggerated, part of the folklore of the place, but the change has occurred in some instances. In the cities there was no woman from down the road to whisper and remember an incident or a face from the past. Over one who made the decision to "passer à blanc," a nagging fear might hang for years, for all of his or her life. Sometimes, too, a tense moment arrived, when a new-found security was at stake. A marriage impended, or some other event that required a certificate with a word or letter opposite a blank space. The man or woman would slip back to the Delta in the evening, to someone who had been a friend of the family, a former official. One such friend has told of it: "They handed me the paper. They did not argue or cry, nor did I bring up the thing that was in the mind of both of us. I perjured myself like a gentleman, and when I prayed to God, I told Him I had acted to the best of my lights."

A family has been known to divide by gradations of color. With the mulattoes in the church a tall woman looks straight ahead as she says her beads. On the opposite side a darker, hulking man gazes in her direction. She ignores him, though they are first cousins. At funerals among the lighter-hued, a black woman will walk in to take a place. She is received with constraint, but she can insist on her right; she is a niece of the dead man. "Everybody pulls from everybody else," nods a much-wrinkled carver of decoy ducks. "They yank so hard they all fall on their backsides." Upon these feelings of separation, many have played to their own advantage. Here, too, politics has been making itself increasingly felt. The bosses use one group against the next; by keeping each in a turmoil of resentment toward the rest, they win over all of them.

At one edge of Buras and at several other points, the middle groups have separate settlements, to which the darker ones are not admitted. In the lines of plain cottages along the road, all of the residents have straight hair, yellowish complexions, and jet-black eyes, and the faces possess a markedly Latin quality. Sometimes the cheekbone is high, and a sharp nose and coppery tone to the skin give evidence of American Indian in the family. Again, a father or grandfather was Filipino, and a distinct, swarthy type results. These people know the lives of hybrids, with ties to two or more groups and full membership in none. Along several canals the settlements multiply, the level of their existence fluctuating with the seasons, now flush, now verging on want. In the deep, luminous eyes of the healthy children, the shadow of a coming melancholy is reflected.

The dark people live quietly along their river. They are farmers, fisherman, and orange growers. Their wives wield the hoe in the gardens when the husbands find jobs as helpers on the shrimp boats and carriers of oyster sacks. The family enjoys its wine and its fish dinners and seems to have taken on an additional slow somnolence from its surroundings. Few can hope to acquire larger homes, as did some of their fathers; "progress" has further reduced their opportunities. Yet they stay on; they go to their churches, Catholic or Baptist, and they have their dances in their orange-packing sheds. Negroes from New Orleans send down three- and four-man bands; rich, quivering notes ring from the bright rooms, and lights flicker upon the ponds of inky water. Throaty laughter echoes over the levee; nothing has taken from these Deltans their capacity for easy joy.

THE STATUS GAP NARROWS, BUT . . .

By Edmond Taylor

BEFORE I WENT TO ASIA I had never paid much attention to the race problem in America. When I thought of it at all I thought of it in terms of the historic struggle between prejudice and progress, with progress, as usual, winning.

When I started looking back on America from Asia it did not seem possible any longer to think that progress was winning. The economic position of the Negro might be slowly improving, his educational level might be gradually rising, the legalistic or terroristic devices which in some states made a farce of the Fifteenth Amendment, might be more discredited, but all this did not necessarily mean that the Negro as a human being was getting happier. It might mean that he was becoming more miserable.

I suspected, from Asia, that the Negro was in fact getting more miserable. If the parallel between India and America held true, if most Americans unconsciously thought of all Negroes in terms of Negro servants—of old-fashioned Negro servants—then the Negro was certain to be getting more miserable. The very fact that his economic and cultural status was rising meant that his capacity for being hurt, his emotional vulnerability, was increasing. If the recognition of his human dignity was not increasing at the same rate, he was getting more hurt than happiness from his progress. The higher he rose from the servant or slave state the more bitterly he would feel the gap between the place he had earned in American society by his own efforts and the recognition accorded him by white Americans. He might be a skilled technician, a great doctor, a renowned artist, an army officer, or a member of Congress, but if he was expected to say 'sir' to a white farmhand, if he could not eat in a restaurant open to any white American who could afford a decent suit and a haircut, then the very scale of his achievement would be the measure of his humiliation.

I did not feel any more confident that racial tensions were diminishing in America than I did that the Negro was making real progress toward the fifth freedom. It seemed likely that the people who never had much race-prejudice now disapproved of race-prejudice more strongly than ever. This was no progress if those who always had race-prejudice were beginning to develop race-hatred.

THE IMPORTANCE OF
NOT BEING LAUGHED AT

By George Orwell

IN MOULMEIN, IN LOWER BURMA, I was hated by large numbers of people—the only time in my life that I have been important enough for this to happen to me. I was sub-divisional police officer of the town, and in an aimless, petty kind of way anti-European feeling was very bitter. No one had the guts to raise a riot, but if a European woman went through the bazaars alone somebody would probably spit betel juice over her dress. As a police officer I was an obvious target and was baited whenever it seemed safe to do so. When a nimble Burman tripped me up on the football field and the referee (another Burman) looked the other way, the crowd yelled with hideous laughter. This happened more than once. In the end the sneering yellow faces of young men that met me everywhere, the insults hooted after me when I was at a safe distance, got badly on my nerves. The young Buddhist priests were the worst of all. There were several thousands of them in the town and none of them seemed to have anything to do except stand on street corners and jeer at Europeans.

All this was perplexing and upsetting. For at that time I had already made up my mind that imperialism was an evil thing and the sooner I chucked up my job and got out of it the better. Theoretically—and secretly, of course—I was all for the Burmese and all against their oppressors, the British. As for the job I was doing, I hated it more bitterly than I can perhaps make clear. In a job like that you see the dirty work of Empire at close quarters. The wretched prisoners huddling in the stinking cages of the lock-ups, the grey, cowed faces of the long-term convicts, the scarred buttocks of the men who had been flogged with bamboos—all these oppressed me with an intolerable sense of guilt. But I could get nothing into perspective. I was young and ill-educated and I had had to think out my problems in the utter silence that is imposed on every Englishman in the East. I did not even know that the British Empire is dying, still less did I know that it is a great deal better than the younger empires that are going to supplant it. All I knew was that I was stuck between my hatred of the empire I served and my rage against the evil-spirited little beasts who tried to make my job impossible. With one part of my mind I thought of the British Raj as an unbreakable tyranny, as something clamped down, in *saecula saeculorum*, upon the will of prostrate peoples; with another part I thought that the greatest joy in the world would be to drive a bayonet into a Buddhist priest's guts. Feelings like these are the normal by-products of imperialism; ask any Anglo-Indian official, if you can catch him off duty.

One day something happened which in a roundabout way was enlightening. It was a tiny incident in itself, but it gave me a better glimpse than I had had before of the real nature of imperialism—the real motives for which despotic governments act. Early one morning the sub-inspector at a police station the other end of the town rang me up on the 'phone and said that an elephant was ravaging the bazaar. Would I please come and do something about it? I did not know what I could do, but I wanted to see what was happening and I got on to a pony and started out. I took my rifle, an old .44 Winchester and much too small to kill an elephant, but I thought the noise might be useful *in terrorem*. Various Burmans stopped me on the way and told me about the elephant's doings. It was not, of course, a wild elephant, but a tame one which had gone "must." It had been chained up, as tame elephants always are when their attack of "must" is due, but on the previous night it had broken its chain and escaped. Its mahout, the only person who could manage it when it was in that state, had set out in pursuit, but had taken the wrong direction and was now twelve hours' journey away, and in the morning the elephant had suddenly reappeared in the town. The Burmese population had no weapons and were quite helpless against it. It had already destroyed somebody's bamboo hut, killed a cow and raided some fruit-stalls and devoured the stock; also it had met the municipal rubbish van and, when the driver jumped out and took to his heels, had turned the van over and inflicted violences upon it.

The Burmese sub-inspector and some Indian constables were waiting for me in the quarter where the elephant had been seen. It was a very poor quarter, a labyrinth of squalid bamboo huts, thatched with palm-leaf, winding all over a steep hillside. I remember that it was a cloudy, stuffy morning at the beginning of the rains. We began questioning the people as to where the elephant had gone and, as usual, failed to get any definite information. That is invariably the case in the East; a story always sounds clear enough at a distance, but the nearer you get to the scene of events the vaguer it becomes. Some of the people said that the elephant had gone in one direction, some said that he had gone in another, some professed not even to have heard of any elephant. I had almost made up my mind that the whole story was a pack of lies, when we heard yells a little distance away. There was a loud, scandalized cry of "Go away, child! Go away this instant!" and an old woman with a switch in her hand came round the corner of a hut, violently shooing away a crowd of naked children. Some more women followed, clicking their tongues and exclaiming; evidently there was something that the children ought not to have seen. I rounded the hut and saw a man's dead body sprawling in the mud. He was an Indian, a black Dravidian coolie, almost naked, and he could not have been dead many minutes. The people said that the elephant had come suddenly upon him round the corner of the hut, caught him with its trunk, put its foot on his back and ground him into the earth. This was the rainy season and the ground was soft, and his face had scored a trench a foot deep and a couple of yards long. He was lying on his belly with arms crucified and head sharply twisted to one side. His face was coated with mud, the eyes wide open, the teeth bared and grinning with an expression of unendurable agony. The friction of the great beast's foot had stripped the skin from his back as neatly as one skins a rabbit. As soon as I saw the dead man I sent an orderly to a friend's house nearby to borrow an elephant rifle. I had already sent back the pony, not wanting it to go mad with fright and throw me if it smelt the elephant.

The orderly came back in a few minutes with a rifle and five cartridges, and meanwhile some Burmans had arrived and told us that the elephant was in the paddy fields below, only a few hundred yards away. As I started forward practically the whole population of the quarter flocked out of the houses and followed me. They had seen the rifle and were all shouting excitedly that I was going to shoot the elephant. They had not shown much interest in the elephant when he was merely ravaging their homes, but it was different now that he was going to be shot. It was a bit of fun to them, as it would be to an English crowd; besides they wanted the meat. It made me vaguely uneasy. I had no intention of shooting the elephant—I had merely sent for the rifle to defend myself if necessary—and it is always unnerving to have a crowd following you. I marched down the hill, looking and feeling a fool, with the rifle over my shoulder and an ever-growing army of people jostling at my heels. At the bottom, when you got away from the huts, there was a metalled road and beyond that a miry waste of paddy fields a thousand yards across, not yet ploughed but soggy from the first rains and dotted with coarse grass. The elephant was standing eight yards from the road, his left side towards us. He took not the slightest notice of the crowd's approach. He was tearing up bunches of grass, beating them against his knees to clean them and stuffing them into his mouth.

I had halted on the road. As soon as I saw the elephant I knew with perfect certainty that I ought not to shoot him. It is a serious matter to shoot a working elephant—it is comparable to destroying a huge and costly piece of machinery —and obviously one ought not to do it if it can possibly be avoided. And at that distance, peacefully eating, the elephant looked no more dangerous than a cow. I thought then and I think now that his attack of "must" was already passing off; in which case he would merely wander harmlessly about until the mahout came back and caught him. Moreover, I did not in the least want to shoot him. I decided that I would watch him for a little while to make sure that he did not turn savage again, and then go home.

But at that moment I glanced round at the crowd that had followed me. It was an immense crowd, two thousand at the least and growing every minute. It blocked the road for a long distance on either side. I looked at the sea of yellow faces above the garish clothes—faces all happy and excited over this bit of fun, all certain that the elephant was going to be shot. They were watching me as they would watch a conjurer about to perform a trick. They did not like me, but with the magical rifle in my hands I was momentarily worth watching. And suddenly I realized that I should have to shoot the elephant after all. The people expected it of me and I had got to do it; I could feel their two thousand wills pressing me forward, irresistibly. And it was at this moment, as I stood there with the rifle in my hands, that I first grasped the hollowness, the futility of the white man's dominion in the East. Here was I, the white man with his gun, standing in front of the unarmed native crowd—seemingly the leading actor of the piece; but in reality I was only an absurd puppet pushed to and fro by the will of those yellow faces behind. I perceived in this moment that when the white man turns tyrant it is his own freedom that he destroys. He becomes a sort of hollow, posing dummy, the conventionalized figure of a sahib. For it is the condition of his rule that he shall spend his life in trying to impress the "natives," and so in every crisis he has got to do what the "natives" expect of him. He wears a mask, and his face grows to fit it. I had got to shoot the elephant. I had committed myself to doing it when I sent for the rifle. A sahib has got to act like a sahib; he has got to appear resolute, to know his own mind and do definite things. To come all that way, rifle in hand, with two thousand people marching at my heels, and then to trail feebly away, having done nothing—no, that was impossible. The crowd would laugh at me. And my whole life, every white man's life in the East, was one long struggle not to be laughed at.

But I did not want to shoot the elephant. I watched him beating his bunch of grass against his knees, with that preoccupied grandmotherly air that elephants have. It seemed to me that it would be murder to shoot him. At that age I was not squeamish about killing animals, but I had never shot an elephant and never wanted to. (Somehow it always seems worse to kill a *large* animal.) Besides, there was the beast's owner to be considered. Alive, the elephant was worth at least a hundred pounds; dead, he would only be worth the value of his tusks, five pounds, possibly. But I had got to act quickly. I turned to some experienced-looking Burmans who had been there when we arrived, and asked them how the elephant had been behaving. They all said the same thing: he took no notice of you if you left him alone, but he might charge if you went too close to him.

It was perfectly clear to me what I ought to do. I ought to walk up to within, say, twenty-five yards of the elephant and test his behavior. If he charged, I could shoot; if he took no notice of me, it would be safe to leave him until the mahout came back. But also I knew that I was going to do no such thing. I was a poor shot with a rifle and the ground was soft mud into which one would sink at every step. If the elephant charged and I missed him, I should have about as much chance as a toad under a steam roller. But even then I was not thinking particularly of my own skin, only of the watchful yellow faces behind. For at that moment, with the crowd watching me, I was not afraid in the ordinary sense, as I would have been if I had been alone. A white man mustn't be frightened in front of "natives"; and so, in general, he isn't frightened. The sole thought in my mind was that if anything went wrong those two thousand Burmans would see me pursued, caught, trampled on and reduced to a grinning corpse like that Indian up the hill. And if that happened it was quite probable that some of them would laugh. That would never do. There was only one alternative. I shoved the cartridges into the magazine and lay down on the road to get a better aim.

The crowd grew very still, and a deep, low, happy sigh, as of people who see the theatre curtain go up at last, breathed from innumerable throats. They were going to have their bit of fun after all. The rifle was a beautiful German thing with cross-hair sights. I did not then know that in shooting an elephant one would shoot to cut an imaginary bar running from ear-hole to ear-hole. I ought, therefore, as the elephant was sideways on, to have aimed straight at his ear-hole; actually I aimed several inches in front of this, thinking the brain would be further forward.

When I pulled the trigger I did not hear the bang or feel the kick—one never does when a shot goes home—but I heard the devilish roar of glee that went up from the crowd. In that instant, in too short a time, one would have thought, even for the bullet to get there, a mysterious, terrible change had come over the elephant. He neither stirred nor fell, but every line of his body had altered. He looked suddenly stricken, shrunken, immensely old, as though the frightful impact of the bullet had paralysed him without knocking him down.

At last, after what seemed a long time—it might have been five seconds, I dare say—he sagged flabbily to his knees. His mouth slobbered. An enormous senility seemed to have settled upon him. One could have imagined him thousands of years old. I fired again into the same spot. At the second shot he did not collapse but climbed with desperate slowness to his feet and stood weakly upright, with legs sagging and head drooping. I fired a third time. That was the shot that did for him. You could see the agony of it jolt his whole body and knock the last remnant of strength from his legs. But in falling he seemed for a moment to rise, for as his hind legs collapsed beneath him he seemed to tower upward like a huge rock toppling, his trunk reaching skywards like a tree. He trumpeted, for the first and only time. And then down he came, his belly towards me, with a crash that seemed to shake the ground even where I lay.

I got up. The Burmans were already racing past me across the mud. It was obvious that the elephant would never rise again, but he was not dead. He was breathing very rhythmically with long rattling gasps, his great mound of a side painfully rising and falling. His mouth was wide open—I could see far down into caverns of pale pink throat. I waited a long time for him to die, but his breathing did not weaken. Finally I fired my two remaining shots into the spot where I thought his heart must be. The thick blood welled out of him like red velvet, but still he did not die. His body did not even jerk when the shots hit him, the tortured breathing continued without a pause. He was dying, very slowly and in great agony, but in some world remote from me where not even a bullet could damage him further. I felt that I had got to put an end to that dreadful noise. It seemed dreadful to see the great beast lying there, powerless to move and yet powerless to die, and not even to be able to finish him. I sent back for my small rifle and poured shot after shot into his heart and down his throat. They seemed to make no impression. The tortured gasps continued as steadily as the ticking of a clock.

In the end I could not stand it any longer and went away. I heard later that it took him half an hour to die. Burmans were bringing dahs and baskets even before I left, and I was told they had stripped his body almost to the bones by the afternoon.

Afterwards, of course, there were endless discussions about the shooting of the elephant. The owner was furious, but he was only an Indian and could do nothing. Besides, legally I had done the right thing, for a mad elephant has to be killed, like a mad dog, if its owner fails to control it. Among the Europeans opinion was divided. The older men said I was right, the younger men said it was a damn shame to shoot an elephant for killing a coolie, because an elephant was worth more than any damn Coringhee coolie. And afterwards I was very glad that the coolie had been killed; it put me legally in the right and it gave me a sufficient pretext for shooting the elephant. I often wondered whether any of the others grasped that I had done it solely to avoid looking a fool.

THE PROBLEM OF SOCIAL ORDER AND SOCIAL CHANGE

By George Herbert Mead

THE CONTROL OVER community life in the past has been a control of situations. The control, as such, has been almost inevitably conservative. It has preserved orders which have established themselves as social habits that we call "institutions." A conscious social control has taken on this form: The law must be obeyed; the constitution must be honored; the various institutions such as the family, school, courts, must be recognized and obeyed; the order which has come down to us is an order which is to be preserved. And, whenever the community is disturbed, we always find this return to the fixed order which is there, and which we do not want to have shaken. It is entirely natural and, in a certain sense, entirely justifiable. We have to have an order of society; and, if what is taking place shakes that order, we have no evidence that we will get another order to take the place of the present one. We cannot afford to let that order go to pieces. We must have it as a basis for our conduct.

The first step consciously taken in advance of this position is that which grew out of the French Revolution, that which in a certain sense incorporated the principle of revolution into institutions. That is, when you set up a constitution and one of the articles in it is that the constitution may be changed, then you have, in a certain sense, incorporated the very process of revolution into the order of society. Only now it is to be an ordered, a constitutional revolution by such and such steps. But, in any case, now you can change the order of things as it is going on.

That is the problem of society, is it not? How can you present order and structure in society and yet bring about the changes that need to take place, are taking place? How can you bring those changes about in orderly fashion and yet preserve order? To bring about change is seemingly to destroy the given order, and yet society does and must change. That is the problem, to incorporate the methods of change into the order of society itself. I do not mean to say that society has not always recognized that change could take place, but it did not undertake to find a process by means of which this should go on. It simply assumed that change was going to take place toward some fixed goal. If you are going to have a society in which everyone is going to recognize the interests of everybody else—for example, in which the golden rule is to be the rule of conduct, that is, a society in which everyone is to make the interests of others his own interest, while actually each person seems to be pursuing his own interest—how can that goal be reached? It was assumed, of course, that this was to be done through a religious current, through a change in the heart of the individual. But in the last analysis that goal was to be reached in the world to come, not in this one. That was the religious solution. The order we find is one given by God for this world and must be preserved. The final perfect

Reprinted from George H. Mead, *Movements of Thought in the Nineteenth Century* (Chicago: University of Chicago Press, 1936), pp. 361–363; copyright 1936 by the University of Chicago and used with the permission of the publisher.

society was to be a New Jerusalem that belonged to another world. The religious goal was one of otherworldliness. We have other conceptions, councils of perfection set up, such as that of a society in which you should bring liberty in the sense of everyone's respecting the rights of everyone else, one's liberty being in that sense only circumscribed by intrenching on others' liberty. That is more or less an abstraction. To take a practical illustration, how are you to determine where the liberty of a man in the control of his property is to be restricted? He needs controlling. We will say that he, or rather a group of men, own shares in a railroad, and that they choose to deal with rates in a fashion which will serve their own interest. Well now, if they are to have complete control over their property, and then the community comes in and says that theirs is property of a different sort, that their acts must have the approval of the community, how are we to determine where the restriction in the control over the property is to take place?

How is society to find a method for changing its own institutions and still preserve the security of those institutions? That is, in general, the problem that presents itself in its most universal form. You want a society that is going ahead, not a fixed order, as the religious solution would have it. You want a society that is progressing. Progress has become essential to intelligent life. Now, how are we to get ahead and change those situations that need changing and yet preserve the security of them? You see this is an advance in which we cannot state the goal toward which we are going. We do not know what the goal is. We are on the way, but we do not know where. And yet we have to get some method of charting our progress. We do not know where the progress is supposed to terminate, where it is going. This is a seemingly insoluble problem.

THE OVEREMPHASIS ON BIOLOGICAL EXPLANATIONS

By William Fielding Ogburn

THERE ARE SEVERAL REASONS why cultural traits tend to be popularly interpreted as biological traits. The effect of culture on an individual is carried around by that individual in the forms of habit, training, education, technique, conditioned reflexes. These acquired ways of doing things are seen as part of an individual as truly as his physiognomy is. The association is almost as close. They become a part of his psychological self and are generally more or less permanently descriptive of the personality. The concept of the original nature of man does not frequently appear in the ordinary judgments of life. It takes

From *Social Change*, 1950, pp. 32–39, by William Fielding Ogburn. Copyright 1922 by B. W. Huebsch, Inc., 1950 by William Fielding Ogburn. Reprinted by permission of the Viking Press, Inc., New York.

some special training and imagination to see the original nature of man beneath his cultural exterior, for it is only in special situations in life where such penetrating observation is called for. Man as nature plus nurture is thus popularly seen as nature. Acquired characteristics are thought to be so integral a part of an individual as to be hereditary. Indeed it required special research to disprove this. So it seems very natural to interpret cultural traits as psychological traits.

In attempting to formulate the concepts of the social heritage and the biological nature of man, it has been seen that a difficulty lies in the confusion of these two ideas due to the general tendency to consider the cultural influence on behavior as biological. There is also another source of confusion. This does not concern behavior so much as the products of behavior. But the results are similar in that the cultural influence is obscured and the biological influence is magnified. Consider, for instance, the appearance of some hitherto undeveloped object of material culture, say, a steam engine. What are the factors that operated to make the steam engine? Obviously one factor is mental ability. Also the formerly invented and prepared materials that go to make up the steam engine, and the existing state of knowledge, are another factor. These two factors are quite different in nature but are quite definitely two general factors operating to produce the steam engine. It could not be produced without the mental ability, nor could it be produced without scientific knowledge and without materials in a certain degree of previous preparation. The factor of mental ability is always recognized. But very often one does not appreciate the cultural factor, that is, one does not think how dependent an invention is on previous inventions and on the previously developed state of knowledge. The steam engine could not have been invented, for instance, without a knowledge of fire, combustion, vaporization, the metals, the wheel, the piston, valves, the screw and numerous other inventions and processes. The existing state of the social heritage is thus a very important factor in the invention of a particular cultural object. The cave man, had he the ability of a modern genuis, could not have invented the steam engine, living as he did on the plane of culture existing during the last ice age. Presented in this manner, it is readily seen that the cultural factor is necessary and as important as is the factor of mental ability. But popularly there is full recognition of mental ability but a neglect of cultural influence. When Edison makes an invention, credit is given to his ability and rightly so because the social heritage is the heritage of many, yet only a few utilize it to make discoveries and inventions. The variable factor is the individual and is therefore thought of as the causative factor. He is not thought of as original nature plus the social heritage.

In a somewhat similar way the culture of Great Britain and her colonies is seen as the product of the ability of the Anglo-Saxon peoples. The dependence of British culture upon the inventions and achievements of other peoples is not called to the attention. To think of this implies a certain historical and cultural knowledge, not possessed by many. Indeed the total knowledge on the origin and diffusion of inventions is quite limited. But many peoples of various periods from different parts of the world have been associated with the development of the modern culture possessed by the British. It has been quite customary to attribute the Greek civilization in a somewhat complete fashion to the genius of the Greek people. Indeed it is only recently that research is establishing how much Greece borrowed from the peoples to the north, the east and the south. Great Britain has borrowed many times as much as she has invented. But even admitting a differentiation between what a people has invented and what borrowed, the concept of cultural evolution is not conceived in any full sense. That is to say, it is not seen that culture would have changed and increased from the time of the Angles and the Saxons until now, more or less irrespective of the particular peoples that may have been associated with this culture. Such an idea is not common, and indeed it is seldom noted in intellectual circles, very largely for the reason that at the present state of our knowledge the laws governing the growth and change of culture are not clearly and quantitatively formulated. Culture grows because of mental ability, but the existing basis of culture is a very important factor in determining the nature and rate of growth of culture.

The prevailing status of general opinion is seen from the fairly complete identification of the state of culture of a people with their abilities. The Egyptians produced the Egyptian culture, the Indian culture is a product of Indian ability, as the European culture is a product of European ability. And the Hottentot culture is an index of the ability of that people. So popular opinion runs. There may be variation in the abilities of peoples but the state of culture is not a good index. The varying social inheritances may be correlated with the abilities of peoples, but the proof is not clear and certainly the correlation is not very close, for the very reason that purely cultural or historical causes are such an important factor in determining a particular culture. These questions of the relations of culture to mental ability and of the causes and laws of the growth and change of culture are far-reaching and will be considered further later on. But enough has been said to show that the purely cultural influence tends to be obscured and overshadowed by the biological factor.

The overemphasis of the biological influence as contrasted to the cultural influence has certain roots in the facts of everyday life. The results of the training are seen through the eyes of youth very much in terms of personal achievement. Honors, prizes, grades, diplomas, emphasize this fact. In the classroom the same culture is presented to all, the variations in results are variations in personal abilities. Honors or diplomas are not given to the textbooks or the teacher. Variations in social opportunity are seen as something to be grasped. And this utilization of opportunity for a greater culture is interpreted in terms of personal ability. Moral training of the young is a matter of doing right or wrong, or praise or blame, an emphasis of the personal and a neglect of the cultural. Achievement reflects the glory of the ego and the hero is given full credit. There is no particular occasion to give the credit to so impersonal a period of prosperity even though it be a matter of crops and rainfall. And factor as culture. The particular political party in power claims credit for a failure, particularly in the other fellow, is a matter of personal inefficiency. Especially among the wealthy classes is it customary to attribute their position almost solely to ability and to make the converse interpretation for those not at the top—a very comfortable theory. In many such simple daily estimations the influence of culture is not appreciated. Thus a mental pattern is ready-made, prepared since youth, and one brings such a ready-made pattern to the study of sociology or to the reading of history, which it may be remarked is also usually written from this same mental pattern.

In intellectual centres, the overemphasis of the biological is in part occasioned by the prevailing status of the various sciences; the prestige of biology among the social sciences has been very great, because of the extraordinary significance of the discovery of natural selection and the emphasis on evolution due to the researches of Darwin and Wallace. The significance was so overshadowing that it seemed to cast something like a hypnotic spell over others doing research. The biological terminology was borrowed quite widely; and it became almost a fad to refer to biological causes and to make biological interpretations for many social phenomena. Of recent years the tendency to get away from this spell is noticeable but the rise of the eugenists has given added emphasis to the importance of biology for sociology.

Eugenics centres attention on biological variation, with the purpose of improving biological ability and eliminating biological inferiority. The eugenists are so impressed with the importance of racial stock that scant attention is given to the social heritage and there is very little understanding of its nature. All through the writings of the eugenists is found the implication that a particular culture is quite simply and directly the ability of the racial stock. They do not seem to realize that cultural growth is caused largely by purely cultural causes. They see inventions and improvement chiefly in terms of mental ability, failing to appreciate the extent of the dependence of future change on existing cultural elements. The result of the spread of the eugenics idea is, like the discovery of natural selection, an overemphasis of the significance of the biological factor in social progress.

INTERRACIAL MARRIAGE AND SOCIAL CHANGE

By Romanzo Adams

WHEN RACIAL contacts are established between the people of two races it usually happens that one of them is more powerful than the other by reason of superior military and economic organization and superior knowledge and technical development and there may or may not be an advantage due to superior numbers. Commonly, the people of superior power undertake to exploit those of inferior power, by means of slavery, peonage, serfdom, trade, or employment at wages. In the beginning the exploitation may be carried on successfully through the superiority of knowledge, technique, and organization, but since some of the exploited race may acquire these advantages they do not

From Romanzo Adams, *Interracial Marriage in Hawaii* (New York: The Macmillan Company, 1937), pp. 50–52. By permission of Mrs. Romanzo Adams.

serve as a permanent basis for profitable exploitation. If the exploitation is to be permanent with race lines, that is, if all of the exploiters are to be of one race and all the exploited of the other, it is necessary that the exploiting race shall be dominant in a political and military sense so that they may make and administer laws which deprive the members of the other race of equal privilege. For, if the exploited possess equal privileges, some of the more able or fortunate will acquire the superior knowledge and technique of the exploiters and, profiting thereby, will rise to the higher economic status. Likewise some of the less capable or less fortunate members of the exploiting race will fall into the exploited class. After this crossing of the line by members of both races takes place for a considerable period of time economic status will not correspond to race. The only way to perpetuate the exploitation of a racial group, as such, is to deny to it equality of privilege, to deny the abler and more fortunate members the privilege which might permit any considerable number to rise out of their class.

The simplest and most obvious and effective way to do this is through slavery,—slavery extended to all the children of slaves. Under some conditions a system of land ownership with serfdom or peonage may accomplish the same results. Discriminatory rules of employment and discriminatory provision for education may be sufficient to maintain race class lines for a long time. If the people of the exploited race have political rights and if they are so numerous as to be able to bring about political compromises with provisions in their favor, it will not be possible to maintain a racially discriminatory organization of sufficient rigidity to be effective. Hence there must be a denial of political rights where numbers are important.

If a dominant racial group is to be successful in its efforts to maintain a system of discriminatory regulations for the purpose of denying the members of the other race equality of privilege, it is necessary to prevent interracial marriage. If some of the members of the dominant race marry members of the dominated race, i.e., form legally and socially sanctioned unions, they will tend to give to their children the advantages reserved to the more privileged people, —wealth, education, political rights, and social status. Gradually there will come into existence a large number of persons of mixed ancestry and of all shades of mixture, some being indistinguishable in appearance from the people of the dominant race. This tends to increase the rate at which miscegenation goes on and finally the race line becomes so obscure that discriminatory race regulations cannot be enforced. Therefore, if the dominant race is to preserve its status as a dominant race it must prohibit by law and sentiment the marriage of its members to members of the dominated race and such illegitimate children of mixed racial ancestry as may be born must be denied the status of the race of superior privilege.

But if intermarriage is to be effectively prohibited it is necessary to prohibit the sorts of social contact that normally lead to marriage or that imply the possibility of marriage. Out of this need a whole code of social relations arises. People of different races must not eat together, entertain each other socially, or attend the same school. The common forms of address must carry the implication of social inequality. There is, in effect, a ritual of race relations through which race is made to appear to be an impassable barrier to marriage. If any member of the dominant race should have the temerity to marry a member of the dominated race the penalty must be certain and severe,—mobbing, perhaps, or at least social ostracism. So strong are the urges and sentiments that influence personal choice in marriage that a weak form of control is ineffective.

A social system, therefore, in which there are racial discriminations denying political and economic equality of privilege and prohibiting interracial marriage may be seen as one that has been evolved in the interest of perpetuating the advantages enjoyed by a dominant racial group. When such a system is adequately supported by sentiment on both sides, i.e., when it has a religious sanction, it is a caste system.

On the other hand, if the social system is such as to involve the recognition of the peoples of both or all races as having equality of political rights, educational opportunity, and economic and social status, freedom of marriage is implied. Prohibition of interracial marriage is associated with a caste system or with tendencies toward a caste system and freedom in marriage is associated with the mores of equality.

GROUP DIFFERENCES IN TIME PERSPECTIVE

By Pars Ram and Gardner Murphy

ESPECIALLY SIGNIFICANT is what Kurt Lewin used to call "time perspective." For the Hindu, events are sketched on an infinite canvas of time; for the Muslim, history is dynamic and even explosive. Important things are occurring at this instant. Without a single clear exception up to the present time, when a Hindu in Aligarh is asked: "What is the most recent example of communal trouble?" he embarks upon a broad historical sketch of Hindu-Muslim relationships down to events of a year or so prior to the interview. "It seems to me," he says, "that there was a scuffle in the streets and somebody was killed 10 or 12 months ago," or, "I think I remember some Muslims leaving at night for Pakistan. That must have been a year ago." Ask any Muslim the same question—and no exception has yet been found among those interrogated—and he tells you of events of a week or two ago, events still burning deeply within him: "Why, last week three men learned that their shops were to be looted and they left for Pakistan at once," or "This very day my children came home from school crying, saying that Hindu children had taunted them." In the same way, for the Hindu the future is a vast open space, for the Muslim a sharply structured region wherein that which is closest is most vivid. Ask any Hindu, "If you had the power, what would you do to stop the communal

Reprinted from Pars Ram and Gardner Murphy, "Recent Investigations of Hindu-Muslim Relations," *Human Organization*, II (Summer, 1952), 15; copyright 1952 by the Society for Applied Anthropology and used with the kind permission of the publisher.

troubles?" and you get this sort of reply, "Well, we've had these troubles a long, long time, and it will be a long, long time before we get rid of them." Ask any Muslim what he would do to stop the difficulties and he replies, "The police can stop them tomorrow if they want to."

Two hypotheses immediately suggest themselves. The first hypothesis is that this difference in time perspective is due to the unstructured nature of time in Hindu culture compared to its highly structured nature in Islamic culture. If this hypothesis is true, we shall find similar responses among Hindus outside of India, notably among those few who are still living in Pakistan. We shall find these same responses characteristic also of a later period of interrogation when the present crisis is past. Similarly, we should get the same responses from Muslims in Pakistan, or indeed in Iran, Jordan, or Egypt. The second hypothesis is that the difference in time perspective is a characteristic difference between majority and minority groups or between secure and insecure people. From this point of view, the secure need not remember crisis incidents nor need they be concerned with the immediacy of their removal. The insecure, subject to continuous threat, must take note of all that threatens them, and recent past and immediate future must be sharply defined.

THE CONCEPT OF MORES AND
RESISTANCE TO CHANGE

By Gunnar Myrdal

WE MUST VOICE OUR GRAVE SKEPTICISM toward the simple explanatory scheme concerning the role of valuations in social life typified by William Graham Sumner's concepts, "folkways" and "mores." Since his time these concepts—or one of their several synonyms—have been widely used by social scientists and have, in particular, determined the approach to the Negro problem. The formula will be found to be invoked with some regularity whenever an author expresses his attitude that changes will be slow, or, more particularly, that nothing practical can be done about a matter. It is closely related to a bias in social science against induced changes, and especially against all attempts to intervene in the social process by legislation. The concept of mores actually implies a whole social theory and an entire *laissez-faire* ("do-nothing") metaphysics, and is so utilized.

Leaving aside for the present the political connotations of Sumner's construction, and focusing our interest only on its usefulness as a scientific tool, our main criticism is the following: By stowing the commonly held valuations

Reprinted from Gunnar Myrdal, *An American Dilemma* (9th ed.; New York: Harper and Brothers, 1944), Appendix I, No. 2 "Theoretical Critique of the Concept 'Mores'." Copyright 1944 by Harper and Brothers and used with the kind permission of the publisher.

into the system of mores, conceived of as a homogeneous, unproblematic, fairly static, social entity, the investigator is likely to underestimate the actual difference between individuals and groups and the actual fluctuations and changes in time. He is also likely to lose sight entirely of the important facts, that even within a single individual valuations are operative on different planes of generality, that they are typically conflicting, and that behavior is regularly the outcome of a moral compromise.

It might be that Sumner's construction contains a valid generalization and offers a useful methodological tool for studying primitive cultures and isolated, stationary folk-communities under the spell of magic and sacred tradition. It might even be that the most convenient definition of such a folk-culture is the applicability of the theory of folkways and mores. The theory is, however, crude and misleading when applied to a modern Western society in process of rapid industrialization, moving in swift trends rippled by indeterminate cyclical waves: a society characterized by national and international mobility, by unceasing changes and differentiations of all valuations and institutions, by spreading intellectualization, by widening intellectual communication and secularization, by ever more daring discussion even of fundamentals and intimacies, and by a consequent virtually universal expectation of change and a firm belief in progress. If Sumner's construction is applied to such a society, except as a contrast conception to mark off some remaining backward cultural isolates which are merely dragged along and do not themselves contain the active factors of social dynamics, it is likely to conceal more than to expose. It conceals what is most important in our society: the changes, the conflicts, the absence of static equilibria, the lability in all relations even when they are temporarily, though perhaps for decades, held at a standstill. The valuation spheres, in such a society as the American, more nearly resemble powder-magazines than they do Sumner's concept of mores.

CHANGING RACE RELATIONS IN MASS SOCIETY

By Joseph Lohman and Dietrich C. Reitzes

THE BASIC SCIENCES slowly and continuously feed their findings and generalizations into the world of practical affairs, but in recent years crises in technology and social relations have been making extraordinary and urgent demands upon scientific knowledge. One such crisis is that precipitated by racial contacts.

Racial relations are no longer a domestic problem which can be solved at

From Joseph Lohman and Dietrich C. Reitzes, "Note on Race Relations in Mass Society," *The American Journal of Sociology*, LVIII (November, 1952), 240–246.

national leisure. They have developed into a problem which greatly affects our relations with other countries. The weaknesses in our domestic race relations provide an extremely effective propaganda tool for the Communists in undermining America's status in those parts of the world which are predominantly nonwhite. This, of course, is the greater portion of the world.

Tragically enough, much of the current research in race relations is of limited usefulness in the face of the "American dilemma." We are in need of more adequate generalizations if our basic knowledge about racial relations is to be employed to implement democratic values.

The shortcomings of our knowledge about racial relations center in two basic and interrelated notions about human behavior in modern society. One is that any specific social relation as such can be theorized *in vacuo;* thus, that *special theories* are appropriate and necessary to an explanation of the behavior of individuals in situations of racial contact.

The other notion is that human behavior in such situations is, for the most part, definitively structured by the attitudes of individuals as such. In consequence collective manifestations of racial relations are interpreted from the perspective of the individuals who constitute the group. And hence the corollary has been adduced that all changes in race relations are brought about through the manipulation of individual attitudes. It is the theme of this paper that these subtle and far-reaching assumptions are questionable and that, moreover, they are limiting much of the current social research.

The behavior of individuals in situations involving contact with members of other racial and ethnic stocks must be regarded as a specific aspect of general human behavior, and, correspondingly, the understanding and analysis of such human behavior are dependent upon the adequacy of our more general theories of human nature and society. They must be related to the social structure inside of which behavior is taking place.

Modern society is increasingly characterized by the fact that individuals participate in specific social situations not as singular and unchanging entities but by playing specifically differentiated roles (i.e., as homeowners, workers, shoppers, merchants, etc.). Such role-playing comes less and less frequently under definitions provided by traditional folkways and mores. It is increasingly structured and defined by the demands and requirements of organizations set up for the purpose of realizing specific objectives. For the most part, the interests of individuals as homeowners, workers, or merchants are now realized within the framework of such institutions.

Mannheim has stressed this aspect of modern society in observing that individuals

are compelled to renounce their private interests and to subordinate themselves to the interests of the larger social units. . . . The attitude produced by competitive action between antagonistic individuals is transformed into a new attitude of group solidarity *though the groups from which it derives are not all inclusive.* . . . The individual today . . . is gradually realizing that by resigning partial advantages he helps to save his own *interests.* . . . Today the individual thinks not in terms of the welfare of the community or mankind as a whole but in terms of that of his own particular groups.

In recent years greater attention has been focused on the fact that we no longer live in a society that is meaningful or understandable in terms of traditional "practices" or established routines of social etiquette. In our time the human community has come to represent, for the most part, great impersonal aggregations of individuals. We live in what has been referred to as "mass society." The term centers attention upon those aspects of current collective life which give it a new meaning and emphasis. It refers to organizations of people who are not held together by informal understandings, beliefs, or practices. However, the immensity of their numbers introduces wide differences of background and opinion; even of disagreements and overt conflict. The groupings are increasingly deliberate, in response to specific needs, and are acting toward the realization of specific interests. The increasing evidence of dependence in modern society upon such deliberately organized groups has been noted by Mannheim:

> [The] stage of spontaneity . . . of groups does not last very long, as in mass society it has to be succeeded by a stage of *strict organization;* for, of the achievements of modern mass society only those can endure which are sponsored by definite organization.

The activities of such deliberately organized groups are necessarily centered in specific interests of individuals and hence are seldom, if ever, inclusive of the whole range of interest and activity of even a single individual. It follows, as Mannheim points out, that "mass society tends to produce the most self-contradictory behavior not only in society but also in the personal life of the individual."

Thus, two observations can be made regarding the nature of modern society. First, that there are a decreasing number of homogeneous, social, or cultural units of which it can be said that their membership directly mirrors, and hence is the individual counter-part of, such collectivities. On the other hand, we observe social life as exhibiting a constant condition of flux, mobility, and change, giving society the appearance of a shapeless mass, whose form and organization are achieved through deliberate and calculated association. It is within the framework of these social developments that the specific phenomena of racial relations should be examined.

In this view of the matter, a view of race relations which centers upon the concept of individual attitudes is severely limited. While there are some situations in which the behavior of persons toward others can be explained individual *qua* individual, in terms of specific attitudes, in the major and significant areas of social life—namely, jobs, business, and the community— this conception is not adequate. Thus most situations of racial contact are defined by the collectively defined interests of the individuals concerned and do not merely manifest their private feelings toward other races, for example, Negroes.

Thus, the residential neighborhood is the special locale in which individuals attempt to realize such specific interests as personal and social deference and the protection of property values; in the commercial districts and in neighborhood shopping centers, it is profits, value received, and convenience; and, on the job, it is wages, security, and working conditions. In terms of these several kinds of interests, the activities of individuals are mobilized and collectively shaped in modern mass society. Of necessity, these interests bring individuals together in organizations and cause the members to reflect in themselves, as individuals, the *raison d'être* of the collectivities. These deliberately organized groups structure and define the situations for the individual and offer him ready and available definitions of behavior. Individual behavior is, for all practical purposes, made a fiction. Hence a distinctly personal attitude toward minority groups may be of little consequence in explaining an individual's behavior.

The reality is the social fact: the key to the situation and the individual's action is the collectivity, and in our time the collectivity is increasingly of the nature of a deliberately organized interest group. The collectivity even supplies the individual with a well-formulated rationale which makes meaningful and even personally justifies his activity; for example, in the acceptance and rejection of minority groups. Thus it is more frequently the policy, strategy, and tactics of deliberately organized interest groups, rather than the folkways, rather than the individual dimensions of personal prejudices or racial amity, which control behavior in specific situations.

It is important to point out, however, that the organizational or collective influences do not work merely as external pressure or force. In the process of accepting collective definition of the situation as to race as in other respects, the individual creates certain self-conceptions, taking over and internalizing roles which are in accordance with the definition of the situation as provided by the collectivity. Since these roles become personal possessions, a part of the self, they are, in effect, principles of conduct for the individual, an authority in their own right. But they do not necessarily reflect general racial attitudes and are frequently even at variance with generalized sentiments and feelings about specific racial groups. They can and do vary with an individual's behavior toward the same object in situations which involve a different self-interest and thus a different self-conception. For example, a person may have a "general attitude" of dislike toward Negroes. But, under certain circumstances, in his role as "property owner," he may join with others to use violence in preventing a Negro from moving into his neighborhood.

However, the same person at the same time may be mobilized and disciplined at his job by his labor union's definition of the situation. In his role as a "union steward," he may even be sympathetic with a Negro who had been insulted by the refusal of a white girl to dance with him at a union dance. Yet he is not necessarily aware of the apparent contradiction. Indeed, his experience is a common one, for it is a distortion of the reality to refer his behavior to some generalized attitude or frame of mind. The question of consistency, which arises when an explanation is sought in individual psychology, is irrelevant in the above context.

What often are characterized as attitudes or tendencies to act are better understood as social myths. These myths, or false beliefs, are, of course, of considerable social significance, since they are an instrumental aspect of the recruitment of individuals in deliberately organized groups. The myths which he adopts and reiterates enable the individual to justify discrimination, both to himself and to others. This is particularly important in a democratic country like the United States, where the individual feels compelled to conform to the ethical tradition expressed in the "American creed."

Since these myths have no basis in fact, they are subject to challenge and exposure. But the destruction of a myth, however, does not necessarily have an effect on behavior, since myths function, in the main, to rationalize actions and are not usually themselves the basis for action. If a myth becomes suspect, it does not follow that a new myth will replace it.

A number of the current racial myths are so ubiquitous and so much taken for granted that they are like the very air we breathe. Their significance in the mobilization of individuals is self-evident, but it is an over-simplification to treat them conceptually as attitudes.

The following are of special current significance in race relations:

1. The myth that acts of racial discrimination are caused by the belief that other races are inferior. This myth is reflected in the other correlative that formal education will bring about changes in racial practices and that logic and information can improve race relations.

2. The myth of "separate but equal"; that absolute equality can be achieved under a system of segregation.

3. The myth that it is impossible to accomplish any change in the tradition-bound South.

4. The myth that we cannot legislate beliefs; that we must conquer individual bigotry and prejudice before we can change the shape of race relations. These notions are the basis for the myth that law cannot be effective in the area of racial relations; we cannot legislate morals.

5. The myth that there is a rank order of rational change; that certain relations must be modified first and others only later.

6. The myth that violence is inevitable if ever and whenever changes in race relations are effected.

7. The myth that in time of crisis we must make progress slowly. It follows that the democratic struggle over the globe can be fought independent of, and without reference to, the local struggle.

The significance of these myths for our research is that behavior is hardly to be understood by studying merely the individual and his generalized attitudes or verbalisms. The individual must be studied in terms of his identification with collectivities, and the terms and conditions of his participation in them, and so the collective framework must be identified and understood before his behavior may be understood. Hence it is of the utmost importance that our studies be oriented toward the collective life, which in our time is characterized by the emergence of the formal and deliberately organized group.

This point of view is the product of the empirical experience and research in various law-enforcement agencies, in a number of situations of community tension, and in a detailed study of segregation in Washington, D. C., which was published in the report, "Segregation in the Nation's Capital."

The Washington study particularly points to the necessity of analyzing racial segregation and discrimination in terms of organizational structure. As it developed, it became increasingly clear that an explanation of the pattern of racial segregation could be found neither in the individual attitudes of the people in Washington nor in the frequently expressed statement that Washington is a "southern city." However, the dynamics of the situation became evident when approached in the perspective of the organizational power structure of Washington.

This power structure applied with like relevance and force to other aspects of race relations in Washington. The racial employment practices of governmental agencies are of three kinds: (a) exclusion of Negroes from employment in any job categories (but Negroes are acceptable for the most menial work which whites will not accept); (b) segregation, Negroes being employed in other than menial ranks, but only in the lower routine jobs and in separately established units; and (c) integration, jobs being open, in principle at least, to Negroes at all levels on equal terms.

There is a tremendous circulation of government employees among the several agencies in Washington, but a person in one agency may be exposed to a quite different pattern of race relations in another agency, if transferred to it. This is the common experience of Washington governmental employees. Moreover, while top-policy directives for the several agencies are the same, actual practices among the agencies differ according to function, internal bureaucratic traditions, and the interpretation of organizational motif by key personnel. The rationalization that differences in practice reflect the disposition of the working force to accept or reject the Negro were widespread, but the evidence that wholesale reorganization from within, or internal redirectives by authoritative personnel, could, overnight, change the policy in an agency was equally ubiquitous.

The same considerations apply in other areas of Washington's social life, public accommodation, housing, and private employment. In each of these critical points of racial contact evidence is plentiful that the terms and conditions of such contact are a function of the interaction of organized collectivities. It becomes increasingly clear that it is irrelevant and an oversimplication to regard bigotry or intolerance or the individual's disposition to accept or reject Negroes as such as the controlling conditions.

The Washington study encompassed the entire community, with a corresponding emphasis upon its organization and structure. Another study designed to throw light upon Negro-white interaction in three situations involving white industrial workers was conducted in Chicago. They were (1) the residential neighborhood; (2) the industrial work situation; and (3) neighborhood shopping centers.

The subjects of the study were selected so as to fulfil these requirements, respectively: (1) residence in a neighborhood area of Chicago which was known to be strongly opposed to the acceptance of Negroes; (2) membership in an industrial union which had a clear-cut and definitely implemented policy of equality of whites and Negroes (Negroes in this union were admitted without reservation as to race and were elected to and held office as union stewards and executive board members; at the time of the study the position of vice-president was held by a Negro); and (3) the white individuals did most of their shopping in stores which served Negroes on the basis of complete equality.

In all three situations it was discovered that the individual's generalized feelings and attitudes toward Negroes were inadequate to explain actual behavior. Such generalized feelings were systematically repressed and subordinated in the face of more specific interests. Thus, in the work situation, the specific interests of wages, working conditions, and job security were identified with the union, and hence the union's position on racial questions was in control. On the other hand, in the neighborhood, such interests as personal and social deference as well as protection of property values were identified with the objectives of the local improvement association. Consequently, the civic organizations' position of completely rejecting Negroes as potential neighbors were determinative.

It is of particular interest to note that there was no statistical correlation between acceptance or rejection of Negroes on the job and acceptance or rejection of Negroes in the neighborhood. That is, there was no evidence to support the common belief that persons who show a high degree of acceptance of Negroes on the job will necessarily show a low degree of rejection of Negroes in their home communities.

These findings have been operationally validated in a number of situations where programs have been inaugurated dealing with outbreaks in race violence. Two situations which were given considerable attention by the newspapers were the following:

In 1949 the Department of the Interior was challenged on its policy of nonsegregation in the public swimming pools of Washington. The immediate result was violence at the Anacostia pool. As a result the pool was closed for the remainder of the 1949 season. Throughout the winter of 1949–50 there was widespread discussion in Washington about the announced policy of the department to again open all the pools without segregation. In April, 1950, the *Washington Post,* in an editorial, stated:

Secretary Chapman has taken an arbitrary stand, in our opinion, by insisting that the six swimming pools under the control of the Interior Department be operated on a nonsegregated basis. . . . The Interior Department could not keep the pools closed all summer without producing a justified explosion in the community. Nor could it operate all of them on a nonsegregated basis without provoking a new racial tension and risking worse disorders than occurred last year. The Department has done its duty in laying down the general principle of nonsegregation, and it can continue to make its influence felt by requiring a gradual approach to that objective. But it cannot take an adamant and extreme stand without injuring the cause that it seeks to promote.

Better race relations are not fostered by dictation in such matters to local committees, nor by the sudden enforcement of rules that are certain to incite interracial animosities. In the absence of agreement, the best thing the Department can do is to turn the pools over to the board for operation in accord with its more realistic policy.

In the meantime, however, the National Capital Parks had conducted a training program of its personnel impressing upon the personnel their duty to follow the official policy. Particularly in the case of the police, their professional status was stressed. No direct attempt was made to change their individual feelings about Negroes. The results can best be judged from another editorial of the *Washington Post* which appeared in September, 1950:

The completion of the first full year of nonsegregated swimming at the six Washington pools controlled by the Interior Department affords an appropriate opportunity for sober re-examination of what has been an overheated community issue. Total attendance at the six pools during the summer months of 1950 was 235,533; of this number, about 90,000 swimmers were colored and about 146,000 were white. No disturbance or unhappy incident of any kind occurred in the course of the season.

The orderliness of the program is attributable in large part, of course, to the care and intelligence with which it was administered by National Capital Parks. Adequate police protection was provided and the police officers assigned to this duty were trained specifically to deal with its problems; in this connection the Metropolitan Police, who took extraordinary care to see that order was maintained in the areas around the pools, deserve a share of the credit. The record demonstrates conclusively that nonsegregated swimming can be handled safely and harmoniously in Washington provided the leadership is sympathic and sensible. Trouble is likely to arise only if, as was the case in 1949, some organized group attempts to foment it.

The lesson of the summer's experience, in our judgment, is that nonsegregated swimming is here to stay; that it can be conducted safely and harmoniously under level-headed leadership; and that along these lines increased swimming facilities should be made available for use next summer. The experience is a credit to the community's good sense. It is a credit especially to the church and civic groups which worked to prevent trouble and to prepare the community for orderly acceptance of the new practice. The outcome is all the more gratifying to The *Washington Post* because last spring we shared the widespread fear that the community was not yet ready to accept nonsegregated swimming without a recurrence of violence.

Similarly, after a serious racial disturbance in Chicago in 1949, known as the Peoria Street Incident, the police lieutenants and sergeants of Chicago were trained in the proper handling of racial disturbances. The results of the course are reflected in the following letter sent by the Chicago Commission on Human Relations to the mayor of Chicago:

About 8:00 P.M. on Sunday evening April 16, 1950 an accident occurred at 63rd Street and Carpenter involving two automobiles, one driven by a Negro woman and the other occupied by a white couple. The occupants of both automobiles reportedly settled matters amicably between themselves. It appeared that both were equally at fault. However, a crowd quickly gathered, tension rose and fighting began among the bystanders with sides quickly taken along racial lines. The area around 63rd and Carpenter is very mixed—63rd Street has for a long time been a dividing line for the Southward movement of Negroes in the Ogden Park community. There are a number of bars along the street, and there have been interracial incidents in this area in previous times.

Police officers from the Englewood station arrived at the scene quickly. The sergeant in charge sensed the potential danger and unhesitatingly requested reinforcements to help clear the streets. . . . This operation was swift and effective. Commission representatives went immediately to the scene, and by the time they reached there, which was less than 20 minutes, the area was found completely under control with no crowds gathered and with no visible sign of tension. . . .

In both the Chicago and the Washington incidents the situations were radically redefined after a sharpening and clarification of public policy and of the role of the law-enforcement agencies in the implementation of it. Considerable apprehension had existed, and with good reason, as to the role of the police and their disposition to countenance acts of violence in opposition to Negroes.

In the absence of a clearly stated and unambiguous policy, further complicated by an absence of a definition of the professional role of the police in such incidents, other organized and conflicting interests take control. This ultimately produces violence. After a program of training of the police, which stressed their role and responsibility in the maintenance of law and order without reference to their personal feelings and beliefs, a new collective fact emerged and took control. The training of the police was not designed to effect changes in their personal attitudes and prejudices but solely to redefine and set forth their role as professional law-enforcement agents in the implementing of public policy.

The performance of the police showed marked differences in these varying collectively defined situations. And similarly, the public's conduct reflects the definition provided by authoritative and unambiguous statements of policy.

It would be a mistake to assume that significant changes have taken place in the racial attitudes, so called, of the individual policemen in Washington or Chicago. Similarly, it is idle to attempt to explain the seemingly contradictory racial behavior of government employees, or urban industrial workers, in terms of their personal feelings and sentiments. In modern mass society, the group continues as the essential reality in human behavior, but the relevant and controlling collectivities are, increasingly, deliberately organized interest groups.

SOCIAL CHANGE, SOCIAL STATUS
AND THE LAW

By Rupert B. Vance

IF CARRIED THROUGH TO COMPLETION, the abolition of public school segregation will mark America's greatest change in social status since the emancipation of the slaves. This may seem a weighty sentence, but as any sociologist can say, its most important word is *If*! The present article proposes to examine this trend toward equalization against doctrines of social status and social change now prevalent in sociological theory. It will be seen that some of these concepts are common to both sociology and law.

Basically, as the sociologist sees it, the Negro has a serious problem of social status—the most drastic facing any group in American life. In a society which thinks of itself as predominantly middle class, with avenues open to mobility for individuals able to achieve, the Negro seems caught in a permanent lower class statue. The remedy is sought in an appeal to the Negro's legal status—an appeal calculated to force social change on the basis of the American ideology of equality and opportunity. The social mechanism by which the Negro is deprived of opportunity is seen as segregation—a segregation in the public sphere, which violates his rights as a citizen. Unaccounted for, in this scheme, are large areas falling within the private sphere of life. Here, also, is a crucial battleground of social change and social status. It is the purpose of this paper to examine these areas in relation to the role of law in social change.

Any attempt to determine the chance of obtaining these social goals by legal action enters the realm of prediction, and must be regarded as estimation. Too, in order to avoid the heat of argument in an area pervaded by emotion, the analysis will be written without apparent ethical commitment. The treatment,

Reprinted from Rupert B. Vance, "Social Change, Social Status, and the Law: A Sociological View," *Journal of Public Law*, III (Spring, 1954), 39–46; copyright 1954 by the Lamar School of Law of Emory University and used with the kind permission of the publisher.

however, will take account of legal and sociological categories representing accepted norms and values. When known, these can be accepted as data. The fact that they vary from one part of the country to another is recognized as setting the problem within a federal-state system of legality.

We may begin by saying that the problem, and paradox, of equality of individuals and groups in our democratic society can be quite simply stated. There is a history of change in legal status and a history of change in social status, and they are not the same. In law, the great transition has been from the *law of many statuses* to the *one status state,* where all members hold the legal status of citizen, with equal rights before the law. In terms that carry understanding to both lawyers and sociologists, Sir Henry Sumner Maine has phrased this great change as an *evolution from the law of status to the law of contract.*

Rights, privileges, and punishment were decreed in Greece, Rome, and the ante-bellum United States on the basis of the individual's status as either freeman, slave, or freedman. After slavery was abolished, the Roman Empire finally created the one-status state when it gave freedmen the status of citizens. After the French Revolution liquidated the survivals of feudalism, there remained one status before the French law—that of citizen. In Brazil this transition was made with remarkable facility, after the emancipation of the slaves in 1888. Negroes, it is true, remained in mass, members of the lowest class, but they gained citizens' rights and exceptional ones rose to high social status.

Democracies have shown no comparable trend toward uniformity of position in the social hierarchy of wealth, power, and prestige. Differential ranking, based on family background and achievement, is a fundamental phenomenon of our social system. Certainly great differences in influence and style of life have continued and increased. It is presumed that these issues are to be settled within the context of class and social stratification, since democracies promote an ideology of "open classes." Here the great goal of most people is not to be one of the few elite of society; rather, it is to be "respectable" middle class instead of lower class. Every opinion poll asking the question brings out the fact that approximately 80 per cent to 90 per cent of our people think of themselves as middle class.

Sociologists recognize that the pressure toward equality in our social system largely represents the drive toward mobility—the desire to climb the economic and social ladder. The spirit behind the transition from Jeffersonian to Jacksonian democracy is epitomized in the frontier feeling: "I am just as good as the next man, if not a darn sight better." Equality is obviously equality of opportunity; the pyramidal structure of social prestige and influence is accepted, and no dead level of stratification is expected or demanded in the society.

The pressure to achieve and to hold middle class status is characterized by stress and strain, so that ambition itself can be seen as a certain mild form of persistent "anxiety." Here, of course, is found the impact of the new education and of the improved economic outlook on major groups in the South. Equality of opportunity now means the chance to advance in the context and symbols of a respectable lower middle class style of life. Avoidance of contact with the less respectable lower class "style of life" is definitely a part of this "anxiety." To the South, the Negro is definitely a lower class symbol.

In the beginning, the Negro—fixed on the bottom rung—was a spectator rather than a participant in this development of the masses and the classes. In the United States, the first American Revolution did nothing to alter his slave status. The "Second American Revolution" made him a freedman. It could not give him social status; no law can do that for any group or individual, but the 14th and 15th Amendments were passed to give him the legal status of citizen. It is unnecessary to remark on the freedman's position at the base of social stratification—unskilled, unpropertied, lacking in prestige—a veritible proletariat.

Inevitably, the hopes of the Negro elite and of the masses turned to education. The principle of universal education, as Reinhold Niebuhr says, was already present as " a product of the democratic movement cultivated by middle class idealists." Schools were accepted as social elevators in a stratified social order. The way to influence and prestige led through the schools and colleges; to be a college graduate marked one as middle class. In Warner and Havighurst's realistic discussion of *Who Shall Be Educated?*, our educational system is seen as a sorting and selecting agency—a conveyor belt where the child is inspected, not only for brains and learning ability, but for skin color, pronunciation, cut of clothes, table manners, and parental bank account.

For the Negro masses, these hopes led to disappointment and frustration; for the Negro elite, they led to achievement, but fell short of prestige and status. The greatest gains from education undoubtedly came in assimilation in language, manners, and style of living—the same process through which the immigrant began his introduction to American life.

The American Negro is now fully convinced that he is confined to the lower class position; he feels this is due to the device of segregation, and that enforcement of legal status will bring the desired changes in his social status. It was not the process of education that failed. It was segregated education that failed.

The reader may well feel that the foregoing discussion represents circular reasoning. The argument does represent a turning upon itself, and the reader is correct in the sense that we have here a sociological *vicious circle*. It can be stated thus: *If the Negro held high social status in our system, his legal rights as a citizen would be enforceable without difficulty. Conversely, the argument runs, if we enforce the legal rights due the Negro as a citizen, Negroes will attain the higher social status desired.* Both these statements may well be valid, but they illustrate the difficulty of selecting an initial factor in the chain of circumstance which, once grasped, is assumed to unroll the sequence of cause and effect.

The danger is that here we overlook the important factors hidden in this sequence. The above statements are highly rational and represent a logical approach to social change. Concealed here may be an irrational factor, highly emotional, and one whose operation may be unconscious. It can be stated thus: *The Negro's distinctive physical traits, his racial uniform, have symbolic value, imputing subordination and low social status.* Our various immigrant stocks and their children, facing a similar situation, have climbed in the social strata pretty much in direct ratio to the length of time they have been in this country and their nearness to the culture of the predominant type, that of the American middle classes. They escape, it is felt, the main handicap which, in spite of his assimilation and long residence, now places the Negro at the foot of the hierarchy. This as we have said is the symbolic impact of racial traits implying low status. The continuance of the Negro in the lower class re-enforces these stereotypes, and thus completes the vicious circle. His origin placed him there; stereotypes help keep him there.

How are these things affected by law? Present laws sanction segregation in many areas. What can law do to change that status? What the lawyers for the NAACP asked of the Supreme Court is a directed change in the Negro's status, in conformity with his rights as a citizen. What are the chances that this will come about? This leads to a consideration of the doctrine of social change.

The trend and sequence of change are imperfectly understood by even the best qualified students of society, but there is general agreement that social change involves a whole context of relations and occurs "all along the line." The classic study, *Social Change* by W. F. Ogburn, made professional sociologists aware of the existence of cultural lag—a phenomenon usually found when change, forced in one institutional sector, moves ahead leaving other sectors unchanged. In Ogburn's view, change moves ahead more rapidly in the technical and economic spheres of life, leaving gaps between innovations here and our customary attitudes and behaviors. President Franklin Roosevelt gave popular currency to this view when he decried what he termed the "horse and buggy" views of the Supreme Court in an automobile age.

In this analysis, law can be seen as the mechanism for closing the lags left by unequal rates of change. The passage of workmen's compensation laws can be seen as a case in point. Thus the introduction of heavy, high speed machinery to replace simple hand tools was a major social change. It left the burden of industrial accidents to be borne by the workers, while society reaped the benefits of low cost production. This lag was closed when, after the passage of workmen's compensation legislation, the principle of insured risks replaced the employers' liability, which had been limited by the doctrines of assumed risk, contributory negligence, and fellow servant. That this offers an example of social change which carried through all along the line is shown by (1) the declining rate of accidents and (2) the collapse of resistance in the various states against the legislation.

National prohibition offers an example of a change in law which did not carry through to change in the collective behavior and attitudes of society. In spite of our respect for the Constitution, resistance increased and law enforcement was insufficient to bring about social change. This resistance assumed the form of violations, as well as evasions, of the law. Under this situation, it can be said that the 18th Amendment was repealed in order to preserve respect for the law. This occurred in spite of the fact that the initial change had the support of public opinion as represented in the (1) affirmative vote of legislatures of the states, and was implemented both by (2) federal legislation, as in the Volstead Act, and (3) supporting legislation in many states. For students of social change, the contrast with a decision of the Supreme Court is impressive.

Thus, while students of law realize that social change can be and has been implemented by legal enactment and judicial decision, it is also realized that resistance to social change is of many types. Here we can say that jurisprudence, as a social science, has shared in the responsibility of determining the extent to which any desired social change is enforceable by law. Laws may be violated, and they may be evaded. Evasion carries the implication of driving a course through gaps in the law, if not actually breaking it. Important to the courts, to public order, and to the profession is the whole field of conflict of laws.

Oftentimes the change ordered by legal enactment and judicial decision is so limited in scope that no actual evasion is drawn upon to block social change. Sometimes modes of adjustment may exist within the choice of individuals and groups—alternatives sanctioned in legal codes. It is in this borderline between public and private spheres of life that the doctrine of social change is of most importance to students of jurisprudence. It must be remembered that issues will be decided, not on the basis of an assumed code of ethics, but on the basis of what is enforceable within the system of legality.

No one can play fair on the issue of school segregation and minimize the role of resistance to change. Evasion has been present throughout this issue, or else the accepted legal doctrine of "separate but equal facilities" would have been implemented in the public schools. The much publicized plans of Georgia and South Carolina to operate their public schools as private institutions also represent forms of evasion, whose legality the courts may be forced to adjudicate.

The public schools as an institution are a weak vehicle on which to place the burden of the drive toward equality. There are several reasons for making this statement: (1) In the early grades and in the high school, the schools function for young children and for adolescents as a primary group, next in intimacy to the family and the playground. It is generally agreed that impersonal and more formal areas of social interaction will be won to racial equality before these more personal areas. (2) The schools are under criticism for their failure to achieve excellence—a criticism that ranges from the schools' lack of influence on juvenile behavior to their failure to achieve excellence in intellectual training. (3) Schools and the school districts are peculiarly local institutions in their control and administration, having strict jurisdictional lines. (4) Public school attendance is not strictly compulsory; any individual has free choice of attending a private school.

The abandonment of public schools by an official body is a direct evasion of law; the abandonment of public schools for private schools by individuals is sanctioned in all our legal codes. In terms of legal alternatives, there is no reason to assume that the courts will allow the use of state funds to support segregated schools conducted under private auspices. On the other hand, there is no conceivable way whereby states and school districts can be forced to support public schools at their present levels if enrollments decline. Nor can it be seen, at the moment, how local school districts can be enjoined from selling or renting school property in districts where pupils no longer attend.

In terms of this situation, the transfer of students from public to private schools should come as no surprise. The pattern is already well-fixed for certain classes and areas in the nation. In the immigrant areas of the Northeast, we have the devotion of the rising middle classes to the private school as a means of holding or achieving higher social status for their children. In addition, association with children of different ethnic backgrounds on the part of the majority is further reduced by the system of parochial schools, leaving the public schools to a group in between. The private school as preparation for high status once was a part of the South's tradition, as it is of New England's today. The South's present devotion to universal education in the public schools represents many things. It is an adjustment to the poverty of many of its people; it also represents a real triumph of the democratic movement in the South.

A movement to parochial schools, now evident among Protestant groups, such as the Lutherans and Presbyterians, is largely motivated by demand for a better quality of education, as well as the desire for religious training. Religious leaders in the South, however, have shown no inclination to allow private schools to be used as public schools in this situation. A flight of students to bona fide private schools, as an individual choice, will depend more on economic circumstances of the aspiring middle classes than on anything else. It would not represent a violation of the law, although it may leave an almost barren public school system to the Negroes and the lower classes.

A second alternative—a flight of teachers from the public schools—is equally sanctioned in law and equally resistant to change. This is already a national problem. In terms of the low income, the low prestige, and the heavy responsibility attached to the occupation of teaching, this condition is to be expected. When young girls, callow youths, and tired functionaries find the nation's race and status problems, with all their community reverberations, dumped in their laps, the flight of teachers from the public schools will be limited only by the extent of alternative opportunities—including marriage. In proportion, the flight of teachers may well exceed that of their pupils. To military service and employment in a prosperous period may be added an increased demand for teachers among the developing private schools.

Unless the new public schools employ the existing corps of Negro teachers for their mixed classes, the loss of teachers will be even greater. Lawyers have the problem of determining whether any form of legal action can be used to enforce the employment of Negro teachers upon the boards of the local school districts. The fact that this can hardly be accomplished in the absence of supporting legislation simply underscores the difficulty of the change. A Supreme Court decision strikes down contrary statutes; it does not guarantee the passage of supporting legislation by either Congress or the states. Would Negro teachers, whose schools are absorbed, have legal recourse in the absence of state or federal FEPC laws?

What of those important officers of administration, the members of local school boards? What alternatives have they? Obviously their alternatives are limited: they cannot resign when they are sued, enjoined, or jailed for the community's noncompliance with the law. But as citizens they can refuse service on school boards. Since there is political capital to be gained in these areas, such refusal to serve may well be selective—exercising negative selection on the more moderate business men and administrators, and bringing forward those types who realize the political rewards to be reaped through the revival of the "Negro baiting" tactics of the recent past.

What tactics will such school boards use? Here it may be said that these tactics are already fairly well developed in the political arena. Here resistance to change may involve either evasion or defiance of the law; this last could lead to litigation of an especially troublesome kind. A persistent evasion, used in politics, already exists—the well-known practice of gerrymandering electoral districts. This practice, along with the failure of state legislatures to reapportion in conformity with constitutional requirements, has rarely proved amenable to legal action. Once the redistricting of school jurisdictions is undertaken, the reorganization of segregated neighborhoods is likely to proceed very rapidly indeed. This also involves alternatives in the field of voluntary action, and thus encounters no applicable legal sanctions. The easement of hardships in permitting whites and Negroes to attend segregated schools outside their districts would represent evasion. The handling of such cases could be most harassing. What legal actions can be taken? Who would sue? And on what grounds? Not those who have been permitted to cross jurisdictional lines, for they are the recipients of special privileges. Not those left behind, for they would thus be asking to violate regulations. The answer, of course, is obvious. In the absence of supporting legislation from the states, the federal judiciary, in the words of counsel John W. Davis before the United States Supreme Court, "will be acting as a glorified Board of Education for the State of South Carolina."

To those who wish to push quickly on to social change, the above discussion may read like a horrifying recital of all the outrages of which the traditional South once proved capable. It should not. Actually it is written in a new context—that of a newly developing "middle-class South" rather than that of the "lower-class South" devoted to violence in race relations. It represents not violations of the law, but alternatives to compliance that are sanctioned in law.

Actually, the recourse to private schools represents the behavior of an aspiring middle class in the avoidance of neighbors who "live across the tracks." Teachers who leave the public schools are simply exercising their right to a choice of occupations. School boards which refuse to hire Negro teachers are exercising their right to a choice of employees. Gerrymandering and the reapportionment of school jurisdictions are not here seen as acts of lower class violence and reprisal. These things, it may be predicted, will be regarded not as white collar criminality but as decent respectable behavior—several cuts, indeed, above the patronizing of bootleggers during the prohibition era. Only the control of these responses by legal action is likely to bring to the community any conviction of wrongdoing.

No doubt there are conditions under which racial violence might flare anew in the South. The abandonment of the public schools in rural areas or in urban slum areas to two groups—the lower classes and the Negro—could be dangerous. Under conditions of compulsory education, it is easy to see how conflict and violence could follow their enforced mingling. Such sequestration of the public schools could raise gerrymandering of school districts to a high level of public policy. This, in the writer's opinion, could well involve conflict with the federal courts.

To keep open the avenues to social status for those who have achieved and for those who are aspiring, is an important component of the "American Dream." To different groups, this ideology means different things. To the Negro, it means the chance of equalizing his social status with his legal status in the American system. To the striving lower middle classes, it has meant a chance to increase their social distance from "lower class" groups who might hinder their children's chances to rise. Here enter the mingled public and private aspects of association in neighborhood, community, and the public school. Equality, which in the American ideology means equal opportunity to rise in the social scale, is seen as relative to groups higher in the hierarchy of status. It thus means different things to different men. As the Negro seeks integration with the common institutions and facilities of American life, the groups with whom he would like to identify himself push on to identify themselves with groups still higher in status.

Decisions in law cannot enforce the major change desired—a higher social status for the nation's "man lower down." Law can be used to enforce citizens' rights only in the use of public facilities. That this is not equivalent to "breaking down segregation" is due to the large area left to the private sphere of social life—areas in which the voluntary action of individuals is legally sanctioned. The problems of social status we have with us always. Change in the "blanket status" of the "man lower down" is social change all along the line. To say that this involves change in the mores is to utter a truism—true because the mores, rather than law, govern in the private sphere of social relations.

ON THE NEED TO BELONG

By Solomon E. Asch

THE RACIAL SENTIMENT OF SOUTHERNERS is only in part directed to Negroes; it is also a function of their most significant ties to family, neighborhood, and group. Earlier we had occasion to show that the individual must in the course of growth establish a relation of trust to his immediate group. The racial outlook derives much of its psychological force from this source. Although the details of the process are obscure, we must suppose that the child's trust in his elders (which has its sensible grounds and is at the same time a condition of his psychological survival) lends a quality of presumptive truth to their sentiments and injunctions about Negroes. These become all the more convincing when his own observations appear roughly to confirm them. The child cannot create a system of beliefs and principles in opposition to the adult environment; at best he can oppose it only in piecemeal ways. Consistent individual opposition under these conditions would require more than resistance to "conformity"; it would need an attitude of systematic distrust toward the social order, suspicion of the closest human figures, and an independently developed social philosophy. The sentiments that a young white finds in his Southern surroundings and eventually adopts are therefore a condition of his solidarity with the human element.

To convey a hint of the importance of group belonging, let us perform a fantastic experiment in imagination and ask how an average Southerner would act if he woke up one morning to find that no one in the white and Negro environment observed or respected the discriminatory racial practices. Disregarding the bewilderment that would follow such a drastic change and the great individual differences in adapting to it, we are inclined to believe that the structure of emotions, beliefs, and habits formed in the course of a lifelong experience would in most instances be undermined and supplanted by the newly prevailing relations, with little need of painful or prolonged "rehabilitation." There might even be many who would experience the change as a great relief.

From Solomon E. Asch, *Social Psychology* (Copyright 1952 by Prentice-Hall, Inc., New York), pp. 577–579. Reprinted by permission of the publisher.

For a Southerner to deny the prevailing views about Negroes requires a drastic intellectual reorientation and a serious snapping of social bonds. It would be tantamount to questioning the perceptions and cherished values of those nearest to him and of casting himself out of the group. We do not say that such reversals are not possible to individuals; they are, and they have occurred. Our task rather is to show the difficulties in the way and the reasons that such a solution is not open to most. It is easier and less threatening to defend an outlook that affirms one's primary relations. It is in these terms that one should understand the fact that Southerners often reject or deny facts and arguments in conflict with their views. The explanation usually offered is that they are "prejudiced," but it is necessary to look more closely. Information that alone or in a different context would point to racial equality has a different meaning in the context of a Southerner's social field. Under the stress of the social pressures the organization of his sentiment has become more tight and rigid than it would have if intellectual factors alone were operating. In defending his views he is in effect defending with all the means at his command the sole social scheme he knows and moves in. Therefore, if you point out to him the achievements of Marian Anderson or George Washington Carver, he will reply that they are exceptions. If you should pursue the argument further, describing the ideas of cultural anthropologists, citing facts on educational facilities for Negro and white in the North and South and on the studies of intelligence, and pointing to the customs of foreign countries, you would observe a variety of reactions. He might question your sources of information, change the subject, state categorically that he disagrees with you, or refuse in some other way to take cognizance of the data you set before him. Such reactions are not necessarily proof of lack of intelligence, or rationalization of prejudice. If one tries to integrate Marian Anderson into an internally consistent picture of white supremacy, the notion of an inexplicable mutation is a fairly sensible solution. Even if the Southerner is a highly intelligent and courageous person, capable of reorienting himself when faced with new facts, it is not likely that he will instantly abandon his entire method of interpreting data on the first evidence that could be interpreted better in another way. The very existence of the first view will prevent him from recognizing the significance of the alien datum upon its first appearance. Under the best conditions the process requires effort and time. If he accepts your evidence he must restructure radically a host of experiences; as new relations begin to dawn on him, he must also sooner or later give up his orientation in many other vital areas that cover a great part of the social scene. To be sure, rejection of data is a breakdown in the orientation process, but to understand why it occurs one needs to consider the alternatives. These carry the danger of disorientation, which, as part of his very nature as a living creature, he will resist with all his resources. His "irrational" reactions to your flawless arguments represent his effort to defend by the most thrifty means the over-all social orientation essential to his functioning. To be surprised at this or to expect otherwise is to entertain unrealistic views about man's faculties for swift reorientation.

THE TRANSMISSION OF RACIAL ATTITUDES AMONG WHITE SOUTHERNERS

By Olive Westbrooke Quinn

WE ARE NOT CONCERNED with the content of racial attitudes which find expression in the behavior of Southern white people toward Negroes, nor with an appraisal of these attitudes; rather, we are interested in discovering, as far as may be, the mechanisms of transmission of racial attitudes among white Southerners. An historical consideration of the problem of the cultural education of the Southern white person would examine those influences which have built up, through time, the accepted white philosophy of race; another approach is through a study of the forces which transmit that philosophy to the individual born into the society. The latter approach is used here in an effort to find how the white child finds his place in relation to the Negro.

Because racial learning is but one aspect of social learning and not a thing apart from it, an understanding of the ways in which the child learns his racial role necessarily involves or presupposes knowledge of the mechanisms of social learning itself. Learning that one is white is part of the process of learning the identity of the self and the symbols and expectations appropriate to the position of that self. The racial role is but one of many which the indivdual must learn, and behavior proper to these roles is socially defined. The society in which a child is reared has ready for him the answer to his question, "Who am I?" The answer is different in different contexts and relationships, and the child must discover, in a variety of ways, the answer appropriate to his immediate situation.

A major task for the developing child is the definition of his relationship to people about him. In answering the question, "Who am I?" he must necessarily answer its corollary, "And who are all of those?" He does not make these definitions alone, of course; most of them are made for him by his society through the medium of his parents, his peers, and others with whom he comes into contact. To say, though, that the child does not make his own definitons does not explain how he learns them, and this is the problem with which we are immediately concerned. We must approach the acquisition of racial attitudes as an aspect of the emergence of a sense of self.

That racial attitudes are involved in a sense of self is demonstrated in the following excerpts from interviews with Southern white young people.

People who say "nigger" say it, I think, to make themselves feel superior. I don't feel superior, but I don't feel inferior, either, and I don't have to belittle other people to make myself big.

I feel a protective attitude toward the Negro; I always have. But I'll have to

Reprinted from Olive Westbrooke Quinn, "The Transmission of Racial Attitudes Among White Southerners," *Social Forces*, XXXIII (October, 1954), pp. 41–47; copyright 1954 by the Williams and Wilkins Company, Baltimore, Md., for the University of North Carolina Press and used with the kind permission of the publishers.

admit that I enjoy being of the Old South, too. I know it is a pose, or at least I think it is; yet it has glamor, and I am afraid I am duped by it.

I can remember in Junior High School being so disgusted with the kind of kid who blustered about, saying, "Why, if a nigger gets fresh with me, I'll break his neck!" Perhaps I am a little more kindly toward them because I so dislike that kind of behavior. I look on it as lower class behavior and lower class attitude . . . I don't like it.

Perhaps my attitude has been altered by the fact that I expect to be a singer. There is no denying that in the field of music there are some great artists who are Negroes. It would be tragic to deny them their rightful place, and so deny all of us the pleasure of their talent. Then, I think that if they are to be allowed to have positions of prominence in my field, there is no reason why they should not be recognized in other fields. I guess everyone starts his thinking from himself.

A young woman who attended a summer school session at a Northern University had this to say about an experience in the classroom:

We were seated in alphabetical order, and a friend of mine and I were in seats next to Negroes. After class we went to the professor and asked to be moved. He wanted to know why. I said, "We are from the South, and we aren't used to sitting by Negroes." He was so mad at us! He said we were prejudiced and ignorant, and he said all kinds of things to us. My friend said, "Yes, I know we are all you say; but that is the way we are, and we aren't used to sitting by Negroes." Well, he raved some more, and finally I said, "I'm sorry that I feel this way, but I do feel this way, and if I can't have a different seat, I'll have to take a different course." He talked to us a long time about how wrong we were, but he moved us, and after that he was real nice to me.

Each of the statements given above is an attempt on the part of the person making it to define his attitude toward race, but it is something more than that, too; it is a public anouncement of the kind of person the speaker thinks of himself as being, a projection of the picture which he has of himself. Racial attitudes, then, seem to be acquired as a part of the individual's attitude toward himself, as one of the areas of definition of his relationships with other people. It is important that we should try to understand how the sense of self arises, and it is to this question that we now turn our attention.

One of the most rewarding approaches to the problem of the emergence of self is that of George Herbert Mead, and it is his concepts and his framework of analysis which we shall use in an effort to understand how the racial role becomes incorporated into the individual's sense of self. Mead points out that we learn who we are (i.e., what kind of person we are) from the reactions of other people toward us. And it is in this way that in any given situation we learn to assess our own behavior. Other individuals indicate to us, by their reactions, the meaning of our behavior; and by taking the role of the other, we are able to make indications to ourselves which serve as guides for future behavior. Sometimes these indications are made in the form of direct verbal responses; often they are but behavioral responses to our own behavior.

Where racial attitudes are concerned, direct instruction seems to play a relatively unimportant part. The most perceptive and self-analytical of the young people interviewed often are unable to produce any memories of direct teaching with respect to racial attitude. For the most part, verbal instruction is avoided, and even when it is given, it is usually justified in other than racial

terms. The one exception to this seems to occur with respect to the term "lady."
Over and over again the young people interviewed told of quite explicit instruction in the use of this word.

Once when we were in the car, I said, "Oh, Mother, look! That colored lady
has on a dress just like yours." Well, Mother was a little upset about the dress, but
she didn't say so. She said, "Agnes, call them colored women. There are no colored
ladies."

I remember when I learned that lesson. I told Mother the washlady was here.
She said to say "woman," and I asked why. Mother explained that you never say
Negro lady. She said "lady" was a term of respect applied to few white ladies and
to no Negroes at all.

About five years ago we were riding through Memphis one day, and I saw a
Negro standing on the street corner. She was all dressed up, and she looked very
pretty. I said to Mother, "Isn't that a pretty Negro lady?" Mother called me down
for it. She told me to say woman. I wanted to know why, and she didn't answer me.
I said, "I don't believe there is any reason. I think you just don't like them—like
Grandmother." Golly, was I sorry I'd said that! Mother lectured me about respect
for my elders, and she said if I ever spoke to her like that again she'd punish me
severely.

It is interesting to note that instruction was given only after a child had erred in
his racial behavior. In the majority of cases reported, no explanation was given
except in general terms, that these are accepted usages. If a child was not satisfied, but sought further reasons, he was told that ladies are always white; and
if he questioned this judgment, he was punished for disrespectful behavior
toward his elders. The rationale for the punishment was given in terms of the
younger-older person relationship, but the association of the punishment with
a transgression of racial patterns did not fail. In the last instance reported above,
this association was strong enough to stop further questioning:

Not long after that I came in late to lunch one day. Everyone had eaten except
the cook, and I started to sit at the table with her and eat. Mother asked her to
move. I didn't understand it, and I was just about to ask why when I remembered
the Memphis incident and decided not to. So I did not protest. But I was embarrassed; I didn't think Mother should have done that. She might have told me
later not to do it again.

In general, it seems that verbal indications that Negroes are different from
whites are used only when the child has violated the racial folkways. Every
instance of explicit verbal instruction, as reported by these young people, was
preceded by some such incident.

One time when I was leaving to go to kindergarten, I kissed my nurse. Father
waited until I was in the car with him, and then he told me not to. I asked why, but
Father is very domineering, and he told me I was too young to understand and that
I'd just have to do as he said.

I don't dare open my mouth on the subject at home. I did once, but I was already
in disgrace. Daddy wasn't speaking to me at the time, but when I said I thought
Negroes should have the vote, he spoke. And he told me never to discuss the subject
in his house again. He thinks the professors and student body at college are all
communists.

While it is generally true that direct verbal instruction is seldom used as a method for teaching racial attitudes, it is not true that verbal indications of an indirect kind are avoided. Indeed, indirect verbal instruction, given by the simple expedient of letting the child "overhear" adult conversation, accounts for most of the stereotyped verbalizations in terms of which young people express their feelings about Negroes. The importance of the kind of adult talk a child is allowed to hear can not be overemphasized. Certainly, it is not accident, except in a few cases, that determines what the child hears. Ordinarily parents are very careful to see to it that their children hear from them only those things considered appropriate to their years. Perhaps these decisions are not always made at a conscious level, but when adults talk freely about sexual looseness and immorality among Negroes, while maintaining a strict silence before their children on the subject of sexual irregularities among white people, it is difficult to escape the judgment that they make this difference because they want their children to believe the one and to disbelieve the other. Stories of Reconstruction days in the South are kept vividly alive, not because of historical interest, but because they provide the emotional set which any good Southerner is supposed to have. Shortcomings and deficiences of Negro servants are paraded, stereotyped, and exaggerated because such a picture of the Negro is appropriate to the treatment accorded him, and this treatment is deemed necessary to "keep the Negro in his place." When a Negro who obviously does not fit the stereotype comes upon the scene, he is explained away as an exception, but for the most part white children simply do not see these exceptional Negroes. Judgments are given the child not in any direct way, but by allowing him to listen to adult talk without participating in it.

I knew Alma lived with men. It's funny, I never heard much talk about the morals of white people; it came to me as a decided shock that white people are often sexually immoral, but I have always known—or nearly always—that colored people are not hampered by morals. I never heard any tales of sexual immorality involving white people until I was considered grown.

I have heard lots of stories about their criminality, about how they cut each other up and cut white people up. I've heard about that lynching a hundred times. What did I hear? Well, they told me that a nigger shot a policeman and they found him and shot him and hanged him on a telephone pole down there by Link's Cafe. They say the Negroes behaved for a long time after that and they were scared to come out for a week or two. Every time the men at the store start talking about how uppity niggers are now, someone tells about that lynching.

I have very vivid recollections of Reconstruction stories. The Negroes were hateful and cruel to white people then. There is much unrest in Memphis at the present time. The Negroes think they can do just anything. They are forming clubs: there is the Bump Club, you know about that, and then all these Eleanor Clubs.

The following excerpt from a diary kept during the collecting of the interviews is revealing on this point:

Tonight I went to Bea's for the evening. She and her mother were very much elated that at last they had found a Negro woman who had agreed to come to the house and do the laundry. All of us were sitting on the front porch, Bea, her mother, Sue and I. Mrs White was laying plans for the morrow. "Bea," she said, "remind me to lock up the silver tomorrow. We don't know a thing about this nigger." Then she turned to me, "You know, you just can't trust any of them. I always lock up my good silver!"

None of Mrs. White's remarks was addressed to her granddaughter, Sue, yet none had escaped her. Listening to the casual conversation of adults, she had been told once again that Negroes are untrustworthy. This lesson has been driven home every time a strange Negro has entered the house. She, like other children, mimics her mother and her grandmother, even in behavior and attitudes of which she is critical. When children seek to identify themselves with others, a common manifestation of this identification is found in imitative behavior. It is not surprising that a young person who has observed that a certan kind of behavior in an adult brings approval from his associates should "try on" this behavior, for this is the way in which a child grows up—by practicing grown-up behavior, seeking to call out in others the desired responses. Such imitation is often the occasion for direct instruction against it, as when children begin to give orders to the servants. Then the parents make it quite clear that giving orders is the special prerogative of adult members of the household. In this case, however, the child's behavior is socially incorrect only in that he has overstepped the boundaries of his age-grade, and he is made to understand that such behavior must wait upon maturity.

Another kind of indirect indication is seen in instructions given to children that they are not to make disparaging remarks about Negroes; rather, they must not let the Negro know that he is considered inferior. Such instruction cannot but make the inferiority an unquestioned fact to the white child.

Servants should be well cared-for, and they should be treated with consideration. We should always be considerate of their feelings; they are human beings. I was always expected to obey my nurse, and I was not allowed to abuse her.

You know, I think from the fact that I was told so often that I must treat colored people with consideration, I got the idea that I could mistreat them if I wanted to.

Here is a very telling clue to the way in which race attitudes are instilled. The first quotation suggests respect for the Negro's feelings and rights, yet the overtone points unmistakably to the essential helplessness, servility, and inferiority which are supposed to characterize the Negro servant. There is a great difference in the respect required of young people for elders of their own family and social rank and the consideration invoked in behalf of serving people. It is one thing to respect the rights of those who hold unquestioned authority; it is another to respect the rights of those who owe those rights to the protection of an authoritative group which claims the child as its own. The white child becomes "Miss" or "Mister" very early to the servant in the home, and while this is not purely a racial phenomenon, it probably occurs earlier when the servants are Negroes than when they are members of the dominant racial group.

It should be pointed out that the servant, himself, having accepted his role in relation to the various members of the family, becomes a teacher to the child. A maid, nurse, cook, or yard man may give very direct training with regard to the expected behavior of the young white person. This is especially true when the Negro undertakes to train the child in "manners."

I had a Negro nurse, Aunt Jennie; she nursed both my brother and me. When the doorbell rang, we wanted to answer the door. She said we were not supposed to. She told me I had to be a lady, and if I wasn't one, she would use the hairbrush on me.

Rosie is scornful of the lack of manners of young Negroes. She calls me "Elsie," and that is all right, but she thinks it is disgraceful when younger colored girls call white girls by their first names.

We have reviewed at some length examples of verbal indications, both direct and indirect, as they relate to the problem of the transmission of racial attitudes. As important as these methods are in teaching the Southern white child his racial role, they account for a very limited proportion of the total racial learning of the white Southerner. It has been pointed out earlier that the occasion for most direct verbal instruction is some kind of infraction of the rules governing the behavior of white people in their relationships with Negroes. It is the behavior itself which is most carefully taught. The prevailing norms of behavior provide a frame of reference within which the child makes his judgments, and the surer he is in the practice of these norms, the more likely he is to find a rationale which defends them.

For the most part the South does not teach attitudes to its white children, nor is such teaching necessary; in establishing practices, by precept, by example, and by law, which separate the races and make distinctions between interracial and intraracial behavior, the South has established a way of life which can have but one meaning for those who diligently practice it. And to escape such practice has, until very recent times, been extremely difficult, for racial etiquette has been woven into the entire institutional fabric of the Southern culture.

A child who is constantly treated with deference by members of a group visibly distinguishable from himself on physical grounds can hardly escape the conclusion that he is superior to members of that group. If, in addition, in learning his various roles, he is able to evoke deference by imitating the dominant example of his elders, this conception of himself is reinforced.

If in public transportation his accommodations are separated from and superior to those of the other racial group, he is likely to take this difference as a matter of course and to accept it as his due. Once the expected behavior is established, the individual can be counted on to defend it, for he must do so if any question arises which threatens his ego, and this will certainly occur if his behavior is called into question. For of what does an individual's ego consist, if not of his conception of himself in relation to others; and this relationship is a behavioral relationship. It happens that in the South great importance is attached to "manners," but manners are, of course, simply the rules which define the relationship of the individual to others and which call for certain specific behaviors as indicating this relationship.

I guess the thing that is stressed most in a Southern girl's training is manners, etiquette. I think it is very important to be sure that your behavior is correct.

You know, where you are makes a lot of difference about how you behave. It's all very well to say I'm for this and against that, but actually, all of us—or I should say most of us—fear criticism from the people we must live with. I sat down by a Negro here in Memphis one time. He was in a funny place; you wouldn't expect to find a Negro there. There were white men across the aisle, and I didn't notice that he was a Negro. I felt very strange, and when a seat opened up across the aisle, I moved. In the North or West it wouldn't have bothered me at all. But many people here were looking at me curiously, some with disgust. I wouldn't have got up if there had been no place to move to, but I'll tell you, it was hard to know what to do.

A ministerial student who can, at a church conference, declare for equal treatment for Negroes on the conference grounds, does not pursue the point in the college diningroom, where he is a student waiter and works with an elderly Negro man.

There is an old Negro who works with us and who has been here for years. We call him "Jones," and he calls me "Mr. Peter." I would not object to calling him Mr. Jones, but it would serve no good purpose to do so. I am sure he would be embarrassed if I did, and all the white people who were not antagonized would certainly be surprised. I'd be set down as a nut.

A militant minister who appeals to the F.B.I. for justice for Negro citizens, and who insists upon preaching what he believes, thereby alienating some members of his congregation, nevertheless submits to the social dictum which requires visits with his Negro friends to be at his instigation and in their homes.

Dr. Sales, the president of the Negro college here, is my personal friend. I like him very much, and he and his wife and my wife and I have many good visits together. I often go to his home to visit, but that is the way the visits must be. He wouldn't dare come to my home to visit.

The parent who would really rather not teach her child the prevailing attitudes with respect to race, yet feels that she must see to it that her child's behavior is correct as judged by the existing norms.

A few weeks ago something came up that was really hard for me to handle. The people next door to us had a little Negro girl come in to wash dinner dishes. They gave her dinner and a little bit of money—I don't know how much, but it was really very little. Well, they decided they didn't need her any longer. She lives in one of those little shacks down near the railroad. Sue came in one night and wanted to know if we couldn't give Janie some dinner. I had noticed that very often the little darkie would call to Sue over the fence. One afternoon she came over and asked for Sue. Fortunately, she was not at home. Well, as I said, Sue came to me and said, "Mother, she is hungry. Can't we give her something to eat?" So I fixed a plate, and the little girl sat on the back steps and ate, and Sue sat and talked with her while she ate. It disturbed me a little. The next day Sue wanted to know if Janie couldn't eat with us and wash our dishes. I told her I was afraid not. She couldn't understand why not. I told her we couldn't do it because we didn't need Janie, that she could get a job somewhere else. I guess actually we could have taken her on and used her very well, but we could also get along without her, and I didn't want her around because it would be so hard to explain to Sue why she must not have a little colored girl for a friend. You know, you hate to bring your child up to be a snob; but you know I couldn't have that. I didn't want the colored child to get any ideas, and I didn't want Sue doing something that other people would question and think queer. It was just an impossible situation.

Attitudes, then, seem to be transmitted not so much by verbal instruction as by providing the kinds of experiences in which the child learns behavior appropriate to his racial role, and by shielding the child from those experiences in which he might learn behavior inappropriate to his position.

An adequate explanation of the means by which racial attitudes are transmitted must take into account and explain failures of transmission. Many observers assert that racial attitudes are changing, that young people today hold attitudes considerably more favorable toward the Negro than those of their parents. If this is so, and it may well be, the change is understandable in terms of our analytical framework.

We have asserted that racial attitudes reflect the behavior of individuals in interracial relationships, that the attitude is, in a sense, the rationale of the act. The racial behavior of earlier generations grew out of a social order that no longer exists. The young white Southerner is no longer brought up in the care of a "mammy"; it is a rare white family that has even one full-time Negro servant, and the behavior appropriate to the "master" class is not an ever-present example in the home. Opportunities for parents to teach racial behavior are fewer than they used to be, and the lessons can not be so thoroughly learned. Since the master-servant relationship and all the practices appropriate to it are so little in evidence, the old verbalizations and stereotypes are losing some of their authority. Perhaps some unconscious awareness of the weaknesses inherent in verbal indications of racial attitudes has accounted for the apparent reluctance of the bearers of the culture to attempt to transmit the attitudes through direct verbal instruction; certainly, without the reinforcement of carefully trained racial behavior, these attitudes are beginning to be altered.

It is customary in the sociological field to talk about relationships between and among different racial groups in terms of social distance. Robert E. Park pointed out that social distance might be either vertical or horizontal, and he thought of the former—with the Negro in the subordinate position—as characterizing racial relationships in the South, as opposed to horizontal social distance—with the Negro relegated to a different sphere of activity—which was characteristic of Northern racial relationships. Economic changes in the South are bringing increased social distance of a horizontal type; it may well be that when this distance is great enough the vertical distance will be negligible. Perhaps this change is an important one for a change in racial attitudes, for it will certainly bring a change in definition of behavioral relationships of Negroes and whites. As more white people find themselves in jobs in which Negroes are their clients and their customers, it is inevitable that the behavior defining these relationships should give rise to new attitudes. A sixteen year-old white girl who lives in a Southern town of about 16,000 population reports:

> You know, I've been working at Wilkie's Shoe Store. A lot of Negroes come in there, and I wait on them. Once I was so startled to hear myself saying "ma'am" to one.

And a seventeen year-old boy from the same town tells:

> Last summer I worked at the ice plant. There was a Negro there I liked. He really was a swell fellow. He was a grown man. Everyone liked him . . . I wouldn't mind working with them. A year ago I might have said I wouldn't like it, but this Negro down at the ice plant did a lot to make me see things differently. I wouldn't particularly like to work under one—no, I shouldn't say that, 'cause I know I wouldn't mind working under the one at the ice plant.

Racial definitions are an inevitable part of the Southerner's point of view because social forces dictate a racial etiquette which can not be ignored. In many instances these social definitions of racial roles are legal definitions as well. Jim Crow is not a folkway only, but a law, and this fact puts a heavy drag on the rate of social change. The white person inclined to protest segregation can be hauled into court if he attempts to make an issue of the principles. Myrdal has observed that liberalism in the South holds an anomalous position in that it runs counter to law. Conservative forces have not only custom, but legal right on their side. Thus, it is extremely difficult for the Southern white person to act against custom, and the social pressures are bulwarked by police and courts. The legal aspects of racial relations lag behind economic and social changes brought about by industrial development and the urgencies of war.

But laws, like attitudes, may be thought of as reflections of already established patterns of behavior, and it seems reasonable to expect that changing racial behavior will be reflected in a new rationale and an accompanying rewriting of legal definitions of racial relationships.

PART VII

Race and Human Nature

INTRODUCTION

THE VARIOUS ECONOMIC and political and racial systems in which men live are of great consequence to their daily actions, but even the most rigid system does not determine social relations and human behavior entirely. There is always an additional something which is a part of every system and, at the same time, a part of none. When men completely commit themselves to a system apart from this additional something they eventually find themselves defenders of the *status quo*. Yet sooner or later the civilizations and empires and racial systems to which they have given their loyalty undergo change and even destruction. But people remain people and beget more people whatever happens; kinships and friendships are forever reforming; and new systems grow up even greater and grander than the old. For behind and suffused into the conventions and forms and laws under which people live for awhile is that thing which evades definition but which appears to give all men a certain commensurable quality. We call this human nature. It is common enough in all people to make possible a minimum communication between them, and to make human behavior in every society intelligible and understandable, up to a point, to every other society. Occasionally, when a rift appears in the customs of a social system, human nature may be caught in the act and clearly observed by anyone. Those who have to live by it, like showmen, politicians, merchants and diplomats, know somewhat more about it. Social scientists make it the object of special and systematic study.

Men of liberal outlook often protest that it is impossible to make sense out of the inconsistent and even contradictory practices to be observed in a racially stratified society. Their perplexity is justified. They might, however, reverse their attention and use the practices to try to make sense out of human nature, the irrational but frequently decisive element in the situation. This element is everywhere, but in the exaggerated practices of an interracial situation it is perhaps more clearly and more accurately observed.

Perhaps the elementary question to be asked when the discussion moves around to the subject of human nature has to do with what we have most in common, that is, our bodies. Voegelin speaks of the idea of race as a "body idea." Body ideas are basic and universal human experiences. In what way or ways is the human body a starting point for the building up of beliefs about 1) a common humanity, and 2) racial and other biological differences? How much like another person is an individual ordinarily willing to be? Is not the thought of being exactly like another person an almost unendurable thought? How different from other people is an individual ordinarily willing to be? Is not the thought of being utterly different from any other human being an equally unendurable thought? What is a race trait? Do race traits change from time to time and from culture to culture? How do people learn about their own traits?

What are the individual and social factors in untouchability, or the avoidance of physical contact? What is the evidence for and against the existence of so-called racial odors? What is the difference between racial antipathy and racial phobia? What do you understand by "the etiquette of race relations" and to what extent, if any, is racial etiquette bound up with racial antipathies and phobias?

There seems to be good reason for suggesting that prejudice is the fundamental attitude operating in the formation of societies if we think of it as "little conflict," or incipient conflict. Prejudice develops from the tendency of human beings to categorize other human beings, and it functions, therefore, to differentiate and isolate groups. Then comes counter-prejudice, the tendency of the group against which there is prejudice to react with prejudice of its own. The kind of society resulting from this dialectic is perhaps determined by the kind of prejudice operating—class prejudice, religious prejudice, race prejudice, etc. When the usual and ordinary prejudices that characterize people in their relation with each other get rationalized in biological terms they become race prejudices, and the member groups of the society become racial groups.

What would a man completely without prejudice be like? Would you disagree with those who say that a man has an "inalienable" right to his prejudices? What positive functions, if any, does prejudice serve? How would you tentatively define race prejudice and how would you set up a plan of investigation or research designed to test your definition? Would you need to distinguish between race prejudice and color prejudice? Is it possible for an individual to hold a prejudice apart from other members of his group? We are said to develop prejudice against those who get out of "place." How can it be determined what the place of a person or a group is? Does there seem to be a relation between numerical race ratios in the community and race prejudice? If so, how would you account for it? Would it be possible to make a map showing the distribution of race prejudice around the world or in a particular country? For such an undertaking what might be used as indexes of race prejudice?

Undoubtedly there is much more to be learned about race prejudice, but it might be suggested that, relatively, this attitude has been overstudied. A number of others deserve attention. When, for instance, one encounters the complaint of a Negro on the American Pacific coast two decades ago that "the indifference of the West is harder to bear than the hatred of the South" one is led to speculate about indifference. There are situations where, paradoxically, "the absence of human relations seems the most human of all relations," where a man has constantly to advertise his race if he wants it noticed. The prestige and the power of Hinduism is said to lie in its self-centered indifference to all other groups. What is the difference between tolerance and indifference? What is the difference between indifference and objectivity? Under what circumstances would racial indifference hurt more than racial prejudice? Compare the white Southerner's attitude toward the Negro with his attitude toward the Indian with reference to the distinction between prejudice and indifference.

Then there is the attitude expressed in the old American frontier saying, "The only good Indian is a dead Indian." Prejudice would keep the other one in his place, but how would you analyze and label the attitude which would wipe out the place altogether along with the individual in it? Is the attitude in the old Russian pogrom against the Jews the same as the attitude in the Southern lynching of a Negro? How would you define contempt, and where would you place it in a continuum of race attitudes? Again, there is the attitude dominant in the Uncle Tom's Cabin type of race fiction of which there is a growing amount. Sumner called it pathos. It is an attitude which sometimes enables minority race members to "sell" or trade upon their race-ness. What is the connection, if any, between prejudice and pathos? How would you distinguish between pity and pathos? between sympathy and pathos? What is respect and how can it be identified as a race attitude?

In any analysis of prejudice, antagonism, pathos, pride, respect, or any of the attitudes, we perhaps miss the most important point unless we see that each is one of those "subtler forms of isolation" about which William I. Thomas wrote. They register themselves not so much in what the person says as in what he assumes is generally understood and taken for granted. But while the attitudes from this point of view isolate those whom they consume, they are not themselves created in isolation. They take form in collective actions and in social movements, and they cannot be understood apart from what actually is going on. It has been suggested, for instance, that when you know the attitude of the white man in America toward the education of the Negro you know his attitude toward the Negro. This formula may be a little too neat to fit all the facts, but it is true that the effort to change the status as well as the condition of the Negro through purposeful education has, ever since colonial days, generated all sorts of different attitudes toward him in America. All these attitudes seem to be common products of the same historical movement, and each attitude seems to be a product of the defining action of each of the others. What are the implications of these remarks for the study of race attitudes generally?

HUMAN NATURE AS ELEMENTAL
COMMUNICATION

By Robert E. Park

THE REAL SIGNIFICANCE of man's interest in the incidents and experiences of other men is not always clearly understood. All animals have a peculiar interest in individuals of their species which they do not manifest toward individuals of other species. Man's "consciousness of kind" differs at least from that of the so-called lower animals in that he has the capacity, through language, to enter more fully than they do into the experiences, the memories, and the aspirations of the members of the human race. This capacity of man to penetrate into and to live in the lives of others is what we mean by human nature. From this basic human trait grows all the distinctive traits of human nature like the impulses of sympathy, decency, romance, morality, and justice. For human beings are interested not only in reliving in imagination the adventures and struggles, the successes and defeats, of others, but they seek vaguely or definitely for their meaning, whether stimulating or boring, customary or divergent, right or wrong, good or bad, as a guide for their own behavior. This interest of man in his fellows is not limited to the sharing of experiences by friends, but it extends throughout the entire range of all human action and thinking.

Man desires to know his past; through history he can relive all recorded events; the building of the Pyramids; the conquest of "the world" by Alexander; the rise and decline of Greece and Rome; the development and decay of feudal society. Through anthropology man seeks to probe beyond the record of man's life upon the planet to the remains of man and his work. Through ethnology he finds and records the strange but always fascinating life of contemporary peoples. Through literature men relive not only all the stirring deeds, heroic and cowardly, magnanimous and mean, noble and base, but in fiction all those that the human mind can imagine and invent. The art of painting and sculpture seeks to portray, in realistic or idealistic forms, the artist's conception of significant events in man's outer or inner life. The plot of the drama is not only derived from life, but it is amusing, melodramatic, serious or tragic, in the way in which it introduces the audience into the lives of its characters as representative of human beings in actual situations.

Man's interest in literature and history does not consist alone in reliving the events and the characters therein portrayed. But in reliving a historical event, as in the case of sharing an experience with another person, one makes that event, that experience, his own. In incorporating this behavior into one's own past life, it takes on meaning and significance. And this meaning thus acquired is the permanent value of the vicarious experience for the person. In like manner the meaning of all a man's past experience is remade by the meaning of each significant new experience.

What was the meaning of the auction of the mulatto girl in New Orleans to Lincoln? Why was the effect of this experience different upon him than upon

Robert E. Park, "Human Nature" (unpublished paper written about 1928).

the other spectators? What is the meaning of Lenin to Russia and to the United States? What is the significance of the Scopes trial in Tennessee to fundamentalists and modernists? These are the types of questions on human nature that are interesting alike to biologists, psychologists, and sociologists, and especially to the historian and the philosopher.

These questions go far to explain why the historian must rewrite the history of the past for every new generation. The events of the past, in an external sense, remain the same, but their meaning changes. In the perspective of the present, George Washington stands in a relation somewhat different to us than to the men of Lincoln's day. So, too, the history of a country gives distinctive meaning to present events. Mussolini assumes a role in Italy that exemplifies the creative function of the Caesars and the memories of the Roman Empire, just as the career of the great Napoleon makes possible events in France that could hardly occur in England. The external aspect of the events and of the characters of the past have not changed; human nature in its essential traits is not different; but because customs and standards of peoples are in constant flux, the experiences of past generations must always be reinterpreted for each succeeding generation.

Religion and philosophy both are concerned with the meaning of life. Religion holds as devine and sacred those objects and relationships that are deemed in any generation or among every people to possess or symbolize the highest human values. Philosophy, whether that of the common man, or in its most comprehensive and systematic forms, attempts to give a formula derived from the realm of all experience of the meaning of life for human conduct.

This disposition of human beings to live in the lives of others has no appropriate word current in English. The term "sympathy" more nearly conveys the meaning, perhaps, than any other, but it implies fellow-feeling rather than actual participation in the experience of the other person, as if it were one's own. The German word *Einfühlung,* employed by psychologists to define the process of artistic appreciation, translated into English as a newly coined term "empathy," may be used to name this basic characteristic of human nature. Just as the artist in the supreme moment of artistic creation, or the art lover at the high tide of aesthetic appreciation of a masterpiece, enters fully into the art object and identifies himself with it, so the person in reliving the extraordinary career of a great leader of mankind like Lincoln, enters more or less completely into his activities, and for the moment becomes Lincoln and feels at one with him.

This identification of the person with another person is seldom or never complete except, perhaps, in insanity, or in hypnotism, or in some exalted state of emotional release or mystical experience. Persons differ as to their capacity to enter into the lives of other persons. In this sense, certain persons are more human than other individuals. To perceive the motives that move a friend is notoriously easier than to appreciate the feelings and attitudes of an enemy.

The relative ability of persons to live in the lives of others and to participate in their memories and hopes is due, in large part, to difference in imagination, and particularly in sympathetic imagination. The extent to which certain individuals live in their own external activities while others live in their imagination must be due largely, but perhaps not entirely, to differences in experience. Sympathetic imagination does not develop from mere external contact with men of many different sorts, but from intimate and personal association with them in person or through biography and fiction. It is, in fact, through sympathetic imagination and appreciation that we are enabled to pass moral judgments upon the conduct of others and upon our own behavior.

Empathy, or the capacity to relive the experiences of other persons, not only makes for appreciation and develops sympathetic imagination, but it gives insight into the motives both of others and of oneself. For as we become aware of the driving forces in the behavior of other men, we tend to arrive at some notion of the nature of the impelling impulses in our own behavior. It is, of course, true, in turn, that as we in this way become apt in detecting our own impulses and attitudes, we gain skill in analyzing the springs of action in others.

Human nature, as empathy, finds expression in sympathetic imagination, appreciation, and insight. Sympathetic imagination and appreciation are essentially subjective aspects of human nature in that the person has the feeling of identification with the other. Insight, on the other hand, while it employs sympathetic introspection into the mind of the other, implies a certain detachment of the person from the other and the emergence of an objective attitude toward him. So, also, with insight into one's own behavior the same detachment is to be observed.

Insight as the objective phase of empathy involves an awareness of the circumstances and the situation under which different types of behavior arise in oneself and others. Gestures, words, and sentences become the labels of situations which have a bearing upon personal and collective action. Through language and rational thoughts human nature transcends insight and develops into intelligence. Insight, like intuition, is the perception of the more subtle aspects of personal experience, while intelligence includes also conceptual knowledge. While human nature is primarily characterized by sympathetic imagination, appreciation, and insight rather than intelligence, it is intelligence and reasoning that differentiate human nature most unmistakably from the nature of the lower animals.

But how does intelligence enable man to make an objective description first of the world of things, and ultimately of the world of persons?

In communicating an experience to another person, there is a disposition to state that experience objectively. An experience should, of necessity, become more or less objective. Spoken language as the medium of thought is a more arbitrary than natural association of sounds with those objects and relationships which have meaning to the social group. What is any sentence but a positive or a negative affirmation of some presumably objective description of an event? All knowledge is verbal, that is, expressed in words, and so incorporated into the fund of objective information possessed by the group.

HUMAN NATURE AND CULTURE

By Romanzo Adams

SOME YEARS AGO Chinese students in Honolulu presented "The Yellow Jacket" to an audience of mixed racial character. Many people unfamiliar with the traditions of Oriental life and art laughed at the wrong places—at moments of tragic climax. A year or two later the Japanese students presented "The Faithful"—and with similar results. Many Caucasians laughed during the scenes of heroic self devotion. Still a few years later an American moving picture was presented at the Mid-Pacific Institute. The audience was made up almost wholly of boys and girls of Chinese and Japanese ancestry. These children, too, laughed at the wrong place. In all the above cited cases the laughter was spontaneous. There was no intent to be rude. It was not the laughter of the over-sophisticated. It was just a case of some people seeing in a situation something incongruous and hence ludicrous while people of a different tradition saw it otherwise. Much seems to depend on custom and on the ethical and aesthetic standards.

The plot of "The Yellow Jacket" turns on the desire of the first wife to see her son inherit the family honors. He is a cripple and so his half-brother, son of the second wife, is expected to succeed to the father's place. The first wife communicates with the spirits of her departed ancestors, asking for help. They inform her that her child may be healed and become the wearer of the yellow jacket—garment of honor—only on condition that she herself join the departed and, from the vantage point of the other world, give help to her son. The tragic climax comes in the scene in which the mother bids farewell to her child and by choice departs this life. So far the audience is emotionally of one mind. Mother-love and ambition speak in a universal language. But the mechanical procedure through which her spirit joins those of the departed ancestors (with the help of the property-man she climbed a ladder into the balcony of heaven) provoked a laugh on the part of Americans unfamiliar with Chinese stage technique.

The property-man according to Chinese custom is always in full view. According to Chinese theory he is invisible, and almost literally so—the Chinese audience ignores him. His behavior is based on the assumption that he actually is unseen. Somewhat bored, nonchalant, he kills time as he pleases when there is no service to render. Because of the novelty of this procedure to a Caucasian audience, he practically divided the honors with the star role when this performance was given in Honolulu.

"The Faithful" is a modern rendering of an ancient plot—one that has been a staple in the Japanese theater for hundreds of years. A noble lord-daimio was forced to commit hara-kiri through the machinations of a contemptible rival who won honor by his treachery. The samurai retainers of the unfortunate daimio made a vow to avenge their lord and after many discouraging years they found opportunity to slay the villain.

A typical American audience here feels that justice has at last triumphed.

Reprinted from Romanzo Adams, "Laughing at the Wrong Place," *Pacific Affairs*, II (July, 1929), 415–417 with the kind permission of the Institute of Pacific Relations.

The slaying of the villain is no more a crime than was the killing of Macbeth. The man got what he deserved. The moral order was vindicated. The whole truth should come out and the loyal samurai should be honored for their loyalty. But not so. For while they have kept utter faith with their immediate overlord they have set themselves against the higher authority—ultimately the authority of the imperial family of divine descent. Here lies the essence of the tragic situation. The duty of a samurai was to be loyal to his lord to the last, even after death to avenge him, but at the same time no man must raise his hand against the higher authority. What could loyal men do under the circumstances? Only one course was open. They must first avenge their lord and then expiate their offense in the only honorable way. Hence when they received written orders to commit hara-kiri they repaired to the tomb of their lord and there, without visible force to compel their action, without hesitation, and with little or no manifestation of emotion, each member of the noble band took his own life. They died as they had lived, according to the ethical standards of bushido—the chivalry of Japan. In an impossible situation their conduct had been most heroic. They had been true to the finest traditions of Japan.

The emotion called forth among Japanese at this point in the drama is one of great exaltation and intensity. One would as little be moved to laughter as would an Englishman by the last act in *King Lear*. And yet many Caucasians laughed. To the Occidental unfamiliar with bushido there is something unnatural in this behavior. The nature of the tragedy is not apparent. He does not realise that hara-kiri is the one way in which the samurai could preserve their honor or extricate themselves from the dilemma of their double loyalty. The apparent lack of the appropriate emotion—the perfect self-control—makes the whole act seem unreal. Herein lies the incongruity which gave rise to the laughter.

The other play, the movie, is one of much less fame. Its name is immaterial. A leading character was a man of wealth and local power. Lacking the finer sort of sentiment, he was contemptuous of the better ideals of his time. A sordid money-getter not too particular as to methods. The one good thing in his life was his sincere love for his daughter. This devotion to the girl humanized him. It revealed something worthy in his character. He was not wholly bad.

The tragedy of the play centers around the accident that causes the daughter's death. The father's grief is mixed with remorse for he sees himself as partly responsible. If he had followed a different course the accident would not have occurred. According to the way of movies, the father registered extreme grief. He was all broken up.

Under the circumstances most Americans would have sympathized with the father. Even if they felt that his loss was a sort of retribution they would not, in the presence of such extreme suffering, have failed to be sympathetically moved by his grief. No occasion for laughter here. But the children of Oriental ancestry did laugh.

Probably, to them, the incongruity lay in the weakness of a man who gave way to his feelings. To Orientals the display of grief is unworthy of a man; it forfeits respect. Here was a supposedly strong, at least ruthless leader who turned out to be only a cheap imitation of a man. Sympathy was impossible. This false note in the would-be tragic ending made the whole affair ludicrous to Oriental minds.

This failure of dramatic situations to call out similar emotional responses on the part of peoples of differing cultural traditions does not stand alone. The whole field of art and of life is replete with similar instances. The harmless witticism of the man of one culture may be a profanation for the man of another culture. What is mere common sense to one is sordidness to the other. What excites the disgust of one is to the other a matter of indifference. What is to one an occasion for the highest emotional exaltation leaves the other cold.

Doubtless differences of a somewhat similar character are found among people who are regarded as the heirs of a common culture. Something depends on temperament as well as on the relation of the individual to the general cultural inheritance of his people. One may utilize only a part of his potential inheritance. But the point to be emphasized here is that each culture tends to produce a type and to the extent that there are diversities of custom and aesthetic and ethical standards there is failure of understanding and a diversity of emotional response.

Because of the multiplied contacts among the peoples of distant regions of our time there is need for a better understanding, a larger appreciation, a more adequate sharing of spiritual values. Not too much reliance should be placed in diplomacy nor in trade nor yet in a knowledge of such facts as can be expressed by columns of figures and graphs. If the peoples of the world would understand each other in the interest of the coming world cooperation they must each give thought to the finer achievements of all the others. Only the liberally educated persons of all lands can have a hand in shaping this world cooperation, and the liberally educated person is one who knows and justly appreciates the poetry, the dramatic literature, the art, the religion and the philosophy of many peoples. Laughter at the wrong place may seem but a symbol, an interesting symptom of cultural difference, but it is a deep offense.

ODOR, ANTIPATHY, AND HUMAN
BEHAVIOR

*

By W. H. Hudson

YEARS AGO—FIFTEEN OR TWENTY, I BELIEVE—in reading an article in a periodical on the progress of Science, or some such matter, I came upon a brief account of a notion put forward by a German scientist about the sense of smell in man. This was that the odours of which we are unconscious do yet serve to inform the mind. Thus, when we conceive a dislike or repulsion to any per-

Adapted from W. H. Hudson, *A Hind in Richmond Park* (New York: E. P. Dutton and Company, 1923), pp. 79–85, 87. Copyright 1923 by E. P. Dutton and Co. and reprinted with the kind permission of the publisher. A later edition is currently available.

son, a stranger to us, it is because he has a bad character or disposition or is for some reason antipathetic to us, and this is revealed to us by his smell.

This notion appeared to me unbelievable and even somewhat fantastic, as I was then quite convinced that it is solely the expression of a new face which reveals the character of the person. Consequently I thought no more about this theory, which does not seem to have received much, if any, attention in any quarter. Now, years later, I find that it throws a sudden bright light into a dim interior in which I had been helplessly, hopelessly groping among vaguely-seen mysterious objects or shapes standing or moving about me. Let me hasten to say that it was, and is, a vast interior, that the sudden light fell upon and revealed only a small number of the dimly-seen shapes about which I must write by-and-by, but I think a good deal must be said first by way of clearing the ground.

We may take it that every object about us, animated and inanimate, has a smell, although our olfactories may not tell us so. We have only to consult a dog to know that the atmosphere teems with scents to which we are insensitive. But we find that by giving a holiday, an idle time, to our olfactories, they recover in some degree their lost or hidden power. Thus, it is a well-known fact that when a person has spent some hours in a deep cavern, like the famous Mammoth Cavè in Kentucky, where in the great rocky chambers, miles under ground, the still atmosphere is free from scent particles, on emerging his nostrils are assailed with a hundred smells—of the soil, of trees and bushes and grass and every object around him. So sharp is the sensation that it is actually painful in some cases. Again, on landing after a sea voyage, the smell of the land and of buildings ís quite powerful, and we smell things strongly too when we come down from a mountain. Even after a day spent on the crest of the South Downs, where I used to take my walks, the various strong smells of the earth and vegetation, and of the village, would come as a surprise and amuse me with the notion that I had recovered a long-lost faculty.

Undoubtedly there is a very considerable difference in the smelling powers of different persons, but the difference appears greater owing to the variety of conditions in which we live, and to the fact that if we live with smells, however pleasing or disagreeable they may be when newly met, we become unconscious of them. I think of the dog's smell in this connection, and note that when I speak to my friends about it they invariably asseverate that the dog, if clean, has no smell at all. The fact that you see dogs in the arms of half the ladies who are out for a drive in their cars, that you find them everywhere in drawing-rooms, not as casual guests, but residents there, as a rule in possession of the most comfortable seats in the room, is taken as a proof that they have no smell. Having become unconscious of the smell themselves from living in it, they imagine it is so with others. Out of doors a dog has no smell for me unless he gets too near by throwing himself on me and trying to lick my face. But in a room I am as conscious of his smell as I am of the smell of a fox, or of rabbits or sheep. It is to me a disgusting smell, and if asked to describe it, I should say that it is a carrion smell—not the smell of carrion lying or drying in the sun, but of a dead animal lying and decomposing in a pool of water in hot weather. Long experience in a wild cattle country, where during the summer droughts old and feeble beasts are always getting stuck and perishing in the muddy water-holes, enables me to make these nice distinctions. It is *the* dog smell, and I find it even in the petted lap-dog, fed delicately and washed and brushed regularly every day by his attendants.

Here I will give a personal experience which illustrates the different way in which the sense of smell affects us, according to our way of life, predilections, and so forth. I went to visit a venerable lady of my acquaintance at her country house, and was told she was laid up with an attack of bronchitis, but wished to see me, and I was taken to her room accordingly and found her in bed, propped up with pillows and breathing with difficulty. Her two favourite dogs, black or dark-grey haired shaggy terriers, were lying on the eiderdown quilt at her feet. Doors and windows were closed, and though it was a large room, the peculiar dog smell described a few lines back was strong enough to make it exceedingly uncomfortable. But she, I knew, was unconscious of it, and I did not venture to suggest the advisability of opening a window lest, coming from me—one, to her thinking, so ignorant and prejudiced as to regard dogs as unclean animals—it should appear like a reflection on her pets. Then the housekeeper came in to consult her about some household matter. She was a stout, or perhaps fat, sonsie little woman with a bright smiling face, and in the light muslin dress she wore looked delightfully cool and fresh—almost flowery. She remained about a minute and a half in the room, standing some distance from the foot of the bed, then withdrew, and no sooner had she closed the door behind her than the sick lady begged me to throw open the front window—wide open to let in plenty of air, as she felt suffocated. Then she added in explanation that she always felt like that when a fat person came into the room; the smell of fat people was intolerable to her!

Many and curious as are the tricks our olfactories play us, I was really surprised on this occasion; but my surprise was nothing to that of a friend of mine at an experience he underwent. He had never previously given a thought to the subject—the smell of the human animal.

He was a young army doctor in India, and at Bombay, his duties being light, he zealously set himself to win a good private practice. He made himself well known in the society of the place, and his servant had strict instructions to come always into the church where he attended Sunday morning service to call him out to a supposed urgent case.

The natives just then were in a state of political excitement, and he was desirous of finding out all he could about their aspirations, intentions, and so on. One day he told his servant that he wished to attend a big meeting about to be held in a quarter of the town he was not well acquainted with, to listen to the speeches of the orators, and he asked his man to take him there and get him admitted. Accordingly they went on an oppressively hot evening, and he sat in a huge densely-packed hall for about half an hour, then came out. After taking a few deep breaths he exclaimed: "What a relief to get out! In another ten minutes I should have collapsed. The smell!"

To which his servant promptly replied: "Ah, Sahib, *now* you will understand what I suffer every Sunday when I have to go right to the middle of the church to call you out!"

Never, he told me, had he been so astonished, so flabbergasted in his life as by this speech, and he could only stare in silence at the man. The extraordinary readiness, the candour, the spontaneity, and even the glee, with which he brought out his words made it impossible for his master to doubt his perfect sincerity. He had taken it for granted that his master *would* understand, and after his own unhappy experience at the native meeting would be ready to sympathise with his servant's sufferings in the performance of that painful Sunday duty. But what an amazing revelation it was! How almost incredible it seemed that a congregation of English ladies and gentlemen, fresh from their morning's ablutions, in their fresh clean clothes, should offend the natives of the country with their European or Caucasian smell, even as they offend us! And what did it mean? Why, that we white-skinned Westerns, lords of creation, have our smell just as the blacks and bi-coloured races and the lower animals have theirs; that we are unconscious of this fact with regard to ourselves—our own race—but are quite conscious of it with regard to the others. And he, a doctor, proud to think himself of a scientific bent of mind, a student above everything of the human subject—how had it come about that he had over-looked so important a matter, that he was so grossly ignorant about man's sense of smell? That others were just as ignorant he soon found, nor could he get any enlightenment from such books as were accessible to him.

That we are not conscious of the smell of people about us is not evidence that it is the same with primitive races; nevertheless, I conclude from my obser-vation of both man and animals that savages are not conscious of the smell of those they consort with, except at certain times, as, for instance, after being separated from them for some time, but that they are always conscious of the smell of a stranger. Also that the mother knows the smell of her own babe, and that there is a double advantage in this—the smell stimulates her maternal feel-ing and prevents infants getting changed by accident, which would otherwise sometimes happen, as the children of savages resemble each other so closely.

* *

By Chester Alexander

INTERACTION, the basic trait of human social life, is a complex of interrelationships. It is considered to be divisible into two major parts, namely, that which is closely related to the biological nature of man and that which con-cerns the multiplicity of activities which constitute cultural patterns. It is, of course, recognized that these have not yet been clearly delineated. While one might use either of them as an approach to a study of society, one might also start by observing human behavior and thus build up classes of acts according to their similarities. This is not necessarily in disharmony with the traditional methods; it could be used to clarify some of their concepts.

Proceeding in this direction, we note that many acts are performed to avoid objects which are unpleasant to the individual. One may call them "negative,"

Chester Alexander, "Antipathy and Human Behavior," *The American Journal of Sociology,* LI (January, 1946), 288–292.

since their most obvious trait is the evasion of the stimulus. This group may be further reduced by including only those which are neither so simple as reflexes nor interpreted by rationalizations.

The nearest approach to a name befitting this group is "antipathy." The definitions which are given in dictionaries and in the social science literature vary considerably, but there is one point of agreement among them, that is, it indicates a "feeling against" an object. Beyond this there is little unanimity regarding the nature of these acts, the range of their intensity, or their social consequences. Therefore, it appeared to be necessary to start the analysis from the initial observation that the primary response to the "feeling" is an avoidance of the object.

In an extended study (1,200 cases) it was found that the antipathetic reaction to objects was not followed by any effort to avoid future encounters. The negative reaction apparently takes place without the intervention of reasoning, for the individual responds almost immediately upon being confronted by the stimulus, while the feeling of aversion vanishes when the act has been completed. It was also quite evident that the reaction is not violent, since one may experience an antipathy while in the presence of other people without giving any conspicuous clues regarding one's feelings. Examples: pictures hanging aslant; woolly things; unpleasant odors; blood; shrill sounds; paper folded unevenly; the taste of marshmallows; a harsh female voice; kissing a baby; "streaky" dishes; women mothering dogs.

From comments gathered during two hundred interviews, the writer concludes that a person is seldom asked to describe his antipathies or to explain related conduct. He does not seek to defend himself or to appeal to socially accepted values. For instance, some of those interviewed stated their antipathy to foods which are of a dark-green color, giving no reasons beyond the dislike of the color and adding that the taste has taken on the same negative tone.

A considerable amount of our data indicates that antipathies are related to primary sense areas. The weight of the evidence favors the single area, although there are cases where individuals were found to be antipathetic through two senses to a single object. The explanation is that these should be regarded as separate antipathies which are set off by the same stimulus.

There is a fairly strong fixation about antipathies, for many people who aided in this study declared that they would not like to experiment with their "dislikes." Examples: the taste of raw fish; oriental coffee; a buzzing sound in the telephone receiver; the odor of boiling liver; the taste of cod-liver oil; the sight of a scab or a sore; "anyone touching the chair I am sitting in"; neckties worn askew; a person singing "flat" notes; a piano that is out of tune; pouting lips; large nostrils; black watery eyes; a familiar hymn sung in a foreign tongue; sight of a wound.

The matter is settled as far as these people are concerned, but it was not found that such sensory experiences are permanently attached to those who hold them. They were not disturbed by the fact that they did not know the origin of their antipathies. Many were not interested in learning whether their feelings of aversion were rare or common, nor did they express any anxiety about getting rid of them.

Another important characteristic of antipathies is that they are marginal to reflective consciousness. This was shown repeatedly by the remarks made by our subjects that they had never thought much about their antipathies, never had tried to analyze them or to discuss them with other people. This might not be significant if antipathies were exceptional phenomena, but this study disclosed an average of 21 per person for the 1,200 cases. We identified 1,256 different antipathies, of which 37.9 per cent were human physical traits and were related to parts of clothing or to mannerisms. Since these were attached to individuals, they appear to be capable of affecting social interaction in proportion to the degree of their intensity. These facts make one realize that antipathies are commoner than we had assumed.

There is a striking similarity between antipathies and allergies. But the differences are even greater.

1. We note that allergies are physiological (or chemical) in nature, while antipathies appear to be psychological, perhaps emotional in some cases.

2. Antipathies are "feelings against" objects but allergies act much too slowly to produce any quick avoidance. In many allergies the negative reaction does not take place at all.

3. A person may be allergic to an object to which he is not antipathetic or vice versa. An individual may, in fact, show a decided liking for the object to which he is allergic. This trait bears no similarity to antipathetic behavior.

4. Often one does not know what causes his allergy, and it must be discovered by medical observation. In contrast to this, one has no difficulty in finding his antipathetic objects, for his senses make them known to him. One may have hay fever and not know what a ragweed looks like, but if he dislikes the odor of fish glue he has no difficulty in locating the object.

5. Allergies often so affect the organism that there is a prolonged and even incapacitating aftereffect. The writer has never found this in the case of antipathies.

6. Some antipathies are picked up from other persons. It is exceedingly doubtful if allergies are learned.

7. Antipathies are directly related to the primary sense areas, but allergies may operate in the organism without irritating any major nerve center.

We tend to underestimate the social role of antipathies because, for one thing, they seldom force us to deal with them on an intellectual level. It is difficult for people to analyze their own antipathies because sensory experiences are nearly always hard to describe; an effort to do so usually results in likening them to something similar. This would fail, however, where two people have not had the same experience. We can also imagine how one who feels our antipathy would simply withdraw, even when it meant avoiding people, and yet fail to realize how they feel about his behavior.

Another factor in our failure to appreciate the social importance of antipathies is that the objects which serve as stimuli are treated by the individual as nonresponding. In consequence, the individual does not see any necessity of setting barriers against the object of antipathy or of making plans to control it.

The individual, furthermore, does not feel that his experiences are subject to ethical evaluation, for he sees neither good nor evil in them. His behavior appears to be without fault, of no social consequence, and of no interest to others. We cannot quite agree with him.

One may wish to ask whether antipathies have any use and, if so, what it is. The answer is in the affirmative: they fit into a set of protective devices. Their particular function is to protect the organism by producing defensive behavior on the sensory level without absorbing attention or calling upon the intellect. A person withdraws from certain objects because they feel, look, taste, or smell unpleasant, or, stated otherwise, the organism moves to shield itself from irritating contacts. Examples: The odor of burning rubber, "whiskey breath," cigar stubs or halitosis; the sight of sharp pointed objects, bowlegged persons, or hands with very stubby fingers; the touch of anything slimy, a cripple, or another's soiled linen; the sound of chalk squeaking on a blackboard or people who sniff nervously when talking.

The mind does not enter into the experience in order to analyze the meaning of the contact or to govern the organism and thereby to decide whether danger is actually present or not. Scores of cases could be presented to show that withdrawals are often from objects which would do the organism no harm; but that would be a logical deduction, and logic does not operate in antipathetic behavior. Through many interviews it became evident that reasoning does not penetrate to the sensory level of antipathies; therefore their voluntary elimination does not appear very probable.

A study of the geographical distribution of antipathetic objects shows that they have a loose but constant relationship to culture areas. This becomes evident when one recalls that people cannot be antipathetic to objects with which they have had no experience. Thus antipathies which are found among preliterates might vary considerably from those known to people in urban areas; some held in the South might not be found in the North. This seems to refute the idea that some antipathies are innate or due to organic peculiarities. Examples: the feel of peaches; the odor of garlic; the color of boiled spinach; the looks of people who have very deep-set eyes; the odor of printer's ink; the sight of gilt on postcards; guttural speech; rice cooked in olive oil; shuffling the feet instead of handclapping to register applause.

We have abundant evidence to show that people are able to take up antipathies from their cultural environment. For instance, antipathies to foods refer to those which are found in a given vicinity, some of which, like garlic, may have been introduced from other cultures.

If one were to judge by the origin of the words "sympathy" and "antipathy," one might say that one is the antithesis of the other. Whether we use the popular understanding of "sympathy" or the more precise sociological meaning, we can readily see that the two are not opposed.

1. Sympathy means a "feeling with" objects; and that distinguishes it from antipathy. Moreover, sympathy involves some reasoning and is thus on a level with social values and above antipathy.

2. Sympathy usually indicates a sharing of the joy or sorrow that another feels. At the least, it leads to an understanding of the other and consequently tends to bring personalities into closer social interaction. One doubts if it could be reduced to the level of "consciousness of kind" or "gregariousness," since they descend too deeply to be called sympathetic relationships. For two organisms to be in sympathetic contact, they must have similar sensory equipment. This neurological likeness may exist only in imagination, as in the case of the little girl who is sad when her doll is ill. This identification of feeling may also

be seen in the story of a woman who sympathizes with her cat when it bears kittens or of the master who sat sadly by his dog as it licked its wounds.

3. In antipathy there is usually no indication that the individual recognizes any sensory equipment at all in the object. This means that an individual is unable to sense the experiences of the object. It holds just as true for the individual bearing a repellent mark as for an inanimate object, and it is one of the chief barriers to the alleviation of prejudice.

4. Sympathy and antipathy both represent an identification with objects, and the attraction or repulsion may be equally strong, but the attitudes behind them differ both in kind and in polarity. An antipathy is not toward a whole person, for it does not invade the realm of personality, even when it appears to do so. It is always directed toward some particular mark. That is why one person can withdraw from another, when the latter bears some disliked trait. This introduces the problem of interpersonal relationships: antipathy may be extended to many people when antipathy is felt to one characteristic. Numerous interviews demonstrate that people may be thus avoided; they may still have likable traits; yet there is no way of avoiding the disliked object without also keeping away from the individual. Examples: persons who are very fat; who have a nasal laugh; who have very oily hair; who chew food audibly; who have a deformed face, crooked teeth, very pale blue eyes, or coal-black eyes; who stutter; "who have a steady fixed gaze when looking at me."

5. Of the two feelings, sympathy is awakened much more slowly, for one may avoid a person who bears an antipathetic trait, then recall later that one should have been sympathetic. It is possible, for instance, to be antipathetic to crossed eyes and yet sympathetic with the individual. However desirable such an awakening may be, it does not happen often: antipathies usually do not arouse sympathetic sentiments. Indeed, they often preclude the development of sympathetic social interaction, as in those cases where race prejudice is supported by antipathies. We would be very close to reality if we spoke of "response" in matters arousing sympathy and of "reaction" where antipathy operates.

6. Sympathy is almost always directed toward human beings, occasionally to pets, rarely to plants, and only in extreme cases to inanimate objects, whereas antipathy is frequently directed to nonliving things or to parts of human beings. Sympathy is ordinarily saturated with sentiment, at least in the popular use of the term, while antipathy clings to sensory experiences. Since they function on different perceptual levels, there is little chance of their meeting. Thus efforts made to reduce prejudices to sympathetic relationships will encounter antipathies which are not readily susceptible to sentimental appeals. For these reasons sympathy and antipathy are not antitheses.

Such marks as shade of pigmentation, prognathism, ulotrichous hair, the epicantric fold, ultra-brachycephalic craniums, or any others which distinguish one group from another may be antipathetically regarded. The sensory effect tends to accentuate group consciousness, but not on an intellectual level. Although people may not openly discuss their own antipathies or those which they hold to given marks of another group, nevertheless their attitudes may be effectively passed from one person to another through gestures, grimaces, puns, intimations, veiled references, and in similar ways. All these act as suggestions, and none of them calls for conversation. Understanding is possible on this lowly level, and behavior on the basis of this accord is also possible, even collective action.

Our data do not as yet show that a particular antipathy may become a prejudice. Both are found in association with human behavior. Antipathies can and do exist separately from prejudice, but it is doubtful whether a prejudice can exist without antipathy. Prejudices are compounds of antipathies, which provide the physiological stimulus, and the "reasons" which make it seem necessary and logical to "keep him in his place." People can talk about these "reasons" but not about antipathies. The latter only reveal their role when a prejudice is dismembered, part by part, reason by reason, and every defense exposed for examination. When the owner of the prejudice has exhausted pseudo-logic, he falls back on the repulsiveness of those to whose traits he is antipathetic. His defenses are designed to protect whatever social value the prejudice shields, and antipathies supply the "feelings against" the prejudicial objects.

Prejudices cannot be permanently removed as long as the roots remain from which new rationalizations may spring. They cannot be touched by reason, argument, logic, sympathy, religion, or threats.

A group that finds it bears cultural traits which are disagreeable to other groups may succeed in time in getting rid of them. Certain food, peculiar articles of clothing or adornment, odd forms of speech, have been known to retard the process of assimilation. Where antipathies are pronounced, they prevent the intimacies which are essential to the fusion of cultures.

Hereditary physical marks can be eliminated only by commixture of the chromosomes. They do not readily vanish during the period of accommodation. Consequently, it is much more difficult for a minority group which is marked by disliked physical traits to become absorbed in a large population than it is for those groups which are distinguished only by cultural differences.

It is of importance to consider the origins of antipathies. We do not have the evidence to call them all innate. We know that some people are exceptionally sensitive in such matters as tone discrimination, and it may be that they would easily take to likes and dislikes.

A second source appears in learning. Parents are not always able to convince their children through persuasion that certain objects are unclean so they transmit sense experiences by wry faces, gestures of disgust, hawking, spitting, vomiting, shivering, shaking off. It is, perhaps, all in mimicry, but it is impressive to a child too young to take words seriously. The same process goes on between adults, but this time by slightly more sophisticated gestures, such as raising the eyebrows, holding the nostrils, jeering, blowing, mimic expectoration, scowling, shrugging—each of which is understood without words. Phrases and scenes in literature and films may have a similar effect.

A third source is in unpleasant or shocking experiences which become associated with some object, whether this be a trait of some conceptualized individual or an inanimate object.

There may be additional sources of antipathies. These three are evident now, and others may make their appearance as the study continues.

Never before have the peoples, the cultures, the races of the earth been thrown into such abrupt and intimate contacts as during the present decade.

Cultural areas which for centuries have grown up in their own manner now find that they are exposed to many others, some familiar and similar, others strange and very different. As people contemplate odd folkways, foreign food, different mannerisms, peculiar dress, unfamiliar speech, novel beliefs, and startling mores, they may be tempted to make ethnocentric comparisons, biased in favor of the familiar, the traditional, the "right." Where prejudices arise, these negative sensory experiences play an important part.

ANTAGONISM

By W. C. Brann

I ONCE SEVERELY SHOCKED the pseudo-philanthropists by suggesting that if the South is ever to rid herself of the negro rape-fiend she must take a day off and kill every member of the accursed race that declines to leave the country. I am not wedded to my plan; but, like the Populists, I do insist that those who object to it are in duty bound to offer something better.

We have tried the restraining influence of religion and the elevating forces of education upon the negro without avail. We have employed moral suasion and legal penalties; have incarcerated the offenders for life at hard labor, and hanged them by the neck in accordance with statutory law. We have hunted the black rape-fiend to death with hounds, bored him with buckshot; fricasseed him over slow fires and flayed him alive; but the despoilment of white women by these brutal imps of darkness and the devil is still of daily occurrence. The baleful shadow of the black man hangs over every Southern home like the sword of Damocles, like the blight of death—an avatar of infamy, a decree of damnation.

There is not to-day in all this land of Christ an aged mother who is safe one single hour unless guarded by watchful sons, a wife who may rest secure beyond the reach of her husband's rifle, a female infant but may be sacrificed to feed some black monster's lust the moment it leaves its father's breast.

In the name of Israel's God, what shall we do?

This condition of affairs is becoming intolerable. A man's first duty is not to an alien and inferior race, but to his family. It is much better to shoot a negro before he commits an irreparable crime against the honor of a family than to hang him afterwards.

Drive out the "nigger"—young and old, male and female—or drive him into the earth! It may be urged that the "good negro" would suffer with the bad. It is impossible to distinguish the one from the other until it is too late. It were better that a thousand "good negroes"—if so many there be—should suffer

---

W. C. Brann, "The Buck Nigger," in *Brann the Iconoclast* (Waco, Texas: Herz Brothers, 1898), I, 24–29.

death or banishment than that one good white woman should be debauched. We must consider ourselves first, others afterwards. The rights of the white man are paramount, and if we do not maintain them at any cost we deserve only dishonor.

During the slavery regime the negro kept his place like any other beast of the field. He no more dreamed of cohabitation with white women than does the monkey of mating with the swan; but when his shackles were stricken off and he was accorded political equality with his old-time master he became presumptuous, insolent—actually imagined that the foolish attempt of fanatics to humanize him had been successful—that a law of nature had been repealed by act of Congress! If we could but restore the negro to his old ante-bellum condition of involuntary servitude and give him time to forget the social fallacies with which he has been inoculated by misguided theorists, all might be well with Sambo; but that is out of the question. We do not want to re-enslave him—he is not worth it. And if we desired to do so, the world, which is crazed with its own foolish cackle of "equality and fraternity," would not permit it.

No, we could not revive old customs if we would. There are too many long-haired men and short-haired women picking up a more or less honest livelihood by experimenting with Sambo at our expense, his wonderful "progress," his divine "rights" and his devilish "wrongs," to permit serious consideration of what is really best for him.

The negro is to the American social organism what a pound of putty would be in the stomach of a dyspeptic. The sooner we realize this fact and spew him out, the better. It were as wise to make the eagle and the cow tenants of the same eyre as the white and black man of the same territory; as sensible to yoke Pegasus and a plow-horse as to make the Caucasian and the African co-rulers of the same country. The attempts of sociologists to "harmonize the races" are as absurd as trying to bring into the same diapason the twanging of a jewsharp and the music of the spheres— the effort to make the negro an element of strength to the nation's energy as misdirected as the labors of Gulliver's scientists at the academy of Lagado. The American nation would be billions of dollars better off to-day had Ham failed to get into the ark. The negro has been the immediate cause of more bitterness and bloodshed than his entire race, from its genesis to the present, is worth, and he will continue the fruitful cause of trouble so long as he is permitted to remain.

The XIVth amendment to the Constitution is a flagrant violation of natural law—of the law that the greater and less cannot be equal, that matter must be subject unto mind, that wisdom was born to rule and ignorance to obey. To deny that the greater shall govern the lesser intellect is to abrogate man's right to rule the beast and God's authority over Adam's sons.

The greatest injury ever done the people of the South was self-inflicted—the introduction of negro slavery. The next greatest was the act of the Federal Government in making the black man co-ordinate sovereign of the State. It would have been a thousand times better for the Southern people had they adopted paganism or polygamy instead of negro slavery—a thousand times better for them and the nation at large had the Federal Government confiscated every foot of soil in the insurgent States, put the torch to every dwelling, destroyed every factory and filled every harbor with the wreck of railroads and the debris of business blocks instead of putting the ballot in the hands of the black.

The ruin wrought by torch and torpedo could have been quickly repaired; the damage done by the XIVth amendment is well-nigh irreparable. Burning with the accursed lust for political power, the Republican party, like another shameless Tarquin, held the knife at the throat of the Southern Lucrece while it robbed her of her honor, made her an object of contempt, her name a byword and a reproach. Pitifullest blunder of all the ages! Most damning infamy ever perpetrated since the dawn of Time! Fearfullest penalty brave men ever paid for daring death for conscience's sake!

This is a republic. The supreme power is, ostensibly at least, vested in the people. The voter is the sovereign. Suppose that it were an absolute monarchy: Would it not be a mistake unparalleled, a crime unspeakable to take from an ignorant, brutal slave his shackles and place upon his stupid head a crown? The Republican party did even worse. A sovereign cannot long oppress a brave and spirited people. Let him issue an edict that meets with general disapproval and it is laughed to scorn. Should he attempt to enforce it he is dragged from the throne. But the Republican party corrupted a sovereign from whose edict there is no appeal. It has debased the great army of voters, poisoned the political organism by injecting into it a vast mass of ignorance destitute of even the saving grace of virtue.

Had the negro been naturally the intellectual peer of the white man, it would have been a grievous blunder to give him the ballot, to force political responsibility upon him until at least a generation after his emancipation. He was an untutored savage in his native land, making no appreciable progress. He was captured, like any other wild beast, brought to America and sold into slavery. Here he was taught, not how to wisely rule, but to servilely obey. It required a thousand years of education to fit the thoughtful Saxon and the quick-witted Celt for the duties and responsibilities of American sovereignty; the stupid Ethiopian was fitted for them by the scratch of a pen and a partisan vote! Transformed from semi-savagery to super-civilization by the power of a political fiat! From slave to sovereign by the magic wand of genie! Fitted for American sovereignty! He was not fitted for it. Ten thousand years of civilization and education could no more qualify the negro for self-government than it could raise to the intellectual level of a lousy ape the piebald jackass who presides over the destinies of the Houston Post. True, it is that there are some negroes with a suggestion of intellect; but they are usually negroes only in name—mongrels in whose veins flows the blood of some depraved Caucasian bum. The pure blood blacks who have exhibited intelectual and moral qualities superior to those of the monkey, are few and far between. And yet the pure-blood Ethiop is generally a much better and safer member of society than the "yaller nigger," who appears to inherit the vices of both races and the virtues of neither.

The negro vote is dangerous because of its ignorance, doubly so because of its venality. It is utterly irresponsible, altogether reckless, knows little of principle, cares less, and will follow wherever the most blatant demagogue or the most liberal purse will lead. Is it any wonder that there is occasional "bulldozing" at the polls in the Black Belt—that men whose ancestors wrung Magna Charta from King John and recognition of American independence from King George, should decline to be dominated by the bastard spawn of white bummers and black bawds?

The presence of the negro in the South has kept this section a century in arrears of what it would otherwise be. It has prevented white immigration; it has kept out capital; it has bred contempt among the Southern whites for labor; it has fomented strife between sections and is still fostering provincial prejudice, fanning the fires of sectional hate. The South could afford to give the negro, black and "yaller," a hundred millions of money to leave the country and never return. The negro is, for a verity, the bete-noire of the South, a millstone about her neck, tending ever to drag her down into the depths of social and political degradation. Every Southern man, every man of whatever clime, long resident here, and not sans eyes, ears and understanding, knows this to be true.

Does the Southern press proclaim it? Not at all. The Southern press, believing the black man a fixture—that the disease is incurable—with a burst of optimism that discounts that of the man who thanked God for the itch because of the luxury of scratching, proclaims his presence an inestimable boon, a transcendent blessing. Every day we are told that the negro is "the natural laborer of the cotton, cane and rice field"—whatever that novel economic theorem may mean. If it meant thereby that white labor is not adapted to those industries, it needs no further refutation than a glance at existing conditions. In every Southern State and county white men are performing identically the same kind of labor as the black, and performing it better. There is not a spot within the broad confines of the United States where the African can live and labor that the Caucasian cannot live as well and labor with more effect.

Remove the negro from the South and this section will quickly become the most populous, prosperous and progressive portion of the American Union. But will the negro be removed? Not at all. The two great political parties need him in their manufacturing industry—the making of political "issues."

The negro will remain right where he is, wear the cast-off clothes of the white man, steal his fowls, black his boots and rape his daughters, while the syphilitic "yaller gal" corrupts his sons. Yes, the negro will stay, stay until he is faded out by fornication—until he is absorbed by the stronger race, as it has absorbed many a foul thing heretofore.

A DEFENSE OF PREJUDICE

By John Grier Hibben

WHAT IS PREJUDICE? Is it always something unreasonable? Is it to be regarded necessarily as an intruder among the more sober activities of the mind? Is it the enemy of clear thinking? Is it the counterfeit of a true judgment? There are many who would give an unqualified assent to these characterizations of the nature of prejudice. I am persuaded, however, that there is a certain form of prejudice that admits of a rational defence. In this defence, moreover, I am not taking merely the part of a devil's advocate; but, on the contrary, I am profoundly convinced that there is a prejudice which has a proper place in the processes of the mind, and must be reckoned with as a natural factor in our thinking, and is not to be regarded in any sense as an abnormal and disturbing element. It is very easy to insist that reason should be free from all taint of prejudice; but no one actually maintains consistently and continuously so high an ideal as this in practice. This is not merely a confession of weakness that prejudices will steal into the deliberations of reason despite our most vigilant guard, and in the face of protest and serious effort on our part to drive them out; there is, on the contrary, substantial ground for the contention that prejudice has a legitimate function to perform amidst the varied activities of the mind.

A prejudice is not always an unreasonable judgment; it may be merely a judgment which is unreasoned. There is a vast difference to be noted in this distinction. An unreasonable judgment is, of course contrary to reason and therefore reason itself must repudiate it. But the judgment which is simply unreasoned may prove in the course of events to be eminently reasonable, and as such even in its unreasoned form may serve a most useful purpose in our thinking.

These unreasoned judgments are absolutely indispensable in the economy of our mental life. If we exclude all judgments which are not accompanied by a satisfactory proof of their validity, a tremendous waste of time and energy would inevitably result. For it is a fundamental law of our intellectual activity that the processes of reason by which we arrive at certain conclusions often drop out of memory: but the conclusions themselves remain as a permanent deposit of knowledge. The proof which we once knew and perfectly understood may be forgotten, but the truth which it served to establish is lodged permanently in the memory. The history of its origin we can no longer recall to mind. It has no recognized ancestry; because much of our knowledge changes form in the processes of assimilation. Its original setting is forgotten. It appears, therefore, as a detached judgment. It is a part of the stored energy of thought. The truth has become ours in a peculiar sense inasmuch as it has been merged into the very texture of our thought. There may also be associated with it the impression, indefinite and vague though it be, that as a reasoned judgment it once passed muster and received the endorsement of reason. The proof is forgotten, the credentials are lost, but the thought remains. Although for the moment it cannot be justified by the law of sufficient reason, it nevertheless is allowed a place in our world of knowledge. The economy of the thought processes not only warrants such a procedure, but demands it as a necessary method in all our thinking. Any impression which we vaguely recognize but cannot justify rationally must certainly be regarded as a form of prejudice.

We have only to examine our store of knowledge in order to discover what a vast amount of it is represented by these remote survivals of past study and travail of mind. The principles of a science, for instance, are remembered and accepted as true, and it may be at times are used by us in some practical emergency; and yet how mysteriously vague and elusive seem the proofs upon which they rest and which we long ago so carefully mastered. We assent with complete confidence to the Newtonian law of universal attraction; we believe that the earth moves around the sun; we are in complete accord with the proposition that the square on the hypotenuse of a right-angled triangle is equal to the sum of the squares on the two sides. There is indeed an uncomfortable familiarity about these utterances. But when we are pressed for a justification of our belief in statements such as these, then all that we can say perhaps is simply that in a general way there is a true ring about them. In other words, they are judgments to which we give assent, but which we cannot prove,—that is, prejudices. And yet the fact that they partake of the hospitality of our minds is not to be regarded necessarily as a weak concession of ignorance on our part, but rather the normal manner in which the laborious processes of past thinking are definitely concentrated and recorded.

I think we will all recognize a similar mental experience if we stop to challenge our opinions concerning the character of a person or of a period in history. There are a few instances, perhaps, concerning which we have recently refreshed our memory or which lie, it may be, in the immediate sphere of our especial study and interest that lend themselves to a satisfactory and adequate interpretation. Outside of an exceedingly circumscribed area, however, we find ourselves unable to justify certain estimates of character, certain impressions of a sense of value and significance, which we nevertheless firmly maintain, and that often with feeling and fervor. We have opinions, possibly very pronounced, regarding the character of the Black Prince, or of Poppaea, or of St. Francis; but would it not be difficult, if not altogether impossible, to justify each judgment by an array of indisputable facts which we could summon upon call from the remote stretches of the memory? If we cannot support our opinions by adequate proof, is it not quite correct to regard them in the light of prejudices? And if we rid our stock of knowledge consistently and thoroughly of all such prejudices, are we not impoverishing our minds for the sake of an ideal which is quixotic and impossible? The rigor of reason must be tempered in this respect to the natural limitations of our mental powers.

There is still another kind of prejudice which is similar to that just considered, namely—the class of judgments which are born of other minds and which nevertheless we come to appropriate as our own. The reasons in which such judgments are grounded we have never examined ourselves,—possibly we could never understand them even if they were presented to us with the most elaborate explanations; and yet these second-hand judgments cannot be eliminated wholly from our body of knowledge without an incalculable loss. The primary sources of knowledge are not available to all persons. There are many truths which are supported only upon expert testimony, and which nevertheless become the common property of mankind. Knowledge comes by reflection as well as by assimilation. And the light that is reflected from another's mind we should never despise; for there is a community in the treasures of thought. We possess far more than we earn. There is a universal liberty of appropriation; for the wealth of knowledge like the bounty of nature is free to all. If, therefore, we exclude these prejudices of reflected opinion from our thinking, no harvest of thought is possible save that of our own sowing and tilling. And this would signify an appreciable shrinking of our world in all of its dimensions; for there is no thought, however original, which does not rest to some extent at least upon a credit basis.

There is another class of judgments which merits the name of prejudice. It comprises those judgments whose source may be traced to the subconscious states of the mind. We must acknowledge that much of our thinking is singularly affected by the processes which are connected with the more obscure activities of thought. There is a secret collaborator within, whose contributions do not seem to bear the stamp of our own creation, but which we have no hesitation in claiming and using as our own. They are ours and yet not ours. We must not fall into the error, however, of characterizing these judgments which spring from the subconscious region of the mind as abnormal. They, on the contrary, are the normal reflex of our conscious activities. They may be trusted to the extent that we trust the judgments which we form through the conscious procedure of reason. The intuitions of a fool are not wisdom. On the other hand however, if the exercise of our faculties at the focal point of consciousness is uniformly true, then it follows naturally that the activities which find play within the penumbral area of our minds will be determined by a like habit. If reason is the controlling factor in the conscious evolution of our opinions generally, then reason will hold sway within the realm of the subconscious operations; but if on the contrary we have formed the habit of following the suggestions of fugitive feelings, of whim and caprice, we may be quite sure that we will discover no trace of any oracle of wisdom within the hidden depths of the mind. We are all aware of the activity of these undercurrents of reason in our thinking. We reach certain conclusions without being conscious of the process of reasoning connected with them. They are so little a part of us that they seem prepared for us rather than produced by us.

We find ourselves, for instance, face to face with a new situation presenting problems which we have never before considered. A quick decision must be made. There is no time for mature deliberation. It is necessary to judge of the trustworthiness of a man, or of the wisdom of a business venture, or of the probable success or failure of a proposed policy. The circumstances force us to make what may seem to be a snap judgment. To state a definite reason as the ground of our decision is altogether impossible. Behind the decision is a play of subtle forces producing a certain total impression which cannot be expressed in words, and which stubbornly resists all attempts on our part to analyze it. It is not amenable to the control of the reason, nor does it appear in any form which enters as a familiar factor in the usual processes of our thinking. It is a prejudice, if you please—a judgment whose force we are constrained to recognize but whose truth we cannot possibly prove. It is sufficient to provoke action, but it is not adequate to justify itself. In such a case the subconscious activities seem to conserve the essential elements of our conscious experiences. A man with a wide knowledge of his fellows has accumulated, day after day, year after year, a wealth of experience which becomes a part of himself—not consciously formulated in maxims of wisdom, but assimilated and stored in the deep recesses of his nature. In every one of us there is a high potential of this kind of unformulated experience. It represents the abiding mood and general disposition of the man; it is a sort of diffused sagacity which eludes all attempts at definition. However, when occasion offers it becomes at once active and efficient. It directs our purposes and gives a final cast to our judgments. We trust it instinctively and yet withal blindly; but who shall say unreasonably?

Our subconscious activities, however, not only serve to mediate a quick decision, but they tend as well to precipitate a delayed decision. One finds himself again and again confronted with a situation wherein he is torn now in one direction, and now in another. The arguments pro and con are nicely balanced. Out of the bewilderment of mind, or even of an agony of spirit, there will come a settling of the will toward one of the rival alternatives, and a decided dip of the scales. In such an experience the mind is aware of a certain compulsion which seems to transcend its conscious autonomy. There is a welling up of the subconscious stream from its source in the depths of that buried life which makes every man a mystery to himself. At times the most momentous decisions of life are reached through the mediation of these influences which, while they may not be contrary to reason, nevertheless transcend it.

It is then that a man seems to be a passive spectator. Something within acts for him. He finds himself determined by a deep-seated prejudice, as he is constrained to confess, if he ever pauses to reflect upon it at all. Is not one's profession, or hobby, or the cause to which he may give his life, or his absorbing pursuits, a revelation in some degree at least of his most deeply rooted prejudices? But will any one maintain, however, that he would wish to be freed from all such influences? Are they not an integral part of his being? And are not the hidden powers of his nature after all the measure of the man?

There is still another function which our prejudices fulfill; they serve to produce the overtones of character. It is the overtone that gives a distinctive quality to sound; and, in a similar manner character may be regarded as having its peculiar timbre. There is a certain ring about a man's character—it is true or false, pleasing or unpleasing, harmonious or discordant, as the case may be. Reason may determine the tone, but it is the prejudice which often produces the overtone. We love a man on account of his prejudices; we hate him also for a like reason. Strip a man of his prejudices, and only the commonplace remains. Individuality is the projection of our prejudices. Remove the prejudices and the individual is merged again with the crowd. He is only one of many. He no longer appeals to our imagination. There is no more of interest or charm or power about him. Character without a dash of prejudice is insipid. A man without a fair amount of prejudice in his nature always lacks intensity of conviction. There may be a glow of intellectual light, but there is a conspicuous absence of fire and driving power. There is often a certain judicial poise of mind which reveals itself in a tolerance that is an indication of weakness rather than strength. Such a man never lets himself go. He always sees two side to every question, and can never commit himself to the one or the other. Freedom from prejudice is often indicated by a vacillation which is pitifully weak and ineffectual. What distinct and striking impresson would the character of Carlyle make upon us, were it to be separated completely from his prejudices? or would it be possible to read Boswell's Johnson, if the work were to be expurgated of everything which savors of a prejudice?

It is also the prejudices underlying character, the prejudices of good sense and of good taste, which often operate as a safeguard against the temptations of the reason; for reason has its temptations as well as the passions—not true reason, but the subtle casuistry of reason. It is easy in the times of extraordinary pressure to convince oneself that the worse cause is really the better, that darkness is light, and light darkness. Then it is that the prejudices which are deeply grounded in our nature tend to steady us. It is possible by plausible sophistries to justify many a course of action wherein our clear vision has been dimmed by the allurements of sense, of selfish interests, of greed and ambition. But at the last we shrink from doing the very thing which we had proposed, and which we had rationally defended. There is something within which gives us pause. We are saved in spite of ourselves, even in spite of reason itself. We find ourselves under the restraint of some undefinable feeling, some fancy, a prejudice indeed, which calls to us from the mass of old-fashioned principles which we had thought forever banished, but which the sophistication induced by an intimate experience with the world had not wholly eradicated. No power which operates upon the human mind is stronger or more permanent in its control than this prejudice of honor. There are certain persons who seem to be almost perversely conscientious; their native shrewdness and the stirrings of the egoistic instincts are constantly overbalanced by their sense of honesty and the overpowering compulsion of their altruistic impulses.

It is in the transition times, when reason is obscured by interest or extinguished by passion, that the commanding voice of prejudice enters its caveat to which it is well to give heed, and instant obedience. Prejudice thus proves in many instances to be a saving grace. It is the instinctive morality after all which is the supreme test of character. There is a calculated virtue, a wisdom always seeking to be justified of her children, which nevertheless does not reveal the man as he really is. His innate tastes and propensities, however, the whole body of his unreasoned predilections and impulses which are the natural soil of prejudice, serve to disclose a man to himself and to others as the very mirror of reality itself. If human nature were devoid of prejudice, the heroics of morality would never be written. That impulsive nobility which is the flower of character is the kind of prejudice which at times flies in the face of reason, following the irresistible lead of its own nature in the scorn of consequence. But is it not in turn approved of reason itself, when we come to pronounce a deliberate judgment upon its moral worth? The prejudice which outstrips reason may nevertheless draw reason after her in her flight, so that the two may eventually meet in mutual recognition and harmony. The prejudice, therefore, which transcends reason, or which anticipates reason, or which is in secret born of reason, is not, necessarily contrary to reason, but may be rationally defended and justified.

THE NATURE OF RACE PREJUDICE

By Herbert Blumer

WHEN ONE VIEWS the recent and present relations between races in different parts of the world he must necessarily be impressed by the magnitude, the tenacity, and the apparent spontaneity of racial prejudice. That it is exceedingly common can scarcely be denied. That it may persist as a chronic attitude

Herbert Blumer, "The Nature of Race Prejudice," *Social Process in Hawaii*, V (June, 1939), 11–20.

over decades of time can be shown by several instances. That it may emerge immediately in new contacts between races can be easily documented, especially in the contacts of whites with other ethnic groups. Indeed, so impressive is its extensiveness, persistency, and apparent spontaneity that many students regard it as inevitable. They believe that it arises from some simple biological tendency —such as an innate aversion of race to race—which is bound to express itself and to dominate race relations.

Interestingly enough, the actual facts of race relations force us to adopt a very different view. For, frequently, racial prejudice may not appear in racial contacts; if present, it may disappear; or, although present, it may not dominate the relations. Instead of thinking of racial prejudice as an invariant and simple matter it must be viewed as a highly variable and complex phenomenon. This is shown, first of all, by the markedly differing character of race relations themselves. There are many instances where members of divergent races may associate in the most amiable and free fashion, intermarrying and erecting no ethnic barriers between them. In other instances there may prevail rigid racial exclusion supported by intense attitudes of discrimination.

Between these extremes there may be other forms of association. Further, the history of any fairly prolonged association between any two ethnic groups usually does not show the continuous existence of any fixed or invariant relation. Instead the association and the attitudes which sustain it usually pass through a variety of form. The markedly differing and variable nature of race relations should make it clear that racial prejudice is not inevitable or bound to dominate the relations. Even though it be very common and very tenacious it must be recognized as merely one form of ethnic relation. It must or may not be present; and even where present, it usually arises inside of a temporal sequence of relations.

Even more important is the realization that racial prejudice is highly variable itself. Instead of always having the same form, nature, and intensity, it may differ a great deal from time to time and from place to place. A comparison of instances of racial prejudice shows that it may differ in intensity, in quality of feeling, in the views by which it is supported, and in manifestation. The prejudice of the American southerner toward the Negro may be great, but it is recognized by many as being less than that of the South Africa white toward his colored neighbors. The attitude of prejudice of the gentile toward the Jew has varied in intensity and form from locality to locality and from time to time. Ethnic prejudice may be bitter in one situation and mild in another. The fact that we generally speak of an increase or decrease of prejudice points to its variability. Thus, while prejudice is very real and obtrusive, and while it is permissible to treat it as a type of phenomenon, recognition must be taken of its changeable and differing character.

The fact that prejudice is not a constant accompaniment of race relations, and that it is variable in its nature, indicates that it is a product of certain kinds of situations and experiences. Two problems are immediately suggested: (1) what are the situations which give rise to racial prejudice, and (2) what experiences account for the variation in its nature and form. Before discussing these two problems it is advisable to consider briefly the nature of race prejudice and point out some of the features by which it is usually identified.

Racial prejudice always exists as a group prejudice directed against another group. This means two important things: (1) it exists as a collective or shared attitude, and (2) it is directed toward a *conceptualized group* or abstract category. Each of these two features requires some explanation. Race prejudice is a collective or shared attitude in the sense that it is held by a number of people, who stimulate one another in the expression of the attitude. Through this form of interaction they build up, sustain, and reinforce the attitude in one another. Through conversation, through the observation of one another's actions, through relating one's experiences, through the expression of one's feelings and emotions before others, through circulating tales, stories and myths, the members of an ethnic group come to build up a common or collectively shared attitude. This shared character of the attitude of racial prejudice raises the interesting question as to how far the attitude is shaped by the inter-transmission of experience rather than by direct contact with the group toward which the attitude is directed. All that needs to be indicated here is that its character will differ in accordance with what enters into these collective experiences.

In speaking of race prejudice as directed toward a "conceptualized group" or abstract category, all that is meant is that the object toward which it is directed represents a classification of individuals and so is an abstract category inside of which we conceptually arrange individuals. For example, we may speak of prejudice against the Jew, the Negro, or the Oriental; in these cases, the Jew, the Negro, and the Oriental stand respectively for certain large classifications or categories in which we conceptually arrange people. The prejudice exists as an attitude toward the classification or is built up around the conceptualized object which stands for the classification. Or, paradoxically, we may say that the prejudice exists as an attitude toward what is logically an abstraction. (This point is of considerable importance because where the object of a group attitude is an abstraction it is possible to build up toward it very weird and extreme notions which may vary widely from the facts of concrete experience.) The prejudice is manifested against a specific individual by identifying the individual with the conceptualized object and then directing towards him the attitude that one has toward the conceptualized object. Thus one may identify an individual as being *a* Negro, and thus be led to direct towards him the attitude that one has toward *the* Negro. If a Negro successfully disguises himself (as by wearing a turban which gives him the appearance of being a Hindu) so that he is not detected or classified as a Negro, he will escape the attitude which is held toward the Negro. Perhaps all this is obvious; but it is important to recognize that racial prejudice is directed toward a conceptualized object, and that individuals come to bear the brunt of this prejudice to the extent to which they are identified with the conceptualized object.

The two features which we have just discussed—the fact that the attitude is a product of collective experience, and that it is directed toward a conceptualized object—are intimately interrelated. Generally we may say (a) that the content of the collective experience determines the form and nature of the conceptualized object, and (b) that the conceptualized object becomes a framework inside of which collective experience may take place. Let us explain each of these two statements. With reference to the first statement it should be pointed out, first of all, that the content of collective experience of one group will determine what classifications they will make of other peoples and so what conceptualized objects they will build up. This gives to the conceptualized objects a somewhat arbitrary character. Thus the American gentile will ordinarily have a concept of the Jew which takes no recognition of the keen conceptual differentiations that the Jews are liable to make among themselves, such as between Spanish Jews, German Jews, Russian Jews, or Polish Jews. Or the American white may conceive the Negro as consisting of individuals who have any trace of Negro ancestry, whereas what the Frenchman means by the Negro is likely to be a very much narrower group. Many other instances could be given; but the illustrations will suffice to show that the particular classifications which are made or which are selected out may vary considerably. The variation seems to be due to the differences of group experience. Not only is the form of the conceptualized object determined by collective experience but the way in which the object is conceived is determined by this experience. This should be self evident. Southern whites with their experiences during slavery and following the civil war formed a conception of the Negro which was necessarily different from that developed by the whites in Brazil, where the line of experience was significantly different.

While the conceptualized object is formed, shaped, and colored by the experiences of the group, it is equally true that the conceptualized object orders, directs and constrains the experiences of the group. So we come to explain statement (b) mentioned above. When a concept of an ethnic group is formed and that group is conceived in a certain way, the concept and the conception will influence to a large extent the kind of experiences that people will have in their association with members of that ethnic group. They will subject this association to the form and framework that is laid down by their concept and conceptions of the ethnic group; accordingly, the kind of experiences they have with members of another ethnic group is largely coerced by this framework. The Southern white in his contact with a Negro acts toward him on the basis of a pretty fixed conception that he has of him, expects from him a certain kind of behavior, is sensitized to perceive certain actions, is prepared to interpret these actions in well-defined ways, and is ready to respond emotionally in a fixed manner. This will suggest how the conceptualized object which is had of a race may largely predetermine the collective experiences that come from association with members of that race. Reasons will be given later to suggest why this predetermination of experience by the conceptualized object may become rigid and extreme, and under what conditions it may be slight and malleable. Here it is sufficient merely to point out that collective experience and conceptualization interact to control one another, and to suggest that this mutual control may become so tight that they become essentially one, or their natures identical.

The experiences of ethnic group A with ethnic group B, built up as they are largely in terms of the interaction inside of group A, will reflect themselves in the conception which group A has of group B; this conception will largely control the nature of the experiences which the members of group A have with group B, and the way in which they digest these experiences in their interaction with one another. The history of race prejudice is a history of the interaction between concept and experience. This is what is involved, then, in the statement that race prejudice is a case of prejudice of one group against another group. (It is clear that whether an individual generalizes his distasteful or thwarting experiences into an attitude or prejudice against a group depends largely on the presence of conceptualized objects in his culture. An American white may have highly distasteful experiences with one or several red-headed people; he is very unlikely to develop an attitude of prejudice against the "red-head," because in American culture there is no conceptualization of the "red-head" which would encourage this.)

It is time now to consider what is peculiar to the attitude of racial prejudice—what distinguishes it from other kinds of racial attitudes. The usual tendency is to regard this attitude as simple or unitary, as if it were made up of a single feeling such as dislike or hatred. Such a view, however, is impossible and cannot be squared with facts. Admittedly, the chief feeling in racial prejudice is usually a feeling of dislike or an impulse of aversion; but it is a mistake to regard such a feeling or impulse as the only one, or even necessarily always the main one. Instead, racial prejudice is made up of a variety of feelings and impulses which in different situations enter into the attitude in differing combinations and differing proportions. Hatred, dislike, resentment, distrust, envy, fear, feelings of obligation, possessive impulses, secret curiosities, sexual interest, destructive impulses, guilt—these are some of the feelings and impulses which may enter into racial prejudice and which in their different combinations give it a differing character. Some of these feelings and impulses may be vivid and easily identified; others are obscure; and still others may be present without their presence being realized. We are forced, I think, to realize that the attitude of racial prejudice is constituted and sustained by a variety of impulses and feelings; and that it gets its peculiar complexion from the peculiar nature of these impulses and feelings. In this way we can account for the differences in racial prejudice that have already been mentioned. The impulses and feelings that come to be embodied in a given instance of racial prejudice have been induced and shaped by the past and present experiences of the given ethnic group. From this point of view we can regard race prejudice as a medium for the expression of various feelings and impulses, some of which may be the consequence of experiences that have no reference to the group against which the prejudice is manifested.

The complexity of the constituent and sustaining elements of an attitude of race prejudice makes it difficult to explain exhaustively the experiences and situations that give rise to racial prejudice. Yet, certain of the more important lines of origin can be pointed out. One of them, undoubtedly, is the general ethnocentrism of groups, showing itself in some aversion to strange and peculiar ways of living, and in a feeling of the inherent superiority of one's own group. There seems to be little doubt that many actions of a strange and alien group may appear uncouth and sometimes repulsive and lead to the formation of an unfavorable impression which may come to be built up into a collective attitude. Such an attitude because it springs from the perception of actions which seem to be offensive and occasionally disgusting may get rooted in the antipathies of people. In addition the general feeling of the superiority of one's own group leads easily to the tendency to disparage other groups, to discriminate against them, and to take advantage of them. There seems to be little doubt that ethnocentrism, in these two phases, is a primitive tendency of group life; as such it must be reckoned with as a nucleus around which an attitude of racial prejudice may develop. And the greater the ethnocentrism, the greater is the likelihood that it may lead to group prejudice. Something of this is to be seen in the frequency with which racial prejudice appears among expanding imperialistic peoples.

Yet, however important ethnocentrism may be as a factor in racial prejudice, it does not seem to be the decisive factor. Of more importance is what amounts to a primitive tribal tendency in the form of fear of an attack, or displacement, or of annihilation. This is suggested by the nature of the situations where racial prejudice is usually most pronounced and serious. Racial prejudice is usually most acute in a social situation which has the following characteristics.

1) The two ethnic groups live together in some degree. The subordinate ethnic group is accepted to some extent, in the sense that it is associated with and depended upon by the dominant ethnic group. The relation between the two groups may be one of mere accommodation or symbiosis, but in any event, the two groups live together inside of a common territory as parts of a unitary society.

2) The acceptance of the subordinate ethnic group, however, is limited and involves various kinds of exclusion and discrimination. There are certain privileges and opportunities which its members are regarded as not being entitled to. In this sense, the subordinate ethnic group is assigned to an inferior status or, as is frequently said, it is expected to keep to a certain place.

The same kind of experiences with Negroes might easily lead him to form a prejudiced attitude against the Negro; in this instance the form of conceptualization would easily permit and justify such a generalization of experience. Further, even if one does develop an attitude of prejudice against a conceptualized group built up out of his own experience it is likely to be weak and ineffective unless shared by his fellows. One is largely sustained in his attitude by the reinforcement which he gets from his fellows.

3) The dominant ethnic group has a fear that the subordinate group is not keeping to its place but threatens to claim the opportunities and privileges from which it has been excluded. As such, it is sensed and felt as a threat to the status, security, and welfare of the dominant ethnic group.

It is in a social situation with these three features that racial prejudice seems to have its primary setting. As the saying goes, as long as the subordinate ethnic group keeps to its place, prejudice toward it is at a minimum. Indications of getting out of its place are felt by the dominant ethnic group as an attack and invoke primitive feelings of tribal protection and preservation. Some of the areas of exclusion have a particularly strong symbolic significance, so that entrance into such areas is an especially acute sign of what is felt to be unwarranted and dangerous aggression and attack. Unaccustomed economic competition ranks high here; also entrance into the more intimate sphere of exclusion. What adds peculiarity to this feeling of being attacked is the fact that the dominant and subordinate ethnic groups, as mentioned above, are usually living together. This means that the attack seems to come from an "inner-enemy"; the resulting apprehension seems to be of peculiar complexity—more abiding, more perplexing, more worrisome and more unstable. The fact that the threatening group must be accepted yields an anomalous and instable character to the feelings of apprehension.

The greater the threat which is *felt,* the greater is likely to be the prejudice. The size of the subordinate ethnic group, its degree of militancy, its degree of clannishness, and the extent of its claims are factors which are likely to determine the extent of the threat. On the side of the dominant ethnic group, the degree of ethnocentrism, the degree of tribal solidarity, the rigidity of the idea of its own status, and the tightness of the lines of exclusion which it lays down are factors which increase the likelihood of its construing actions as an attack upon it.

The foregoing discussion should make clear the general character of racial prejudice and the lines along which it is formed. If ethnic contacts are attended by feelings of ethnocentrism, and if the ethnic group in the dominant position feels that its common status is insecure and is under the threat of an attack by a subordinate ethnic group, prejudice seems to be the inevitable result. Ethnocentrism helps to set and sustain patterns of social exclusion. Failure to observe these patterns by the excluded group are felt as threats and attacks to tribal status, security, and welfare. Feelings of aversion, fear, and hostility— all more or less in a state of suspension—seem to be the result.

It cannot be too strongly emphasized that the formation of racial prejudice is not an immediate or inevitable matter but that, instead, it is a product of collective experience, and is dependent upon the extent to which this collective experience fits the conditions which have been specified. The initial conditions of ethnic contact may or may not be conducive to the development of racial prejudice; if the framework of ethnocentrism is not laid down along ethnic lines, racial prejudice is not likely to get started. (As in the case of the early expansion of Mohammedanism which, while involving extensive ethnic contacts, was organized on the basis of *religious* ethnocentrism and gave rise to religious prejudices.) Further, the incidents of experience in the association between ethnic groups may or may not lead a dominant group to feel that it is being threatened.

When specific instances of racial prejudice are traced through it will usually be found that the prejudice has followed upon a series of experiences or incidents which are resented by a dominant ethnic group and construed as affronts, unwarranted aggressions and attacks—usually as signs of a possibly more abiding and more threatening attack. The history of race prejudice could be written (and would have to be written) in terms of such incidents, especially the more exciting ones. For it is such incidents that stir people, arouse feelings, and initiate that interchange of experience that we can speak of metaphorically as a process of collective digestion. Such collective experiences yield the new meaning and content that become fused into the "conceptualized object" which the one ethnic group has made of the other. Since these collective experiences are an outgrowth of primitive and deep seated feelings, it is not surprising that the conceptualized object becomes emotional and fixed in nature, and that in acquiring such a form it exercises a coercive control over subsequent collective experience. (It should be realized that an attitude of racial prejudice, once formed, is transportable. It may be brought into a situation where it has not previously existed; or communicated to those whose own experiences have not given rise to it; in this way, racial prejudice may occur in situations which do not have the features which we have been discussing.) A social situation favoring (and attended by) a run of incidents, especially of a critical nature, which make a dominant ethnic group *feel* that its position is being jeopardized and its security seriously threatened easily conduces to tenacious racial prejudice. A very powerful complex of feelings and sentiments may develop, under the influence of collective experience, and become fused into the conceptualized image of an ethnic group.

(It is appropriate to note that the conditions that give rise to prejudice may likewise give rise to prejudice in other kinds of groups. Many instances are provided in American history, especially in the case of European immigrant groups. Usually, such groups were regarded as inferior by the native whites; their effort to improve their economic and social position was frequently regarded as undue encroachment and as a threat expressing themselves in discrimination and occasionally in violence. What is of crucial significance in such instances, as students have frequently noted, is that members of such a group which is incurring prejudice, in not being ethnically distinct, may avoid much prejudice and move into other groups. Group prejudice is difficult to maintain under such conditions. Where prejudice arises against people who are racially distinct and recognizable, the prejudice is more persistent and less easily escaped. This seems to be the chief reason for the greater tenacity of race prejudice as against other forms of group prejudice.)

It is not surprising that the attitude of racial prejudice should become deeper embedded in the individual as the collective feeling becomes more intense and the conceptualized object more emotionally forbidding. It may even get deeply rooted in the individual's antipathies so that the individual's organism rebels at even the thought of entering into certain kinds of relations—especially intimate touch relations—with members of the other ethnic group. Such antipathies seem to be in the nature of strong defense reactions which seem *to be symbolic* of the collective feelings of exclusiveness and fear of invasion. Indeed, although it might seem incredible, the primitive feeling of tribal preservation may become transferred to the antipathies so that some of them become more important than existence itself. The Southern whites would probably prefer the thought of annihilation to the thought of their women becoming the consorts of Negroes.

The analysis of racial prejudice which has been made should throw some light on the viciousness of behavior in which racial prejudice may at times express itself, and on the ease with which it may become a scape goat mechanism. Since the attitude of prejudice is rooted in a primitive feeling of tribal preservation and may, under the influence of historical experience, become highly symbolical of such a tribal position, it is not surprising that in response to a critical incident, it might express itself in vicious and brutal behavior. Deep rooted fears, restrained and simmering hatreds, strong defense feelings, and strongly felt antipathies may all gain an expression at such a time. Indeed, many other feelings and impulses which enter into the structure of the attitude—especially the more unconscious ones—may gain expression at this time. (It is well to remember, as stated previously, that a variety of impulses and feelings may enter into the attitude of racial prejudice as a result of the collective experiences of the group.)

Light is also thrown on the ease with which racial prejudice may become a scape goat mechanism. Mention has already been made of the fact that the interexchanging of experience between members of an ethnic group may be more influential in the formation of their attitude than actual experience with the group toward which prejudice is developed. This makes ample room for the development of myths and for the focussing on a given race of feelings that have nothing intrinsically to do with it. In this way the attitude toward an ethnic group may come to be the carrier of feelings and impulses aroused in other areas of experience. This can be done with special ease in the case of race prejudice, since the ethnic group is sensed as an "inner enemy," as a more or less persistent threat to vital security and existence. At times of critical distress, disturbance, or calamity it is easy to hold it responsible for the insecurity and woes that are experienced.

Before ending the discussion, some attention may be given to the interesting problem of the breaking down of racial prejudice. First of all, it should be noted again that racial prejudice is not inevitable in ethnic contacts. Racial prejudice may not even appear; or if it does appear, it may not take root; or, if it does take root, it may not grow. All depends upon the nature of the social situation and upon the incidents which occur; for these will influence the collective experience of the group and the resulting conceptualizing of the racial object. In the association of races first of all, it is quite possible for people to classify one another on other bases than that of ethnic makeup in making their important group differentiations. In this event, the important group oppositions may easily cut across ethnic lines. This is to be seen historically in religious movements, in nationality opposition, and in some present day radical movements. Indeed, it might be declared that the widespread racial prejudice that exists in the world today is but a historical accident; that it is an expression of a historical epoch in which there is present at the same time heightened ethnocentrism on the part of groups that happen to be *ethnically distinct,* and a vast increase in contacts between such groups. Racial prejudice seems to have followed definitely in the swing toward modern nationalistic expansion. It may happen in the future, as it has at times in the past, that ethnic makeup will be of little meaning in the important group classifications that people make of one another, and consequently in the "tribal units" with which they identify themselves.

Where racial prejudice already exists, its disappearance or mitigation seems to turn on the condition that the subordinate ethnic group is no longer felt as a threat. This may be brought about in a number of ways. The subordinate ethnic group may keep fastly to an assigned status or to what the dominant group regards as its proper places; hence it is no longer felt as a threat. Or the subordinate group may retire into a segregated position, reducing its contacts with the dominant group, and building up a bilateral society. Both of these adjustments have gone on, and are going on today, in different parts of the world; but they seem to be only temporary appeasements—under modern conditions of communication and contact such adjustments can scarcely be expected to solidify or endure. The other way by which the subordinate group is no longer felt as a threat is by the dominant group changing its conceptualization of the subordinate groups, so that the group no longer is regarded as offensive and unacceptable. To the extent to which the group is regarded as acceptable and assimilable, to this extent it ceases to be regarded as a threat. Where the acceptance is full, the meaning of the original ethnic classification has disappeared.

Modern intentional efforts to break down racial prejudice are usually always along this third line, that is they try to change the *idea* which people of one race have toward another. We see this effort in the case of some churches, some educational agencies, and some humanitarian groups and individuals, all of whom try to point out the injustice and absurdity of a prevailing view of racial prejudice. The importance of such efforts is not to be minimized, but it is questionable whether they do have or can have much influence where racial prejudice is pronounced, or where the "conceptualized racial object" is strongly set. For the prejudice is certain to be rooted in the antipathies; and these do not change easily even though it be shown that the conceptualization is false and unjustifiable. Efforts to have members of different races appreciate their common human character by entering into personal contact are likely to be more fruitful; for where people have an opportunity to identify themselves with one another and to learn each other's personal experiences, a collective conceptualization is difficult to maintain. But even such efforts are limited in possibility and run counter again to antipathies. Any profound change in antipathies is likely to come only as a result of a new body of collective experience built up either around new issues in which the ethnic factor is of no import, or based on a shift in the social scene (such as an extensive population change) in which races are brought into new forms of interdependency.

In closing this paper I wish merely to note that no discussion has been given in it to the topic of counter-prejudice—the defensive prejudice of the subordinate ethnic group against the dominant one. In many ways this counter-prejudice is more complicated, interesting and important than direct racial prejudice. It has been little studied.

JEWISH-ARAB PREJUDICE

By Alexander Goldenweiser

I WANT TO GIVE YOU a recent illustration of the insidiousness of race prejudice. I refer to the Jews in Palestine. Here for once, the tables are reversed, and the Jew turns into a racial snob. The Jews, the eternally persecuted ones, who through tragic ages have learned the horrors of persecution, have felt the sting of racial hatred, have at last returned to their old home, Zion. They have established a community, they want to have a democratic government. There are a certain number of Jews there, and ten times as many Arabs. The proportion is about that of the Negro to the white in this country, the Jews standing for the Negro. What would we think of a situation in the United States in which the white population would have to submit to government dominated by the

Alexander Goldenweiser, "Race and Culture in the Modern World," *The Journal of Social Forces*, III (November, 1924), p. 133.

Negro? Now look at Palestine! In the "democratic" organization of the new Jewish state, the Arab is outvoted and ruled against his will by the Jewish people with the assistance of foreign British police. This is the situation in Palestine. Of course, those enthusiastic about Palestine say that all of this will change in the future. The fact that Zion has been established, they claim, will stimulate a great many rich Jews all over the world to give money in order that others may go there, and then there will ultimately be more Jews in Palestine than Arabs, and a truly democratic rule will be established.

All this may be so, but meanwhile we have before us the little edifying picture of a state ruled by Jews, heretofore victims of race prejudice, over the heads of the majority of the local population.

Nor is this all. Some time ago I had a conversation with a gentleman who came from Palestine, where he had been an inspector of schools. As he was proceeding with his story, I noticed something strange in his attitude toward the Arabs. I asked: "You do not mean to say that you teach the children in your schools that the Arabs represent an inferior race?" "Oh, no," he replied, "we do not have to tell them that. They can see it for themselves." So there we are! Those same Arabs who centuries ago brought many elements of what is now our civilization with them to Spain, the very same Arabs, because today they are in a state of decay, because they are dirty, etc., etc., are regarded by the Jews as inferior, as a primitive race.

OUT OF PLACE

By H. C. Brearley

A NEGRO YOUTH yet in his teens seats himself upon a much whittled bench in front of a tottering general store near the railway tracks. Ceremoniously he adjusts his hat at a rakish angle, picks up his banjo, and sings to an approving circle of listeners:

> I'se Wild Nigger Bill
>   Frum Redpepper Hill,
> I never did wo'k, an' I never will.
> I'se done kill de boss;
>   I'se knocked down de hoss:
> I eats up raw goose widout apple sauce!

Such folk-songs, expressing the Negro's admiration for recklessness and bravado, may be heard almost any day on the back streets of the villages and towns of the lower South. In Negro folk literature the "bad" man plays a role

Reprinted from H. C. Brearley, "Ba-ad Nigger," *South Atlantic Quarterly*, XXXVIII (January, 1939), 75–81; copyright 1939 by Duke University Press and used with the kind permission of the publisher.

hardly secondary to that of the trickster, so well exemplified by the Br'er Rabbit of Joel Chandler Harris's *Uncle Remus*.

In all folk tales the daredevil is a constantly recurring character. From primitive champions like Beowulf to train-robbers like Jesse James and killers like John Dillinger the imagination of men has often cast an aura over the lives of those who dare to rebel against fate or authority or law.

In many Negro communities, however, this emphasis upon heroic deviltry is so marked that the very word *bad* often loses its original significance and may be used as an epithet of honor. This use of *bad* as a term of admiration is quite likely an importation from Africa, for Herskovitz has found a similar terminology among the blacks of the Surinam district of Dutch Guiana, among the Negroes of the West Indies, and among the natives of the province of Dahomey in West Africa. In some parts of the South, however, there is a change in pronunciation to indicate whether or not the word carries approval. If the speaker wishes to use the term with the ordinary connotation, he pronounces it after the manner of Webster. But if he is describing a local hero, he calls him "ba-ad." The more he prolongs the *a*, the greater is his homage.

If this esteem for "bad" men is really African in origin, contact with the whites has not destroyed it. On the contrary, it has doubtless been strengthened by the traditional European approbation of rebels and outlaws. Besides, the Negro's love of derringdo may be partly an overcompensation for the generally observed docility of the natives of central West Africa and for the enforced servility of slavery and later Jim Crow-ism.

But regardless of its origin, the tradition of the glory of the "bad" man still flourishes and definitely motivates the conduct of many Negroes, especially in the rural South. Even Jesus Christ has been portrayed by a Negro circuit rider as a man "who wouldn't stand no foolin' wid. Why, he could pop off a lion's head jus like he was a fryin' size chicken!" No one in the congregation would fail to understand this tribute or to admire such courage and power.

The songs of Lead Belly, the tough troubadour brought to notice by Lomax, are exceptional chiefly for their high quality. On every holiday hundreds of other boastful songsters arouse the envy of Negro audiences by similar ballads and tales of amorous and murderous exploits.

The geographical extent of this tradition of the "bad" Negro is, however, difficult to state with exactness. Evidences of it have been found from Texas to Virginia. Dabney's reminiscences show it to have been prevalent among Cincinnati Negroes during the eighties and nineties, but several competent observers deny its importance among present-day Northern city dwellers. In West Virginia, according to Laing, Negroes native to the state look with disfavor upon those moving in from farther South because "they brag about how mean they is" and because "they'll kill you in a minute." This pattern of behavior is, then, more characteristic of the Negro of the lower South, since it is well known throughout the Cotton Belt.

Open expression of admiration for a "ba-ad nigger" is doubtless a comparatively recent development. Even if his type existed during slavery, the singing of ballads in his honor was not a very politic method of securing the favor of masters and overseers. Besides, his lawless activities were greatly circumscribed by the authority of the owners and the watchfulness of the "patterollers." Occasionally, however, a "bad" slave resisted punishment and fled to the swamps or the hills. This was a desperate recourse and usually led to his death or recapture and sale to a distant plantation.

The "bad" Negro of today has, however, an almost unlimited field of operations. One of his most effective methods of demonstrating his prowess is to "break up" a picnic, ball game, or "frolic." In Odum's *Rainbow Round My Shoulder* a Negro rowdy vividly describes the exploits of one "Graveyard Kid" and comments enviously, "Thought I was bad enough, but he sho got me beat." One rainy day this Graveyard Kid, disgusted with his duties as stable boy in a construction camp, went to his shack and "git in one hand a thirty-eight special an' in other a ortermatic an' jump up on that table while about fohty of us boys was eatin' supper an' go trompin' down the middle of it, steppin' in beans and bread, an' every other kind o' food his big feet hit." Meanwhile he announced loudly, "Now, boys, any of you don't like this don't have to take it, 'cause it ain't no doctor's 'scription. Nobody got to take it. If anybody meaner than I is don like it, jes let me know." Intimidated by the two revolvers, "nobody never open his mouth."

Such dramatic exhibitions of recklessness and egotism have been enacted hundred of times. If successful, they are sure to raise the status of the desperado. Bad-Lan' Stone understood his audience when he threatened,

> Don't you never dare slight my repertation,
> Or I'll break up this jamberee.

If the bravo is often able to terrorize the onlookers, he may become more than a local celebrity and may even have ballads sung in his honor, such as those telling of the deeds of Stagolee, Roscoe Bill, Eddy Jones, and other heroes. Many bloody affrays are, of course, occasioned by these attempts to secure prestige. Songs portraying this motive are very common.

> I went down town de yudder night,
> A 'raisin' san' an' a-wantin' a fight;
> Had a forty-dollar razzer an' a gatlin' gun
> Fer to shoot dem niggers down one by one.

Usually, however, the days of boasting are few. A rival "bad" Negro comes upon the scene. Shortly afterwards money is being collected to provide funeral expenses for one of the combatants, as is described in one of the ballads about Stagolee:

> Some give a nickel, some give a dime;
> I didn't give a red copper cent, 'cause
> He's no friend o' mine:
> Stagolee done kill dat bully now.

> Fohty dollar coffin, eighty dollar hack,
> Carried po' man to cemetery but failed
> to bring him back;
> Lawdy, Lawdy, one mo' rounder gone.

As the stanzas above suggest, there are other character types that resemble in one way or another the true "bad" Negro. The "bully" is generally one who secures his reputation at the expense of unarmed men or of those of inferior strength. The "rounder" is usually a ne'er-do-well, depending more upon chicanery than courage. He is often, however, a favorite with the women, as is the "nachel bohn Eastman," who boasts that he does not have to work— " 'cause I got it writ on the tail o' my shirt." Such near heroes are, none the less, distinctly inferior in status to the genuine "ba-ad nigger."

Negro women, like their sisters the world over, give the "bad" man his full share of praise. Indeed, the desire for feminine approval is one of the strongest motives for attempting this role. As one ballad puts it:

> I'm de rough stuff o' dark-town alley,
> I'm de man dey hates to see.
> I'm de rough stuff o' dis alley,
> But de womens all falls for me.

Many "bad" Negroes confine their bravado strictly to members of their own race. Often a man who is the very personification of arrogance in his dealings with other Negroes will be quite deferential in his treatment of whites. But others consider their triumph incomplete if they are unable to flaunt themselves in the face of a white man, especially of one who is known to go armed or to be "rough on niggers." On the other hand, the white, especially if he is of inferior social status, feels that any slight from a Negro is a humiliation that must be instantly revenged. These antagonistic attitudes make frequent interracial slayings difficult to avoid.

Two Negro women had a fight. A white man living nearby interfered. One of the women, according to her report, "cussed him out. And he took it." The next day she spent several hours going through the Negro village proudly describing her intimidation of the white man. If he had picked up a stick and knocked her unconscious, as the folkways demanded, she would have had far more regard for him.

The would-be "bad" Negro has, needless to say, little difficulty in arousing the anger of the whites. The interracial situation is so loaded with explosive prejudices that a triviality may easily lead to hostilities. A Negro may enrage a white man merely by calling him by his given name or by asking him a simple question in a sneering voice. Again, he may resort to bartering wit, at which he is an adept, as when a colored fisherman replies to a passerby's question, "What are you catching?" with the saucy rejoinder, "Catching cold." Besides such verbal affronts, there is always the possibility of more overt conflicts, as collisions on the sidewalk, insulting gestures, and minor obscenities.

The white overseer is a favorite target for these more or less subtle shafts. In a Louisiana cane field a laborer replied to the young foreman's rebuke by asking, "Who taught you to cut cane?" Had the foreman attempted to ignore this indignity, he might as well have resigned his position. This method of securing prestige by "sassing the boss" is not, of course, confined to the Negro. It has been observed among the Shanty Irish, Italian miners, and other groups of day laborers. Essentially, it is an unsophisticated form of egotism, but among Negroes it serves also as an expression of racial antagonism and as a means of developing the reputation of being "ba-ad."

The policeman rather than the foreman provides, however, the supreme test of daring. Here is a white man, armed, the embodiment of authority. Whoever gets the better of him has reached the highest goal of the "bad" Negro.

In a small town a Negro man choked the local constable into insensibility. Immediately the hero was dubbed "Jack Johnson," after the famous Negro boxer. This admiration made him overbold. Shortly afterwards, possibly to maintain his reputation, he killed a policeman with a baseball bat and ended his life in the electric chair.

Perhaps the most famous of all "bad" Negroes is Railroad Bill, about whose career dozens of ballads have been composed. This hero, whose real name was Morris Slater, shot a policeman with a rifle and escaped on a freight train. Sheriff McMillan went to capture the desperado, but

> Railroad Bill was de worst ole coon,
> Killed McMillan by de light o' de moon;
> It's lookin' fer Railroad Bill.

As Carl Carmer says, "Railroad Bill is a god of Negro mythology. A rifle was the symbol of his godhead. A freight train was his chariot. The white gods pursued him—but he escaped." Not for long, however. The bullets of "the law" finally found their mark and "laid him down" on the "coolin' board" of the undertaker.

Such a hostile attitude toward officers of the law is one of the important causes of killings involving both whites and Negroes. In the more than thirteen hundred cases of interracial homicide studied by the writer approximately fifty per cent concern police officials, either as the slain or as the slayer. The "bad" Negro pattern of behavior is certainly one reason for this bloodshed, although there are such contributing causes as the arrogance of officers and the Negro's fear of the third degree and "the white folks' law."

In defense of the "bad" Negro it should be added, however, that he rarely premeditates interracial murder. He prefers to arouse the fury of the whites and then "get away with it." This is no easy task, for the Southern white who in such a matter does not take the law into his own hands loses the respect of both Negroes and whites. If the disturber becomes too bold, the community may seize upon some relatively unimportant incident as a pretext for "quieting" the offender. This is the explanation of not a few seemingly unprovoked lynchings.

In spite of these "miscalculations" the "bad" Negro enjoys so much prestige that he has imitators even among the whites, especially in sections where the Negroes predominate in number. The white who essays this role often feels it incumbent upon him to "shoot up the town" once or twice a year, preferably during the Christmas celebrations. In one Southern village the lone policeman is said to run ahead of the desperado, shouting to bystanders, "Get out of the way; a bad man's coming!"

Usually the "bad man," white or black, is less formidable than he seems. Vanity is his compelling motive, not revenge. Loudly he boasts of the killing power of his weapons, but rarely does he use his "thirty-eight special" or his "fohty fo." If his name is commonplace, he feels moved to adopt a more colorful one—"Cottoneyed Joe," "Big Bad Wolf." Hardly ever is he of the killer type. With him the risk of slaying or of being slain is but a part of the price to be paid for prestige and glory.

The person of mixed blood, it is generally believed, is more likely than the black to attempt the part of the "bad" Negro. This is probably true, for the average mulatto feels superior to the blacks and often welcomes a chance to demonstrate his importance. Besides, he resents even more than does the black the racial discriminations practiced by the whites. His "almost but not quite" status is a precarious one and needs to be bolstered by public approval. If he has luck and courage, he may, by playing successfully the role of the "bad" Negro, be assured of the prestige he yearns for.

This pattern of conduct is, consequently, a very significant one in the life of the South. As a local hero and a racial demigod the "bad" Negro not only enjoys an esteem far out of proportion to his social worth, but he also induces the young and suggestible to imitate his recklessness and criminality. To understand the rural Negro of the lower South, it is necessary to keep in mind the potency of his desire to be known as a "ba-ad nigger."

THE FEAR OF GANGSTERS AND THE
FEAR OF SWINDLERS

By Gustav Ichheiser

FROM OUR CHILDHOOD on we feel threatened in our social relations by two basic kinds of real or potential dangers. On the one hand, we fear that somebody may harm us by using, or threatening to use, *physical force* (violence). On the other hand, we fear that someone may harm us by using some kind of *fraud, deception, or manipulation*. Violence and fraud, therefore, constitute two fundamental forms of dangers in inter-human relations towards which we react with fear and hostility. They deeply affect the whole framework of our social experience.

In order to have a catchword, we wish to call the first type of fear the *fear of gangsters,* the second the *fear of swindlers.* "Gangsters" and "swindlers" may be considered, in this context, as two *personified symbols* of those two fundamental forms of danger in social life.

Our thesis is that the predominance of the one or the other type of fear and hostility affects deeply the make-up of a given personality, and, especially in times of increased insecurity, determines the character of its social and political attitudes.

The predominance of the one, or the other, form of fear and hostility may, obviously, be conditioned both by individual and by social (situational) factors. The question is: what kind of individual or social factors have to be considered as *relevant* in this respect? Without pretending to be able to give an exhaustive answer to this question, we shall attempt to indicate some of the probably most important factors here under discussion.

Reprinted from Gustav Ichheiser, "Fear of Violence and Fear of Fraud," in *Diagnosis of Antisemitism: Two Essays* (Sociometry Monograph. No. 8, New York: Beacon House, 1946); copyright 1946 by Beacon House and used with the kind permission of the publisher.

Whether our predominant fear and hostility refers rather to the dangers of brutality and violence ("gangsters"), or rather to the dangers of fraud and manipulation ("swindlers"), depends probably,

A) On whether, in the course of our life, we have experienced stronger emotional shocks of the one or of the other kind. The trauma of having been deceived, or fallen victim of some kind of manipulation, especially by those in whom we have had full confidence, can affect the make-up of our personality as deeply as the trauma of having been physically mistreated. This experience of having been deceived marks often the end of a phase in the development of a given personality. It terminates the phase of a naive attitude to life in which things have been confidently taken at their face value. It initiates a new phase characterized by a rather suspicious (critical, sceptical) attitude which splits the until then one-dimensional experience of life into the two dimensions of "reality" and "sham." It depends further,

B) On whether we feel ourselves better equipped, bio-psychologically, to cope with the dangers created by violence or with the dangers created by fraud. The physically strong and courageous, other things being equal, will rather fear the "swindlers" than the "gangsters," especially if he does not feel able to handle very well the different defensive counter-measures against fraud and manipulation. On the other hand, the shrewd and crafty, but lacking in physical strength and courage, will rather tend to fear the "gangsters." It depends finally,

C) On whether, and to what degree, an individual is sensitized with regard to the truth, the sincerity, the loyalty, in social relationships. It is of no importance in this context, whether the form and degree of this sensitivity depends on the personality type, or on some other factors. Important here is the fact that actually certain individuals feel, emotionally as well as morally, more comfortable in facing *overt* even if otherwise unpleasant relationships, whereas other individuals prefer to have unpleasant or antagonistic relationships *covered up,* by politeness, or hypocrisy, or whatever it may be. It has been noticed, for instance, that certain personality types feel more comfortable, and even psychologically more "free," in relationships of an overt subordination, like those existing in an army, than in relationships of a covert subordination, like those existing in an office, or a factory. People of this type may also feel disguised hostility or coercion to be more painful than overt forms of antagonism and struggle.

These, then, are, if we are not mistaken, some of the more important factors which may influence emotional attitudes and reactions towards the two main types of social dangers: towards the "gangsters" as symbols of violence and brutality, and towards the "swindlers" as symbols of fraud and deception.

It is reasonable to assume that sex and age also play an important part in conditioning the two types of fear. However, it may be advisable to consider, psychologically, the influence of sex and age under the three aspects outlined above.

We shall limit ourselves to consideration of two kinds of social factors which appear to be of great importance with regard to the problems here under discussion.

A) It is quite obvious that certain types of societies, or certain particular conditions prevailing in a society at a given time, such as, for instance, actual or probable wars or revolutions on the one hand, economic insecurities on the other, tend to generate respectively the fear of violence and brutality, or the fear of fraud and deception ("manipulation behind the scenes").

Now it is equally obvious that in modern society, under normal conditions, in everyday life the danger of overt violence plays an infinitely smaller role as compared with the more indirect, and often disguised, forms of social danger. Conflicts and antagonisms, oppression, discrimination, exploitation in "civilized societies" are generally carried out by using covert, indirect forms of action: by deceptive manipulations and strategems of every description on the one hand, by "non-violent," especially economic pressures, on the other. Especially, in times like our own, characterized by deep economic insecurities, ideological confusion, fluidity and impenetrability of intricate social processes, by propaganda, advertising, adulteration of goods, the man in the street feels himself far more deeply threatened by those rather "invisible" social dangers than by overt coercion and violence. And he is getting more and more suspicious that those invisible processes by which he is threatened are intentionally, and for someone's advantage, manipulated by some kind of swindlers "behind the scenes." Consequently, the swindler—the manipulator behind the scene—*becomes the main symbol of the predominant fear*.

Furthermore, the swindler, and the forces and dangers which he represents, is more *intangible* and, therefore, more *uncanny* than the gangster, and the forces which the latter represents. The former cannot, as can the latter, be faced and grasped and battled in an open way. He is everywhere and nowhere, he can neither be faced nor grasped, he evades any definite and clearcut showdown. Thus, the average person feels profoundly helpless and powerless when confronted by this kind of "enemy."

B) Of great importance, too, is the fact that in our society it is the *overt* form of hostility and struggle which is, more than anything else, stigmatized and morally condemned. In all forms of antagonistic relationships, individuals as well as groups have, under normal conditions, to be very careful to use, as far as possible, only non-violent techniques of coercion, either economic means of pressure, or some disguised forms of manipulation. Otherwise, they face the risk of provoking an indignant reaction of "public opinion." As a consequence, a state of affairs is established in interpersonal and intergroup relations according to which only those means of coercion, discrimination, and exploitation are admitted by the mores which *cannot be overtly perceived as a form of hostility*. The actual hostility and struggle which permeates interhuman relationships has to remain hidden. The appearance has to be maintained that there is no struggle and no hostility at all but only "harmony of interests" and "friendly cooperation."

The individual, therefore, who in times of social disorganization and ideological disintegration tends to fear more than anything else the invisible, intangible, indirect social dangers as personified, and allegedly manipulated, by swindlers, sees himself caught in the following *emotional dilemma*.

His moral standards impel him to take the most negative and condemning attitude towards any form of overt brutality and violence. At the same time, however, certain experiences of everyday life arouse in him the feeling that brutality and violence are by no means always the worse of the evils. For the real "enemy" to be feared and to be hated is the disguised form of coercion, oppression, exploitation, and the symbol as well as manipulator of those dangers: the "swindler." And there are many people in many lands whose not quite admitted, and often repressed, emotions are not without sympathy with the "gangsters," who, although using the morally condemned violence, appear to be at least "open" and "sincere."

Originally, power and leadership had its basis in *bio*-psychological superiority of an individual: in his *physical force*. The individual who was *biologically strong* was, by this very fact, also *socially strong*.

However, the progress of civilization, the transformation of forms of social organization, and of moral values has brought about a decisive shift in the personal and social conditions of power. This shift has proceeded in two main directions:

A) The originally predominant importance of the *biological* equipment of the individual with regard to his power-ability has been gradually replaced by the importance of his psychological equipment. Not the physically strong (the "soldier") but the shrewd, the clever, and the master of social strategy becomes the predominant power type. The "lions" are being replaced more and more by the "foxes."

B) The predominance of the *immediate personal,* be it physical or mental equipment, is being more and more replaced or supplemented by socially acquired and transmitted *indirect* means of power: by privileges of any description, especially money. The lions as well as the foxes are being replaced by owners of power-producing social symbols: by the privileged and the rich.

This double shift in the basis of power is, therefore, characterized by the replacement of *biological* means of coercion and power (physical force), firstly by bio-*psychological* means (cleverness, shrewdness, etc.), and secondly, by *social* means (different power symbols, like money). Both, the power of the "clever" and the power of the "rich," represent a departure of the means of power from the original biological basis.

Concomitant to this shift in the actual basis of power in interhuman relations, a transformation of *moral* standards is taking place with reference to the evaluation of different types of coercion. Whereas the overt (physical) types of coercion are being more and more stigmatized and eliminated, the psychological and indirect types of coercion are being either treated as "nonexistent," or at least tolerated as "legitimate." Consequently, the whole fabric of coercive mechanisms *departs more and more from the original biological basis* and grows more and more indirect and disguised. Finally, the "law of force" is replaced by the more respectable "law of deception."

Under normal conditions, these indirect and disguised forms of coercion, legalized by tradition and by mores, are accepted and taken for granted. If they are completely interiorized, they may even cease to be sensed as "coercion." However, in times of an acute social disorganization and ideological disintegration, the growing insecurities and the feeling of being trapped in an invisible but nonetheless unbreakable network of coercion and dependence, of being helpless and powerless to cope with those *evasive* social dangers and pressures, in such times there emerges among the masses the vague, and often repressed, conviction that, after all, it would be perhaps better, and less tantalizing, if all those disguised hostilities and concealed forms of dangers would at last be drawn into the open. It grows and spreads the conviction that those invisible and intangible forms of social relations are sometimes much more dangerous and more monstrous than even the most brutal forms of hostility and coercion. For the latter are, at least, overt and "sincere." Once this stage of social disorganization and ideological confusion is reached, then *not the violence and brutal force but hypocrisy, deception and manipulation may easily become the main target of the hostility of the masses.* And, under such conditions, the fact that those repressed hostilities and disguised forms of coercion are being drawn into the open may even have, psychologically, the effect of a releasing catharsis.

Only against the background of those social experiences and emotional reactions can certain aspects of the psychology of antisemitism be fully understood. In the following section we shall attempt to make explicit the sociopsychological relation which obtains between the "fear of swindlers," predominant in our age, and the "modern" form of antisemitism.

"Politics, as a practice, whatever its profession, had always been the systematic organization of hatred," said Henry Adams in *The Education of Henry Adams*. Antisemitism, as a political weapon, is one of the psychologically most effective forms of a "systematic organization of hatred." Its effectiveness is the consequence of the fact that it appeals to the deep-seated *fear of fraud* which permeates the feeling and thinking of the masses, especially in our age."

The Jews, namely, for various reasons *lend themselves extremely well to be used as an impressive symbol of the "swindler."* In this context it is of no importance to determine what, and how, the Jews "really are." We are trying only to explain why they lend themselves to be used as symbol and target of the "fear of fraud." On the one hand, the Jews by not being either workers, or peasants, or soldiers, symbolize the type of people who although not working in a visible and tangible way, are nevertheless successful, and getting ahead, by performing more or less "mysterious" and "surreptitious" manipulations "behind the scene." On the other hand, the peculiar history of Jews, the lack of their own country, their own state, their own army, the predilection, for whatever reasons it may be, toward living in cities in an industrialized and commercialized atmosphere, has engendered the Jewish attitudes of "worshipping the false intellectual values" of shrewdness and cleverness, and disparaging the "original biological values" of physical strength and physical courage. Thus, in the hands of a diabolically clever propagandist, the Jews became an impressive and convincing symbol of the "up-rooted swindler"—the countersymbol of the "straightforward soldier-peasant-gangster-hero" who is "solidly rooted in blood and soil."

If, therefore, our psychological hypothesis is correct, one of the deeper causes of the political effectiveness of the modern forms of antisemitism is to be found in the fact that it appeals to the widespread and deep-seated, conscious or sub-conscious, fear of, and hostility against the "swindlers" as a personified symbol of all kinds of deception, fraud, manipulation, intrigue, of disguised coercion and intangible oppression. It dramatizes, therefore, the experiences of everyday life in terms of a battle of the straightforward "soldier-hero-gangster" against those uncanny and evasive forces and dangers by which the masses feel themselves threatened, and with which, just because of their evasiveness, they are unable to cope. Thus, the vague fears are released, the focus of identification as well as a personal object of hostility is defined, and the until now invisible and evasive enemy can be at last faced, grasped, and battled.

PATHOS

By William Graham Sumner

SUGGESTION IS POWERFULLY AIDED BY *pathos,* in the original Greek sense of the word. Pathos is the glamour of sentiment which grows up around the pet notion of an age and people, and which protects it from criticism. The Greeks, in the fourth century before Christ, cherished pathos in regard to tyrannicide. Tyrants were bosses, produced by democracy in towns, but hated by democrats. Tyrannicides were surrounded with a halo of heroism and popular admiration. Something of the same sentiment was revived in the sixteenth century, when it appeared that a tyrant was any ruler whose politics one did not like. It cost several rulers their lives. Pathos was a large element in the notions of woman and knighthood (twelfth and thirteenth centuries), of the church (thirteenth century), of the Holy Sepulcher (eleventh and twelfth centuries). In the thirteenth century there was a large element of pathos in the glorification of poverty. A great deal of pathos has been expended on the history and institutions of Greece and Rome in modern times. Classical studies still depend largely on it for their prestige. There is a pathos of democracy in the United States. In all English-speaking countries marriage is an object of pathos. The pathos is cultivated by poetry and novels. Humanitarianism is nourished by pathos and it stimulates pathos. The "poor" and the "laborers" are objects of pathos, on account of which these terms, in literature, refer to a conventional and unreal concept. Consequently there is no honest discussion of any topic which concerns the poor or laborers. Some people make opposition to alcohol an object of pathos.

Whenever pathos is in play the subject is privileged. It is regarded with a kind of affection, and is protected from severe examination. It is made holy or sacred. The thing is cherished with such a preëstablished preference and faith that it is thought wrong to verify it. Pathos, therefore, is unfavorable to truth. It has always been an element in religion. It is an element now in patriotism, and in regard to the history of one's own country. The coercion of pathos on the individual comes in popular disapproval of truth-telling about the matter in question. The toleration for forgery and fraud in the Christian church until modern times, which to modern people seems so shocking and inexplicable, was chiefly due to pathos about religion and the church. If a forgery would help the church or religion, any one who opposed it would seem to be an enemy of religion and the church and willing to violate the pathos which surrounded them.

Reprinted from William Graham Sumner, *Folkways* (Boston: Ginn and Co., 1906), pp. 180–181; copyright 1906 by William Graham Sumner and used with the kind permission of the publisher.

EDUCATION AND THE ATTITUDES

By Harry Lee Swint

[MANY NORTHERNERS who came to the South to teach Negro freedmen immediately after the War Between the States were contemptuous of white Southerners and Southern conditions.] A Georgia teacher wrote her sister that she should be thankful that she was

not a poor *secesh* lady, going about peddling your old 'before the war' clothes, as I often see them doing here, and trying to get plain sewing of the 'Yankee' ladies. Alas! for the poor F. F. G's. What a *glorious* fall they have had—while the 'unbleached American Nobility' are on the topmost round of Fortune's ladder! I am just at this time feeling as if it would be pleasant, had I the power, and an *iron heel* strong enough, to grind every one of the Secessionists deep into the earth. I am feeling more than usually *ugly* toward them as I have just received a visit from an 'Aunty' who has been telling me how our Union prisoners were treated. . . . Tell my friends I am A four-fold Abolitionist. I have seen the effect of slavery in all its forms.

Some of the teachers were especially bitter. One diatribe reveals a strong undercurrent of personal animosity:

What a magnificent revenge Massachusetts has now an opportunity to have upon South Carolina, and especially Boston upon Charleston, for all the sneers and insults heaped upon them by this Southern State and city,—for the expulsion of Judge Hoar, for the betrayal of Daniel Webster, for the beating of Charles Sumner, and for the numberless indignities which the oligarchs of Carolina have delighted to cast upon the sons of the old Bay State.

Oh for one hour of the wizard's cunning, to evolve the spirit of Calhoun from the trance of death, and show him the thronging thousands of the people he despised as brutes, crowding around the school-house doors. . . .

And then to show him the stores of goods sent down from the friendly hands busied around countless firesides at the North, proving that love is the inspiration of liberty, and *brotherhood* the basis of Christian civilization.

And then to tell him that these things come from the New England which he hated; from Boston, which he reviled; and from the abolitionists whom he detested; and that this is the answer Massachusetts makes to South Carolina.

Would this punishment be too severe even for his crimes? Not greater at any rate than that which his *misguided disciples* are suffering here every day. . . .

Not all the teachers looked upon the South with such a completely disapproving eye. One South Carolina teacher was charmed with the South, particularly the picturesque beauty of the pines, Spanish moss, and luxuriant flowers. The Negroes she also found interesting. "The negroes," she wrote, "sang to us in their wild way as they rowed us across— I cannot give you the least idea of it. Indeed, I can't give you the least idea of anything, and you must not expect it."

Adapted from Harry Lee Swint, *The Northern Teacher in the South, 1862–1870* (Nashville: Vanderbilt University Press, 1941), pp. 63–105; copyright 1941 by the Vanderbilt University Press and used with the kind permission of the publisher.

The attitude of the teacher toward the Negro was a continuation of the traditional abolitionist, equalitarian, individualist philosophy. A man was an individual, and his color or race must not be considered. Every trace of racial distinction must be eradicated. The terms "freedman" and "Negro" must be dropped from the national vocabulary. Individuals must be considered simply as individuals, as component units of society, as brothers in the great family, not as members of races, classes, or groups. The humanitarian and educational work of the various societies must deal simply with "*men,* as fellow creatures, fellow citizens, or fellow members of the household of faith." The teacher must "educate not whites nor blacks specifically, but all men equally as members of the same great commonwealth."

This attitude had neither its origin nor its termination in the mind of the Northern teacher. The controversy between the advocates of "racial distinction," or "racial discrimination," and those who bitterly oppose either distinction or discrimination has remained to trouble the relations of the Negro and his white neighbors.

Practically all the teachers seem to have agreed that the Negro was very intelligent and that he learned very quickly. One declared that his "sable friends" journeyed up "the hill difficulty . . . quite as rapidly as our *white* boys and girls." Another declared that if there was any difference in intellect between the Negroes and the whites of Virginia, "the advantage is on the side of the colored people." A third said that the Negroes of Virginia were far more intelligent than the whites. The general opinion seems to have been that the Negro children compared favorably with white children of the North, the older pupils learning even more rapidly than white children because they put forth more effort.

There were some teachers whose enthusiasm led them to make statements so extreme as to raise doubt as to the value of their letters as evidence. One said that in twenty years experience in the schools of Massachusetts and New York he had never seen such "rapid advances made in reading and spelling" as had been made in his school. "The blessing of God seems to be again descending upon the people here," he said. Another asserted that "no class of human beings" had ever developed faster, "in every desirable (*sic*) sense," than the freedmen. "No children learn faster, and but few so fast as these poor plantation children," he wrote. Such statements as these were common:

After several years spent in teaching in *white* schools at the North, I feel no hesitation in saying that these children learn the alphabet, the figures and rudiments of arithemtic, more readily than the whites.

In seven years of teaching at the North. I have not seen a parallel to their appetite for learning, and their active progress.

I have taught white pupils for the last twelve years . . . and never did I see more rapid progress in any school.

In some ten year's experience in the schools of my native state I have never seen greater advancement in the same time. I have never known children commit to memory more readily.

One teacher, who evidently had come into contact with a skilled trader, assured her friends in the North that the "African brethren" were quite capable of caring for themselves. "They are exceedingly keen in their financial calculations. A Wall Street broker would scarcely get ahead of some of them," she said. The Negro studied arithmetic in order to avoid being cheated in business and to learn to detect counterfeit money, said another. One admitted that the Negro might be lazy and grasping, but asserted that the white man was not less so. The tendency toward greed and aggressiveness should be encouraged, as an evidence of the ability of the Negro to take care of himself. Now that he was "relieved from the necessity of supporting (his) master's family" he should be given an opportunity to show what he could do. Their real ability was not understood, even at the North. In fact, they were the equals, if not the superiors, of even the Northern whites, so great was their mental capacity and energy.

Contact with them was stimulating in the extreme. The work was "wholly absorbing," yet even that phrase was inadequate to express the intensity with which mind and soul engaged in the work. Every day revealed some new development of character, some new flash of nobility in the Negro. The Negro had attained a higher moral and spiritual level, a "purer and more vital" nature, than the white. He was unspoiled by civilization. God had richly endowed him, and his nature would expand to a wondrous beauty under "a tender and general culture." The teacher was conscious of a strong "sense of obligation to devote every mental and physical power" to teaching the Negro, and many were determined to "consecrate the brief years of a lifetime" to this work.

These were the expressions of theoretical abolitionists, whose contact with the Negro had been either entirely vicarious, or had been confined to aiding some fugitive in his effort to escape. An awakening was inevitable. No group, whatever its merits, powers, or potentialities, could have realized the expectations of the radical abolitionists. No large group of white people, North or South, could have measured up to the standard which they set. Certainly it was not to be expected that the Negro, who had lived only a few generations in America, could have reached that standard.

Gradually, as continued contact forced upon them the realization that they had overestimated the Negro, the teachers began reluctantly to admit their error. By 1865 some of the most enthusiastic friends of the Negro admitted that it would "take many years to make an economical and thrifty man" of the freedman. There was even doubt whether the educational work of the societies need be carried on any longer. It was a "laudable and a noble work," but could not be sustained "after the novelty" was over. By this time there was "a lethargy" among the Northern people, a general agreement that the Negro "must make the most of his chances and pick up his a, b, c's as he can." "Of course," said E. S. Philbrick, "there is not much enthusiasm about sending teachers South to teach the poor whites, so the negro suffers from the magnitude of the undertaking, from his remoteness from view, and the general disposition among mankind to let everybody hoe their own weeds so long as they don't shade one's own garden."

Less philosophical and even more definite opinions were expressed by other teachers and agents. In discussing a group of 120 laborers a superintendent declared that the satisfaction derived from the honesty of thirty was insufficient to atone for the anxiety caused by the remaining ninety "who lie by habit and steal on the least provocation." "From them," he declared, "all the artifices of a lawyer cannot draw a fair statement of fact, even when it is obviously for their own interest to tell the whole truth. 'Wherefore he is called the everlasting Niggah.' " Their dishonesty was most discouraging. They were, he declared, "almost incorrigible." During the winter of 1865 and 1866 the Sea Island Negroes were "stealing cotton at a fearful rate," and the superintendents felt "such rascality" to be "more discouraging than caterpillars and drought." The "untrustworthiness" of the Negroes was a source of great annoyance to their Northern friends. "Their skill in lying, their great reticence, their habit of shielding one another (generally by silence), their invariable habit of taking a rod when you, after much persuasion, have been induced to grant an inch . . . joined with an amazing impudence in making claims—these are the traits which try us continually," wrote an agent.

One disillusioned abolitionist and teacher published a very critical article. Contrary to his expectations, he said, he had never seen parents "more apathetic." "Certainly the expression of affection is rare to any children who are old enough to get out of the way." The children were frequently whipped, but the whippings were evidently less painful than "the usual New England chastisement." After careful consideration of the subject, this writer doubted that the slaves, "as a class," had suffered as much, "body and mind together," as did the laboring classes in "our Northern cities," who suffered from "want, anxiety and responsibility."

When the teachers first entered the South they found the whites suspicious, cold, but not bitter toward them. There was no active persecution, no physical assault. They were not harmed, but were "entirely passed by, and looked upon with contempt." They were not accepted socially; and they received neither visits nor invitations. At some places even the Unionists refused to associate with them. A teacher at Portsmouth, Virginia, complained that there were "supposed to be some white Unionists" there, but she could not find one who would "shelter a teacher of the 'contrabands.' " As late as 1865 a North Carolina teacher could say: "The whites treat us so-so; the men now and then lift their *hats* while the ladies for variety almost invariably *lift* their *noses*. But we pay little or no attention to either, and 'work goes marching on.' " At Lexington, Virginia, the teachers were the objects of the ribald laughter and taunts of college students and small-town hangers-on. One wrote that on her first visit to town some college students followed her into a store, and then called to their companions to "come take a look at the Yankee, at .25 (*sic*) a look." Corner louts sneered and laughed at her and her companions when they appeared on the street. "From one set of students, whose boarding-house I was compelled constantly to pass, I habitually received the polite salutation of 'damned Yankee bitch of a nigger teacher,' with the occasional admonition to take up my abode in the infernal regions."

The possibility that they were being persecuted as missionaries rather than as Yankees does not seem to have occurred to the teachers. The fact that the members of any group feel a keen resentment toward those who come into their midst as missionaries was well stated by a Republican tax assessor in Georgia, who was also a trustee of Atlanta University. His testimony before the Congressional Committee on Affairs in the Insurrectionary States is rather remarkable. He said that the Negroes were, in many cases, "insolent," and that they had demanded "certain rights without knowing exactly what their rights" were. The white people had been "exceedingly arrogant" and unwilling even to hear the requests of the Negroes. Sentiment was, in general, opposed to Negro education, and he had "heard of" the burning of schoolhouses.

It was his opinion that teaching in a Negro school would exclude any individual from "what is called society" in Georgia.

"Even Republican families of reasonably good standing" would not recognize such teachers, for "by so doing they would exclude themselves from society." In response to the question, whether "people who go as missionaries to the heathen, even to the lowest type of heathenism, would not lose caste thereby," he said, "They would not lose caste at home, neither would these teachers from New England lose caste in New England, but the missionaries might lose caste in China."

WHAT'S RACE AMONG FRIENDS?

By Samuel McChord Crothers

IT IS PLEASANT not only to know what wise men have thought about friendship, but how friendly souls have actually felt. There must be a vast variety in the incidents of friendships and a unity in its essential nature. No abstract or philosophical description can satisfy us in regard to an intimate personal experience which we all have felt.

I can imagine a warm-hearted friend reading Emerson's Essay on Friendship, and wondering what it is all about.

"Why should we desecrate noble and beautiful souls by intruding on them? Why insist on rash personal relations with your friend? Why go to his house and know his mother or brother or sisters? Why be visited by him at your own? Are these material to our covenant? Leave this touching and clawing. Let him be to me a spirit." . . . "The hues of the opal, the light of the diamond, are not to be seen if the eye is too near. To my friend I write a letter and receive a letter. That seems to you a letter. It suffices me. It is a spiritual gift worthy of him to give and of me to receive. It profanes nobody." . . . "I do then with my friends as I do with my books. I would have them where I can find them, but I seldom use them. We must have society on our own terms and admit or exclude on the slightest cause. I cannot afford to speak much with my friends."

To the ordinary person there is something chilly in all this. But if we cannot feel, or desire to feel in just this way toward those whom we call our friends, we can at least try to understand what Emerson meant. To him friendship was something sacred. The friend was the elect soul who stood always for the ideal best. For him to fall short of the ideal was to forfeit his sacred office. Friendship and Duty were from this point of view identical; for it is the friend who points the way and keeps us in it.

It is a far cry from Emerson's ethereal friendship with its fastidious with-

Reprinted from Samuel McChord Crothers, *The Book of Friendship* (New York: The Macmillan Company, 1910), pp. vi–xii, and used with the kind permission of the publisher.

drawal from all personal contact, to the friendship of Huckleberry Finn and Negro Jim as they lie sprawling on the raft in the middle of the Mississippi. Neither of them would have understood the high moods of the spirit. Neither of them illustrated the dignity of human nature. One was a specimen of the "poor white trash" as it existed on the great river, and the other was a runaway slave. They had not chosen one another; they had literally been "thrown together" as by a careless Fate. They had shared the same crusts, they had smoked together and fished off the same log, and lied and stolen in the common cause of self-preservation. In all this there was nothing consciously ethical or inspiring. When Huckleberry Finn's conscience did assert itself, it was by way of protest against this friendship. His conscience was vague on most points, but one thing he knew to be wrong. Whatever other form of stealing might be condoned, he was clear in regard to the heinousness of the sin of stealing a slave from his lawful owner. When he slipped off the raft determined to give the information that would send Jim back to slavery, he felt that he was about to do a noble act.

Then he lost his nerve. He refused to obey his inward monitor and sneaked back to his companion. "I got aboard the raft feeling bad and low, because I knowed very well I had done wrong, and I see it warn't no use for me to learn to do right: a body that don't get *started* right when he's little ain't got no show —when the pinch comes, there ain't nothing to back him up and keep him to his work, and so he gets beat. Then I thought a minute, and says to myself, hold on, s'pose you'd a done right and give Jim up, would you have felt better than what you do now? No, says I, I'd feel bad—I'd feel just the same way I do now. Well, then, says I, what's the use you learning to do right when it's troublesome to do right and ain't no trouble to do wrong, and the wages is just the same? I was stuck. I couldn't answer that. So I reckoned I wouldn't bother no more about it, but after this always do whichever come handiest at the time."

Huckleberry Finn was unable to apologize for the impulse upon which he acted. It seemed to him a weakness—which he accepted just as he accepted his other manifold weaknesses. He was used to yielding to temptation, and here was another. He was aware that he ought to give Jim up, and he would have done it if he hadn't known him so well, and if Jim hadn't trusted him. He couldn't quite make up his mind to go back on his friend.

Better heads than Huckleberry Finn's have been puzzled over the problems of friendship and have failed as ignominiously when they have attempted a formal solution. For a friend is always an exception to the abstract laws which our reason accepts. We confess this when we say that we are "partial" to certain persons. We are not willing to hand them over to the tender mercies of universal law. We want to shield them, and to give them a little better chance.

It is not that our friends are wiser and better than other people, but that we know them better. The accident of contiguity may have first given them a place in our affections, but now they cannot be removed from that place without causing us pain. They make our familiar world. They are a part of our environment to which we have become happily wonted. We take them as they are, with the frank acknowledgment that to us they are not as other men are, but form a privileged class. We find it easy to forgive their shortcomings, and their good points are all the better because they belong to them. Nor are we satisfied with thinking of them as unrelated personalities. We take them into our hearts with all their natural belongings. We want to know their brothers and their sisters, and to have them drop in to see us.

But after all, Emerson's idea of friendship and Huckleberry Finn's meet at the essential point. Friendship is "attachment" and not detachment. A friend is one to whom we are pleasantly drawn. "It wasn't any trouble" to have old Jim on the raft, and it would have been very lonesome to have him taken away.

A friend is one whom you like to have with you when you are doing what you most like to do. If what you most like to do is to dwell upon the ideally perfect, your friend is the one who meets you in these rare moments. The vision of spiritual beauty is not more than half real till it is shared with him. In the consciousness that another mind reflects your thought, you find the keenest satisfaction. Here is the high office of a friend, and in these high experiences is the point of attachment.

But because thou art virtuous, shall Friendship have no cakes and ale for those less highly endowed? Happily, Friendship is the most accommodating of all the virtues. She is easy to be entreated and has something for all sorts and conditions of men. Personal attachments are within the reach of the humblest. If our idea of perfect bliss is to go fishing, and loaf in the woods, and float down a river on a raft, we may still have a friend. He is the one whose presence is no intrusion, and whose conversation conveys no reproach. Are we lazy, so is he; are we hungry, he also enjoys his victuals. If the world be against us, all the more do we draw together. To hate the same people and to reject their advice is a real bond.

Friendship rises into the heights of disinterested virtue, but it begins where life begins. It is mingled with the earliest experience, and it exists among the ferocities of the primitive struggle for existence. St. Augustine, referring to Virgil's story of the unsocial giant Cacus dwelling in his dreary cavern without wife or child or friend, said: "It is better to believe that such a man, or semi-man, never existed, and that this in common with many other fancies of the poets is a mere fiction. For the most savage animals encompass their own species with a ring of protecting peace." . . . What tigress does not gently purr over her cubs and lay aside her ferocity to fondle them. What kite, solitary as he is when circling over his prey, does not seek a mate to build the nest and maintain peace.

Friendships have been formed not alone by the fireside of the home or in some sacred place, but by soldiers on the march, by wanderers on the highways, by boys roving the streets in gangs, by pirates upon the high seas, by scholars, and by men of affairs. Wherever there is "something doing," the law of friendship asserts itself. The laws of evolutionary progress favor it. The unfriendly deed is barren. Friendly coöperation multiplies power. A company of friends conscious of a common purpose, trusting each other, and subordinating individual preferences can achieve success.

In the third and fourth centuries, piety took an unsocial, not to say a morose, form. The idea was to get away from the wicked world and renounce one's natural relations. Hundreds of ascetics fled from their homes to the deserts of Egypt in search of a solitary goodness. The sand hills were honeycombed with the cells of these hermits. But by and by human nature asserted itself. The anchorite who had fled from his neighbors couldn't prevent them from following his example. The desert began to be populous. It was a great experience for the unsocial saint when he discovered that the other saint whom he met every morning at the well was not such a bad fellow after all. So after a while all the cells came to be under one roof, and spiritual isolation gave way to the organized friendliness of the monasteries.

Human life, like all other life, has from some standpoints a sinister aspect. There seems to be a natural hostility between all living creatures. Their interests seem necessarily to conflict. One species devours another. One individual of the species crowds out others who are less fit for the struggle. Friendship at first seems but a feeble and futile protest against a grim reality. It is the expression of a personal preference. Before the bar of Necessity it pleads for tender treatment for a few whom we may have happened to know intimately. "These are my friends, deal gently with them." As if it mattered.

But the wonderful thing is that it does matter. Friendship, at the beginning so narrow in its scope and so fitful in its action, grows at last into a world power. If conditions are hard, it creates new conditions. It becomes a creative force. What are we working for but to make the world a better place for our friends to live in?

> "Love from its awful throne of patient power
> In the wise heart,"

is all the time working toward this end. Already human institutions have a more friendly aspect. There is a world-wide conspiracy against those cruel powers which have for ages held sway. We are coming to believe that the friendly way is also the strong and wise way.

It is because of this that a Book of Friendship is a Primer of Civilization. It contains the first lessons which must be learned by those who would work for a better social order. All the high loyalties rest on one discovery—the discovery of the worth of a friend. It is surely worth our while to learn as much as possible of the lore of the heart.

PART VIII

The Study and Control

of Race Relations

INTRODUCTION

THE SCIENTIFIC STUDY of race relations, and the effort to effect some degree of rational control over these relations, are recent phases of a long historical movement which must have begun with the contact and mutual curiosity of peoples strange to the sight and to the ways of each other. Perhaps no combination of exotic peoples anywhere or anytime has been stranger or any more remarkable than the combination of Englishmen and Negroes in contact with native Indians on the shores of colonial Virginia. Among them there must have been, originally, a great deal of speculative conversation such as that which we know developed later over the "wellnigh inscrutable Negro soul." However, in the generality of such situations where different peoples mingle on the same soil, things tend to settle down and men come to take each other more or less for granted until and unless some kind of issue develops. In America the issue came to be over the enslavement of labor. Until the Civil War there was a great deal of discussion about the morality of Negro slavery but not nearly so much about race as such except as it figured in the justification of slavery. Slavery was destroyed by the Civil War but the Negro remained, and then the discussion moved down to the more fundamental question of race. The enormous amount of this discussion has not solved the race problem, but perhaps it is at last beginning to raise among the generality of people, and not just among students and scholars, the question of just what society, the business of collective living, is all about.

America is now in a period of *Aufklärung,* a period of clearing up, in which

[513]

everything is being questioned as in the days of Socrates in Greece. Among other things, we are trying to clear up some things about race. In this field, as in others, our oral traditions are being superseded by a large and growing literature most of which is controversial in character. A great deal of this literature does not tell us much about race, but it does reveal the intensity of the racial conflict and the nature of the passions involved.

It was inevitable that interest in the subject of race should find its way into academic institutions. During the past several decades American college courses on immigration have given place to courses on the Negro and other minority groups, and there seems to be a tendency at present for these in turn to give way to more general courses on race and race relations. In Europe this subject is more likely to be studied under the rubric of colonial sociology. American teachers drew originally upon the large literature and upon their personal experiences and knowledge. Now the textbooks are beginning to appear. What, in your opinion, are the changes incident to the introduction of textbooks into a field of study and especially into a field such as that of race relations? What changes occur when the professors begin to quarrel among themselves as German, French, English and American professors have quarreled over the nature and meaning of race?

Popular and academic discussion of the race problem has contributed to its secularization, and it is this which has led students to seek such a statement of the problem as would stimulate, not more discussion, but inquiry and research. What do you regard as the central theoretical problem involved in the study of race? In the study of race relations? Can you suggest a research project in race relations which seems to you to promise more light on this central problem? Do you have any suggestions on how comparative census and tax data from different race relations regions might be more effectively used in the study of race relations? What might be done to increase the comparability of future census data? Discussing the census in the *Encyclopedia Brittanica* Sir Percival Vivian said, "The whole field of statistics can be viewed as concerned with either personnel or material. . . . The census as an instrument for the collection of information is predominantly concerned with aspects of personnel. . . . It is unable to elucidate any subject except as an attribute of the individual man or woman. . . . It is useless to make any inquiry respecting which individuals may have any conscious motive, real or fancied, for suppressing or distorting the facts." What are the implications of these remarks for the use of the census in the study of race and race relations? Does a census count help authenticate the existence of a race, or does it contribute toward breaking down a race into a collection of individuals? To what extent do governmental and industrial regulation and administration require increasing census classification and discriminaton?

What are the 1) advantages and 2) the disadvantages of personal involvement in any particular study of race relations? In what way or ways can the race of the investigator influence or effect research and the outcome of research in race relations? What can be learned by members of the dominant group that cannot be learned by members of the subordinate group, and vice versa? What advantage, if any, does the so-called marginal man have as investigator in the study of race relations? What advantage, if any, does the outsider, *e.g.,* Myrdal, Schrieke, Dollard, and others, have in the study of race relations?

What do you understand by "the sociology of racial knowledge"? What is the connection, if any, between the popular knowledge and the scientific knowledge of race and race relations? Is popular racial knowledge merely a random collection of beliefs and practices, or does it contain some fairly well-organized and consistent theory of race, the nature of man and social relationships generally, and human nature? What is likely to be the difference between the racial knowledge of those who look down upon, and those who look up to, the members of another race? What kind of racial knowledge would you expect the governmental administrator, the employer of labor, the missionary, the trader, and the competitor to have? In various situations and associations who emerges as the "expert" on the subject of race? Does not the planter differ from the ordinary farmer as one who is presumed to have some special knowledge of the nature of his labor of another race as well as knowledge of how to grow the crop? When Southern whites claim to "know" the Negro, what is the nature of the knowledge involved? One widely distributed brochure described the experiences of a white newspaper reporter who, passing as a Negro, moved freely inside the social world of Negroes in the South. What is the conception of race which leads to investigation by disguise? To what extent have the values of American society determined the problems and even the conclusions of research in race relations in this country? To what extent is the "science" of race relations in American "science"? Is there a separate "science" of race relations?

What areas of control reveal inadequacies in the theory of race relations? Upon what theories of race do modern organizations, agencies and programs for the amelioration and control of race relations rest? What is the conception of race and race relations which views 1) eugenics, 2) strict subordination and segregation, 3) return to Africa, 4) amalgamation, 5) assimilation and integration as the best solution of the problem? Can you suggest some acceptable face-saving formula for both whites and Negroes as a way of easing present social changes in America? What are the chances for engineering overt race conflict into a sort of secularized race politics proceeding according to the rules of American politics generally?

THE UNKNOWABLE NEGRO

By Reed Smith

THE NEGRO is a superlative actor and pantomimist, and lets the white man see and know just what the Negro wishes him to—and no more.

Failure to take this into account leads to strange conclusions. It is the reason why so many visiting observers, even though earnest and sincere, have received and recorded impressions of the Negro in the South that are highly plausible—and more highly erroneous.

Following are three well-balanced expressions on this point, two looking to the present, the third looking toward the past:

(1) William Pickens, himself a Negro, says: "Till this day the Negro is seldom frank to the white man in America. He says what he does not mean; he means what he does not say. . . . This is one reason for the great misconception in the white race respecting the desires, ambitions and sentiments of the black." *The New Negro, His Political and Civil Status and Related Essays,* p. 37.

(2) Mr. Gonzales says: "Of all the inscrutable peoples of the Eastern world, none is more secretive than the Negro, nor any so puzzling to the psychologist, for while it is easy to know that deceit lurks behind the mask of engaging frankness with which he seeks to disarm those who doubt him, the exact nature of the deceit can seldom be discerned. Review of Charles C. Jones, *Negro Myths From the Georgia Coast.*

(3) Dr. Stanhope Sams, literary editor of "The State," looks to the Negro's past: "There is a dark region beyond the mind and soul of the Negro of the slave plantation that may never be explored. No trained and well equipped psychologist, so far as I know, has ever attempted this magnificent research. Certainly none of the Negro students of the race has seemed to get even so near as white students have approached. So far as I have ever seen in their writings or heard in their speech, DuBois and Booker Washington did not enter that primeval jungle. And it is not possible now, perhaps, to 'restore' this primitive jungle race and lore. It would be a far more difficult task than the restoration of Kish or Ur, or to bring back to earth some semblance of the mysterious Sumerians. There we have at least a tablet or stele or monument to help; but we must decipher the Negro of the days of the Pharaohs and of Carthage and of the impenetrable backward and abysm of time that stretches like an uncharted sea behind the African Negro from the modern Negro in America or Africa.

"At all events, as it seems, the contact he must have had with cultured Egyptians and Carthaginians left no enduring record. It is possible—despite some vague beginnings of civilization in certain parts of Black Africa—that the only lasting betterment in conditions the Negro has yet known or held has been received during and since he became a slave in the Southern States.

Reprinted from Reed Smith, *Gullah* (Columbia: Bureau of Publications, University of South Carolina, 1926), pp. 11–12, with the kind permission of the publisher.

"It remains an alluring, but a chimerical adventure—this attempt to learn what the Negro was before his contact with us.

"On their own part, the Negroes seem to have formed a conspiracy of silence. Possibly they suffered too profoundly, were hurt too bitterly, to tell us their own story. They preferred, doubtless, to leave it behind them in the engulfing and obliterating jungle. They must have known, must have remembered, those first slaves, and they have always had the genius for story-telling and singing. Yet they tell no stories that reveal their previous march, sing no songs—except with borrowed music, and fill their mythologies with the animals and beings of the world that bound and enslaved them."

THE PLANTER AS EXPERT IN MATTERS OF RACE

UPON A QUESTION, whether a person is a *free negro,* it is competent for one, who says he is the owner and manager of slaves, and has been for twelve years, that he has given much attention to the effects of the intermixture of the races, and believes he can distinguish between the descendants of the negro and white person and negro and Indian, and whether a person has more or less African blood in him, to testify as an *expert.*

INDICTMENT against the defendant, as a free negro, for carrying firearms, against the form of the Act of Assembly, tried before *Heath, J.,* at BRUNSWICK.

The State introduced one Pritchett, who swore that he knew the defendant, and had known him as long as he had known any one; that he had never seen any of defendant's ancestors, and knew nothing of them from reputation. Thereupon the solicitor, with a view of showing that witness was qualified to speak as an expert, inquired of him what business and occupation he followed, and what knowledge and observation he had, if any, of the effect of the intermixture of negro or African blood with that of other races. The counsel for the defendant objected that, as the witness did not profess to have any knowledge of defendant's ancestry by actual knowledge or reputation, he could not be permitted to testify as to whether the defendant was a free negro or not. The Court held that the witness might be permitted to answer the question propounded, in order that it might be seen whether he was qualified to testify as an expert.

The witness then stated that he was a planter, an owner and manager of slaves, and had been for more than twelve years; that he had paid much attention to and had had much observation of the effects of the intermixture of negro or African blood with the white and Indian races, and that from such attention and observation he was well satisfied that he could distinguish be-

From "State v. Asa Jacobs," 51 *North Carolina Reports,* 282–286 (1859).

tween the descendants of a negro and a white person, and the descendants of a negro and Indian; and further, that he could therefrom also say whether a person was full African or negro, or had more or less than half negro or African blood in him, and whether the cross or intermixture was white or Indian blood.

The witness was admitted to testify, and stated his opinion to be that the defendant was what is called a mulatto—that is, half African and half white. The defendant's counsel excepted to the admission of this evidence, and upon defendant's conviction, appealed to this Court.

Attorney-General and *K. P. Battle,* for the State.

Baker, for the defendant.

BATTLE, J. The sole question presented on the record is whether the witness, Pritchett, was competent to testify as an expert, that the defendant was a descendant of an African ancestor. An expert, in the strict sense of the word, is defined to be "a person instructed by experience." But more generally speaking, the term includes "all men of science"; as it was used by *Lord Mansfield,* in *Folkes v. Chadd,* 3 Doug., 157, "or persons conversant with the subject matter, on questions of science, skill, trade, and others of the like kind." Best's Principles of Evidence, sec. 346; 1 Gr. Ev., note to sec. 440. The rule on this subject is stated by Mr. Smith in his note to *Carter v. Boehm,* 1 Smith Lead. Cas., 286: "On the one hand it appears to be admitted that the opinion of witnesses, possessing peculiar skill, is admissible whenever the subject matter of inquiry is such that inexperienced persons are unlikely to prove capable of forming a correct judgement upon it without such assistance; in other words, where it so far partakes of the nature of science as to require a course of previous habit or study in order to the attainment of a knowledge of it; while, on the other hand, it does not seem to be contended that the opinion of witnesses can be received when the inquiry is into a subject matter, the nature of which is not such as to require any peculiar habits or study in order to qualify a man to understand it." In support of the principles thus announced, it has been decided that seal-engravers may be called to give their opinion upon an impression, whether it was made from an original seal, or from another impression. *Folkes v. Chadd,* Doug., *ubi supra.* So the opinion of an artist in painting is evidence of the genuineness of a picture. *Ibid.* It has been said that the genuineness of a postmark may be proved by the opinion of one who has been in the habit of receiving letters with that mark. *Abbey v. Hill,* 5 Bing., 299. A shipbuilder may give his opinion as to the seaworthiness of a ship, on facts stated by others. *Thornton v. The Royal Exch. Ass. Co.,* 1 Peake, 25. Merchants and bankers, who are daily engaged in handling the notes of particular banks, and have thus become thoroughly acquainted with their whole appearance, may prove whether a particular note is genuine or counterfeit. *State v. Harris,* 27 N.C., 287. Persons accustomed to observe the habits of a certain kind of fish have been permitted to give in evidence their opinions as to the ability of the fish to overcome certain obstructions in the rivers which they were accustomed to ascend. *Cottrill v. Myrick,* 3 Fairf., 222. Many other instances of the application of the principle might be given, but those to which we have referred are sufficient to show that it is extensive enough to embrace the case now before us. The effect of the intermixture of the blood of different races of people is surely a matter of science, and may be learned by observation and study. Nor does it require a distinguished comparative anatomist to detect the admixture of the African or Indian with the pure blood of the white race. Any person of ordinary intelligence, who, for a sufficient length of time will devote his attention to the subject, will be able to discover with almost unerring certainty the adulteration of the Caucasian with the negro or Indian blood. This is incidentally implied in the following extract from the work of Nott & Gliddon on the "Types of Mankind," which will be found on page 260: "Mr. Lyell, in common with tourists less eminent, but on this subject not less misinformed, has somewhere stated that the negroes in America are undergoing a manifest improvement in their physical type. He has no doubt that they will in time show a development in skull and intellect quite equal to the whites. This unscientific assertion is disproved by the cranial measurements of Dr Morton." After admitting some physical improvements on account of the increased comforts with which the negroes are here supplied, the authors add, "One or two generations of domestic culture effect all the improvement of which negro organism is susceptible. We possess thousands of the second and many more of negro families of the eighth or tenth generations in the United States, and (where undulterated with white blood) they are identical in physical and intellectual characters. No one in this country pretends to distinguish the native son of a negro from his great-grandchild (except through occasional and ever apparent admixture of white or Indian blood), while it requires the keen and experienced eye of such a comparative anatomist as Agassiz to detect structural peculiarities in our few African-born slaves. The improvement among Americanized negroes noticed by Mr. Lyell, in his progress from South to North, are solely due to those ultra-ecclesiastical amalgamations, which, in their illegitimate consequences, have deteriorated the white element in direct proportion that they are said to have improved the black." It is here clearly implied that even a common observer may discover from the outward appearance the intermixture of the white and black races, and on that account it may perhaps be said that to be able to do so is not a matter of science or skill. It may well be admitted that simply to be able to detect the presence of African blood by the color or other physical qualities of the person, is not a matter of science, but it will by no means follow that a qualification to ascertain the extent of the negro blood is not so. On the contrary, we believe that it would often require an eye rendered keen by observation and practice to detect, with any approach to certainty, the existence of anything less than one-fourth of African blood in a subject. A free negro, so far as he is noticed as such in our law, is defined (Rev. Code, ch. 107, sec. 79) to be one who is "descended from negro ancestors to the fourth generation inclusive, though one ancestor of each generation may have been a white person." He may, therefore, be a person who, as we said in *State v. Chavers,* 50 N.C., 11, has only a sixteenth part of African blood in his veins. The ability to discover the infusion of so small a quantity of negro blood in one claiming the privilege of a white man, must be a matter of science, and, therefore, admitting of the testimony of an expert; and we think that the witness, Pritchett, proved in the present case that he possessed the necessary qualification to testify as such.

PER CURIAM.   Judgement affirmed.

THEY KNEW THEY WERE HUMAN ALL THE TIME

By Gunnar Myrdal

THE SPLIT IN THE AMERICAN SOUL HAS BEEN, and still is, reflected in scientific thought and in the literature on the Negro race and its characteristics. Thomas Jefferson, the author of the Declaration of Independence and the supreme exponent of early American liberalism, in his famous *Notes on Virginia* (1781–1782) deals with the Negro problem in a chapter on "The Administration of Justice and the Description of the Laws." He posits his ideas about race as an argument for emancipating the slaves, educating them, and assisting them to settle in Africa:

> Deep-rooted prejudices entertained by the whites; ten thousand recollections, by the blacks, of the injuries they have sustained; new provocations; the real distinctions which nature has made; and many other circumstances, will divide us into parties, and produce convulsions, which will probably never end but in the extermination of the one or the other race.

He goes on to enumerate the "real distinctions" between Negroes and whites and gives a fairly complete list of them as they were seen by liberal people of his time: color, hair form, secretion, less physiological need of sleep but sleepiness in work, lack of reasoning power, lack of depth in emotion, poverty of imagination and so on. In all these respects he is inclined to believe that "it is not their condition, then, but nature, which has produced the distinction." But he is cautious in tone, has his attention upon the fact that popular opinions are prejudiced, and points to the possibility that further scientific studies may, or may not, verify his conjectures.

This guarded treatment of the subject marks a high point in the early history of the literature on Negro racial characteristics. In critical sense and in the reservation for the results of further research, it was not surpassed by white writers until recent decades. As the Civil War drew nearer, intellectuals were increasingly mobilized to serve the Southern cause and to satisfy the Southern needs for rationalization. After Reconstruction their theories were taken over by the whole nation. Biology and ethnology were increasingly supplanting theology and history in providing justification for slavery and, later, caste. Even the friends of the Negroes assumed great racial differences, even if, out of charity, they avoided elaborating on them. The numerous enemies of the Negro left a whole crop of pseudo-scientific writings in the libraries, emphasizing racial differences. Robert W. Shufeldt's book, *America's Greatest Problem: the Negro* which had considerable influence for a time—illustrating the inferiority argument by a picture of a Negro lad between two monkeys and filled with an imposing mass of presumed evidences for Negro inferiority— is a late example of this literature at its worst.

Reprinted from Gunnar Myrdal, *An American Dilemma* (9th ed.; New York: Harper and Brothers, 1944), pp. 89–97; copyright 1944 by Harper and Brothers and used with the kind permission of the publisher.

Without much change this situation continued into the twentieth century. At this time the heavily prejudiced position of science on the race problem was, however, beginning to be undermined. Professor Franz Boas and a whole school of anthropologists had already come out against these arguments for racial differences based on the primitive people's lack of culture. The outlines of a radically environmentalistic sociology were being drawn by W. G. Sumner, W. I. Thomas and C. H. Cooley. The early research on intelligence pronounced that there were considerable racial differences but it had already encountered some doubts as to validity. Improved techniques in the fields of anatomy and anthropometry had begun to disprove earlier statements on Negro physical traits.

The last two or three decades have seen a veritable revolution in scientific thought on the racial characteristics of the Negro. This revolution has actually a much wider scope: it embraces not only the whole race issue even outside the Negro problem, but the fundamental assumptions on the nature-nurture question. The social sciences in America, and particularly sociology, anthropology, and psychology, have gone through a conspicuous development, increasingly giving the preponderance to environment instead of to heredity.

As creators of original scientific theories and as independent research workers in the field of social science, as in other fields, the Negroes came late and are even now rather exceptional. This is a consequence of the American caste system. But for a much longer time they have had gifted essayists well in touch with the trends in social sciences. From the beginning, Negro writers took the stand that the American dogma of racial inequality was a scientific fake. The late Kelly Miller, particularly, knew how to present the Negro's case effectively. In *Out of the House of Bondage* (1914) he had well digested the anthropological criticism against the argument that the Negroes had never produced a culture of their own in Africa and knew how to turn it around:

Because any paricular race or class has not yet been caught up by the current of the world movement is no adequate reason to conclude that it must forever fall without the reach of its onward flow. If history teaches any clear lesson, it is that civilization is communicable to the tougher and hardier breeds of men, whose physical stamina can endure the awful stress of transmission. To damn a people to everlasting inferiority because of deficiency in historical distinction shows the same faultiness of logic as the assumption that what never has been never can be. The application of this test a thousand years ago would have placed under the ban of reproach all of the vigorous and virile nations of modern times.

Concerning the physical disabilities of the Negro, he was full of scorn:

Do you recall the school of pro-slavery scientists who demonstrated beyond doubt that the Negro's skull was too thick to comprehend the substance of Aryan knowledge? Have you not read in the now discredited scientific books of that period with what triumphant acclaim it was shown that the shape and size of the Negro's skull, facial angle, and cephalic configuration rendered him forever impervious to the white man's civilization? But all enlightened minds are now as ashamed of that doctrine as they are of the one-time dogma that the Negro had no soul.

If at the time when he was writing, he could have seen the modern development of intelligence research he would have had still more arrows for his bow.

Miller has been quoted at some length here because his attitude is typical of the thinking of the intellectual Negroes on this issue for several decades, in fact, from the first time the Negro people had a group of individuals trained to independent scholarly thinking. These early Negro intellectuals were in all certainty just as much driven by their rationalization interests as their white colleagues. Only their interest went in the opposite direction. In the development of intelligence research it is apparent that Negroes and members of other minority groups always had a tendency to find environmental explanations for differences in intelligence performance, while the "American" scientists and, particularly, Southerners and other Americans who for one reason or other felt tender toward the Southern cause, for a long time labored under the bias of expecting to find innate differences.

From one point of view it is, of course, merely an historical accident that modern research has tended to confirm the Negroes' view and not the whites'. The Negro writers constantly have proceeded upon the assumption, later formulated by Du Bois in *Black Reconstruction:* ". . . that the Negro in America and in general is an average and ordinary human being, who under given environment develops like other human beings. . . ." This assumption is now, but was not a couple of decades ago, also the assumption of white writers. Negro writings from around the turn of the century, therefore, sound so much more modern than white writings. It is mainly this historical accident which explains why, for example, Du Bois' study of the Philadelphia Negro community, published in the 'nineties, stands out even today as a most valuable contribution, while white authors like H. W. Odum and C. C. Brigham have been compelled—and have had the scientific integrity and personal courage—to retreat from writings of earlier decades even though they were published after Du Bois' study. The white authors have changed while the Negro authors can stand by their guns. It is also apparent, when going through the literature on the Negro, that the whole tone, the "degree of friendliness" in viewpoints and conclusions, has been modified immensely in favor of the Negro since the beginning of the 'twenties. This trend is, of course, intimately related to the general trend in social sciences and to the still broader political and social development in the American nation.

The Negro intellectuals' resistance to the white race dogma has been widely popularized among the Negro people through the Negro press, the Negro school and the Negro pulpit. As it corresponds closely to Negro interests, it will now be found to emerge as a popular belief in all Negro communities in America, except the backward ones. It may be assumed that formerly the Negroes more often took over white beliefs as a matter of accommodation.

The spread of the same conclusions from modern research has been much slower among whites, which is also natural, as they do not coincide with their interest in defending the caste order, and in any case, do not have the same relevance to their own personal problems of adjustment. One most important result is, however, that *it is now becoming difficult for even popular writers to express other views than the ones of racial equalitarianism and still retain intellectual respect.* This inhibition works also on the journalists, even in the South and even outside of the important circle of Southern white liberals. The final result of this changing might, in time, be considerable. Research and education are bolstering the American Creed in its influence toward greater equalitarianism.

FROM SACRED TO SECULAR IN THE LITERATURE OF RACE RELATIONS

By Edward B. Reuter

THE TITLE OF THIS VOLUME implies a degree of social unity and racial solidarity among American Negroes that is not a fully accomplished fact. The time may come—conceivably, it may come soon—when the Negroes will be fused into a race-conscious minority, animated by a common wish and presenting a united front in a struggle for clearly defined objectives. But in the present both the strength and the weakness of the Negroes' position lie in the fact that they are not a fully organized and self-conscious minority. They are held together by external factors restricting their participation in the communal life rather than by exclusive sentiments and internal bonds. What the Negro wants can be stated only in terms that would be largely or wholly unintelligible to the mass of the Negroes. To be realistic, and at the same time to do full justice to the contributors to this symposium, it is necessary to read the title as "What Negroes Want."

Most of the contributors to the volume are not professional students of social or racial relations, but each is a person of note in some field of Negro endeavor. Mary McLeod Bethune is president of the National Council of Negro Women; Sterling A. Brown is in the English department and Rayford W. Logan is in the history department of Howard University; W. E. B. Dubois is director of special research and Roy Wilkins is assistant secretary of the National Association for the Advancement of Colored People; Gordon B. Handcock is a teacher of economics; Leslie Pinckney Hill, Frederick D. Paterson, and Charles H. Wesley are college presidents; Langston Hughes is a poet and writer; A. Philip Randolph is president of the Brotherhood of Sleeping Car Porters; George S. Schuyler is a newspaper editor; Willard S. Townsend is president of the "Red Caps"; and Doxey A. Wilkerson is vice-president of the International Workers' League.

The Negroes want what all other men of comparable experience and status want. The masses want food, shelter, a cessation of gratuitous physical abuse, and other elementary necessaries of a tolerable animal existence. From this level, the desires increase in number and kind and, through varying stages and combinations, to those that characterize sensitive and civilized men. As stated by the contributors to this symposium, they want nothing new or startling, nothing that could be reasonably denied them. They ask for such things as freedom, the Four Freedoms, participation in American life, first-class citizenship, protection of civil rights, equal work opportunities, equal protection under the law, equal education, equal health and hospital services, abolition of public segregation, and end to mob violence, and the elimination of restrictions on

Review of Rayford W. Logan (ed.), *What the Negro Wants* (Chapel Hill: University of North Carolina Press, 1944) by Edward B. Reuter in *The American Journal of Sociology*, L (January, 1945), 317–318.

voting. They have no ideology other than that of democracy, and they want the rights, priviliges, and responsibilities possessed by other Americans. But the contributors are little concerned with what Negroes want. Each states his conception of the desires briefly—some do so in general terms, others with a variety of concrete detail; some state them bluntly and without quibbling, others are cautious and conciliatory—and moves on to what interests him, to race problems and solutions, to means by which the Negroes can get what they want, to racial activities and programs and movements.

The volume is in no sense a scholarly or profound analysis of race relations or of the race problem; it is, nevertheless, a significant contribution if it is seen as a pamphlet in a racial controversy and as an index of the current stage of the race-relations cycle. One stage in the cultural advance of an excluded group is characterized by vague discontent and restless behavior, by unorganized protests and rebellious outbursts and other random activity, which express a widespread dissatisfaction and misery but show no real appreciation of the causal factors or genuine understanding of effective means of control. It is at this point that leaders may arise—leaders who are able to articulate the unrest, inspire the confidence, and arouse the enthusiasm of the masses; define appealing objectives; formulate programs of action; and mobilize the group to various forms of collective behavior. When, and in the degree that this is done in America, the Negro-white relations will change in character; the race problem will move into a new phase of the racial cycle. The book does not do this; but it does, in its expression of various objectives and descriptions of various tentative and preliminary efforts at organization, indicate that a new phase of the Negro-white problem may not be far away.

Certainly these movements, when and as they come, will do little or nothing to control the course of events or to change the future of the Negro or of race relations. On the contrary, the nature of the movements will be defined and guided by the course of events. The efforts of the Negroes and the conflicting efforts of the white southerners are analogous to the competition of rival boatmen rowing upstream while the swift current is carrying both to their ultimate destination. The future of the Negro, as of the white population of the South, will be determined by impersonal factors or by fortuitous events—soil depletion, machine agriculture, competing crop areas, federal policies, conservation movements, and the like—rather than by the Negroes' wishful thinking or the whites' indulgence in nostalgic fantasies.

But efforts such as those described in the volume and others yet to come should not be undervalued. Such efforts, in and of themselves, are seldom impressive; generally they are futile, obviously destined to fail. They have, however, a very real value apart from their avowed purpose; they are educative experiences. It is apparently in just such efforts that men become in a measure civilized; it is in their efforts, aside from anything achieved by the efforts, that men acquire initiative and self-confidence and develop new conceptions of themselves. The Negroes, like other men, will advance through their efforts and their failures.

The book has another value aside from its specific content. Every effort of the Negroes to improve their social status, as every vigorous verbal or other protest against sub-American conditions and treatment, does its bit to bring the racial situation out of the realm of sacred phenomena and into the arena of public discussion, where it can be examined on it merits and modified by rational techniques. In a rational world the statement of the Negroes' wants must be faced and it must be answered—and it can be answered only in terms of counterfacts and logical argument. It is for this reason that one regrets that this is not a better book; the Negroes' position still lacks a definitive and masterly statement.

RACIAL THEORY

By Edward B. Reuter

FIFTY YEARS is a very brief period in which to observe changes in social thought and to distinguish basic and enduring trends from the ephemeral fluctuations of local incidence. Folk beliefs and sentiments, rooted in traditional and customary adjustments, are transmitted and flourish for decades and centuries after they are shown to be fallacious and inefficient; it is only when the utilitarian advantage of the new is obvious or immediately demonstrable or when the refusal to substitute the new for the old acts selectively in the population that folk thought changes with scientific discovery. At the level of ideas, where superiority is never obvious and rarely completely demonstrable, the customary modes of thought are not displaced; folklore persists beside scientific understanding and often prevents the acceptance of the new. The genuine contributions to human understanding are sometimes slow to be recognized as such; they are likely to be less colorful and more difficult than the currently familiar doctrines, and they often demand a mental reorientation that meets great resistance. At the academic level the new often meets with violent and persistent opposition. Some students, well indoctrinated in the prevailing system of thought, are unable to understand and appreciate the strange ideas and analyses; others, sensing the significance of the new for the system of thought to which they are committed, are stimulated to activity in defense of the old or in opposition to the new. The gracious acceptance of significant ideas is not a uniform practice of jealous contemporaries; the fruitful exploration of new insights is more commonly the work of a later academic generation from whom they reach the popularizers and ultimately the literate elements of the population.

These familiar facts are exemplified in detail in the study of race relations. Serious study and competent analysis have gone on in the midst of an elaborate, emotionally deep-seated, and continuing body of popular philosophy. New understandings have not displaced old beliefs; more often they have revitalized the old doctrines and brought them to new periods of activity. In some cases,

From Edward B. Reuter, "Fifty Years of Racial Theory," *The American Journal of Sociology*, L (May, 1945), 452–461.

the persisting conceptions of earlier decades and centuries compete for acceptance with the findings of modern scholarship; in other cases fragments of ancient theories and dogmas are interwoven with and concealed in what purports to be careful and sophisticated analysis. Aristotle's common sense generalization to the effect that other races are slaves by nature has a wider currency today than it had twenty-three hundred years ago. Moreover, the contact of races and peoples is an area in which cold and disinterested analysis is not widely approved; it is, rather, an area in which conflicting interests and emotional attitudes determine behavior. Numerous individuals and organizations are zealously engaged in promoting action programs designed to accomplish the impossible; other individuals and groups are struggling with equal zeal to prevent or delay changes that are manifestly inevitable. Each group, in its efforts to prevail, elaborates and propagates a philosophy justifying its position and program. In consequence, the prevailing body of popular ideas on race and race relations is a confusion compounded of the lumber of folklore and naïve and Machiavellian justifications of present and traditional sentiments, practices, and relations. The traditional ideas and current beliefs, as well as the sophisticated rationalizations of profitable status arrangements, vie with the body of science and sometimes prevent the emergence, or delay the acceptance, of research findings.

Nevertheless, some notable contributions to racial theory have been made in the past half-century. It would, perhaps, be no exaggeration to say that objective racial theory is a development of the second half of that period; certainly, the contributions made in the past quarter-century are more numerous and of greater significance than those of all previous time. Some of these contributions are sufficiently well established to be set out with some degree of assurance. The scholarly interest has been shifted from political activity to scientific analysis; the point of view has been shifted from phenomena to process, thereby substituting scientific analysis for historical and literary methods of study; the problem of race relations has been in some measure isolated from the confused reality of common sense experience and defined objectively and abstractly, and some aspects of the problem have been made the objects of empirical research.

While racial differences have perhaps nowhere escaped observation and comment and have often been made the basis for differential treatment, scientific study appears to have had its beginning with the publication of Linnaeus' classification of species in 1758. His division of mankind into the *Sapiens*, the *Ferus*, and the *Monstruosus*—the wise, the wild, and the vicious—gave no new concept of race or race relations. It was grounded in common sense observations and the questions it raised were relevant to race, not to race relations. But it set a pattern of interest and defined a method of study; for well over one hundred years discussion was concerned exclusively or primarily with racial differences and problems of biological descent, and research was limited to the use of biological or pseudo-biological methods. In some measure the continued interest in racial classification must be understood in terms of its practical usefulness; particularly as subsidiary techniques developed, it gave an apparently objective basis for the reasoning in support of the differential treatment of racial groups. In 1854, a century after Linnaeus, Count Arthur Gobineau published a study, *The Inequality of Human Races,* which seemed to justify the dominant races of Europe in extending their control over other peoples.

In America racial discussion took a peculiarly concrete form that precluded any theoretically significant contribution. It was chiefly concerned with the Negro as a unique phenomenon, not with race or even with races; hence it could not rise to a truly scientific level. During the first one-half and particularly during the second one-quarter of the nineteenth century, race, as typified by the Negro, was a matter of political controversy rather than an object of analysis and research. The northern writers, generally uniformed and doctrinal, had little interest in research findings and objective realities except as these could be used in the political controversy; the southern social students were equally not interested in cautious analytical procedure: they were occupied in elaborating rationalizations of the institution of slavery. Following the emancipation of the slaves, an extensive racial literature concerned itself with the so-called Negro problem, but, except for a few scattered literary items, it made remarkably little contribution to an understanding of racial relations.

In a later period, racial comment shifted from the Negroes to the immigrants and the foreign-born elements of the population. But here the interest was in political or practical problems; the discussion was chiefly concerned with the concrete historical phenomena, hence made little contribution to an understanding of basic racial realities. The popular prejudices toward Orientals, as toward European and other immigrants supposed to differ racially from the established population, were fostered and inflamed in the promotion of political and economic interests. Discussion emphasized racial and cultural differences, deplored the inevitable decline in the biological quality of the stock, and the slender possibility of preserving national and cultural unity in a racially heterogeneous population. There were some scientific studies and some changes in theoretical conceptions, particularly in the period of the first World War, but they had little influence on public attitudes or national policy. The legislation defining a changed immigration policy was based on the tacit assumption that fundamental racial differences separated the old from the new immigrants and on the belief that the racial traits of the later immigrants made their assimilation difficult and undesirable.

In the decades around the end of the century, the formative years of sociology, social thought was almost completely dominated by the biological concepts and points of view. The idea of organic evolution was the common property of all literate people and was reaching the stage of general public acceptance; the Darwinian concepts of universal competition, lethal selection, and species adaptation seemed to provide an explanation of social organization and assure a continuous social evolution. Social Darwinism—the body of social theories called forth by the Darwinian principle—got its first coherent statement in Walter Bagehot's *Physics and Politics* which was published in 1872 and read by all social students in England and America for a full generation. It undertook, by the application of the principles of natural selection and inheritance, to give a natural history of political society. Ludwig Gumplowicz' *Der Rassenkampf* appeared in 1883 and his *Grundriss der Soziologie* in 1885. Gustav Ratzenhofer's *Wesen und Zweck der Politik* was published in 1893 and *Die Soziologische Erkenntniss* in 1898 Benjamin Kidd's *Social*

Evolution, which appeared in 1894, was a widely read and influential publication.

Certain prominent social Darwinians, notably G. Vascher de Lapouge, *Les selections social* (1896), were proponents of the doctrine that Nordic or Aryan races are inherently superior and that progress and civilization are dependent upon the racial composition of the population. This doctrine was further popularized by Houston Chamberlain's *Foundations of the Nineteenth Century* (1899), which exploited the Germans as a superior type of chosen people, and achieved complete vulgarization in popular American books by Madison Grant, *The Passing of the Great Race* (1916), Lothrop Stoddard, *The Rising Tide of Color Against White World Supremacy* (1920), and other writers to the present day.

Another exploitation of the currently popular mode of thought appeared in the anti-democratic philosophy of eugenics, a pseudo-biological exploitation of individual, class, and racial differences. In psychology, the biological point of view received expression in the doctrine of human instincts which, carried over into sociology, helped to delay the appearance of profitable methods for the study of human behavior and social phenomena. At a later date, it reappeared in psychology in the form of mental testing; here the assumptions were that the obvious differences in performance and social behavior arise from differences in innate capacities, and that the isolation and measurement of the native traits will provide the explanation of individual, cultural, and racial differences. This position was widely recognized as untenable in the second decade of the century but was not given up for another decade.

The dominance of the biological point of view was not conductive to serious and objective racial study; it directed attention along lines that prevented the emergence of significant questions and productive procedures. Classification emphasized differences; this led to the definition and measurement of physical and mental traits. But these racial traits had no meaning, or at least the meaning was not clear without interpretation. Interpretation involved the dubious procedure of explaining social reality in biological terms.

In the decades at the end of the nineteenth and the beginning of the twentieth centuries there was a growing realization that the social significance of race could not be discovered and understood by the enumeration and definition of physical characters and mental differences or through an examination of biological processes. The attempts to classify races had finally brought a realization of the fact that there are no pure races and that no valid classification of the empirical groups was possible. In a biological sense, pure races are hypothetical entities. There is no known group of men whose culture can be differentiated on the basis of any specific complex of racial traits. In civilized life, probably in all stages of culture, the significant differences among peoples are those of language, belief, custom, technology, and other items in the mode of life. These cultural acquisitions are quite independent of race; they are learned, used, transmitted, and discarded without changes in the germ plasm.

The cultural differences among peoples are wide and conspicuous, and they are not easily eradicated. Moreover, they excite prejudices and lead to antagonisms; the conflicting attitudes in the contact of culturally diverse peoples are quite as intense as those that arise in the contact of racially different groups. Such considerations suggested the study of the social heritage as a profitable approach in the analysis of racial realities. The emphasis on culture in the study of race definitely changed the locus of the problem; it moved racial study out of a biological and into a cultural frame of reference.

Social and cultural study developed slowly. It did not abruptly displace the biological methods and points of view, rather it grew up beside the older modes of analysis and report. In the theory of Durkheim, Tarde, and others, the emphasis was placed on cultural rather than on biological facts in account-ing for differences among peoples. The extensive, and in many ways admirable, ethnological writings of the later decades of the nineteenth century, drawing heavily on the accumulated store of travelers' tales and other descriptive accounts, extended the historical and factual information of the customs and institutions of strange and distant peoples. As ethnology came to be called "social anthropology" at the end of the century, it gave special attention to the invention, accumulation, diffusion, and transmission of behavior patterns. Culture came to be treated, at least by one dominant school, as a distinct and self-determining realm, the culture traits operating as a new set of race de-terminers.

The more genuinely sociological point of view and contribution came considerably later. If the publication of Ward's *Dynamic Sociology* in 1883 is taken as marking the beginning of a continuing scholarly interest in sociology in the United States, ethnological and cultural studies began a good generation earlier; they were numerous and important during the final quarter of the cen-tury. Moreover, sociology was slow to become a profitable research instrument: it was handicapped by its biological viewpoint and, until about 1920, by its humanitarian legacy of philanthropic ideas and sentiments and their expression in social reform interests and movements.

As sociological study approached the status of scientific procedure, its emphasis shifted from the description of social structures to the study of social processes. The interest in differences was replaced by an interest in uniformities; the interest in traits, whether inherited or acquired, whether biological or cultural, gave way to an interest in relationships. Social traits were seen to form and change in the experience of living together; the problem of social re-search was seen to lie, not in the biological characters or cultural traits which get whatever meaning they have in social relations and their changes, but in the social and human attitudes, values, and experiences.

The development of racial theory followed closely the emergence of scien-tific sociology, it was promoted by and contributed to the growth of general theory. In some very large part the development of each was the work of the same men. The early conception of race in terms of concrete phenomena—the Negroes, the Orientals, or other physically divergent types—gave way, in the second and later decades of the century, to generalized and impersonal conceptions. The efforts to examine racial realities objectively forced students to face and redefine the field with the result that the problem became one of interaction, and the relevant data became relations rather than traits. The traditional common sense ideas were in a measure replaced by abstract and generalized conceptions of race and race relations which, for the first time, provided a framework and a basis for empirical research of a productive order.

In the period under discussion, there has been a persistence of earlier interests and modes of thought, there have been various sporadic movements in response to new doctrines and methods in more or less related fields, and there have been some negative reactions to the direction of thought and efforts to counteract the movement toward objective analysis. But the trend of racial theory has been reasonably consistent: it has been away from physical concepts and biological processes, through cultural analysis, and into a sociological and social-psychological study of social interrelations. The progression may, perhaps, be further clarified by an enumeration and brief descripton of some significant aspects of the change in interests and conceptions that mark the advances in racial theory. The items to be mentioned cannot in all cases be stated in a disconnected serial order nor as independent developments. They are, in reality, different phases of the same body of thought as it moved from a biological to a sociological frame of reference; they are often divergent offshoots of the same insights.

The interest in racial prejudice, which had its beginning around the turn of the century and has continued intermittently to the present time, requires only brief comment. It was a step away from the earlier preoccupation with physical traits, but, so far as the interest remained in the body of phenomena, it was not productive of results. Other efforts to explain the prejudices as instinctive reactions to strange and divergent types contributed little or nothing to social understanding. But some studies of prejudicial attitudes undertook an examination of the conditions and factors associated with their rise and persistence. Here the findings supplemented those of other research and blended with it in the emergence of modern racial theory. Race prejudice came to be seen and treated as a subjective aspect of competition and conflict, as a subjective barrier interrupting, or accompanying the interruption of, the processes of racial and cultural fusion.

Racial consciousness, race movements, racial ideologies, and other social-psychological and collective phenomena have received some study. Particularly in the later and recent periods, there has been considerable attention given to personality development in racial groups and to the general problem of racial relations in the American social order. But for the most part the points of view have been dictated by practical, rather than scientific, considerations, and the publications have been informative rather than enlightening.

The natural history of group contacts is not well defined. The knowledge is still more incomplete where the contacts are between peoples sharply contrasted in physical characters, historical experiences, cultural heritages, or social values. The variability in the external conditions of such contacts—the relative population numbers, the types of economy, the stages of technological advance, the nationalistic sentiments, the purposes and interests of the invading groups, and other factors—determines the types of dominance, the nature, speed, and duration of the stages of acculturation, the ease of assimilation, and other items in the concrete historical sequence. However the social research and racial study of the last two or three decades have defined the general forms of contact with reasonable clarity.

Two or more groups, whether closely similar or widely divergent in physical or cultural characteristics, may occupy the same general area as relatively independent units. They may exist side by side with a minimum of biological fusion, cultural exchange, or social contact. Conflicts may arise in the event of trespass, but otherwise a high degree of isolation may be maintained over very considerable periods of time. The attitudes remain mutually hostile and intolerant; each group holds the other in contempt as something short of real men. The contacts are physical, geographic, and territorial, essentially the contacts that obtain among animals of different species occupying the same general area. The spacial distribution of each such group is determined in some part by the presence of the other groups, but only in the ecological sense of being an adjustment to their presence as to other external facts of the habitat.

Peoples unlike in physical type or culture may live and intermingle in a common area in a way that is symbiotic or mutually helpful, but with few or no personal contacts and social relations. The economies are separate, the adjustments are essentially biotic, the relations are exploitative or mutualistic but quite impersonal; each regards the other as of a different species. Such interactions as exist are characteristically non-social; there is no mutual understanding or personal sympathy; there is no inter-penetration of personalities, hence no genuine human understanding.

Contrasted racial groups may establish and maintain economic and competitive relations which are in no real sense social or racial. Such tends to be the case where the Europeans, interested in trade and exploitation rather than in the occupation and settlement of an area, establish and maintain contacts with native peoples. If the traders desire goods that lie outside the orbit of the indigenous economy, the ecological order of the native peoples—the balance of population and cultural resources—may for a time remain undisturbed. The repercussions of contact are indirect. The introduction of strange artifacts may change the native order by creating new wants external to the traditional culture. The withdrawal of natives from the indigenous economy to supply commodities to exchange for the traders' goods presently disrupts the ecological balance. Particularly in the case of the alienation of land, the closed native economy gives way to a money economy, and values come to be defined by competition in the market rather than by tradition. In the process, the native economy is demoralized and the natives are in a measure acculturated. But the contacts are economic and exploitative rather than social; no race relations exist and no race problems arise.

In other situations, in order to profit quickly and in full measure from the resources of the area, it may be in the interests of the militaristically dominant group to exploit the vital power of a weak but numerous people. In these circumstances slavery or some other form of forced labor is used to develop a plantation economy or exploit other resources, or coercion through systematic impoverishment may bring the native people into the new economy. In such colonial areas there are numerous and often difficult problems of administration, but in general there are no race problems. The contacts of the natives with their exploiters may be friendly or they may be hostile; in either case they are external and impersonal. The natives are completely dominated, and a habit of collective obedience is established; in time they become accommodated to a semi-service status and a body of understanding and expectations develops which defines and supports the system and promotes harmonious working relations.

In areas of racial contact the native peoples become in varying degrees acculturated and, in larger or smaller numbers, assimilated. They gain a command of the language of the conquerors and conform in other respects to the culture standards of the ruling group. As they acquire the European heritage, they seek to penetrate the European world; they aspire to new and equal status in the culture area; they consider themselves as integral parts of the life of the area and feel entitled to the same treatment and opportunities as others of like attainment. As their developing social and political aspirations are denied, they become racially self-conscious, develop a sense of unity and solidarity, become a conflict group engaged in a struggle for status. It is at this stage in the contact of peoples that race problems, as distinct from economic and administrative problems, make their appearance and that race contacts take on the character of race relations.

The isolation and definition of race relations and race problems as distinct from prior and non-social forms of contact, was a major step in racial theory. As the distinction came to be appreciated, racial studies entered a new phase. The relations of contrasted groups, seen as adjustments of ideas and aspirations, became meaningful; the contact of peoples could be separated from specific concrete phenomena, could be conceived as a natural process amenable to scientific analysis. It became generally clear that race relations, like all social and human relations, begin with language communication involving the inter-penetration of personalities and result, inevitably, in a degree of unity, in a new society.

The recognition of diverse types of racial contacts and their appearance in some sort of a temporal sequence was a first step in the statement of a natural history. It differentiated biotic, economic, administrative, and other contacts from one another and indicated the type of unity or integration to which each gave rise. In doing so it differentiated each from a racial order, that is, an order among peoples of diverse physical or biological traits which is based on human and social relations.

The isolation of race relations from the various forms of non-social contact set new problems of a similar order. In the concrete reality, race relations are a confused complex, in varying degrees, of opposition and agreement, friction and harmony, conflict and cooperation. To work out the cycle of relations— the sequence of steps from the emergence to conflict to its disappearance in new and unified attitudes—was an obvious task if the study of race was to maintain or achieve scientific reputability. The problem was one of major dimensions and the studies so far made or in progress, while suggestive and useful, are, for the most part, in the nature of preliminary and tentative explorations.

The definition of an ecological interest and point of view, chiefly a development of the third decade of the century, was a distinctive contribution to social and racial theory. Human ecology was less the emergence of a new hypothesis than it was a reformulation of existing modes of analysis and their extension and use in a new area of study. The prompt prosecution of a series of studies developed the conceptual framework and defined a methodological procedure which, by isolating independent but coincident processes, contributed to the definition of the racial cycle and otherwise brought a measure of clarity into a confused area of social study.

Ecology came into social analysis from the biological sciences and, in lesser degree, from classical economics. In biology it was concerned to describe the spacial distribution of living forms and to define the factors and the impersonal process determining the placement. In the biological struggle for existence, success is determined by superior competitive ability; the survivors are those who have the traits that fit them to succeed in the existing conditions. The inevitable end result of competition, in the presence of diverse characters and variable external conditions, is a distributional pattern: each form occupies, to the exclusion of competing forms, the area to which it is best adapted—the area in which, because of its specialized needs and distinctive traits, it can survive and propagate its kind. Ecology is then a description of distributional patterns and of the simple impersonal processes that create and maintain them.

In the human world, ecology includes all this and something more. The spatial distribution of human populations is rather obviously determined by impersonal factors; men live where they can secure the means of subsistence. Competition and survival, operating in and below the level of a social order, are the mechanisms that determine their placement. In civilized life the gross and direct aspects are in a measure concealed by cultural factors and human activities, and some new factors determining survival make their appearance. But man never escapes the universal principle. Its application is wider in the human than in the simpler orders of life. It determines the distribution and survival of forms of culture, its operation dictates the class structure, and the occupational placement of individuals and groups is a result of competitive struggle. The factors determining success in competition are numerous and they differ with the social situation; their operation is often indirect and sometimes subtile, but the process is continuous and universal. The isolation of impersonal factors and processes made it possible to discuss them in objective rather than in personal terms, hence made possible a search for rational and effective controls.

The development of the ecological studies provided a useful tool in racial analysis. Some of the superior studies were pieces of racial research. Their general influence was to increase the emphasis on natural factors and processes, reduce the emphasis on human prejudices and other personalized explanations of status, and make a larger area of racial phenomena understandable in mechanistic and impersonal terms.

Human hybridization with the associated body of social and cultural phenomena, long an area of confused and conflicting doctrines, has received some sociological study and clarification in the recent decades. The problem has been redefined, the physical and the cultural phenomena have been differentiated, and some of the social aspects have been analyzed and made generally intelligible. The studies made important contributions to racial and social theory: they provided valuable new insights, and they opened several new and productive lines of sociological research. From these studies, in a brief period, there emerged the generic sociological concept of marginality with its great contribution to the study and understanding of culture development and personality organization.

Certain facts in regard to racial miscegenation have long been matters of common knowledge. The historians have made it generally clear that all the great civilizations of record have been the work of heterogeneous and racially mixed groups and, with catholic impartiality, they have often attributed the decline of nations to the mongrelization of their population stock. Anthropological and other study of the skeletal remains of early man made it evident that racial crossings were common some thousands of years before the era of modern man. Further, it was commonplace knowledge that all the contemporary peoples are of mixed racial origin. In some measure, at least, it was recognized that racial mixture was a mathematical function of mobility, apparently an invariable consequence of racial contact and its amount was determined by numbers. Throughout the historic period, intermixture has been rapid in vicinal areas and regions of conquest and occupation; it has been relatively slow in isolated areas and continental interiors. The areas of advanced civilization and fractional contacts, the cities and other centers of trade and commerce, have been areas of rapid intermixture and the loci of disorganized and troublesome hybrids.

In areas of racial contact and intermixture, the individuals of mixed ancestry are, in numerous cases, persons of mixed heritage. In the same way, populations of mixed blood are populations of mixed social heritage. As the study of race came within the sociological framework of analysis and interpretation, the personal and group experiences tended to displace hybridization as the basis for understanding; the superiority, like the disorganization, of the hybrid persons and heterogeneous groups was sought in social contacts and cultural experiences. The mixed ancestry of the hybrid, by giving at least a partial entree to both ancestral groups, increased his mobility, hence his intelligence, and freed him as an individual. The disorganization of traditional and oppressive cultural forms, resulting from cultural contacts, gave opportunity for fruitful new combinations. The point of view thus brought the superiority, leadership, and disorganization of the hybrids, as well as the cultural superiority and advance of mixed groups and the disorganized character of evolving cultures, into a common frame of reference.

The insights gained in the sociological study of hybrids were clarified and extended in studies of the Jew and other personality types that emerge in the fluid and fractional contacts of civilization as dstinct from the stable and personal relations that characterize cultural groups. Presently they got conceptual generalization in the term "marginality." At this point racial theory became virtually freed from the biological modes of thought. The hybrids, like other marginal men, were seen to mirror the conflict of culture and civilization.

It would be rash to attempt to forecast future trends in racial theory and research. There is urgent need for a body of science as a guide in the formulation of public policy, and it would be relatively easy greatly to increase the amount of fundamental research. But there are no present indications that the development of racial theory will be rapid: there are very few competent scholars working on racial problems, and the encouragement of scholarship and the support for theoretical research is very small. Without engaging in any way in hazardous historical prophesy, it is possible to enumerate some present scholarly interests and activities, to indicate some types of needed study, and to display some areas that are open and awaiting analysis.

There is a need in the present for a basic ecological study of race problems that would competently define the order of race contacts and race problems that exist in the various bi-racial and multi-racial areas. At present there is only a very sketchy body of comparable data; most of the reports of areas of racial contact have been made without the guidance of a body of racial theory, or against outmoded theories, and by different methods and for different purposes. The need is for a coordinated series of monographic studies based on concrete empirical investigation in the various places of contact and conflict, carried on by comparable methods, and similarly related to the present body of tentative theory. The natural history of race relations has been blocked out in its main lines only. Race relations have been clearly differentiated from the logically antecedent economic, administrative, and colonial contacts. But neither the social nor the pre-social relations have been adequately analyzed, and both exist coincidentally in numerous areas of racial contact. A series of comparative area studies is a present prime need.

Racial relations themselves are incompletely analyzed and imperfectly described. They seem to begin at the point where partly acculturated and imperfectly assimilated members of the excluded group, aspiring to membership in the superior group and seeking to participate in its culture life, are repulsed and their wishes denied. The excluded individuals become racially self-conscious and develop into conflict groups that are at once dependent upon and potentially at war with the group in whose culture they desire to participate. In the struggle for rights that they feel are unjustly denied them, they develop organization, initiate movements, construct ideologies, and otherwise evolve the complex machinery that goes with organized political activity. The details of the procedure apparently display the whole collective behavior process. A body of careful research in the field of racial movements is a prerequisite to an understanding of the natural history of race relations. Incidentally, such studies would make an important contribution to the general theory of collective behavior—an important area of sociology that has received little serious study.

The practical value of such study is perhaps too obvious to mention. Without a knowledge of the race relations process, no genuinely statesmanlike control measures are possible; until the natural history of race relations is worked out, efforts to mediate racial conflict cannot be expected to rise above the level of unenlightened good intentions.

Every race-conscious group displays a rich variety of collective behavior phenomena that offer a fertile field for social-psychological study. Race and racial status are at the focus of attention; they are the subjects of endless talk, misdirected effort, and futile procedure. The groups are burdened with racial activities, organizations, movements, and programs. Some of the behavior is spontaneous and self-directed; some of it is created and fostered by groups seeking to improve interracial relations; some of it comes from persons seeking an emotional outlet and some from others seeking a basis for a professional career. The objective examination of these racial activities would provide an exceptionally enlightening group of preliminary studies. They would lead, inevitably, to a problem of basic importance. If it be granted that these folk movements and action programs are futile, pathetic, and destined to failure, the question still remains as to whether or not they are not the only means by which culturally backward groups ever reach a modicum of civilization. Apparently, the development of intelligence and personality has always come in the collective process of struggle for group ends—generally a collective struggle for ends manifestly absurd, useless, undesirable, and impossible of achievement.

Finally, racial theory would profit greatly by more fundamental analysis and restatement of the process by means of which minority and excluded groups are incorporated into a dominant culture. The doctrinal preconceptions of the present-day action groups lead to programs designed to overcome or override existing attitudes and thereby bring the excluded racial minorities into unobstructed participation in the culture life of the dominant group. Even at the theoretical level, much of racial thought seems to rest on imperfectly analyzed assumptions concerning the fusion of cultures and the integration of foreign elements. There is much reason to believe that the process is less easy and simple than is commonly thought.

In the mixture of racial stocks the hybrids do not appear as a new race; they represent new and strange combinations of heritable traits which they do not transmit to succeeding generations. They will develop into a stable racial type, if at all, only through a prolonged period of selection and inbreeding. In an analogous, though in a somewhat less simple, way the mixture of culture heritages seems not to produce a new culture; it seems to result, through the borrowing and use of conveniences and in less obvious ways, in a mechanical mixture and corruption of both heritages, in a hybrid rather than in an integrated culture. In certain favorable conditions, an indigenous culture may emerge from a culturally heterogeneous area and presently displace the corrupted fragments of an earlier period. It is impossible, for example, to bring the Negro into the present-day culture of the American South, since no genuine culture exists. If, and when, an indigenous culture emerges it will displace the present disjointed, conflicting, and corrupted heritages of past eras.

In any case, a more coherent analysis of the way in which societies actually emerge from the broken fragments of earlier organization would increase the fruitfulness of racial study. It would, to mention a single way, clarify the significance of the mixed bloods and the marginal man and, by doing so, would make it possible to study more profitably the organization of the human personality. And through the personality study of the mixed blood and the marginal man, the emerging society may be seen from a subjective point of view. Thus, as racial study becomes meaningful it blends with, disappears into, and becomes an integral part of sociological science.

CENSUS PROBLEMS OF RACIAL ENUMERATION

*

By Calvin L. Beale

RACE IS A USEFUL ITEM of demographic classification in multi-racial societies, but operational definitions for the precise determination of race are hard to come by. The federal censuses of the United States have attempted to follow prevailing social usage in classifying race. In this system a person may be classified as a member of the majority white race only if he has no known Negro or Oriental ancestry. A degree of Indian ancestry complicates matters because of the peculiar relationship of legally defined Indians to the federal government, and because a small degree of Indian ancestry does not carry the same social stigma among the white race as does Negro or Oriental descent. Consequently an Indian is defined in several ways. He is a person who is of ¼ or more Indian origin, or who is enrolled in an Indian agency or reservation roll, or who is recognized as an Indian in the community in which he lives. This is a wide definition. At one extreme it embraces some persons of only ¼₅₆ part Indian who are recognized as Indian on the tribal rolls of the Five Civilized Tribes in Oklahoma. At the other extreme it rejects persons of sub-stantial Indian blood who do not exhibit sufficient Indian physical or cultural characteristics to be regarded as Indian in their communities.

Further rules are provided for the classification of persons of mixed non-white descent, such as Indian-Negro or Chinese-Negro. However, one may wonder with Shelley, "What is all this sweet work worth?", since in the actual enumerative process race is determined on the observation and opinion of the enumerator and not by the application of agreed criteria through direct questioning. Enumerators are empowered to inquire about race when in doubt, but in practice they may refrain from doing so because of the sensitive nature of the subject. Thus uniform practices in the counting of minority or mixed-blood groups are difficult to achieve from one enumerator to another, let alone from one census to another. The fruits of this difficulty are especially evident in the statistics for Indians and multi-racial groups, and the remainder of this discussion will consider these two racial classes.

Although there is little Indian immigration or emigration, no notion of the biological natural increase of Indians can be gained from the data for successive censuses. At a given census the size of the Indian population count appears to depend largely upon whether or not a special Indian schedule is used (and publicized) for obtaining statistics such as tribal stock and language spoken.

In the 1950 Census, the tabulated Indian population was 343,000. Of this number about 292,000 were living on reservations or in Indian agency areas.

Reprinted from Calvin L. Beale, Agricultural Marketing Service, U.S. Department of Agriculture, *The Enumeration of Mixed-Blood Racial Groups in the Census of 1950* (Revised version of a paper read before the annual meeting of the Population Association of America, at Cincinnati, Ohio, May 3, 1953, and prepared while the writer was employed by the Bureau of the Census.)

The identity of the reservation groups is relatively well-known to enumerators, and, judging from corroborative records of the Bureau of Indian Affairs, their count is practically complete. On the other hand, persons living off-reservation may frequently not be recognized as Indian unless they so identify themselves to the enumerator. There is little incentive for them to go to this trouble. However, the off-reservation Indian may be very particular about registering as Indian in vital statistics records because of the role of such records in securing tribal membership and federal benefits. If the excess of Indian births over deaths since 1930 is added to the rather complete count of Indians in the 1930 Census, the Indian population of 1950 should have been about 390,000 rather than the enumerated 343,000. Considering coverage of Indians on reservations to be complete, the 51,000 enumerated nonreservation Indians probably represent little more than ½ the number who should have been counted. This coverage problem will undoubtedly be aggravated as the current urban movement of Indians continues.

Indians may also pass into other population stocks, particularly the white, as their Indian blood and culture are diluted by intermarriage and assimilation. In Oklahoma, where both of these phenomena are well advanced, there are many persons living in long established Indian localities with obviously Indian surnames—such as Wildcat, Fivekiller, Sixkiller, Doublehead, and Roastingear—who are now enumerated as white, whereas their parents or even they themselves were listed as Indian 20 years ago.

Problems of race classification are even more acute among the various communities of mixed-blood people who live as distinct social or racial groups in the eastern United States. The great majority of these groups have, either in fact or by tradition, tri-racial, white, Indian, and Negro ancestry. They are found most generally to be very socially disadvantaged and geographically isolated. Legal disputes over school and selective service questions, and vital statistics registration, have been numerous among groups living in Southern or Border States. Their current racial status shows wide variations, both as it is viewed by their neighbors and in the minds of the mixed bloods themselves. Some occupy perhaps no more than a peculiar status among the Negro population. Some are regarded as a separate race, known either as Indian or by a local colloquial name. Others have achieved some measure of acceptance as white persons. Under such circumstances it is not surprising that the mixed bloods have been the source of vexing problems of enumeration from one census to another.

Some recorded examples from the Census of 1930 will illustrate the point. The so-called "Issues" of Amherst County, Virginia, wished to be counted as Indians in 1930. Some of their white neighbors and the State Registrar of Vital Statistics insisted they be listed as Negro. The controversy waxed so hot that the census taker refused to give them a race entry at all. He turned their schedules in with the race column blank and passed the problem on to the district office, where a decision was made to count them as Indian.

The mixed bloods of Rockingham County, North Carolina, declared themselves as white to the enumerator. According to the statement of one of their leaders, the enumerator listed them as white in their presence but changed the race entry to Indian after leaving their homes. This they resented very much.

The Rappahannock Indians, a mixed-blood group of Caroline County,

Virginia, were enumerated as Negro, whereupon a body of them visited the census office and asked to have the record changed to Indian. The request was granted, but at the insistence of the Virginia Bureau of Vital Statistics a footnote was appended to the statistics of Indians in Virginia in the 1930 Census reports, declaring that the status of many of these people as Indian had been questioned.

Robeson County, North Carolina, shows the most extreme example of unreasonable statistical changes caused by inconsistency of race coding. There were 174 Indians in that county in the Census of 1890. By 1940 the number had multiplied 95 times to a figure of 16,629. The change was not caused by migration and although the mixed bloods of Robeson County are among the most prolific people in the United States, a 95-fold increase in 50 years connotes a fertility exploit far beyond imagination.

In an effort to bring some consistency of reporting into effect, and in view of the fact that some of the mixed-blood communities live as separate racial groups—even to the point of having their own special public schools—the Census Bureau attempted in the 1950 Census to have enumerators list mixed-blood groups by local race names, and then in publication to include them in the category, "Other nonwhite races."

To assess the results of this policy and to supply comparable data on the numbers of the various groups, the writer made a survey of the enumeration status in 1950 of all known native, tri-racial, mixed-blood groups in the eastern United States. On the basis of information regarding the surnames and localities of the groups, the mixed bloods were located in the 1950 schedules and data were recorded on their numbers and their racial classification. The method of identification by surname is generally effective because of the high degree of endogamy practiced by most of the mixed bloods and the localized nature of many of their settlements. In many localities the surnames of the mixed bloods are unique to them.

In all, groups in 109 counties were checked. Some small or ill-defined groups had to be omitted. By race entry the mixed bloods fall into four categories: (1) Those listed as white, (2) Those listed as Indian or by some local race term, (3) Those listed as Negro, and (4) Those receiving more than one type of race entry. The entry of colloquial race names on the census schedules other than the use of the term "Indian" as a euphemism was found to be limited to the partial use of the terms "Turk" in South Carolina, "Cajan" and "Creole" in Alabama, "Moor" in Delaware, and "Portugese" in North Carolina.

The terms "Redbone," "Dominicker," "Turk," "Creole," "Croatan," and "Portuguese" all appear at some time in past censuses when no instruction regarding mixed bloods was given. Thus, the instruction to enumerators to use local race terms in 1950 had little or no effect. It should be noted however that the 1950 instruction was not mentioned in the enumerator training program but was simply included as a rule in the Enumerator's Reference Manual. Some enumerators may have refrained from using local terms because more frequently than not they constitute terms of social stigma regarded with great opprobrium by those so called.

Large groups receiving a variable race listing were the "Cajans" of Alabama, "Brass Ankles" and related groups of South Carolina, "Guineas" of West Virginia, and "Jackson Whites" of New Jersey and New York. Among these groups the varying or uncertain opinions of the white enumerators were quite evident. Thus for example, one enumerator would list all West Virginia Guineas in his district as Negro, a neighboring enumerator would list them as white, while a third would distinguish between families, listing one family as Negro and the next as white, and occasionally in a state of complete indecision leaving the race entry blank. The Alabama Cajans were listed by different enumerators as white, Negro, Indian, and Cajan.

Although there is a good deal of random fluctuation in race entries from one census to another caused by the employment of different enumerators, it is obvious from an examination of schedules over the last hundred years that the race status of a number of mixed-blood groups as reflected in the census is not static. In censuses prior to the Civil War the majority of the "Melungeon" groups appeared as free colored. In Tennessee they were deprived as free colored of the right to vote. At various censuses after the Civil War Melungeons in many counties were classified as Indian in the census. By 1950 all but a few Melungeons were listed as white and are known to be accepted as white in their local communities. The Red Bones of Louisiana, who are distantly related to the Melungeons, went from a generally free colored stage before the Civil War to an almost all-white stage today without an intermediate Indian stage. The phenomenon of race passing is generally associated with the actions of people acting as individuals, but it is clear from the cases just cited, and from others that could be given were there space, that whole families or clans of mixed-blood peoples have passed over *en masse* from a colored status into the white population in certain areas of the Nation. Other former free colored groups, either unable to acquire white status or undesirous of pressing for it, have acquired a rather stable non-Negro status as Indians. The Croatans and "Cubans" of North Carolina are examples of such groups.

The total estimated number of mixed bloods in the counties checked was 72,994 in 1950, of whom 28,804 were enumerated as white, 32,863 as Indian, 10,261 as Negro, and 1,066 under other race names or with the race entry blank. The problem of the proper racial classification of mixed-blood groups is a difficult one from the standpoint of public relations, particularly because few of these groups possess a socially acceptable race name. The Census Bureau's experiment in classifying the mixed bloods in 1950, though conceived completely without social malice, was sharply criticized by an important chain of Negro newspapers as being an instrument of race prejudice.

In view of the wide variation in race status found among the mixed bloods, and the changing status of some groups, it is the writer's opinion that no overall instruction regarding their classification in the census can be effective. Separate instructions can be effectively issued in certain areas, but problems of race classification promise to vex census takers and demographers for many years to come.

**
By C. A. Vlieland

THE TERM "RACE" IS USED, for the purposes of a Malayan census, in a peculiar sense, which requires explanation. The information, which it is desired to obtain from the results of enquiries under this heading, is of importance for a variety of purposes, and the word "Race" is used, for lack of a more approprate term, to cover a complex set of ideas of which race, in the strict or scientific sense, is only one small element. It would be of little use to the administrator or the merchant to attempt a classification of the population by race in the ethnographic sense, to say nothing of the fact that any such tentative classification would be highly controversial. An attempt at classification by "nationality," or, more exactly, by national status or political allegiance, would be almost equally open to controversy, and of little, if any, greater practical value. It is, in fact, impossible to define the sense in which the term "Race" is used for census purposes; it is, in reality, a judicious blend, for practical ends, of the ideas of geographic and ethnographic origin, political allegiance, and racial and social affinities and sympathies. The difficulty of achieving anything like a scientific or logically consistent classification is enhanced by the fact that most Oriental peoples have themselves no clear conception of race, and commonly regard religion as the most important, if not the determinant, element. The Malay, for instance, habitually regards adherence to Islam in much the same light as a European regards a racial distinction, and will speak of a Muhammadan Indian and a Hindu (even if the two are of precisely similar origin), as though the distinction between them were similar in nature and magnitude to that between a Frenchman and a German. Again, the term "Jawi-Pekan," which to the European implies a mixture of Indian and Malay blood, is frequently applied to an Indian who has in fact no Malayan blood in his veins, but is a Muhammadan who has settled and married in Malaya. The confusion of ideas has even affected current English usage of terms, and the European will frequently use the name "Sikh" instead of "Punjabi" (since the majority of Punjabis he knows of profess the Sikh religion).

In default of anything resembling a definition of the term "Race" as used in this report, perhaps the best way of conveying its meaning in a few words is to say that, in asking the question of an individual "What is your race?" the census authority is trying to obtain an answer of the same nature as we expect when we ask in ordinary non-technical conversation "What is that man?"— assuming that the context makes it clear that we are not enquiring as to his occupation. In such circumstances, we should be surprised, and possibly annoyed, to be told that a Madras Indian was British or Dravidian, when we wanted to know whether he was a Tamil or a Telegu; yet either of these answers might well be correct. We should be more shocked to receive the information that a given white man was Teuto-Erse, when we wanted to know whether he was in fact an American, and not a Canadian, Australian or Englishman.

Adapted from C. A. Vlieland, *British Malaya: A Report on the 1931 Census and on Certain Problems of Vital Statistics* (London: The Crown Agents for the Colonies, 1932), Chapter VIII, and pp. 88–89.

At this census, following precedent, the population was first classified under six main racial heads, Europeans (including Americans and all white races), Eurasians, Malaysians, Chinese, Indians and "Others." These primary classes were subsequently sub-divided, with considerable departures from precedent, into over seventy races. It may be noted, in passing, that, as against the difficulties in classification indicated above, the problem is simplified by the very small extent to which intermarriage occurs between the different races which make up the peculiarly heterogeneous population of British Malaya. The great bar to such intermarriage is of course Islam, but, even where there is no religious bar, there is very little tendency to fresh racial mixture of blood. Even the Eurasian element in the population receives very small accessions to-day from inter-marriage of European and Asiatic, or European and Eurasian, individuals. The Eurasian community in Malaya forms, in the main, a settled endogamic section of the population with its own manners, customs and traditions, and its increase is essentially the "natural increase" characteristic of a separate and distinct people.

In subdividing "Europeans," an attempt was made to ascertain what proportions of persons of ultimate European origin and British nationality hailed from each of the principal parts of the British Empire. This classification was rendered difficult by the large number of cases in which individuals insisted on describing themselves as "British," but the writer feels that the distinction between "English," "Scottish," "Australian" and so forth, however unscientific, is of sufficient practical interest and importance to justify the attempt.

The term "Malaysian" is used to include all indigenous peoples of the Malay Peninsula and Archipelago, and the term "Malay" to include only those Malaysians (excluding aboriginals) who belong to British Malaya. No immigrants born in Java, Sumatra or other parts of the Malay Archipelago, are numbered amongst "Malays," and the children and later descendants of the original immigrants are only treated as "Malays" when definitely so returned. Thus, children born in Malaya of Javanese immigrant parents if returned as Javanese as they normally are, are classed in this report as "Other Malaysians," and the same is true in general of Banjarese, Boyanese or Dyaks. On the other hand, the children born in Malaya of Sumatran parents are normally returned as "Malay" and so classified. This procedure is designed to reflect the persistence of separate race consciousness, customs and language in the case of Javanese and other immigrant peoples from the south and west of the archipelago, as contrasted with the ready assimilation of the Sumatran Malay. At the same time, the writer considers it well to maintain the rule that individuals born outside British Malaya should not be classed with the native Malay. This is an illustration of the inclusion of the idea of political status amongst the census criteria of race.

The classification of Chinese is a matter of considerable difficulty, and, whatever list of divisions is adopted, the census authority cannot hope to escape a considerable measure of expert criticism. The writer's plea is that the classification adopted in this report represents a tolerable compromise between the conflicting views of different authorities who were consulted and the practical considerations which weighed with him as the authority responsible for the census. The classification is admittedly based on an inconsistent blend of political, geographic and linguistic, rather than ethnographic criteria, but is intended to reflect those broad divisions with which a non-specialist administrator is mainly concerned *in Malaya*. By way of marking the peculiar nature of this classification, the word "tribe" is used in place of "race" for the subdivisions of the Chinese element in the population—not that it is a particularly appropriate term.

There are many millions of Muhammadans amongst the Chinese in parts of northern China, but the China immigrant into Malaya comes from the South, and it may be safely assumed that practically all Chinese Muhammadans enumerated at this census have been locally converted to Islam. The inducement to conversion is nearly always marriage, not religious conviction. A Malay woman cannot marry any but a Muhammadan, and a Chinese in a remote Malay village, where there are often no women of his own race available, has no option but to embrace Islam if he wishes to take a wife from amongst the local people, and settle permanently in the locality. It is also not uncommon for a childless Malay in prosperous circumstances to adopt a Chinese child, and bring it up in the Muhammadan faith. Race and religion are conceptions not readily separable by the oriental mind, and this is especially true of the Muhammadan Malay mind. It is therefore probable that, in not a few cases, "Maalap," or Chinese converts to Islam, are returned as "Malay," while children of mixed Chinese and Malay blood, brought up in a Muhammadan atmosphere and to all appearances Malay in habit of life and general characteristics, would almost invariably be so returned. Several cases of Maalap, and a few of undoubted mixed blood, were brought to the notice of the writer during compilation, and it was found exceedingly difficult to persuade a Malay sorter that such individuals should not be classed as Malays proper.

For these reasons, it is not unlikely that the number of Chinese (to say nothing of Sino-Malay) Muhammadans in Malaya, and particularly in the Unfederated States, is in reality appreciably higher than the figures show. The percentages returned as Muhammadans are naturally considerably higher in the Malay States than in the Straits Settlements, since the inducement to intermarriage indicated above is far greater where Chinese women are few, and the population so predominantly Malay that the Chinese immigrant is bereft of association with his own kind and tends to become more and more intimately associated with, and assimilated to, the people of the country. The extreme cases are Singapore, where there are only 9 Muhammadan Chinese in 10,000, and Trengganu where there are at least 256, and probably considerably more, in view of the source of error indicated above.

The problem of racial classification in the case of Indians is at least as formidable as it is in the case of Chinese immigrants into Malaya, though it is of lesser importance since the Indian component is far smaller than the Chinese, and the difficulties are relatively small in the case of Madrasis who form the bulk of the Indian immigrant population. These Madrasis, and other southern Indians, can be tolerably classified as either Tamil, Telegu or Malayali. Over half these southern Indians were enumerated by managers of estates who could generally be relied upon to classify them satisfactorily, and a considerable proportion of the remainder were recorded by employers of labour, and other responsible persons, whose reliability in such a matter was greater than could be expected of the average Malay or Chinese enumerator.

* * *

By Everett C. Hughes

"RACIAL CLASSIFICATION of People Who Married in 1938." In the summer of 1953, my eye fell by chance upon this heading of a table in the Statistical Yearbook of the German Reich for 1941–1942, the last published by the Nazi regime. From earlier work with German official statistics, I was practically certain that the pre-Nazi German had had a religion, but not a race. The statistical German was the opposite of the statistical American, who had a race but no religion. The accident of noticing this change of categories in the German census led me to ask a question: What changes did the statistician of the German Reich have to make in his official Yearbook when the Nazis came to power? Behind it lie more general questions for professional statisticians: How politically neutral is their work? To what extent are the very categories in which they report their data subject to political demands?

I do not known the answers to these general questions. But I did go through all of the German statistical yearbooks from the last one of the pre-Nazi Weimar republic, 1932, through the Nazi period, and including the first post-war volume, to see what changes of category and of reporting occurred along with the radical political changes. I don't know how deeply the Nazis dug into the private opinions of the Reich statistician, or whether Party people were put in his office to watch over him. I have only the internal evidence of the Statistical Yearbooks themselves. The last Weimar volume, and all of the Nazi Yearbooks except the last are signed by one Dr. Reichardt of the Reich Statistical Office. The last Nazi volume, 1941–42, is signed Godlewski. Whether Dr. Reichardt simply reached the age of retirement about the end of 1940 or whether he finally turned out to be not sufficiently *gleichgeschaltet* (coordinated), I don't know. Many a man did try to get on with his work by making little compromises, only to find one day that it was impossible to continue and fatal to quit. I must add that I do not know what happened to Godlewski either; he certainly did not sign the first Yearbook of the new Bonn republic.

The Foreword to the last pre-Nazi Yearbook, 1932, is the exact, dull little statement one expects of a faithful public servant who is accustomed to going modestly on with his work while prime ministers and cabinets come and go. It contains no word about parties or government polices. It uses no political symbol. When, in November, 1933, Dr. Reichardt signed the next Yearbook, Hitler had been Reichs-chancellor for the better part of a year. The Foreword takes no notice of the change. It is the same little business-like statement about the contents of the book. In the next Foreword, 1934, however, Dr. Reichardt feels called upon to tell the reader that the Yearbook now contains a series of "German economic curves, showing the economic events since the taking over of power by the Nationalsocialist regime." In 1935, the mention becomes a plug, "In the many tables of the Yearbook there come to expression the powerful accomplishments made by the New State in all fields of folk and

Reprinted from Everett C. Hughes, "The Gleichschaltung of the German Statistical Yearbook," *The American Statistician,* IX (December, 1955), 8–11; copyright 1955 by the American Statistical Association and used with the kind permission of the publishers.

economic life in the three years since the taking over of power by the National-socialist regime." He especially notes the great success of measures against unemployment. In passing he mentions some new family statistics, and tables on the Special Census of the Occupational and Social Distribution of *Glaubensjuden* (Jews by faith) and Foreigners.

From 1935 on, the Foreword always tells how many years it has been since the Nationalsocialists took power, and reports in more and more glowing terms the accomplishments of the New State. The statement is typically like this "The Yearbook gives an accounting in sober, but eloquent figures of the measures taken by the New State in all fields of folk and economic life, and the results in population, economics and in cultural and political affairs." Dr. Reichardt even notes that the Yearbook has to be bigger because of the increased activity of the New State. From 1936 on, curves showing economic progress are put on the inside of the front cover where they are the first thing to be seen when one opens the book. In 1938 the flyleaf shows a map entitled "Folk and Space since the Assumption of Power." It shows how the empire has been expanded by the assimilation of Austria and Sudetenland. In 1939–40, a similar map shows most of Western Europe under German "protection." Under the map is a summary table showing the increase of territory and population accomplished by the New State. Dr. Reichardt tells us in his 1938 Foreword that the Yearbook now reports the Greater German Reich; he regrets that not many of the tables take account of the new territories, since comparable statistics do not yet exist. The last two books, done in war time, no longer bother to plug for the New State. A brief Foreword says that the Yearbook was produced under difficulties, "because the needs of the State and the Party require it." Readers are enjoined, under penalty, to keep copies in metal safes and to divulge the contents to no one not in government service.

The 1932 Yearbook shows the results of all Reichstag elections from 1919 to 1932, with the number of votes for each party. The most recent election, that of July 31, 1932, was reported in even greater detail. The 1933 book gives the same summary of past elections, and includes the detail of two new elections. One was the election of November, 1932, in which there was a considerable decline of the Nazi vote. In spite of that, Hindenburg had called upon Hitler to form a government. The other was the election of March, 1933, the only free election in the Hitler time; in it the Social-Democrats held their own, the Catholic Centre gained a little, and the Nazis gained tremendously. The Communists apparently contributed most to the Nazi increase, since they lost a million votes from November, before Hitler came in, to March, just after he came to power. But this is an aside. The Yearbook merely reports the figures. In 1934 and after, each Yearbook reports only the new-style Yes and No elections of the current year. I do not know whether Dr. Reichardt was told to stop reporting the elections of the late Weimar republic, or whether he gave it up for purely technical reasons. It would make no sense to try to compare the results of free elections in which a dozen or more parties struggled for slight gains in their popular vote and for more seats in parliament with those of the new style, high-pressure plebiscites in which the choice was to be for or against Hitler. Maybe Dr. Reichardt was not coordinated on this point; it was sufficient that the elections were coordinated.

But this Yearbook did not even bother to compare the Nazi elections with one another. Perhaps the Nazis missed a propaganda chance here; for it is quite an accomplishment to increase a party's vote from 43.9% of the total to 95.3% in the course of a few months, as did the Nazis between March and November, 1933. Of course, the percentage for the Fuehrer dropped back to 89.9% in August, 1934, but they soon got it up again. In 1936, 99.5% of all qualified voters did their duty, and 98.8% did it right by casting ballots "For the List and for the Fuehrer." There were by now so few negative votes that the statistical office simply lumped them together with the invalid ballots. After the great success in getting an expression of the people's will to follow the leader in 1936, there was no new plebiscite until the empire had expanded to take in more of the German folk. In April, 1938, the Austrians were allowed to show how devoted they were to the Fuehrer and how glad to be absorbed by the New State. The Sudeten Germans were given the same privilege in due time. After that there were no plebiscites. The war was on. But in the reporting of 1938 elections in the 1939 Yearbook a slight change was made. What had been called Austria in 1938 was now called "former Austria." One must remember that the German name for Austria means Eastern Empire, obviously not a fit name for a rather insignificant part of the all-inclusive eternal Greater German Empire.

Race, in the pre-Nazi Yearbooks, was a characteristic of stallions. The number of their registered services for the propagation of their respective races was faithfully recorded in the agricultural part of the book. Men, on the other hand, had religion. They were Christians of Protestant or Roman-Catholic confession, or they were Israelites. That took in most Germans; a handful of others were lumped together. The 1932 book showed how many of each of these categories had lived in various parts and in the whole of Germany in 1910 and in 1925. The only other tables of religion are those which show the religion of each partner in all marriages of the previous year. Religion is indirectly shown in the tables of membership in trade unions and professional organizations, for some such organizations were Catholic or Protestant. None was specifically Jewish. In the first Hitler Yearbook, 1933, the references to religion are exactly as before—with one exception. The trade unions had already been dissolved. The book listed the divisions of the new Labor Front, but regretted that membership figures were not yet available. They were not in the next book, or the one after that, or ever. Perhaps, since all workers belonged to the Labor Front by definition, it would have been silly to give figures; they would have been the same as the figures of people employed in each occupation and industry.

The expressions Jew, Jewess, and Jewish do not occur in the pre-Nazi books or in the first Hitler Yearbook, 1933. Some people were of Israelite religion; some men and women of Israelite religion were married to women and men of the same religion or of Protestant, Roman Catholic or other faiths. That was all. The 1934 Yearbook reports a new religious Census made in 1933, and compares the religious composition of the population of that year with that of 1925. The 1910 comparison was dropped. The same words are still used for the various religions. But in 1935, although the same figures and the same words were used, there is a whole new set of tables which tell us all about some people called "Glaubensjuden," of whom a special census had been taken on the 16th of June, 1933. They must be the same people who were formerly of

Israelite religion, because there are exactly as many of them. But the change is more than one of name. The 1935 Yearbook picks these Glaubensjuden out for special attention not given people of other religions. We are shown what per cent Jews form of the population in all geographic divisions; how many of them live in cities of more than 100,000, more than 50,000 and so on. The Jewish populations of Berlin, Hamburg, Frankfurt, Breslau and a few other large cities are shown in a separate table. The places of birth of Jews are tabulated, also the number and per cent of them who are of German or foreign birth, and subjects of Germany or of other countries.

By this time, the Nuremberg laws had made a distinction between people who are subjects of Germany and those who are citizens. The Jews were subjects but could not be citizens. No such facts are presented for the population at large, or for Protestants or Catholics. It is clear that statistics on the Jew are of special interest to the government. We may fairly assume that the statistician had been told to prepare special data on Jews—and to change their names. The name Glaubensjuden (Jews by faith) is still one without racial connotation. Only in the tables on marriages and the religion of people who were born or who died in Prussia were there still people of Israelite religion. In fact, Israelites continued to be born, get married, and to die right down until 1939–40, while people called "Jews by faith" had occupations and lived in various places. In the 1939–40 Yearbook this name is dropped, and tables give us some new categories which take account of the finer distinctions of the Nuremberg laws: Jews, Jewish mixtures of the first degree and Jewish mixtures of the second degree in all parts of Germany, including Austria, for 1939. The same book still gives a table on the religion of the people, including Israelite. But in 1941–42, there is no longer an Israelite religion in German statistics. The religious categories are Protestant, Roman Catholic, Believers in God, and others. The Gleichschaltung of the statistics is complete. Jews are a race, not a religious group. German statistical segregation is also complete. Jews appear nowhere as simply another category of people in tables which include other Germans. There is one little exception: the good old Prussian vital statistics still show that people of Israelite religion are born and die. The Prussian civil servant is a stubborn fellow. He does his duty, come what may. Or maybe no one issued a new form for recording births and deaths in Prussia, and the officials just had to go on using the old ones.

Of all Israelite women married in 1930, one in eight married a Christian; of Israelite men, one in four married a Christian. From 1933 on, these proportions constantly decreased. In 1936, about one in fifty married out. The people of Germany were being *gleichgeschaltet;* but the statistical Yearbook stuck to its old form of reporting marriages by religion. Only in 1939–40 does racial reporting take the place of religious in marriage tables. There is in the book of that year a table showing the "Racial Classification of People Who Married in 1938." Marriage partners are now of five kinds: German-blooded, Jewish mixtures of the first degree, Jewish mixtures of the second degree, Jews and Jewesses, and persons of other foreign blood. Twenty-five German-blooded men married Jewesses, and thirty-three Jewish men married German-blooded women in that year. But these traitors to German blood were nearly all of foreign nationality; in 1939, no German-blooded subject of the Reich married a Jew or Jewess. Gleichschaltung both of marriage and marriage statistics was complete.

The Reichstatistician was prodded, I suspect, into setting up tables and graphs to show at a glance the progress of the New State's program of prosperity and territorial expansion. He never showed in a summary and graphic way the success of the program to rid the country and the folk of foreign (Jewish) blood. One has to dig the facts out from many tables. In 1910 there were 538,909 people of Israelite religion in the Reich; 564,379 in 1925; 499,-682 in 1933. One can also figure it out that in 1939 there were 451,451 of the people called Jews, Jewish mixtures of the first degree and Jewish mixtures of the second degree in the new Greater Germany. The Nazi regime could have taken credit for most of the decrease of Jewish people between 1925 and 1933, and certainly they could claim as their own the whole decrease of 48,000 between 1933 and 1939. They could have made their success more impressive by reminding the reader that the new Germany of 1939 included new eastern territory in which many Jews had lived. They could have shown in a more prominent place the reduction in percentage of Jewish population. In 1910 and 1925 nearly one German in a hundred had been a Jew; in 1939, only about one in 190. The Yearbook could also have made a better story out of emigration. It reported only those emigrants who went overseas, and failed to tell how many of them were Jews rather than people of true German blood. This was corrected in later books; for the years 1937, 1938, and 1939 Jewish overseas emigrants are shown separately from others. Until then the total number of overseas emigrants per year had remained between 12,000 and 15,000 since before the Nazi time. Emigration overseas was 14,203 in 1937; 22,986 in 1938; 25,818 in 1939. One can see in a separate table that 7,155 of the emigrants in 1937 were Jews; 16,561 in 1938, and 22,706 in 1939. The reader has to figure out for himself that while in 1937 only half the emigrants were Jews, over 90% of them were Jews in 1939. In still another table, the reader could learn that true Germans were actually coming home from overseas in greater number than they were leaving. In 1939, only 3,112 people not of Jewish blood emigrated overseas, while 10,455 came back to live or die under the New Order. The statistician could have put these things all together so that a person could follow with pride the purifying of his folk. But no; he reported it only bit by bit, grudgingly.

He did a little better for Prussia. Prussia, in its old-fashioned way, kept right on reporting births and deaths by religion, and persisted in considering that there was an Israelite religion—a fallacy that the New State had given up. If this kind of reporting had been done for all of Germany, one could have had an ideal record of the progress of the liquidation of the Jews. As it is, we do know from various tables that there were 370,348 Prussian Israelites in 1910; 404,446 in 1925; 361,826 Prussian Jews by faith in 1933; and 233,727 Jews, Jewish mixtures of the first and second degrees in the larger Prussia in 1939. Some measure of success is seen in the fact that actually one person in a hundred was a Jew in 1925 in Prussia, but only about half a person in a hundred in 1939. But how was the success achieved? Through encouraging emigration and the death rate? Or by discouraging the birth rate? One has to work hard to get some idea of the weights of these various methods. By using a lot of tables and making some assumptions of the kind that statisticians make, one can estimate that about 42,000 Prussian Jews emigrated overseas from 1933 to the end of August, 1939. As to the births, 2,100 children were born to Jewish mothers in Prussia in 1933, and about 100 to other mothers but of Jewish fathers. The births decreased steadily until 1939, when only 478 were born to Jewish mothers and less than fifty to other mothers and Jewish fathers. This was a good solid reduction of 75% in the number of Jews being produced by birth. But that is a slow method of liquidation. It depends too much upon the life-span. In the meantime, in spite of the smaller number of Jews left in Prussia, the death figure held up very well. In 1933, when there were 361,826 Jews in Prussia, 5,565 died. The number of deaths remained above 5,000 a year right along. In 1938, for instance, 5,632 died.

In 1939 the number of deaths weakened a little to 5,182. But since there were then only 233,727 Jews and mixtures left in Prussia, the death rate was more than holding its own. Just think of it: the Jewish population was down 128,099 in six years, a good 35%, without making a dent in the number of Jews who died every year! A pretty good record, all in all, when one remembers that the big campaign had not really started yet. But the statistician should have saved the reader all this trouble. He should have coordinated his statistics about this program of the New State, just as for others. I begin to think he wasn't really *gleichgeschaltet* at all. It is too late for him to make it good now. The 1941–42 Yearbook was the eighth and last put out by the 1,000-Year Reich.

To be sure, a new series of Yearbooks has been started. The first is out: Statistical Yearbook of the German Federal Republic, 1952. It looks a lot like the old ones. The Foreword, signed by one Dr. Gerhard Fuerst, is short and businesslike. He tells of the technical difficulties caused by loss of records and by changes in boundaries. A lot of the tables are devoted to the many refugees from the east. The New State of the Nazis, like the new eastern-zone Democratic German Republic, exported refugees. The new western Federal Republic of Germany receives refugees.

The new western statistical German has lost his race and got back his religion. Some of them even belong to "the Jewish religious community." Not many; just 17,116 as compared with 103,293 in the same territory in 1939.

BIAS IN THE STUDY OF RACE RELATIONS

By John Dollard

IT HAD NEVER OCCURRED TO ME to consider my own bias until I got into the field. Here, however, one harsh experience brought it sharply to mind. One hot morning I made bold to present a letter of introduction to a well-known southern writer. He met me on his porch and, after an exchange of formalities,

Reprinted by permission from *Caste and Class In A Southern Town*, by John Dollard, Harper and Brothers, New York, 1949, pp. 33–40.

inquired what I was doing. I told him briefly. He responded at once that I had little chance of learning anything about the personality of Negroes; he had lived among them for years and had not learned much; so what hope could there be for me? Since I had heard this before, I did not take it too seriously. Then he said something, however, which made me angry but which eventually I took very seriously. I had the idea in the back of my mind, he told me, that he was prejudiced and untrustworthy, and I came prepared not to believe what he had to say. I assumed unconsciously that he was blinded by race prejudice, as it is called in the North. I must feel this way, he said, because all northerners come south with this idea, no matter what their formal protestations may be. At this point, I decided that he had taught me enough and went my way, but I marveled at his candor and his insight. He had not been in essence discourteous, merely uncomfortably frank.

Returning to my research, I examined the material I had already collected and found abundant evidence of the attitude attributed to me—an attitude which had safely survived my sociological graduate training. An example from my notes written before this meeting will demonstrate the point.

These white people down here are very charming and really exert themselves to do friendly things once you are accepted, but they seem very much like the psychotics one sometimes meets in a mental hospital. They are sane and charming except on one point, and on this point they are quite unreliable. One has exactly the sense of a whole society with a psychotic spot, an irrational, heavily protected sore through which all manner of venomous hatreds and irrational lusts may pour, and —you are eternally striking against this spot.

This excerpt reveals an obvious bias in the form of an invidious comparison of southern white people with psychotics, and it further indicates disbelief in what they say, exactly as my informant asserted.

The shock of this experience sufficed to bring about a serious reconsideration of the subject of bias and a conscious awareness of it which persisted during the entire data-gathering period. The example just cited illustrates clearly the sectional bias on the part of northerners of which southern white people are so conscious. There has been a long history of bitter and aggressive men going into the South from the northeast, and the newcomer is appropriately classified at once, especially when his avowed motive is "to study the Negro." One attempt to escape such a classification is to refer to oneself as a "student of society" and imply thereby a lack of bias. Actually, however, there was no escaping the fact that I was a northerner making a study of the South. At first I wanted to escape it; I preferred to hold up an image of myself as without affect and objective. This illusion could not be maintained and for the reason above alleged, namely, that southerners did not believe it and that it was not true. Northern readers and students need to be reminded of their sectional bias and of the necessity of reckoning with it in all dealings with the South or southerners. Most of us still take pride in the fact that "we" saved the Union and freed the slaves and rebuked properly the arrogance of South Carolina and the rest. Many of us can recall our schoolroom thrills in singing "Tenting Tonight," "John Brown's Body," and other Civil War songs. Many of us can experience vicariously the anxiety of four long years of war and the relief at knowing that "the right" was upheld even at such a price. Many, too, vaguely remember stories of ancestors who died or were wounded in the War. Behind the romantic legend which now conceals the realities of the conflict, considerable anti-southern sentiment can still be mobilized today. We inherit an abolitionist tradition, which has soaked into our frame of social perception. The visitor is brought up short when he first hears of the "War between the States," a name which stresses the independence and autonomy once claimed by the individual southern states. Southern writers and scientists have not been lacking in appreciation of northern regional bias. The scholarly A. H. Stone has made the point clearly, as Thomas N. Page had done even earlier, and more recently Howard W. Odum has referred to the "emotional set" of northern intellectuals.

The only possible conclusion from this experience was that I had the typical sectional bias to be expected of a northerner, and I thereupon set out to isolate and discount it. For one thing, I began to pay serious attention to what southern white people told me about the interracial situation, and although I did not always agree with them, I always learned from them. The persistence of an unacknowledged and unresisted sectional bias might have barred me from much indispensable information. The discovery of sectional bias had another advantage, namely, that I realized I was irrevocably a northerner and ended my attempts to pass for anything else. This was a healthier rôle and permitted a much more honest interaction with southern white people. The shock of being a "Yankee," instead of a sociologist, soon wore off and compensatory advantages were revealed.

A second form of bias which cannot be ignored is personal bias. A notion that there might be such in my case dawned upon me when I realized that people were forever asking overtly or by implication: "What is this particular Yankee sociologist among all possible Yankee sociologists doing down here studying niggers?" On several occasions this question was directly and impolitely asked, more often indirectly and courteously, but it seemed to be in everyone's mind. It finally occurred to me to ask myself: What *was* I doing down there? Sectional bias supplied part of the answer. I was there on the old northern errand of showing up the evils of the southern system in its treatment of the Negro, and the suspicion could not be avoided that I wanted to make my research come out that way. The personal aspect of my interest, however, derived from another source, not necessarily a discreditable one, but still a bias. It was what might be called a strong feeling for the underdog, a feeling grounded in my own life history and to some extent previously revealed in self-examination. This resulted recognizably in a tendency to feel with Negroes, to be specially accessible to unusual incidents recording oppressive treatment of them, and to stand with them against the dominance of the white caste. Whatever may be the advantage of such a tendency to the social reformer, it is out of place in the researcher, whose business is to see clearly and report correctly. A pro-Negro bias generates disbelief in the statements of southern white people and supports the wish to pillory and humiliate them. From this form of bias, no doubt, came the abolitionists' idealization of Negroes and the lack of realism in their social action with reference to Negroes.

There is another form of personal bias and it pulls in quite another direction. The fact of being a socially mobile person and a member of a middle-class university group inevitably creates a bias tending to make one's research come out in such a way as to be acceptable to members of one's social class;

the possible penalty is rejection or isolation by them. The words we use and the thoughts we think, even in research, are likely to label us as loyal or disloyal members of our own class. Further, the middle-class researcher could easily make the mistake of assuming that all Negroes are disciplined middle-class persons like himself, undoubtedly an immortal error in northern perception of the Negro. He might attribute to all Negroes his own restless urges toward mobility and postulate on their behalf an unhappiness which they do not feel in their lot. He will certainly exaggerate the desirability of his own class position and underestimate the frustrations and sacrifices entailed by it. The best chance of avoiding these erroneous forms of perception is to have a clear understanding of one's own class position, past and present. Undoubtedly many researchers who have gone south unaware of this bias have been seduced by the hospitality of the middle- and upper-class southern white people, have formed agreeable ties with them, and have thereupon been pulled into the southern mode of perception of the racial problem. This is to some extent unavoidable since southern white people are often courteous hosts and one inevitably identifies with them. One feels the implied stipulation: "If you like me, think as I do." Unconsciously the researcher wants to please those who have displayed cordiality and generosity by seeing eye-to-eye with them at all points. He is in like danger of being influenced by friendly relations with cultivated Negroes. In referring to the race question Stone has specifically stressed the necessity of examining one's own bias.

In talking with informants I noticed constantly the different manner in which we viewed various daily incidents, such as a suicide, a divorce, or a dream. This difference can be attributed to a psychological mode of perception resulting from my psychoanalytic training. Psychological observation deserves to be classed as a bias, because its utility is not generally conceded in the social science field. The analyst is concerned with individual meanings, with the affect which accompanies any act, with the position of an item of observed behavior in the character and life history of the informant. In particular he is trained to watch for the reservations with which people carry out formally defined social actions, the repression required by social conformity, and, in general, to see, behind the surface of a smooth social façade, the often unknown and usually unacknowledged emotional forces which drive and support social action. This point of view gives a solid sense of man as an animal and tends to stress the biological driving forces of human action. Culture is seen as a device for modeling and remodeling a recalcitrant animal and as performing the remarkable feat of his socialization. We learn from this view, for example, that while animals may be made docile in social life by reducing drive forces (i.e., by actual castration), men are made tractable by culture (i.e., by internalizing social prohibitions). Psychological perception or bias makes the problem more complex but permits explanations which are impossible on the institutional-historical level of perception; it fosters a tendency to watch details of behavior, to ponder on them, and to try to make systematic sense of whatever fragments of the individual life one can get hold of.

A fourth attitude, the sociological, perhaps deserves least of all to be called a bias; yet from the standpoint of Southerntown it was definitely regarded as such, and it is still far from widespread enough to have the agreement necessary for a tested method. First and foremost, it involves distance from the object of study, an intellectual distance provided by the many comparisons one is able to make with any given community. It challenges the sense of absoluteness and rightness with which all culture bearers view their social habits. One sees the community comparatively and historically, and in this perspective it seems historically determined and relative. By using this view also one sees not a mere forest of individuals, but rather a collectivity interacting—something more than an aggregate of individual animals. When we speak of a "society," we refer to the central object of study. Conceptualization takes place in terms of groups and group relations and not in terms of a specious isolation of individuals. As one of my teachers expressed it, one sees the individual as a specimen of a group rather than as one of a mere aggregate of individuals.

Another feature of the sociological bias is its insistence upon fully utilizing the social heritage in explaining human action before having recourse to biological factors. Taken by itself this frequently leads to a kind of sociologism which excludes the biological life altogether. It is probably a truly biased view if used apart from a valid mode of psychological perception. Southerntowners certainly found the sociological point of view very irritating when it was occasionally brought to the fore; as, for example, in denying the categorical inferiority of Negroes and explaining their present status in terms of historical circumstances.

RESEARCH AS AN EXPERIENCE IN HUMAN RELATIONS

*

By Thomas Gordon

A WELL-KNOWN RESEARCH PSYCHOLOGIST once advised me about the inappropriateness of including in a research report an account of the troubles and bad luck I had encountered on a research project. His argument was that colleagues, and especially the sponsors of the project, are primarily interested in results and may interpret a report of your troubles as an excuse for not obtaining results. Although I have had occasion to see the wisdom of his judgment, I am also convinced that there are certain values in looking behind the scenes at some of the troubles encountered in doing research.

I see value in calling the attention of investigators who may do work in the same area in the future to the problems one encounters and the mistakes one

Reprinted from Thomas Gordon, "Research As An Experience in Human Relations," *Human Development Bulletin*, 6, (January, 1950), 6–10, published by the Human Development Organization under the sponsorship of the Committee on Human Development, the University of Chicago.

makes in meeting them. Furthermore, it is becoming more apparent to me that as social scientists we must place the act of doing research itself under scientific scrutiny. When we do, we will not only do better research but we are apt to discover psychological principles which are just as fruitful as those derived from research on other problems involving human behavior.

There perhaps may be still another value in a behind-the-scenes report of the research process. I have long felt that from the typical research articles in scientific journals students may learn facts, figures and findings, but they are denied the opportunity to learn how to conduct research. Here I am suggesting to the faculties of graduate training programs in social science that in our emphasis upon imparting the *results* of research to our students we may be overlooking an opportunity for them to begin to learn the *skills* of conducting research. By skills, I do not mean the technical skills required for the construction of tools and statistical analysis of data. Rather, I refer to the social skills required in dealing with people.

* *

By Everett C. Hughes

THE RESEARCH PART of what is reported in *French Canada in Transition* (Chicago: University of Chicago Press, 1943), was not designed, if by design one means a blue-print complete before the work was begun. It has been a growth of some twenty-five years. One might speak of it as a social movement, for eventually many people have been drawn into it. This memorandum will be a sort of natural history of this movement.

In the late 1920's, Carl A. Dawson began to study the process of settlement of the frontier, as seen in the growth and changes of a number of communities in the western provinces of Canada. Some of these communities were experiments in settling British urban workers on the land; many were created by people of Continental European origin; others, by sects who sought on the distant prairie a haven where they could practice a peculiar faith in peace and prosperity. Dawson had thus chosen as his own one of Canada's great problems (C. A. Dawson, *The Settlement of the Peace River Country,* [Toronto: The Macmillan Company of Canada, Ltd., 1934]).

He had just begun this work when I joined him in the still new department of sociology at McGill University. I had had no previous interest in Canadian problems, and but little knowledge of the country. In the several months between my appointment and my departure from Chicago for Montreal, I read a good deal about the French Canadians whom, I knew, were to be found in Montreal in large number. I decided to study the French Canadians simply

Everett C. Hughes, "The Natural History of a Research Project: French Canada." Unpublished paper.

because their presence seemed the most interesting thing about Montreal and that region. By so slight a joining of circumstances, I picked Canada's other great problem, that of the adjustment to each other of the two major ethnic groups.

The baggage I took with me from graduate school to Montreal included two conceptions of a people such as the French Canadians. They were: 1) that of an immigrant group in course of being assimilated, and 2) that of a national minority.

In the United States, sociologists had devoted much of their effort to study of European immigrants who had come to America more recently than themselves. From simple talk of loyalty and Americanization, some of the sociologists had gone on to seek a more general set of concepts for describing the changes which take place when diverse peoples meet in the same community (country or region). Park adapted the socialization cycle of Simmel to this problem; contact was followed successively by conflict, accommodation and assimilation. Application of this set of concepts to the contact of peoples rested upon the assumption that one people was more ephemeral than the other, that one would disappear into the other. Although other Canadians knew well that the French Canadians were not an immigrant people, but a "charter member" group, I think that generally they thought that the French would, and ought eventually, to disappear; that the English Canadian group would and ought to outlast the French Canadians as an ethnic entity. A few studies appeared now and again on the number of French who spoke English, or who otherwise appeared to be abandoning their culture. Without going into why I think the measurement of change of individual cultural traits is a false way to study the relations between ethnic groups, I will simply say that for some reason I did not in fact accept this model of the assimilation cycle and resisted the desire of some of my students to proceed with studies on that model.

The second conception was that of a territorial national minority, such as one finds in Europe where a political boundary is shoved over in such a way as to leave some people in the wrong country. The people thus marooned may then seek to have the boundary put right so that their citizenship and ethnic identity will again correspond; or, if a whole people has been deprived of sovereignty, they may seek to found a new and separate state. The French Canadians were made into a people and a minority in precisely this way; but there was no movement among them to join France, and there appeared to be no major or persistent movement to seek political separation from Canada. They did show minority behavior in their insistence on a certain autonomy, and in their constant resistence to alleged encroachment on their rights. I found the national minority model of use, but as I read the voluminous literature, it appeared to me that political objectives, as such, were relatively unimportant to French Canadians. The most constant plaint was that French Canadians get less than their fair share of good positions, wealth and power in the economic and political institutions. The great battle cry, along with that for cultural autonomy, was *parity*,—a share in all positions commensurate with the French proportion in the population. But parity implied not separation, but integration into a larger whole. I find in my notes that I quite early came to the idea of studying just what the place of French and English was in the larger whole of which both are part, and especially of discovering the ethnic division of labor (or of economic function), both in its major outlines and in its subtleties.

In the course of following up this lead, I read a good deal on the establishment of industries in Quebec. That led to the labor movement. Now the Catholic Church had early tried to keep the French labor of Quebec out of unions, and especially out of unions which were "neutral" as to religion. A few good pieces of work had been done on the movement to organize Catholic labor syndicates. This led me to a literature I had known nothing of—that on the various attempts to establish a separate Catholic labor movement in various parts of Europe. A good deal of this literature dealt with the German Rhineland, where Protestant entrepreneurs from outside the region had brought heavy industry to utilize local resources and had mobilized local Catholic peasants as their labor force. Protestant labor leaders had followed the entrepreneurs to organize the local labor (exactly as in Quebec). As I followed up this case, I got more clearly into my mind the model of the region or community industrialized by outsiders, cultural aliens. The local region furnishes labor and/or raw materials and/or power. The newcomers furnish capital, enterprise and technical knowledge. In course of the development, the native non-industrial middle and/or upper class finds many of its functions usurped by the alien industrial leadership. In fact, the community now has two sets of leaders, one traditional and "spiritual," the other new, secular and technological. The strain between the two has many repercussions in politics and in local institutions. To rise in the new order of things requires new skills; but the educational institutions are geared to produce those qualities and skills valued in the pre-industrial regime. To re-tool the schools and universities for the new order quickly would require the calling in of even more cultural aliens. Similar dilemmas occur in other institutions: trade and labor organizations, local government, religious organizations, charities, and even in families and cliques. As I got into this it appeared to me there were essentially two kinds of industrial communities (or regions): 1) those in which by some social and economic chemistry local people themselves initiated the great changes of industrialization, eventually drawing a supply of labor from outside (this is the kind of situation to which the assimilation cycle concept may be applied with some reason); and 2) those to which industry is brought by outsiders who exploit local labor, and who undertake as many social changes as they think necessary for their purposes, within the limits of their power as counterbalanced by that of the local society. England and New England are of the first kind; the Rhineland and French Canada are of the second. Since the agents of social change in the Rhine country differed from the native people in religion but not in language, it seemed promising to examine this region so that I might better sort out the aspects due to ethnic difference from those due to the industrial invasion and to differences of religion. I did, in fact, spend more than a year in Germany digging up the story of industrialization there, and trying out with data of the German occupational and religious censuses various schemes of tabulation which I might use in analyzing the division of labor between French, English and others in Canada. The study of the Rhine case did indeed fix in my mind more clearly the model of a whole region undergoing that series of changes known as industrialization, with one ethnic element as the active, enterprising agent of change, and another in the position of having to adjust itself, although resisting them, to these changes.

When I got back to Montreal after the German excursion, I started a few students on the ethnic division of labor there. William Roy went to a number of industrial concerns and got the data which he worked up into tables showing the proportions of French and English among their employees of different kinds and ranks. From these tables we got several characteristic patterns. In heavy machine industries, a solid core of old-country British skilled workmen apparently could keep the French out of apprenticeships. In industries with mass production, and with great use of semi-skilled operators, the working force was almost completely French. Fiduciary functions were apparently kept closely in English hands, even including the faithful pensioners so often kept on as night watchmen. If there was need for extensive contact with the public, and especially the little people of the city and region, the French got their chance.

Stuart Jamieson worked on the professions, and found that not only were there marked differences in choice of profession as among French, English and Jewish, but that in the same profession each of the groups tended to practice in a certain way, the professionals of each group performing not only the peculiar services wanted by their own peoples but also some special part of the professional services of the larger system of which all were part. Thus French and Jewish lawyers tended to practice in small firms, while a very large majority of the English lawyers were gathered into a few huge firms. A leading figure in each such large firm was a member of the boards of a group of powerful corporations. Each such English firm had, however, one or two French members, apparently to act as liaison with French people and to plead before French judges. It thus became clear to me that it was much too simple merely to say that the French preferred certain occupations and the English preferred others, and that the English discriminated against French in appointing people to positions of authority in industry (although these things were doubtless true). One had to regard the whole thing as a system in which the interaction of the two peoples had brought about a division of function which was, in some points, quite subtle.

While we were working away on this line, I had some conversations with my close friend and associate, Robert Redfield, who had a crew working on a series of communities in Yucatan; he hoped to learn something of the change from what he called folk culture to urban civilization by studying simultaneously a series of communities each of which was assumed to present a point in this kind of change. It seemed to me that if we were to understand fully what was happening in metropolitan Montreal, we had to find a base line from which to gauge changes in French-Canadian culture and institutions. I began to think of a series of community studies with a village with no English people in or near it at one end, and with Montreal (where about one-fifth of all French Canadians live) at the other. Each community was to be picked for some special combination of the forces which might be at work on French Canadian institutions and mentality.

Somehow, in the midst of this, Horace Miner, an enterprising graduate student of anthropology at the University of Chicago, got himself a field fellowship to study the base-line rural community. After much search of statistics and maps a community—St. Denis de Kamouraska—was picked as being likely to show traditional French-Canadian institutions operating in full force. It was remote, but not back-woodsy or poor. This turned out to be an excellent choice, for it became clear that many of the traditional customs and practices depended on prosperity. A daughter of the house could not be kept at home spinning and weaving, on her own loom and with wool and flax from the family farm, unless the family land was plentiful and fertile. Farmers on back-country, poor and hilly farms had to go out to work in lumber-camps and their daughters had to go to towns to work, too; thus the common phenomenon of proud preservation of traditions by a prosperous peasantry after they are lost by the agricultural laboring class. Mr. Miner's work is published and well-known (*St. Denis: A French-Canadian Parish,* [Chicago: University of Chicago Press, 1939]). A couple of years ago he spent a few weeks there and published some notes on change since his first study in the *American Journal of Sociology* entitled "A New Epoch in Rural Quebec" (July, 1950, LVI: 1–10).

It was our intention to study a series of rural communities, at various distances from the cities and from English people, with varying terrain and soil. The notion was that each kind of situation would tend to produce its own pattern of functional connections with the larger industrial and urban world outside. Léon Gérin, a French-Canadian sociologist who studied under LePlay, had done a series on rural communities some forty years earlier, and Raoul Blanchard, the French geographer, had given a basic description of the soil and terrain, modes of agriculture, and movements of populations (Etudes canadiennes, 2e serie. *Revue de géographie alpine,* (I., XXIV, 1936, 1–189), (II., XXV, 1937, 1–210), (III., XXVI, 1938, 1–183)). We used these works in tentative choice of kinds of communities to be studied. Some rather superficial studies of new northern settlements have been made since then, but no detailed studies to determine the flow of people and goods from country to city and from farm to industry, or the flow of fashion and other changes from city to country.

The middle term of the series was to be a small industrial city. Now there were many such in the province of Quebec. We worked over government and business statistics with great care before choosing the first town, which my wife and I were to study ourselves. In the north and on the mountainous fringes of Quebec are towns with pulp-mills, company towns where various non-ferrous ores are mined, and a few where colossal power developments have brought aluminum smelters (which require cheap power) far out into the backwoods of yesterday. In some of these the industry created the town. Some are seasonal; some hire men only, and so on. Since we wanted to see what effect the newer industry had on French-Canadian institutions, we chose as the starter a community in which those institutions had all been in existence well before industry came and in which there were local French families of a wide variety of occupations and of all the commoner social classes, and in which consequently there were French Canadians accustomed to the roles of political and economic leadership. The problem was not defined primarily in terms of English and industrial influence of, let us say, the language spoken by people, but in terms of the operating social structure.

It may perhaps be well to tell the plan of *French Canada in Transition.* In the foreword and first chapter I say some of the things I have enlarged upon in this memorandum. Then I describe briefly the rural family and parish, for these are the cradle of the industrial labor force of the cities, and are the institutions which undergo change under the influence of industry and the English. After considering the larger series of industrial towns and cities, I go on to our chosen community. In order to understand the industrial town of today, it seemed to me that we had to know its past, the rise and decline of enterprises, institutions and families through more than a century. With this setting in the reader's mind, we took him directly to the division of labor, in and outside industry. In the case of industry, we were able to describe pretty exactly, I think, the division of labor, and to account for the details of it. Subsequent studies in other industries and cities have revealed very little deviation from these patterns.

In the section on non-industrial occupations I attempted to set up a scheme for analyzing what will happen in an inter-ethnic community to those services and business enterprises which are subject to daily small choices of customers and clients, rather than to the major policy-choices of large executives. It seemed to me that one could posit that there are some services and goods wanted by both ethnic elements in identical form, while others are wanted by one more than by the other. Further one can suppose that there are some things which people insist on getting from people of their own kind, while they are relatively indifferent about the hands from which they get other things.

From there we go on to consideration of institutions, distinguishing those areas of life in which there is but one set of going concerns (institutions) operated by and for both elements of the population, and noting the changes brought about in them by industrializing, and the part played in them by French and English. Business, sports and government showed but a single set of institutions. In religion and education, there was almost complete separation of the two ethnic elements, but it turned out that the English as well as the French schools and churches had been profoundly affected by the new people of industry. The Catholic parishes and their auxiliary institutions have shown great modification to suit industrial and urban conditions.

In the later chapters we presented the less formal aspect of things; or perhaps I should say the livelier side, for the French have a rich ceremonial calendar; informal social contacts, public gatherings, amusements and fashions. The book closes with reference to Montreal, the metropolis. It was our aim to continue with studies in Montreal, but I left Canada at this point.

There are some bad lacunae in the study and in the book. While we present some data concerning cliques in the chapter on Social Contacts, and have a good deal more in our field notes, we did not adequately analyze the operation of small and informal groups in the town and in the industries. I am reasonably sure that there were no inter-ethnic small groups to speak of in the industries, but we should have got the data on small-groups and informal understandings and controls. Our knowledge of informal organization of industry was confined to the upper levels of the hierarchy.

The analysis of the more intimate life of the masses of the people of the town is sketchy. The story of the working-class family,—the internal stresses and strains of such a family newly come from farm to town and factory,—is not more than touched upon. We did not get adequate case material on this point. In fact, what the family as a going concern is in Cantonville, what crises it meets in its ongoing life, we did not find out. M. Jean-Charles Falardeau of Université Laval, is in the midst of studying the families of a large working-class parish in Quebec City. He has already published one article on the contingencies and life-cycle of urban French-Canadian families (Jean C. Falardeau, "Changes in Community Organization, Group Attitudes and Collective Behavior," *Symposium: The Social Impact of Industrialization in the Province of Quebec,* Laval University, 1952). We still do not have adequate knowledge of the changes in consumption patterns of individuals and families of the various classes of urban French-Canadians. Such knowledge is necessary to an understanding of family objectives and of conflict between the family and its individual members.

Just before I left Montreal, I began to have some conversations with a psychiatrist who was analyzing some young people of the sophisticated classes of French Canadians. Although he had some rather ready clichés about them, he was really interested in learning the structure of French-Canadian personalities. I had run into a number of restless, uneasy French young men, who knew they had been trained for a world that was passing, and that they had not the nerve to break away from their protective families far enough to start over and take the ego risks of a new kind of learning and a new kind of career; the contingency of being bred a gentleman a little too late had caught them. This aspect of the industrialization of this region has not been studied; the personality problems, the psychological risks. The most recent information I have shows that the French graduates of the French-Canadian engineering schools still tend to seek the cover of semi-bureaucratic jobs. Whether they do it before or after a rebuff or two in industry, before or after a minor failure,— I don't know. But the whole structure of the famliy, the church-controlled educational system, etc., as they operate to produce people geared to certain patterns of risk and security, with certain balances with respect to reaching out and travelling far as against digging in and staying near home, with certain capacities for aggressive interaction and tolerating criticism, this should all be studied. And it should be studied by some combination of observing and analyzing personal careers with use of the devices now available for delving deep into the dreams and nightmares of people. The question may be this: Will the French-Canadian middle class personality ever gear into the interactional systems of industrial line organizations; or will they skirt the edges catching a slight hold only in certain liaison or staff positions which they hold precisely because they are French? In that case, it might be that if French-Canadians do rise in the line organization of industry they may be people of some new class created by industry itself. The story of the individual in French Canada, of the forming of his personality, and of his meeting the new big world as a series of career-crises demanding fateful decisions on his part, that has not been told either in my study or in any other.

The program for studying a whole series of industrial communities was not carried through. The great recent development in Quebec has been that of new towns around new industries in the far north. In such towns there is no established French middle class, no set of local businesses and institutions, around them is no established *habitant,* or farm-owning class. It might be argued that we should have studied a north-country boom town in the first place, but I still think it served our purpose better to start with a town in which the French-

Canadian institutions and a French-Canadian society were in full operation before English people brought industry. Yet, the whole region will not be understood until someone takes a good look at what kinds of social and political structure grow up where the new industry with an English management builds a town with French labor, but no counter-balancing French social élite except the clergy.

Even on the rural front, the full variety of typical communities has not been studied. Aileen Ross of McGill University has done one good study of the social processes of ethnic succession on the frontier between French and English in the eastern townships of Quebec.

The third kind of community was to be metropolitan, Montreal. I had started there, and most of the work done by the few students I got interested (they were just beginning to flock my way when I left) was centered there. I carried some of the material to Chicago with me and with the aid of a research assistant whom I brought along,—Margaret McDonald—a couple of articles got published on the ethnic division of labor. A few students came along and carried out small bits of work which fitted into the general scheme.

The plan was to work out the whole scheme of division of labor with as much detail and subtlety as we could. It had already become clear that the Jewish people had to be drawn into the scheme. The fact that the English and French are so clearly marked off from each other, and that they have so many separate institutions made the Jews and Jewish institutions more visible than in many communities; they are a kind of third term in the local system. We also planned to watch changes in the larger institutional systems (philanthropy, education, etc.,) of the French world in Montreal, and to see what kinds of connections might grow up between French and English institutions as the city grew.

My hypothesis concerning charitable institutions, for instance, was that the French would adopt the English institutional forms—raising money by city-wide campaigns, distribution of money and services by professional social workers, etc.,—but that the French-Catholics and English-Protestants would continue to maintain fully separate systems of going-concerns in this field. The English Protestant institutions are those developed to replace, under urban and industrial conditions, the earlier parochial charitable institutions. It seemed almost inevitable that the French, finding their own parochial institutions inadequate to the new conditions, would follow the only available model. Aileen Ross has been studying further the English philanthropic structure, but I do not believe anyone is studying the further adaptation of the French. I do know that French and English are sharing some of the faculty of their schools of social work.

Some parts of the study as originally conceived are being carried out by Prof. Oswald Hall and his students. They are studying hospitals and one of his students, M. Jacques Brazeau, did a penetrating study of the career contingencies of French-Canadian physicians. This group and some other people are studying the inner organization of industries which have personnel of the two ethnic groups. (Incidentally, a little observation in a large company in Montreal suggested that the reason all their dieticians had nervous breakdowns in a few months after being hired was simply that they hired progressive English dieticians to feed French-Canadian pères de famille. Think of a compulsive English-speaking protestant spinster dietitian trying to feed a bunch of hearty peasoupers.) They are also studying the induction of French and English recruits into the Canadian Army, with emphasis on small group formation as a factor in adjustment. But there is not quite, I think, a studied and persistent effort to build out the model of study of Montreal that we had thought of.

But a most interesting and unforeseen thing has happened. I had early concluded that the future of French Canada lay very much in the great national headquarters city, Montreal, and that Quebec City, the older and more purely French headquarters of French Canada, would have a minor role in the new industrial society. I visited down there occasionally, because it was picturesque and because I wanted statistics from provincial bureaus. But I did not take Quebec City seriously.

No sooner had I got settled in Chicago than I began, in one way or another, to meet people from Quebec City. Eventually I was invited down there for a semester as visiting professor at the Université Laval (I had never been invited in any way to the Université de Montreal, although I had tried to make contacts there). Laval had established a very live faculty of social sciences. I found there an active group of people engaged in a variety of movements of a "take the bull by the horns" spirit with respect to the industrialization of Quebec. A metropolicentric (sic) Montrealer, I knew almost nothing of the people or the movements in Quebec. Since then my contacts have been with the young social scientists of this faculty, nearly all of whom are continuing work on the economic and social changes accompanying industrialization of the province. I certainly did not create this group, nor did I design their research. Yet I have been a part of the movement of which they are also part, and the general design worked out in course of my study has been, in general, followed out in their work. What interests me much more than the influence of this model on their work or on any one's work, is an incidental implication of some importance for applied social scientists. At a certain point in the history of Quebec, an outsider came there under circumstances which made it a most intriguing and natural thing to start study of the bi-ethnic community and region, and to turn that study toward the changes wrought by industrialization. I, the outsider, for a long time got little or no interest from English students of the region. The first to work with me on the problem was a New England boy, born of French Canadian parents; he looked at the whole thing with interest but as from a slight distance; the next was a Western Canadian who looked on the whole world from a slight distance. This combination kept the work going for some time. Perhaps it was inevitable that, if the work was to be continued, it should be done by the French Canadians themselves, the people most affected by the changes. What good is a research design which does not include some reference to those who will execute it?

SOCIAL SCIENCE AND SOCIAL ENGINEERING

By Louis Wirth

PROGRAMS FOR THE IMPROVEMENT of race relations have enlisted wide popular interest and substantial material support. Hundreds of national, state, and local public and private organizations are at work pursuing activities designed to solve practical problems in this field. It must be admitted, however, that perhaps to a greater degree than in other problem areas, practice far outruns reliable scientific knowledge. The thousands of men and women of good will who are engaged in improving the relations between racial, religious, and cultural groups that comprise America have been guided by moral, religious, or patriotic convictions, by common sense, and by such expert knowledge as chance has made available to them. They trust that what they do makes a difference and leads to improvement; but they are not certain.

Most of the present programs assume that it is possible to change human behavior by teaching, preaching, propaganda, and legislation or by exposing people to new experiences and altering their conditions of life. The assumptions upon which these efforts rest, however, have not been critically and systematically examined. Only the first steps toward testing the validity of the theories underlying practical action have been taken. In view of the acuteness of the problems, their importance for national well-being and the future of America's position in the world, the impatience of the action agencies is understandable. They want practical results and they want the research workers to deliver them now. Some of the more impetuous of the action agencies are either convinced that they already have all of the answers or so sceptical or naive about the ability of social science to give them valid answers to their questions as to be inclined to ignore research altogether.

The ability of the social sciences to furnish answers to questions of policy and techniques in the field of racial and cultural relations is limited by many obstacles. In this field, as in so many other areas of social life, the research worker labors under the handicaps that every layman considers himself an expert and that controlled experimentation is difficult and costly. Competition between agencies is keen and there is a tendency to claim that such beneficent changes as take place are due to one's own program whether or not such claims are justified. The very multiplication of agencies and programs, however, and the more critical attitude of the supporters of these programs have led to some degree of coordination of effort and have given impetus to concerted programs of research both in the action agencies themselves and in the universities and research centers.

Progress in the development of more effective techniques for analyzing and treating problems of inter-group relations has been aided by the more general

Reprinted from Louis Wirth, "Research in Racial and Cultural Relations," *Proceedings of the American Philosophical Society,* XCII (November 12, 1948), 381–386, with the kind permission of Mary Wirth.

acceptance among research workers of a number of common assumptions, notably the following:

(1) That problems of race relations can be more adequately understood if they are viewed generically, i.e., if Negro-white relations are seen as not fundamentally different from the minority-dominant group relations involving Catholics, Jews, Spanish-Americans, and Japanese-Americans.

(2) That racial and cultural relations are not a realm apart from the rest of social life but manifest themselves in the normal routines of living, such as business and industry, the school, the church, the labor union, the courts, the army, the professions, in recreation, health, housing, welfare, and in community affairs.

(3) That the problems of racial and cultural relations are the product of the loosening of local ties, of widened and intensified human contacts incident to mass migration, mass communication, industrialism, and urbanism and to the world-wide diffusion of the democratic ideal which has inspired the quest for freedom and equality among many peoples who formerly accepted their lot without protest, and hence could not be considered minority peoples.

(4) That race relations are not essentially different from other inter-group relations such as industrial relations and international relations, and that they must be approached as we approach other interpersonal and intergroup attitudes, prejudices, antipathies, tensions, and conflicts, keeping in mind, of course, the complicating factor of racial and cultural differences.

(5) That racial and cultural relations are affected by the character of the society, its traditions and laws, its resources, its stability, its stratification, its economy and the composition, distribution, and succession of its component population groups, and

(6) That, although there has always been and probably will always be intergroup conflict, not all of this conflict is inevitable, and that, given the will and the intelligence, much of it is subject to prevention and control.

Despite the enormous volume and great variety of practical activity in this field there is at present no reliable evidence to show what, if any, contribution this prodigious effort is making to improve the situation. In view of the serious nature of the problems and in the light of the result obtained by scientific study of other fields it would seem, therefore, that if even an infinitesimal proportion of the total resources now devoted to action programs were diverted to the ascertainment of the effectiveness or ineffectiveness of these programs, both the field of race relations and that of social science might be well served.

Lest anyone think that race relations is merely an *ad hoc* area of applied social science or of social engineering, let me say that although I would not be ashamed to admit it, if it were true, such a view, in my opinion, involves a fundamental misunderstanding of the social sciences. Our task is to study social reality, i.e., the life of man in society, and racial and cultural relations are one phase of this life. There is no other realm of existence for us to study, although we can approach this as well as all other phases of social existence on varying levels of generality, abstractness, or remoteness from the scene of action and policy.

There is scarcely an aspect of race relations which social scientists might not study with profit and there is no social science discipline which does not in some manner bear upon the problems of race relations. To arrive at sound social policies we need, to be sure, all the relevant knowledge that the social sciences have to offer, and more; we need wisdom, courage, freedom, and the power to put our knowledge to use. We may not be able to answer all the pressing immediate problems at once, but if we are skillful we can define our subject of inquiry in such a way as to make it both scientifically valuable and practically useful. I know of no rule in science which says that we must halt our investigations whenever they threaten to have important practical consequences. On the other hand there is no rule of practical conduct which dictates that all action must cease until science has given us a complete and final answer to our questions. We know that *all* the facts will never be in, and meanwhile we must act on the basis of such knowledge and wisdom as we have. I for one am willing to start with common sense, for that, contradictory as it may be, is all that we have to start with; and I shall be content if, for some time to come, while we are trying to improve upon the accumulated empirical wisdom of the human race by means of science, we can assure ourselves of achieving an even slightly better than fifty per cent probability of correct answers.

At present, however, the conflagrations reported all about us keep us busy trying to put out fires when we are not at all certain as to whether the hose that we use is filled with water or with gasoline. In discussing his program with a leader of a national organization in the race relations field recently I suggested that the time might have come to evaluate the effectiveness of his program. He was frank enough to tell me that, even if an objective appraisal showed that the money they spent did no good, they might still continue to carry it on because probably it did no harm. Fortunately, however, both for race relations and for social science, there is increasing interest among the technicians and executives of the race relations agencies as well as among the donors of their funds in a critical appraisal of the assumptions upon which they proceed, the methods they use, and the results they achieve.

One of the serious obstacles to the improvement in race relations has been the ambiguity of the objectives to be attained. There is a disposition to assume that, if only the people of our community, our nation, and the world were to forget about the different racial, religious, and cultural groups in their midst and were to treat them all as human beings, all would be well. But the fact is that different racial, ethnic, religious, and cultural groups are a stark reality or at least a fairly rugged product of our imagination and they complicate our lives and trouble our consciences. We shall probably never live in a world without having to take cognizance of these differences, although most humane and enlightened people that I know wish that they could live with others in peace, order, and under freedom retaining their own integrity and recognizing others on the basis of their personal qualities and achievement rather than their race, creed, or national origin. If you happen to live in the southern part of the United States or in South Africa, however, your conception of proper race relations is circumscribed by a deeply rooted etiquette of racial relations which prescribes strict segregation, a belief in white supremacy, and grossly unequal opportunities. Hence many otherwise enlightened Southerners are for the present unable to share our professed ideal of non-segregation and equality of opportunity, to which, let it be said, we ourselves do not always adhere.

This calls attention to the fact that what is a problem of race relations in one area and one culture may not be a problem in another area or culture and that even in any one community the values that are to be striven for are not always unambiguous and mutually compatible. Since social problems arise out of the recognition of a discrepancy between norms and practices, between aspiration and realization, or as Mr. Myrdal has put it, between our creed and our performance, the social scientist seeking to understand these problems cannot afford to ignore the factors that make them problems, namely the value system of the community or society in question.

It is the social scientist's business not merely to ascertain what the dominant values of the society are, but to show their compatibility with each other, the extent to which they are realized or realizable and at what social cost. It will become quite clear in the course of such investigations, whether carried out through historical studies, life histories, community surveys, intensive interviews, or mass attitude and opinion polls, that not all alleged values are actually cherished and that they are not all equally fervently sought. From the standpoint of the strategy of race relations such studies might be crucial for they might reveal, for instance, that what the Southern whites most fear and are most reluctant to concede, namely Negro-white social equality, especially intermarriage, is not what the Negro most wants; and that what the Negro wants most, namely equality before the law, equal job opportunities, and educational opportunities, is precisely what the whites would be most likely to yield.

Thus, while the social scientist does not set the values of society, it is his proper role to discover what they are, how they are structured, by whom and how genuinely they are held and what the consequences are of the attempt to realize them upon other values, upon various segments of society, and upon society as a whole. By making the prevailing values explicit the social scientist can use them to discover what society takes for granted and obtain a more reliable view of the tacit assumptions underlying thought, feeling, and action.

BIBLIOGRAPHY

I. THE NEED TO KNOW WHO WE ARE

A. THE RACIAL SELF

Balint, Alice. "Identification." *International Journal of Psychoanalysis,* XXIV, (1943), 97–102.

Cantril, Hadley. "Identification With Social and Economic Class." *Journal of Abnormal and Social Psychology,* XXXVIII (1943), 74–80.

Clark, Kenneth B. and Clark, Mamie K. "The Development of Consciousness of Self and the Emergence of Racial Identification in Negro Preschool Children." *The Journal of Social Psychology,* X (November, 1939), 591–599.

Faris, Robert E. L. *Social Psychology.* New York: Ronald Press Company, 1952.

Foote, Nelson N. "Identification as the Basis for a Theory of Motivation." *American Sociological Review,* XVI (February, 1951), 14–21.

Goodman, M. E. *Race Awareness in Young Children.* Cambridge, Mass.: Addison-Wesley Press, 1952.

Horowitz, Ruth E. "Racial Aspects of Self-Identification in Nursery School Children." *Journal of Psychology,* VII (1939), 91–99.

Kaplan, Bernice A. "Ethnic Identification in an Indian Mestizo Community." *Phylon,* XIII (Second Quarter, 1953), 179–186.

Klausner, S. Z. "Social Class and Self-Concept." *Journal of Social Psychology,* XXXVIII (November, 1953), 201–205.

Mead, George H. "The Social Self." *Journal of Philosophy,* X (1913), 374–380.

——. "The Genesis of the Self and Social Control." *International Journal of Ethics,* XXXV (1924–1925), 251–277.

——. *Mind, Self and Society.* Chicago: University of Chicago Press, 1934.

Memmi, Albert. *The Pillar of Salt.* Translated by Edouard Roditi. New York: Criterion Books, 1955.

Murphy, Gardner. *Personality: A Biosocial Approach to Origins and Structure.* New York: Harper and Brothers, 1947.

Sprague, Theodore W. "The Rivalry of Intolerance in Race Relations." *Social Forces,* XXVIII (October, 1949), 68–76.

B. RACIALLY MARGINAL PERSONS AND GROUPS

1. The Marginal Man

A Half Chinese. "Persecution and Oppression of Me." *Independent,* LXXI (August 24, 1911), 421–426.

Allingham, Margery. *The Galantrys.* Boston: Little, Brown and Company, 1943.

Barker, Roger G., Wright, Beatrice A., and Gonick, Mollie R. *Adjustment to Physical Handicap and Illness: A Survey of the Social Psychology of Physique and Disability.* New York: Social Science Research Council, 1953. 2nd ed.

Browne, Lewis. *That Man Heine.* New York: The Macmillan Company, 1927.

Ferber, Edna. *A Peculiar Treasure.* New York: Doubleday, Doran and Company, Inc., 1939.

Ginsburg, Solomon L. *A Wandering Jew in Brazil.* Nashville, Tenn.: Sunday School Board, Southern Baptist Convention, 1922.

Goldberg, M. M. "Qualification of the Marginal Man Theory." *American Sociological Review,* VI (February, 1941), 52–58.

Golovensky, David I. "The Marginal Man Concept." *Social Forces,* XXX (March, 1952), 333–339.

Green, Arnold W. "A Re-Examination of the Marginal Man Concept." *Social Forces,* XXVI (December, 1947), 167–171.

Hedrick, Helen. *The Blood Remembers.* New York: Alfred A. Knopf, 1941.

Herbert, Xavier. *Capricornia.* New York: D. Appleton-Century Co., Inc., 1943.

Johnson, James Weldon. *The Autobiography of an Ex-Coloured Man.* New York: The New American Library, 1948.

Kipling, Rudyard. *Kim.* New York: Charles Scribner's Sons, 1902.

Lewisohn, Ludwig. *Up Stream.* New York: Boni and Liveright, 1923.

——. *The Island Within.* New York: Harper and Brothers, 1928.

Lourié, Anton. "The Jew as a Psychological Type." *American Imago,* VI (1949), 119–155.

Masters, John. *Bhowani Junction.* New York: Viking Press, 1954.

Morton, Leah. *I Am a Woman and a Jew.* New York: J. H. Sears and Company, 1926.

Park, Robert E. "Migration and the Marginal Man," in E. W. Burgess (ed.), *Personality and the Social Group.* Chicago: University of Chicago Press, 1929, pp. 64–77.

Riesman, David. "Some Observations Concerning Marginality." *Phylon,* XII (September, 1951), 259–278.

Slotkin, J. S. "Status of the Marginal Man." *Sociology and Social Research,* XXVIII (September, 1943), 47–54.

Sone, Monica. *Nisei Daughter.* Boston: Little, Brown and Company, 1953.

Stern, E. G. *My Mother and I.* New York: The Macmillan Co., 1937.

Stonequist, Everett V. *The Marginal Man: A Study in Personality and Culture Conflicts.* New York: Charles Scribner's Sons, 1937.

Tillery, Carlyle. *Red Bone Woman.* New York: John Day Company, 1950.

Toller, Ernst. *I Was A German.* New York: W. Morrow & Company, 1934.

Warren, Robert Penn. *Band of Angels.* New York: Random House, 1955.

Wasserman, Jakob. *My Life as German and Jew.* New York: Coward-McCann, Inc., 1933.

2. Marginal Groups

Berry, Brewton. "The Mestizos of South Carolina." *The American Journal of Sociology,* LI (July, 1945), 34–41.

Bond, H. M. "Two Racial Islands in Alabama: Creoles and Cajuns." *The American Journal of Sociology,* XXXVI (January, 1931), 552–567.

Brotz, Howard M. "Negro 'Jews' in the United States." *Phylon,* XII (Fourth Quarter, 1952), 324–337.

Child, Irvin L. *Italian or American?* New Haven: Yale University Press, 1943.

Cressey, Paul Frederick. "The Anglo-Indians: A Disorganized Marginal Group." *Social Forces,* XIV (December, 1935), 263–268.

Day, Caroline Bond. *A Study of Some Negro-White Families in the United States.* Cambridge, Mass.: Peabody Museum of Harvard University, 1932.

De Vos, P. J. "Die Dunns Van Zoeloeland." *Journal for Social Research* (South Africa), II (June, 1951), 43–53.

Dover, Cedric. *Half-Caste.* London: M. Secker and Warburg, Ltd., 1937.

Embree, Edwin Rogers. *Brown America: The Story of a New Race.* New York: The Viking Press, 1931.

Estabrook, Arthur Howard and McDougle, Ivan E. *Mongrel Virginians: The Win Tribe.* Baltimore: The Williams and Wilkins Company, 1926.

Fischer, Eugen. *Die Rehobother Bastards und das Bastardierungsproblem-beim Menschen.* Jena: G. Fischer, 1913.

Gallaher, Art, Jr. *A Survey of the Seminole Freedmen.* Norman: University of Oklahoma, M.A. thesis, 1951.

Gilbert, William Harlen, Jr. "The Wesorts of Southern Maryland: An Outcasted Group." *Journal of the Washington Academy of Sciences,* XXXV (August 15, 1945), 237–246.

——. "Memorandum Concerning the Characteristics of the Larger Mixed-Blood Racial Islands of the Eastern United States." *Social Forces,* XXIV (May, 1946), 438–447.

Gillin, John. "Mestizo America," in Ralph Linton (ed.), *Most of the World.* New York: Columbia University Press, 1949.

Gold, Michael. *Jews Without Money.* New York: H. Liveright, 1930.

Graeber, Isacque and Britt, Steuart Henderson (eds.). *Jews in a Gentile World.* New York: The Macmillan Company, 1942.

Halford, Samuel James. *The Griquas of Griqualand: A Historical Narrative of the Griqua People.* Capetown, South Africa: Juta, 1950.

Hedin, E. L. "The Anglo-Indian Community." *American Journal of Sociology,* XL (September, 1934), 165–179.

Hofmeyr, Stefanus. *Twintig Jaren in Zoutpansberg.* Capetown: J. H. Rose and Co., 1890.

Icaza, Jorge. *Cholos.* Quito, Ecuador: 1938.

Johnson, Guy B. "Personality in a White-Indian-Negro Community." *American Sociological Review,* IV (August, 1939), 516–523.

Lam, Margaret M. *Six Generations of Race Mixture in Hawaii.* Honolulu: University of Hawaii, M.A. thesis, 1932.

Lamson, H. D. "The Eurasian in Shanghai." *American Journal of Sociology,* XLI (January, 1936), 642–648.

Leslau, Wolf. "The Black Jews of Ethiopia." *Commentary,* VII (March, 1949), 216–224.

—— (translator). *Falasha Anthology.* Yale Judaica Series, VI. New Haven: Yale University Press, 1951.

Marais, J. S. *The Cape Coloured People, 1652–1937.* London: Longmans Green & Co., 1939.

Marshall, C. E. "Birth of the Mestizo in New Spain." *Hispanic American Historical Review,* XIX (May, 1939), 161–184.

Martinez, Enrique Naranjo. "White Indians." *Hispanic American Historical Review,* XIV (February, 1934), 95–98.

"Mestizo." *Enciclopedia Universal Ilustrada Europeo-Americana.* Barcelona: Espasa-Calpe, S. A., 1905–1933, XXXIV, pp. 1090–1094.

Millin, Sarah Gertude. *God's Stepchildren.* New York: Boni and Liveright, 1924.

——. *King of the Bastards.* New York: Harper and Brothers, 1949.

Nathan, Robert. *Road of Ages.* New York: Alfred A. Knopf, 1935.

Parenton, Vernon and Jones, Joseph Hardy, Jr. "The People of Frilot Cove: A Study of Racial Hybrids." *American Journal of Sociology,* LVII (September, 1951), 145–149.

—— and Pellegrin, Roland J. "The 'Sabines': A Study of Racial Hybrids in a Louisiana Coastal Parish." *Social Forces,* XXIX (December, 1950), 148–154.

Pearse, Hugh Wodehouse. *The Hearseys: Five Generations of An Anglo-Indian Family.* London: W. Blackwood and Sons, 1905.

Price, Edward T. "The Melungeons." *Geographical Review,* XLI (1951), 256–271.

——. "A Geographical Analysis of White-Negro-Indian Racial Mixtures in Eastern United States," *Association of American Geographers, Annals.* XLIII (1953), 138–155.

Reuter, Edward Byron. *The Mulatto in the United States.* Boston: R. G. Badger, 1918.

Saxon, Lyle. *Children of Strangers.* Boston: Houghton Mifflin Company, 1937.

Shapiro, Harry L. *The Heritage of the Bounty: The Story of Pitcairn Through Six Generations.* New York: Simon and Schuster, 1936.

Sigmund, Sameth, *Creek Negroes: A Study of Race Relations.* Norman: University of Oklahoma, M.A. thesis, 1940.

Sombart, Werner. *The Jews and Modern Capitalism.* Translated by M. Epstein. Glencoe, Ill.: The Free Press, 1951.

Taylor, Douglas MacRae. *The Black Caribs of British Honduras.* New York: Wenner-Gren Foundation for Anthropological Research, Inc., 1951.

Van der Veur, Paul W. "The Eurasians of Indonesia: Castaways of Colonialism." *Pacific Affairs,* XXVII (1954), 124–137.

Weslager, C. A. *Delaware's Forgotten Folk.* Philadelphia: University of Pennsylvania Press, 1943.

White, William Charles and Williams, Ronald James. *Chinese Jews.* Toronto, Canada: University of Toronto Press, 1942, 3 vols.

Wood, Margaret Mary. "The Russian Creoles of Alaska as a Marginal Group." *Social Forces,* XXII (December, 1943), 204–208.

C. POPULAR CLASSIFICATION AND NAMING

Adamic, Louis. *What's Your Name?* New York: Harper and Brothers, 1942.

Anonymous. "I Changed My Name." *The Atlantic.* CLXXXI (February, 1948), 72–74.

Barnouw, Adriaan J. *Language and Race Problems in South Africa.* The Hague: Martinus Nijhoff, 1934.

Cahnman, Werner. "Religion and Nationality." *American Journal of Sociology,* XLIX (May, 1944), 524–529.

Cohn, David L. "I've Kept My Name." *The Atlantic Monthly,* CLXXXI (April, 1948), 42–44.

Dominian, Leon. *The Frontiers of Language and Nationality in Europe.* New York: Henry Holt and Company, 1917.

Dunlap, A. R. and Weslager, C. A. "Trends in the Naming of Tri-Racial Mixed Blood Groups in the Eastern United States." *American Speech,* XXII (April, 1947), 81–87.

Freeman, Edward A. "Race and Language." *Historical Essays,* Third Series, 1879.

Ghurye, G. S. *The Aborigines—"So-Called"—and Their Future.* Poona: Gokhale Institute of Politics and Economics, 1943.

Hale, Horatio. "Race and Language." *Popular Science Review,* VII (April 30, 1886), 399–401.

Handman, Max. "Conflict and Equilibrium in a Border Area," in E. B. Reuter (ed.),

Race and Culture Contacts. New York: McGraw-Hill, 1934, Chapter VI.

Hughes, Everett C. and Hughes, Helen. *Where Peoples Meet: Racial and Ethnic Frontiers.* Glencoe, Ill.: The Free Press, 1952. Chapter IX, "What's in a Name?"

The Immigration Commission Report. *Dictionary of Races or Peoples.* United States Senate Document No. 662. Washington: Government Printing Office, 1911.

Kephart, W. M. "Negro Visibility." *American Sociological Review,* XIX (August, 1954), 462–467.

Lefèvre, André. *Race and Language.* London: International Scientific Series, 76, 1894.

Mencken, Henry L. "Designations for Colored Folk." *American Speech,* XIX (October, 1944), 161–174.

Michel, Francisque. *Histoire des Races Maudites de la France et de l'Espagne.* Paris: A. Franck, 1847.

Müller, F. Max. *Lectures on the Science of Language.* New York: Charles Scribner's Sons, 1868–1869.

——. *Three Lectures on the Science of Language.* Chicago: The Open Court Publishing Company, 1899.

Nelson, Lowrie. "Speaking of Tongues." *American Journal of Sociology,* LIV (November, 1948), 202–210.

Parrish, Charles Henry. *The Significance of Color in the Negro Community.* Chicago: University of Chicago, 1944. Ph. D. thesis.

——. "Color Names and Color Notions." *Journal of Negro Education,* XV (1946), 13–20.

Powell, Raphael P. *Human Side of a People and the Right Name.* New York: Philemon Company, 1937.

——. *Are We Negroes or Colored People?* New York: Philemon Company, 1938.

Shaler, N. S. *The Neighbor: The Natural History of Human Contacts.* Boston: Houghton, Mifflin Company, 1904.

Shapiro, Harry L. *From the Neck Up.* New York: Man and Nature Publications, American Museum of Natural History, 1947.

Talbert, Robert H. *Spanish-Name People in the Southwest and West: Socioeconomic Characteristics of White Persons of Spanish Surname in Texas, Arizona, California, Colorado, and New Mexico.* Forth Worth: Texas Christian University Press, 1955.

Vandiver, Marylee Mason. "Racial Classifications in Latin American Censuses."

Social Forces, XXVIII (December, 1949), 138–146.

Wirth, Louis. "Foreword," in Erich Rosenthal, *The Jewish Population of Chicago, Illinois.* Chicago: The College of Jewish Studies, 1952.

Woodbridge, Hensley C. "Glossary of Names Used in Colonial Latin America for Crosses Among Indians, Negroes, and Whites." *Journal of the Washington Academy of Sciences,* XXXVIII (November 15, 1948), 353–362.

D. ETHNICS, MINORITY GROUPS, AND PEOPLES

Atamian, Sarkis. *The Armenian Community.* New York: Philosophical Library, 1955.

Braunstein, Baruch. *The Chuetas of Majorca.* Scottdale, Pa.: Mennonite Publishing House, 1936.

Brogan, D. W. *The English People, Impressions and Observations.* New York: Alfred A. Knopf, 1943.

Crooke, W. "The Stability of Caste and Tribal Groups in India." *Journal of the Royal Anthropological Institute of Great Britain and Ireland,* XLIV (1914), 270–279.

Fishberg, Maurice. *The Jews: A Study of Race and Environment.* New York: Charles Scribner's Sons, 1911.

Francis, E. K. "The Nature of the Ethnic Group." *The American Journal of Sociology,* LII (March, 1947), 393–400.

——. "The Russian Mennonites: From Religious to Ethnic Group." *American Journal of Sociology,* LIV (September, 1948), 101–107.

——. "Minority Groups—A Revision of Concepts." *The British Journal of Sociology,* II (September, 1951), 219–230.

Hodge, Frederick. *Handbook of American Indians North of Mexico, Part II.* Washington: Government Printing Office, 1907–1910.

Kautsky, Karl. *Are the Jews a Race?* New York: International Publishers, 1926.

Lane-Poole, Stanley. *The Story of the Moors in Spain.* New York: G. P. Putnam's Sons, 1897.

Lea, Henry Charles, *The Moriscos of Spain: Their Conversion and Expulsion.* Philadelphia: Lea Brothers and Company, 1901.

Leyburn, James G. *World Minority Problems.* New York: Public Affairs Committee, 1947. Pamphlet No. 132.

Levy, Reuben. *Introduction to the Soci-*

ology of Islam. London: Williams and Norgate, Ltd., 1930.

Ninomiya, Shigeaki. "Inquiry Concerning the Origin, Development and Present Situation of the Eta in Relation to the History of Social Class in Japan." *Transactions of the Asiatic Society of Japan,* X (December, 1933), 51–154.

Philip, E. M. *The Indian Church of St. Thomas.* Nagercoil: London Mission Press, 1950.

Roth, Cecil. *A History of the Marranos.* Philadelphia: The Jewish Publication Society of America, 1932.

Weber, Max. "Ethnic Segregation and Caste," in Max Weber, *Essays in Sociology.* New York: Oxford University Press, 1946, pp. 188–190.

——. "Ethnische Gemeinschaften," in Max Weber, *Wirtschaft und Gesellschaft.* Tübingen: J. C. B. Mohr, 1922, Vol. 1, Part 2, Chapter 3, pp. 217–226.

E. THE SOCIOLOGY OF RACE

Anonymous. "An Analysis of Jewish Culture." In Isacque Graebner and Steuart Henderson Britt, *Jews in a Gentile World: The Problem of Anti-Semitism.* New York: The Macmillan Company, 1942, Chapter LX, pp. 243–263.

Ashley Montagu, M. F. *Man's Most Dangerous Myth: The Fallacy of Race.* New York: Columbia University Press, 1942.

Benedict, Ruth. *Race: Science and Politics.* New York: Modern Age Books, 1940.

Brearley, H. C. "Race as a Sociological Concept." *Sociology and Social Research,* XXIII (July, 1939), 514–518.

Brotz, Howard M. "The Definition of a Jew," in Maurice Freedman (ed.), *A Minority in Britain: Social Studies of the Anglo-Jewish Community.* London: Vallentine, Mitchell and Company, Ltd., 1955.

Comas, Juan. *Racial Myths.* Paris: UNESCO, 1951.

Corrigan, Joseph M. and O'Toole, G. Barry (eds.). *Race, Nation, Person: Social Aspects of the Race Problem: A Symposium.* New York: Barnes and Noble, Inc., 1944.

Cox, Oliver C. "Race and Caste: A Distinction." *The American Journal of Sociology,* L (March, 1945), 360–368.

——. *Caste, Class, and Race: A Study in Social Dynamics.* Garden City, N. Y.: Doubleday and Company, 1948.

Dover, Cedric. *Know This of Race.* London: Secker and Warburg, 1939.

Freedman, Maurice. "Race Against Time." *Phylon,* XIV (Fourth Quarter, 1953), 401–409.

Hayakawa, S. I. "The Semantics of Being Negro." *ETC, A Review of General Semantics,* X (Spring, 1953), 163–175.

Herskovits, Melville J. "When is a Jew a Jew?" *The Modern Quarterly,* IV (June–September, 1927), 109–117.

Hook, Sidney. "Reflections on the Jewish Question." *Partisan Review,* XVI (May, 1949), 463–482.

Isaacs, William and Kolodny, Jules. "What is a Jew?" *Common Sense,* XV (January, 1946), 9–13.

Kertzer, Morris Norman. *What is a Jew?* Cleveland: The World Publishing Company, 1953.

Klineberg, Otto. *Race and Psychology.* Paris: UNESCO, 1951.

——. *Race Differences.* New York: Harper and Brothers, 1935.

Lea, Henry Charles. *A History of the Inquisition of Spain.* New York: The Macmillan Company, 1906–1907. Vol. II. Book IV, Ch. IV, "Limpieza."

Leiris, Michel. *Race and Culture.* Paris: UNESCO, 1951.

Lewisohn, Ludwig. "The Art of Being a Jew." *Harper's Magazine,* XL (May, 1925), 725–729.

Manasse, Ernst Moritz. "Max Weber on Race." *Social Research,* XIV (June, 1947), 191–221.

Radin, Paul. *The Racial Myth.* New York: Whittlesey House, McGraw-Hill Book Company, Inc., 1934.

Ramos, Arthur. "The Question of Race and the Democratic World." *UNESCO's International Social Science Bulletin,* I, 1949.

Redfield, Robert. "What We Do Know About Race." *Scientific Monthly,* LVII (September, 1943), 193–201.

F. THE BIOLOGY AND PHYSICAL
ANTHROPOLOGY OF RACE

Ashley Montagu, M. F. *Statement on Race.* New York: Schuman, 1951.

Beals, Ralph L. and Hoijer, Harry. *An Introduction to Anthropology.* New York: The Macmillan Company, 1953.

Boas, Franz. "Race." *Encyclopaedia of the Social Sciences,* XIII, pp. 25–36.

——. *Race, Language and Culture.* New York: The Macmillan Company, 1940.

Boyd, W. C. "Critique of Methods of Classifying Mankind." *American Journal of Physical Anthropology,* XXVII (December, 1940), 333–364.

——. *Genetics and the Races of Man.* Boston: Little, Brown and Co., 1950.

Bradley, John Hodgdon. *Patterns of Survival: An Anatomy of Life.* New York: The Macmillan Company, 1938.

Coon, Carleton S., Garn, Stanley M. and Birdsell, Joseph B. *Races: A Study of the Problems of Race Formation in Man.* Springfield, Ill.: C. C. Thomas, 1950.

Count, Earl W. (ed.). *This is Race.* New York: Henry Schuman Inc., 1950.

Cressey, Paul F. "Chinese Traits in European Civilization: A Study in Diffusion." *American Sociological Review,* X (October, 1945), 595–604.

Dahlberg, Gunnar. *Race, Reason and Rubbish.* New York: Columbia University Press, 1942.

Dixon, Roland B. *The Racial History of Man.* New York, London: Charles Scribner's Sons, 1923.

Dunn, L. C. *Race and Biology.* Paris: UNESCO, 1951.

Hankins, Frank Hamilton. *The Racial Basis of Civilization.* New York: Alfred A. Knopf, 1926.

Huxley, Julian and Haddon, A. C. *We Europeans.* New York: Harper and Brothers, 1936.

Jennings, H. S. *The Biological Basis of Human Nature.* New York: W. W. Norton and Company, 1930.

Jennings, H. S. et al. *Scientific Aspects of the Race Problem.* Washington: The Catholic University of America Press; New York: Longmans, Green and Company, 1941.

Krogman, Wilton M. *A Bibliography of Human Morphology, 1914–1939.* Chicago: University of Chicago Press, 1941.

——. "What We Do Not Know About Race." *Scientific Monthly,* LVII (August, 1943), 97–104.

——. "The Concept of Race," in Ralph Linton (ed.), *The Science of Man in the World Crisis.* New York: Columbia University Press, 1945.

Linton, Ralph. *The Study of Man.* New York: Appleton-Century Company, 1936.

Penniman, Thomas Kenneth. *A Hundred Years of Anthropology.* New York: The Macmillan Company, 1936.

Royal Anthropological Institute and the Institute of Sociology. *Race and Culture.* London: Le Play House Press, 1935.

Shapiro, H. L. *Migration and Environment.* New York: Oxford University Press, 1939.

Slotkin, James Sydney. "Racial Classifications of the Seventeenth and Eighteenth Centuries." *Wisconsin Academy of Sciences, Arts and Letters, Transactions, 1944.* XXXVI, 459–467.

Snyder, Louis L. *Race: A History of Modern Ethnic Theories.* New York: Longmans, Green and Company, 1939.

United Nations Educational, Scientific and Cultural Organization. *The Race Concept: Results of an Inquiry.* Paris: UNESCO, 1952.

Vallois, Henri V. "Race," in A. L. Kroeber et al., *Anthropology Today.* Chicago: University of Chicago Press, 1953, pp. 145–162.

II. THE GEOGRAPHY OF RACE AND OF RACE RELATIONS

A. THE RACE REGION

Boas, Franz. "Changes in Bodily Form of Descendants of Immigrants." *United States Immigration Commission Reports,* XXXVIII. Washington: Government Printing Office, 1911.

Boyd, William C. *Genetics and the Races of Man: An Introduction to Modern Physical Anthropology.* Boston: Little, Brown and Company, 1950.

Coon, Carleton S. *The Races of Europe.* New York: The Macmillan Company, 1939.

Dixon, Roland B. *The Racial History of Man.* New York: Charles Scribner's Sons, 1923.

Fleure, Herbert John. "Racial Distribution in the Light of Archaeology," in *John Rylands Library Bulletin,* XVII. Manchester, England, 1933, pp. 247–263.

Gerland, Georg. *Atlas der Völkerkunde.* Gotha, 1892.

Goldstein, Marcus. *Demographic and Bodily Changes in Descendants of Mexican Immigrants.* Austin: Institute of Latin-American Studies, The University of Texas, 1943.

Haddon, A. C. *The Races of Man and Their Distribution.* New York: The Macmillan Company, 1925.

Hettner, Alfred. *Grundzüge der Länderkunde.* Leipzig: B. G. Teubner, 1923–24.

Kroeber, A. L. *Anthropology*. New York: Harcourt, Brace and Company, 1948, new edition revised, Chapter IV.

Lasker, Gabriel Ward. "Migration and Physical Differentiation: A Comparison of Immigrant with American-Born Chinese." *American Journal of Physical Anthropology*, IV (1946), 273–300.

Lundborg, Herman and Linders, F. J. (eds.). *The Racial Characters of the Swedish Nation*. Stockholm: The Swedish State Institute for Race Biology, 1926.

Mill, Hugh R. (ed.). *The International Geography*. New York: D. Appleton and Company, 1909.

Pittard, Eugene. *Race and History: An Ethnological Introduction to History*. New York: Alfred A. Knopf, 1926.

Reclus, Élisée. *The Earth and Its Inhabitants*. New York: D. Appleton and Company, 1876–1894.

Ripley, William Z. *The Races of Europe: A Sociological Study*. New York: D. Appleton and Company, 1923.

Shaler, N. S. *Nature and Man in America*. New York: Charles Scribner's Sons, 1891.

Spier, Leslie. *Growth of Japanese Children Born in America and Japan*. University of Washington Publications in Anthropology, III. Seattle, Wash.: Univ. of Washington Press, 1929.

Ware, C. F. "Ethnic Communities." *Encyclopedia of the Social Sciences*, V.

Wissler, Clark. "Ethnic Types and Isolation." *Science*, XXIII (January 26, 1906), 147–149.

——. *Indians of the United States: Four Centuries of Their History and Culture*. New York: Doubleday, Doran and Company, 1940.

B. THE RACE RELATIONS REGION

Chicago Commission of Race Relations. *The Negro in Chicago: A Study of Race Relations and a Race Riot*. Chicago: The University of Chicago Press, 1922.

Claude, Inis L., Jr. *National Minorities: An International Problem*. Cambridge: Harvard University Press, 1955.

Clark, Kenneth B. "Candor About Negro-Jewish Relations." *Commentary*, I (February, 1946), 8–14.

Comhaire, Jean Louis Leopold. "Urban Segregation and Racial Legislation in Africa." *American Sociological Review*, XV (June, 1950), 392–397.

——. "Some African Problems of Today." *Human Organization*, X (Summer, 1951), 15–18.

——. (Comp.) *Urban Conditions in Africa. Select Reading List on Urban Problems in Africa*. London: Oxford University Press, 1952.

Conant, Melvin. *Race Issues on the World Scene: A Report on the Conference on Race Relations in World Perspective*. Hawaii: University of Hawaii Press, 1955.

Cooper, Eunice. "Urbanization in Malaya." *Population Studies*, V (November, 1951), 117–131.

Dean, Vera Micheles. *The Nature of the Non-Western World*. New York: New American Library, 1957.

Dingwall, Eric John. *Racial Pride and Prejudice*. London: Watts and Company, 1946.

Donald, Henderson H. "The Urbanization of the American Negro," in George Peter Murdock (ed.), *Studies in the Science of Society Presented to A. G. Keller*. New Haven: Yale University Press, 1937, pp. 181–199.

Ekwensi, Cyprian. *People of the City*. London: Andrew Dakers Ltd., 1954.

Epstein, A. L. *The Administration of Justice and the Urban African*. London: H. M. Stationery Office, 1953.

Frazier, E. Franklin. "Race Contacts and the Social Structure." *American Sociological Review*, XIV (February, 1949), 1–11.

Hancock, W. K. *Survey of British Commonwealth Affairs*. London: Oxford University Press, 1942. Vol. II, pt. 2.

Harris, Chauncy D. "Ethnic Groups in Cities of the Soviet Union." *Geographical Review*, XXXV (July, 1945), 466–473.

Hoselitz, Bert F. (ed.). *The Progress of Undeveloped Areas*. Chicago: The University of Chicago Press, 1952.

Kattsoff, L. O. "Definition of a Situation: The Jew in America." *Social Forces*, XXVII (May, 1949), 461–464.

Kennedy, R. "The Colonial Crisis and the Future," in Ralph Linton (ed.), *The Science of Man in the World Crisis*. New York: Columbia University Press, 1945.

Krige, Eileen Jensen. "Changing Conditions in Marital and Parental Duties among Urbanized Natives." *Africa*, IX (January, 1936), 1–23.

Lebeuf, Jean-Paul. "Centres Urbains d'Afrique Equatoriale Française."

Africa, XXIII (October, 1953), 285–297.

Leyburn, James G. "Urban Natives in South Africa." *American Sociological Review,* IX (October, 1944), 495–502.

Lind, Andrew W. (ed.). *Race Relations in World Perspective.* Honolulu: University of Hawaii Press, 1955.

Masuoka, J. "Race and Culture Contacts in the Emporium." *American Journal of Sociology,* L (November, 1944), 199–204.

——. "The City and Racial Adjustment: A Definition and Hypothesis." *Social Forces,* XXVII (October, 1948), 37–41.

Miller, Harry. *The Communist Menace in Malaya.* New York: Frederick A. Praeger, 1954.

Mitchell, J. Clyde. *African Urbanization in Ndola and Luanshya.* Lusaka: Rhodes-Livingstone Institute, 1954.

Munger, Edwin S. "Geography of Sub-Saharan Race Relations," in Charles G. Haines (ed.), *Africa Today.* Baltimore: Johns Hopkins Press, 1955, pp. 175–196.

Park, Robert E. "The Nature of Race Relations," in Edgar T. Thompson (ed.), *Race Relations and the Race Problem.* Durham: Duke University Press, 1939.

Phillips, Ray E. *The Bantu in the City: A Study of Cultural Adjustment on the Witwatersrand.* Lovedale, South Africa: The Lovedale Press, 1938.

Reuter, E. B. "Why the Presence of the Negro Constitutes a Problem in the American Social Order." *Journal of Negro Education,* VIII (July, 1939), 291–298.

Russell, Alan Gladney. *Colour, Race and Empire.* London: Victor Gollancz, 1944.

Sanders, Irwin T. et al. *Societies Around the World.* Lexington: University of Kentucky, 1950–1953. 2 vols.

Schuyler, George S. "The Caucasian Problem," in Rayford W. Logan (ed.), *What the Negro Wants.* Chapel Hill: University of North Carolina Press, 1944.

Sensing, Thurman. "The South has No Race Problem." *Manufacturers Record,* CXIII (July, 1944), 28ff.

Sheppard, Harold L. "The Negro Merchant: A Study in Negro Anti-Semitism." *American Journal of Sociology,* LIII (September, 1947), 96–99.

Smith, Marian W. (ed.). *Indians of the Urban Northwest.* New York: Columbia University Press, 1949.

Wood, Margaret Mary. *The Stranger: A Study in Social Relationships.* New York: Columbia University Press, 1934.

C. REGIONAL VARIETIES OF RACE RELATIONS

1. *Africa: General*

Balandier, Georges. *Les Villages Gabonais: Aspects Démographiques, Économiques, Sociologiques, Projects de Mordernisation.* Mémoires de l'Institut d'Études Centrafricaines, Brazzaville (A. E. F.) no. 5, 1952.

——. *Sociologie des Brazzavilles Noires.* Paris: Armand Colin, 1954.

——. "Race Relations in West and Central Africa," in Andrew W. Lind (ed.), *Race Relations in World Perspective.* Honolulu: University of Hawaii Press, 1955. Chapter VII.

Bartlet, James Vernon. *Struggle for Africa.* New York: Frederick A. Praeger, 1953.

Bascom, William R. "West and Central Africa," in Ralph Linton (ed.), *Most of the World.* New York: Columbia University Press, 1949.

Buell, Raymond Leslie. *The Native Problem in Africa.* New York: The Macmillan Company, 1928. 2 vols.

Cary, Joyce. *Mister Johnson.* New York: Harper and Brothers, 1951.

Conrad, Joseph. "Heart of Darkness," in *Youth and Two Other Stories.* Garden City, N. Y.: Doubleday, Page and Company, 1929.

Davidson, Basil. *The African Awakening.* London: Cape, 1955.

Dougall, James W. C. *Christianity and the Sex Education of the African.* London: Society for Promotion of Christian Knowledge, 1937.

Du Bois, W. E. B. *Color and Democracy: Colonies and Peace.* New York: Harcourt, Brace and Company, 1945.

Fanon, Frantz. *Peau Noir Masques Blancs.* Paris: Éditions du Seuil, 1952.

Giesebrecht, Franz. *Die Behandlung der Eingeborenen in den Deutschen Kolonieen.* Berlin: S. Fischer, 1898.

Hailey, William Malcolm. *An African Survey.* London: Oxford University Press, 1938.

Haines, Charles G. (ed.). *Africa Today.* Baltimore: Johns Hopkins Press, 1955.

Huxley, Elspeth and Perham, Margery. *Race and Politics in Kenya.* London: Faber and Faber, 1944.

Jackson, Mabel V. *European Powers and South-East Africa.* New York: Longmans, Green and Company, 1942.

Kingsley, Mary H. *West African Studies.* New York: The Macmillan Company, 1901.

Kuper, Hilda. *The Uniform of Colour: A Study of White-Black Relationships in Swaziland.* Johannesburg: Witwatersrand University Press, 1947.

Lanham, Peter. *Blanket Boy.* New York: Thomas Y. Crowell Company, 1953.

Leakey, L. S. B. *Mau Mau and the Kikuyu.* New York: The John Day Company, 1954.

Little, K. L. "The Significance of the West African Creole for Africanist and Afro-American Studies." *African Affairs,* XLIX (1950), 308–319.

Maran, René. *Batouala.* Monaco: Imprimerie Nationale, 1950.

Monsarrat, Nicholas. *The Tribe that Lost Its Head.* New York: William Sloane Associates, 1956.

Olivier, Sydney Haldane. *The Anatomy of African Misery.* London: Hogarth, 1927.

Rankin, F. Harrison. *The White Man's Grave.* London: Richard Bentley, 1836.

Ruark, Robert. *Something of Value.* Garden City, N. Y.: Doubleday and Sons, 1955.

Simons, J. H. "Race Relations and Politics in Southern and Eastern Africa." in Ralph Linton (ed.), *Most of the World.* New York: Columbia University Press, 1949.

Smith, E. W. *The Golden Stool.* London: Holborn Publishing House, 1926.

Thurnwald, Richard. *Black and White In East Africa: The Fabric of a New Civilization.* London: George Routledge and Sons, Ltd., 1935.

Wallbank, T. Walter. *Contemporary Africa.* Princeton, N.J.: Van Nostrand Press, 1956.

Wilson, Godfrey. *An Essay on the Economics of Detribalization in Northern Rhodesia.* Livingstone, Northern Rhodesia: The Rhodes-Livingstone Institute, 1941–42, Nos. 5–6, Parts I, II.

2. *Africa: South*

Barnes, John A. "Race Relations in the Development of Southern Africa," in Andrew W. Lind (ed.), *Race Relations in World Perspective.* Honolulu: University of Hawaii Press, 1955. Chapter VIII.

Brookes, Edgar. *South Africa in a Changing World.* Capetown: Oxford University Press, 1953.

Calpin, G. H. *Indians in South Africa.* Pietermaritzburg: Shuter and Shooter, 1949.

——. (ed.). *The South African Way of Life.* New York: Columbia University Press, 1953.

Davidson, Basil. *Report on Southern Africa.* New York: British Book Centre, 1952.

De Kiewiet, C. W. *A History of South Africa: Social and Economic.* Oxford: Clarendon Press, 1941.

——. *The Anatomy of South African Misery.* New York: Oxford University Press, 1957.

Du Plessis, I. D. *The Cape Malays.* Johannesburg, South Africa: Institute of Race Relations, 1946.

Dvorin, Eugene P. *Racial Separation in South Africa: An Analysis of Apartheid Theory.* Chicago: University of Chicago Press, 1952.

Evans, Maurice S. *Black and White in Southeast Africa: A Study in Sociology.* New York: Longmans, Green and Company, 1911.

Gordimer, N. *The Lying Days.* New York: Simon and Schuster, 1953.

Hatch, John. *The Dilemma of South Africa.* London: Dennis Dobson, Ltd., 1952.

Kuper, Leo. "South African Native: Caste, Proletariat or Race." *Social Forces,* XXVIII (December, 1949), 146–153.

——. "Some Demographic Aspects of White Supremacy in South Africa." *The British Journal of Sociology,* I (June, 1950), 114–153.

Hellmann, Ellen (ed.). *Handbook on Race Relations in South Africa.* New York: Oxford University Press, 1949.

Hoernle, R. F. Alfred. "Race-Mixture and Native Policy in South Africa," in I. Schapera (ed.), *Western Civilization and the Natives of South Africa.* London: George Routledge and Sons, 1934.

Houghton, D. Hobart. *Summary of the Findings and Recommendations of the Tomlinson Commission.* Johannesburg: South African Institute of Race Relations, 1956.

MacCrone, I. D. *Race Attitudes in South Africa.* London: Oxford University Press, 1937.

Macmillan, W. M. *The Cape Colour Question: A Historical Survey.* London: Faber and Gwyer, 1927.

Marquard, Leopold. *The Peoples and Policies of South Africa.* New York: Oxford University Press, 1952.

Paton, Alan. *Cry the Beloved Country: A Story of Comfort in Desolation.* New York: Charles Scribner's Sons, 1948.

——. "South Africa Today." *Public Affairs Pamphlet,* No. 175. New York: Public Affairs Committee, Inc., 1951.

Patterson, Sheila. *Colour and Culture in South Africa.* London: Routledge and Paul, 1953.

——. *The Last Trek: A Study of the Boer People and the Afrikaner Nation.* London: Routledge and Paul, 1956.

Peattie, Roderick. *Struggle on the Veld.* New York: The Vanguard Press, Inc., 1947.

Robertson, H. M. "150 Years of Economic Contact between Black and White." *South African Journal of Economics,* II (December, 1934), 402–425; III (March, 1935), 3–25.

Roux, Edward. *Time Longer Than Rope: A History of the Black Man's Struggle for Freedom in South Africa.* London: Victor Gollancz, 1948.

Sachs, E. Solly. *The Choice Before South Africa.* London: Turnstile Press, 1952.

Sachs, Wulf. *Black Anger.* Boston: Little, Brown and Company, 1947.

Sampson, Anthony. *Drums: A Venture into The New Africa.* London: Collins, 1956.

Schapera, I. (ed.). *The Bantu-Speaking Tribes of South Africa: An Ethnographical Survey.* London: George Routledge and Sons, Ltd., 1937.

Sundkler, B. G. M. *Bantu Prophets in South Africa.* London: Lutterworth Press, 1948.

Tingsten, Herbert. *The Problem of South Africa.* Translated by Daniel Viklund. London: Victor Gollancz, 1955.

Van Eck, H. J. *Some Aspects of the South African Industrial Revolution.* Johannesburg, South Africa: Institute of Race Relations, 1953.

3. Asia: General

Colbert, Evelyn. *The Left Wing in Japanese Politics.* New York: International Secretariat, Institute of Pacific Relations, 1952.

Ekvall, Robert B. *Cultural Relations on the Kansu-Tibetan Border.* Chicago: University of Chicago Press, 1939.

Freeman, Andrew A. *Brown Women and White.* New York: The John Day Company, 1932.

Furnivall, John Sydenham. *Colonial Policy and Practice: A Comparative Study of Burma and Netherlands India.* Cambridge, England: University Press in Cooperation with the International Secretariat, Institute of Pacific Relations, 1948.

Landon, Kenneth Perry. *The Chinese in Thailand.* London: Oxford University Press, 1941.

Lattimore, Owen. *Manchuria: Cradle of Conflict.* New York: The Macmillan Company, 1932.

Lindgren, Ethel John. "An Example of Culture Contact Without Conflict: Reindeer Tungus and Cossaks of Northwestern Manchuria." *American Anthropologist,* n.s., XL (October-December, 1938), 605–621.

Rama Rau, Santha. *East of Home.* New York: Harper and Brothers, 1950.

Smythe, H. H. "Note on Racialism in Japan." *American Sociological Review* XVI (December, 1951), 823–824.

4. Asia: India

Forster, Edward Morgan. *A Passage to India.* London: E. Arnold and Company, 1931.

Foster, William. *The English Factories in India.* Oxford: The Clarendon Press, 1906–1927. 12 vols.

Ghurye, G. S. *Caste and Race in India.* London: Kegan Paul, Trench, Trubner and Company, Ltd., 1932.

Hutton, J. H. *Caste in India.* New York: Oxford University Press, 1951.

Majumdar, D. N. *Races and Cultures of India.* Lucknow, India: Universal Publishers, 1956.

Menen, Arthur. "The Last Nabob," in *Dead Men in the Silver Market.* New York: Charles Scribner's Sons, 1953.

Murphy, Gardner. *In the Minds of Men: The Study of Human Behavior and Social Tensions in India.* New York: Basic Books, 1953.

Ram, Pars and Murphy, Gardner. "Recent Investigations of Hindu-Muslim Relations in India." *Human Organization,* XI (Summer, 1952), 13–16.

Redding, J. Saunders. *An American in India.* Indianapolis: The Bobbs-Merrill Company, 1954.

Risley, Sir Herbert H. *The People of India.* London: W. Thacker and Company, 1915.

Rowan, Carl T. *The Pitiful and the Proud.* New York: Random House, 1956.

Senart, Émile. *Caste in India.* Translated by

Sir E. Denison Ross. London: Methuen and Co., Ltd., 1930.

Spear, Thomas George. *The Nabobs: A Study of the Social Life of the English in Eighteenth Century India.* London: Humphrey Milford, Oxford University Press, 1932.

Taylor, Edmond. *Richer by Asia.* Boston: Houghton Mifflin Company, 1947.

Thorner, Daniel and Alice. "India and Pakistan," in Ralph Linton (ed.), *Most of the World.* New York: Columbia University Press, 1949.

5. Asia: China

Brown, Philip Marshall. "Extraterritoriality: General." *Encyclopaedia of the Social Sciences,* VI, 36–37.

Eldridge, Frank R. *Oriental Trade Methods.* New York: D. Appleton and Company, 1923.

Fishel, Wesley R. *The End of Extraterritoriality in China.* Berkeley: The University of California Press, 1952.

Holcombe, A. N. "Exterritoriality: China." *Encyclopaedia of the Social Sciences,* VI, 37–39.

Keeton, George Williams. *The Development of Extraterritoriality in China.* New York: Longmans, Green and Company, 1928.

Lattimore, Owen. *Inner Asian Frontiers of China.* New York: American Geographical Society, 1940.

Schwartz, Benjamin I. *Chinese Communism and the Rise of Mao.* Cambridge: Harvard University Press, 1951.

Shin, Shun Liu. *Extraterritoriality: Its Rise and Decline.* Columbia University Studies in History, Economics and Public Law, CXVIII (1925), no. 2.

Willoughby, Westel W. *Foreign Rights and Interests in China.* Baltimore: The Johns Hopkins Press, 1927. Revised and enlarged edition. 2 vols.

6. Asia: Southeast

Ball, William MacMahon. *Nationalism and Communism in East Asia.* Carlton, Australia: Melbourne University Press, 1956.

Boeke, Julius Herman. *The Structure of Netherlands Indian Economy.* New York: International Secretariat, Institute of Pacific Relations, 1942.

——. *The Evolution of the Netherlands Indies Economy.* New York: Netherlands and Netherlands Indies Council, Institute of Pacific Relations, 1946.

Freedman, M. *The Sociology of Race Relations in South-East Asia with Special Reference to British Malaya.* London: London University, 1948. Ph.D. thesis.

——. "The Chinese in Southeast Asia," in Andrew W. Lind, (ed.), *Race Relations in World Perspective,* Honolulu: University of Hawaii Press, 1955. Chapter XVII.

Furnivall, John Sydenham. *Netherlands India: A Study of Plural Economy.* Cambridge, England: The University Press, 1939.

——. *Progress and Welfare in Southeast Asia: A Comparison of Colonial Policy and Practice.* New York: Secretariat, Institute of Pacific Relations, 1941.

——. *Educational Progress in Southeast Asia.* New York: International Secretariat, Institute of Pacific Relations, 1943.

——. *Colonial Policy and Practice: A Comparative Study of Burma and Netherlands India.* Cambridge, England: University Press, 1948.

Hogbin, H. Ian. *Transformation Scene: The Changing Culture of a New Guinea Village.* London: Routledge and Paul, 1951.

Keith, Agnes Newton. *Land Below the Wind.* Boston: Little, Brown and Company, 1939.

Kennedy, Raymond. "Southeast Asia and Indonesia," in Ralph Linton (ed.), *Most of the World.* New York: Columbia University Press, 1949.

Lasker, Bruno. *Peoples of Southeast Asia.* New York: Alfred A. Knopf, 1944.

Mills, Lennox A. and Associates. *The New World of Southeast Asia.* Minneapolis: University of Minnesota Press, 1949.

Morrisson, I. "Aspects of the Racial Problem in Malaya." *Pacific Affairs,* XXII (September, 1949), 239–253.

Palma, Rafael. *The Pride of the Malay Race: A Biography of José Rizal.* New York: Prentice-Hall, 1949.

Pearn, B. R. *The Indian in Burma.* Race Relations Studies in Conflict and Cooperation, No. 4. Herefordshire, England: Le Play House Press, 1946.

Purcell, Victor. *The Chinese in Malaya.* New York: Oxford University Press, 1948.

——. *The Chinese in Southeast Asia.* New York: Oxford University Press, 1951.

Schrieke, Bertram Johannes Otto (ed.). *The Effect of Western Influence on Native*

Civilisations in the Malay Archipelago. Batavia, Java: G. Kolff and Company, 1929.

Smith, T. E. *Population Growth in Malaya: An Analysis of Recent Trends*. London: Royal Institute of International Affairs, 1952.

Suyin, Han. *And the Rain My Drink*. Boston: Little, Brown and Company, 1956.

Thayer, Philip W. (ed.). *Southeast Asia in the Coming World*. Baltimore: Johns Hopkins Press, 1953.

Thompson, Virginia McLean and Adloff, Richard. *The Left Wing in Southeast Asia*. New York: Sloane, 1950.

Van der Kroef, Justus M. "Social Conflict and Minority Aspirations in Indonesia." *American Journal of Sociology*, LV (March, 1950), 450–463.

——. "The Eurasian Minority in Indonesia." *American Sociological Review*, XVIII (October, 1953), 484–493.

Wertheim, W. F. "The Indo-European Problem in Indonesia." *Pacific Affairs*, XX (September, 1947), 290–298.

7. *Australia and New Zealand*

Beaglehole, Ernest. "Race Relations in the Pacific." *International Social Science Bulletin*, II (Winter, 1950), 479–496.

——. "Some Sociological Aspects of Race Relations in New Zealand." *International Social Science Bulletin*, III (Summer, 1951), 253–258.

Berndt, Ronald M. and Catherine H. *From Black to White in South Australia*. Chicago: University of Chicago Press, 1952.

Borrie, W. D. *Italians and Germans in Australia: A Study of Assimilation*. Melbourne: F. W. Cheshire, 1954.

Dale, William S. *New Zealand: A Socio-Educational Study in Race Relations*. New Haven: Yale University, 1936. Ph.D. thesis.

Dark, Eleanor. *The Timeless Land*. New York: The Macmillan Company, 1941.

Elkin, A. P. "Reaction and Interaction: A Food-Gathering People and European Settlement in Australia." *American Anthropologist*, LIII (April-June, 1951), 164–168.

Forsyth, W. D. *Governor Arthur's Convict System: Van Diemen's Land, 1824–1836: A Study in Colonization*. New York: Published for the Royal Empire Society by Longmans, Green and Company, 1935.

Lyng, J. *Non-Britishers in Australia: Influence on Population and Progress*. Melbourne: Melbourne University Press, 1935.

Mair, L. P. *Australia in New Guinea*. London: Christophers, 1948.

Park, Ruth. *The Witch's Thorn*. London: M. Joseph, 1952.

Sacchi, F. "Queensland's Olive Peril." *Living Age*, CCCXXVI (August 29, 1925), 439–442.

Thonemann, H. E. *Tell the White Man: The Life Story of an Aboriginal Lubra*. London: Collins, 1949.

Willard, Myra. *History of the White Australia Policy*. Melbourne: Melbourne University Press, 1923.

8. *Brazil*

Amado, Jorge. *The Violent Land*. Translated by Samuel Putnam. New York: Alfred A. Knopf, 1945.

Cahnman, Werner J. "Brazil: Rule by Miscegenation." *Jewish Frontier*, (October, 1947), 29–31.

Chamberlain, Henriqueta. *Where the Sabiá Sings: A Partial Autobiography*. New York: The Macmillan Company, 1947.

Cunha, Euclydes da. *Rebellion in the Backlands*. Chicago: The University of Chicago Press, 1944.

Frazier, E. Franklin. "Some Aspects of Race Relations in Brazil." *Phylon*, III (Third Quarter, 1942), 287–295.

——. "A Comparison of Negro-White Relations in Brazil and in the United States." *Transactions of the New York Academy of Sciences*, Series 2, VI (May, 1944), 251–269.

Freyre, Gilberto. *Sobrados e Mucambos*. São Paulo: Companhia editora nacional, 1936.

——. *Brazil, An Interpretation*. New York: Alfred A. Knopf, 1945.

——. *The Masters and the Slaves: A Study in the Development of Brazilian Civilization*. New York: Alfred A. Knopf, 1946.

Graça Aranha, José Pereira da. *Canaan*. Boston: The Four Seas Company, 1920.

Kelsey, Vera. "The Man of Color," in *Seven Keys to Brazil*. New York: Funk and Wagnall's Company, 1940, pp. 60–62.

Oliveira Vianna, Francisco José de. *Evolucão do Povo Brasileiro*. São Paulo: Companhia Editora Nacional, 1938. Third edition.

Pierson, Donald. "The Negro in Bahia, Brazil." *American Sociological Review,* IV (August, 1939), 524–533.

——. *Negroes in Brazil: A Study of Race Contact at Bahia.* Chicago: The University of Chicago Press, 1942.

——. "The Brazilian Racial Situation." *The Scientific Monthly,* LVIII (March, 1944), 227–232.

Ramos, Arthur. *The Negro in Brazil.* Translated by Richard Pattee. Washington, D. C.: Associated Publishers, Inc., 1939.

——. *O Negro Brasileiro.* São Paulo: Companhia Editora Nacional, 1940.

——. "The Negro in Brazil," in T. Lynn Smith, *Brazil: Portrait of Half a Continent.* New York: Dryden Press, 1951, chapter 5.

Sayers, Raymond S. *The Negro in Brazilian Literature.* New York: Hispanic Institute in the United States, 1956.

Wagley, Charles. "Brazil," in Ralph Linton (ed.), *Most of the World.* New York: Columbia University Press, 1949.

——. (ed.). *Race and Class in Rural Brazil.* Paris: UNESCO, 1952.

Willems, Emilio. "Racial Attitudes in Brazil." *American Journal of Sociology,* LIV (March, 1949), 402–408.

9. Canada

Bie, Pieree. *Le Fait Canadien Francais: Étude Comparative des Nationalismes Flamand et Canadien Francais.* Louvain: Institut de Recherches Economiques et Sociales, 1948.

Ducharme, Jacques. *The Shadows of the Trees; The Story of the French-Canadians in New England.* New York: Harper and Brothers, 1943.

Giraud, Marcel. *Le Métis Canadien: Son Rôle dans l'Histoire des Provinces de L'Ouest.* Paris: Institut d'Ethnologie, 1945.

Howard, Joseph Kinsey. *Strange Empire.* New York: Morrow, 1952.

Hughes, Everett C. "The French-English Margin in Canada." *American Journal of Sociology,* XXXIX (July, 1933), 1–11.

——. *French Canada in Transition.* Chicago: The University of Chicago Press, 1943.

Jenness, Diamond. "Canada's Indians Yesterday. What of Today?" *Canadian Journal of Economics and Political Science,* XX (February, 1954), 95–100.

La Violette, Forest E. *The Canadian Japanese and World War II.* Toronto: University of Toronto Press, 1948.

MacLennan, Hugh. *Two Solitudes.* New York: Duell, Sloan and Pearce, 1945.

Rambaut, Thomas D. "The Hudson's Bay Half-Breeds and Louis Riel's Rebellions." *Political Science Quarterly,* II (1887), 135–166.

Reid, A. P. "The Half-Breed Races of Northwest Canada." *The Journal of the Anthropological Institute of Great Britain and Ireland,* IV (1874).

Ross, Aileen D. *Ethnic Relations and Social Structure.* Chicago: University of Chicago, 1950. Ph.D. thesis.

——. "Ethnic Group Contacts and Status Dilemma. *Phylon,* XV (Third Quarter, 1954), 267–275.

Sandwell, B. K. "The French Canadians." *Annals of the American Academy of Political Science,* CCLIII (1947), 169–175.

Stanley, George F. G. *The Birth of Western Canada: A History of the Riel Rebellions.* Toronto: Longmans, 1936.

——. "The Métis and the Conflict of Cultures in Western Canada." *The Canadian Historical Review,* XXVIII (December, 1947), 428–433.

Valentine, V. F. "Some Problems of the Métis of Northern Saskatchewan." *Canadian Journal of Economics and Political Science,* XX (February, 1954), 89–95.

Wade, Mason. *The French-Canadian Outlook.* New York: The Viking Press, 1946.

10. Europe

Aubrey, Pièrre. *Milieux Juifs de la France Contemporaine à travers leurs Écrivains,* Paris: Plon, 1957.

Bienenfeld, F. R. *The Germans and the Jews.* New York: F. Ungar, 1944.

Coon, Carleton. *The Races of Europe.* New York: The Macmillan Company, 1939.

Drake, St. Clair. *Value Systems, Social Structure and Race Relations in the British Isles.* Chicago: University of Chicago, 1954. Ph.D. thesis.

Fleure, Herbert J. *The Peoples of Europe.* London: Oxford University Press, H. Milford, 1922.

Freedman, Maurice (ed). *A Minority in Britain; Social Studies of the Anglo-Jewish Community.* London: Vallentine, Mitchell, 1955.

Gayda Virginio. *Modern Austria*. London: T. F. Unwin, 1915.

Little, Kenneth Lindsay. *Negroes in Britain: A Study of Racial Relations in English Society*. London: Kegan Paul, Trench, Trubner and Company, 1948.

Morant, Geoffrey McKay. *The Races of Central Europe: A Footnote to History*. London: G. Allen and Unwin, Ltd. 1939.

Ottley, R. *No Green Pastures*. New York: Charles Scribner's Sons, 1951.

Ripley, William Z. *The Races of Europe*. New York: D. Appleton and Company, 1923.

Strakhovsky, Leonid I. (ed). *A Handbook of Slavic Studies*. Cambridge: Harvard University Press, 1949.

11. Israel

Eisenstadt, S. N. "The Oriental Jews in Israel." *Jewish Social Studies*, XII (July, 1950), 199–222.

——. "Youth, Culture and Social Structure in Israel." *British Journal of Sociology*, II (June, 1951), 105–114.

——. "Delinquent Group-Formation Among Immigrant Youth." *British Journal of Delinquency*, II (July, 1951), 1–12.

——. "The Place of Elites and Primary Groups in the Absorption of New Immigrants in Israel." *American Journal of Sociology*, LVII (November, 1951), 222–231.

——. *The Absorption of Immigrants*. Glencoe, Ill.: The Free Press, 1955.

Infield, Henrik F. "The Concept of Jewish Culture and the State of Israel." *American Sociological Review*, XVI (August, 1951), 506–514.

Murphy, H. B. M. "The Resettlement of Jewish Refugees in Israel, with Special Reference to Those Known as Displaced Persons." *Population Studies*, V (November, 1951), 153–174.

Neumann, Robert. *By the Waters of Babylon*. New York: Simon and Schuster, 1940.

Parkes, James William. *End of an Exile; Israel, the Jews and the Gentile World*. London: Vallentine Mitchell, 1954.

Patai, Raphael. *Israel Between East and West: A Study in Human Relations*. Philadelphia: Jewish Publication Society of America, 1953.

Voss, Carl Hermann. *The Palestine Problem Today; Israel and Its Neighbors*. Boston: The Beacon Press, 1953.

12. The Moslem World

Antonius, George. *The Arab Awakening: The Story of the Arab National Movement*. London: H. Hamilton, 1938.

Bowles, Paul. *The Spider's House*. New York: Random House, 1955.

Brinton, Jasper Yeates. *The Mixed Courts of Egypt*. New Haven: Yale University Press, 1930.

Byng, Edward J. *The World of the Arabs*. Boston: Little, Brown and Company, 1944.

Cahnman, Werner J. "France in Algeria—A Problem of Culture Contact." *The Review of Politics*, VII (July, 1945), 343–357.

Coon, Carleton. "North Africa," in Ralph Linton (ed.), *Most of the World*. New York: Columbia University Press, 1949.

——. *Caravan: The Story of the Middle East*. New York: Henry Holt and Company, 1951.

Ellis, Harry B. *Heritage of the Desert: The Arabs and the Middle East*. New York: The Roland Press Company, 1956.

Hoskins, Halford L. *The Middle East: Problem Area in World Politics*. New York: The Macmillan Company, 1954.

Hourani, A. H. *Syria and Lebanon: A Political Essay*. Issued under the auspices of the Royal Institute of International Affairs. New York: Oxford University Press, 1946.

——. "The Decline of the West in the Middle East." *International Affairs*, XXIX (January, 1953), 22–42; (April, 1953), 156–183.

——. *Minorities in the Arab World*. New York: The Oxford University Press, 1947.

——. "Race and Related Ideas in the Near East," in Andrew W. Lind (ed.), *Race Relations in World Perspective*, Honolulu: University of Hawaii Press, 1955. Chapter VI.

Izzeddin, Nejla. *The Arab World. Past, Present, and Future*. Chicago: Henry Regnery Company, 1953.

Julien, C. A. *L'Afrique du Nord en Marche: Nationalismes Musulmans et Souveraineté Francaise*. Paris: R. Julliard, 1952. Second Edition.

Jurkat, E. and Kiser, Louise P. "The Peoples of the Mohammedan World." *Annals of the American Academy of Political and Social Science*, CCXXXVII (January, 1945), 94–106.

Landau, Rom. *France and the Arabs*.

Toronto: Canadian Institute of International Affairs, 1954.

Morrison, S. A. *Middle East Tensions: Political, Social and Religious.* New York: Harper and Brothers, 1955.

Nuseibeh, Hazem Zaki. *The Ideas of Arab Nationalism.* Ithaca, N. Y.: Cornell University Press, 1956.

Richardson, F. L. W., Jr. and Batal, James. "The Near East," in Ralph Linton (ed.), *Most of the World.* New York: Columbia University Press, 1949.

Sanger, Richard H. *The Arabian Peninsula.* Ithaca: Cornell University Press, 1954.

Stevens, Edmund. *North African Powder Keg.* New York: Coward-McCann, 1955.

Von Grunebaum, Gustave E. *Unity and Variety in Muslim Civilization.* Chicago: University of Chicago Press, 1955.

13. The Soviet Union

Cohen, Elliot E. (ed.). *The New Red Anti-Semitism: A Symposium.* Boston: The Beacon Press, 1953.

Fedorova, Nina. *The Family.* Boston: Little, Brown and Company, 1940.

Hrdlička, Aleš. "The Peoples of the Soviet Union." *Smithsonian Institution, War Background Studies No. 3,* 1942.

Hula, Erich. "The Nationalities Policy of the Soviet Union." *Social Research,* XI (May, 1944), 168–201.

Kolarz, Walter. *Russia and Her Colonies.* London: G. Philip, 1952.

——. *The Peoples of the Soviet Far East.* New York: Frederick A. Praeger, 1954.

Lamont, Corliss. *The Peoples of the Soviet Union.* New York: Harcourt, Brace and Company, 1946.

Lorimer, Frank. *The Population of the Soviet Union: History and Prospects.* Geneva: League of Nations, 1946.

Meyer, Peter. *The Jews in the Soviet Satellites.* Syracuse, New York: Syracuse University Press, 1953.

Phinney, Archie. "Racial Minorities in the Soviet Union." *Pacific Affairs,* VIII (September, 1935), 321–327.

Robinson, Jacob. "The Soviet Solution of the Minorities Problem," in R. M. MacIver (ed.), *Group Relations and Group Antagonism.* New York: Harper and Brothers, 1944.

Schwarz, Solomon M. *The Jews in the Soviet Union.* Syracuse, N. Y.: Syracuse University Press, 1951.

14. Spanish America

Alegría, Ciro, *Broad and Alien is the World.* New York: Farrar and Rinehart, Inc., 1941.

Beals, Ralph L. "Indian-Mestizo-White Relations in Spanish America," in Andrew W. Lind (ed.), *Race Relations in World Perspective.* Honolulu: University of Hawaii Press, 1955. Ch. XVIII.

Biesanz, John. "Cultural and Economic Factors in Panamanian Race Relations." *American Sociological Review,* XIV (December, 1949), 772–779.

——. "Race Relations in the Canal Zone." *Phylon,* XI (First Quarter, 1950), 23–30.

—— and Mavis. *The People of Panama.* New York: Columbia University Press, 1955.

Borah, W. "Race and Class in Mexico." *Pacific Historical Review,* XXIII (November, 1954), 331–342.

Bryce, James. *South America: Observations and Impressions.* New York: The Macmillan Company, 1916. Chapter xiii, "The Relations of Races in South America."

de la Fuente, Julio. "Ethnic and Communal Relations," in Sol Tax et al., *Heritage of Conquest: Ethnology of Middle America.* Glencoe, Ill.: The Free Press, 1952.

Humphrey, N. D. "Race, Caste and Class in Colombia." *Phylon,* XIII (Second Quarter, 1952), 161–166.

Icaza, Jorge. *En Las Calles.* Buenos Aires: Publicaciones Atlas, 1936.

Mendieta y Nuñez, Lucio. "Racial and Cultural Tensions in Latin America." *International Social Science Bulletin,* IV (1952), 442–451.

Nash, Roy. *The Conquest of Brazil.* New York: Harcourt, Brace and Company, 1926.

Rosenblat, Angel. *La Población Indígena y el Mestizaje en América, 1492–1952.* Buenos Aires: Editorial Nova, 1954, 2nd edition, 2 vols.

Service, Elman R. *Spanish-Guarani Relations in Early Colonial Paraguay.* Ann Arbor: University of Michigan Press, 1954.

Stewart, Watt. *Chinese Bondage in Peru.* Durham: Duke University Press, 1951.

Tax, Sol. "Ethnic Relations in Guatemala." *American Indigena.* Mexico, D. F.: Instituto Indigenista Interamericano, II (October, 1942), 43–48.

Tumin, Melvin M. *Caste in a Peasant Society: A Case Study in the Dynamics of Caste.* Princeton: Princeton University Press, 1952.

Wagley, Charles. *Amazon Town.* New York: The Macmillan Company, 1953.

15. *The United States: General*

Aginsky, Burt W. "The Interaction of Ethnic Groups: A Case Study of Indians and Whites." *American Sociological Review,* XIV (April, 1949), 288–293.

Anderson, Elin L. *We Americans.* Cambridge: Harvard University Press, 1937.

Archambault, Alberic A. *Mill Village.* Boston: Bruce Humphries, Inc., 1943.

Cole, Stewart G. and Mildred Wiese. *Minorities and the American Promise.* New York: Harper and Brothers, 1954.

D'Agostino, Guido. *Olives on the Apple Tree.* New York: Doubleday, Doran & Co., Inc., 1940.

Drake, St. Clair and Cayton, Horace R. *Black Metropolis: A Study of Negro Life in a Northern City.* New York: Harcourt, Brace and Company, 1945.

Ellison, Ralph. *Invisible Man.* New York: Random House, 1952.

Frazier, E. Franklin. *The Negro in the United States.* Chicago: University of Chicago Press, 1949.

——. *Black Bourgeoisie,* Glencoe: The Free Press, 1957.

Gorer, Geoffrey. *The American People.* New York: W. W. Norton, 1948. Chapter viii, "More Equal Than Others."

Handlin, Oscar. *Boston's Immigrants, 1790–1865: A Study in Acculturation.* Cambridge: Harvard University Press, 1941.

——. "Group Life Within the American Pattern." *Commentary,* VIII (November, 1949), 411–417.

——. *Race and Nationality in American Life.* Boston: Atlantic-Little, Brown, 1956.

Hartshone, Richard. "Racial Maps of the United States." *Geographical Review,* XXVIII (April, 1938), 276–288.

Herskovits, Melville Jean. "The Social History of the Negro," in C. Murchison, (ed.), *A Handbook of Social Psychology.* Worcester, Mass.: Clark University Press, 1935, pp. 207–267.

Higham, John. *Strangers in the Land: Patterns of American Nativism, 1860–*

1925. New Brunswick, N. J.: Rutgers University Press, 1955.

Landes, Ruth. "Biracialism in American Society: A Comparative View." *American Anthropologist,* LVII (December, 1955), 1253–1263.

McWilliams, Carey. *Brothers Under the Skin.* Rev. ed. Boston: Little, Brown and Company, 1951.

Myrdal, Gunnar. *An American Dilemma: The Negro Problem and Modern Democracy.* New York: Harper and Brothers, 1944. 2 vols.

Nichols, Lee. *Breakthrough on the Color Front.* New York: Random House, 1954.

Nolan, William A. *Communism Versus the Negro.* Chicago: H. Regnery Company, 1951.

Potts, John. *Look in Your Mirror: A Study in Human Behavior.* New York: Vantage Press, 1952.

Record, Wilson. *The Negro and the Communist Party.* Chapel Hill, N. C.: University of North Carolina Press, 1951.

Reuter, Edward Byron. *The American Race Problem: A Study of the Negro.* New York: Thomas Y. Crowell Company, 1938. Revised edition.

Schermerhorn, R. A. *These Our People.* Boston: D. C. Heath, 1949.

Warner, W. Lloyd and Srole, Leo. *The Social Systems of American Ethnic Groups.* New Haven: Yale University Press, 1945.

16. *The United States: Alaska and Hawaii*

Adams, Romanzo Colfax. *Interracial Marriage in Hawaii: A Study of the Mutually Conditioned Processes of Acculturation and Amalgamation.* New York: The Macmillan Company, 1937.

Hormann, Bernhard L. "Racial Complexion of Hawaii's Future Population." *Social Forces,* XXVII (October, 1948), 68–72.

Inn, Henry. *Hawaiian Types.* New York: Hastings House, 1945.

Kuykendall, R. S. *The Hawaiian Kingdom.* Honolulu: University of Hawaii, 1938.

Lind, Andrew W. *Hawaii's Japanese: An Experiment in Democracy.* Princeton: Princeton University Press, 1946.

——. *Hawaii's People.* Honolulu: University of Hawaii Press, 1955.

Marshall, Robert. *Arctic Village.* New York: H. Smith and R. Hass, 1933.

Scott, John Carver. *Race and Culture Con-*

tact in Southeastern Alaska. University of Chicago, 1953. Ph.D. thesis.

17. The United States: South

Adams, Samuel C., Jr. *The Changing Organization of a Rural Negro Community and Its Implications for Race Accommodation.* University of Chicago, 1947. Ph.D. thesis.

Aptheker, Herbert. *A Documentary History of the Negro People in the United States.* New York: Citadel Press, 1951.

Ashmore, Harry S. *The Negro and the Schools.* Chapel Hill: The University of North Carolina Press, 1954.

Baker, Ray Stannard. *Following the Color Line: An Account of Negro Citizenship in the American Democracy.* New York: Doubleday, Page and Company, 1908.

Brown, Ina Corinne. *Race Relations in a Democracy.* New York: Harper and Brothers, 1949.

Collins, Charles Wallace. *Whither Solid South? A Study in Politics and Race Relations.* New Orleans: Pelican Publishing Company, 1947.

Davis, Allison; Gardner, Burleigh B.; and Gardner, Mary R. *Deep South: A Social Anthropological Study of Caste and Class.* Chicago: The University of Chicago Press, 1941.

Dollard, John. *Caste and Class in a Southern Town.* New Haven: Yale University Press, 1937.

Doyle, Bertram Wilbur. *The Etiquette of Race Relations in the South.* Chicago: University of Chicago Press, 1937.

Frazier, E. Franklin. *The Free Negro Family; A Study of Family Origins Before The Civil War.* Nashville, Tenn.: Fisk University Press, 1932.

——. *The Negro Family in the United States.* Chicago: University of Chicago Press, 1939.

Harris, A. L. and Spero, S. D. "Negro Problem." *Encyclopaedia of the Social Sciences,* XI, pp. 335–355.

Key, Valdimer Orlando, Jr. *Southern Politics in State and Nation.* New York: Alfred A. Knopf, 1949.

McIlwaine, Shields. *The Southern Poor-White from Lubberland to Tobacco Road.* Norman, Oklahoma; University of Oklahoma Press, 1939.

Moore, W. E. "Stratification in the Ante-Bellum South." *American Sociological Review,* VII (June, 1942), 343–351.

O'Brien, Robert W. "Status of Chinese in the Mississippi Delta." *Social Forces,* XIX (March, 1941), 386–390.

Phillips, Ulrich Bonnell. *Life and Labor in the Old South.* Boston: Little, Brown and Company, 1929.

——. "The Central Theme in Southern History." *American Historical Review,* XXXIV (October, 1928), 30–43. Reprinted in E. Merton Coulter (ed.), *The Course of the South to Secession: An Interpretation by Ulrich Bonnell Phillips.* New York: D. Appleton-Century Company, 1939.

Powdermaker, Hortense. *After Freedom: A Cultural Study in the Deep South.* New York: The Viking Press, 1939.

Raper, Arthur F. "A Day at Police Court." *Phylon,* V (Third Quarter, 1944), 225–232.

Stone, Alfred Holt. *Studies in the American Race Problem.* New York: Doubleday, Page and Company, 1908.

Thompson, Edgar T. (ed.). *Race Relations and the Race Problem: A Definition and an Analysis.* Durham, N. C.: Duke University Press, 1939.

—— and Alma Macy Thompson. *Race and Region: A Descriptive Bibliography Compiled With Special Reference to the Relations Between Whites and Negroes in the United States.* Chapel Hill, N. C.: University of North Carolina Press, 1949.

Walker, Harry J. "Changes in the Structure of Race Relations in the South." *American Sociological Review,* XIV (June, 1949), 377–383.

Warner, W. Lloyd. "American Caste and Class." *American Journal of Sociology,* XLII (September, 1936), 234–237.

18. The United States: Southwest

Burma, John H. *Spanish-Speaking Groups in the United States.* Durham: Duke University Press, 1954.

Crichton, Kyle Samuel. *The Proud People, A Novel.* New York: Charles Scribner's Sons, 1944.

Fergusson, Erna. *Our Southwest.* New York: Alfred A. Knopf, 1940.

——. *New Mexico: A Pageant of Three Peoples.* New York: Alfred A Knopf, 1951.

Fergusson, Harvey. *Followers of the Sun.* New York: Alfred A. Knopf, 1936.

Laughlin, Ruth. *Caballeros.* Caldwell, Idaho: The Caxton Printers, 1947.

Lawrence, Lars. *Morning, Noon and Night.* New York: G. P. Putman's Sons, 1954.

Lipsky, Eleazar. *Lincoln McKeever.* New York: Appleton-Century-Crofts, 1953.

Lummis, Charles F. *The Land of Poco Tiempo.* New York: Charles Scribner's Sons, 1897.

McWilliams, Carey. *North From Mexico: The Spanish-Speaking People of the United States.* Philadelphia: J. B. Lippincott Company, 1949.

——. "The Spanish-Americans of New Mexico, U. S. A.," in Margaret Mead (ed.), *Cultural Patterns and Technical Change.* Paris: UNESCO, 1953, pp. 168–193.

Reid, Jesse Taylor. *It Happened in Taos.* Albuquerque: University of New Mexico Press, 1946.

Rusinow, Irving. *A Camera Report on El Cerrito: A Typical Spanish-American Community in New Mexico.* Miscellaneous Publications, No. 479. Washington: Bureau of Agricultural Economics, United States Department of Agriculture, January, 1942.

Sanchez, G. I. *Forgotten People.* Albuquerque, New Mexico: University of New Mexico Press, 1940.

Saunders, Lyle. *A Guide to Materials Bearing on Cultural Relations in New Mexico.* Albuquerque: University of New Mexico Press, 1944.

——. "The Social History of Spanish-Speaking People in Southwestern United States Since 1846." *Proceedings of the First Congress of Historians from Mexico and the United States.* Monterrey, September 4–9, 1949. Editorial Cultura, Mexico, 1950.

——. *Cultural Difference and Medical Care,* New York: Russel Sage Foundation, 1954.

Schulman, Irving. *The Square Trap.* Boston: Little, Brown and Company, 1953.

Scotford, John R. *Within These Borders. Spanish-Speaking Peoples in the U. S. A.* New York: The Friendship Press, 1953.

Taylor, Paul Schuster. *An American-Mexican Frontier. Nueces County, Texas.* Chapel Hill, N. C.: The University of North Carolina Press, 1934.

Tuck, Ruth D. *Not With the Fist. A Study of Mexican-Americans in a Southwest City.* New York: Harcourt, Brace and Company, 1946.

Zeleny, Carolyn. *Relations Between the Spanish-Americans and Anglo-Americans in New Mexico: A Study of Conflict and Accommodation in a Dual Ethnic Relationship.* New Haven: Yale University, 1944. Ph.D. thesis.

19. The United States: West Coast.

Bloom, Leonard and Riemer, Ruth. *Removal and Return.* Berkeley: University of California Press, 1949.

Cox, Oliver C. "The Nature of the Anti-Asiatic Movement on the Pacific Coast." *Journal of Negro Education,* XV (Fall, 1946), 603–614.

Grudzins, Morton. *Americans Betrayed.* Chicago: University of Chicago Press, 1949.

Konvitz, Milton R. *The Alien and the Asiatic in American Law.* Ithaca, N. Y.: Cornell University Press, 1946.

Lea, Homer. *The Valor of Ignorance.* New York: Harper and Brothers, 1909.

McKenzie, R. D. "The Oriental Invasion." *Journal of Applied Sociology,* X (November-December, 1925), 120–130.

——. *Oriental Exclusion.* Chicago: University of Chicago Press, 1928.

McLeod, Alexander. *Pigtails and Gold Dust.* Caldwell, Idaho: The Caxton Printers, Ltd., 1947.

Miyamoto, Shotaro Frank. *Social Solidarity Among the Japanese in Seattle.* University of Washington Publications in the Social Sciences, Vol. 11, no. 2 (December, 1939), 57–130.

Orientals and Their Cultural Adjustment. Nashville, Tenn.: Social Science Institute, Fisk University, 1946.

Rodman, W. Paul. "The Origin of the Chinese Issue in California." *Mississippi Valley Historical Review,* XXV (1938), 181–196.

Sandmeyer, Elmer C. *The Anti-Chinese Movement in California.* Urbana: University of Illinois Press, 1939.

Steiner, Jesse Frederick. *The Japanese Invasion: a Study in the Psychology of Interracial Contacts.* Chicago: A. C. McClurg and Co., 1917.

Thomas, Dorothy Swaine. *Japanese-American Evacuation and Resettlement.* Berkeley, Calif.: University of California Press, 1946–54. 3 vols.

20. The West Indies and Adjacent Areas

Campbell, Albert A. *St. Thomas Negroes; A Study of Personality and Culture.*

Evanston, Ill.: The American Psychological Association, Inc., 1943.

Curtin, Philip D. *Two Jamaicas. The Role of Ideas in a Tropical Colony, 1830–1865.* Cambridge: Harvard University Press, 1955.

Gordon, Maxine W. "Cultural Aspects of Puerto Rico's Race Problem." *American Sociological Review,* XV (June, 1950), 383–392.

Hadley, C. V. D. "Personality Patterns and Aggression in the British West Indies." *Human Relations,* II (1949), 349–362.

Henriques, Fernando. "Colour Values in Jamaican Society." *British Journal of Sociology,* II (June, 1951), 115–121.

——. *Family and Colour in Jamaica.* London: Eyre and Spottiswoode, 1953.

Kerr, Madeline. *Personality and Conflict in Jamaica.* Liverpool: University Press, 1952.

Lamming, George, *In the Castle of My Skin.* London: M. Joseph, 1953.

Leyburn, James G. *The Haitian People.* New Haven: Yale University Press, 1941.

——. "The Making of a Black Nation," in George Peter Murdock, *Studies in the Science of Society.* New Haven: Yale University Press, 1937.

Lobb, John. "Caste and Class in Haiti." *American Journal of Sociology,* XLVI (July, 1940), 23–34.

Mills, Charles Wright; Goldsen, Rose K. and Senior, Clarence. *The Puerto Rican Journey.* New York: Harper and Brothers, 1950.

Mittelhölzer, Edgar. *The Life and Death of Sylvia.* London: Secker and Warburg, 1953

Olivier, Sydney Haldane. *Jamaica: The Blessed Land.* London: Faber and Faber Ltd., 1936.

Ortiz Fernández, Fernando. *Cuban Counterpoint: Tobacco and Sugar.* New York: Alfred A. Knopf, 1947.

Reuter, E. B. "Culture Contacts in Puerto Rico." *American Journal of Sociology,* LII (September, 1946), 91–101.

Rogler, C. "Morality of Race Mixing in Puerto Rico." *Social Forces,* XXV (October, 1946), 77–81.

Simey, T. S. *Welfare and Planning in the West Indies.* Oxford: The Clarendon Press, 1946.

Smith, Raymond T. *The Negro Family in British Guiana.* London: Routledge and Kegan Paul, 1956.

Williams, Eric. *The Negro in the Carib-*
bean. Washington, D. C.: Associates in Negro Folk Education, 1942.

——. *Capitalism and Slavery.* Chapel Hill, N. C.: University of North Carolina Press, 1944.

——. "Race Relations in Puerto Rico and the Virgin Islands." *Foreign Affairs,* XXIII (January, 1945), 308–317.

——. "The Historical Background of British Guiana's Problems." *Journal of Negro History,* XXX (October, 1945), 357–381.

BIBLIOGRAPHY, Chapter III

III. The Ecology of Race Relations

A. human ecology: general

Davis, Kingsley. "The World Demographic Transition." *American Academy of Political and Social Science, Annals,* CCXXXVII (January, 1945), 1–11.

Hawley, Amos H. "Ecology and Human Ecology." *Social Forces,* XXII (May, 1944), 398–405.

——. *Human Ecology: A Theory of Community Structure.* New York: The Ronald Press, Company, 1950.

Hughes, Everett C. and Hughes, Helen M. *Where Peoples Meet: Racial and Ethnic Frontiers,* Glencoe, Ill.: The Free Press, 1952. Chapter IV, "Ecology: Land, Numbers and Survival."

Kuske, Bruno. "The Relationship of Race and Nationality Groups to the Historical Formation of World Economy." (Die Beziehung von Rassen und Völkergruppen zur historischen Gestaltung des weltwirtschaftlichen Raumes.) *Weltwirtschaftliches Archiv,* XLIX (May, 1939), 489–509.

McKenzie, Roderick D. *The Evolving World Economy.* Reports of the Albert Kahn Foundation for the Foreign Travel of American Teachers. Vol. V. New York: 1928.

——. "Industrial Expansion and the Interrelations of Peoples," in E. B. Reuter (ed.), *Race and Culture Contacts.* New York: McGraw-Hill Book Company, Inc., 1934, Chapter II.

Park, Robert E. "Human Ecology." *American Journal of Sociology,* XLII (July, 1936), 1–15.

——. "Symbiosis and Socialization: A Frame of Reference for the Study of Society." *American Journal of Sociology,* XLV (July, 1939), 1–25.

——. *Human Communities,* Glencoe, Ill.: The Free Press, 1952.

Quinn, James A. *Human Ecology.* New York: Prentice-Hall, 1950.

Ratzel, Friedrich. "Der Lebensraum. Eine Biogeographische Studie." in *Festgaben für Albert Schaeffle,* Tuebingen, 1901, pp. 101–189.

Strausz-Hupé, Robert. *Geopolitics; The Struggle for Space and Power.* New York: G. B. Putnam's Sons, 1942.

Wirth, Louis. "Human Ecology." *American Journal of Sociology,* L (May, 1945), 483–488.

B. MIGRATION

Brown, John W. *World Migration and Labour.* Amsterdam, 1926.

Calef, Wesley C. and Nelson, Howard J. "Distribution of Negro Population in the United States." *Geographical Review,* XLVI (January, 1956), 82–97.

Citroen, H. A. *European Emigration Overseas Past and Future.* The Hague: Martinus Nijhoff, 1951.

Dixon, Rowland B.; Halphen, Louis and Ferenzi, Imre. "Migrations." *Encyclopaedia Of the Social Sciences,* X, 420–441.

Ferenzi, Imre. *International Migrations.* New York: National Bureau of Economic Research, 1929. 2 vols.

Gladwin, Harold Sterling. *Men Out of Asia.* New York: Whittlesey House, 1947.

Guthrie, W. B. "Migration." *The Catholic Encyclopaedia,* (1911), X. 291–298.

Haddon, A. C. "Migration." *Encyclopaedia Britannica.* 14 ed., 1929.

Handlin, Oscar. *The Uprooted; The Epic Story of the Great Migrations that Made the American People.* Boston: Little, Brown and Company, 1951.

Heberle, Rudolf. *Über die Mobilität der Bevölkerung in den Vereinigten Staaten.* Jena: G. Fischer, 1928.

——. "Types of Migrations." *South Western Social Science Quarterly,* XXXVI (June, 1955), 65–70.

Hobbs, Albert Hoyt. *Differentials in Internal Migration.* Philadelphia: University of Pennsylvania Press, 1942.

Isaac, Julius. *Economics of Migration.* New York: Oxford University Press, 1947.

Jacobs, Joseph. "Migration." *The Jewish Encyclopedia,* (1904), VIII, 583–585.

Keller, Albert G. *Colonization: A Study in the Founding of New Societies.* Boston: Ginn and Company, 1908.

Kondapi, C. *Indians Overseas.* New Delhi: Indian Council of World Affairs, 1951.

Lasker, Bruno. *Filipino Immigration to Continental United States and to Hawaii.* Chicago: University of Chicago Press, 1931.

Lestschinsky, Jakob. "Jüdische Wanderungen im letzten Jahruhundert." *Weltwirtschaftliches Archiv,* 25 Band, Heft I, January, 1927, pp. 69–86.

McKenzie, R. D. "Movement and the Ability to Live," in Carl C. Leebrick and J. E. Harley (eds.), *Proceedings of the Institute of International Relations.* First Session, December 5–12, 1926. Los Angeles: University of Southern California Press, 1927.

——. "Oriental Immigration." *Encyclopedia of the Social Sciences,* XI, pp. 490–494.

Mukerjee, Radhakamal. *Migrant Asia.* Rome: Tipografia Failli, 1936.

Numelin, Ragnar. *The Wandering Spirit: A Study of Human Migration.* London: The Macmillan Company, 1937.

Park, Robert E. "Human Migration and the Marginal Man." *American Journal of Sociology,* XXXIII (May, 1928), 881–893.

Reid, Ira DeA. *The Negro Immigrant: His Background, Characteristics and Social Adjustment, 1899–1937.* New York: Columbia University Press, 1939.

Ross, Frank Alexander and Kennedy, Louise Venable. *A Bibliography of Negro Migration.* New York: Columbia University Press, 1934.

Spears, John Randolph. *The American Slave-Trade: An Account of Its Origin, Growth, and Suppression.* New York: Charles Scribner's Sons, 1900.

Swanstrom, Edward E. *Pilgrims of the Night: A Study of Expelled Peoples.* New York: Sheed and Ward, 1950.

Taft, Donald R. *Human Migration: A Study of International Movements.* New York: The Ronald Press, 1936.

Taylor, Thomas Griffith. *Environment and Race: A Study of the Evolution, Migration, Settlement and Status of the Races of Men.* London: Oxford University Press, 1927.

Teggart, Frederick J. *The Processes of History.* New Haven: Yale University Press, 1918.

Vance, Rupert. *Research Memorandum on Population Redistribution Within the United States.* New York: Social Science Research Council, Bulletin 42, 1938.

C. SUCCESSION

Beynon, Erdmann D. "Occupational Succession of Hungarians in Detroit." *American Journal of Sociology,* XXXIX (March, 1934), 600–610.

Blanchard, Raoul. "Etudes Canadiennes: 2e Série. II Les Cantons de l'est." *Revue de Geographie Alpine.* Tome XXV (1937), 1–210.

Clark, Andrew H. *The Invasion of New Zealand by People, Plants and Animals.* New Brunswick, N. J.: Rutgers University Press, 1949.

Condliffe, John B. *New Zealand in the Making; A Survey of Economic and Social Development.* London: George Allen and Unwin, Ltd., 1930.

Cressey, Paul F. "Population Succession in Chicago, 1898–1930." *American Journal of Sociology,* XLIV (July, 1938), 59–69.

Davis, Kingsley (ed.). "World Population in Transition." *The Annals of the American Academy of Political and Social Science,* CCXXXVII (January, 1945), especially Davis, "The World Demographic Transition." pp. 1–11.

Duncan, Otis D. and Duncan, Beverly. *The Negro Population of Chicago: A Study of Residential Succession.* Chicago: The University of Chicago Press, 1957.

Evans, Maurice S. *Black and White in South East Africa.* New York: Longmans, Green and Company, 1911.

Ford, Richard G. "Population Succession in Chicago," *American Journal of Sociology,* LVI (September, 1950), 156–160.

Goldenweiser, E. A. "Walker's Theory of Immigration." *American Journal of Sociology,* XVIII (November, 1912), 342–351.

Hawgood, John A. *The Tragedy of German-America.* New York: G. P. Putnam's Sons, 1940.

Hollingshead, A. B. "Changes in Land Ownership as an Index of Succession in Rural Communities." *American Journal of Sociology,* XLIII (March, 1938), 764–777.

Lind, Andrew W. *An Island Community: Ecological Succession in Hawaii.* Chicago: University of Cricago Press, 1938.

McKenzie, R. D. *Oriental Exclusion: The Effect of American Immigration Laws, Regulations, and Judicial Decisions Upon the Chinese and Japanese on the American Pacific Coast.* Chicago: University of Chicago Press, 1928.

———. "Ecological Succession in the Puget Sound Region." American Sociological Society, *Publications,* XXIII (1929), 60–80.

McPhee, Allan. *The Economic Revolution in British West Africa.* London: G. Routledge and Sons, Ltd., 1926.

Murphy, R. C. "Racial Succession in the Colombian Choco." *Geographical Review,* XXIX (July, 1939), 461–471.

Park, Robert E. "Succession, and Ecological Concept." *American Sociological Review,* I (April, 1936), 171–179.

Price, A. Grenfell. *White Settlers and Native Peoples: An Historical Study of Racial Contacts Between Whites and Aboriginal Peoples in the United States, Australia and New Zealand.* Melbourne: Georgian House, 1950.

Ross, Aileen D. "The Cultural Effects of Population Changes in the Eastern Townships." *The Canadian Journal of Economics and Political Science,* IX (November, 1943), 447–462.

Schietinger, E. F. "Racial Succession and the Value of Small Residential Properties," *American Sociological Review,* XVI (December, 1951), 832–835.

Taylor, P. S. and Vasey, Tom. "Historical Background of California Farm Labor." *Rural Sociology,* I (September, 1936), 281–295.

Vance, Rupert B. "Racial Competition for the Land," in Edgar T. Thompson (ed.), *Race Relations and the Race Problem.* Durham: Duke University Press, 1939, Chapter IV.

Younge, Eva R. "Population Movements and the Assimilation of Alien Groups in Canada." *Canadian Journal of Economics and Political Science,* X (August, 1944), 372–380.

D. RACIAL SURVIVAL

Allen, Ruth. *The Labor of Women in the Production of Cotton.* Austin: University of Texas, 1931.

Barr, Stringfellow. *Let's Join the Human Race.* Chicago: University of Chicago Press, 1950.

Cahnman, Werner. "The Mediterranean and Caribbean Regions." *Social Forces,* XXII (December, 1943), 209–214.

Cook, S. F. *The Conflict Between the California Indian and White Civilization.* Berkeley: University of California Press, 1943. 4 vols.

Coulter, Charles W. "Problems Arising from Industrialization of Native Life in Central Africa." *American Journal of Sociology*, XL (March, 1935), 582–592.

Frazier, C. and Hung-Chiung. *Racial Variations in Immunity to Syphilis; A Study of the Disease in the Chinese, White and Negro Races*. Chicago: University of Chicago Press, 1948.

Holmes, S. J. "Changing Effects of Race Competition." *Science*, n. s., LXXV (February 19, 1932), 201–208.

———. *The Negro's Struggle for Survival*. Berkeley: University of California Press, 1937.

Hörmann, Bernard Lothar. *Extinction and Survival: A Study of the Reaction of Aboriginal Populations to European Expansion*. University of Chicago, Ph.D. thesis, 1949.

———. "Rigidity and Fluidity in Race Relations," in Andrew W. Lind (ed.), *Race Relations in World Perspective*. Honolulu: University of Hawaii Press, 1955. Chapter II.

Johnson, Charles S. "The Place and Importance of Population Studies in Relation to the Negro Population of the South." *Social Forces*, XX (October, 1941), 26–31.

Kroeber, A. L. *Anthropology*. New York: Harcourt, Brace and Company, 1948, pp. 182–190.

Lambert S. M. *The Depopulation of Pacific Races*. Honolulu: The Bernice Bishop Museum, Special Publication 23, 1934.

Park, Robert E. and Burgess, E. W. *Introduction to the Science of Sociology*. Chicago: University of Chicago Press, 1924. Chapter VIII, "Competition."

Pearl, Raymond. *Studies in Human Biology*. Baltimore: Williams and Wilkins Company, 1924.

Rakower, Joseph. "Tuberculosis Among Jews. Mortality and Morbidity Among Different Jewish Ethnic Groups, Tuberculosis Among Yemenite Jews. Etiologic Factors." *American Review of Tuberculosis*. LXVII (January, 1953), 85–93.

Reynolds, C. N. "Competition and Conflict Between Races of Differing Cultural Standards." *Publications of the American Sociological Society*, XXV (May, 1931), 81–89.

Rumyaneck, J. "An Urbanized Community." *American Journal of Sociology*. XXXVIII (January, 1933), 523–535.

Sayers, James Denson. *Can the White Race*

Survive? Washington: The Independent Publishing Company, 1929.

Simmons, James Stevens. *Global Epidemiology: A Geography of Disease and Sanitation*. Philadelphia: J. B. Lippincott Company, 1944.

Stearn, E. Wagner and Stearn, Allen E. *The Effect of Smallpox on the Destiny of the Amerindian*. Boston: Bruce Humphries, Inc., 1945.

Stitt, E. R. "Our Disease Inheritance from Slavery." *United States Naval Medical Bulletin*, XXVI (October, 1928), 801–817.

Stoddard, Theodore Lothrop. *The Rising Tide of Color Against White World-Supremacy*. New York: Charles Scribner's Sons, 1922.

Zinsser, Hans; Enders, John F. and Fothergill, Leroy D. *Immunity: Principles and Application in Medicine and Public Health*. New York: The Macmillan Company, 1939. Fifth edition, pp. 110–112.

E. SEGREGATION

Buck, Paul H. "The Poor Whites of the Ante-Bellum South." *American Historical Review*, XXXI (October, 1925), 41–54.

Carnegie Commission of Investigation. *The Poor White Problem in South Africa*. Stellenbosch: Pro Ecclesia-Drukkery, 1932. 5 vols.

Deutsch, K. W. "Some Economic Aspects of the Rise of Nationalistic and Racial Pressure Groups." *Canadian Journal of Economics and Political Science*, VIII (February, 1942), 109–115.

Emerson, Frederick V. "Geographical Influences in American Slavery." *Bulletin of the American Geographical Society*, XLIII (January-March, 1911), 13–26, 106–118, 170–181.

Frazier, E. Franklin. "Human, All Too Human." *The Survey Graphic*, XXXVI (January, 1947), 74ff.

Hancock, W. K. *Survey of British Commonwealth Affairs*. New York: Oxford University Press, 1937. Vol. II, Chapter I, Part II, "White Man's Country."

Hartshorne, Richard. "Racial Maps of the United States." *Geographical Review*, XXVIII (April, 1938), 276–288.

Hawley, Amos. "Dispersion Versus Segregation Apropos of a Solution of Race Problems," in *Papers of the Michigan Academy of Science, Arts and Letters,*

XXX (1944), 667–674. Ann Arbor: University of Michigan Press, 1945.

Hollander, A. N. J. Den. *De Landelijke Arme Blanken in het Zuiden der Vereenigde Staten: een Sociaal-Historische en Sociografische Studie.* Groningen: J. B. Wolters', 1933.

——. "The Tradition of 'Poor Whites'," in William Terry Couch (ed.), *Culture in the South.* Chapel Hill, N. C.: University of North Carolina Press, 1935, Chapter XX.

Huxley, Mrs. E. J. *White Man's Country: Lord Delamere and the Making of Kenya.* London: Macmillan and Company, Ltd., 1935. 2 vols.

Kahn, S. "Ghetto." *The Jewish Encyclopedia,* (1903), V, 652–655.

Lestschinsky, Jakob. "Ghetto." *Encyclopedia of the Social Sciences,* VI, 646–650.

Lohmann, J. D. *Segregation in the Nation's Capital.* Chicago: National Committee on Segregation in the Nation's Capital, 1949.

McIlwaine, Shields. *The Southern Poor White From Lubberland to Tobacco Road.* Norman, Oklahoma; University of Oklahoma Press, 1939.

McKenzie, R. D. "The Oriental Invasion." *Journal of Applied Sociology,* X (1925–1926), 120–130.

Mell, Mildred Rutherford. "Poor Whites of the South." *Social Forces,* XVII (December. 1938), 153–167.

Price, A. Grenfell. *White Settlers in the Tropics.* New York: American Geographical Society, 1939.

Randall, R. J. "Some Reflections on the Financial Policy of Certain Municipalities Toward the Natives Within Their Boundaries." *The South African Journal of Economics,* VII (June, 1939), 149–171.

Raper, Arthur F. *Preface to Peasantry: A Tale of Two Black Belt Counties.* Chapel Hill, N. C.: University of North Carolina Press, 1936.

Smythe, Hugh H. "The Concept 'Jim Crow'." *Social Forces,* XXVII (October, 1948), 45–48.

Tolmshee, Stanley J. "The Origin of the First 'Jim Crow' Law," *Journal of Southern History,* XV (March, 1949), 235–247.

Weaver, Robert. *The Negro Ghetto.* New York: Harcourt, Brace and Company, 1948.

Wirth, Louis. *The Ghetto.* Chicago: University of Chicago Press, 1928.

——. "Segregation." *Encyclopaedia of the Social Sciences,* XIII, 643–646.

Woodward, C. Van. *The Strange Career of Jim Crow.* New York: Oxford University Press, 1955.

F. COMPETITION AND THE RACIAL DIVISION OF LABOR

Anderson, H. Dewey and Davidson, Percy E. *Occupational Trends in the United States.* Stanford University, California: Stanford University Press, 1940.

Arendt, Hannah. "The Jew as Pariah. A Hidden Tradition." *Jewish Social Studies,* VI (April, 1944), 99–122.

Beynon, Erdmann Doane. "The Gypsy in a Non-Gypsy Economy." *American Journal of Sociology,* XLII (November, 1936), 358–370.

——. "Social Parasitism in a Foreign Language Colony," *Sociology and Social Research,* XX (November-December, 1935), 103–116.

Bhandarkar, D. R. (ed.). "India." *Annals of the American Academy of Political and Social Science,* CXLV (September, 1929), Supplement–203.

Block, Martin. *Gypsies, Their Life and Their Customs.* London: Methuen and Company, 1938.

Brown, William G. "The White Peril: The Immediate Danger of the Negro." *North American Review,* CLXXIX (December, 1904), 824–841.

Blunt, E. A. H. *The Caste System of Northern India.* London: The Oxford University Press, 1931. Chapter IX.

Collins, Orvis. "Ethnic Behavior in Industry, Sponsorship and Rejection in a New England Factory," *American Journal of Sociology,* LI (January, 1946), 293–298.

Cox, Sir Edmund C. *Police and Crime in India.* London: Stanley Paul and Company, 1911. Chapter XVII, "Criminal Tribes."

Davenport, H. J. "Non-Competing Groups." *Quarterly Journal of Economics,* XL (November, 1925), 52–81.

Dewey, Donald. "Negro Employment in Southern Industry." *The Journal of Political Economy,* LX (August, 1952), 279–293.

——. *Selected Studies of Negro Employment in the South: Four Studies of Negro Employment in the Upper South Prepared for the NPA Committee of the South.* Washington: National Planning Association, 1953.

Evans, Kenneth. "Some Occupational Trends in the South." *Social Forces,* XVII (December, 1938), 184–190.

Feldman, Herman. *Racial Factors in American Industry.* New York: Harper and Brothers, 1931.

Frazier, E. Franklin. "Occupational Classes Among Negroes." *American Journal of Sociology,* XXXV (March, 1930), 718–738.

Gillin, John Lewis. *Taming the Criminal.* New York: The Macmillan Company, 1931. Chapters IV–V.

Glick, Clarence E. "The Position of Racial Groups in Occupational Structures." *Social Forces,* XXVI (December, 1947,) 206–211.

Goldberg, Nathan. "Occupational Patterns of American Jews." *The Jewish Review,* III (April, 1945), 3–24; (October-December, 1945), 162–186; (January, 1946), 280–290.

Grierson, P. J. H. *The Silent Trade.* Edinburgh. 1903.

"The Gypsie, Symposium." *The Survey,* LIX (October 1, 1927).

Handlin, Oscar. "International Migration and the Acquisition of New Skills," in Bert F. Hoselitz (ed.), *The Progress of Underdeveloped Areas,* Chicago: The University of Chicago Press, 1952, pp. 54–59.

Handman, Max S. "Gypsies." *Encyclopaedia of the Social Sciences,* VII, 231–232.

Hatt, Paul K. "Occupation and Social Stratification." *American Journal of Sociology,* LV (May, 1950), 533–543.

Holmes, S. J. "The Changing Effects of Race Competition." *Science,* LXXV (February, 1932), 201–208.

Hughes, Everett C. and McDonald, Margaret L. "French and English in the Economic Structure of Montreal." *Canadian Journal of Economics and Political Science,* VII (November, 1941), 493–505.

Hughes, Everett C. *French Canada in Transition.* Chicago: University of Chicago Press, 1943. Chs. VII–VIII.

——. "The Knitting of Racial Groups in Industry." *American Sociological Review,* XI (October, 1946), 512–519.

Katoaka, W. T. "Occupations of Japanese in Los Angeles." *Sociology and Social Research,* XIV (September-October, 1929), 53–58.

Kephart, William M. "What is the Position of Jewish Economy in the United States?" *Social Forces,* XXVIII (December, 1949), 153–164.

Koenig, Samuel. "Ethnic Factors in the Economic Life of Urban Connecticut." *American Sociological Review,* VIII (April, 1943), 193–197.

——. "Ethnic Groups in Connecticut Industry." *Social Forces,* XX (October, 1941), 96–105.

Lestschinsky, Jacob. "The Position of Jews in the Economic Life of America," in Isacque Graebner and Steuart H. Britt (eds.), *Jews in a Gentile World.* New York: The Macmillan Company, 1942, Chapter XV.

Lind, Andrew W. "Occupational Trends Among Immigrant Groups in Hawaii." *Social Forces,* VII (December, 1928), 290–299.

McKenzie, R. D. "Cultural and Racial Differences as Bases as Human Symbiosis," in Kimball Young (ed.), *Social Attitudes.* New York: Henry Holt and Company, 1931. Chapter VI.

Nieboer, H. J. *Slavery as an Industrial System.* The Hague: Martinus Nijhoff, 1910.

Noland, E. William and Bakke, E. Wight. *Workers Wanted: A Study of Employers' Hiring Policies, Preferences and Practices in New Haven and Charlotte.* New York: Harper and Brothers, 1949.

Olivier, Sydney. *White Capital and Coloured Labour.* London: L. and V. Woolf, 1929.

Putnam, Patrick. "The Pygmies of the Ituri Forest," in Carleton S. Coon, *A Reader in General Anthropology.* New York: Henry Holt and Company, 1948, pp. 322–328.

Reuter, Edward B. "Competition and the Racial Division of Labor," in Edgar T. Thompson (ed.), *Race Relations and the Race Problem.* Durham, N. C.: Duke University Press, 1939. Chapter II.

Ring, H. H. and others. *Negroes in the United States: Their Employment and Economic Status,* United States Bureau of Labor Statistics Bulletin No. 1119, 1953.

Ross, Malcolm H. *All Manner of Men.* New York: Reynal and Hitchcock, 1948.

Ruchames, Louis. *Race, Jobs and Politics: A Story of F. E. P. C.* New York: Columbia University Press, 1953.

Smythe, Hugh H. "The Eta: A Marginal Japanese Caste." *American Journal of*

Sociology, LVIII (September, 1952), 194–196.

Tinley, J. M. *The Native Labor Problem of South Africa.* Chapel Hill, N. C.: The University of North Carolina Press, 1942.

Van der Horst, Sheila T. *Native Labour in South Africa.* London: Oxford University Press, 1942.

Vance, Rupert B. "Racial Competition for the Land," in Edgar Thompson (ed.), *Race Relations and the Race Problem.* Durham, N. C.: Duke University Press, 1939, Chapter IV.

Weslanger, C. A. "The Delaware Indians as Women." *Journal of the Washington Academy of Sciences,* XXXIV (1944), 381–388.

Wilson, Logan and Gilmore, Harlan. "White Employers and Negro Workers." *American Sociological Review,* VIII (December, 1943), 698–705.

G. ECONOMIC INSTITUTIONS

Boeke, J. H. *Economics and Economic Policy of Dual Societies as Exemplified by Indonesia.* New York: Institute of Pacific Relations, 1953.

——. *The Structure of Netherlands Indian Economy.* New York: Institute of Pacific Relations, 1942.

Dunlop, W. R. "Economic Research in Tropical Development With Special Reference to British Guiana and British Malaya." *Journal of the Royal Society of Arts,* LXXIII (1925), 311–334.

——. "Queensland and Jamaica: A Comparative Study in Geographical Economics." *Geographical Review,* XVI (October, 1926), 548–567.

Greaves, I. C. *Modern Production Among Backward People.* London: G. Allen and Unwin, Ltd., 1935.

Hughes, Everett C. "Race Relations in Industry," in William F. Whyte (ed.), *Industry and Society.* New York: McGraw-Hill, 1946, Chapter VI.

——. "Queries Concerning Industry and Society Growing out of the Study of Ethnic Relations in Industry." *American Sociological Review,* XIV (April, 1949), 211–220.

——. and Hughes, Helen M. *Where Peoples Meet: Racial and Ethnic Frontiers.* Glencoe, Ill.: The Free Press, 1952. Chapter VI, "How They Work for Each Other."

International Labour Organization, Committee on Work on Plantations. Basic *Problems of Plantation Labour.* Geneva: International Labour Office, 1950.

Keller, Albert Galloway. *Colonization: A Study of the Founding of New Societies.* Boston: Ginn and Company, 1908. Chapter I.

McBride, George McCutchen. "Plantation." *Encyclopaedia of the Social Sciences,* XII, 148–153.

McWilliams, Carey. *Factories in the Field; The Story of Migratory Farm Labor in California.* Boston: Little, Brown and Company, 1939.

Miller, Delbert C. and Form, William H. *Industrial Sociology.* New York: Harper and Brothers, 1951.

Moore, W. E. *Industrial Relations and the Social Order.* New York: The Macmillan Company, 1946.

——. *Industrialization and Labor.* Ithaca, N. Y.: Cornell University Press, 1951.

Rottenbert, S. "Income and Leisure in an Underdeveloped Economy." *Journal of Political Economy,* LX (April, 1952), 95–101.

Simpson, Lesley Byrd. *The Encomienda in New Spain.* Berkeley: University of California Press, 1950.

Sofer, Cyril. *Some Aspects of Race Relations in An East African Township.* Ph.D. thesis. London: London School of Economics and Political Science, 1952.

Thompson, E. T. "The Natural History of Agricultural Labor in the South," in David K. Jackson (ed.), *American Studies in Honor of William Kenneth Boyd.* Durham, N. C.: Duke University Press, 1940.

——. "Comparative Education in Colonial Areas, With Special Reference to Plantation and Mission Frontiers." *American Journal of Sociology,* XLVIII (May, 1943), 710–721.

——. *The Plantation: A Bibliography.* Washington: Pan American Union, Social Science Monographs, IV, 1957.

IV. THE IDEA OF RACE

A. THE NATURE AND HISTORY OF THE IDEA OF RACE

Andrezejewski, Stanislaw. "Are Ideas Social Forces?" *American Sociological Review,* XIV (December, 1949), 758–764.

Arendt, Hannah. "From the Dreyfus Affair to France Today." *Jewish Social Studies,* IV (July, 1942), 195–240.

——. *The Origins of Totalitarianism.* New

York: Harcourt, Brace and Company, 1951.

Bailey, Thomas P. *Race Orthodoxy in the South*. New York: The Neale Publishing Company, 1914.

Barzun, Jacques. *The French Race: Theories of Its Origins and Their Social And Political Implications Prior to the Revolution*. New York: Columbia University Press, 1932.

——. *Race; A Study in Modern Superstition*. New York: Harcourt, Brace and Company, 1937.

Baumer, Franklin Le Van (ed.). *Main Currents of Western Thought; Readings in Western European Intellectual History From the Middle Ages to the Present*. New York: Alfred A. Knopf, 1952.

Beardsley, Mrs. Grace Hadley. *The Negro in Greek and Roman Civilization*. Baltimore: The Johns Hopkins Press, 1929.

Beazley, C. R. *The Dawn of Modern Geography*. London: J. Murray, 1897–1906. 3 vols.

Belloc, Hilaire. "Talking (and Singing) of the Nordic Man," in *Short Talks With the Dead and Others*. London: Johnathan Cape, 1928, pp. 104–116.

Bodin, Jean. *Methodus*. Amstelaedmi, Joannis Ravesteiny, 1650.

Boulainvilliers, Henri, Comte de. *Histoire de l'Ancien Gouvernement de la France*. A la Haye and a Amsterdam: Aux dépends de la compagnie, 1727. 3 vols.

Brady, Robert. *The Spirit and Structure of German Fascism*. New York: The Viking Press, 1937.

Brennecke, Fritz. *The Nazi Primer*. Translated by Harwood L. Childs. New York: Harper and Brothers, 1938.

Brinton, Clarence Crane. *Ideas and Men: The Story of Western Thought*. New York: Prentice-Hall Company, 1950.

Bryce, James. *The Relations of the Advanced and Backward Races of Mankind*. Oxford, England: Clarendon Press, 1902.

——. "Race Sentiment as a Factor in History." Creighton Lecture, London, 1915.

Buffon, George Louis Leclerc, Comte de. *Natural History, General and Particular*. London: A. Strahan and T. Cadell in the Strand, 1791.

Bunche, Ralph J. *A World View of Race*. Washington, D. C.: The Associates in Negro Folk Education, 1936.

Carroll, Charles. "*The Negro a Beast*"; or, "*In the Image of God*." St. Louis, Missouri: American Book and Bible House, 1900.

Cassirer, Ernest. *The Myth of the State*. New Haven: Yale University Press, 1946. Chapter XVI, "From Hero Worship to Race Worship."

Casson, Stanley, *The Discovery of Man: The Story of the Inquiry into Human Origins*. New York: Harper and Brothers, 1939.

Castro, Americo. *The Structure of Spanish History*. Translated by Edmund L. King. Princeton: Princeton University Press, 1954.

Count, Earl W. "The Evolution of the Race Idea in Modern Western Culture During the Period of the Pre-Darwinian Nineteenth Century." *Transactions of the New York Academy of Sciences*, VIII, Ser. 2 (February, 1946), 139–165.

Fouillée, Alfred. "Race From the Sociological Standpoint," in G. Spiller (ed.), *Papers on Interracial Problems*. London: P. S. King and Son, 1911, pp. 24–29.

Gobineau, Joseph Arthur de. *The Moral and Intellectual Diversity of Races, With Particular Reference to Their Respective Influence in the Civil and Political History of Mankind*. Philadelphia: J. B. Lippincott, 1856.

——. *The Inequality of Human Races*. London: Heinemann, 1915.

Grant, Madison. *The Passing of the Great Race, or, The Racial Basis of European History*. New York: Charles Scribner's Sons, 1918.

Greene, John C. "Some Early Speculations on the Origin of Human Races." *American Anthropologist*, LVI (February, 1954), 31–41.

——. "The American Debate on the Negro's Place in Nature, 1780–1815." *Journal of the History of Ideas*, XV (June, 1954), 384–396.

Herskovits, Melville J. *The Myth of the Negro Past*. New York: Harper and Brothers, 1941.

Hertz, Frederick. *Nationality in History and Politics: A Psychology and Sociology of National Sentiment and Nationalism*. London: Routledge and Kegan Paul, Ltd., 1951.

Honigsheim, Paul. "The Philosophical Background of European Anthropology." *American Anthropologist*, N. S. XLIV (July-September, 1942), 376–387.

Hourani, Albert H. "The Concept of Race Relations, Thoughts After a Conference." *International Social Science Bulletin*, VII (1955), 335–340.

Huxley, Julian and Haddon A. C. *We Europeans*. New York: Harper and Brothers, 1936.

Jernegan, Marcus W. "Slavery and Conversion in the American Colonies." *American Historical Review*, XXI (April, 1916), 504–527.

Jonassen, Christen T. "Some Historical and Theoretical Bases of Racism in Northwestern Europe." *Social Forces*, XXX (December, 1951), 155–161.

Kohn, Hans. *The Idea of Nationalism: A Study in Its Origins and Background*. New York: The Macmillan Company, 1948.

Lasswell, Harold D. *Politics: Who Gets What, When, How*. New York: P. Smith, 1936, Chapters II, IX.

Lovejoy, Arthur O. and Boas, George. *Primitivism and Related Ideas in Antiquity*. Baltimore: The Johns Hopkins Press, 1935.

MacIver, Robert M. "Man and Government," in *The Web of Government*. New York: The Macmillan Company, 1948. Chapter I.

Mandeville, Sir John. *The Travels of Sir John Mandeville*, in Alfred William Pollard, (ed.), *The Library of English Classics*. New York: The Macmillan Company, 1905. Especially chapter XXII.

Merton, R. K. "The Self-Fulfilling Prophecy." *Antioch Review*, VIII (June, 1948), 193–210.

Myrdal, Gunnar. *An American Dilemma*. New York: Harper and Brothers, 1944. I, chapter IV; II, chapter XXXVIII and pp. 956–966.

Paget, Violet (Vernon Lee, pseud.). *Vital Lies: Studies of Some Varieties of Recent Obscurantism*. New York: John Lanne, 1912.

Ptolemy (Ptolemaeus, Claudius). *Tetrabiblos*. Edited and translated by F. E. Robbins. Cambridge: Harvard University Press, 1940.

Redfield, Robert. "Ethnic Relations, Primitive and Civilized," in J. Masuoka and Preston Valien (eds.), *Race Relations: Theories and Problems* (to be published).

Rivers, W. H. R. "The Sociological Significance of Myth." *Folk-Lore*, XXIII (September, 1912), 306–331.

Schuyler. George S. *Black No More: Being an Account of the Strange and Wonderful Workings of Science in the Land of the Free, A. D. 1933–1940*. New York: The Macaulay Company, 1931.

Seger, Gerhart and Marck, Siegfried K. *Germany: To Be or Not To Be?* New York: The Rand School Press, 1943.

Simar, Théophile. *Étude critique sur la fondation de la doctrine des races au 18e et son expansion au 19e siecle*. Brussels: 1922.

Simon, Yves. *La grande crise de la République française; observations sur la vie politique des Français de 1918 à 1937*. Montréal: Editions de l'Arbre, 1941.

——. "Secret Sources of the Success of the Racist Ideology." *The Review of Politics*, VII (January, 1945), 74–105.

Sorel, Georges. *Reflections on Violence*. New York: B. W. Huebsch, 1912.

Spitz, D. "The Concept of Racial Aristocracy," in *Patterns of Anti-Democratic Thought*. New York: The Macmillan Company, 1949. Chapter VI.

Starkey, Marion L. *The Devil in Massachusetts: A Modern Inquiry into the Salem Witch Trials*. New York: Alfred A. Knopf, 1949.

Taylor, J. H. "The Restriction of European Immigration and the Concept of Race." *South Atlantic Quarterly*, L (January, 1951), 25–37.

Trachtenberg, Joshua. *The Devil and the Jews: The Medieval Conception of the Jew and Its Relation to Modern Anti-semitism*. New Haven: Yale University Press, 1943.

Tumin, M. J. "The Idea of 'Race' Dies Hard." *Commentary*, VIII (July, 1949), 80–85.

Vaihinger, Hans. *The Philosophy of "As If": A System of the Theoretical, Practical and Religious Fictions of Mankind*. Translated by C. K. Ogden. New York: Harcourt, Brace and Company, 1924.

Victoria, Francisci de. *De Indis et de Ivre Belli Relectiones*. Edited by Ernest Nys. Washington: Carnegie Institution of Washington, 1917.

Voegelin, Erich. *Die Rassenidee in der Geistesgeschichte von Ray bis Carus*. Berlin: Junker und Dünnhaupt, 1933.

——. "The Growth of the Race Idea." *The Review of Politics*, II (July, 1940), 283–317.

Wethered, Herbert Newton. *The Mind of the Ancient World: A Consideration of Pliny's Natural History*. London: Longmans, Green and Company, 1937.

Whitehead, Alfred North. *Adventures of Ideas*. New York: The Macmillan Company, 1933.

Windelband, Wilhelm. *A History of Philosophy: With Especial Reference to the Formation and Development of its Problems and Conceptions.* New York: The Macmillan Company, 1923.

Wright, John Kirkland. *The Geographical Lore of the Time of the Crusades: A Study in the History of Medieval Science and Tradition in Western Europe.* New York: American Geographical Society, 1925.

B. PASSING

Anonymous. "White, but Black: A Document on the Race Problem." *Century Magazine,* CIX (February, 1925), 492–499.

———. "I Was a Jew." *Forum,* CIII (January, 1940), 8–11.

Burma, John H. "The Measurement of Negro 'Passing.' " *American Journal of Sociology,* LII (July, 1946), 18–20.

Davis, Arthur P. "The Gentle Art of 'Passing'." *Negro Digest,* III (October, 1945), 33–34.

Eckard, E. W. "How Many Negroes 'Pass'." *American Journal of Sociology,* LII (May, 1947), 498–500.

Lee, Reba. *I Passed for White.* New York: Longmans, Green and Company, 1955.

C. INTERRACIAL MARRIAGE AND
MISCEGENATION

Adams, Romanzo. *Interracial Marriage in Hawaii: A Study of the Mutually Conditioned Processes of Acculturation and Amalgamation.* New York: The Macmillan Company, 1937.

Anonymous. "My Daughter Married a Negro." *Harper's Magazine.* CCIII (July, 1951), 36–40.

Baber, R. "Study of 325 Mixed Marriages." *American Sociological Review,* II (October, 1937), 705–716.

Barron, Milton L. *People Who Intermarry: Intermarriage in a New England Industrial Community.* Syracuse, N. Y.: Syracuse University Press, 1946.

Champly, Henry. *White Women, Coloured Men.* London: John Long, Ltd., 1936.

Das, Frieda. *A Marriage to India.* New York: The Vanguard Press, 1930.

Davis, Kingsley. "Intermarriage in Caste Societies." *American Anthropologist,* XLIII (July-September, 1941), 376–395.

Dixon, Thomas. *The Sins of the Fathers.*

New York: D. Appleton and Company, 1912.

Eskelund, Karl. *My Chinese Wife.* New York: Doubleday, Doran and Company, 1945.

Findlay, George. *Miscegenation.* Pretoria: The "Pretoria News" and Printing Works, Ltd., 1936.

Franking, Mrs. M. T. *My Chinese Marriage.* New York: Duffield and Company, 1921.

Frisbie, Robert Dean. *The Island of Desire.* New York: Doubleday, Doran and Company, 1944.

Garnett, David. *The Sailor's Return.* London: Chatto and Windus, 1925.

———. *Pocahontas; or, The Nonparell of Virginia.* New York: Harcourt, Brace and Company, 1933.

Golden, Joseph. "Patterns of Negro-White Intermarriage." *American Sociological Review,* XIX (April, 1954), 144–147.

Graham, Gwethalyn (Pseud.). *Earth and High Heaven.* Philadelphia: J. B. Lippincott, 1944.

Hirschfeld, Magnus. *Racism.* London: Victor Gollancz, Ltd., 1938.

Hoggan, Frances. "The Negro Problem in Relation to White Women," in G. Spiller (ed.), *Papers on Inter-Racial Problems.* London: P. S. King and Son, 1911, pp. 364–366.

Lattimore, Owen D. *The Gold Tribe, "Fishskin Tatars" of the Lower Sungari.* Menasha, Wis.: American Anthropological Association, publication no. 40, 1933.

Lévy, Sarah. *Beloved!* New York: Simon and Schuster, 1930.

Marcson, Simon. *The Prediction of Intermarriage.* University of Chicago, Ph.D. thesis, 1950.

———. "A Theory of Intermarriage and Assimilation." *Social Forces,* XXIX (October, 1950), 75–78.

Merton, Robert K. "Intermarriage and the Social Structure: Fact and Theory." *Psychiatry: Journal of the Biology and the Pathology of Interpersonal Relations,* IV (August, 1941), 361–374.

Minard, Ralph D. "Race Relationships in the Pocahontas Coal Field." *The Journal of Social Issues,* VIII (1952), 29–44.

Panunzio, Constantine Marie. "Intermarriage in Los Angeles, 1924–1933." *American Journal of Sociology,* XLVII (March, 1942), 690–701.

Report of the Commission on Assaults on

Women. Capetown, Union of South Africa: U. G. 39–1913.

Resnik, Reuben B. "Some Sociological Aspects of Intermarriage of Jew and Non-Jew." *Social Forces,* XII (October, 1933), 94–102.

Reuter, Edward B. *Race Mixture: Studies in Intermarriage and Miscegenation.* New York: McGraw-Hill Book Company, 1931.

——. "Amalgamation." *Encyclopaedia of the Social Sciences,* II, 16–17.

Rogers, Joel A. *Sex and Race.* New York: J. A. Rogers Publications, 1940, 1942, 1944, 3 volumes.

Schuyler, Josephine. "An Interracial Marriage." *American Mercury,* LXII (March, 1946), 273–277.

Shapiro, Harry L. *Race Mixture.* Paris: UNESCO, 1953.

Smith, Bradford. *This Solid Flesh: A Novel of Intermarriage Between East and West.* New York: Bobbs-Merrill Company, 1937.

Sofer, Cyril. "Some Aspects of Inter-Racial Marriages in South Africa, 1925–46." *Africa,* XIX (July, 1949), 187–203.

Sokolsky, G. E. "My Mixed Marriage." *Atlantic Monthly,* CLII (August, 1933), 137–146.

Stern, Bernhard J. "Intermarriage." *Encyclopaedia of the Social Sciences,* VIII, 151–154.

Woodson, C. G. "The Relations of Negroes and Indians in Massachusetts." *Journal of Negro History,* V (January, 1920), 45–57.

D. THE RACE-MAKING FRONTIER

Balandier, Georges. "La Situation Coloniale: Approche Théorique." *Cahiers Internationaux de Sociologie,* XI (1951), 44–79.

Baldwin, James. "Stranger in the Village." *Harper's Magazine,* CCVII (October, 1953), 42–48.

Barker, Ernest. "The Contact of Colours and Civilisations." *Contemporary Review,* CXXXVIII (November, 1930), 578–587.

Beach, Harlan P. and Fahs, Charles H. (eds.). *World Missionary Atlas.* New York: Institute of Social and Religious Research, 1925.

Billington, Ray Allen. *Westward Expansion.* New York: The Macmillan Company, 1949. Chapter XXXII.

Cromer, Earl of. *Ancient and Modern Imperialism.* London: J. Murray, 1910.

Ekvall, Robert B. "An Instance of Sino-Tibetan Race and Culture Contact." *Bulletin of the Society for Social Research,* XXVII (1938), 11–12.

Hancock, William Keith. "The Evolution of the Trader's Frontier: West Africa." *Survey of British Commonwealth Affairs,* Vol. II, *Problems of Economic Policy, 1918–1939.* New York: Oxford University Press, 1937. Part II, Chapter II.

——. *Argument of Empire.* New York: Penguin Books, 1943.

Handlin, Oscar. *The Uprooted.* Boston: Little, Brown and Co., 1951.

Harmand, J. *Domination et Colonisation.* Paris: E. Flammarion, 1910.

Hogbin, H. Ian. *Transformation Scene: The Changing Culture of a New Guinea Village.* London: Routledge and K. Paul, 1951. Chapter XIII.

Hughes, Everett C. and Hughes, Helen M. *Where Peoples Meet: Racial and Ethnic Frontiers.* Glencoe, Ill.: The Free Press, 1952. Chs. III and V.

——. "The Nature of Racial Frontiers," in J. Masuoka and Preston Valien (eds.), *Race Relations: Theories and Problems* (to be published).

Hunter, Monica. *Reaction to Conquest. Effects of Contact with Europeans on the Pondo of South Africa.* London: Humphrey Milford, 1936.

Keller, Albert G. *Colonization: A Study of the Founding of New Societies.* Boston: Ginn and Company, 1908.

Kennedy, J. H. *Jesuit and Savage in New France.* New Haven: Yale University Press, 1950.

Knight, M. M. "Backward Countries." *Encyclopaedia of the Social Sciences,* II, 379–381.

Latourette, K. S. "Missions." *Encyclopaedia of the Social Sciences,* X, 536–546.

Leyburn, James G. *Frontier Folkways.* New Haven: Yale University Press, 1935.

Lind, Andrew W. "Occupation and Race on Certain Frontiers," in Andrew W. Lind (ed.), *Race Relations in World Perspective,* Honolulu: University of Hawaii Press, 1955, Chapter III.

——. "Race Relations Frontiers in Hawaii," in J. Masuoka and Preston Valien (eds.), *Race Relations: Theories and Problems,* (to be published).

Locke, Alain and Stern, Bernhard J. (eds.). *When Peoples Meet: A Study in Race and Culture Contacts.* New York: Hinds, Hayden and Eldredge, 1946.

McLeod, William Christie. *The American Indian Frontier.* New York: Alfred A. Knopf, 1928.

Maldonado de Guevara y Andrés, Francisco. *El primer contacto de blancos y gentes de color en América.* Valladolid: Universidad de Valladolid, 1924.

Mannoni, Dominique O. *Prospero and Caliban.* Translated by Pamela Powesland. New York: Praeger, 1956.

Marchant, Alexander. *From Barter to Slavery: The Economic Relations of Portuguese and Indians in the Settlement of Brazil, 1500–1580.* Baltimore: The Johns Hopkins Studies in Historical and Political Science, Series LX, no. 1, 1942.

Masuoka, Jitsuichi. "Racial Symbiosis and Cultural Frontiers: A Frame of Reference." *Social Forces,* XXIV (March, 1948), 348–353.

——. "The City as a Racial Frontier. With Special Reference to Colonialism and Urbanism in Africa," in J. Masuoka and Preston Valien, (eds.), *Race Relations: Theories and Problems* (to be published).

Maunier, René. *The Sociology of Colonies.* Translated by E. O. Lorimer. London: Routledge and Kegan Paul, 1949. 2 volumes.

Munch, Peter A. "Cultural Contacts in an Isolated Community—Tristan da Cunha." *American Journal of Sociology,* LIII (July, 1947), 1–8

Muntz, Earl Edward. *Race Contact.* New York: The Century Company, 1927.

Park, Robert E. *Race and Culture.* Glencoe Ill.: The Free Press, 1950. Chapter VII and chapter IX.

Priestley, Herbert I. *The Coming of the White Man, 1492–1848.* New York: The Macmillan Company, 1929.

Reed, Stephen Winsor. *The Making of Modern New Guinea, With Special Reference to Culture Contact in the Mandated Territory.* Philadelphia: American Philosophical Society, 1943.

Reuter, E. B. (ed.). *Race and Culture Contacts.* New York: McGraw-Hill Book Company, 1934.

Smith, Bradford. *Yankees in Paradise.* New York: J. B. Lippincott Co., 1956.

Thompson, Edgar T. "Language and Race Relations," in J. Masuoka and Preston Valien (eds.), *Race Relations: Theories and Problems* (to be published).

Thurston, Lucy G. *Life and Times of Lucy Thurston.* Ann Arbor: S. C. Andrews, 1882.

Williams, Eric. *Capitalism and Slavery.* Chapel Hill, N. C.: University of North Carolina Press, 1944.

Woodruff, Douglas. *The Relations of European With Non-European Peoples.* Vol. VII of Eyre, Edward (ed.). *European Civilization: Its Origin and Development.* New York: Oxford University Press, 1934–39.

E. SITUATIONS AND FACTORS

Brady, Alexander. *Democracy in the Dominions: A Comparative Study in Institutions.* Toronto: University of Toronto Press, 1952.

Cahnman, Werner. "Religion and Nationality." *American Journal of Sociology,* XLIX (May, 1944), 524–529.

Carnegie Commission of Investigation on the Poor White Question in South Africa. *The Poor White Problem in South Africa.* Stellenbosch: Pro-Ecclesia-Drukkery, 1932. 5 volumes.

Cooley, C. H. *Social Organization.* New York: Charles Scribner's Sons, 1929. Chapter XIX.

Dakin, A. *Calvinism.* Philadelphia: The Westminster Press, 1946.

Deutsch, Karl W. "The Economic Factor in Intolerance," in *Approaches to National Unity.* New York: Conference on Science, Philosophy and Religion in their Relation to the Democratic Way of Life, 1945, pp. 368–386.

Donnan, Elizabeth (ed.). *Documents Illustrative of the History of the Slave Trade to America.* Washington, D. C.: Carnegie Institution of Washington, 1930. 4 volumes.

Gates, Charles M. (ed.). *Five Fur Traders of the Northwest.* Minneapolis: University of Minnesota Press, 1933.

Gillin, John. " 'Race' Relations Without Conflict: A Guatemalan Town." *American Journal of Sociology,* LIII (March, 1948), 337–343.

Handlin, Oscar and Mary F. "Origins of the Southern Labor System." *William and Mary College Quarterly,* 3rd series. VII, (April, 1950), 199–222.

Heitz, Hilda. *Language and the Social Situation: A Study in Race Relations.* Ph.D. dissertation, Duke University, 1950.

Hudson, W. H. *Idle Days in Patagonia.* New York: E. P. Dutton and Company, 1923. Chapter VIII.

Kristov, Cyril. "Baba Meglena," in Arthur

E. Christy and Henry W. Wells (eds.), *World Literature: An Anthology of Human Experience.* New York: American Book Company, 1947, pp. 519–522.

MacKay, Douglas. *The Honourable Company.* Indianapolis: Bobbs-Merrill Company, 1936.

Melville, Herman. "The Whiteness of the Whale," in *Moby Dick.* New York: Albert and Charles Boni, Inc., 1933, pp. 167–175.

Moller, Herbert. "Sex Composition and Correlated Culture Patterns of Colonial America." *The William and Mary College Quarterly,* 3rd series, II, (April, 1945), 113–153.

Unknown French Author. Translated by Andrew Lang. "Aucassin and Nicolete," in Arthur E. Christy and Henry W. Wells (eds.), *World Literature: An Anthology of Human Experience.* New York: American Book Company, 1947, pp. 505–519.

Wolff, W. H. "Les Conquistadors et leurs femmes indigenes." *Revue Politique et Litteraire,* LXXVII (May, 1939), 201–203.

Wyndham, Hon. Hugh A. *The Atlantic and Slavery.* London: Oxford University Press, 1935.

F. RACE IDEOLOGIES

Chamberlain, Houston Stewart. *Foundations of the Nineteenth Century.* New York: John Lane Company, 1913.

Copeland, Lewis C. *The Function of Racial Ideologies with Special Reference to the Beliefs About the Negro.* Ph.D. Thesis, Duke University, 1939.

Fitzhugh, George. *Sociology for the South.* Richmond: Morris, 1854.

Park, Robert E. *Race and Culture.* Glencoe, Ill.: The Free Press, 1950. Chapter XXIII, "Race Ideologies."

Roucek, Joseph S. "A History of the Concept of Ideology." *Journal of the History of Ideas,* V (October, 1944), 479–488.

Tansill, Charles C. "Racial Theories in Germany from Herder to Hitler." *Thought,* XV (September, 1940), 453–468.

V. RACE CONFLICT

A. CONFLICT GENERALLY

Coser, Lewis. *The Functions of Social Conflict.* Glencoe, Ill.: The Free Press, 1956.

Ellis, Havelock. "On a Certain Kind of War." *Living Age,* CCXCVI (February, 1918), 432–435.

MacIver, Robert M. (ed.). *Group Relations and Group Antagonisms.* New York: Harper and Brothers, 1944.

Parsons, Talcott. "Certain Primary Sources and Patterns of Aggression in the Social Structure of the Western World," in *Essays in Sociological Theory, Pure and Applied.* Glencoe, Ill.: The Free Press, 1949.

Simmel, Georg. *Conflict.* Glencoe, Ill.: The Free Press, 1955.

Singer, Kurt, *The Idea of Conflict.* Melbourne: Melbourne University Press, 1949.

Wright, Quincy. "The Nature of Conflict." *Western Political Quarterly,* IV (June, 1951), 193–209.

B. THE WAR OF THE RACES

Angle, Paul M. *Bloody Williamson: A Chapter in American Lawlessness.* New York: Alfred A. Knopf, 1952.

Aptheker, Herbert. *American Negro Slave Revolts.* New York: Columbia University Press, 1943.

Barnes, Leonard. *Caliban in Africa: An Impression of Colour-Madness.* London: V. Gollancz, Ltd., 1930.

Bloom, Harry. *Episode in the Transvaal.* Garden City, N.Y.: Doubleday and Sons, 1955.

Brearley, H. C. "The Negro's New Belligerency." *Phylon,* V (Fourth Quarter, 1944), 339–445.

Brown, J. Cudd. *The Ghost Dance and Mau Mau: A Comparative Study of Colonial Administration.* Eugene: The University of Oregon. Ph.D. thesis, 1956.

Chicago Commission on Race Relations. *The Negro in Chicago: A Study of Race Relations and a Race Riot.* Chicago: University of Chicago Press, 1922.

Clinchy, Everett Ross. *All in the Name of God.* New York: John Day Company, 1934.

Cox, O. C. "Lynching and the Status Quo." *The Journal of Negro Education,* XIV (Fall, 1945), 576–588.

Dahlke, H. O. "Race and Minority Riots— a Study in the Typology of Violence." *Social Forces,* XXX (May, 1952), 419–425.

Detweiler, F. G. "The Rise of Modern Race Antagonisms." *American Journal of Sociology,* XXXVII (March, 1932), 738–747.

Dollard, John. "Hostility and Fear in Social Life." *Social Forces*, XVII (October, 1938), 15–26.

Gregory, J. W. *The Menace of Colour*. London: Seeley, Service & Co., Ltd., 1925.

Grow, Oscar. *The Antagonism of Races: or The Functions of Human Institutions in the Struggle for Existence*. Waterloo, Iowa: St. Louis, Press of Nixon-Jones Printing Company, 1912.

Gumplowicz, Ludwig. *Der Rassenkampf*. Innsbruck: Wagner, 1928.

Haimowitz, Morris L. *The Development and Change of Ethnic Hostility*. Ph.D. Thesis, University of Chicago, 1951.

Hersey, John. *The Wall*. New York: Alfred A. Knopf, 1950.

Huie, William Bradford. "The Ordeal of Roosevelt Wilson," in Louis L. Snyder and Richard B. Morris, *A Treasury of Great Reporting*. New York: Simon and Schuster, 1949, pp. 750–757.

Janowitz, Morris. *Mobility, Subjective Deprivation and Ethnic Hostility*. Ph.D. Thesis, University of Chicago, 1948.

Johnson, Guy B. "Patterns of Race Conflict," in E. T. Thompson (ed.), *Race Relations and the Race Problem*. Durham, N. C.: Duke University Press, 1939, Chapter V.

——. "The Course of Race Conflict and Racial Movement in the South," in J. Masuoka and Preston Valien (eds.), *Race Relations: Theories and Problems*. (To be published.)

Jordan, Joe. "Lynchers Don't Like Lead." *The Atlantic Monthly*, CLXXVII (February, 1946), 103–108.

Katz, Irwin. *Conflict and Harmony in an Adolescent Interracial Group*. New York: New York University Press, 1955.

Killian, L. M. "The Effects of Southern White Workers on Race Relations in Northern Plants." *American Sociological Review*, XVII (June, 1952), 327–331.

Kluckhohn, Clyde. "Group Tensions: Analysis of a Case History," in L. Bryson et al. (eds.), *Approaches to National Unity*. New York: Conference on Science, Philosophy and Religion in Their Relation to the Democratic Way of Life Inc., 1945.

Kohn, Hans. "Race Conflict." *Encyclopedia of the Social Sciences*, XIII, 36–41.

Lee, Alfred McClung and Humphrey, Norman Daymond. *Race Riot*. New York: The Dryden Press, Inc., 1943.

Mason, Philip. *An Essay on Racial Tension*. New York: Royal Institute of International Affairs, 1954.

Mathews, Basil. *The Clash of Colour: A Study in the Problem of Race*. New York: Missionary Education Movement of the United States and Canada, 1924.

Miller, Herbert A. *Races, Nations, and Classes*. Philadelphia: J. B. Lippincott Company, 1924.

Money, Leo Chiozza. *The Peril of the White*. London: W. Collins Sons and Company, Ltd., 1925.

Mukerjee, Radhakamal et al. *Inter-Caste Tensions: A Survey Under the Auspices of the UNESCO*. Lucknow, India: University of Lucknow, 1951.

Percival, Arthur Ernest. *The War in Malaya*. London: Eyre and Spottiswoode, 1949.

Raper, Arthur F. *The Tragedy of Lynching*. Chapel Hill: University of North Carolina Press, 1933.

Ratliff, B. A. "In the Delta: The Story of a Man Hunt." *Atlantic Monthly*, CXXV (April, 1920), 456–461.

Reichmann, Eva G. *Hostages of Civilization: The Social Sources of National Socialist Anti-Semitism*. Boston: The Beacon Press, 1951.

Robinson, Bernard F. "The Sociology of Race Riots." *Phylon*, II (Second Quarter, 1941), 162–171.

——. "War and Race Conflicts in the United States." *Phylon*, IV (Fourth Quarter, 1943), 311–327.

Samuel, Maurice. *You Gentiles*. New York: Harcourt, Brace and Company, 1924.

——. *The Great Hatred*. New York: Alfred A. Knopf, 1940.

Sancton, Thomas. "Race Clash." *Harper's Magazine*, CLXXXVIII (January, 1944), 135–140.

Simpson, B. L. *The Conflict of Colour*. New York: The Macmillan Company, 1910.

Stoddard, Lothrop. *The French Revolution in San Domingo*. Boston: Houghton Mifflin Company, 1914.

——. *The Rising Tide of Color Against White World-Supremacy*. New York: Charles Scribner's Sons, 1922.

Willcox, Walter F. "Is Race Friction Between Blacks and Whites in the United States Growing and Inevitable?" *American Journal of Sociology*, XIII (May, 1908), 820–823.

C. RACIAL POLITICS

Ashmore, Harry S. *The Negro and the Schools.* Chapel Hill.: University of North Carolina Press, 1954.

Brogan, D. W. *Politics in America.* New York: Harper and Brothers, 1954. Chapter III, "Race and Politics."

Chapman, Guy. *The Dreyfus Case: A Reassessment.* London: R. Hart-Davis, 1955.

Gosnell, Harold F. *Negro Politicians; The Rise of Negro Politics in Chicago.* Chicago: University of Chicago Press, 1935.

Gregory, John Walter. *Race As A Political Factor.* London: Watts and Company, 1931.

Halasz, Nicholas. *Captain Dreyfus. The Story of a Mass Hysteria.* New York: Simon and Schuster, 1955.

Haldane, J. B. S. *Heredity and Politics.* New York: W. W. Norton & Co., 1938.

Hancock, Carolyn Lois, *L'Affaire Bassett.* M.A. thesis, Duke University, 1950.

Hankins, Frank H. "Race as a Factor in Political Theory," in Charles Merriam and Harry Elmer Barnes, *A History of Political Theories, Recent Times.* New York: The Macmillan Comany, 1924, vol. IV, pp. 508–548.

Kesselman, Louis. *The Social Politics of FEPC.* Chapel Hill: University of North Carolina Press, 1948.

Kirwan, Albert D. *Revolt of the Rednecks: Mississippi Politics, 1876–1925.* Lexington: University of Kentucky Press, 1951.

Lewinson, Paul. *Race, Class and Party; A History of Negro Suffrage and White Politics in the South.* New York: Oxford University Press, 1932.

Nowlin, William F. *The Negro in American National Politics.* Boston: The Stratford Company, 1931.

Riesman, David. "The Politics of Persecution." *Public Opinion Quarterly,* VI (Spring, 1942), 41–56.

Ruchames, Louis. *Race, Jobs, and Politics.* New York: Columbia University Press, 1953.

Shugg, Roger W. *Origins of Class Struggle in Louisiana: A Social History of White Farmers and Laborers During Slavery and After, 1840–1875.* Baton Rouge: Louisiana State University Press, 1939.

D. INTERRACIAL SOCIETIES

Arendt, Hannah. "Concerning Minorities." *Contemporary Jewish Record,* VII (August, 1944), 353–368.

Bercovici, Konrad. *Around the World in New York.* New York: The Century Company, 1924.

Bernard, Jessie. "The Conceptualization of Intergroup Relations With Special Reference to Conflict." *Social Forces,* XXIX (March, 1951), 243–251.

Bernstein, Peretz F. *Jew-Hate as a Sociological Problem.* New York: Philosophical Library, 1951.

Cahnman, Werner J. "An American Dilemma." *The Chicago Jewish Forum,* III (Winter, 1944–45), 92–96.

Devereux, George and Loeb, E. M. "Antagonistic Acculturation." *American Sociological Review,* VIII (April, 1943), 133–147.

Drake, St. Clair. "The International Implications of Race and Race Relations." *The Journal of Negro Education,* XX (Summer, 1951), 261–278.

Frank, Lawrence K. "World Order and Cultural Diversity." *Free World,* III (June, 1942), 83–86.

Gayda, Virginio. *Modern Austria: Her Racial and Social Problems.* London: T. F. Unwin, Ltd., 1915. Chapter III.

Gluckman, Max. *Custom and Conflict in Africa.* Oxford: Blackwell, 1955.

Golightly, Cornelius L. "Race, Values and Guilt." *Social Forces,* XXVI (December, 1947), 125–139.

Lee, Alfred McClung. "A Sociological Discussion of Consistency and Inconsistency in Intergroup Relations." *The Journal of Social Issues,* V (1949), 12–18.

Locke, Alain. "The Negro's Contribution to American Culture." *Journal of Negro Education,* VIII (July, 1939), 521–529.

Loewenstein, Rudolph M. *Christians and Jews: A Psychoanalytic Study.* New York: International Universities Press, 1951. Chapter V.

Mead, George H. "National-Mindedness and International-Mindedness." *The International Journal of Ethics,* XXXIX (July, 1929), 385–407.

Montgomery, Isaiah. "Speech in the Mississippi Constitutional Convention of 1890." *The New York World,* (September 27, 1890).

Murphy, Edgar Gardner. *The Basis of Ascendency: A Discussion of Certain Principles of Public Policy Involved in the Development of the Southern States.* New York: Longmans, Green and Company, 1910.

Oppenheimer, Franz. *The State.* New York: Vanguard Press, 1926.

Tannenbaum, Frank. "An American Dilemma." *Political Science Quarterly*, LIX (September, 1944), 321–340.

Thompson, Edgar T. "The Plantation: The Physical Basis of Traditional Race Relations in the South," in Edgar T. Thompson (ed.), *Race Relations and the Race Problem*. Durham, N. C.: Duke University Press, 1939. Chapter VII.

——. "Race in the Modern World." *The Journal of Negro Education*, XIII (Summer, 1944), 270–279.

E. RACE CONSCIOUSNESS AND RACE MOVEMENTS

Balandier, Georges. "Messianismes et Nationalismes en Afrique Noire." *Cahiers Internationaux de Sociologie*, XIV (1953), 41–65.

Baber, Bernard. "Acculturation and Messianic Movements." *American Sociological Review*, VI (October, 1941), 663–669.

Barton, Rebecca Chalmers. *Race Consciousness and the American Negro: A Study of the Correlation Between the Group Experience and the Friction of 1900–1930*. Copenhagen: A. Busck, 1934.

Brown, W. O. "Emergence of Race Consciousness." *Sociology and Social Research*, XV (May, 1931), 428–436.

——. "The Nature of Race Consciousness." *Social Forces*, X (October, 1931), 90–97.

——. "Race Consciousness Among South African Natives." *American Journal of Sociology*, XL (March, 1935), 569–581.

Cohn, Helen F. *Tactics and Ideologies as They Affect the Growth of Selected Southern Social Movements*. M.A. thesis, Tulane University, May 1949.

Cronon, Edmund D. *Black Moses, The Story of Marcus Garvey and the Universal Negro Improvement Association*. Madison: University of Wisconsin Press, 1955.

Glick, Clarence E. "Collective Behavior in Race Relations." *American Sociological Review*, XIII (June, 1948), 287–294.

Halsey, Margaret, *Color Blind: A White Woman Looks at the Negro*. New York: Simon and Schuster, 1946.

Herskovits, Melville J. *The Myth of the Negro Past*. New York: Harper and Brothers, 1941.

Hughes, Everett C. "New Peoples," in Andrew W. Lind (ed.), *Race Relations in World Perspective*. Honolulu; University of Hawaii Press, 1955. Chapter V.

Kohn, Hans. "Pan Movements." *Encyclopaedia of the Social Sciences*, XI, 544–553.

——. *Pan-Slavism: Its History and Ideology*. Notre Dame, Ind.: University of Notre Dame Press, 1953.

Kuper, Leo. "The Background to Passive Resistance (South Africa, 1952)." *The British Journal of Sociology*, IV (September, 1953), 243–256.

——. *Passive Resistance in South Africa*. London: Jonathan Cape, 1956.

Linton, Ralph. "Nativistic Movements." *American Anthropologist*, n. s., XLV (April-June, 1943), 230–240.

Mooney, James. *The Ghost Dance Religion and the Sioux Outbreak of 1896*. Fourteenth Annual Report of the Bureau of American Ethnology, Part 2. Washington: Government Printing Office, 1896.

Park, Robert E. "Negro Race Consciousness as Reflected in Race Literature," in Robert E. Park, *Race and Culture*. Glencoe, Ill.: The Free Press, 1950. Chapter XXII.

Reade, Winwood. *The Martyrdom of Man*. London: Kegan Paul, Trench, Trübner and Company, Ltd., 1912.

Roback, A. A. "Is Psychoanalysis a Jewish Movement?" in *Jewish Influence in Modern Thought*. Cambridge: Sci-Art Publishers, 1929. Chapter IX.

Salz, Beate. "Indianismo." *Social Research*, XI (November, 1944), 441–469.

Sartre, Jean-Paul. "Orphee Noir," in Léopold Sédar Senghor, *Anthologie de la Neuvelle Poésie Nègre et Malgache de Langue Française*, Paris: Presses Universitaires de France, 1948, pp. ix-xliv.

Standing, T. G. "Nationalism in Negro Leadership." *American Journal of Sociology*, XL (September, 1934), 180–192.

——. "Race Consciousness as Reflected in the Negro Press." *Southwestern Social Science Quarterly*, XIX (December, 1938), 269–280.

Sundkler, Bengt G. M. *Bantu Prophets in South Africa*. London: Lutterworth Press, 1948.

Van der Kroef, Justus M. "The Messiah in Indonesia and Melanesia." *The Scientific Monthly*, LXXV (September, 1952), 161–165.

Wirth, Louis. "The Problems of Minority

Groups," in Ralph Linton (ed.), *The Science Of Man in the World Crisis.* New York: Columbia University Press, 1945.

F. ETHNOCENTRISM

Carter, Wimoth A. "Nicknames and Minority Groups." *Phylon,* V (Third Quarter, 1944), 241–245.

Copeland, Lewis C. "The Negro as a Contrast Conception," in Edgar T. Thompson (ed.), *Race Relations and the Race Problem.* Durham, N. C.: Duke University Press, 1939. Chapter VI.

Cothran, Tilman C. "Negro Conceptions of White People." *American Journal of Sociology,* LVI (March, 1951), 458–467.

Cozart, Winfield Forrest. *The Chosen People.* Boston: The Christopher Publishing Company, 1924.

Crookshank, F. G. *The Mongol in Our Midst: A Study of Man and His Three Faces.* London: K. Paul, Trench, Trubner & Co., Ltd., 1931.

Cuber, John Frank. *Sociology: A Synopsis of Principles.* New York: D. Appleton-Century Company, Inc., 1947. Chapter VII and Part IV.

Davie, Maurice R. *The Evolution of War: A Study of Its Rôle in Early Societies.* New Haven: Yale University Press, 1929. Appendix A, "Ethnocentrism and Tribal Names," pp. 234–236.

Grant, Madison. *The Passing of the Great Race: or, The Racial Basis of European History.* New York: Charles Scribner's Sons, 1918.

Haar, Francis Ter. *Mixed Marriages and Their Remedies.* Translated by the Rev. Aloysius Walter. New York and Cincinnati: Frederick Pustet Company, 1933.

Haarhoff, T. J. *The Stranger at the Gate: Aspects of Exclusiveness and Cooperation in Ancient Greece and Rome, with Some Reference to Modern Times.* Oxford: Blackwell, 1948.

James, William. "On a Certain Blindness in Human Beings," in *Talks to Teachers on Psychology: and to Students on Some of Life's Ideals.* New York: Henry Holt and Company, 1929, pp. 229–242.

Kent, Donald P. and Burnight, Robert G. "Group Centrism in Complex Societies." *American Journal of Sociology,* LVII (November, 1951), 256–259.

Kolnai, Aurel. *The War Against the West.* London: J. Gollancz, Ltd., 1938.

La Violette, Forest and Silvert, K. H. "A Theory of Stereotypes." *Social Forces,* XXIX (March, 1951), 257–262.

Lips, Julius. *The Savage Hits Back.* New Haven: Yale University Press, 1937.

Mace, C. A. "Beliefs and Attitudes in Class Relations," in T. H. Marshall (ed.), *Class Conflict and Social Stratification.* London: Le Play House Press, 1938. Pp. 157–160.

Murdock, George P. "Ethnocentrism." *Encyclopaedia of the Social Sciences,* V, 613–614.

Roback, A. A. *A Dictionary of International Slurs.* Cambridge, Mass.: Sci-Art Publishers, 1944.

Rosenberg, Alfred. *Der Mythus des 20. Jahrhunderts; eine wertung der seelischgeistigen gestaltenkämpfe unserer zeit.* München: Hoheneichen-verlag, 1933.

Schapera, I. (ed.). *Western Civilization and the Natives of South Africa: Studies in Culture Contact.* London: Routledge and Sons, Ltd., 1934.

Sumner, William G. *Folkways.* Boston: Ginn and Company, 1907. "Ethnocentrism," pp. 13–15.

Voegelin, Erich. *Rasse und Staat.* Tübingen: J. C. B. Mohr, 1933, pp. 181–208.

Wesley, Charles H. "The Concept of Negro Inferiority in American Thought." *Journal of Negro History,* XXV (October, 1940), 540–560.

VI. STATUS AND CHANGE

A. RACE AS A SOCIAL STATUS

Anderson, C. Arnold and Bowman, Mary Jean. "The Vanishing Servant and the Contemporary Status System of the American South." *American Journal of Sociology,* LIX (November, 1953), 215–230.

Bendix, Reinhard and Lipset, Seymour Martin (eds.). *Class, Status and Power: A Reader in Social Stratification.* Glencoe, Ill.: The Free Press, 1953.

Benoit-Smullyan, Emile. "Status, Status Types and Status Inter-Relationships." *American Sociological Review,* IX (April, 1944), 151–161.

Berger, Morroe. *Equality by Statute: Legal Controls Over Group Discrimination.*

New York: Columbia University Press, 1952.

Bryson, Lyman, et al. (eds). Aspects of Human Equality. Fifteenth Symposium of the Confernce on Science, Philosophy and Religion. New York: Harper and Brothers, 1956.

Buck, Pearl S. "The Future of the White Man in the Far East." Foreign Affairs, XIX (October, 1940), 22–33.

Cahn, Edmond N. The Sense of Injustice. New York: New York University Press, 1949.

Cattell, Raymond B. "The Concept of Social Status." Journal of Social Psychology, XV (May, 1942), 193–308.

Coughlin, R. J. "The Status of the Chinese Minority in Thailand." Pacific Affairs, XXV (December, 1952), 378–389.

Dollard, John. Caste and Class in a Southern Town. New York: Harper and Brothers, 1949. Chapter VIII, "The Prestige Gain."

Dorfman, Ben. "White Russians in the Far East." Asia, XXXV (March, 1935), 166–172.

Frazier, E. Franklin. Black Bourgeoisie. Glencoe, Ill.: The Free Press, 1956.

Gilbreath, Olive. "Where Yellow Rules White." Harper's Monthly Magazine, CLVIII (February, 1929), 367–374.

Ginsberg, M. "The Problem of Colour in Relation to the Idea of Equality." Journal of Philosophical Studies, I (April, 1926), 213–224.

Glick, Clarence. "The Relation Between Position and Status in the Assimilation of Chinese in Hawaii." American Journal of Sociology, XLVII (March, 1942), 667–679.

Goldhamer, Herbert and Shils, Edward A. "Types of Power and Status." American Journal of Sociology, XLV (September, 1939), 171–182.

Grygier, Tadeusz. Oppression. A Study in Social and Criminal Psychology. London: Routledge and Kegan Paul, 1954.

Hatt, Paul K. "Class and Ethnic Attitudes." American Sociological Review, XIII (February, 1948), 36–43.

Heinrich, J. C. The Psychology of a Suppressed People. London: George Allen and Unwin, Ltd., 1937.

Hill, M. C. and McCall, B. C. "Social Stratification in 'Georgia Town'." American Sociological Review, XV (December, 1950), 721–729.

Hughes, Everett C. "Position and Status in a Quebec Industrial Town." American Sociological Review, III (October, 1938), 709–717.

——. Where Peoples Meet: Racial and Ethnic Frontiers. Glencoe, Ill.: The Free Press, 1952. Chapter VII.

Humphrey, Norman D. "American Race Relations and Status Structure." Social Science, XXII (January, 1947), 19–22.

Huszar, George Bernard de. Equality in America. New York: W. H. Wilson Company, 1949.

Hyman, Herbert H. "The Psychology of Status." Archives of Psychology, XXXVIII, No. 269, (June, 1942).

Kane, Harnett T. Deep Delta Country. New York: Duell, Sloan and Pearce, 1944. Chapter XVII.

Landry, Stuart O. The Cult of Equality; A Study of the Race Problem. New Orleans: Pelican Publishing Company, 1945.

Linton, Ralph. The Study of Man. New York: D. Appleton-Century Company, Inc., 1936. Chapter VIII, "Status and Role."

Lloyd, R. Grann. White Supremacy in the United States: An Analysis of Its Historical Background, with Especial Reference to the Poll Tax. (Annals of American Research) Washington, D. C.: Public Affairs Press, 1952.

McCloy, Shelby T. "The Cagots: A Despised People in France." The South Atlantic Quarterly, LIV (January, 1955), 44–55.

Maine, Henry James Sumner. Ancient Law, Its Connection with the Early History of Society and its Relation to Modern Ideas. London: J. Murray, 1930.

Miller, Herbert. "The Oppression Psychosis," in Races, Nations and Classes. Philadelphia: J. B. Lippincott Company, 1924. Chapter IV.

Muller, H. S. "The Soviet Master Race Theory." The New Leader, XXXII (July 30, 1949), 3.

Myers, Henry A. Are Men Equal? An Inquiry into the Meaning of American Democracy. New York: G. P. Putnam's Sons, 1945.

Myrdal, Gunnar. An American Dilemma. New York: Harper and Brothers, 1944. Appendix 5, "A Parallel to the Negro Problem."

Orwell, George. Shooting an Elephant and Other Essays. New York: Harcourt, Brace and Company, 1950, pp. 3–12.

Park, Robert E. "The Concept of Social Distance." Journal of Applied Sociol-

ogy, VIII (July-August, 1924), 339–344.

Perbal, Albert. "La Race Nègre et la Malédiction de Cham." *Revue de L'Universite D'Ottawa,* X (1940), 156–177.

Poston, Ted. "The Revolt of the Evil Fairies." *The New Republic.* CVI (April 16, 1942), 458–459.

Radin, Max. "Status." *Encyclopaedia of the Social Sciences,* XIV, 373–377.

Ratcliffe, S. C. "Social Structure and Status." *Sociology and Social Research,* XIV (November-December, 1929), 156–165.

Simmel, Georg. "Superiority and Subordination as Subject-Matter of Sociology." *American Journal of Sociology,* II (September, 1896), 167–189, (November, 1896), 392–415.

Spitz, D. *Patterns of Anti-Democratic Thought.* New York: The Macmillan Company, 1949. Chapter VI and chapter VII.

Tawney, R. H. *Equality.* London: George Allen and Unwin, Ltd., 1931.

Taylor, Councill Samuel. *Color and Class: A Comparative Study of Jamaican Status Groups.* Ph.D. thesis, Yale University, 1955.

Thomson, David. *Equality.* Cambridge: Cambridge University Press, 1949.

Warner, W. L. and Lunt, P. S. *The Status System of a Modern Community.* New Haven: Yale University Press, 1942.

Wertheim, W. F. *Indonesian Society in Transition: A Study of Social Change.* The Hague, Netherlands: W. Van Hoeve, 1956. Chapter VI.

Westie, F. R. "Negro-White Status Differentials and Social Distance." *American Sociological Review,* XVII (October, 1952), 550–558.

Williams, Roger John. *Free and Unequal: The Biological Basis of Individual Liberty.* Austin: University of Texas Press, 1953.

Young, Jefferson. *A Good Man.* Indianapolis: The Bobbs-Merrill Co., 1953.

B. SOCIAL CHANGE AND RACE RELATIONS

Brearley, H. C. "Culture Change and Race Relations." *Social Forces,* XX (December, 1941), 260–263.

Burke, Kenneth. *Permanence and Change. An Anatomy of Purpose.* New York: New Republic, Inc., 1935.

Furnivall, J. S. *Educational Progress in Southeast Asia.* New York: International Secretariat, Institute of Pacific Relations, 1943.

Gallagher, Buell G. "What Would Constitute Progress?" *Journal of Negro Education,* VIII (July, 1939), 571–582.

Hughes, Everett C. "Social Change and Status Protest: An Essay on the Marginal Man." *Phylon,* X (First Quarter, 1949), 58–65.

Huxley, Julian. *Heredity East and West: Lysenko and World Science.* New York: Henry Schuman, 1949.

——. *Soviet Genetics and World Science.* London: Chatto and Windus, 1949.

Johnson, Charles S. (ed.). "Education and the Cultural Process: A Symposium." *American Journal of Sociology,* XLVIII (May, 1943), No. 6.

——. "Race Relations and Social Change," in Edgar T. Thompson (ed.), *Race Relations and the Race Problem.* Durham, N.C.: Duke University Press, 1939. Chapter X.

Kluckhohn, Clyde. *Mirror for Man: The Relation of Anthropology to Modern Life.* New York: Whittlesey House, 1949. Chapter V.

Lohman, Joseph D. "Race Relations in a Mass Society," in *Implementing Civil Rights.* Nashville: Fisk University, 1949, pp. 65–67.

——. and Reitzes, Dietrich C. "Note on Race Relations in Mass Society." *American Journal of Sociology,* LVIII, (November, 1952), 240–246.

Long, H. H. "Race Prejudice and Social Change." *American Journal of Sociology,* LVII (July, 1951), 15–19.

McCully, B. T. *English Education and the Origins of Indian Nationalism.* New York: Columbia University Press, 1940.

McWilliams, Carey. "Race Discrimination and the Law." *Science and Society,* IX (Winter, 1945), 1–22.

Malherbe, E. G. (ed.). *Educational Adaptations in a Changing Society.* Capetown, South Africa: Juta and Company, Ltd., 1937.

Masuoka, Jitsuichi. "Can Progress in Race Relations be Measured?" *Social Forces,* XXV (December, 1946), 211–217.

Ogburn, William F. *Social Change: With Respect to Culture and Original Nature.* New York: The Viking Press, 1950.

Wilson, Godfrey and Wilson, Monica. *The Analysis of Social Change.* Cambridge: The University Press, 1945.

C. MAINTAINING THE RACIAL ORDER

Bibby, Harold Cyril. *How Life Is Handed On.* New York: Emerson Books, 1947.

Davis, Allison and Dollard John. *Children of Bondage.* Washington: American Council on Education, 1940.

Davis, Allison. "American Status Systems and the Socialization of the Child." *American Sociological Review,* VI (June, 1941), 345–354.

——. "Child Training and Social Class," in R. G. Barker et al, (eds.), *Child Behavior and Development.* New York: McGraw-Hill Book Company, 1943. Chapter XXIV.

——. "Socialization and the Adolescent Personality." *Adolescence, Forty-Third Yearbook of the National Society for the Study of Education,* XLIII. Chicago: Department of Education, University of Chicago, 1944, pp. 198–216.

——. and Havighurst, Robert J. "Social Class and Color Differences in Child-Rearing." *American Sociological Review,* XI (December, 1946), 698–710.

Goodman, Mary Ellen. *Race Awareness in Young Children.* Cambridge: Addison-Wesley Press, 1952.

Haardt, Sarah. "Little White Girl." *Scribner's Magazine,* XCV (April, 1934), 259–262.

Horowitz, Eugene L. "The Development of Attitude Toward the Negro." *Archives of Psychology,* XXVIII (January, 1936), No. 194.

Simmel, Georg. "The Persistence of Social Groups." Translated by Albion W. Small. *The American Journal of Sociology,* III (March, 1898), 662–698; (May, 1898), 829–836; IV (July, 1898), 35–50.

Trager, Helen G. and Yarrow, Marian Radke. *They Learn What They Live: Prejudice in Young Children.* Bureau for Intercultural Education Series, VIII. New York: Harper and Brothers, 1952.

Warner, W. Lloyd; Junker, B. H. and Adams, W. A. *Color and Human Nature.* Washington: American Council on Education, 1941.

Westbrook, Olive Elizabeth. *The Transmission of Racial Patterns Among White Southerners.* M.A. thesis, University of Chicago, 1945.

VII. RACE AND HUMAN NATURE

A. GENERAL

Adams, Romanzo. "Laughing at the Wrong Place." *Pacific Affairs,* II (July, 1929), 415–417.

Aginski, Burt W. "An Indian's Soliloquy." *American Journal of Sociology,* XLVI (July, 1940), 43–44.

Berkerley-Hill, O. A. R. "The Color Question from a Psychoanalytic Standpoint." *Psychoanalytic Review,* XI (July, 1924), 246–253.

Boas, Franz. *The Mind of Primitive Men.* New York: The Macmillan Company, 1938.

Botkin, B. A. (ed.). *Lay My Burden Down: A Folk History of Slavery.* Chicago: University of Chicago Press, 1946.

Brann, W. C. "The Buck Negro," in *Brann the Iconoclast: A Collection of the Writings of W. C. Brann.* Waco, Texas: Hertz Brothers, 1898. Vol. I, pp. 24–29.

Brearley, H. C. "Ba-ad Nigger." *South Atlantic Quarterly,* XXXVIII (January, 1939), 75–81.

Christy, Arthur E. and Wells, Henry W. *World Literature: An Anthology of Human Experience.* New York: American Book Company, 1947. Part 14, "Contacts of Races."

Clemens, Samuel (Mark Twain, pseud.). *Huckleberry Finn.* New York: Harper and Brothers, 1912.

Crothers, Samuel McChord. *The Book of Friendship.* New York: Macmillan Company, 1910.

——. *Among Friends.* Boston: Houghton Mifflin Company, 1914, pp. 1–24.

Eddy, G. Norman. *The Human Face: A Study in Culture and Social Interaction.* Ph.D. thesis, Duke University, 1943.

Eells, Kenneth Walter et al. *Intelligence and Cultural Differences: A Study of Cultural Learning and Problem-Solving.* Chicago: University of Chicago Press, 1951.

Evarts, A. B. "Colour Symbolism" *Psychoanalytic Review,* VI (April, 1919), 124–157.

Faris, Ellsworth. "The Nature of Human Nature," in *The Nature of Human Nature and Other Essays in Social Psychology.* New York: McGraw-Hill Book Company, 1937. Ch. II.

Heather, P. J. "Colour Symbolism." *Folk Lore,* LIX (4th. Quarter, 1948), 165–183; LX (1st Quarter, 1949), 208–216; (2nd. Quarter, 1949), 266–276; (3rd. Quarter, 1949), 316–331.

Heyward, Dubois. *Mamba's Daughters.* New York: Doubleday, Doran and Company, 1929.

Huber, Ernst. *Evolution of Facial Muscula-*

ture and Facial Expression. Baltimore: The Johns Hopkins Press, 1931.

Hughes, Everett C. "Principle and Rationalization in Race Relations." *American Catholic Sociological Review*, VIII (March, 1947), 3–11.

Hurston, Zora Neal. "The 'Pet Negro' System." *American Mercury*, LVI (May, 1943), 593–600.

Hutchinson, Harry. "Shades of Color and of Meaning." *Courier* (UNESCO), V, nos. 8–9 (August–September, 1952), 11.

Ichheiser, Gustav. "Sociopsychological and Cultural Factors in Race Relations." *American Journal of Sociology*, LIV (March, 1949), 395–401. Comment by Louis Wirth.

Jennings, Herbert S. *The Biological Basis of Human Nature*. New York: W. W. Norton and Company, Inc., 1930.

Johnson, Charles S. "From Race Relations to Human Relations," in J. Masuoka and Preston Valien (eds.), *Race Relations: Theories and Problems* (to be published).

King, A. R. "Status Personality Change in Northern Negroes in the Southern United States." *Social Forces*, XXVI (December, 1947), 153–166.

Murray, Gilbert. "Satanism and the World Order." *The Century Magazine*, C (July, 1920), 289–299.

Park, Robert E. "Behind Our Masks." *Survey Graphic*, XVI (May, 1926), 135–139; Reprinted in Robert E. Park, *Race and Culture*. Glencoe, Ill.: The Free Press, 1950. Chapter XIX.

———. *Race and Culture*. Glencoe, Ill.: The Free Press, 1950. Chapter XIII. "The Etiquette of Race Relations in the South."

Parrish, Charles Henry. *The Significance of Color in the Negro Community*. Ph.D. thesis, University of Chicago, 1944.

Redfield, Robert. "Race and Human Nature: An Anthropologist's View." *Fiftieth Foreign Mission Conference of North America*. New York: Foreign Missions Conference of North America, 1944, pp. 179–186.

Riesman, David. *The Lonely Crowd: A Study of the Changing American Character*. New Haven: Yale University Press, 1950.

Riezler, Kurt. *Man, Mutable and Immutable: The Fundamental Structure of Social Life*. Chicago: Henry Regnery Company, 1950.

Sachs, Wolf. *Black Hamlet: The Mind of an African Negro Revealed by Psychoanalysis*. London: G. Bles, 1937.

Schilder, Paul. *The Image and Appearance of the Human Body; Studies in the Constructive Energies of the Psyche*. London: Kegan Paul, Trench, Trubner and Company, Ltd., 1935.

Seid, Ruth (Sinclair, Jo, pseud.). *Wasteland*. New York: Harper and Brothers, 1946.

Strong, Samuel M. "Human Nature and the Color of Skin." *Prairie Schooner*, XX (Fall, 1946), 164–176.

Warner, W. L.; Junker, Buford H. and Adams, Walter A. *Color and Human Nature; Negro Personality Development in a Northern City*. Washington: American Council on Education, 1941.

B. RACIAL ATTITUDES

Ackerman, Nathan W. and Jahoda, Marie. *Anti-Semitism and Emotional Disorder: A Psychoanalytic Interpretation*. New York: Harper and Brothers, 1950.

Adorno, T. W. et al. *The Authoritarian Personality*. New York: Harper and Brothers, 1950.

Alexander, Chester Stephen. *Antipathy and Prejudice: A Study of the Distinctions Between These Two Phenomena*. Ph.D. thesis, University of Chicago, 1942.

———. "Antipathy and Social Behavior," *American Journal of Sociology*, LI (January, 1946), 288–292.

Allport, Gordon W. "Prejudice: A Problem in Psychological and Social Causation." *The Journal of Social Issues*, VI Supplement Series, No. 4, (November, 1950), 4–23.

———. *The Nature of Prejudice*. Cambridge: Addison-Wesley Publishing Company, 1954.

Anonymous. "The Arabs' Peculiar 'Anti-Semitism': An Old Hostility Takes a New Form." *Commentary*, VII (February, 1949), 162–165.

Belfrage, Cedric. *A Faith to Free the People*. New York: The Dryden Press, 1944.

Bettelheim, Bruno and Janowitz, Morris. *Dynamics of Prejudice; A Psychological and Sociological Study of Veterans*. New York: Harper and Brothers, 1950.

Bissell, Benjamin. *The American Indian in English Literature of the Eighteenth Century*. New Haven: Yale University Press, 1925.

Blumer, Herbert. "The Nature of Race

Prejudice." *Social Process in Hawaii,*
V (June, 1939), 11–20.

——. "Attitudes and the Social Act." *Social Problems,* III (October, 1955), 59–65.

——. "Race Prejudice as a Sense of Group Position," in J. Masuoka and Preston Valien (eds.), *Race Relations: Theories and Problems* (to be published).

Brown, Fred. "A Socio-Psychological Analysis of Race Prejudice." *Journal of Abnormal and Social Psychology,* XXVII (January–March, 1933), 364–374.

Bryant, Sophie. "Antipathy and Sympathy." *Mind,* IV, n.s. (July, 1895), 365–370.

Burns, Sir Alan C. *Colour Prejudice; With Particular Reference to the Relationships Between Whites and Negroes.* London: George Allen and Unwin, Ltd., 1948.

Clark, Francis Edward. "Our Dearest Antipathies." *Atlantic Monthly,* CXXVII (February, 1921), 239–243.

Cooper, Eunice and Jahoda, Marie. "The Evasion of Propaganda: How Prejudiced People Respond to Anti-Prejudice Propaganda." *Journal of Psychology,* XXIII (January, 1947), 15–25.

Cox, Oliver C. "Race Prejudice and Intolerance—A Distinction." *Social Forces,* XXIV (December, 1945), 216–219.

Deutsch, Karl W. "Anti-Semitic Ideas in the Middle Ages: International Civilizations in Expansion and Conflict." *Journal of the History of Ideas,* VI (April, 1945), 239–251.

Dewey, John. "Racial Prejudice and Friction." *Chinese Social and Political Science Review,* VI (March, 1922), 1–17.

Faris, Ellsworth. "The Natural History of Race Prejudice," in *The Nature of Human Nature.* New York: McGraw-Hill Book Company, 1937. Chapter XXXII.

Foreman, Carolyn Thomas. *Indians Abroad, 1493–1938.* Norman: University of Oklahoma Press, 1943.

Goldenweiser, Alexander. "Race and Culture in the Modern World." *Journal of Social Forces,* III (November, 1924), 127–136.

Hellenbach, Lazar Baron. *Die Vorurtheile der Menschheit.* Leipzig: Mutze, 1893. Third edition. 3 volumes.

Hibben, John Grier. "A Defence of Prejudice," in *A Defense of Prejudice and Other Essays.* New York: Charles Scribner's Sons, 1921, pp. 1–17.

Hogben, Lancelot. "Race and Prejudice," in *Dangerous Thoughts.* New York: W. W. Norton, 1940. Chapter III.

Horowitz, E. L. "'Race' Attitudes," in Otto Klineberg (ed.), *Characteristics of the American Negro.* New York: Harper and Brothers, 1944 pp. 139–247.

Ichheiser, Gustav. *Diagnosis of Antisemitism: Two Essays. Sociometry Monographs,* No. 8. New York: Beacon House, 1946.

Keith, Arthur. *The Place of Prejudice in Modern Civilization.* New York: John Day Company, 1931.

Lowenthal, Leo and Guterman, Norbert. *Prophets of Deceit: A Study of the Techniques of the American Agitator.* New York: Harper and Brothers, 1949.

Mekeel, Scudder. "Concerning Race Prejudice." *American Journal of Orthopsychiatry,* XIV (October, 1944), 699–705.

Menen, Aubrey. "My Grandmother and the Dirty English," in *Dead Men in the Silver Market.* New York: Charles Scribner's Sons, 1953, pp. 22–39.

Myers, Gustavus. *History of Bigotry in the United States.* New York: Random House, 1943.

Nanavati, Manilal B. and Vakil, C. N. (eds.). *Group Prejudices in India, A Symposium.* Bombay: Vora and Company, Ltd., 1951.

O'Connell, William Henry. *Recollections of Seventy Years.* Boston: Houghton Mifflin Company, 1934. Chapters II–IV.

Olivier, Sydney. "Colour Prejudice." *Contemporary Review,* CXXIV (October, 1923), 448–457.

Pinson, Koppel S. (ed.). *Essays on Anti-Semitism.* New York: Conference on Jewish Relations, 1946.

Ribot, Theodule A. "L'Antipathie." *Revue Philosophique,* CXXVIII (July, 1939), 5–16.

Robb, J. H. *Working-Class Anti-Semite: A Psychological Study in a London Borough.* London: Tavistock Publications, 1954.

Rose, Arnold M. (ed.). *Race Prejudice and Discrimination: Readings in Intergroup Relations in the United States.* New York: Alfred A. Knopf, 1951.

Saenger, Gerhart. *The Social Psychology of Prejudice: Achieving Intercultural Understanding and Cooperation in a Democracy.* New York: Harper and Brothers, 1953.

Smith, Ruth. *White Man's Burden: A Personal Testament.* New York: The Vanguard Press, 1946.

Vickery, William E. and Morris, Edward Opler. "A Redefinition of Prejudice for Purposes of Social Science Research." *Human Relations*, I (1948), 419–428.

C. SOCIAL AND PERSONALITY TYPES

Adorno, T. W. and others. *The Authoritarian Personality*. New York: Harper and Brothers, 1950.

Christie, Richard and Jahoda, Marie (eds.). *Studies in the Scope and Method of "The Authoritarian Personality."* Glencoe, Ill.: The Free Press, 1955.

Dai, Bingham. "Minority Group Membership and Personality Development," in J. Masuoka and Preston Valien (eds.), *Race Relations: Theories and Problems* (to be published).

Glick, Clarence. "Social Roles and Types in Race Relations," in Andrew W. Lind (ed.), *Race Relations in World Perspective*. Honolulu: University of Hawaii Press, 1955. Chapter XI.

Kardiner, Abram and Ovesey, Lionel. *The Mark of Oppression; A Psychosocial Study of the American Negro*. New York: Norton and Company, 1951.

Quinn, Olive Westbrooke. *Racial Attitude and the Conforming Personality*. Ph. D. thesis, University of Chicago, 1950.

Strong, S. M. "Negro-White Relations as Reflected in Social Types." *American Journal of Sociology*, LII (July, 1946), 23–30.

Sutherland, Robert Lee. *Color, Class and Personality*. Washington: American Council on Education, 1942.

D. COLLECTIVE BEHAVIOR

Black, Percy. "Racial Prejudice and Sociocultural Contexts." *Phylon*, XI (Second Quarter, 1950), 156–158.

Reitzes, Dietrich C. *Collective Factors in Race Relations*. Ph.D. thesis, University of Chicago, 1950.

VIII. THE STUDY AND CONTROL OF RACE RELATIONS

A. THE SOCIOLOGY OF RACIAL KNOWLEDGE

Blumer, Herbert. "Reflections on Theory of Race Relations," in Andrew W. Lind (ed.), *Race Relations in World Perspective*. Honolulu: University of Hawaii Press, 1955. Chapter I.

Logan, Rayford W. (ed.). *What the Negro Wants*. Chapel Hill: University of North Carolina Press, 1944.

Moton, Robert R. *What the Negro Thinks*. Garden City, N.Y.: Doubleday, Doran and Company, 1929.

Myrdal, Gunnar. *An American Dilemma: The Negro Problem and Modern Democracy*. New York: Harper and Brothers, 1944. Volume I, pp. 40–42; 89–97.

Radin, Paul. *The Racial Myth*. New York: Whittlesey House, McGraw-Hill Book Company, 1934.

Reuter, Edward B. "Southern Scholars and Race Relations." *Phylon*, VII (Third Quarter, 1946), 221–235.

Saunders, Lyle. *Cultural Differences and Medical Care*. New York: Russell Sage Foundation, 1954. Appendix A, "Demographic Characteristics of the Spanish-Speaking Population of the Southwest."

Sprigle, Ray. "In the Land of Jim Crow." *The Pittsburg Post-Gazette*, (August, 1948).

B. THE SYSTEMATIC CONSIDERATION OF RACE RELATIONS, SCIENTIFIC AND POLITICAL

Bloom, Leonard. "Concerning Ethnic Research." *American Sociological Review*, XIII (April, 1948), 171–177.

Frazier, E. Franklin. "Sociological Theory and Race Relations." *American Sociological Review*, XII (June, 1947), 265–271.

——. "Race Contacts and the Social Structure." *American Sociological Review*, XIV (February, 1949), 1–11.

Hill, Mozell C. and Ackiss, Thelma D. "The 'Insight Interview' Approach to Race Relations." *Journal of Social Psychology*, XXI (May, 1945), 197–208.

Hooton, E. A. "Methods of Racial Analysis." *Science*, LXIII (January, 1926), 75–81.

House, F. N. "Viewpoints and Methods in the Study of Race Relations." *American Journal of Sociology*, XL (January, 1935), 440–452.

——. "Some Methods of Studying Race and Culture." *Social Forces*, XV (October, 1936), 1–5.

Hughes, Everett C. "Principle and Rationalization in Race Relations." *American Catholic Sociological Review*, VIII (March, 1947), 3–11. Also in Everett C. and Helen M. Hughes, *Where Peoples Meet*. Glencoe, Ill.: The Free Press, 1952, Appendix, pp. 145–155.

——. "The Study of Ethnic Relations." *The Dalhousie Review,* XXVII (January, 1948), 477–482. Also in Everett C. and Helen M. Hughes, *Where Peoples Meet.* Glencoe, Ill.: The Free Press, 1952. Appendix, pp. 155–162.

Jahoda, Marie; Deutsch, Morton and Cook, Stuart. *Research Methods in Social Relations.* New York: The Dryden Press, 1951.

Kahin, George M. *The Asian-African Conference, Bandung, Indonesia, April, 1955.* Ithaca: Cornell University Press, 1956.

Mann, Floyd C. "Human Relations Skills in Social Research." *Human Relations,* IV (November, 1951), 341–353.

Moore, George Edward. "Relations, Properties and Resemblance," in *Some Main Problems of Philosophy.* New York: The Macmillan Company, 1953. Chapter XVIII.

Park, Robert E. Review of John Dollard, *Caste and Class in a Southern Town. Annals of the American Academy of Political and Social Science,* CXCIII (September, 1937), 210–211.

——. *Race and Culture.* Glencoe, Ill.: The Free Press, 1950. Chapter X, "Experience and Race Relations," and Chapter XI, "A Race Relations Survey."

Redfield, Robert. "The Art of Social Science." *American Journal of Sociology,* LIV (November, 1948), 181–190.

Reuter, Edward B. "The Relation of Biology and Sociology." *American Journal of Sociology,* XXXII (March, 1927), 705–718.

——. "The Field and Problems of Biological Sociology." *Publications of the American Sociological Society,* XXVII (1932), 35–45.

——. Review of Rayford W. Logan (ed.). *What the Negro Wants* (1944), *American Journal of Sociology,* L. (January, 1945), 317–318.

——. "Racial Theory." *American Journal of Sociology,* L (May, 1945), 452–461.

Riesman, David. "Marginality, Conformity, and Insight." *Phylon,* XIV (Third Quarter, 1953), 241–257.

Romulo, Carlos P. *The Meaning of Bandung.* Chapel Hill: University of North Carolina Press, 1956.

Smith, Samuel Stanhope. *An Essay on the Causes of the Variety of Complexion and Figure in the Human Species.* New York: Williams and Whiting, 1810.

Stouffer, Samuel A. "Quantitative Methods in the Study of Race Relations," in J.

Masuoka and Preston Valien (eds.), *Race Relations: Theories and Problems* (to be published).

Thomas, William I. "The Relation of Research to the Social Process," in W. F. G. Swann et al, *Essays on Research in the Social Sciences.* Washington: The Brookings Institution, 1931, pp. 175–194.

——. "The Comparative Study of Cultures." *American Journal of Sociology,* XLII (September, 1936), 177–185.

White, Leslie A. Review of Franz Boas, *Race and Democratic Society* (1945), *American Journal of Sociology,* LII (January, 1947), 371–373.

Wirth, Louis. "Research in Racial and Cultural Relations." *American Philosophical Society Proceedings,* XCII (November, 1948), 381–386.

——. "Problems and Orientations of Research in Race Relations in the United States." *British Journal of Sociology,* I (June, 1950), 117–125.

Wright, Richard. *The Color Curtain: A Report on the Bandung Conference.* Cleveland: The World Publishing Company, 1956.

C. TEXTBOOKS AND GENERAL WORKS

Barron, Milton L. (ed.). *American Minorities: A Textbook of Readings in Intergroup Relations.* New York: Alfred A. Knopf, 1957.

Berry, Brewton. *Race Relations; The Interaction of Ethnic and Racial Groups.* New York: Houghton Mifflin Company, 1951.

Brown, Francis J. and Roucek, Joseph S. (eds.). *Our Racial and National Minorities: Their History, Contributions and Present Problems.* New York: Prentice-Hall, Inc., 1937.

Campbell, Byran. *American Race Theorists: A Critique of Their Thoughts and Methods.* Boston: Chapman and Grimes, 1952.

Davie, Maurice R. *Negroes in American Society.* New York: McGraw-Hill Book Company, 1949.

Dowd, Jerome. *The Negro in American Life.* New York: The Century Company, 1926.

Frazier, E. Franklin. *The Negro in the United States.* New York: The Macmillan Company, 1949.

——. *Race and Culture Contacts in the Modern World.* New York: Alfred A. Knopf, 1957.

Locke, Alain, and Stern, Bernhard J. (eds.). *When Peoples Meet: A Study in Race and Culture Contacts.* New York: Committee on Workshops, Progressive Education Association, 1942.

McDonagh, Edward and Richards, Eugene. *Ethnic Relations in the United States.* New York: Appleton-Century-Crofts, Inc., 1953.

MacIver, R. M. *Society: An Introductory Analysis.* New York: Rinehart and Company, 1949. Chapter XV, "Ethnic and Racial Groups."

Marden, Charles F. *Minorities in American Society.* New York: American Book Company, 1952.

Redfield, Robert. "The Ethnological Problem," in George B. de Huszar (ed.), *New Perspectives on Peace.* Chicago: University of Chicago Press, 1944. Chapter IV.

Reuter, Edward B. *The American Race Problem: A Study of the Negro.* New York: Thomas Y. Crowell Company, 1938.

Rose, Arnold M. (ed.). *Race Prejudice and Discrimination: Readings in Intergroup Relations in the United States.* New York: Alfred A. Knopf, 1951.

Simpson, George Eaton and Yinger, J. Milton. *Racial and Cultural Minorities: An Analysis of Prejudice and Discrimination.* New York: Harper and Brothers, 1953.

Soper, Edmund D. *Racism: A World Issue.* New York: Abbingdon-Cokesbury Press, 1947.

Spiller, Gustav (ed.). *Papers on Inter-Racial Problems Communicated to the First Universal Races Congress Held at the University of London, July 26–29, 1911.* London: P. S. King and Son, 1911.

Stone, Alfred Holt. *Studies in the American Race Problem.* New York: Doubleday, Page and Company, 1908.

Thompson, Edgar T. (ed.). *Race Relations and the Race Problem.* Durham, N.C.: Duke University Press, 1939.

——. and Thompson, Alma Macy. *Race and Region: A Descriptive Bibliography Compiled with Special Reference to the Relations Between Whites and Negroes in the United States.* Chapel Hill: University of North Carolina Press, 1949.

Walter, Paul A. F., Jr. *Race and Culture Relations.* New York: McGraw-Hill Book Company, Inc., 1952.

Work, Monroe N. *A Bibliography of the Negro in Africa and America.* New York: The H. W. Wilson Company, 1928.

Young, Donald. *American Minority Peoples: A Study in Racial and Cultural Contacts in the United States.* New York: Harper and Brothers, 1932.

D. THE CONTROL OF RACE RELATIONS

Allport, Gordon W. "Catharsis and the Reduction of Prejudice." *Journal of Social Issues,* I (August, 1945), 3–10.

——. *The Resolution of Intergroup Tensions.* New York: National Conference of Christians and Jews, 1951.

Brown, William O. "Interracial Cooperation: Some of the Problems." *Opportunity,* XI (September, 1933), 272ff.

Burgess, Ernest W. "Social Planning and Race Relations," in J. Masuoka and Preston Valien (eds.), *Race Relations: Theories and Problems* (to be published.)

Chatto, Clarence I. and Halligan, Alice L. *The Story of the Springfield Plan.* New York: Barnes and Noble, Inc., 1945.

Clinchy, Russel J. *Human Rights and the United Nations.* Irvington-on-Hudson, N.Y.: Foundation for Economic Education, 1952.

Dean, John P. and Rosen, Alex. *A Manual of Intergroup Relations.* Chicago: University of Chicago Press, 1955.

Krech, David and Crutchfield, Richard S. *Theory and Problems of Social Psychology.* New York: McGraw-Hill Book Company, 1948. Chapter XII, "Racial Prejudice in the United States," and chapter XIII, "Controlling Racial Prejudice."

LaFarge, John. *The Race Question and the Negro: A Study of the Catholic Doctrine on Interracial Justice.* New York: Longmans, Green and Company, 1943.

Lewin, Kurt. *Resolving Social Conflicts. Selected Papers on Group Dynamics.* New York: Harper and Brothers, 1948.

Marcson, Simon. "The Control of Ethnic Conflict." *Social Forces,* XXIV (December, 1945), 161–165.

Mekeel, Scudder. "Cultural Aids to Constructive Race Relations." *Mental Hygiene,* XXIX (April, 1945), 177–189.

Merton, R. K. "Discrimination and the American Creed," in R. M. MacIver,

Discrimination and the National Welfare. New York: Harper and Brothers, 1949. Chapter XI.

Redfield, Robert. "Race and Religion in Selective Admission." *The Journal of the American Association of Collegiate Registrars,* XXI (July, 1946), 527–542.

Williams, Robin. *The Reduction of Intergroup Tensions: A Survey of Research on Problems of Ethnic, Racial and Religious Group Relations. Social Science Research Council Bulletin, No. 57.* New York: Social Science Research Council, 1947.

Wirth, Louis. "Race and Public Policy." *Scientific Monthly,* LVIII (April, 1944), 302–312.

——. *Community Life and Social Policy: Selected Papers.* Chicago: University of Chicago Press, 1956.

CONTRIBUTORS

EDWARD CLARKSON LEVERETT ADAMS (b. 1876) was a physician, planter, and writer of Columbia, South Carolina.

ROMANZO ADAMS (1868–1942) was Professor of Sociology at the University of Hawaii. He wrote *Taxation in Nevada* (1918) and *The Peoples of Hawaii— a Statistical Study* (1925), in addition to *Interracial Marriage in Hawaii* (1937).

CHESTER ALEXANDER is Professor of Sociology and Statistics at Westminster College, Fulton, Missouri. In addition to his interest in race studies, he is interested in research in longevity as affected by biological inheritance, natural environment, and culture. He has published numerous papers.

WILEY B. ALFORD (1923–   ) is Assistant Professor of Sociology at Wake Forest College, North Carolina.

RUTH ALICE ALLEN (1889–   ) is Professor of Economics at the University of Texas. She also is editor of the *Southwest Social Science Quarterly* and author of *The Great Southwest Strike* (1942) and chapters in *The History of Organized Labor in Texas* (1941).

HANNAH ARENDT (1906–   ) is a German born author and former Director of the Conference on Jewish Relations and Jewish Cultural Reconstruction. She is the author of *Six Essays* (1948) and *The Origins of Totalitarianism* (1951).

SOLOMON ELLIOT ASCH (1907–   ) has been Professor of Psychology at Swarthmore College since 1947. He has specialized in social and experimental psychology, the psychology of thinking and learning, and perception. He is the author of *Social Psychology* (1952).

GEORGES BALANDIER (1920–   ) is Director of Studies at L'École Pratique des Hautes Études at the Sorbonne and Professor at the Institute d'Études Politiques. He has conducted research in French West Africa and is the author of *Sociologie des Brazzavilles Noires* (1955) and *Sociologie de l'Afrique Noire* (1955).

STRINGFELLOW BARR (1897–   ) has been active in world government organizations since 1940 and is the author of *Citizens of the World* (1952) and *The Pilgrimage of Western Man* (1949).

CALVIN LUNSFORD BEALE (1923–   ) is Acting Head, Farm Population Section, Farm Population and Rural Life Branch of the U.S. Department of Agriculture. He is the author of several papers on population distribution and trends. His most recent paper is "Farm Population as a Useful Demographic Concept," published in *Agricultural Economics Research* in 1957.

KOVOOR THOMAS BEHANAN was born in India and educated in India and in the West. The studies and experimental researches which form the basis of his book *Yoga* (1937) were done in part under the direction of the Graduate Department of Psychology at Yale University. He is also author of *Realities and Make-Believe* (1952).

KONRAD BERCOVICI (1882–   ) is a writer and former staff member of the New York *World* and the New York *Post*. He has written *The Exodus* (1947), *It's the Gypsy in Me* (an autobiography, 1941), and several other books.

[611]

HEBERT BLUMER (1900–   ) is Professor of Sociology at the University of California at Berkely. He has written *Movies, Delinquency and Crime* (1933), *Movies and Conduct* (1933), and several articles and chapters in the field of social psychology.

WILLIAM COWPER BRANN (1855–1898) was the Illinois-born Texas editor of *Brann's Iconoclast*. His numerous writings are collected in *The Complete Works of W. C. Brann* (1929) and Charles Carver has recently produced *Brann and the Iconoclast* (1957).

HARRINGTON COOPER BREARLEY (1893–   ) has been Professor of Sociology at George Peabody College in Nashville, Tennessee, since 1939. He is the author of *Homicide in the United States* (1932).

LEONARD BROOM (1911–   ) is Professor of Sociology at the University of California at Los Angeles and author of *Removal and Return* (with Ruth Reimer, 1949) and *The Managed Casualty: the Japanese-American Family in World War II* (1956).

WILLIAM O. BROWN (1899–   ) is Director of the African Research and Studies Program and Professor of Sociology at Boston University. He edited "Contemporary African Trends and Issues," *Annals of the American Academy of Political and Social Science,* Vol. 298 (1955).

WILMOTH ANNETTE CARTER (1916–   ) is Associate Professor of Sociology at Shaw University, Raleigh, N.C. She is the author of *Colloquial Language as an Index of Social Adjustment.*

AIMÉ CÉSAIRE (1913–   ) was born at Pointre-à-Pitre in Martinique. He is now a deputy of Martinique in the French National Assembly. He has published several volumes of verse, one of which, *Corps Perdu,* is illustrated by Picasso.

MRS. HENRIQUETA CHAMBERLAIN is the daughter of a Jewish missionary of the Southern Baptist Church to Brazil and was born in that country. She is the translator of *Inocência* (1945) by Alfredo d'Escragnolle Taunay. *Where the Sabiá Sings* (1947) is a partial autobiography.

HOUSTON STEWART CHAMBERLAIN (1855–1927) was a well-known Englishman who lived in Germany and admired all things German. His best known work is *Die Grundlagen des Neunzehnten Jahrhunderts* (1902).

HERBERT COLLINS (1920–   ) is Assistant Professor of Sociology at North Carolina State College. He is the author of "The Sedentary Society" in *The Scientific Monthly* and "The Ideological Assessment of Negroes," *Journal of Human Relations.*

MELVIN CONANT (1924–   ) is Director of the Pacific and Asian Affairs Council, Honolulu, and author of Occasional Papers on Far Eastern Studies, Harvard University.

SAMUEL McCHORD CROTHERS (1857–1927) was a Unitarian minister who served as preacher to Harvard University. He wrote biographies of Emerson and Oliver Wendell Holmes. His numerous essays are written with insight and charm.

JAMES DARMESTETER (1849–1894), French scholar, writer, and translator, was the author of *Essais Orientaux* (1883). The translator of Darmesteter's *Selected Essays,* Morris Jastrow Jr., was one time Professor of Semitic Languages at the University of Pennsylvania.

JOHN DOLLARD (1900–   ) is Professor of Psychology at Yale University and part author of *Personality and Psychotherapy* (1950) and *Steps in Psychotherapy* (1953).

CEDRIC DOVER (1904–   ), born in Calcutta, India, is the author of *Hell in the Sunshine* (1943), *Know This of Race* (1939), *Half Caste,* and numerous articles and reviews.

WILLIAM EDWARD BURGHARDT DuBOIS (1868–   ), American Negro writer and lecturer, was formerly Professor of Sociology at Atlanta University, where he directed what was probably the first field research in race relations in the South. He wrote *The World and Africa* (1947), *In Battle for Peace* (1952), and several other books.

KATHLEEN TAMAGAWA ELDRIDGE (Mrs. F. R. Eldridge) (1893–   ) is the daughter of a Japanese father and an Irish mother. *Holy Prayers in a Horse's Ear* (1932) is the story of her own life.

JOHN FRANKLIN ENDERS (1897–   ) is Chief of the Research Department on Infectious Diseases, Children's Hospital, Boston, winner of a Nobel prize in medicine and physiology (1954), and editor of *The Journal of Immunology*.

MAURICE FISHBERG (1872–1934), Russian-born American citizen of Jewish ancestry, was deeply interested in the anthropology and the sociology of his people. After becoming a doctor of medicine at New York University he worked with the Bureau of Immigration. He is the author of *The Jews: A Study of Race and Environment* (1911), *Rassenmerkmale der Juden* (1912), and he produced a treatise on tuberculosis.

LeROY DRYDEN FOTHERGILL (1901–   ) is adviser to U.S. military departments on biological warfare and onetime Professor in Harvard Medical School.

ALFRED JULES ÉMILE FOUILLÉE (1838–1912), French philosopher and psychologist, is the author of *Descartes* (1893), *Esquisse Psychologique des Peuples Européens* (1903), and several other works.

EMERICK K. FRANCIS (1906–   ) is Professor of Sociology at Notre Dame University and author of *In Search of Utopia: The Mennonites in Manitoba* (1956).

EDWARD AUGUSTUS FREEDMAN (1823–1892) was a distinguished English historian. His *Life and Letters* was edited by Dean Stephens and published in 1895. Freedman's *History of the Norman Conquest* is one of the great works of English historical learning.

WILLIAM S. GILBERT (1836–1911) was of the famous Gilbert and Sullivan comic opera team.

JOHN PHILIP GILLIN (1907–   ) is Professor of Anthropology at the University of North Carolina and the author of *The Culture of Security in San Carlos* (1951), *Moche; a Peruvian Coastal Community* (1947), and several other works.

CLARENCE GLICK (1906–   ) is Professor of Sociology at the University of Hawaii. He has written numerous articles dealing with race relations, including "Race Relations in World Perspective" for UNESCO.

ALEXANDER GOLDENWEISER (1880–1940) was a distinguished American anthropologist. Among his best known works are *Early Civilization* (1922) and *History, Psychology and Culture* (1933).

THOMAS GORDON (1918–   ) is a Psychological Consultant, with special interest in individual and group therapy and leadership, to business and industry. He is the author of *Group-Centered Leadership* (1955).

MARION BESSANT HAMILTON (Mrs. Thomas Hamilton) is a graduate student at Duke University.

FRANK HAMILTON HANKINS (1877–   ) is a specialist in population and social and race theory, and former Professor of Sociology at Smith College. He is the author of *Introduction to the Study of Society* (rev. ed., 1935), other books and numerous articles.

AMOS H. HAWLEY (1910–   ) is a sociologist at the University of Michigan and author of *Demography and Public Administration* (1954), *Population Distribution Within Metropolitan Areas, 1900–1950* (1955), and *The Changing Shape of Metropolitan America* (1956).

JOHN GRIER HIBBEN (1861–1933) was president of Princeton University and the author of *A Defense of Prejudice, and Other Essays* (1911) and *The Higher Patriotism* (1915).

WILLIAM E. HOCKING (1873–   ), Professor Emeritus of Philosophy at Harvard since 1943, has since that time lectured at the University of California, University of Leiden, and under the Office of Military Government in Bavaria. He is the author of *Science and the Idea of God* (1944), *Experiment in Education* (1954), *The Coming World Civilization* (1957), and other books.

REINHOLD FRIEDRICH ALFRED HOERNLE (1880–1943), late Professor and Head of the Department of Philosophy, University of Witwatersrand, Johannesburg, Union of South Africa, is the author of *Studies in Contemporary Metaphysics* (1920), *Idealism as a Philosophy* (1924), and *South African Native Policy and the Liberal Spirit* (1939).

EVERETT CHERRINGTON HUGHES (1894–   ), Professor of Sociology at the University of Chicago, is the author of *French Canada in Transition* (1943) and *Where Peoples Meet* with Helen McGill Hughes (1952).

GUSTAV ICHHEISER (1897–   ) is an Austrian by birth who did teaching and research in Austria, Poland, and at the Institute of Sociology in London. He came to the United States in 1940 and he is Professor of Psychology and Sociology at Talladega College. He is the author of "Misunderstandings in Human Relations: A Study in False Social Perception" (Number 2, Part 2, Vol. LV of *The American Journal of Sociology* for September, 1949).

WILLIAM JAMES (1842–1910) was a distinguished philosopher at Harvard University and author of *Principles of Psychology, Varieties of Religious Experience, The Will to Believe,* and other well-known works.

CHRISTEN T. JONASSEN (1912–   ), Norwegian-born American, is Associate Professor of Sociology at Ohio State University and Director of International House in Columbus, Ohio.

HARNETT T. KANE (1910–   ), New Orleans journalist, is the author of *Bayous of Louisiana* (1943), *Deep Delta Country* (1944), and *Miracle in the Mountains* (1956).

V. O. KEY, JR. (1908–   ) is Professor of Government at Harvard University and author of *Politics, Parties and Pressure Groups* (1942) and *A Primer of Statistics for Political Scientists* (1954).

WALTER KOLARZ (1912–   ) is in charge of the Central Research Unit of the British Broadcasting Company, European Service. He is the author of *Peoples of the Soviet Far East* (1954), *Russia and Her Colonies* (1952), and *Myths and Realities in Eastern Europe* (1946).

FORREST E. LAVIOLETTE (1904–   ) is Professor of Sociology at Tulane University in New Orleans and author of *Americans of Japanese Ancestry* (1946), *Canadian-Japanese and World War II* (1948), and other sociological and ethnological papers.

ANDREW W. LIND (1901–   ) is Professor of Sociology at the University of Hawaii and author of *An Island Community: Ecological Succession in Hawaii* (1938), *Hawaii's Japanese: An Experiment in Democracy* (1946), and several papers dealing with race relations in Hawaii.

JOSEPH DEAN LOHMANN (1910–   ) is the Sheriff of Cook County, Illinois, with varied experiences in the fields of education, sociology, criminology, penology, and labor-management relations. He is the author of *Principles of Police Work with Minority Groups* (1950), "Segregation in Washington," National Committee on Segregation in the Nation's Capital (1948), *The Police and Minority Groups* (1946), and numerous articles.

MARVIN LOWENTHAL (1890–   ) is a lecturer, editor of *The American*

Zionist, and author of *A World Passed By* (1933) and *This Was New York* (1945).

IAN DOUGLAS MACCRONE (1898–   ) is Professor of Psychology at the University of Witwatersrand, Johannesburg, Union of South Africa. In addition to his well-known work *Race Attitudes in South Africa* which was reprinted in 1957, he is the author of several monographs on aspects of race relations.

CECIL ALEC MACE, Professor of Psychology and Dean of the Faculty of Science, Birkbeck College, England, is the author of *Incentives* (1952) and *The Principles of Logic* (1933).

WILLIAM CHRISTIE MCLEOD was an Assistant Professor in the Department of Finance in the Wharton and Graduate Schools of the University of Pennsylvania at the time *The American Indian Frontier* was published in 1928. He later published *The Origin and History of Politics* (1931).

REUBEN HENRY MARKHAM (1887–1949) was a teacher, journalist, foreign correspondent, and lecturer. Markham lived in Europe many years and covered Southeastern and central Europe for the *Christian Science Monitor.* He is the author of *The Wave of the Past* (1941), *Tito's Imperial Communism* (1947), *Rumania Under the Soviet Yoke* (1949), and several other books.

ROBERT MARSHALL (1901–1939), one time Director of Forestry of the Bureau of Indian Affairs and later Chief of the Division of Recreation and Lands in the U.S. Forestry Service, was the founder of the Wilderness Society. Papers left by Marshall were published in 1956 under the title *Arctic Wilderness.*

JITSUICHI MASUOKA (1903–   ), an American citizen of Japanese ancestry, is Professor of Sociology at Fisk University and author of many articles in the field of race relations.

GEORGE HERBERT MEAD (1863–1931) was a distinguished philosopher and professor at the University of Chicago. His lectures were brought together and published after his death as *Mind, Self and Society* (1934), *Movements of Thought in the Nineteenth Century* (1936), and *The Philosophy of the Act* (1938).

GEORGES MESNARD was a French demographer at the University of Paris at the time the article on Algeria used in this book was written. He has published a number of articles on population in *La Nature.* None have appeared in this periodical since 1938.

HERBERT MOLLER (1909–   ), a German-born American citizen, is Associate Professor of History at Boston University. He is interested in the social history of Europe and in the history of population.

MONTAGUE FRANCIS ASHELY MONTAGU (1905–   ), English-born American citizen, is Professor of Anthropology at Rutgers University. He is the author of *Human Development* (1955), *The Natural Superiority of Women* (1955), and *Man: His First Million Years* (1957).

GARDNER MURPHY (1895–   ), Psychologist and Director of Research at the Menninger Foundation, Topeka, Kansas, is the author of several books including *Introduction to Psychology* (1951) and *In the Minds of Men* (1953).

ROBERT CUSHMAN MURPHY (1887–   ), Lamont Curator of Birds at the American Museum of Natural History and the recipient of numerous awards and medals, is a contributing Editor of The Geographical Review.

GUNNAR MYRDAL (1898–   ), a distinguished Swedish economist and Director of the Study of the American Negro Problem for the Carnegie Corporation of America, 1938–1942, which produced *The American Dilemma* (1944), has been Executive Secretary of the United Nations Economic Commission in Europe since 1947.

WILLIAM FIELDING OGBURN (1886–   ), former Sewell L. Avery Distin-

guished Professor of Sociology at the University of Chicago, is now Visiting
Professor of Sociology at Florida State University. He is the author of *Social
Change* (1922) and editor of a series on *Recent Social Changes*.

GEORGE ORWELL (pseudonym of Eric Blair, 1903–1950) is the author of *Animal Farm* (1945), *Nineteen Eighty-Four* (1949), and other books and stories.

ROBERT EZRA PARK (1864–1944) was Professor of Sociology at the University
of Chicago and later Visiting Professor at Fisk University. With Ernest W.
Burgess he was the author of *An Introduction to the Science of Sociology*. His
papers have been collected and published as *Race and Culture* (1950), *Human
Communities* (1952), and *Society* (1955).

TALCOTT PARSONS (1902–   ) is Professor of Sociology at Harvard University and the author of numerous articles and several books including *The Social
System* (1951) and *Economy and Society* (1956).

SALME PEKKALA of Helsinki, Finland, is a former graduate student of Duke
University.

WILLIAM MATTHEW FLINDERS PETRIE (1853–1942), one of the greatest of
modern Egyptologists and Professor of Egyptology at University College, London, until 1933, is the author of *Seventy Years of Archaeology* (1931) and *The
Making of Egypt* (1939).

ULRICH BONNELL PHILLIPS (1877–1934) was Professor of American History
at Yale University at the time of his death. Phillips was born and reared in the
South and was deeply interested in its history. He wrote *American Negro Slavery* (1918), *Life and Labor in the Old South* (1929), and many articles.

GEORGE HENRY LANE-FOX PITT-RIVERS (1890–   ), an English ethnologist, is the owner-director of the Pitt-Rivers Museum and author of *The Clash
of Cultures and the Contact of Races* (1927).

PATRICK TRACEY LOWELL PUTNAM (1904–1953) was an anthropologist
who, in 1925, went to Africa for the Peabody Museum. The statement on
Negro-Pygmy relations used in this book was actually written by Professor
Carleton S. Coon from information furnished by Putnam of whom Coon says:
"He was a complete non-conformist and a man of originality second to none."

MRS. OLIVE WESTBROOK QUINN (1914–   ) is Research Sociologist at the
Laboratory of Socioenvironmental Studies of the National Institute of Mental
Health at Bethesda, Maryland. With Leila C. Deasy, she is the author of "The
Wife of the Mental Patient and the Hospital Psychiatrist" which appeared in
Vol. XI of *The Journal of Social Issues*.

PARS RAM (1902?–1952) was born in India and educated at the University of
Calcutta. He was influential in the establishment of child guidance centers in
India. At the time of his death, he was Director of the BM Institute of Child
Development in Ahmedabad. He is the author of *A UNESCO Study in Social
Tensions in Aligarh*, edited by Gardner Murphy and published in 1956.

ROBERT REDFIELD (1897–   ) is Robert Maynard Hutchins Distinguished
Service Professor of Anthropology at the University of Chicago and author of
The Primitive World and Its Transformation (1953) and *The Little Community* (1955).

STEPHEN WINSOR REED (1912–   ) is Associate Professor of Sociology at
Yale University and Director of Southeast Asia Studies.

DIETRICH C. REITZES (1916–   ) is Assistant Professor of Sociology at Calumet Center, Indiana, with special interest in race relations and criminology.

EDWARD BYRON REUTER (1882–1946) was Professor of Sociology at the
State University of Iowa and Visiting Professor at Fisk University, editor of
Race and Culture Contacts (1934), and author of a number of books in
several sociological fields.

ALBION ROSS is a New York *Times* correspondent formerly stationed at Johannesburg, South Africa.

MAURICE SAMUEL (1895–) was born in Roumania and educated in England. He is now an American citizen. Mr. Samuel has been in contact with "practically every Jewish community between Jordan and the Golden Gate, between Manchester and Cape Town." He is the author of twelve books and the translator of fifteen others.

THOMAS SANCTON (1915–) was a Rosenwald Fellow and former Managing Editor of *The New Republic*. He is the author of *A Whole New World to Build* (1944).

BUDD SCHULBERG (1914–) is an American novelist, columnist for *Sports Illustrated*, and author of *The Disenchanted* (1950) and *On the Waterfront* (1954).

ELLEN CHURCHILL SEMPLE (1863–1932) was Professor of Geography at Clark University. She is the author of *American History and Its Geographic Conditions* (1903), *The Influences of Geographic Environment on the Basis of Ratzel's System of Anthropo-Geography* (1911), and *The Geography of the Mediterranean Region* (1931).

NATHANIEL SOUTHGATE SHALER (1841–1906) was an American geologist and at one time in charge of the Atlantic Division of the U.S. Geological Survey. In addition to books in his main field he wrote on aspects of social life, including *The Neighbor* (1904) and *Man and the Earth* (1905). His autobiography, with a supplementary memoir by his wife, was published in 1909.

THOMAS SPENSLEY SIMEY (1906–) is Professor of Social Science at the University of Liverpool, England. He is the author of *Welfare and Planning in the West Indies* (1946).

REED SMITH (1881–1943) was Professor of English Literature and Dean of the Graduate School at the University of South Carolina. He is the author of *American Anthology of Old-World Ballads* (1937) and *Learning to Write in College* (1939).

THOMAS GEORGE SPEAR, bursar and steward in Selwyn College, Cambridge, England, is the author of *Twilight of the Muhghuls* (1951) and *India, Pakistan and the West* (1952).

OSWALD SPENGLER (1880–1936), German philosopher and historian, is the author of *The Decline of the West* (1923), *The Hour of Decision: Germany and the World* (1934), and other books.

GEORGE MALCOLM STRATTON (1865–), Professor Emeritus of the University of California, is the author of *International Delusions* (1936) and *Man, Creator or Destroyer* (1952).

WILLIAM GRAHAM SUMNER (1840–1910) was a distinguished pioneer American sociologist. He was Professor of Political Science at Yale at the time of his death. His best known work, *Folkways*, was copyrighted by Sumner in 1906, and his voluminous materials were later brought together, and added to, and published by his colleague A. G. Keller under the title *The Science of Society*.

HENRY LEE SWINT (1909–) is Assistant Professor of History at Vanderbilt University in Nashville, Tennessee, and author of *The Northern Teacher in the South, 1862–1870* (1941).

FRANK TANNENBAUM (1893–) is an Austrian-born American citizen and Professor of Economics at Columbia University. He has shown a special interest in Latin American affairs and international relations. He is the author of *Mexico* (1948), *A Philosophy of Labor* (1951), and *American Tradition in Foreign Relations* (1955).

EDMOND LAPIERRE TAYLOR (1908–) is a journalist, lecturer, and author of *The Strategy of Terror* (1940).

THE REV. FRANCISCUS TER HAAR (1857–1939) was a Dutch-born Professor of Moral Theology, first in The Netherlands and later in Rome. At the time of his death, he was Adviser to the Superior General of the Congregation of the Most Holy Redeemer in Rome. In addition to *De Matrimoniis Mixtis,* he is the author of a two-volume work *Casus Conscientiae* and *De Occasionariis,* and other books and articles dealing with the problem of morals and the history of moral theology.

EDGAR T. THOMPSON (1900–   ) is Professor of Sociology at Duke University. He is editor of, and contributor to, *Race Relations and the Race Problem* (1939, and compiler (with Alma Macy Thompson) of *Race and Region: A Bibliography* (1948), and author of various articles dealing with race relations and plantation systems.

LUCY GOODALE THURSTON (1795–1876) was the wife of the Rev. Asa Thurston, pioneer Protestant missionary to the Hawaiian Islands from New England. In 1882 her letters and journals, extending over a period of more than fifty years, were published as *The Life and Times of Lucy G. Thurston.* The book was republished in 1921.

ARNOLD JOSEPH TOYNBEE (1889–   ) is a well-known English historian and editor of *The Political History of World War II* for the Royal Institute of International Affairs. He is the author of *A Study of History,* originally in 10 volumes (1934–1954), *The World and the West* (1953), and other books.

RUPERT BAYLESS VANCE (1899–   ) is Kenan Professor of Sociology at the University of North Carolina and Associate Editor of *Social Forces.* He is the author of *All These People* (1945), *Human Factors in Cotton Culture* (1929), *Human Geography of the South* (1932), other books and numerous articles.

JUSTUS MARIA VAN DER KROEF (1922–   ), an Indonesian-born citizen of Dutch parentage, is Assistant Professor of Foreign Studies at Michigan State College. He is the author of *Dutch Policy in Indonesia* (1950) and *Indonesia in the Modern World* (1954–56).

C. A. VLIELAND (1890–   ) is a former member of the Malayan Civil Service and was Undersecretary of the Straits Settlements at the time of his retirement in 1941. In addition to his report on the 1931 Malayan Census, he is the author of "The Population of the Malay Peninsula: A Study in Human Migration," published in *The Geographical Review,* Vol. XXIV.

ERIC VOEGELIN (1901–   ) is a German-born American citizen who is Professor of Political Science at Louisiana State University. He is the author of *The New Science of Politics* (1952), *Order and History* (Vol I, 1956), and other books and articles.

CHARLES WAGLEY (1913–   ) is Professor of Anthropology at Columbia University and author of *Race and Class in Rural Brazil* (1952) and *Amazon Town: A Study of Man in the Tropics* (1953).

THE REV. ROBERT WALSH (1772–1852) is the author of *A Journey from Constantinople* and *Notices of Brazil in 1828 and 1829* (1830, 2 vols.). The latter book was written while the author was chaplain at the British Embassy in Brazil "for the amusement and information of a friend in England."

CLINTON ALFRED WESLAGER (1909–   ) is an American archaeologist and ethnologist who has worked with East Coast Indian material in Delaware, Maryland, and Pennsylvania. He is the author of *Delaware's Forgotten People* (1947) and *The Nanticoke Indians* (1948).

LOUIS WIRTH (1897–1952) was Professor of Sociology at the University of Chicago and active in several social agencies and organizations. He is the author of *The Ghetto* (1928), and numerous papers many of which have been brought together and published under the title *Community Life and Social Policy* (1956).

HUGH ARCHIBALD WYNDHAM (1877–   ) is Fourth Baron of Leconfield
and author of *The Atlantic and Emancipation* (1937), *Britain and the World*
(1944), and *Sutton and Dunstan Manors* (1956).

HANS ZINSSER (1878–1940) was Professor of Immunology at Harvard Medical
School and author of *A Textbook of Bacteriology* (1934), *Rats, Lice and History* (1935), and a thinly veiled autobiography entitled *As I Remember Him*
(1940).